BASIMOV'S GUIDE TO THE BIBLE

THE OLD TESTAMENT

ISAAC ASIMOV

BASIMOV'S GUIDE TO THE BIBLE

VOLUME ONE

THE OLD TESTAMENT

Maps by Rafael Palacios

AVON
PUBLISHERS OF BARD, CAMELOT, DISCUS AND FLARE BOOKS

AVON BOOKS
A division of
The Hearst Corporation
959 Eighth Avenue
New York, New York 10019

First Avon Printing, November, 1971

AVON TRADEMARK REG. U.S. PAT. OFF. AND
FOREIGN COUNTRIES, REGISTERED TRADEMARK—
MARCA REGISTRADA, HECHO EN U.S.A.

Printed in the U.S.A.

DON 20 19 18 17 16 15 14 13 12

To
Lawrence P. Ashmead
who has faith

CONTENTS

INTRODUCTION

The most influential, the most published, the most widely read book in the history of the world is the Bible. No other book has been so studied and so analyzed and it is a tribute to the complexity of the Bible and the eagerness of its students that after thousands of years of study there are still endless books that can be written about it.

I have myself written two short books for young people on the earlier books of the Bible* but I have long wanted to take on a job of more ambitious scope; one that I can most briefly describe as a consideration of the secular aspects of the Bible.

Most people who read the Bible do so in order to get the benefit of its ethical and spiritual teachings, but the Bible has a secular side, too. It is a history book covering the first four thousand years of human civilization.

The Bible is not a history book in modern sense, of course, since its writers lacked the benefit of modern archaeological techniques, did not have our concept of dating and documentation, and had different standards of what was and was not significant in history. Furthermore, Biblical interest was centered primarily on developments that impinged upon those dwelling in Canaan, a small section of Asia bordering on the Mediterranean Sea. This area makes only a small mark on the history of early civilization (from the secular viewpoint) and modern histories, in contrast to the Bible, give it comparatively little space.

Nevertheless, for most of the last two thousand years, the Bible has been virtually the only history book used in Western civilization. Even today, it remains the most popular, and its view of ancient history is still more widely and commonly known than is that of any other.

So it happens, therefore, that millions of people today know of

* *Words in Genesis* and *Words from the Exodus.*

Nebuchadnezzar, and have never heard of Pericles, simply because Nebuchadnezzar is mentioned prominently in the Bible and Pericles is never mentioned at all.

Millions know of Ahasuerus as a Persian king who married Esther, even though there is no record of such an event outside the Bible. Most of those same millions never suspect that he is better known to modern historians as Xerxes and that the most important event in his reign was an invasion of Greece that ended in utter defeat. That invasion is not mentioned in the Bible.

Millions know certain minor Egyptian Pharaohs, such as Shishak and Necho, who are mentioned in the Bible, but have never heard of the great conquering Pharaoh, Thutmose III, who is not. People whose very existence is doubtful, such as Nimrod and the queen of Sheba, are household words because they are mentioned in the Bible, while figures who were colossal in their day are sunk in oblivion because they are not.

Again, small towns in Canaan, such as Shechem and Bethel, in which events of the Bible are described as taking place, are more familiar to us today than are large ancient metropolises such as Syracuse or Egyptian Thebes, which are mentioned only glancingly in the Bible, or not at all.

Moreover, usually only that is known about such places as happens to be mentioned in the Bible. Ecbatana, the capital of the Median Empire, is remembered in connection with the story of Tobit, but its earlier and later history are dim indeed to most people, who might be surprised to know that it still exists today as a large provincial capital in the modern nation of Iran.

In this book, then, I am assuming a reader who is familiar with the Bible, at least in its general aspects, but who knows little of ancient history outside the Bible. I assume a reader who would be interested in filling in the fringe, so to speak, and who would expect much of the Bible to become easier to understand if some of the places and people mentioned in it are made less mysterious. (After all, those places and people were well known to the original readers of the Bible, and it would be sad to allow so important a book to grow needlessly murky with the passing of the centuries because the periphery has grown dim and indistinct.)

I am attempting to correct this, in part at least. I will, for instance, speculate on who Nimrod might have been, try to define the time in which Abraham entered Canaan, place David's kingdom in its world setting, sort out the role played by the various monarchs who are only mentioned in the Bible when they fight against Israel and Judah, and work out the relationships among the Herods encountered by Jesus and the Apostles.

I am trying, in short, to bring in the outside world, illuminate it in terms of the Biblical story and, in return, illuminate the events of the Bible by adding to it the non-Biblical aspects of history, biography, and geography.

In doing so, there will be the constant temptation (born of the modern view of history) to bring in dates though few can be definitely assigned to individual events in the Bible. It will be convenient then to make use of a more or less arbitrary set of "periods" which will chop history into sections that will make for easy reference.

The period from the beginning of the earliest civilizations, say 4000 B.C. to 100 A.D., can be lumped together as "the Biblical period." Of this the period to 400 B.C. is "the Old Testament period," from 400 B.C. to 4 B.C. is the "inter-Testamental period," while the A.D. section is "the New Testament period."

The Biblical period can be broken down into smaller sections as follows:

4000 B.C. to 2000 B.C. — The Primeval period
2000 B.C. to 1700 B.C. — The Patriarchal period
1700 B.C. to 1200 B.C. — The Egyptian period
1200 B.C. to 1000 B.C. — The Tribal period
1000 B.C. to 900 B.C. — The Davidic kingdom

Thereafter, it is most convenient to name periods after the peoples who did, in fact, dominate western Asia. Thus:

900 B.C. to 600 B.C. — The Assyrian period
600 B.C. to 540 B.C. — The Babylonian period
540 B.C. to 330 B.C. — The Persian period
330 B.C. to 70 B.C. — The Greek period
70 B.C. to 100 A.D. — The Roman period

During the last century of the Greek period, the Jews won a brief independence under the Maccabees, so that the century from 170 B.C. to 70 B.C. might be called "the Maccabean period."

I cannot pretend that in writing this book I am making any significant *original* contribution to Biblical scholarship; indeed, I am not competent to do so. All that I will have to say will consist of material well known to students of ancient history. (There will, however, be a few places where I will indulge in personal speculation, and label it as such.)

Nevertheless, it is my hope that this material, well known though it may be in separate bits, will now be presented in a newly useful way, since it will be collected and placed within the covers of a moderately sized book, presented in one uniform manner, and in a style and fashion which, it is hoped, will be interesting to the average reader of the Bible.

I intend to be completely informal in this book, and to adhere to no rigid rules. I won't invariably discuss a place or person at its first appearance in the Bible, if it seems to me I can make more sense out of it by bringing the matter up in a later connection. I will not hesitate to leave a discussion incomplete if I plan to take it up again later on. I will leave out items toward which I don't feel I can contribute anything either useful or interesting, and I will, without particular concern, allow myself to digress if I feel that the digression will be useful.

Again, since this book is not intended to be a scholarly compendium, I do not plan to burden its pages with such extraneous appurtenances as footnotes giving sources. The sources that I use are, after all, very general and ordinary ones.

First of all, of course, are various versions of the Bible:

a) The Authorized Version, originally published in 1611 and familiarly known as the "King James Bible." This is the Bible used in the various Protestant churches. It is the version which is most familiar to most Americans and it is from this version that I quote, except where otherwise indicated.

b) The Revised Standard Version, Thomas Nelson & Sons, 1946, 1952, and 1959.

c) Saint Joseph "New Catholic Edition," Catholic Book Publishing Co., 1962.

d) The Jerusalem Bible, Doubleday and Co., Inc., 1966.

e) The Holy Scriptures according to the Masoretic text, The Jewish Publication Society of America, 1955.

f) I have leaned particularly heavily on those volumes of the Anchor Bible (Doubleday) so far published, since these represent some of the latest and most profound thinking on the Bible.

Much of the Apocrypha is contained in the "New Catholic Edition" and, in addition, I have made use of the King James Version and the Revised Standard Version of these books.

I have also consulted, quite steadily, A *New Standard Bible Diction-ary*, Third Revised Edition, Funk and Wagnalls Company, 1936, *The Abingdon Bible Commentary*, Abingdon Press, 1929, and "Dictionary of the Bible" by John L. McKenzie, S.J., Bruce Publishing Company, 1965.

In addition, I have turned to general encyclopedias, dictionaries, histories, geographies, and any other reference books available to me which could in any way be useful to me.

The result—well, the result can begin to be seen when you turn the page.

1. GENESIS

Genesis

The Bible begins at the logical place—the beginning. The very
first verse starts:

Genesis 1:1. *In the beginning . . .*

The phrase "In the beginning" is a translation of the Hebrew word
bereshith. In the case of several of the books of the Bible, the first
word is taken as the title of the whole (much as Papal bulls are
named for the two Latin words with which they begin.) The Hebrew
name of the first book is, therefore, *Bereshith*.

The Bible was first translated into another language in the course of
the third century B.C. and that other language was Greek. This Greek
version was, according to tradition, based on the work of seventy
learned scholars, and it is therefore known as the Septuagint, from a
Latin word meaning "seventy."

In the Septuagint, the various books of the Bible were, naturally

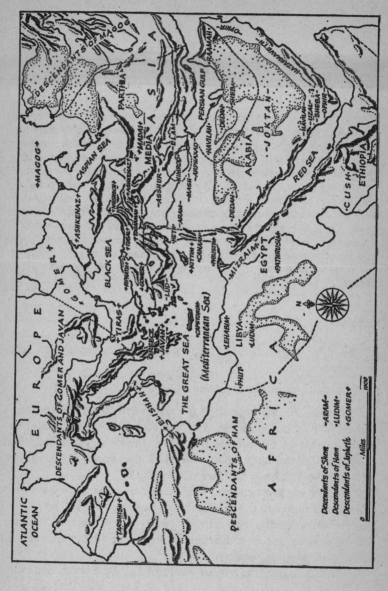

The Nations of Genesis

enough, given Greek names. The Hebrew habit of using the first words as the name was not followed, and descriptive names were used instead.

The first book was named "Genesis," which means, literally, "coming into being." It implies a concern with births and beginnings which is appropriate for a book that begins with the creation of heaven and earth.

By ancient tradition, the first five books of the Bible were written by Moses, the folk hero who, according to the account given in the second through fifth books, rescued the Israelites from Egyptian slavery. Modern scholars are convinced that this theory of authorship is not tenable and that the early books of the Bible are not the single work of any man. Rather, they are the combined and carefully edited version of a number of sources. Despite this, the full name of the first book of the Bible as commonly given in English translation remains "The First Book of Moses, Called Genesis."

The first five books of the Bible give not only the traditional history of the ancestors of the Israelite people, but also describe a legal code as having been given to Moses by God and by Moses to the Israelites generally. Because of Moses' traditional role in what was, in actual fact, a set of laws that developed slowly over the centuries, the whole is termed the "Mosaic law" or, more simply still, "the Law." The Hebrew word for the first five books is "Torah," which is the Hebrew word for "law."

The Greek word for the first five books is "Pentateuch" ("five books"). In recent times, it has been recognized that the sixth book of the Bible is closely connected with the first five and is derived from similar sources. All six books may be referred to as the "Hexateuch" ("six books").

God

The Bible centers about God, and God is brought into the tale at once:

Genesis 1:1. *In the beginning God created the heaven and the earth.*

The Hebrew word, translated here as God, is "Elohim" and that is a plural form which would ordinarily (if tradition were defied) be translated "gods." It is possible that in the very earliest traditions on which the Bible is based, the creation was indeed the work of a plurality of gods. The firmly monotheistic Biblical writers would carefully have eliminated such polytheism, but could not perhaps do anything with the firmly ingrained term "Elohim." It was too familiar to change.

Some hints of polytheism seem to have survived the editing. Thus, after the first created man disobeys God's injunction not to eat of the tree of knowledge, God is quoted as saying:

> Genesis 3:22. . . . Behold, the man is become as one of us, to know good and evil . . .

Then, too, still later, when God is concerned over mankind's arrogance in attempting to build a tower that would reach to heaven, He is quoted as saying:

> Genesis 11:7. Go to, let us go down, and there confound their language . . .

It is possible to argue that this is not true evidence of early polytheism. God might be viewed as using the royal "we"; or as speaking to an angelic audience; or even, in the Christian view, as speaking in the persons of the Trinity.

Nevertheless, as far as we know the history of religion outside the Bible, early beliefs were always polytheistic and monotheism was a late development in the history of ideas.

The Seventh Day

Carefully and sparely, and with great vigor and beauty, the first thirty-four verses of the Bible tell the story of creation. Six acts of creation are described as taking place on six successive days:

> Genesis 2:2. And on the seventh day God ended his work . . . and . . . rested . . .
> Genesis 2:3. And God blessed the seventh day, and sanctified it . . .

This marks the traditional establishment of the Sabbath—a day separated from the ordinary days of the week and dedicated to God.

The role played by the Sabbath in Judaism was quite small at first, and quite enormous in the end. The dividing line comes at one of the great watersheds in Jewish history—the Babylonian Exile. This took place in the sixth century b.c. and will be dealt with extensively later in the book. It is that sixth-century dividing line to which I will refer when I say something is pre-Exilic or post-Exilic.

In pre-Exilic times the Sabbath is barely mentioned and seems to have been of little consequence among the Israelites. In post-Exilic times, its observance was of the greatest importance and Jews died rather than violate that observance.

It is tempting to suppose that the Sabbath was Babylonian in origin, and that it gained new significance to the Jews in exile (see page 576). Nor can one fairly use the first chapters of Genesis as evidence for the great antiquity of the Sabbath in its holiest form, since it is widely accepted these days that the creation tale received its present shape after the Babylonian Exile and was, in fact, a version of the Babylonian creation myth, purified of polytheism and grossness, and put into the loftiest and most abstract terms of which the Jewish priesthood was capable.

The creation tale is typical of those portions of the first few books of the Bible that were put into final form by priestly hands soon after the time of the Exile. Such portions are part of the "Priestly document" and are usually designated as P by Biblical scholars. The Priestly document is characterized by impersonality and by a heavy reliance on statistics and genealogies.

The Lord God

Once the P version of creation is ended, a new version begins:

Genesis 2:4. *These are the generations of the heavens and of the earth when they were created, in the day that the Lord God made the earth and the heavens.*

The distinctive feature here is the sudden use of the term "Lord God," where throughout the first thirty-four verses the Deity had been referred to as simply "God."

The Hebrew word, here translated as "Lord," is made up of four Hebrew letters, which can be written in English as YHVH, and which are expressed, traditionally but mistakenly, as "Jehovah" for reasons to be given later (see page 135). Modern scholars believe "Yahveh" is the more accurate presentation.

Where "god" is a general term for any deity, and where the capitalized form "God" expresses the one Deity of the Bible, Yahveh is the specific name of that specific Deity. Names were of considerable importance to ancient man, for they were considered an extension of personality. To be able to pronounce the name was to be able (according to folklore) to control the being named. Names were therefore tools of magic and Jews of post-Exilic times disapproved of magic, not because they did not believe in its reality, but because the magic was usually performed in the names of heathen idols.

The name of God came to be avoided on principle, therefore. When it did occur in some of the traditional sources of the early books of the Bible or in the writings of the prophets of pre-Exilic times, pious Jews took to saying *Adonai* ("Lord") instead. This euphemism was accepted in English translation and what might have been given as "the God, Yahveh" is given as "the Lord God" instead.

The use of the term "the Lord God" ("Yahveh Elohim") in place of God ("Elohim") is characteristic of a particular early strand of tradition which was incorporated into the Hexateuch. This strand is known as the "J document" because of its characteristic use of "Jehovah" ("Yahveh") in connection with God.

There is another strand of early tradition which like the P document uses simply Elohim for God, and it is the "E document." Both J and E are much more personal than P, tell stories with circumstantial detail and do not greatly interest themselves in the more formal aspects of the matter.

The J document may have been put into written form as early as the ninth century in the more southerly of the two kingdoms into which the Israelites were then divided. This was the kingdom of Judah. The E document was put into written form a century later in the northern kingdom of Israel.

The dominant tribe in the northern kingdom was Ephraim and that was sometimes used as a poetic synonym for Israel. There is thus the interesting coincidence that the J document can stand for

Judah as well as Jehovah, and the E document for Ephraim as well as Elohim.

The northern kingdom was destroyed toward the end of the eighth century B.C. and the priests of Judah incorporated E into their own J tradition. This made the primitive history of their ancestors more complete, but also introduced occasional duplications, with the same tale told twice, once with a northern orientation and once with a southern. Despite the careful dovetailing of verses, such duplicate versions can be dissected and identified.

During and after the Babylonian Exile, the priesthood took this combined JE version, added P material of their own, and produced Genesis as we have it now. It is not my purpose, in this book, to untwine Genesis and identify the source of each verse (something that is done in the Anchor Bible, for instance) but it is well to know that different sources do exist.

Man

In J's tale of creation (more primitive than that of P) God does not call human beings into existence by spoken command alone. Rather, he shapes them out of clay as a sculptor might:

Genesis 2:7. *And the Lord God formed man of the dust of the ground, and breathed into his nostrils the breath of life; and man became a living soul.*

The word "man" is a translation of the Hebrew word *adam*, which is a general expression rather akin to what we mean when we say "mankind." (The Hebrew word for an individual man is *ish*.)

The word *adam*, used in reference to this first created man, came to be a proper name, Adam. The King James version slips into this usage later in the chapter:

Genesis 2:19. . . . *the Lord God formed every beast . . . and every fowl . . . and brought them unto Adam . . .*

Actually, the Hebrew does not seem to make use of Adam as a proper name until the beginning of the fifth chapter:

Genesis 5:1. *This is the book of the generations of Adam . . .*

and the Jerusalem Bible, for instance, is careful to translate *adam* as "man" up to that very point.

After forming man, God breathes life into him, a reminder that in primitive times, the breath was often equated with life for what seemed obvious reasons.

Dead creatures no longer breathed, and breath was invisible and impalpable and therefore seemed a fitting representation of that mysterious something that left the body at the moment of death. Indeed, the word "soul" used in Genesis 2:7 is a translation of the Hebrew *nephesh*, which means "breath."

Eden

Having formed man, God also prepares a dwelling place for him and that involves the mention of the first definite place name in the Bible:

> Genesis 2:8. *And the Lord God planted a garden eastward in Eden . . .*

Notice that it is not the garden itself that is named Eden. One cannot speak of "Eden" as though it were synonymous with the garden, any more than one can speak of "California" as though it were synonymous with Yosemite Park.

The garden is planted somewhere in a land called Eden and the location of that land is "eastward"; eastward, that is, from Canaan, which is the focal point of reference of the Biblical story and the home of both the writers and the original readers of Genesis.

The question, then, is: Where is Eden?

There have been numerous answers to this question, some of them exceedingly farfetched, and no definite answer acceptable to all is possible. And yet, if we were to try the simplest and most direct possible line of thought, a reasonable solution will offer itself.

In the first place, suppose we consider the geography of the region not as it was at the time the ancient Jews believed creation to have taken place (roughly 4000 B.C. by modern dating convention) but as it was in the much later time when the material in the Book of Genesis was reduced to writing.

Genesis is based, to some extent, on very ancient traditions, but these

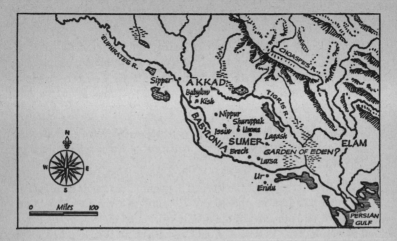

The Garden of Eden

traditions were not reduced to writing until the ninth century B.C. at the earliest. Some strands of the book were not written until several centuries later and the whole was not unified and put together into the form we now have until the fifth century B.C.

The geographical references in Genesis must therefore refer to the situation as it was from the ninth to the fifth centuries B.C. (the Assyrian period and somewhat later) if they were to have meaning to the writer and reader.

Thus, if someone were to write a book, today, about the fourteenth-century American Indians, he might well write of "the Indian tribes that inhabited what is now the United States." To save space, he might speak elliptically of "the Indians of the United States," taking it for granted that the readers would realize the United States did not actually exist in the fourteenth century and would not be confused. In ancient times, when every copy of a book was produced by hand and not by the printing press, the need to be economical with words was far greater. It was not to be expected that anyone would write, "And the Lord God planted a garden eastward in the land which we now call Eden."

So we must ask ourselves where Eden was during the Assyrian period; and the Bible tells us that quite plainly. It refers to Eden several times— not as a mystical primeval site of a garden in which Adam and Eve roamed, but as a prosaic everyday land which was conquered by the Assyrians in the eighth century B.C.

Thus, when the Assyrian hosts of Sennacherib were laying siege to Jerusalem in 701 B.C., they sent a message to the men guarding the walls of the city, warning them not to rely on their God for salvation, as the gods of other nations had not saved those nations from conquest by the Assyrians:

> 2 Kings 19:12. *Have the gods of the nations delivered . . . Gozan, and Haran and Rezeph, and the children of Eden which were in Thelasar?*

Thelasar ("Tel-assar" in the Revised Standard Version) is the name of an Assyrian province, mentioned as "Til-asuri" in Assyrian inscriptions. It extended on both sides of the middle reaches of the Euphrates River and so was, indeed, "eastward" from Canaan—about four hundred miles due east, in fact.

And yet, even so, it is not necessary to suppose that the Biblical writer intended the specific, relatively small, area of Eden in the province of Thelasar. Place names have a tendency to broaden out and grow diffuse with time. Thus "Asia," which originally referred to the western section of what is now the nation of Turkey, spread out to include an entire vast continent, while "Africa," originally signifying the northern portion of the modern nation of Tunisia, spread out to include a continent almost as vast.

Consequently, Eden might well have been used not only as a specific geographical term, but also as a rather general one for the entire valley of the Euphrates River. This makes sense, too, for if the Bible makes Eden the original home of the human race, archaeology has revealed that on the banks of the Euphrates River there arose one of the earliest (if not *the* earliest) of civilizations.

By 3000 B.C., powerful cities dotted the banks of the Euphrates, an elaborate network of irrigation canals was in use, writing had been invented, and, in general, man as a civilized being was in existence.

The Euphrates River

By the time the Book of Genesis was being reduced to writing in its final form, the editor who was arranging the various source materials

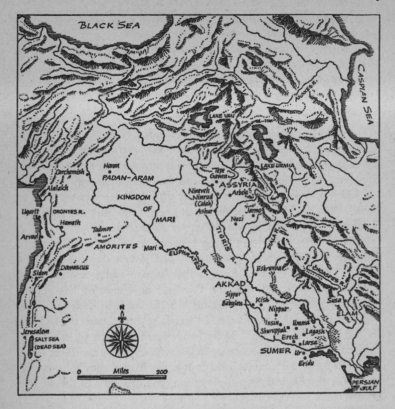

The Tigris and Euphrates Rivers

must have realized that "Eden" had become a vague term and he set about defining the location of the garden more precisely in terms that undoubtedly made sense at the time, but that have become much less clear with the passage of over two thousand additional years.

He set up his definition by placing Eden and its garden at or near the junction of important rivers:

> Genesis 2:10. *And a river went out of Eden to water the garden; and from thence it was parted, and became into four heads.*
> Genesis 2:11. *The name of the first is Pison: that is it which compasseth the whole land of Havilah, where there is gold;*

Genesis 2:12. *And the gold of that land is good: there is bdellium and the onyx stone.*

Genesis 2:13. *And the name of the second river is Gihon: the same is it that compasseth the whole land of Ethiopia.*

Genesis 2:14. *And the name of the third river is Hiddekel: that is it which goeth toward the east of Assyria. And the fourth river is Euphrates.*

The rivers are listed in order of increasing familiarity to the writer so that the fourth river, the Euphrates, is merely mentioned. No need is felt to locate it by describing the regions it traverses. This is understandable since the Euphrates was familiar to the Jews of the Assyrian period and before and parts of it were not very distant. Indeed, in the time of David, when the Jewish kingdom was at its most extensive and powerful, its northern boundary lay on the upper Euphrates.

The Euphrates was known to the Assyrians as "Pu-rat-tu" from a still earlier term which meant "great river." The Hebrew term used in the Bible is "Perath," clearly a form of the Assyrian name, and our word "Euphrates" originated with the Greeks, who converted the strange Assyrian syllables into a set that made more sense to their own ears.

(The English Bible has reached us, to a large extent, from the Hebrew, via first Greek, then Latin. Many Hebrew names reach us in Graeco-Latin form therefore. In general, the Catholic version of the Bible clings more closely to the Graeco-Latin, where the King James Version and even more the Revised Standard Version tend to return to the original Hebrew.)

The Euphrates is indeed a "great river." It is the longest river in southwestern Asia, flowing for seventeen hundred miles. Two streams rise in eastern Turkey, the more northerly only seventy-five miles south of the Black Sea. They flow west separately for about two hundred miles, then join to form the Euphrates. Flowing south now, the river approaches within a hundred miles of the Mediterranean Sea, enters Syria and turns southeast, leaving Syria and passing through Iraq until it finally pours its waters into the Persian Gulf. Though rising and passing so closely to seas that open into the Atlantic Ocean, the river reaches the Indian Ocean at last.

It is a sluggish river that is navigable for quite a distance. During the spring the melting of snow in the mountainous source area causes its level to rise in a slow, potentially useful flooding. Properly controlled, this water supply can be used to turn the nearby land into a garden of fertility and productivity, and throughout the Biblical period irrigation canals were used in this manner.

The third river of Eden is the Hiddekel, which is the Hebrew version of the Assyrian "i-di-ik-lat." It is described in Genesis 2:14 as going "toward the east of Assyria"; that is, forming the eastern boundary of Assyria, and this assuredly was not so. Assyria was an extensive domain in the centuries when Genesis was written and lay on both sides of the river. However, Assyria is the Greek form of the Hebrew "Ashur," which applied not only to the nation, but to its original capital city. It is the city that is meant here and the Hiddekel does indeed skirt the city on the east.

The Hiddekel is not as long as the Euphrates, but its length is quite respectable just the same—1150 miles. It is more turbulent than the Euphrates and is not really navigable except for small boats and rafts. It is perhaps because of the savage danger of its turbulence that the Greeks gave it the name "Tigris" ("tiger"), the name by which we know it to-day.

The fact that the Biblical description of the rivers of Eden mentions "a river [that] . . . was parted, and became into four heads" might lead one to think that the Tigris and Euphrates (along with the other two rivers mentioned) must have a single source. This is almost so. One of the sources of the Tigris River is a lake in eastern Turkey that lies only a dozen miles south of one of the streams that go to make up the Euphrates.

There might therefore be a strong temptation to attempt to locate the garden of Eden specifically in eastern Turkey, except that there is no need to suppose that the writers of Genesis felt obliged to make use of our modern geographical conventions.

When we say that a river parts into two or more streams, we take it for granted that we are imagining ourselves to be moving downstream. But suppose two rivers join as they move downstream. If you follow the joined river upstream you will find it will part into the two rivers.

Let's see how this applies to the Euphrates and the Tigris. The two rivers flow southeastward in almost parallel fashion. At one point, about 350 miles from the Persian Gulf, they approach within twenty-five miles of each other, then move apart before approaching again.

In the time of the earliest civilizations that rose in the region, the Euphrates and the Tigris entered the Persian Gulf by separate mouths, that of the Tigris being almost a hundred miles east of that of the Euphrates.

At that time, however, the Persian Gulf extended about 175 miles further northwestward than it now does. The rivers, flowing southwestward from the Turkish mountains, carried mud and silt with them, slowly forming a delta that filled in the upper end of the narrow Persian Gulf, moving the seacoast 175 miles southeastward in six thousand years.

The Tigris and Euphrates had to continue flowing over the new land as it formed. As it happened, the Tigris flowed south and the Euphrates east. Eventually they met to form a single joined river, now known as the Shatt-al-Arab, which is 120 miles long.

At the time the Book of Genesis was reduced to writing, the Tigris and the Euphrates had already joined to form the common stream and surely the reference in Genesis 2:10 is to the parting (working upstream) of the Shatt-al-Arab into the Tigris and the Euphrates. The reference to the garden of Eden would then be, specifically, to the lower stretches of those two rivers, near where they come together and as it happens, it was precisely there (in the days before the two rivers had yet come together) that civilization arose.

That leaves the first and second rivers of the garden, the Pison and the Gihon. Neither river can be identified, though glamorous guesses have been made for each. Thus, the Pison ("Pishon," in the Revised Standard Version) "compasseth the whole land of Havilah, where there is gold . . . bdellium and the onyx stone." (The Anchor Bible has "lapis-lazuli" in place of the onyx stone.)

Havilah is thus pictured as a land of wealth, where one can find gold and other precious material. In searching for a fabled land of wealth that will represent Havilah, later Europeans had a tendency to fix upon India with its proverbial "wealth of the Indies." In that case, the Pison (or Pishon) might be the Indus River, the long river—as long as the Euphrates—that drains what is now Pakistan, flowing into the Arabian Sea.

As for the Gihon, that seems to be clearly described as compassing "the whole land of Ethiopia." Ethiopia was, in ancient times, a land to the south of Egypt, and a nation bearing that name is still located about five hundred miles south of Egypt nowadays. A tributary of the Nile River rises in Ethiopia and it seems logical to suppose, then, that the Gihon is the Nile River.

If we go no farther in our reasoning, then, the four rivers of Eden would be the Indus, the Nile, the Tigris, and the Euphrates, in that order. This is an intriguing guess. There are only two civilizations, as far as is known, that compete in age with that in the Tigris-Euphrates region. One arose on the banks of the Nile and the other on the banks of the Indus.

And yet the picture cannot be correct. Neither the Indus nor the Nile comes anywhere near the Tigris and Euphrates. The closest approach of the Indus to the Tigris-Euphrates is twelve hundred miles and the closest approach of the Nile is nine hundred, and this certainly does not gibe with the Biblical statement that the four rivers all come together. (While not everything in the Bible can be taken literally, it must certainly be supposed that the Biblical writers could tell when four rivers came together in a region of the world known to them.)

Let's consider the land of Havilah first. Whatever it is, it can't be India, since a word for India does occur in the Book of Esther and, in Hebrew, it is "Hoddu." Havilah itself is mentioned elsewhere, notably in Genesis 25:18 where it is described as part of the region in which the descendants of Ishmael live:

Genesis 25:18. *And they dwelt from Havilah unto Shur, that is before Egypt, as thou goest toward Assyria* . . .

It is reasonably certain that the Ishmaelites were tribes of the Arabian borderland, southeast of Canaan and southwest of the Tigris-Euphrates and so, without trying to pin it down too carefully, we can suppose that Havilah was somewhere south of the Euphrates River.

If this is so, then the Pison (Pishon) may have been a tributary of the Euphrates, flowing into its lower stretches from Havilah to the south and west. It may not have been an important stream and, in the gradual desiccation of the area that has taken place in recent ages, it may have disappeared. (It may even have been a man-made canal, confused by the Biblical writer with a natural stream.)

And what about Ethiopia? That is far off in Africa. The Hebrew word, which is here translated as Ethiopia in the King James Version, is "Cush." Undoubtedly, there are occasions in the Bible where Cush does indeed refer to the region south of Egypt and where it is justifiably translated as Ethiopia. Very likely, this is not one of those places. Indeed, in the Revised Standard Version, the Gihon is described as flowing around the "land of Cush." The word is left in its Hebrew form and no attempt is made to equate it with Ethiopia.

More often than not, the Biblical Cush refers to some Arabian tribe.

There is a reasonable possibility that the word "Cush" in Genesis 2:13 refers to the land of the people whom the ancient Greek geographers spoke of as the Kossaeans, and whom modern historians refer to as the Kassites. They dwelt east of the Tigris and had a period of greatness in the centuries before the rise of Assyria, for between 1600 and 1200 B.C., the Kassites controlled the great civilization of the Tigris-Euphrates.

If this is so, then the Gihon may have been a tributary (now gone) of the Tigris, flowing in from the east—or, possibly, another man-made canal.

We are thus left with the following situation. The Pison (Pishon) joins the Euphrates near its ancient mouth and the Gihon joins the Tigris near its ancient mouth. The two double rivers then join in the new land gradually formed afterward. The four rivers all come together over a reasonably small area and the very ancient civilization that rose in that area may represent the historical kernel within the story of the garden of Eden.

This region was called, in the primeval period, by a name which we now render as "Sumer" or "Sumeria." In the Sumerian language, the word *eden* means "plain." No one knows where, exactly, the Sumerians came from, but if, as seems likely, they originally entered the area from the hilly regions to the east, they may well have thought of themselves as coming "to Eden"; that is, "to the plain."

If so, then the term "Eden" may point specifically at Sumeria, and its identification with the later Eden farther up the Euphrates may be accidental (even though it pointed us in the right direction).

In Hebrew, *eden* means "delight" or "enjoyment," which seems appropriate for the garden, but this is, in all likelihood, merely a fortunate etymological accident since Hebrew and Sumerian are not related languages. (In fact, Sumerian is not related to any known language.) Nevertheless, the accidental Hebrew meaning helped crystallize the feeling that Eden might be a mystical term without actual geographic meaning and that the place originally inhabited by mankind was merely "the garden of delight" with no place name at all.

One more speculation is possible. By 2500 B.C., centuries before Abraham was born, the Sumerians had already passed their peak. New tribes from the north, the Akkadians, took over "the plain" and harder times must have come for the Sumerians, who were now a conquered people. They must have looked back nostalgically to the great days of "the plain."

Can the Biblical tale of the glorious garden of Eden, lost forever, have been a reflection, at least in part, of the Sumerian longing for a past that had vanished?

The Serpent

After Adam is settled in the garden of Eden, God grants him the right to full enjoyment of its delights, with one exception. He says:

Genesis 2:17. *But of the tree of the knowledge of good and evil, thou shalt not eat* . . .

God creates a woman as a companion for Adam, forming her out of the man's rib. Presumably the two might have lived in the garden in eternal happiness as long as they respected God's prohibition. There was, however, a spoiler in the garden:

Genesis 3:1. *Now the serpent was more subtil than any beast of the field* . . .

The serpent is portrayed as able to speak and as maneuvering the naïve woman into eating the forbidden fruit in defiance of God's prohibition. The woman then encouraged Adam to eat it as well.

As told here, the serpent's evil is motiveless or, at best, arises out of mere delight in mischief. The Jews of post-Exilic times made this seem more reasonable, however, by equating the serpent with Satan, who is the spirit of Evil as God is the spirit of Good. (This notion was derived from Persian religious thought—see page 409.)

Actually, the tale of the serpent is quite un-Biblical in atmosphere. Only here and in one other case (that of Balaam's ass, see page 184) do the Hebrew scriptures mention talking animals. It seems quite likely that the tale of the serpent is extremely primitive and represents a remnant of nature myth (see page 175).

Eve

Because of the disobedience of the man and woman, who ate of the fruit of the tree despite prohibition, God drives them out of Eden. They may no longer live easily by food gathering but are condemned to the heavy labor of agriculture.

Several thousand years before the dawn of recorded history, agriculture had been invented somewhere in southwestern Asia. Agriculture gave man a more plentiful and more dependable food supply and made possible a large increase in population in those areas where it was practiced. Because crops were immobile and had to be cared for, farmers had to remain in one place. For mutual protection, they gathered in villages which gradually became cities and thus arose "civilization" (from a Latin word for "city-dweller").

Despite the material benefits brought to man by agriculture, it is quite likely that those who were used to the free wandering irresponsibility of hunting and food gathering (a life that probably seemed a great deal more fun in retrospect than in reality) could not help but view agriculture as a kind of detestable slavery.

Might it not be, then, that a second strand of historical significance to the tale of the expulsion from Eden includes a dim memory of the unfavorable aspects of the changeover to agriculture?

Once the man and his wife took up their life outside the garden, the man gave his wife a name:

Genesis 3:20. *And Adam called his wife's name Eve; because she was the mother of all living.*

At the time these traditions were being reduced to writing, it was customary for Jews to give names with straightforward Hebrew meanings (usually with religious significance.) Thus, Jehoshaphat means "Yahveh has judged"; Ezekiel means "God strengthens"; Hananiah means "Yahveh is gracious" and so on.

The names of the men and women in the earliest traditions were often not in Hebrew and, therefore, were not of clear significance. The Biblical writers, searching for the meaning they felt ought to be in all names, would spot a resemblance to some Hebrew word or phrase and invent an explanation around it.

Thus the Hebrew name equivalent to our own Eve is Havvah, which has a similarity of sound to *hayah*, meaning "to live." (Actually, the initial "h" is a guttural sound not found in our language but similar to the German "ch.") Since Eve is regarded as the mother of the human race, it is tempting to equate Havvah and *hayah* and say that she received the name because she was the mother of all living. This is an example of "folk etymology," in which the Bible abounds. The real meaning of Havvah or Eve is, of course, unknown.

Cain and Abel

Adam and Eve had children:

Genesis 4:1. *And . . . Eve . . . bare Cain, and said, I have gotten a man from the Lord.*

Genesis 4:2. *And she again bare his brother Abel. And Abel was a keeper of sheep, but Cain was a tiller of the ground.*

The name Cain ("Kayin" in Hebrew) is usually taken to mean "smith." In the early days of civilization, the use of metals was introduced and the new material became exceedingly important both in ornamentation and in the manufacture of weapons for hunting and warfare. Men who could prepare the metals and work them into the necessary shapes were important and highly regarded artisans. To be a smith and be called one was a matter of honor, and to this day "Smith" is a common surname among the English and Americans.

This meaning of Cain seems clearer in a later use of the word, in the same chapter, as part of the name of a descendant of Cain:

Genesis 4:22. *And Zillah . . . bare Tubal-cain, an instructor of every artificer in brass and iron . . .*

"Tubal-cain" means "smith of Tubal," where Tubal is a district in Asia Minor. In the centuries immediately preceding the period during which the legends in Genesis were reduced to writing, the techniques for obtaining iron from its ore were worked out in Asia Minor. The smiths of Tubal would therefore have become famous for producing iron weapons superior to anything that had been seen before, and the smiths of Tubal, "Tubal-cain," might well have entered legend as the founders of metallurgy.

Nevertheless, during the Exilic period, some clearly Hebrew meaning for the word was sought for and found in the similarity of *kayin* to *kanah*, meaning "to get." Eve was therefore made to say "I have gotten a man of the Lord" and to name her son something that was reminiscent of her first words on learning of his birth. Thus, the etymology was set.

Cain and Abel seem to represent the farmer and the herdsman (or nomad) respectively. The early histories are written from the standpoint of the farmers, the settled city-men, and in them the nomads are viewed as barbaric raiders, ruthless and bloodthirsty.

It was the farmers who multiplied, however, and it was civilization that spread. Nomads could triumph when internal dissensions weakened the city-men, but in the long run, civilization had the men, organization, and the intricate weapons that could be produced in quantity only by an elaborate technology. (Cain was not only a farmer, he was also a smith.)

In the end, civilization won completely, and that eventual and inevitable victory must have been foreseen long before it came to pass. The tale (briefly and obscurely told) of how Cain grew jealous of Abel and killed him may be, in part, a remnant of some nomadic lament over the all-encroaching tentacles of settled civilization.

In fact, the very name Abel ("Hebel" in Hebrew) means "a puff of air," seeming to imply the briefness and instability of the nomadic way of life against the steady push of the farmer. (We experienced a similar period in American history toward the end of the nineteenth century when the nomadic "cowboy" of the West had to give way, at last, to the plodding farmer and his barbed-wire fences.)

The name Abel may also be related to the Babylonian *aplu*, meaning "son." This would indicate a possible Sumerian origin for the tale.

Nod

After Cain murders Abel, he is driven away:

Genesis 4:16. *And Cain went out from the presence of the Lord, and dwelt in the land of Nod, on the east of Eden.*

No one has tried to identify the "land of Nod" with any actual specific region and it is usually taken to be a metaphorical expression. The Hebrew word "Nod" is related to the term meaning "wanderer"; therefore to dwell in the land of Nod is taken to mean that one takes up a wandering life and becomes a nomad.

Here we seem to have a second strand incorporated into the ancient tale. Now we are dealing not with Cain the farmer and smith, but with Cain the nomad.

If Eden is taken to be Sumeria, then the region "east of Eden" would be that known as Elam. Elam, in what is now southwestern Iran,

Perhaps this is a dim reference to the ancient transition of a pastoral Elam to the ways of civilization. There is no record of any city named Enoch, but it is conceivable that this might be the city that eventually became known to later history as Susa. This dates back to the Stone Age and for thousands of years was the chief city of Elam.

The remainder of the fourth chapter deals quickly with the succeeding descendants of Cain, including Tubal-cain. The book of Genesis then returns to Adam to follow the line of descent that leads to the Israelites.

Seth

Adam has a third son:

Genesis 5:3. *And Adam lived an hundred and thirty years, and begat a son . . . and called his name Seth.*

This chapter is a portion of P again, and as generation after generation is given, the statistical data is carefully included. The age of each individual is given at the time of the birth of his first son, and at the time of his death.

Genesis 5:5. *And all the days that Adam lived were nine hundred and thirty years: and he died.*

These ages were legendary, reflecting parts of earlier Babylonian tales picked up by the Jews during the Exile and modified by the priesthood according to some unknown principle of their own. Nevertheless, those who feel every word of the Bible to be literally true have tried to make use of these figures (and of others given here and there in the Bible) to calculate the year in which Adam was born, and the universe created.

The Jews of the Middle Ages calculated the date of the creation to have been October 7, 3761 B.C., and this is still used in calculating the number of the year in the Jewish calendar. Thus, September 1968 A.D. is the beginning of the year 5729 by that calendar.

Christian theologians have come up with a variety of dates for the eation. The most familiar of these is one worked out by James Ussher, Anglican archbishop of Armagh, Ireland. In 1654, he decided that creation had taken place in 4004 B.C. (at 9 A.M. of October 23 of ..at year, according to some). The date 4004 B.C. is often found at the head of the first pages of the Bible in editions of the King James version.

Actually 4004 B.C. isn't a bad date for the establishment of historic times. Man began to have a history in the proper sense only after writing had been invented, and writing was invented a little before 3000 B.C. However, the first cities had been organizd as early as 8000 B.C. and prehistoric man (or creatures recognizably similar to man) have left remains that are well over a million years old.

The earth itself is some five billion years old and the universe as a whole perhaps fifteen billion years old.

Enoch [of Seth]

The descendants of Adam, through Seth, are then listed through eight generations (ten, counting Adam and Seth themselves) somewhat less hastily than those of Cain were mentioned. As a group, these are the antediluvian patriarchs. (A patriarch is the head of a tribe and by "antediluvian" is meant "before the Flood.")

The names of the line of Seth are suspiciously like those of the line of Cain, however. Both include an Enoch and a Lamech, and other names, if not identical, are very similar. It is possible that the two lines represent the same legendary material, one given by J and the other by P.

The antediluvian patriarchs are notable for their ages. Several, including Adam himself, lived nearly a thousand years. The record holder is Methuselah (whose name has become a byword for age) who attained the age of 969 years.

These patriarchs cannot be associated with any historical personages and nothing is known of them beyond this bare Biblical mention. They seem, however, to be a reflection of Sumerian legend. At least, the Sumerians had lists of nine or ten kings who reigned before the Flood, each of them living for many thousands of years. One was listed as having reigned nearly 65,000 years. The writer of this portion of Genesis, far from imposing on credibility by making use of extended life spans, apparently took legendary material and did his best to cut those ages down to reasonable size.

What's more, throughout the Hexateuch, the writers kept steadily reducing the ages attained by the chief figures in the tales though even at the end these were still boasting life spans somewhat in excess of a hundred years.

Of the antediluvian patriarchs, one attains an age markedly different from the others. This is Enoch, the father of Methuselah.

Genesis 5:23. *And all the days of Enoch were three hundred sixty and five years:*

Genesis 5:24. *And Enoch walked with God: and he was not; for God took him.*

The fact that Enoch is described as living 365 years, whereas his father Jared lived 962 years and his son Methuselah lived 969 years, seems odd. Is it a coincidence that there are 365 days in a year; that is, in the complete circuit of the sun across the skies? Is it possible that the verses given over to Enoch are all that remains of some Babylonian sun myth?

What is meant by saying that Enoch walked with God and was not is uncertain, but later traditions made it clear that the usual interpretation was that he was taken up alive into heaven as a reward for unusual piety.

It was supposed by the Jews of post-Exilic times that in heaven, Enoch was able to see the past and future of mankind. Between 200 B.C. and 50 B.C., several books were written purporting to have come from the pen of Enoch, describing this past and future. They are purely legendary and are a form of "religious fiction" which was fairly common in the post-Exilic period. (Some of it, as we shall see, found its way into the Bible.)

The books attributed to Enoch did not gain entry into the Bible, but there is a mention of them in the New Testament. In the Epistle of Jude, the writer says:

> Jude 1:14. *And Enoch also, the seventh from Adam, prophesied of these . . .*

Ararat

If one adds up the ages of the antediluvian patriarchs at the time of the births of their respective sons, one finds that Noah, the great-great-great-great-great-great-great-great-grandson of Adam was born 1056 years after the creation or (accepting Ussher's figures) about 3000 B.C. When he was six hundred years old, that is, about 2400 B.C., there came the Flood.

This, according to the Bible, was a world-wide deluge, but there is no record of any such phenomenon, of course. The Egyptian civilization, for instance, was in a particularly flourishing state at this very time and was building its pyramids. Nor do the Egyptian records speak of any floods other than the annual overflow of the Nile, as far as we know.

This is not to say, however, that the Biblical story of the Flood was not based on some actual, but local, flood in Sumerian history.

Sumeria was a flat land between two large rivers. As is true of any large river (we have only to think of our own Missouri and Mississippi) unusual rises will bring about flooding conditions. In a country as flat as Sumeria, it would not take much of a flood to cover large portions of the entire region.

A particularly bad flood would live on in the memory of later generations, and particularly bad floods undoubtedly occurred. In 1929, the English archaeologist Sir Charles Leonard Woolley reported finding water-deposited layers as much as ten feet thick in his excavations near the Euphrates. Such deposits were not found everywhere in the region and Sumerian culture showed no over-all break. Nevertheless, the evidence exists that somewhere about 3000 B.C. there were indeed drastic floods of at least a local nature.

With time, as the story is told and retold it is dramatically inevitable that a flood which spreads out over parts of Sumeria and neighboring regions with great loss of life will be said to have covered "all the world," meaning the entire region. It is further inevitable that later genera-

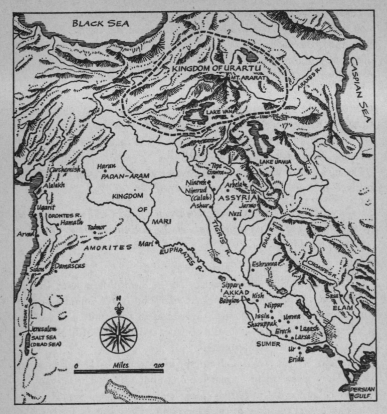

The Flood and the Kingdom of Urartu (Ararat)

tions, with a much broader knowledge of geography, would accept the phrase "all the world" literally and reduce themselves to needless speculations on the impossible.

(A well-known example of this is the statement frequently met with among the ancient historians that Alexander the Great "conquered the world" and then wept for "other worlds to conquer." What was meant was merely that Alexander had conquered a large part of those sections of the world which were well known to the Greeks of the time. Actually, Alexander conquered only 4 or 5 per cent of the earth's land surface and had plenty of room in which to extend those conquests.)

The people of Sumeria and of Akkadia (lying to the northwest of

Sumeria) told and retold the tale of one particular flood, which may have been produced by unusually heavy rains on the region. Some people suspect the flood to have been too serious to be accounted for by rain alone and think there may have been a sudden rise in the water level of the Persian Gulf, leading to a disastrous influx from the sea.

It has occurred to me recently that a possible explanation for such an invasion of the sea would be the unlucky strike of a large meteorite in the nearly landlocked Persian Gulf. The splash that would result would take the form of a huge wave that might move inland catastrophically, sweeping away everything in its path.

The invasion of water from the sea (for whatever reason) is, indeed, involved in the Biblical description of the Flood:

> Genesis 7:11. *In the six hundredth year of Noah's life . . . were all the fountains of the great deep broken up, and the windows of heaven were opened.*

A tidal wave plus rain, in other words.

In 1872, an English archaeologist, George Smith, deciphered ancient tablets from the remains of a royal Assyrian library and found a description of a flood in which one man saves himself, his family, and samples of animal life on board a ship. The story is based on still older tales dating back to Sumerian times.

The hero of this tale is Gilgamesh, king of the Akkadian town of Erech. He is in search of eternal life and finds Ut-Napishtim, who has the secret. Ut-Napishtim tell his story. It appears that he was king of a Sumerian city at the time of the Flood and rode it out in a large ship. Gilgamesh obtained the secret of eternal life from him, nearly obtained the necessary conditions, and through misadventure lost it.

The details of this Sumerian flood story are very similar in a number of points to the story in the Bible. It seems quite likely that the Biblical story of the Flood is a version of this much earlier tale.

In the Biblical story, Noah's ark floats on the floodwaters for months. The waters slowly recede—

> Genesis 8:4. *And the ark rested . . . upon the mountains of Ararat.*

Notice that a specific mountain peak is not named. There is no mention of a "Mount Ararat." Instead the Bible clearly states "the mountains of Ararat," implying Ararat to be a region or nation within which there was a mountain range on which the ark came to rest. The Anchor Bible translates the phrase as "the Ararat range."

If further Biblical evidence is needed that Ararat is a region and not a mountain, it can be found in the fifty-first chapter of Jeremiah. The prophet is reporting God's promise to destroy Babylon, which at that time was on the point of conquering Judah:

> Jeremiah 51:27 . . . *call together against her* [Babylon] *the kingdoms of Ararat, Minni, and Ashchenaz . . .*

But where and what was Ararat? Remember that in searching for it one must consider geography as it was known to those who reduced Genesis to writing and not necessarily as it was known in the time of the Sumero-Akkadians.

In Assyrian times there was a kingdom among the mountains in which the Tigris and Euphrates rose, in what is now eastern Turkey. It centered about Lake Van (a salt lake about the size and shape of our own Great Salt Lake) and is sometimes called the "kingdom of Van" in consequence. This kingdom extended from the lake to the Caucasus Mountains, and in Assyrian inscriptions is referred to as the kingdom of Urartu—of which name Ararat is clearly a version.

The kingdom of Urartu was greatly weakened by Assyrian attack and by 612 B.C. it had ceased to exist, at a time when Assyria itself was also being destroyed. In the area in which it had existed, new tribesmen arrived and a new name (of Persian origin) was given to the land, which became Armenia.

In those sections of the Bible which were reduced to writing after the end of Urartu, the term Armenia is used instead. Thus, in the Second Book of Kings, there is the tale of the assassination of the Assyrian king, Sennacherib, by his two sons, in 681 B.C., and of their rapid flight thereafter:

> 2 Kings 19:37. . . . *and they escaped into the land of Armenia . . .*

What is really meant, of course, is Urartu, since Armenia did not yet exist, and in the Revised Standard Version, the phrase is indeed changed to "the land of Ararat."

The tradition that the ark came to rest in Ararat some six hundred miles northwest of Sumeria again speaks in favor of the tidal-wave theory of the Flood. Ordinary river flooding would sweep floating objects downstream—southeastward into the Persian Gulf. A huge tidal wave would sweep them upstream—northwestward toward Ararat.

Despite all evidence, most people insist on thinking of Ararat as the name of a definite mountain peak and indeed the name Ararat was eventually applied to one. Mount Ararat is a mountain in the eastern-most region of Turkey about seventy miles northeast of Lake Van. It has two peaks, Great Ararat and Little Ararat, the former being the higher, reaching 16,873 feet (3.2 miles) above sea level. The tradition remains firmly fixed that Noah's ark came to rest somewhere on Great Ararat and every once in a while there are expeditions there to find traces of it.

Ham

Once the Flood story is done, the writers of Genesis turn to the task of giving the names of the descendants of Noah. These, in almost every case, represent tribes or nations. It was common for ancient tribes to call themselves after the name of an ancestor (real or mythical). In fact, if a tribe was known by some name, it was assumed that it was because the members were descended from an ancestor of that name. (An ancestor from whom a tribe receives its name is an eponym of that tribe.)

Related tribes could be described as descending from eponyms who were brothers, and whose father was a still broader eponym. The Greeks, for instance, called themselves Hellenes and recognized them-selves to exist as groups of related tribes called Aeolians, Dorians, Achaeans, and Ionians. They therefore supposed themselves all to be descended from a man named Hellen. Hellen was described as having two sons named Aeolus and Dorus, and a third son, Xuthus, who had twin sons named Ion and Achaeus.

In this spirit, the Book of Genesis describes the immediate descend-ants of Noah:

> Genesis 9:18. *And the sons of Noah . . . were Shem, and Ham, and Japheth: and Ham is the father of Canaan.*

The three sons of Noah represent the three great divisions of the peo-ples known to the ancient writers of the Bible.

In general, the descendants of Shem are pictured as occupying the Arabian peninsula and the regions adjoining it to the north, including the Tigris-Euphrates region, which is the center of interest in the early

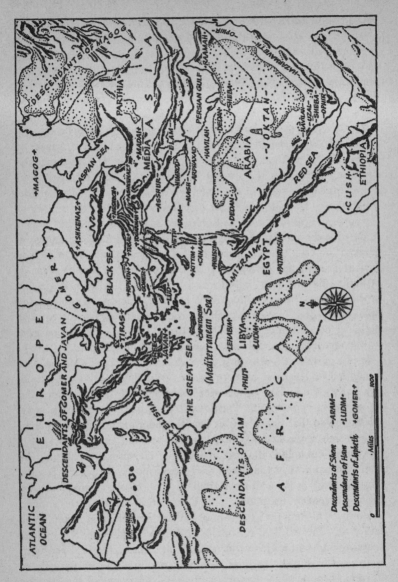

The Hamites

portions of Genesis. Since this includes the Hebrews themselves, Shem is given the post of honor and is made the eldest son of Noah. At least, he is mentioned first.

It is for this reason that the languages of the people dwelling in this region are referred to as "Semitic." ("Sem" is the Graeco-Latin form of Shem.) These languages include Hebrew, Assyrian, Aramaean, and, as the most important living example, Arabic.

The descendants of Ham are described as inhabiting chiefly the corner of Africa adjacent to Asia. For this reason the original languages of the peoples of northeastern Africa are called "Hamitic." This includes Coptic (derived from the ancient Egyptian), the Berber languages of North Africa, and some of the languages of Ethiopia, such as Amharic.

The descendants of Japheth are described as inhabiting the regions to the north and east of the Tigris-Euphrates. Sometimes "Japhetic" is used to describe certain obscure languages in the northern mountainous regions of the Caucasus. Occasionally, it is used more broadly to include ancient Persian, for example. Since the language of the Persians is related to those spoken in India and in Europe, this book is (in the broader sense) being written in a Japhetic language. However, the importance of Europe is such (modern students of comparative philology being European in culture) that the broad classification gave way to the more geographically intelligible "Indo-European."

It is a mistake, though, to suppose that the writers of Genesis were influenced by language. Modern notions of philology are strictly modern. Rather, the Biblical writers were guided by political connections and by geographic propinquity. Such connections often did bespeak racial relatedness so that terms such as Semitic and Hamitic did turn out to make much sense, linguistically, but this was not true in every case.

A prime example is the case of Canaan. The people inhabiting the land (Canaanites) at the time the Hebrews moved in spoke a Semitic language and had a culture related to that of the Tigris-Euphrates region. By modern terminology, the Canaanites were distinctly Semites.

However, Genesis 9:18 goes out of its way to specify that "Ham is the father of Canaan." The reason for that is a simple one. Some three centuries prior to the Hebrew occupation of Canaan, the land had been conquered by Egyptian armies and for a long time formed part of the Egyptian Empire. Since Egypt was the most important of the Hamitic nations it seemed reasonable, according to the standards of the time, to describe Canaan as a son of Ham.

The end of the ninth chapter of Genesis relates a tradition in which

Noah, offended by his second son, Ham, curses him and condemns him and his son, Canaan, to servitude to his brothers. This reflects the fact that at the time Genesis was being reduced to writing, the Canaanites were indeed reduced to servitude to the Israelites, who were descendants of Shem.

Some moderns seem to think that Ham represents the Negro peoples and that this chapter can be used to justify Negro slavery. This is the purest piffle. Neither Ham, Canaan, nor any of their named descendants were viewed as Negroes by the Biblical writers.

Japheth

The Greeks, it seems, must be considered—in Biblical terms—to be among the descendants of Japheth. The writers of Genesis may even in this respect have been influenced by Greek traditions, reaching them dimly from the west.

For instance, Japheth himself has been identified by some with the Titan Iapetus in the Greek myths. (Since the initial "J" in Hebrew names is pronounced like a "Y" in Hebrew, as is the initial "I" in Greek names, the similarity between Japheth and Iapetus is greater than it appears to be in print.) According to the Greek myths, Iapetus was the father of Prometheus who, in turn, fathered the human race by molding them out of clay. For this reason, Iapetus was considered by the Greeks to be the ancestor of mankind; and, to the Hebrews, Japheth was the ancestor of that portion of mankind to which the Greeks belonged.

The sons and grandsons of Japheth are listed in the tenth chapter of Genesis:

Genesis 10:2. *The sons of Japheth; Gomer, and Magog, and Madai, and Javan, and Tubal, and Meshech, and Tiras.*

Genesis 10:3. *And the sons of Gomer; Ashkenaz, and Riphath, and Togarmah.*

Genesis 10:4. *And the sons of Javan; Elishah, and Tarshish, Kittim, and Dodanim.*

We must remember that such genealogies reflect the geographic and political situation of the Assyrian period, when the various parts of Genesis were reduced to writing.

Of the sons of Japheth, Gomer seems to be identical with the people who, in Assyrian inscriptions, were the "Gimirrai" and these in turn were the people known in Latin spelling as the Cimmerians. In earlier times they lived north of the Black Sea but in the seventh century B.C., pushed on by new bands of barbarians in the rear, they invaded Asia Minor and met the Assyrians there in earth-shaking battles. They were eventually defeated, to be ours, but Assyria was badly wounded in the process. The Cimmerians would certainly be in prominent view at the time the tenth chapter was being written and their eponym, Gomer, would, very reasonably, be viewed as the first-born of Japheth.

As for Magog, that may represent "the land of Gog" where Gog is the ruler known to us from the Greek historians as Gyges. He was king of the Lydians, a people in western Asia Minor, and was one of the important adversaries of the invading Cimmerians. In fact, he died in battle against them about 652 B.C.

Madai is supposed to refer to the Medes, who inhabited the territory east of Assyria, and who were soon to be among the final conquerors of Assyria. Tubal, Meshech, and Tiras are all thought to represent minor tribes of Asia Minor. The name Tiras bears some similarities to the Greek "Tyrsenoi," which was applied to a people who, it was thought, dwelt originally in Asia Minor but migrated to Italy. If so, Tiras could represent the Etruscans.

The most interesting of the sons of Japheth is Javan. This name is almost certainly identical with an archaic form of the Greek "Ion," who was the eponym of the Ionian Greeks. The Ionians had, about 1000 B.C., migrated eastward to occupy the islands of the Aegean Sea and the coasts of Asia Minor. Of the various Greek tribes they were the nearest to Canaan and would be best known to the Israelites of Assyrian times. Their tribal name would be naturally applied to the Greeks generally.

Of Gomer's sons, Ashkenaz may be identical with the name "Ashguza" found among Assyrian inscriptions. This seems to refer to the peoples known to the Greeks, and therefore to ourselves, as the Scythians. The Scythians were nomadic tribes who entered Europe from somewhere in central Asia some time before 1000 B.C. It was their pressure southward against the Cimmerians that drove the Cimmerians into Asia Minor. The Scythians took their place in the steppelands north of the Black Sea, and from that standpoint, Ashkenaz (Scythia) might well be considered the eldest son of Gomer (Cimmeria).

For some reason, the later Jews viewed Ashkenaz as the ancestor of the Teutonic people. For this reason German-speaking Jews were called "Ashkenazim" as contrasted with the Spanish-speaking "Sephardim."

It would be expected that the sons of Javan listed in Genesis 10:4 would refer to those Greek-speaking regions closest to Israel. Elishah seems to be similar to the "Alashiyah" found in Assyrian documents and this refers to the island of Cyprus. This had already been colonized by Greeks in Assyrian times, and it was the closest of all Greek-speaking lands to Canaan, being only two hundred miles to the northeast.

Indeed, Cyprus is mentioned twice, for Kittim surely represents Kition (Citium in Latin), a city on the southern coast of the island, the name of which was often used for the entire island.

Dodanim is widely thought to be a misprint for Rodanim; in fact, it is given as Rodanim in some early copies of the Bible. If the name is Rodanim then it is tempting to equate it with the island of Rhodes, two hundred miles west of Cyprus.

Tarshish, on the basis of references later in the Bible, is usually taken to represent a city in Spain. However, it occurs to me that in this one instance, it might represent Tarsus, an important Greek town, a hundred miles north of Cyprus, on the southern coast of Asia Minor. It was an important city in Assyrian times and might represent the Greeks of Asia Minor generally.

Cush

The most notable confusion in this tenth chapter, describing the nations of the Near East, occurs in connection with Cush, which I said earlier (see page 29) could be used to represent the Ethiopians, south of Egypt, and also the Kossaeans, east of the Tigris.

Genesis 10:6. And the sons of Ham; Cush, and Mizraim, and Phut, and Canaan.

Genesis 10:7. And the sons of Cush; Seba, and Havilah . . .

In Genesis 10:6, Cush clearly means the Ethiopians, south of Egypt, who, indeed, speak a Hamitic tongue. Phut (better, "Put," as given in the Revised Standard Version) is usually thought to represent the peoples west of Egypt whom the Greeks called Libyans. These also spoke a Hamitic language.

Mizraim is the Hebrew word for "Egypt," so he is the eponym of that nation. Wherever else it occurs in the Bible, Mizraim is translated into "Egypt" (a term of Greek origin). If such translations were done here, the verse might read: "And the sons of Ham; Ethiopia, and Egypt, and Libya, and Canaan," which would accurately reflect the area dominated by Egypt in the days of her greatness.

In the very next verse, however, Cush is described as the father of Seba, Havilah, and a series of other sons, all of whom are clearly eponyms of Arabian tribes. This Cush must be the one representing the Kossaeans, and not the Hamitic Cush of Ethiopia.

Nimrod

This confusion of Cushes leads to a section of obviously Semitic ethnology being included under Ham:

> Genesis 10:8. And [the Semitic] Cush begat Nimrod: he began to be a mighty one in the earth.
> Genesis 10:9. He was a mighty hunter . . .
> Genesis 10:10. And the beginning of his kingdom was Babel, and Erech, and Accad, and Calneh, in the land of Shinar.
> Genesis 10:11. Out of that land went forth Asshur, and builded Nineveh, and the city Rehoboth, and Calah,
> Genesis 10:12. And Resen between Nineveh and Calah . . .

Nimrod is the only name in Chapter 10 of Genesis who is clearly an individual and not an eponym. Who, then, is Nimrod? Can he be identified at all and equated with any historic personage? Or is he lost forever in the primeval mists?

There is no question but that whoever he was, he is described as ruling over the Tigris-Euphrates region, for that is where all the cities named are known (where they are known at all) to have been located. Furthermore the "land of Shinar" is accepted as being the Biblical term used for what we would call "Sumeria."

Genesis 10:10 appears, then, to make Nimrod an important king of the Tigris-Euphrates region, with his power based on the four cities

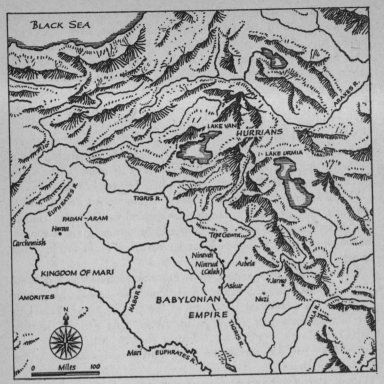

The Empire of Nimrod

of Babel, Erech, Accad, and Calneh. The location of Calneh is unknown and there is general agreement now that its inclusion is an error and that the word is not the name of a city but is Hebrew for "all of them." The verse is made to read in the Revised Standard Version: "The beginning of his kingdom was Babel, Erech, and Accad, all of them in the land of Shinar."

The three cities that remain are no mystery. Erech corresponds to the city known as "Uruk" in the ancient inscriptions of the region. The city was first excavated in the 1850's and showed every sign of having once been an extensive metropolis, with large temples and a library. It dates back to 3600 B.C. at least. It was located on the Euphrates River about forty miles from its ancient mouth. The Euphrates River has since changed its course somewhat and the ruins of Erech are now several miles east of the present course of the river.

The mythical Gilgamesh (see page 40) was king of this city and this city was also ruled by a historical conqueror. This was Lugal-Zaggisi, king of Erech, who ruled shortly after 2300 B.C. He conquered other Sumerian city-states and was the first individual we know of to govern a sizable empire in the Tigris-Euphrates. His realm may even have reached the Mediterranean. His triumph was short-lived, however, thanks to another conqueror, associated with Accad, the second of the cities mentioned in Genesis 10:10.

Accad, or Akkad, is, in the ancient inscriptions, Agade. Its exact site is unknown but it was probably also on the Euphrates, about 140 miles upstream from Erech. The city gave its name to the upper portion of the Tigris-Euphrates region, which became known as Akkad.

The Akkadians who inhabited these upstream regions were not identical with the Sumerians, although they adopted the Sumerian culture. The Akkadians spoke a Semitic language, for instance, while the Sumerian language was non-Semitic (and, indeed, had no known linguistic affiliations).

The Akkadians were at first under Sumerian domination but about 2280 B.C., a man named Sharrukin ("righteous king" in Akkadian) came to power and established his capital in the city of Agade. That king has become Sargon of Agade to us. About 2264 B.C., he defeated Lugal-Zaggisi and founded an Akkadian Empire. Sargon's grandson, Naram-Sin, extended the empire even farther and about 2180 B.C. it was at its height.

About 2150 B.C., however, soon after Naram-Sin's death, barbarians from the eastern mountains invaded and conquered the Tigris-Euphrates region and brought the Akkadian Empire to an end. After a century of barbarian domination, the Sumerians won their freedom and, about 2000 B.C., experienced a last period of power. After that, the remaining city mentioned in Genesis 10:10 comes in.

The town of Babel was located on the Euphrates River about 40 miles downstream from Agade. It existed as a small and unremarkable place for over a thousand years while the Sumerian city-states still further downstream flourished and the Akkadian Empire rose and fell.

While the Sumerians were in their final period of glory, however, another group of peoples from the middle Euphrates, the Amorites, seized control of Babel about 1900 B.C., and made it the capital of an expanding empire.

Under the sixth king of the Amorite dynasty, Hammurabi, who reigned about 1700 B.C., Babel became a world metropolis and remained so for two thousand years, despite the fact that it was frequently conquered and ravished. Indeed, it was the glamor city of the East throughout Old Testament times and is best known to us by the Greek version of its name—Babylon. The entire Tigris-Euphrates region is commonly known as Babylonia after this city.

Under Amorite domination, the Sumerians finally broke and declined rapidly, losing their identity, though their culture remained to be inherited and elaborated by conqueror after conqueror. The language died out as a living vehicle for communication but remained as part of religious liturgy (like Latin in the modern Catholic Church) for some 1500 years, not dying out completely till 300 B.C.

The Amorites did not long survive the glories of Hammurabi. About 1670 B.C. the Kassites or Kossaeans invaded Babylonia from the East and established a "dark age" that lasted for nearly five hundred years.

With southern Babylonia thus in eclipse, the cities of the far northern reaches of the river valley had their chance to gain prominence. Whereas Genesis 10:10 concerns itself with southern Babylonia, verse 10:11 turns to the north.

The King James Version begins the verse by saying "Out of that land went forth Asshur." This is now generally accepted as a mistranslation of the Hebrew. The Revised Standard Version has the verse begin: "Out of that land he [Nimrod] went forth into Asshur."

Asshur is the region along the upper courses of the Tigris River, in what is now northern Iraq. The town of Asshur (or Ashur), which gave its name to the region, was located on the Tigris River about 230 miles north of Babylon and was founded (by Sumerian colonists, perhaps) as early as 2700 B.C. Asshur is far better known by the Greek version of its name—Assyria.

Assyria was part of the Akkadian Empire and then later part of the Amorite Empire. The Assyrian inhabitants of that region, however, maintained their identity and had periods of great prosperity. The capital of the region was moved from Ashur to cities further upstream on the Tigris, first to Calah, then finally to Nineveh. (The site of the town of Resen, described in verse 10:12 as lying between these two cities, is not known, but the word, like "Calneh," may not signify a town at all.)

The turning point in Assyrian history may have come during the reign of Shalmaneser I, about 1250 B.C. He is reputed to have built Calah and he may have witnessed the introduction into Assyria of the art of smelting iron from Asia Minor, where it seems to have been developed.

The use of iron weapons gives an army a great advantage over one that is armed only with bronze weapons. Iron can be made harder than bronze and iron edges are sharper and less easily blunted. Shalmaneser's son, Tukulti-Ninurta I, used his iron-armed warriors to make himself the first of Assyria's conquering monarchs.

Despite occasional setbacks, Assyria grew stronger and stronger, displaced the Kassites, and established their rule over all of Babylonia, then spread far beyond. By the time the traditions of Genesis were being reduced to writing, Assyria was the most powerful nation the world had yet seen.

It would appear, then, that the verses 10:8–12 are a brief résumé of 2500 years of the history of the Tigris-Euphrates region, from the period of the Sumerian city-states, through the Akkadian Empire, the Amorite Empire, and, finally, the Assyrian Empire.

And where in this long history are we to find Nimrod?

The Biblical passage concerning him seems to telescope the deeds of Lugal-Zaggisi, Sargon of Agade, Hammurabi, and Shalmaneser I (and perhaps even Gilgamesh) and to make his single person reflect the greatness of the Sumerians, Akkadians, Amorites, and Assyrians.

And yet to the writers of Genesis, the Assyrians were the latest and greatest of the empires of the Tigris-Euphrates and their glory tended to dim the memory of what had gone before. To the first conquering king of Assyria might then go the credit not only for establishing Assyrian might, but of performing all the deeds of the preceding kingdoms as well. (It is as though a child receiving some garbled notice of America's early history but understanding full well that George Washington was the first President of the United States would then write: "George Washington crossed the Atlantic Ocean in the Mayflower, discovered America, conquered Mexico, built Washington, D.C., and became first President of the United States.")

The first Assyrian conqueror of note was, as I have said, Tukulti-Ninurta I. It seems very likely that he served as the original inspiration for the Greek legend of Ninus. ("Ninurta" with a few letters dropped and the Greek final -s, almost invariably used in their own names, becomes "Ninus.") In the Greek legend, Ninus singlehandedly founds Nineveh, conquers all of Babylonia and Armenia (Urartu), and the nomadic regions to the east as well, founding the Assyrian Empire.

It seems quite possible that, in analogous fashion, "Ninurta" became "Nimrod" to the editors of Genesis. Indeed, the short picture of Nimrod in these few Biblical verses seems to point to an Assyrian monarch in particular. Assyrian art was powerful and cruel and one of the favorite objects of portrayal was that of the Assyrian kings in pursuit of big game. Hunting was undoubtedly a favorite and well-publicized sport of those monarchs and this is undoubtedly the reason for describing Nimrod as "a mighty hunter."

Then, too, the Assyrians succeeded the Kassites (Cush) as the dominant power in Babylonia, which makes it natural to have Nimrod described as the son of Cush.

Aram

With Nimrod out of the way, the writers of Genesis go on to complete the genealogy of Ham, by giving the descendants of Ham's sons, Mizraim [Egypt] and Canaan. Some of these have no particular interest and others will be more conveniently dealt with later.

Genesis then goes on to discuss the line of Shem:

Genesis 10:22. *The children of Shem; Elam, and Asshur, and Arphaxad, and Lud, and Aram.*

. . . .

Genesis 10:24. *And Arphaxad begat Salah; and Salah begat Eber.*

The first two sons of Shem are Elam and Asshur, the eponyms of the Elamites and the Assyrians, which at the time that Genesis was reduced to writing were the most powerful nations of the "Semitic" world. I put "Semitic" in quotes because actually Elam was not Semitic in the modern sense; its language being of uncertain affiliation, and certainly not Semitic. However, its propinquity to Semitic Babylonia and Assyria and its long connection with both (if only through perennial war) fulfilled the Biblical criterion of the word. Almost to the very end of the Assyrian period, Elam was the great unconquered adversary of Assyria, so that it deserved being listed as an independent son of Shem. And since it was clearly the more ancient it deserved being listed as the eldest.

The other three sons of Shem might conceivably represent other areas at the borders of the Assyrian Empire, still unconquered in the eighth century B.C.

Aram is clearly the eponym of the Aramaean tribes. These emerged from northern Arabia about the twelfth century B.C., and infiltrated the fertile regions round about. Aramaean raids helped weaken the Assyrian Empire after its first round of conquests under Tukulti-Ninurta I, and Tiglath-Pileser I, the latter of whom died about 1100 B.C. For two centuries thereafter, the Assyrian Empire remained almost in a state of suspended animation, Western Asia was given a respite and smaller states were allowed to establish themselves.

Even when the Assyrian Empire had recovered and, after 900 B.C., began expanding again, an independent Aramaean kingdom nevertheless maintained itself north of Canaan until 732 B.C. To the writers of Genesis, then, it deserved notice as an independent son of Shem.

Lud is much more controversial. The similarity of sound gives rise to the thought that Lud is the eponym of Lydia, already mentioned in connection with Magog (see page 46). Lydia, in western Asia Minor, maintained its independence against Assyria although it paid tribute at times.

That leaves the two small kingdoms of Israel and Judah, which, at the time that Genesis was reduced to writing, also maintained a precarious independence. Surely, since it was in Israel and Judah that the two chief strands of Genesis were compiled, these would be noticed as independent sons of Shem.

In a way they were. Arphaxad (better, "Arpachsad," as the Revised Standard Version has it) is a complete puzzle linguistically and does not even seem to be a Semitic name. However, Genesis 10:24 states that Arphaxad was the grandfather of Eber and Eber is the eponym of the Hebrew people, which would include the inhabitants of both Israel and Judah (as well as certain other related peoples).

Babel

With the genealogies taken care of, the Book of Genesis goes on to relate one last tale centered about Babylonia.

While the descendants of Noah were still a relatively small group, all speaking a single language, they came to Shinar (Sumeria) and decided to build a huge tower there, with which to "reach unto Heaven."

However, God defeated their purpose by giving each man a different language, making it impossible for them to understand each other.

Unable to continue their complex building activities, they had to leave off, and this tale is used to explain the name of the city in which the tower was built:

Genesis 11:9. *Therefore is the name of it called Babel; because the Lord did there confound the language of all the earth* . . .

In other words, the writers of Genesis derived "Babel" from the Hebrew word *balal*, meaning "mixed," "confused," or "confounded." This derivation is, however, a false one, for in the Babylonian language, the name of the city is "Bab-ilu," meaning "gate of God." From this is derived the Hebrew "Babel" and the Greek "Babylon."

There was, as it happens, a tower in Babel; indeed, there were towers in most Sumerian and Babylonian cities. The temples to the gods in these cities took the form of stepped pyramids which were ascended by inclined planes about the outside. These were called ziggurats.

A large ziggurat in Babylon was begun by a Sumerian king and was left unfinished perhaps as a result of the disorders involved in the southward march of Sargon of Agade. For many centuries, the ziggurat remained incomplete and perhaps gained fame because of its shortcoming (as does the Leaning Tower of Pisa or Schubert's Unfinished Symphony). It served as the model, one might assume, for the Biblical tale of the unfinished tower in Babel.

However, in the sixth century B.C., Nebuchadnezzar, king of Babylon, finished the largest ziggurat ever built. It was formed in seven diminishing stages (one for each of the planets). The bottommost stage was 300 feet by 300 feet and the whole structure reared 325 feet into the air.

This would scarcely make a respectable skyscraper now, and it was much smaller than the tremendous pyramids built by the Egyptians. It was, however, the largest structure in southwestern Asia and, more remarkable still, it was what is now so familiar to us as the "tower of Babel"—finished at last.

Ur of the Chaldees

The eleventh chapter of Genesis concludes with a quick listing of the descendants of Shem and Arphaxad. Again the age of each postdiluvian patriarch is given at the time of the birth of the successor. The years he lived after this birth are also given. The total age given for these patriarchs gradually decreases. The age of Shem at the time of his death is given as 602 years (itself a fall-off from Methuselah's 969), but Terah, eight generations later, lives only 205 years, and his immediate descendants have lifetimes of less than 200 years.

If we add up the ages, it would seem that Abram, the son of Terah, was born 292 years after the Flood, or, roughly, 2100 B.C There is no way of checking this from any source outside the Bible, but it would better fit the dates of the later events of the Bible if his birth were placed a bit later in history—perhaps soon after 2000 B.C.

It is impossible, now, to tell whether Abram and his immediate descendants represent actual individuals or, as in the case of Nimrod, a telescoping of several. If we take the Biblical story at its face value, however, he is an individual and a well-depicted individual, too. Genesis makes him *sound* historical whether he is or not.

Abram (whose name was later altered to the now better-known Abraham) is the first of the patriarchs from whom the later Jews traced their descent not only physically but spiritually. The importance of Abraham over those that came before him, if we follow the Biblical story, was that he was the first to travel to Canaan and, according to legends which do not appear in the Bible, that he publicly abandoned the worship of idols and became a staunch monotheist. (The legends explain that his father, Terah, was a manufacturer of idols and that Abram broke them in anger.)

The tale of Abram begins in the Tigris-Euphrates region which has been the focus of the first eleven chapters of the Bible:

> Genesis 11:27. . . . *Terah begat Abram, Nahor, and Haran; and Haran begat Lot.*
> Genesis 11:28. *And Haran died before his father Terah in the land of his nativity, in Ur of the Chaldees.*

Ur, therefore, can be taken as the home of Abram's family, and the birthplace of Abram himself.

Ur was a Sumerian city, founded no later than 3500 B.C. and possibly much earlier. It was located on the right bank of the Euphrates River about 140 miles southeast of Babylon and right at what was then the coastline of the Persian Gulf. It was an important city in Sumerian days, a center of worship of the moon-god, Sin, possessor of an impres-

Ur of the Chaldees

sive ziggurat, and probably enriched by an important seagoing commerce, situated as it was on the seacoast.

About 2500 B.C., Ur experienced a period of considerable power under its "first dynasty." This, however, came to an end after two and a half centuries, when Ur fell under the triumphant armies of Lugal-Zaggisi and, later, Sargon of Agade.

The inhabitants and historians of Ur must have viewed these conquerors in a harshly unfavorable light. If it is true that Nimrod represents a dim memory of Lugal-Zaggisi and Sargon, among others, then it is interesting that in Jewish legend Nimrod is represented as king of Babylonia at the time of Abram's birth and is described as having sought, unsuccessfully, to kill Abram.

After the fall of the Akkadian Empire, Ur entered another period of greatness and commercial prosperity under its "third dynasty." This final period of Sumerian power lay between 2050 B.C. and 1950 B.C. and it was during that period that Abram was born.

Ur continued to exist throughout Old Testament times and it is mentioned in documents as late as 324 B.C. However, by the time Genesis was being reduced to writing, Ur was nothing but a decayed and obscure village. The writers of Genesis, in mentioning a town which, thanks to the birth of Abram there, was of surpassing interest to their readers, felt called upon to identify it somewhat. They therefore called it "Ur kasdim," which is translated as "Ur of the Chaldees" or, better, "Ur of the Chaldeans," as in the Revised Standard Version.

The Chaldeans were an Arabian tribe who pressed into Babylonia from the south, on the heels of the Aramaeans (see page 54), about 1150 B.C. It was not until nearly a thousand years after Abraham's time, then, that Ur really became part of the Chaldean territory. Nevertheless, during the Assyrian period, the Chaldeans were the most important tribal component of the Babylonian population, and "Ur of the Chaldees" was the most economical way of identifying the town, regardless of the anachronism of the phrase.

Haran

The period of Ur's prosperity was coming to an end during Abram's youth. The silting-up of the mouths of the Tigris and Euphrates meant that Ur could maintain its maritime prosperity only by constant labors. The continuing struggles among the Sumerian cities, however, sapped its energies and helped ruin Ur as a seaport. Furthermore, the rising might of the Amorite rulers of Babylon was gradually bringing all the Sumerian city-states to a common end.

It is not surprising, then, that Abram's family could see little future in remaining in Ur and left Sumeria altogether.

Genesis 11:31. . . . *they went forth . . . from Ur of the Chaldees . . . and they came unto Haran, and dwelt there.*

In doing this, the family was following the normal trade routes from Sumeria to the Mediterranean. The Mediterranean lies five hundred miles due west of Ur, but if one were to travel due west one would have to cross the northern reaches of the Arabian desert, and that would be impractical. Instead, one would follow the rivers to the northwest and then turn south, marking out a great crescent that would carry one over a distance of more than a thousand miles. The greater distance is made up for by the fact that one travels over fertile, settled territory and can rely on obtaining food and supplies for men and animals over the route. Indeed, the regions traversed by Abram make up what is familiarly termed "the Fertile Crescent."

Abram and his family stopped at Haran, at the northern peak of the crescent, and remained there for several years. Haran is located on the eastern bank of the Balikh River, which flows south into the upper Euphrates, sixty miles away. Haran is about 170 miles east of the northeastern corner of the Mediterranean and is located in what is now southeastern Turkey, just north of the Syrian border.

It was, in Abram's time, an important commercial center and therefore a good place to settle down, at least for a while, and catch one's breath. Like Ur, it was a center of the worship of the moon-god, Sin.

The Anchor Bible points out certain difficulties in accepting the phrase "Ur of the Chaldees" and wonders if it might not possibly be better given as "land of the Chaldees." In that case, Haran itself might be the place of birth of Abram's family, rather than Ur, and the two might have been confused through the common moon-worship.

Birth in Haran rather than Ur would make Abram an Aramaean (or at least the native of a region that later became Aramaean) rather than a Sumerian. This would square with the description in the Book of Deuteronomy of the ancestor of the Israelites, presumably Abraham.

In the Revised Standard Version, this reads: "A wandering Aramaean was my father."

It might seem at first glance that it is significant that Abram's younger brother, who had died early, was named Haran. It cannot be taken, however, that he could possibly have been named for the city, for the two names are alike only in English. In Hebrew, the name of the city does not really begin with the sound represented by out "H" but by that represented by the German "Ch."

But it is not likely that this view will win out. The birth of Abram at Ur is not only firmly embedded in tradition, but has its attractive features as well.

Ur is one of those places in which excavation reveals thicknesses of silt resulting from a severe flood. It may be that emigrants from Ur, with Abram prominent among them, brought tales of this flood to Canaan, where it entered the traditional story of early man and remained there. Other Sumerian legends, such as that of the garden of Eden, of Cain and Abel, of the tower of Babel, may also have arrived with them.

The city of Haran enters into history as more than merely a place of which one might say "Abram slept here." It is the site of three dramatic battles. It was an important bastion of the Assyrian Empire and when that empire fell, it was at Haran that its forces made their last stand—and were destroyed. To the Romans, Haran was known as Carrhae. There, in 53 B.C., a Roman army under Crassus was defeated by the Parthians, a crucial check to the expanding empire. In 296 A.D., the Roman Emperor Galerius was defeated there by the Persians in another dramatic battle.

Canaan

Abram's father, Terah, died in Haran, and it was time for Abram to move on.

> Genesis 12:5. *And Abram took Sarai his wife, and Lot his brother's son . . . and into the land of Canaan they came.*

Canaan is the name of that section of the Mediterranean coast of Asia that lies south of Asia Minor. The use of the name in that sense is found in Egyptian inscriptions dating back to 1800 B.C.

Canaan was the center of a late Stone Age civilization with distinct towns by 4000 B.C. By 3200 B.C., metalworking had been introduced and it entered the Bronze Age.

People speaking a Semitic language entered Canaan as early as 3000 B.C. and for the next thousand years, they benefited from contact with the expanding culture of the Tigris-Euphrates region and by renewed immigration. By the time of Abram's arrival, then, Canaan already had a long history of civilization and was occupied by a mixture of peoples, lumped together in the Bible as the "Canaanites."

Despite the Bible's characterization of Canaan as a son of Ham (see page 44) because of Egyptian domination of the land, most Canaanites not only spoke a Semitic language, they actually spoke Hebrew. The Israelites who eventually conquered the land spoke or adopted the language of the people they overcame but—and this is the essence of Israel's importance in history—made and, in the end, held to their own values in religion.

Egypt

While Abraham had gone on a thousand-mile journey, he had, in a sense, never left home, for the culture that had originated in Sumeria filled all the Fertile Crescent in his day. Canaan, however, represented the western limit of that culture. When Abram traveled southwestward out of Canaan, he emerged into a new world altogether.

Genesis 12:10. *And there was a famine in the land* [Canaan]: *and Abram went down into Egypt to sojourn there . . .*

This was natural enough, for Egypt depended upon the annual flooding of the Nile for its fertility and this rarely failed. Consequently the famines that plagued semi-arid lands whenever the rainfall dipped below normal usually left Egypt untouched.

Egypt shares with Sumeria the honor of being the earliest home of human civilization. By 3000 B.C., civilization was well advanced, writing had been developed (borrowed from Sumeria, most likely), art and literature flourished.

Egypt benefited by its location. In all directions it was isolated by desert or by sea and it could develop its own way without interference. Whereas western Asia saw a succession of different cities or tribes rise

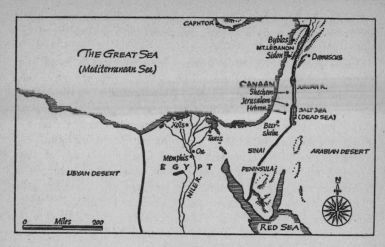

The Egyptian Kingdom

to dominance and fall to ruin, with prosperity and disaster alternating, Egyptian history was comparatively calm.

On the other hand, Egypt suffered in its earliest age from that same geography. Egypt is a long, thin nation, a veritable thread of a country. Only the immediate banks of the Nile receive the life-giving water of the flood and the Egyptians found themselves cultivating some 550 miles of riverside with an average width of just about twelve miles. This linearity and lack of regional compactness meant that the country naturally broke itself into isolated fragments.

Toward the end of the fourth millennium B.C. these had coalesced into two portions. In the north, where the Nile approached the Mediterranean, it built up a delta (as the Tigris and Euphrates did) and into this delta the Nile poured, breaking up into a series of sluggish streams that fertilized an area in the rough shape of an equilateral triangle about one hundred miles on each side. (The Greek letter "delta" in its capital form is an equilateral triangle and it is that which gave the Nile delta, and, eventually, all river deltas whatever their shape, its name.) This Nile delta made up "Lower Egypt."

South of the delta is the river itself with its thin strip of fertile land along either bank. That is "Upper Egypt."

About 3100 B.C., a ruler of upper Egypt named Narmer, but better known by the Greek version of his name, Menes, made himself king

over both Egypts and established his capital at Memphis, just about
fifteen miles south of the beginning of the delta. The site of the
capital was probably selected deliberately because it was nearly at the
point of junction of the two earlier kingdoms, so that neither appeared
to be dominating.

Menes was the first king of the 1st dynasty (where a dynasty signifies
a ruling family with members following each other in, usually, unbroken
succession) of united Egypt. Eventually, thirty dynasties were recorded
as ruling Egypt, though some of the later ones represented foreign
conquerors.

Egypt's first period of high prosperity is referred to as the "Old Kingdom." It endured during the 3rd to the 6th dynasties inclusive, from
2664 B.C. to 2181 B.C., a period of nearly five hundred years that
neatly brackets the traditional date of the Flood. The first ruler of
the 3rd dynasty was Zoser and, according to tradition, it was in his
reign that the first pyramid was built.

The pyramids were large stone structures that were intended as vast
tombs for the ruler. The Egyptian religion was strongly death-centered
and it was felt that the route to eternal life lay in the physical
preservation of the body. A vastly complicated system of embalming
was developed and the production of mummies (some of which have
survived many centuries into our own time) was carried through with
care. The mummy of the ruler was buried with vast riches (to serve
him in the next world) and care had to be taken to prevent sacrilegious
thieves from rifling the tombs. The pyramids were attempts to prevent
such thievery by sheer bulk and strength, together with hidden exits
and cunningly contrived passages. These failed, almost entirely, although
in 1922, the British archaeologists, the Earl of Carnarvon and Howard
Carter, discovered the unrifled tomb of Tutankhamen, a ruler who died
in 1343 B.C., and created a sensation.

The pyramid madness reached its peak in the 4th dynasty with Khufu,
the second king of that dynasty (better known by the Greek version
of his name, Cheops). He ruled from 2590 B.C. to 2568 B.C., just a
trifle earlier than the first dynasty of Ur. He constructed what is
now known as the "Great Pyramid," a monster of an edifice built
from a square base 756 feet on each side and rising to a point 481½
feet above the level of the base. It is built out of huge granite blocks
averaging 2½ tons in weight, and 2,300,000 such blocks went into the
structure. According to Herodotus, it took 100,000 men thirty years
to build the structure. Maybe that's not too exaggerated. Relative to

the technology of the time, the Great Pyramid is the most ambitious project of man with the possible exception of the Great Wall of China; and it is certainly the most useless, without exception.

After the end of the 6th dynasty, a period of virtual anarchy followed. Egypt fell apart into separate segments as a result of the slow decline of central authority during the later years of the Old Kingdom and the steady rise to power of the feudal lords of the various towns and regions. During a century and a quarter five different dynasties ruled, overlapping perhaps. It was only Egypt's isolation that allowed it the luxury of this anarchy; otherwise it would certainly have fallen prey to some outside enemy.

It was not until 2052 B.C. that central authority under the 11th dynasty began to make itself felt again. By 1991 B.C. (about the time of Abram's birth), Amenemhet I, first king of the 12th dynasty, came to the throne. This initiated the "Middle Kingdom," a second period of high civilization and culture. It was then that Abram entered.

Pharaoh

In Egypt, Abram eventually found himself in an uncomfortable position when the beauty of his wife attracted unwelcome attention:

Genesis 12:15. *The princes . . . of Pharaoh saw her . . . and the woman was taken into Pharaoh's house.*

The name "Pharaoh," uniformly used as a title of respect for the Egyptian ruler, comes from the Egyptian *pero*, meaning "great house"; that is, the ruler's palace. (One might similarly speak obliquely of "the White House" when one means the American President, or of the "Kremlin" when one means the Soviet ruling body.)

The difficulty of this respectful practice is that it makes it quite impossible to tell which Pharaoh is being referred to very often. If one asks which Pharaoh it was that tried to add Abram's wife to his harem, we can only answer that while we might guess, we can never know.

I would like to suggest that it was Sesostris I, the second king of the 12th dynasty, who ruled from 1971 B.C. to 1928 B.C. He extended Egypt's power to the south and west and under him Egypt experienced a prosperity that might have seemed very attractive to a "wandering Aramaean."

In fact, Abram did well in Egypt. If, eventually, he got into trouble with Pharaoh and received back his wife only after considerable unpleasantness, and if he decided it was the better part of valor to return to Canaan, he at least did so as a rich man.

Jordan River

On his return to Canaan, Abram found his herds so multiplied that there was insufficient forage for both them and the herds of his nephew, Lot. It seemed reasonable to separate and generously, he allowed Lot first choice of territory.

> Genesis 13:10. *And Lot lifted up his eyes, and beheld all the plain of Jordan, that it was well watered everywhere, before the Lord destroyed Sodom and Gomorrah, even as the garden of the Lord, like the land of Egypt . . .*
> Genesis 13:11. *Then Lot chose him all the plain of Jordan . . .*
> Genesis 13:12. . . . *and pitched his tent toward Sodom.*

Canaan is largely a semi-arid country and the one place where water was (and is) unfailingly available was in the valley of the Jordan River. The fertility is described in this verse as being like that of the land of the two great river civilizations: Sumeria ("the garden of the Lord," that is, Eden) and Egypt.

For its size, the Jordan River is certainly the most famous river in the world, thanks entirely to its Biblical associations. It rises from the mountains that run along the line where the modern states of Lebanon, Syria, and Israel meet, and flows directly south about 135 miles, flowing into an inland sea without an outlet. The waters of the Jordan never reach the ocean. The river winds and meanders so, however, that its full length if straightened out would be 250 miles.

In one respect, the Jordan River is quite unusual. Its level descends rapidly and, in its relatively short length, that level drops from source to mouth about three thousand feet, or well over half a mile. In fact, it is sometimes suggested that the name of the river is derived from this fact and from a Hebrew word meaning "to go down." This, however, may be mere coincidence and the name may arise from pre-Semitic sources.

The result of this descent is that the water level in the river, over

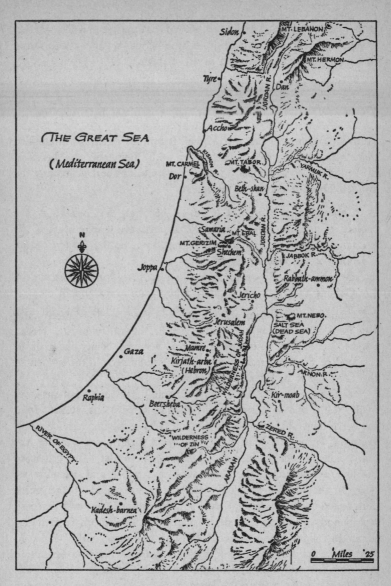

The Jordan River

the lower two thirds of its course, is actually below sea level. As far as is known, this is true of no other river in the world.

The reason for this is that the Jordan River occupies the northern tip of the Great Rift Valley, a gigantic downfaulted block in the earth's crust which continues southward past the mouth of the Jordan River, into the long, narrow Red Sea (which fills that section of the rift), and in a large arc through eastern Africa. The deep and narrow lakes: Rudolf, Albert, Tanganyika, and Nyasa, fill sections of the African portion of the rift. All told, the Great Rift Valley is some four thousand miles long.

Despite Lot's opinion, the Jordan is not a very attractive river. It is not navigable and it is steaming hot in the summer, with temperatures not uncommonly reaching 110° in the shade. The general unattractiveness of the Jordan valley is recognized in Genesis 13:10, which carefully explains that Lot's estimate was before the destruction of Sodom and Gomorrah (the story of which is told later in Chapter 19).

In modern times, the Jordan has gained new kinds of importance. First, it is a national boundary. After World War I, what had once been Canaan was freed from Turkish control and was set up as a separate area, Palestine, under British control. The Jordan River served as part of its eastern boundary and to the east was another region, Trans-Jordan, ("beyond the Jordan") also under British control.

Trans-Jordan became an independent kingdom in 1946. Then in 1948, a portion of Palestine was set up as an independent Jewish state, which adopted the name of Israel. There was war at once between Israel and the surrounding Arab states. Trans-Jordan occupied and annexed a portion of the land to the west of the Jordan River and changed its own name to Jordan. (That portion of Jordan west of the river was occupied by Israel after the Six-day War of 1967.)

Hebron

After Lot left, Abraham contented himself with the less fertile and apparently less desirable region southwest of the Jordan.

Genesis 13:18. *Then Abram removed his tent, and came and dwelt in the plain of Mamre, which is in Hebron . . .*

Actually, "plain of Mamre" is a mistranslation and, in the Revised Standard Version, it is "oaks of Mamre" with a footnote to the effect

that it might be "terebinths of Mamre." In either case, the reference
is, apparently, to a sacred grove of trees located (according to tradition)
about two miles north of Hebron.

Hebron itself is twenty miles south of Jerusalem and is one of the
oldest towns in Canaan. Although it is called Hebron here, that being
its name at the time Genesis was placed in final form, it was apparently called Kirjath-arba in Canaanite times (as stated later in Genesis 23:2):

> Genesis 23:2. . . . *Kirjath-arba; the same is Hebron* . . .

Hebron still exists and has a population of about twenty-five thousand. Its Arabic name is "El-Khalil" ("the friend") in honor of Abraham, "the friend of God." Various ancient oaks in its vicinity are
pointed out as the "oaks of Mamre" but it is not possible that any of
them are really four thousand years old.

Amraphel

After the separation of Abraham and Lot, the "cities of the plain"
with which Lot had cast his lot were subjected to invasion by armies
from the east. The heads of the invading force are named:

> Genesis 14:1. . . . *Amraphel king of Shinar, Arioch king of Ellasar,
> Chedorlaomer king of Elam, and Tidal king of nations;*

This seems to picture the situation as it existed in the days of the
final decay of Sumeria.

Elam, the constant enemy of Sumeria (see page 35) now has
the upper hand. It had been conquered by Sargon of Agade and for
centuries had remained more or less under Sumero-Akkadian rule. After
Ur's final gasp of power had faded away, however, Elam moved in.
In fact, Elamite onslaughts may have helped bring Ur to final ruin.
(I would like to imagine that the news of this reached Abram in
Haran or Canaan. If so, it might have seemed as though Cain were
slaying Abel at last—see page 34—and helped fix that legend in the
mind of those who traced their descent from Ur.)

Ellasar may well be the city referred to in Babylonian records as
Larsa. This was a city on the Euphrates about twenty miles upstream
from Ur. Ur's decline meant its temporary rise. Tidal is sometimes

identified with Tudhaliya I, the ruler of some Hittite tribe. (I will have more to say about the Hittites later.)

The ruler mentioned in this verse who has received the lion's share of attention from Biblical scholars is, however, Amraphel king of Shinar. At this time—about 1900 B.C.—the Amorites (see page 50) had taken over Babylon. Eventually, they were to take over all of Sumeria, so that Amraphel, possibly a local ruler and no more, is already called, a little prematurely, the king of Shinar.

The greatest ruler of the Amorite line was, as I have said earlier, Hammurabi, who ruled about 1700 B.C. and is best known for the code of laws issued in his reign. A copy was discovered in modern times on a diorite stele eight feet high. Hammurabi eventually conquered Larsa, which, under its powerful king Rim-Sin, had made things hot for him for a while. He also conquered Elam. (Nevertheless, Elam had its recurrent periods of power later. The column on which the code of Hammurabi was inscribed was found in Susa, the Elamite capital, where it may have been taken after a successful Elamite raid on Babylon during one of the periods of weakness of the latter city.)

It has long been customary to say that Amraphel was Hammurabi, but this seems quite out of the question. Hammurabi reigned some centuries after the events of this chapter of Genesis must have taken place. The Biblical story has Chedorlaomer of Elam the leading element of the coalition (even though Amraphel is mentioned first in 14:1) and this would be unthinkable in Hammurabi's reign.

The picture, then, is of a Sumeria on the decline, with Babylon and Larsa acting as a pair of city-states under the domination of Elam, with whom some Hittite elements are allied (or are perhaps serving as mercenaries).

Apparently, Elam, having secured the Tigris-Euphrates, is now reaching westward for the rest of the Fertile Crescent, which for some centuries has been under the domination of whatever power had ruled in the east.

The Vale of Siddim

Against the invaders stood the forces of what were then the most populous and prosperous cities of Canaan, the five "cities of the plain":

Sodom, Gomorrah, Admah, Zeboiim, and Zoar, concerning which there will be more to say later.

Apparently, they had paid tribute for twelve years but now they refused further payment and prepared to resist.

> Genesis 14:3. *All these were joined together in the vale of Siddim, which is the salt sea.*

The "salt sea" is the inland sea into which the Jordan empties and a most unusual body of water it is. It is not large in size, only about forty-seven miles long and not more than ten miles wide. Its area is 370 square miles, which makes it only slightly larger than the five boroughs of New York City.

The descending Jordan River is at 1286 feet below sea level when it finally enters the "salt sea," the shores of which are thus lower than any other land area in the world.

If the depression in which the salt sea rests could be filled to sea level, it would form a much larger inland sea some two hundred miles long and twenty miles wide, almost as large as the state of Connecticut.

The reason why the salt sea does not fill the depression is simple. The amount of water it receives—that of the Jordan River carrying to it the rainfall upon the mountains in southern Syria and Lebanon—is small. Its temperature is high (readings of up to 140° F. are recorded in its neighborhood) and the loss of water by evaporation is high. The salt sea represents a puddle, so to speak, which has partly dried.

The water brought in by the Jordan River is fresh but it does contain small amounts of chemicals dissolved from the soil it passes over and the banks it passes between. These chemicals accumulate in the salt sea. If the salt sea had an opening to the ocean the chemicals would be washed out as fast as they came in and the waters of the sea would remain fresh. But there is no opening and the sea loses water only by evaporation. The chemicals do not evaporate and remain behind; more is constantly being added and none is removed. As a result, the sea is now from 23 to 25 per cent dissolved chemicals, mostly sodium chloride (common salt) and magnesium chloride, plus smaller quantities of a variety of other substances. It is rightly named the salt sea.

So heavy is the salt concentration (seven times that of the ocean) that nothing can live in the waters of the sea. For that reason, the Greek geographers took to calling it the Dead Sea, and it is by that name that it is best known to us. The name Dead Sea does not, however, occur in the Bible.

Despite the fact that the Dead Sea is a partly dried puddle resting at the bottom of a depression, we must not get the idea that it is almost all gone and that another little push will cause it to disappear altogether in a final burst of evaporation. Remember that the water of the Dead Sea fills part of the Great Rift Valley. This allows the Dead Sea, low though its level has fallen, to be one of the deepest lakes in the world. Its average depth is 1080 feet and its greatest depth is 1310 feet. The volume of water it contains is considerably greater than that in some apparently much larger lakes (in terms of surface area) which are very shallow. The Dead Sea contains about twelve times as much water, for instance, as does our own Great Salt Lake, although the latter, in terms of area, is four times as large.

The Dead Sea is a major source of chemicals and indeed plants now exist in its neighborhood for the extraction of potassium chloride from its waters. Chemicals that kill life in too great a concentration can act as fertilizers in proper dosage. Nowadays, the Dead Sea lies between the nations of Jordan and Israel.

The Dead Sea is divided into two unequal parts by a small peninsula that extends into it from the eastern shore. The northern part, making up about two thirds of the whole area, is the deep portion. The southern part, making up the remaining third, is quite shallow, with depths of from three to thirty feet. It is possible that the "vale of Siddim" mentioned in Genesis 14:3 refers to the neighborhood of this southern portion of the Dead Sea particularly.

Rephaims

The army of Chedorlaomer, on its way down the western half of the Fertile Crescent, quickly subdued the regions east and south of the Dead Sea:

Genesis 14:5. . . . *Chedorlaomer, and the kings that were with him, . . . smote the Rephaims . . . and the Zuzims . . . and the Emims . . .*

The use of the expression "Rephaims," by the way, is an example of a false plural. The "-im" suffix is itself the Hebrew plural, and to add a further "-s" is superfluous. The Revised Standard Version speaks, therefore, of the Rephaim, Zuzim, and Emim. (The Zuzim are often identified with the "Zamzummim" mentioned later in the Book of Deuteronomy.)

These people predated those who arrived six or seven centuries after the time of Abraham—the Israelites and related tribes. The tradition is strong that the pre-Israelite inhabitants of Canaan, the Rephaim in particular, were giants. Indeed, the tradition of the one-time existence of giants, with sizes that are magnified as the tales are passed on from generation to generation, are very common in the folklore of all nations. The Bible states flatly in one much-discussed passage:

Genesis 6:4. *There were giants in the earth in those days . . .*

However, the Hebrew term here translated as "giants" is *Nephilim* and there is no way of being certain that giants is what is actually meant. It may simply have meant a race of mighty warriors, without particular reference to gigantic physical size. The Revised Standard Version evades the issue by leaving the Hebrew word untranslated and saying "The Nephilim were on the earth in those days."

Again in the Book of Numbers, in retailing the report of the spies sent into Canaan by Moses, the Bible has them say:

Numbers 13:33. *And there we saw the giants, the sons of Anak, which come of the giants . . .*

Here also the term is *Nephilim* and the Revised Standard Version reads: "And there we saw the Nephilim (the sons of Anak, who come from the Nephilim) . . ."

At least one reason for the persistent tales of giants may rest in the wonder felt by barbarian invaders at the sight of the works of the civilizations they replaced. Thus, when the Dorian Greeks invaded the Peloponnesus they were struck with astonishment at the thick walls of towns such as Mycenae and Tiryns, which had been strongholds of the defeated Mycenaean civilization. Viewing the tremendous stone blocks that made up those walls, the Dorians decided that they could only have been built by giants and the Greek myths do indeed say that the huge one-eyed Cyclopes built those walls. (And such walls, made up of large stone blocks, held by their own weight without cement or mortar, are still called "cyclopean walls.")

Similarly, the Israelite invaders of 1200 B.C., viewing the elaborate fortifications of the Canaanite cities, may have felt they were fighting giants. The term must have been used metaphorically at first, as a dramatic expression of the technological advancement of the enemy. Thus, the verse in Numbers already cited goes on to say:

Numbers 13:33. . . . *and we were in our own sight as grasshoppers, and so we were in their sight.*

which is about how an unarmed man might feel facing a man with a loaded rifle, or how the latter might feel facing a man in a tank.

Nevertheless, all such expressions came to be accepted literally and in later rabbinical legends, the Rephaim, Emim, Zuzim, Zamzummim, Nephilim, and Anakim all became giants of absolutely tremendous size. It would certainly be strange if they were, however, since they were easily defeated by Chedorlaomer and also by the later Israelite invasion.

It is almost needless to say that archaeologists have come across no traces of giant races in historic times. To be sure, there are a very few fossil remains, mostly teeth, indicating the one-time existence of a manlike being even larger than the modern gorilla. These must, however, have lived a hundred thousand years ago and more, and it is unlikely in the extreme that any existed as recently as Abraham's time.

Salem

Chedorlaomer's army then turned the southern flank of the Dead Sea region, fell upon the forces of the cities of the plain, and defeated them. The city of Sodom was sacked and Lot, Abram's nephew, was one of those who were carried off to enslavement.

Abram (pictured in Chapter 14 of Genesis as a powerful desert sheik), on hearing of this, immediately gathered his men and set off in pursuit. He defeated a contingent of the army of Chedorlaomer and liberated Lot, together with much of the taken loot.

As Abram returned from this victorious raid:

Genesis 14:18. . . . *Melchizedek king of Salem brought forth bread and wine: . . .*

Genesis 14:19. *And he blessed him, and said Blessed be* Abram . . .

Melchizedek is Hebrew for "righteous king" and is thus the Canaanite equivalent of the Akkadian name "Sargon." Nowhere else in the Bible is Melchizedek mentioned except in reference to this single incident.

Naturally, there has been considerable speculation as to where Salem might be located. The later Jews decided that Salem (a Hebrew word meaning "peace") was a shortened form of Jerusalem. In the 76th Psalm, for instance, this shows up:

> Psalm 76:2. *In Salem also is his* [God's] *tabernacle, and his dwelling place in Zion.*

As is the fashion in Hebrew poetry, the same thing is said twice, so that Salem must be synonymous with Zion. Zion is a poetic way of referring to Jerusalem and therefore it seems very likely that Salem must be another reference to that city.

There have been objections to this interpretation on the grounds that before the Israelite conquest, Jerusalem was the home of a Canaanite tribe called the Jebusites and that the city itself was called Jebus.

Yet references in Egyptian chronicles dating back to well before the Israelite conquest refer to a city called "Urusalim" which seems almost certainly to be Jerusalem. It would seem then that Jerusalem is indeed a very ancient name (of which the derivation is unknown despite the correspondence of the last two syllables to the Hebrew word for "peace") and that Jebus is actually a late derivation from Jebusite.

If Salem is indeed Jerusalem, as seems most likely, it is the first appearance of that city, later so famous as the seat of the Temple, in the Bible. In fact, one reason the legend may have been retained and recorded in Genesis was to show that Abram himself paid tithes at the future site of the Temple.

Damascus

Abram's great sorrow at this time was the lack of a son and heir; a terrible situation in a family-centered tribal society. He bemoaned the fact that only some servant, not part of his bloodline, could inherit his accumulated property:

Genesis 15:2. . . . I go childless, and the steward of my house is this Eliezer of Damascus.

Damascus had already been mentioned earlier in the previous chapter as a place name used to describe the extent of Abraham's northward raid in pursuit of Chedorlaomer:

Genesis 14:15. . . . he . . . pursued them unto Hobah, which is on the left hand of Damascus.

In Genesis 14:15, the reference might be merely to a place where later the city of Damascus was built, but Genesis 15:2 refers to an actual city, one with native sons. And, indeed, Damascus was in existence at the time of Abraham and even a thousand years earlier perhaps. It is believed to be the oldest continuously occupied city in the world.

It is about 150 miles north of Jerusalem, centered in a verdant, well-watered area. Indeed, its name ("Dammesek" in Hebrew) is derived, apparently, from the Aramaic phrase *di masqya,* meaning "having water resources." It is an important city even today. It is the capital of the modern nation of Syria and has a population of about 475,000.

The Hittites

Nevertheless, God promises Abram a son and also promises him that his descendants shall inherit the land of Canaan and that the people then, or soon to be, living in the land shall be displaced. (This promise is repeated on several occasions in the Book of Genesis.) The tribes dwelling in Canaan are then enumerated, as they are to be enumerated on a number of occasions later in the Bible. They were also enumerated in the "Table of Nations" in the tenth chapter of Genesis, as children of Canaan. The details of the enumeration change from place to place. Here it is given as:

Genesis 15:19. The Kenites, and the Kenizzites, and the Kadmonites,
Genesis 15:20. And the Hittites, and the Perizzites, and the Rephaims,

The Hittite Kingdom

Genesis 15:21. *And the Amorites, and the Canaanites, and the Girgashites, and the Jebusites.*

There is wide variety in these names. The Kenites, Kenizzites, and Kadmonites are all desert tribes of the south and southeast. The Jebusites are the inhabitants of Jerusalem and its environs. Virtually nothing is known of the Perizzites and Girgashites, except that they are mentioned among the inhabitants in several of the lists. The Rephaim I have discussed earlier (see page 72).

The Canaanites are, obviously, a general term for the inhabitants of Canaan and the Amorites are used as an almost synonymous general term. This may be because in Abraham's time, the Amorites had become the most important of the west Semitic tribes. They had taken over Babylon and were on the way to the control of all the Tigris-Euphrates (see page 50).

By far the most interesting of the groups listed, however, is the Hittites.

The Hittites are sometimes referred to as the "sons of Heth" and Heth (the eponym of the tribe) is referred to in the tenth chapter of Genesis as the second son of Canaan:

Genesis 10:15. *And Canaan begat Sidon his firstborn, and Heth . . .*

Because the Hittites are invariably mentioned in the Bible as among the tribes of Canaanites, the feeling arose that they were a minor people, no more important than, let us say, Girgashites, who have never been heard of outside those few verses in the Bible in which they are mentioned. And yet the fact that Heth is Canaan's second-born bespeaks a certain importance.

The old Egyptian and Babylonian records do speak of the "Kheta" and the "Khatti" respectively (quite similar to "Heth") as a powerful people north of Canaan and the thought grew that these might be the Biblical Hittites and that they might not be an unimportant group of Canaanites after all. Archaeological findings in the nineteenth century seemed to point to a hitherto unknown empire that had once flourished in Syria and Asia Minor.

Finally, in 1906, a German archaeologist, Hugo Winckler, uncovered a store of cuneiform tablets near the village of Bogazkoy in central Turkey, about ninety miles east of the present Turkish capital, Ankara.

It turned out that the tablets were found on the site of the capital of what had indeed been a Hittite Empire.

Further investigation showed that the Hittites had ruled a powerful realm, had introduced the use of iron and of horse-drawn chariots (something which the Assyrians were later to improve on), and, for a few centuries, had disputed the mastery of western Asia with Egypt when the latter kingdom was at her most powerful.

How then could this great empire go unnoticed in the Bible and be mentioned only as an unimportant tribe?

Actually, this is an accident of history. In the time of Abraham and his immediate descendants, the Hittites had not yet reached the fullness of their strength. Indeed, Tidal, an early Hittite leader, is mentioned only as a confederate of Chedorlaomer (see page 68) and as of no more importance than a Sumerian city-state.

It was not until 1750 B.C., well after Abraham's time, that the Hittite "Old Kingdom" was founded and that a conquering Hittite king spread its power outside Asia Minor. And by that time, Abraham's descendants were on their way into Egyptian bondage and the focus of the Bible moves away for some centuries from Canaan.

After a century of Hittite decline between 1500 and 1400 B.C., there followed a period of even greater power, and the Hittite "New Kingdom" was established. Under Shubbiluliu, who reigned from 1390 B.C. to 1350 B.C., the Hittites reached the peak of their power and for a moment seemed on the point of establishing their dominion over all the civilized world. In the end, however, a long war with Egypt wore them out; they declined first slowly and then more rapidly, and by 1200 B.C. the Hittite Empire came to a final end.

When the Israelites invaded Canaan and the Biblical focus was restored to that land, the remnant of the Hittites remaining here and there in Canaan and to the north could be viewed as an unimportant tribe.

In short, the Bible talks of Canaan before the Hittites rose to power and after the Hittites fell from power, but never while the Hittites were in their full glory. And since the Bible was, until the nineteenth century, the chief source of historical knowledge concerning the ancient East, the great Hittite Empire vanished from sight. Only with Winckler's work did archaeological finds in the Middle East restore it to the knowledge of man.

Ishmael

At the suggestion of his wife, Sarai, Abram takes her servant, Hagar, as his concubine.

Genesis 16:15. *And Hagar bare Abram a son: and Abram called his son's name . . . Ishmael.*

Ishmael is the eponym of a group of tribes, collectively known as Ishmaelites in the Bible, who dwelt on the border of the Arabian desert south and southeast of Canaan. The Israelites recognized the kinship of these Arabian tribes to themselves by tracing the descent of those tribes from Abraham. It was a descent through a concubine, however, indicating the view (from the standpoint of the writers of Genesis) that the Ishmaelites were of subordinate importance in the scheme of things.

The Arabians in later centuries came under the influence of Judaism and even after the establishment of Islam in the seventh century A.D. accepted many parts of the Bible and embroidered the legendary material of Genesis in their own fashion. They considered themselves to be descended from Abram and Ishmael and the Arabic versions of those names, Ibrahim and Ismail, remain favorites among Moslems. According to Moslem legend, both Hagar and Ishmael are buried in Mecca.

Circumcision

Ishmael is not, however, the son through whom the descendants will arise to whom Canaan is promised. God now renews the promise, entering into a covenant with Abraham; something that in human terms would be a legal, binding agreement.

In return for the divine right to Canaan, Abraham, in his own name and that of his descendants, agrees to accept God as the national deity. God says:

Genesis 17:7. *And I will establish my covenant between me and thee and thy seed after thee . . . to be a God unto thee, and to thy seed after thee.*

As his "signature" to this agreement, Abram (now renamed Abraham—a change in name to signify the new situation) agrees to accept the rite of circumcision. (The Hebrew term for it is *berith*, meaning "covenant.") God says:

> Genesis 17:10. *This is my covenant, which ye shall keep . . . Every man child among you shall be circumcised.*

Circumcision is the removal of the foreskin of the penis; a loss which in no way hampers the sex act, and does not result in any inconvenience at all.

The custom is, actually, far older than Abraham and its origins are lost in prehistoric antiquity. It was practiced by the Egyptians and by the Canaanites, who were under the political and cultural domination of Egypt in Abraham's time. The rite was not practiced in the Tigris-Euphrates region, and the tale of Abraham's circumcision may represent a memory of the adoption of certain phases of Egyptian and Canaanite culture by the westward-wandering nomads.

Circumcision does not seem to have been particularly important among the pre-Exilic Jews. It was practiced, of course, and uncircumcised people (such as the Philistines) were looked down upon; but the overwhelming religious significance of the rite seemed to arise during the Exile.

When the Jews in Babylon were trying to maintain their national existence and to keep themselves separate from the much greater numbers of the Babylonians, circumcision grew important. It marked off the Jews from the uncircumcised Babylonians.

It was comforting, further, to interpret that mark of separation as the legal witness that the Promised Land, from which the Jews had been torn by the Babylonian conquerors, was Jewish by divine agreement, and would therefore be theirs again someday. The Book of Genesis, which was being put into its final form at the time, was naturally so edited as to stress this point.

The land was indeed restored and the importance and prestige of circumcision was thus fixed. Through all the Greek and Roman period, it continued to be the fundamental rite marking the entry of the infant (or the adult convert) into Judaism. It was partly over the rite of circumcision that Christianity and Judaism parted company in the time of the Apostle Paul.

Although many people nowadays attempt to interpret the operation as a measure intended for the purpose of hygiene or cleanliness, it is likely that to primitive man (innocent of our modern notions of hygiene) the act had magical overtones. It may, for instance, have been intended to ensure fertility.

Sodom and Gomorrah

But while the promised heir is awaited, the focus shifts again to the outside world.

Abraham learns that the cities of the plain—of which Sodom and Gomorrah were the most important—are to be destroyed in a great catastrophe. It had been in Sodom that Lot had chosen to live (see page 65) and it had been Sodom that had led the rebellion against Chedorlaomer (see page 70).

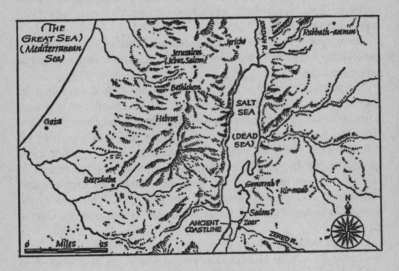

Sodom and Gomorrah

Abraham intercedes on behalf of those of the inhabitants of the cities who might be righteous and his nephew Lot is allowed to escape in time to the smallest of the cities of the plain, Zoar (although Lot's wife is lost, being turned into a pillar of salt, according to the story).

Genesis 19:23. . . . *Lot entered into Zoar.*

Genesis 19:24. *Then the Lord rained upon Sodom and upon Gomorrah brimstone and fire . . .*

Genesis 19:25. *And he overthrew those cities, and all the plain, and all the inhabitants of the cities, and that which grow upon the ground.*

The description of the catastrophe could match that of a volcanic eruption, combined with an earthquake; or, conceivably, a large meteorite strike. Certainly such events have proved catastrophic enough even in recent times. In 1883, a volcanic eruption on the island of Krakatoa in the strait between the Indonesian islands of Java and Sumatra killed 36,000 people in Java.

The question is, though, where Sodom and the other cities of the plain might have been located before the destruction. The "plain" seems to refer to the entire depression occupied by the Jordan River and the Dead Sea, which, according to Genesis 13:10, was "well watered everywhere."

Certainly the shores of the Dead Sea are bleakly infertile now but conceivably that might have been the result of the very catastrophe described here.

The most interesting possibility follows from certain signs that indicate that in Abraham's time, the level of the Dead Sea may have been some feet lower than it is today. It might therefore have been that the Dead Sea was at that time confined only to its deep portion, the northern two thirds (see page 71). The shallow, southern third might have been the dry, or perhaps marshy, plain on which Sodom and its sister cities were located, with a fresh-water table that kept the area fertile as it drained northward into the Dead Sea. This area might, indeed, have been the very "vale of Siddim" referred to in Genesis 14:3.

It might then have been that the catastrophe which overwhelmed Sodom and the other cities, whether a volcano or earthquake or meteorite strike, led to a slight subsidence of the land, so that the waters of the Dead Sea flooded southward; and this flood might have been made the worse as the result of a rise (for some reason) of the general water-level of the Sea. If all this were so, what was left of the cities (and considering the size and make-up of Canaanite cities of 1900 B.C., it wouldn't be much) would be covered by the waters of the Dead Sea.

It is only fair to say, however, that no extra-Biblical evidence of such a catastrophe is known and there are no reports of any remains of civilization buried under the waters of the southern end of the Dead Sea.

Although not mentioned here, two of the other cities of the plain were also destroyed, according to Deuteronomy:

> Deuteronomy 29:23. . . . *like the overthrow of Sodom, and Gomorrah, Admah, and Zeboim, which the Lord overthrew in his anger . . .*

Zoar, the last city of the plain, and the refuge of Lot, was spared. In the Book of Jeremiah, the prophet inveighs against Moab, mentioning Zoar among its cities:

> Jeremiah 48:33. *And joy and gladness is taken from the . . . land of Moab; . . .*
> Jeremiah 48:34. . . . *from Zoar even unto Horonaim . . .*

From the known location of Moab, this would place Zoar, most likely, southeast of the Dead Sea, perhaps nearly at the edge of the present shore, just far enough from the other cities to have escaped the catastrophe and inundation. No trace of Zoar remains in modern times.

During medieval times, by the way, when few Europeans ever saw the Dead Sea, impressions of it, arising out of the nineteenth chapter of Genesis, were most horrible. Its waters were thought to be black; the vapors above it poisonous; birds could not fly over it. None of this is true, of course. Its climate is miserable and its waters are bitter and contain no life, but it is not poisonous externally, and men can swim in it if they choose. (Such swimming is a remarkable experience, for the salt concentration makes the water unusually dense and one cannot sink in it even if one tries.)

Moab and Ammon

Lot's two daughters escaped with him from the destruction of Sodom. While hiding in a cave near Zoar, the daughters, at least, are depicted as convinced that the destruction had been universal. Feeling themselves to be the only possible mothers of future humanity, they made use of the only man available, their father, after making him drunk.

Genesis 19:37. *And the firstborn bare a son, and called his name Moab: the same is the father of the Moabites unto this day.*

Genesis 19:38. *And the younger, she also bare a son, and called his name Ben-ammi: the same is the father of the children of Ammon unto this day.*

The Moabites and Ammonites were peoples related to the Israelites in terms of language and culture, and the Biblical writers recognized this relationship by having them descended from Lot, the nephew of Abraham.

The Moabites and Ammonites descended upon Canaan from the eastern desert some five centuries after Abraham's time and perhaps a century before the Israelites themselves did. The Bible says this in its own fashion by placing the time of birth of the eponyms of Moab and Ammon before the time of birth of the eponym of Israel.

The actual origins of the names Moab and Ammon are not known, but they can be twisted to imply incestuous origin. "Moab" may mean "from father" and "Ben-ammi" seems to mean "son of my people." If this is taken to read "from [my own] father" and "son of my [own] people" nothing more is needed. Since for centuries after the Israelite conquest of Canaan, Moab and Ammon remained perennial enemies of the Israelites, the writers of Genesis were probably only too pleased to record the folk tale of their scandalous origin.

Gerar

After the destruction of Sodom, Abraham apparently felt the need of moving away from unpleasant associations and of making a new start.

Genesis 20:1. *And Abraham journeyed from thence . . . and sojourned in Gerar.*

Gerar is about forty miles west of Hebron and a little to the south. It is only about ten miles from the Mediterranean coast and not more than twenty miles northeast of what would now be considered the boundary of Egypt.

The writer of Genesis speaks of Gerar as being in Philistine territory for its king, on returning to his city, is recorded as having:

Genesis 21:32. *. . . returned into the land of the Philistines.*

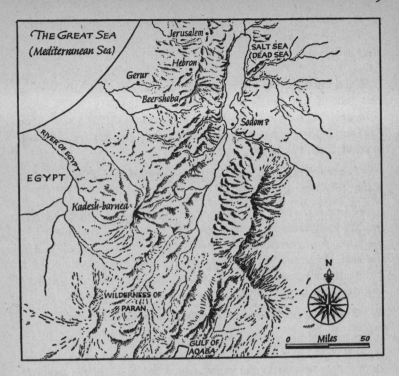

Canaan in the Time of the Patriarchs

Again, at the end of the description of happenings during Abraham's stay at Gerar, a summary, as follows, is presented:

> Genesis 21:34. *And Abraham sojourned in the Philistines' land many days.*

This should not be taken to mean that the Philistines actually occupied the territory of Gerar in Abraham's time. Gerar was in the area which eventually became Philistine, to be sure, some five centuries immediately preceding the time that Genesis was reduced to writing so it was best identified in that fashion. The anachronism was similar in nature to that involved in "Ur of the Chaldees" (see page 58).

Beersheba

While Abraham was in southern Canaan, a son was finally born to him and his wife, Sarah, and he was named Isaac.

In order that there might be no confusion as to who was to be Abraham's heir, Hagar, Abraham's concubine, and her son, Ishmael, were, at Sarah's insistence, cast out.

> Genesis 21:14. . . . *and she* [Hagar] *departed, and wandered in the wilderness of Beersheba.*

Wilderness is a term referring to uninhabited territory and presumably the city itself had not yet been founded. Its founding is attributed in the same chapter to Abraham, who is recorded as having dug a well in the area. He established the ownership of that well by coming to a formal agreement with the king of Gerar, an agreement involving an oath rendered inviolate by the ritual sacrifice of seven lambs.

> Genesis 21:31. *Wherefore he called that place Beersheba* . . .

The name of the town can be said to mean either "well of the oath" or "well of the seven" or, perhaps, "seven wells." In any case it is the water supply that marks the importance of the place. In the semi-arid land of Canaan, a reliable well or wells is essential for a permanent community and Genesis therefore deals in some detail with traditions concerning the digging of wells.

Beersheba, about twenty-eight miles southwest of Hebron, is about as far south as one can go and expect to find a reliable water supply. It is therefore the southernmost sizable town in Canaan and is usually taken by the Biblical writers as representing the southern boundary of the land. Farther south is the desert, or Negev (which is simply a Hebrew word for "south").

When Palestine was under Turkish rule prior to World War I, Beersheba was a small village with the Arabic name of Bir-es-saba. Some of its wells were still in existence and the largest was called the "Well of Abraham." In 1917, the British invaded Palestine from Egypt and won a victory over the Turks at Beersheba, one which led to the rapid conquest of Palestine.

Beersheba is now part of Israel, has a population of about 32,000, and is still the southernmost sizable town in the land (except for Elath, the Red Sea port). Its present importance depends upon the fact that it is an industrial and manufacturing center, thanks in part to its nearness to the chemicals produced at the Dead Sea, a little over thirty miles to the east.

Paran

Ishmael, after being cast out, made his home in the desert regions south of Canaan:

Genesis 21:21. *And he dwelt in the wilderness of Paran: and his mother took him a wife out of the land of Egypt.*

Paran is an ill-defined area usually marked on the maps as including the northern portion of the triangular peninsula of Sinai, which lies between Canaan and Egypt. The nomadic tribes wandering there, and in the portions of Arabia neighboring it, are the Ishmaelites par excellence.

The region, thanks to its closeness to Egypt, would be under Egyptian influence even when Canaan itself was free, so that the fact that Ishmael had an Egyptian mother and an Egyptian wife seems to express the geographical and political situation in the personal terms appropriate for an eponym.

Moriah

There follows then the well-known story of Abraham's rocklike faith and his readiness to offer his son, Isaac—his long-awaited son—as a human sacrifice at God's order. At the last minute, however, Abraham is held back from the deed, and a ram is sacrificed in Isaac's place.

The place of the near sacrifice of Isaac is not closely specified. God's instructions are:

Genesis 22:2. . . . *get thee into the land of Moriah; and offer him* [Isaac] *there for a burnt offering upon one of the mountains . . .*

There seems no way of determining where the land of Moriah might be. It is not mentioned elsewhere in the Bible or anywhere outside the Bible. It is over two days' journey from Beersheba for Abraham sighted it on the third day, but the direction in which he was traveling is not given.

Among the later Jews, the tradition grew that the place of the near sacrifice of Isaac was destined to be the very place at which the Temple of Solomon was to be built. This place is referred to as Zion in every Biblical reference but one. The exception is a late-written reference:

2 Chronicles 3:1. *Then Solomon began to build the house of the Lord at Jerusalem in mount Moriah . . .*

Actually, the chance that the place of Isaac's ordeal and that of Solomon's Temple are the same may be flattering to later Jewish nationalism but is not at all likely to be true. Even in Abraham's time, the hill in Jerusalem was occupied and was within a well-fortified city. Abraham would not have had entry into it without careful negotiation that Genesis would surely have detailed.

Aram and Chesed

Meanwhile, Abraham's brother Nahor was back in Haran and news concerning him was brought to Abraham:

Genesis 22:20. . . . *Milcah . . . hath also born children unto thy brother, Nahor;*
Genesis 22:21. *Huz his firstborn, and Buz his brother, and Kemuel the father of Aram,*
Genesis 22:22. *And Chesed, and Hazo, and Pildash, and Bethuel.*
Genesis 22:23. *And Bethuel begat Rebekah . . .*

These are eponyms, of course, and the most important are Aram and Chesed. Aram is the eponym of the Aramaeans and, earlier in Genesis, is presented as a son of Shem. This apparent contradiction may be the result of the effort of the final editors of Genesis to keep each of two well-known traditions.

The two separate births of Aram also serve two separate functions if Aram is viewed as an eponym representing a people, rather than as an individual human being. In the tenth chapter, Aram is presented as a son of Shem to indicate that the Aramaeans were independent of Assyria at the time Genesis was reduced to writing (see page 23). Here, in the twenty-second chapter, Aram is presented as a son of Nahor, brother of Abraham, to indicate the kinship of the Aramaeans to the Israelites.

As for Chesed, he is probably the eponym of the Chaldeans ("Kasdim" in Hebrew). This is rather appropriate historically, since the Aramaeans and Chaldeans emerged from the desert into the Fertile Crescent at nearly the same time (see page 58).

The other names mentioned undoubtedly represent various Aramaean or Chaldean tribes and speculation about them is fruitless now. Huz (better "Uz" as in the Revised Standard Version) and Buz are of some interest with respect to the Book of Job, a matter which will be taken up in the appropriate place.

This short genealogy is also of direct interest to the Israelite readers of Genesis since Rebekah is listed as a daughter of Bethuel, who is himself first cousin to Isaac. Since Rebekah is later to marry Isaac, she is one of the ancestresses of the Israelites.

Machpelah

Eventually, Abraham's wife, Sarah, died at a time when she and Abraham were living in Hebron once more (referred to here at first by its Canaanite name of Kirjath-arba). Abraham bought a burial plot of "the children of Heth." This is usually interpreted as meaning "Hittite" though there is some argument about that which is not easily resolved. The transaction is carefully detailed.

Genesis 23:19. *And after this, Abraham buried Sarah . . . in the cave of the field of Machpelah before Mamre . . .*

Eventually, Abraham himself was buried in the cave (Genesis 25:9) as well as Isaac and his wife, and Isaac's younger son and one of his wives (Genesis 49:30-31; 50:13), all direct forebears of the Israelites.

By New Testament times, a tradition had arisen that a particular spot in Hebron represented the Cave of Machpelah. The Moslems (who were to be in occupation of Hebron for thirteen hundred years) respect the tradition and improve on it. The traditional site is enclosed in stone walls like a fortress and the enclosure is called the "Haram" (the "forbidden" place). One end is taken up by a mosque and the whole is treated with the deepest awe.

Mesopotamia

The time had now come for Abraham to be concerned over finding a wife for Isaac. Proud of his ancient lineage, he did not wish to have Isaac intermarry with any of the Canaanite peoples among whom he lived. He decided, therefore, to send his steward to Haran where his brother, Nahor, and his family still lived. A wife was to be selected from among that family.

> Genesis 24:10. *And the servant . . . arose, and went to Mesopotamia, unto the city of Nahor.*

The word "Mesopotamia" is Greek and not Hebrew. It is used as a translation of the Hebrew term "Aram-Naharaim" with reference to the country surrounding Haran. The Revised Standard Version retains "Mesopotamia" but the Catholic and Jewish versions in my possession use "Aram-Naharaim" without translation, as does the Anchor Bible.

Of course, Aram-Naharaim is rather an anachronism as the use of the term "Philistine" was earlier (see page 85). The Aramaeans were not actually in possession of that region until some centuries after the time of Abraham.

Mesopotamia means "between the rivers" and was applied by the Greeks to the land between the Tigris and Euphrates, at first only to the portions north of Babylonia and then to the whole region. In that sense, Haran, and all of Aram-Naharaim (which means "Aram on the rivers"), is in Mesopotamia. The term "Mesopotamia" remained popular in the west down to World War I, and was the most used name for what I have been calling the Tigris-Euphrates region, and Babylonia.

Prior to World War I, Mesopotamia was a possession of Turkey. It was taken from Turkey after World War I and became a British mandate. At that time, the native name of the land, Iraq, came into favor and is now used exclusively. In 1932, Iraq was recognized as an independent nation. Although Iraq includes most of the ancient Mesopotamia, it is not quite extensive enough to include Haran within its borders.

Syria

A bride was indeed found for Isaac. She was Rebekah, earlier mentioned as the daughter of Bethuel and granddaughter of Nahor (see page 89). She had also a brother, Laban, with whom the negotiations for marriage were carried on, and who was to play an important part later in Genesis.

The matter is summarized:

Genesis 25:20. *And Isaac was forty years old when he took Rebekah to wife, the daughter of Bethuel the Syrian of Padan-Aram, the sister to Laban the Syrian.*

Padan-Aram (or "Paddan-Aram" in the Revised Standard Version) is clearly a term synonymous with Aram-Naharaim.

The term "Syrian" is the Greek version of "Aramaean" and throughout the King James Version, the terms "Aram" and "Aramaean" are translated as "Syria" and "Syrian" respectively. The Revised Standard Version speaks of "Bethuel the Aramaean" and "Laban the Aramaean" in this verse—although even to call them Aramaeans is anachronistic.

The term "Syria" stems back to a Babylonian word, "Suri," for a district along the upper Euphrates. In later times, the Greeks, pushing eastward, encountered this portion of the Aramaean lands first. The name Syria (in Latin spelling) came to apply to the eastern shores of the Mediterranean generally.

In the Bible, once that was translated into Greek, Syria came to be applied, in particular, to the region north of Canaan, which retained its independence of Assyria in the ninth and eighth centuries B.C. This became the Syria, with Damascus as its capital, which plays so important a role in the First and Second Books of Kings.

The region north of Canaan has remained Syria ever since, through Greek, Roman, and Moslem occupation. After World War I, Syria was freed of Turkish rule and was put under French mandate. In 1945, after World War II, the French also left and Syria became an independent republic, again with Damascus as its capital. It includes Haran near its northern border.

Midian

Before Genesis turns to a consideration of Isaac's descendants, however, it cleans up the matter of the various Abrahamic lines through
concubines. Thus:

> Genesis 25:1. *Then again Abraham took a wife, and her name was*
> *Keturah.*
> Genesis 25:2. *And she bare him . . . Midian . . . and Shuah.*

Other descendants, over a dozen, are listed, but most are names
only. All are eponyms, one would assume, of various Arabian tribes,
of whom Midian is by far the best known. Midian is the eponym of the
Midianites who ranged over the land of Midian. This is usually marked
on the maps as occupying the northwest corner of Arabia, separated
from Sinai by a narrow arm of the sea, and thus quite close to the
"wilderness of Paran" occupied by the Ishmaelites. Indeed, the Midianites and Ishmaelites are used almost synonymously in the Bible.

Shuah is of some interest in connection with the Book of Job, a matter
which will be taken up later.

The descendants of Ishmael are given later in the chapter, all of whom
are now only names. Twelve of them are given, representing twelve
tribes, analogous perhaps to the twelve tribes of Israel. One of the tribal
eponyms is Massa, a name with some significance when the time comes
to take up the Book of Proverbs.

Abraham is recorded, then, as dying at the age of 175, and as being
buried in the cave at Machpelah by Isaac and Ishmael. A half century
later, Ishmael died at the age of 137 and now with all loose ends carefully knotted, Genesis turns to Isaac and his descendants.

Edom

Isaac and Rebekah have twin sons, Esau and Jacob. The characters
of the two are contrasted: Esau is a rough hunter, an unsubtle man
of the outdoors, loved and admired by his father. Jacob is a quiet,
shrewd man living at home and the favorite of his mother.

Esau is the elder by a few minutes and is therefore entitled to the birthright; that is, to the inheritance of the main portion of his father's property. He is also entitled to a father's blessing as his chief heir and such a blessing had great legalistic value in the society of that time.

Jacob managed, however, to outmaneuver his older brother. At one point, when Esau was returning faint and weary from a hunt, he asked for some of the soup of red lentils which Jacob was preparing.

> Genesis 25:30. . . . *Feed me, I pray thee, with that same red pottage; for I am faint: therefore was his name called Edom.*

Jacob allowed him to eat but only after demanding the cession of the birthright in exchange, and receiving it.

The writer of Genesis thus gives Esau the alternate name of Edom ("red"), connecting that with the soup of red lentils that he desired. This made Esau (Edom) the eponymous ancestor of the Edomites, who, in centuries to come, were to occupy the territory south of Moab.

On the other hand, Jacob, who later in Genesis is given the alternate name of Israel, is the eponymous ancestor of the Israelites.

Throughout Old Testament times, there was continuing enmity between the Israelites and the Edomites. This is reflected backward into an enmity between the eponymous twin brothers.

Such enmity arose not only over the enforced sale of the birthright, but also as a result of a second successful deceit on the part of Jacob. Isaac, now blind and awaiting death, decided to give Esau the final blessing. To forestall this, Jacob dressed himself in Esau's clothes and put goatskins on his arms to imitate Esau's hairiness, and, pretending to be Esau, obtained his father's blessing.

Both these tales show a younger brother achieving hereditary dominance over an older. This forecast the actual historic situation—well established at the time Genesis was reduced to writing. The Israelites entered Canaan only after the Edomites had become well established on the outskirts, so that the Israelites were the "younger brother." On the other hand, through the centuries that followed the rise of David, the Israelites ruled over the Edomites.

Bethel

To prevent the possible murder of Jacob by a naturally resentful older brother, Rebekah decided to send her younger son away, at least temporarily. She persuaded Isaac to order him to Haran to get a wife for himself from the descendants of Nahor (as had been done in the case of Isaac himself).

On his nearly five-hundred-mile journey northward, Jacob slept at a certain place and dreamed of a ladder extending to heaven, with angels ascending and descending. He determined this to be a vision of God's dwelling place and decided that the ground on which he was standing was holy. (The Anchor Bible suggests that the vision of a ladder was really that of a ziggurat, which is built with steps working up along its outer walls.)

Genesis 28:19. *And he called the name of that place Bethel* . . .

The name "Bethel" means "house of God," an obvious reference to a temple, or even a ziggurat, which may have stood on the site quite early in Canaanite times.

The sacred traditions of Bethel were to have important consequences in the days of the divided kingdom a thousand years later, and to be a source of heresy among the Israelites. The city itself is located about fifty miles northeast of Beersheba and about eleven miles north of Jerusalem. It is now represented, according to general belief, by a village named Beitin.

Reuben and His Brothers

Jacob reached Haran safely and obtained not one wife, but two: Leah and Rachel, the daughters of Laban, who was the brother of his mother Rebekah. The girls were therefore his first cousins.

Carefully, the writers of Genesis record the birth of his children, beginning with his first:

Genesis 30:32. *And Leah conceived and bare a son, and she called his name Reuben* . . .

Jacob went on to have thirteen children listed by name: seven by Leah, two by Rachel, two by one concubine, Bilhah, and two by another concubine, Zilpah. Of these, twelve were born during his twenty-year stay with Laban and one was born after his return to Canaan.

These may be listed as follows:

Leah: Reuben, Simeon, Levi, Judah, Issachar, Zebulun, Dinah;
Rachel: Joseph, Benjamin;
Bilhah: Dan, Naphtali;
Zilpah: Gad, Asher.

All of these were sons, except for the one daughter, Dinah. It was Benjamin, the youngest child, who was born after Jacob's return to Canaan.

Each of the twelve sons was the eponym of a tribe of Israelites, though Joseph was, to be more accurate, the ancestor of two tribes, of which his sons were the eponyms.

It is sometimes tempting to interpret this in terms of a confederation of tribes uniting for the purpose of conquering Canaan and continuing to form a loose union (at times very loose) afterward. The tradition of descent from a single man, Jacob, would then be a way of marking off that confederation (binding it legally, in the family sense) as opposed to other related tribes—those of Edom, Moab, and Ammon, for instance—who did not join the confederation or even opposed it.

Furthermore, the division into four groups according to the maternal ancestress might indicate closer interrelationships. The "Leah tribes" may have formed the initial confederation, to which a pair of "Rachel tribes" later joined and the others still later.

However, such interpretations must remain guesswork. The only information we have concerning the early history of the Israelite tribes is what can be found in the Bible and this is not enough for the purpose.

It is interesting, though, that most of the sons of Jacob remain only names in the Book of Genesis. The only two who really appear as individuals are Judah and Joseph, the former eventually playing the chief role among the Leah tribes and the latter the chief role among the Rachel tribes. Moreover, when the Israelite kingdom was divided, the Joseph tribes (there were two of them) dominated the northern kingdom, while the tribe of Judah dominated the southern kingdom.

Genesis is built up chiefly of a pair of traditions, one developed in the northern kingdom, with tales of Joseph prominent; the other developed in the southern kingdom, with tales of Judah prominent.

While members of all twelve tribes are Israelites, it is the members of the tribe of Judah only that are, strictly speaking, Judeans, or Jews.

Seir

Jacob prospered in Haran and finally, after long-drawn-out quarreling with his father-in-law, Laban, left with his wives, his children, his cattle, and his goods. His next problem was to face his estranged brother, Esau. He had to prepare the way for such a meeting:

> Genesis 32:3. *And Jacob sent messengers before him to Esau his brother unto the land of Seir, the country of Edom.*

Esau is pictured as already dwelling in the area which, centuries later, was to be occupied by the Edomites. Seir is an alternate name of the land which is more usually called Edom.

More specifically, Seir is the name given to the range of mountains that covers much of Edom. This range runs in a north-south direction from the Dead Sea to the Gulf of Aqaba, the northeastern arm of the Red Sea. Directly to the west of this range is a deep, narrow depression, which is now called Wadi el-Arabah, a continuation of the Great Rift Valley.

The Wadi el-Arabah starts below sea level at the Dead Sea, but rises, and at its highest point, just about halfway between the Dead Sea and the Gulf of Aqaba, it rises to some seven hundred feet above sea level, though even at that point it is flanked by considerably higher ground, east and west.

Sometimes the name Seir is applied specifically to the highest mountain peak of the Seir range, which is known as Mount Seir. It is located about thirty miles south of the Dead Sea and is about 4400 feet high.

An alternate name of Mount Seir is Mount Hor. This reflects the fact that prior to the occupation of the land by the Edomites, it was occupied by a group of people called Horites. Thus, in the description of the peoples defeated by Chedorlaomer, the account includes:

> Genesis 14:6. *And the Horites in their Mount Seir . . .*

The Horites were, apparently, a non-Semitic people related to the Hittites. It was only a relatively small segment of these that had found their way so far south. Their main concentration was farther north and they are more frequently called "Hurrians." (The Horites to the south may, however, have been a distinct people with a name that only coincidentally resembled that of the Hurrians of the north.)

Like the Hittites, the Hurrians (Horites) had not yet reached the period of their greatness in patriarchal times. About 1475 B.C., however, they formed the kingdom of Mitanni along the northern Euphrates, taking up the area referred to in the Bible as Aram-Naharaim. For a while, Mitanni was one of the great powers of western Asia and held out against a conquering Egypt. A century later, however, it was overshadowed by the Hittite New Kingdom and by 1275 B.C. it was defeated and absorbed by the Assyrians.

When the Israelites were conquering Canaan, the great days of Mitanni were over. Like the Hittites, they had flourished during the interval when the Bible's attention is absent from Canaan, and their deeds are therefore not recorded.

The Hurrians had, apparently, more of an influence over the early customs of the patriarchal period than had been expected. The Anchor Bible painstakingly analyzes the tales of the marriages of the patriarchs, of the position of concubines, of questions concerning birthright, and so on, and finds that much that would otherwise be puzzling in the stories of Abraham, Isaac, and Jacob becomes clear in the light of Hurrian custom.

Earlier I had explained that the Anchor Bible expressed doubt as to whether Abraham's origins were in Ur or in Haran (see page 59) and whether the Israelites could trace their ancestry to Sumerians or to Aramaeans. If Haran were the origin, it would perhaps be at a point in time before the coming of the Aramaeans but not before the coming of the Hurrians (or the people from whom the Hurrians had borrowed their culture). Perhaps one might properly have the Israelites say: "A wandering Hurrian was my father." The fact that the Hurrians were not Semitic is not a crucial argument against this theory. It seems clear that the Israelites adopted the Canaanite language when they occupied Canaan; who can tell what their language might have been earlier. It might have had strong Hurrian components.

Israel

Esau came to meet Jacob and the two approached each other east of the Jordan. Jacob made ready for the meeting in considerable fear. His company, including his wives and children, were most vulnerable. The mere act of traveling with them, of getting the company across rivers, for instance, was difficult.

> Genesis 32:22. *And he rose up that night . . . and passed over the ford Jabbok.*

The Jabbok River is a tributary of the Jordan, flowing into it from the east at a point about twenty-five miles north of the Dead Sea.

After Jacob had supervised the crossing of the Jabbok on the part of his company and while he yet remained alone on the other side "there wrestled a man with him until the breaking of the day." In the morning, Jacob's adversary said:

> Genesis 32:28. . . . *Thy name shall be called no more Jacob, but Israel . . .*

and thus he became the eponym of the Israelites. The descendants of Jacob are regularly called "the children of Israel" in the Bible. Once the Israelites conquered Canaan, it becomes the "land of Israel." When the kingdom of David and Solomon breaks up, the northern part, which is the greater in area, population, and power, is called Israel.

Finally, when the modern Jewish state was established in Palestine in 1948, it took the name Israel.

Shechem

Fortunately, Esau seemed to hold no grudge against Jacob, but treated him graciously and generously. Nevertheless, Jacob, not completely trusting the good will of his brother, managed to persuade Esau to return to Seir and to leave him and his family to their own devices. Jacob then settled down in Canaan:

> Genesis 33:18. *And Jacob came to Shalem, a city of Shechem . . . and pitched his tent before the city.*

Shalem is not mentioned, as a city, elsewhere in the Bible. It is the Hebrew word for "peace" and the passage as it stands in the King James Version is clearly a mistranslation. The Revised Standard Version has it: "And Jacob came safely to the city of Shechem." In other words he did not come to Shalem, a city of Shechem; he came "in peace" to the city of Shechem.

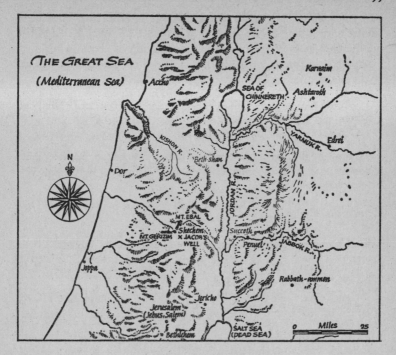

The City of Shechem

Shechem is about thirty miles north of Jerusalem and is considerably farther north than the areas where Abraham and Isaac dwelt. It was more than a hundred miles north of Seir, and no doubt Jacob felt that this was the sort of comfortable distance he wanted between himself and Esau.

Shechem is located in a narrow valley, not more than a hundred yards wide, between two mountains; a most strategic position, for it controls the road from the Jordan River to the sea, and from southern Canaan to northern. Through much of Biblical times, therefore, it was the most important city north of Jerusalem.

For forty years after the division of the Davidic kingdom, Shechem served as the capital of the northern kingdom. After that, when the capital of the northern kingdom was moved to Samaria, five miles northwest of Shechem, the importance of the older city began to decline.

After the destruction of Judea by Rome, the Emperor Vespasian initiated the rebuilding of a town near the site of what had once been Shechem, renaming it Neapolis ("new city"). This has been distorted into Nablus, its present name. It has a popultion of about 42,000.

Shechem was an important religious center, too. The first altar built by Abraham after he entered Canaan was near Shechem:

> Genesis 12:6. And Abram passed through the land unto the place of Sichem [Shechem] . . .
> Genesis 12:7. . . . and there builded he an altar unto the Lord . . .

All through Biblical times, Shechem retained its sacred character and it served as a rival at times even to the Temple at Jerusalem.

Hamor the Hivite

Jacob's stay in Shechem was, however, marked by tragedy:

> Genesis 34:1. And Dinah, the daughter of Leah . . . went out to see the daughters of the land.
> Genesis 34:2. And when Shechem the son of Hamor the Hivite, prince of the country, saw her, he took her . . . and defiled her.

The inhabitants of Shechem are here spoken of as Hivites. These are mentioned chiefly in connection with Shechem in the present instance and, in the Book of Joshua, as inhabiting Gibeon, a city some twenty-five miles south of Shechem. It is usual, therefore, to consider the Hivites another petty Canaanite tribe, concentrated in central Canaan. The Anchor Bible suggests, however, that the Hivites are a Hurrian people. Indeed, there may be some confusion, here and there in the Bible, between Horites, Hivites, and Hittites, and it is not really practical to try to untangle the matter completely.

Shechem wanted to marry Dinah after the rape, but the sons of Jacob agreed to permit this only if Shechem and all the males of the city would agree to be circumcised. (The lack of circumcision would seem to indicate that the Shechemites were not Semitic and this is a point in favor of the Hurrian theory.) After the circumcision, while the Shechemites were sore and uncomfortable, the sons of Jacob struck at them to avenge the rape.

> Genesis 34:25. . . . Simeon and Levi, Dinah's brethren . . . came upon the city boldly, and slew all the males.

This chapter of Genesis breaks into the personal story of Jacob and his sons and seems to describe a bit of early tribal history. It is not likely that two individual human beings would attack a city. Rather, this is a war of tribes, represented by their eponyms. Even Shechem, the rapist, is an eponym.

What may have happened is that three tribes in alliance attempted an assault on central Canaan prior to the general Israelite conquest of the land. The tribe of Dinah was defeated at Shechem and virtually destroyed and was then avenged by the tribes of Simeon and Levi, who themselves however, must have suffered badly and retired greatly weakened, eventually to join the Israelite confederacy when it gathered to assault Canaan.

That this is so is suggested by the fact that during the tribal period during and after the conquest of Canaan, Simeon and Levi were among the weakest of the tribes. Simeon occupied land in the far south and was absorbed by Judah soon after the conquest. Levi was never even assigned any coherent district but merely held certain isolated towns. The Levites in later times served a priestly function and were never again noted as warriors.

That the assault on Shechem was really a failure is indicated by the fact that Jacob is recorded as protesting bitterly against the raid and as finding himself forced to leave the area for fear of reprisal.

Nevertheless, the stay of Jacob in the area brought on certain patriarchal associations with Shechem. A mile and a half east of the city is still to be found "Jacob's Well," and a bit farther east, the tomb of Joseph. Indeed, the tradition arose in New Testament times that all of Jacob's sons were buried near Shechem.

Ephrath

Jacob and his family, after the troubles at Shechem, traveled southward about forty miles, passing through Bethel with its awe-inspiring memories for Jacob and then on to a point somewhere between Jerusalem and Hebron.

En route, the caravan had to stop for Rachel was giving birth to her second son, Benjamin, Jacob's youngest and the only son to be born in Canaan. With this birth, however, came tragedy again, for Rachel did not survive.

Genesis 35:19. *And Rachel died, and was buried in the way to Ephrath, which is Bethlehem.*

This is the first mention of Bethlehem in the Bible, Ephrath being its earlier, Canaanite name, or perhaps being the name of the tract of land in which the town itself was located.

Bilhah

While Jacob and his family dwelt in the region between Bethlehem and Hebron, still another variety of unpleasantness took place.

Genesis 35:22. *And it came to pass, when Israel dwelt in that land, that Reuben went and lay with Bilhah his father's concubine: and Israel heard it . . .*

Nothing further is said about this, as though the writers of Genesis found the matter too repulsive to pursue.

And it may be that this, too, reflects early tribal history. The tribe of Reuben must have been quite powerful at first. Since Reuben is listed as the oldest son of Israel, it may have been the leader of the confederacy when it was first formed.

The episode described above may mirror an attempt by Reuben to make its leadership absolute. (One of the methods by which a usurper attempted to dramatize and legitimize his position in Old Testament times was to take over the harem of his predecessor. Absalom did this when he rebelled against David, his father.) There may have followed a civil war ("Israel heard it") in which Reuben was defeated. Certainly, Reuben's primacy was lost and when the Israelites conquered Canaan, Reuben played a minor role. Nor did the tribe survive long afterward.

Amalek

Before going on with the tale of Jacob's sons, the writers of Genesis again pause to tie up some loose ends. The death of Isaac at the age of 180 is described, and then the genealogy of Esau is given and disposed of. Notably:

Genesis 36:10. *These are the names of Esau's sons; Eliphaz . . .*

Genesis 36:11. *And the sons of Eliphaz were Teman . . .*

Genesis 36:12. *And Timna was concubine to Eliphaz . . . and bare . . . Amalek . . .*

Eliphaz and Teman are of interest in connection with the Book of Job and this will be discussed when that book is taken up.

As for Amalek, he is the eponym of the Amalekites, a tribe apparently considered by the Israelites to be related to the Edomites, since they lived south of Canaan near the Edomite territory.

Amalek is the last of the eponyms of the non-Israelite nations. Genesis has mentioned up to this point a number of tribes as having descended from Terah. All of these may, in a very general sense, be classified as Hebrews, since all are descended from Eber, the great-great-great-grandfather of Terah. The relationships can be made clear from the accompanying simplified genealogical table.

Seir the Horite

The Book of Genesis then goes on to make a quick list of the rulers of Edom. They list first the Horite rulers who preceded the Edomites:

Genesis 37:20. *These are the sons of Seir the Horite . . .*

Seir is the Horite eponym of the nation as Edom is the Hebrew eponym. It is very likely, of course, that the Edomites did not replace the Horites root and branch, but, as is customary in the case of such conquests, settled among them and intermarried with them.

Thus, although Esau is earlier described as having married "daughters of Heth" (Genesis 26:34), one of his wives is, in this present chapter, described as "Adah the daughter of Elon the Hittite," and another as:

Genesis 36:2. . . . *Aholibamah the daughter of Anah the daughter of Zibeon the Hivite.*

(The second "daughter" in the verse is changed to "son" in the Revised Standard Version.)

By Hivite, here, is probably meant Horite. For that matter, it is not entirely beyond the bounds of possibility that by "Elon the Hittite" is

THE RELATIONSHIP OF THE VARIOUS "HEBREW" TRIBES
AS PRESENTED IN GENESIS

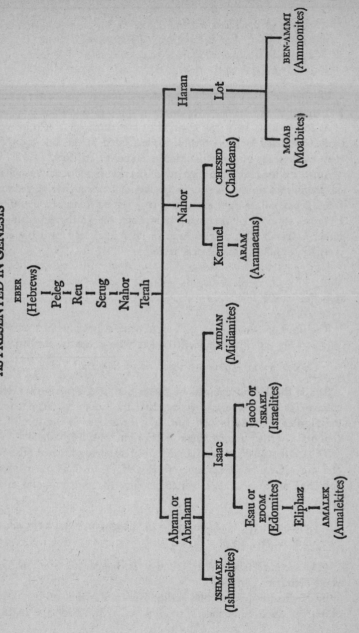

meant Elon, the Horite. As I said earlier, the Hittite-Hivite-Horite situation is hopelessly confused at times. It seems very likely, however, that these passages of the Bible indicate an intermingling of the Edomite invaders with the Horites already dwelling in the land.

Bela and Jobab

The chapter ends with a list of the successive kings that reigned over Edom before the kingship had been established in Israel. The Edomite kingship was not hereditary, since each new king seems to be unrelated to the one before, so that an elective monarchy may have been evolved. The first two kings are of interest.

Genesis 36:32. *And Bela the son of Beor reigned in Edom . . .*
Genesis 36:33. *And Bela died, and Jobab . . . reigned in his stead.*

Bela the son of Beor is sometimes equated with Balaam the son of Beor, who shows up in the Book of Numbers as an adversary of the Israelites, while Jobab is sometimes equated with Job, the hero of the book of that name.

The first identification is very unlikely and arises only through the probably accidental similarity of names. The second identification may also be unlikely, but it is a more attractive one for there are other connections between this chapter of Genesis and the Book of Job. For instance, among the names given in the Horite genealogy is one reminiscent of Job's native land, Uz.

Genesis 36:28. *The children of Dishan are these; Uz, and Aran.*

Potiphar

Genesis now enters its last section and deals with the story of Joseph, who is described as Jacob's favorite son and who is more than a little spoiled by the fact. He earns the hatred of his brothers by acting as a talebearer against them and by telling of dreams he has had which seem to foreshadow a day when he will be supreme over the family.

One day, Jacob sent Joseph to inquire after the welfare of his brothers, who were grazing the family's flocks in the neighborhood of Shechem (another reason for patriarchal associations—particularly that of Joseph and his brothers—with that city).

They had left Shechem by the time he arrived and had passed on to Dothan, a town about fifteen miles farther north. Joseph followed them there. The brothers spied him from the distance and conspired to kill him. At the intervention of Reuben or Judah (there are two traditions here, one stemming from the northern tribes and the other from the southern, and both are included by the final editors of Genesis) he is not killed but is sold to passing nomads. Jacob is then told Joseph was killed by wild beasts and the old father goes into deep mourning.

Joseph is carried southward, then westward to Egypt:

> Genesis 37:36. And the Midianites sold him into Egypt unto Potiphar, an officer of Pharaoh's . . .

Except for the short episode of Abraham's stay in Egypt (see page 64) this is the first appearance of this land as the scene of the Biblical story. Where Abraham's stay involves no details except for the mention of Pharaoh and his harem, the description of Joseph's stay is much more circumstantial. It begins immediately with the mention of the name of an Egyptian which, indeed, is a thoroughly Egyptian name. Potiphar is the shortened form of "Potiphera" meaning "he whom Ra gave." (This is analogous to the name "Theodore" in our own Western world.)

Pharez and Zarah

In view of the overwhelming importance of Judah among the tribes in later history, the writers of Genesis felt it necessary to incorporate some Judean genealogy. This seemed to them to be the logical point—Joseph had disappeared and the lapse of time could be emphasized by a shift in focus.

In circumstantial detail, it is told how Judah was tricked into consorting with Tamar, a woman who had originally been married to two of his sons, each of whom had died young and childless. Tamar then gave birth to twins, presenting them as new heirs to Judah.

During the childbirth, one of the twins began to emerge and the midwife tied a scarlet thread about the finger, declaring him to be the first-born. However:

Genesis 38:29. . . . *he drew back his hand . . .* [and] *his brother come out: and . . . his name was called Pharez.*

Genesis 38:30. *And afterward came out his brother . . . and his name was called Zarah.*

The two brothers are called Perez and Zerah in the Revised Standard Version and these names are preferable.

The twin brothers are eponyms who mark the two chief clans of the tribe of Judah, the Zerahites (or Zarthites) and the Perezites (or Pharzites). The tale told here undoubtedly reflects some early tribal history.

Apparently, within the tribe of Judah, the Zerahites achieved early dominance after two clans, represented by Judah's older sons, had died out. Therefore Zarah (Zerah) is listed here as technically the first-born. In time, however, the Perezites achieved the leadership, as is indicated by the fact that Zarah drew back and allowed his twin the actual primacy of birth.

If the importance of the Perezite clan needed reinforcement in the eyes of the later Jews, it is only necessary to point out that the great hero-king, David, and therefore all the subsequent Judean kings were Perezites, a fact made clear in the Book of Ruth.

Pharaoh [of Joseph]

In Egypt, Joseph, through his diligence and intelligence, prospers and is made steward of Potiphar's household. However, Potiphar's wife attempts to seduce the young man and, on failing, accuses him to her husband of having tried to rape her. Joseph is cast into prison.

There, again by his diligence and intelligence, he gains the favor of the jailer. He also gains the respect of his fellow prisoners by showing himself to be an ingenious interpreter of dreams. In particular, Pharaoh's butler, temporarily imprisoned, is gratified by Joseph's dream interpretation and promises to mention the matter to Pharaoh, but forgets.

Nor is it only the prisoners who dream:

Genesis 41:1. *And it came to pass . . . that Pharaoh dreamed, and behold, he stood by the river.*

Pharaoh dreamed that seven fat cows emerged from the river, but that seven lean cows emerged after them, ate the fat cows but remained as lean as before. He woke, then fell asleep and dreamed similarly about seven good ears of grain and seven bad ones.

Pharaoh's wise men were unable to interpret the dream to the monarch's satisfaction. Now Pharaoh's butler finally remembered the Hebrew slave who had been in prison with him.

Joseph was called for and interpreted the dreams at once. The seven fat cows and seven good ears of grain, he said, meant seven prosperous years, while the seven lean cows and seven bad ears of grain represented seven years of famine to follow, years of famine that would consume the land. The grain of the good years should therefore be carefully preserved and stored against the bad years to come.

Pharaoh was struck favorably by the interpretation and suggestion and placed Joseph in complete charge. Quickly he became the all-powerful prime minister of Egypt.

The question is, then, who was this Pharaoh, who was so favorable to a Hebrew slave and who, later, was to be benevolent to the family of Jacob generally? He could not very well be the usual run of Pharaohs for Egypt had so long been isolated that they were quite xenophobic; hostile at worst and patronizing at best to foreigners. The Egyptian Pharaoh was considered as a god by the Egyptians and by Pharaoh himself and he was not likely to delegate power to Asian foreigners. —Unless he himself were an Asian foreigner.

If we turn to Egyptian history, we find that the Middle Kingdom of Abraham's time (see page 64) lasted for two hundred years, from 1991 B.C. to 1786 B.C., enduring through much of the patriarchal period.

When the Middle Kingdom decayed there followed a new period of anarchy in Egypt, with weak dynasties ruling different portions of the kingdom.

About 1730 B.C. Egypt's weakness made it possible for Asian invaders to begin moving into the land. The Semitic invaders who, for a century and a half, were to rule the Nile delta and, on occasion, parts of the upper reaches of the Nile also, are called the Hyksos, which seems to be derived from Egyptian words meaning "foreign kings."

The Hyksos, making up the 15th and 16th dynasties in the ancient (more or less mangled) lists of Egyptian kings, established their capital at the northeastern edge of the delta, the point closest to Asia.

There is little record of the Hyksos and their rule remaining today, for later Egyptian historians apparently found the story of Egypt's defeat and subjection too unpleasant to talk about. The only account we have is that to be found in a book by Josephus, a Jewish historian who lived in the first century A.D. and who quoted from Manetho, an Egyptian historian who lived three centuries before Josephus' time.

From this, we might judge that the Hyksos ruled not only over the Nile delta, but also over part of the western half of the Fertile Crescent. If so, this is important.

Until the story of Joseph, the Book of Genesis had ignored Egypt except for a ten-verse description of Abraham's visit there. This was natural. Canaan had been, from the time of Sargon of Agade at least, and perhaps even from the time of Lugal-Zagissi of Erech, under the influence of the Tigris-Euphrates region. For much of the period, indeed, the Fertile Crescent had been a single realm, politically. This meant that movement was free between all parts of the Fertile Crescent. Abraham had come from Ur; his servant, and later Jacob, had returned to Haran temporarily; Sodom and its allies fought against invading armies from the Tigris-Euphrates.

Egypt, however, was another civilization and another world and was separated from the Fertile Crescent by a more or less permanent political boundary. Beginning in 1730 B.C., however, that political boundary was erased and the same power—the Hyksos—ruled over Canaan and over Egypt. Travelers between the two regions could move freely and when the Midianites purchased Joseph in Canaan it was easy to sell him as a slave in Egypt.

The picture of the friendly and gracious Pharaoh of Joseph's time may therefore be that of one of the Hyksos rulers. He would find Joseph a fellow Semite and would consider it perfectly thinkable to place the Egyptians under a Semitic viceroy.

Even this much is conjecture, of course, although it is *reasonable* conjecture, for the Bible makes no mention of the Hyksos as such, and no historical source outside the Bible (or those derived from the Bible) makes any mention of Joseph or of the dramatic events described in Genesis concerning his stay in Egypt. And even if Joseph's Pharaoh were indeed one of the Hyksos kings, it seems, on the basis of present knowledge at least, to be beyond hope to pin down which particular one of the line he might be.

According to Josephus, the tale of the Hyksos is the Egyptian version of the coming of Joseph and, later, of his family, to Egypt. The Hyksos, according to Josephus' views, *were* the Israelites, but this is not taken seriously by anyone nowadays.

The River [Nile]

In Genesis 41:1, when the description of Pharaoh's dream begins, it is stated "he stood by the river."

In Egypt, it was never necessary to describe what was meant by "the river." There was only one river and it virtually *is* Egypt. Egypt is a desert land where it virtually never rains. What water there is comes from the single river that threads its length from south to north. What communication and trade there was in Biblical times came through the boats that passed up and down the Nile; what population existed, lived by virtue of the food that could be grown in the land that was flooded each summer by the life-giving waters of the Nile. The Greek historian Herodotus, in a famous phrase, called Egypt "the gift of the Nile" and so it was.

(Modern Egypt is still the gift of the Nile today. Fully twenty-seven million people crowd the narrow banks of the river while the land to east and west is virtually empty.)

It is not surprising that in Pharaoh's dream, he imagined that:

Genesis 41:2. . . . *there came up out of the river seven well-favoured kine and fatfleshed . . .*

Cattle do not literally emerge from a river, but if these cattle represent seven years of good harvest, it is only fitting they come out of the Nile, for all harvests depended upon its water. And seven lean cows would emerge from the Nile, if the Nile floods fell below normal height as once in a while they disastrously did.

The word "Nile" is neither Egyptian nor Hebrew, but is a Greek word of unknown derivation. "Nile" does not occur anywhere in the King James Version of the Bible, although it is used in the Revised Standard Version, which has Pharaoh "standing by the Nile," for instance, in Genesis 41:1.

The Egyptian word for the Nile was "Hapi," a sacred name used to represent the god of the river. In ordinary usage, the Nile was simply "the river," a phrase which in Egyptian is "Yor" and in its Hebrew form "Yeor."

The Nile is about four thousand miles long, a hair longer perhaps

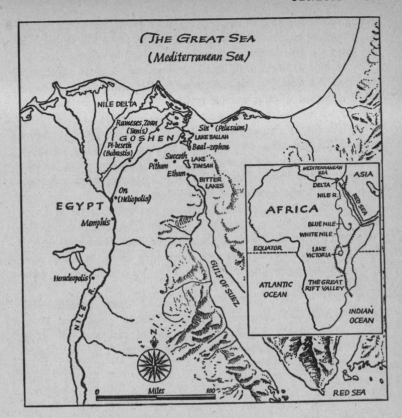

The Nile River

than the Missouri-Mississippi and the Amazon. That would make it the longest river in the world.

Its remotest headwaters are in Tanganyika, where the Kagera River rises and flows 429 miles (forming a bit of the western boundary of Tanganyika) and then discharges into Lake Victoria, which in terms of surface area is the second largest fresh-water lake in the world. (Our own Lake Superior is the largest.) From the northeastern corner of Lake Victoria emerges the White Nile, which flows northward through Kenya, the Sudan, and Egypt and into the Mediterranean at last.

The main tributary is the Blue Nile. This rises in Lake Tana in northern Ethiopia. It flows east to begin with but makes a huge circle, joining the White Nile, at last, in Khartoum, the capital of the Sudan. The stretch of river downstream from the junction of the White Nile and the Blue Nile is the Nile itself, unqualified by adjective.

Two hundred miles north of Khartoum, another smaller tributary joins the Nile from the east and thereafter the river flows a thousand miles to the sea without a single further tributary, flowing through a solid stretch of desert in doing so.

The Nile flood is derived from the annual rains that fall not in Egypt but in east central Africa far upstream. The flood waters carry rich muck from the Ethiopian and Kenyan highlands. The Blue Nile, though shorter than the White Nile, is the more important in this respect, contributing much more to the flood volume.

The great length of the Nile, stretching southward as far as Egyptian, Greek, or Roman eyes could see, presented the ancient world with a mystery. Where was the far-off source of the Nile? Occasional reports that the Nile had its origin in great lakes were spread by Greek and, later, by Arabic merchants, and this seems to have reflected successful exploring expeditions.

It was not, however, until the 1870's that the African expeditions of the Anglo-American explorer Henry Morton Stanley placed east Africa and its lakes on the map in the full light of day, and only then was the Nile traced completely from source to sea.

On

With Joseph now a high official, Pharaoh bestowed on him a highborn wife:

> Genesis 41:45. . . . *and he gave him to wife Asenath, the daughter of Potipherah priest of On* . . .

Joseph's new father-in-law bore the same name as his old master, but the two need not necessarily be one man. Different men do bear the same name.

On, or Anu, was a city of great religious importance to the Egyptians. It was located at the southern base of the delta just about six miles northeast of modern Cairo. It was an important center for the worship of the Egyptian sun-god, Ra, so that the Egyptians called it "Pa-ra" ("house of Ra"). In the Book of Jeremiah, a direct Hebrew translation of Pa-ra is used for the city. Jeremiah in thundering against Egypt warns of the destruction that will follow a Babylonian invasion and says:

Jeremiah 43:13. *He shall break also the images of Beth-she-mesh . . .*

where "Beth-shemesh" means "house of the Sun."

The Greeks also used a translation of Pa-ra as the name of the city, calling it Heliopolis ("city of the Sun") and it is by that name that it is best known to posterity. It remained a center of Egyptian religion and learning throughout Old Testament times. It was well known for its obelisks and the Revised Standard Version changes the passage in Jeremiah 43:13 and makes "images of Beth-shemesh" into "obelisks of Heliopolis." Cleopatra's Needles, two great obelisks, taken out of Egypt and erected, one in London and one in New York's Central Park, are from Heliopolis.

After 300 B.C., when the Macedonian dynasty, the Ptolemies, took over Egypt and made Alexandria (about 220 miles northwest of Heliopolis) their capital, Heliopolis declined. Only a few ruins remain.

Goshen

Joseph's rule over Egypt was successful. The produce of the seven good years was carefully stored against the coming famine and two sons, Manasseh and Ephraim, were born to him. Then, when the famine came, Egypt was prepared.

Canaan was not, however. Jacob and his sons suffered from lack of food and the sons were sent to Egypt to buy grain. Joseph used the occasion to test them. He treated them harshly and demanded they bring Benjamin (whom Jacob had solicitously kept at home) with them if they ever came for food again.

They did so and Joseph maneuvered matters so that he seemed to have a legitimate reason for taking Benjamin captive and putting him to death. Once before the brothers had been willing to sacrifice one of themselves, regardless of the pain they might cause their father. Had they changed? Apparently, they had. They refused to abandon Benjamin, and Judah, in one of the most touching speeches of literature, offers himself as a slave in place of Benjamin since otherwise "thy servants shall bring down the gray hairs of thy servant our father with sorrow to the grave."

And then Joseph finally revealed himself and there was a grand reconciliation.

Since Joseph was now Egypt's all-powerful viceroy and since his successful handling of the crisis of famine must have made him popular throughout the land, he had no hesitation in inviting his entire family into Egypt; nor had Pharaoh any hesitation in welcoming them. The word Joseph sent to his father was:

> Genesis 45:10. *And thou shalt dwell in the land of Goshen, and thou shalt be near unto me* . . .

Goshen is usually represented as being located on the eastern border of the Nile delta. This would be the first portion of Egypt reached by settlers from Canaan. Furthermore, if all this were indeed taking place during the period of Hyksos rule, the Egyptian capital of Tanis, where Joseph would be holding office, would be right at the western borders of the district. Jacob and his sons would thus indeed be "near unto" Joseph.

Jacob, transfigured with joy, prepares to obey. Genesis lists the males who accompany him to Egypt, his sons, grandson, and great-grandsons, and counts all the males of the company (including Joseph and his sons) at the round figure of seventy.

They arrive, are introduced to Pharaoh, and then:

> Genesis 47:11. . . . *Joseph . . . gave them a possession in the land of Egypt . . . in the land of Rameses* . . .

By "land of Rameses" is meant Goshen. It is an anachronistic name for it refers to a city of the region which was not built in the Hyksos period but only some centuries later.

Ephraim and Manasseh

Jacob was 130 years of age when he entered Egypt and lived there seventeen years. Then came the time when he felt himself to be dying. In his last days he asked Joseph to bring his sons to him. Joseph brought his young sons for their grandfather's blessing, and Jacob adopted them as his own:

Genesis 48:5. *And now thy two sons, Ephraim and Manasseh . . .*
are mine; as Reuben and Simeon, they shall be mine.

Joseph thus came to be the ancestor of two of the tribes of Israel,
those of Ephraim and Manasseh, and sometimes they are lumped together as the "Joseph tribes."

Since Jacob had twelve sons and since one of them, Joseph, was
the ancestor of two tribes, there turned out to be thirteen tribes altogether. However, the tribe of Levi never received any distinct tract
of land in Canaan in later centuries, but formed a priestly caste that
lived scattered through the land. The twelve tribes of Israel, as
represented in a later age by definite pieces of Canaanite territory,
were: Reuben, Simeon, Judah, Dan, Gad, Issachar, Zebulun, Asher,
Naphtali, Benjamin, Ephraim, and Manasseh.

The fact that Joseph fathered two tribes while the rest only fathered
one each indicates that he received the birthright (a double share of
the inheritance) in place of Reuben, who would ordinarily have
received it as the eldest son. Joseph's inheritance of the birthright
is made plain, at least in the King James Version, when Jacob tells
him:

Genesis 48:22. *Moreover I have given to thee one portion above*
thy brethren . . .

This is not a clear verse, however. The Hebrew word *shekem*,
translated here as "portion," usually means "shoulder" and therefore
perhaps a mountain slope. In the Revised Standard Version, Jacob
is made to say "Moreover I have given to you rather than to your
brothers one mountain slope . . ." On the other hand, it might refer
to the city of Shechem, and the Anchor Bible translates it, "I give you
as the one above your brothers, Shechem . . ."

As a matter of fact, when Canaan was apportioned among the tribes,
centuries later, Ephraim received one portion and Manasseh, the
second Joseph tribe, received another portion—including Shechem and
its environs.

When Jacob prepared to bless Ephraim and Manasseh, Joseph carefully arranged matters so as to have Manasseh, the first-born, within
reach of Jacob's right hand, since the old man, like his father before
him, was blind with old age and could not tell them apart, unaided.

Nevertheless, Jacob crossed his arms, placing his right hand upon the head of Ephraim, the younger.

This again probably reflects early tribal history and suggests a situation parallel to that involving Pharez and Zarah (see page 107). At the start, Manasseh may have been the dominating group within the Joseph tribes, so that tradition has him Joseph's first-born. At some later date, however, Ephraim obtained and kept the upper hand.

Judah

Jacob then ordered his sons to gather round his deathbed while he forecast the future of each to them. There follows the "Testament of Jacob," which seems to reflect the situation as it existed in the time of David, so that the forty-ninth chapter of Genesis probably received its final form in that time.

The language used is oracular and, while possibly easily understood as referring to known historical events by the men of the time, has become obscure to us with the passage of time.

The first three sons are dismissed quickly. Their early domination had faded completely by David's time:

Genesis 49:3. *Reuben, thou art my firstborn* . . .

Genesis 49:4. *Unstable as water, thou shalt not excel; because thou wentest up to thy father's bed* . . .

Genesis 49:5. *Simeon and Levi are brethren; instruments of cruelty are in their habitations.*

. . . .

Genesis 49:7. *Cursed be their anger* . . .

The traditional reasons for their failure are Reuben's seduction of Bilhah, and the attack by Simeon and Levi on Shechem (see pages 100 and 102).

Turning then to his fourth son, Jacob is depicted as becoming enthusiastic.

Genesis 49:8. *Judah, thou art he whom thy brethren shall praise* . . .

. . . .

Genesis 49:10. *The sceptre shall not depart from Judah, nor a lawgiver from between his feet* . . .

This reflects the fact that when a stable and powerful kingdom was established over the land of Israel, it was David of the tribe of Judah that established it. Israel had by then defeated all its enemies and had established its domination over the entire western half of the Fertile Crescent. It seemed to have brought the story of Israel to a triumphant climax, a kind of "happy ending" that suffuses this part of the Testament.

To be sure, less than a century after David's coming to power, the kingdom was split in two and the Judean dynasty of David retained only the lesser half. Presumably the forty-ninth chapter was placed in its final form before the split had taken place.

Of course, the kingship over the southern portion of the land remained in the Davidic line without real interruption until 586 B.C., so that at no time for over four centuries did the sceptre "depart from Judah."

The remaining brothers are, with one exception, noted briefly and cryptically, and, on the whole, favorably. The exception is, of course, Joseph, who is praised exuberantly and lengthily. This is a reflection of the importance of the tribes of Ephraim and Manasseh during the tribal period before the establishment of David's kingdom.

It might also have been a matter of diplomacy. The northern tribes did not take kindly to Judean dominance and indeed broke away quickly enough. It would not have been politic to withhold praise from their outstanding representative.

Jacob then died at the age of 147, and was brought back by his sons to Canaan that he might be buried in the Cave of Machpelah where were already buried his grandparents, Abraham and Sarah, his parents, Isaac and Rebekah, and one of his wives, Leah.

About half a century later, Joseph died too, at the age of 110, and with that the Book of Genesis comes to an end at a date which might be estimated to be 1650 B.C. The curtain drops over an Egypt in which the Hyksos are still in firm control and the Israelites are still welcome guests of the nation.

When the curtain rises again, with the opening of the next book, some four centuries have passed, and conditions have changed drastically.

2. EXODUS

Exodus

Between the first two books of the Bible there is a long chronological gap of some four centuries following the entry of Jacob and
his sons into Egypt. To bridge the gap, the second book begins with
a hasty summary, listing the names of the heads of families who
entered Egypt:

> Exodus 1:1. *Now these are the names of the children of Israel . . .*

The phrase "Now these are the names" is a translation of the
Hebrew *ve-elleh shemoth*. The Jews use that phrase as the name of
this second book, usually reducing the phrase to the single word
"Shemoth" ("names"). The Septuagint named the book "Exodos"
(or, in the Latin equivalent, "Exodus"), meaning "going out," because it deals with the departure of the Israelites from Egypt.

Ephraim

Though the sons of Jacob are listed at the beginning of Exodus,
the Bible makes no further mention of the eponymous patriarchs of
the tribes as individuals, with a single exception.

In the First Book of Chronicles, which quickly reviews the genealogies of early history as viewed by the Jews of the post-Exilic

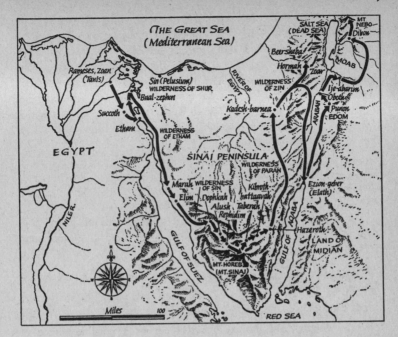

The Exodus

period, there is a passing mention that some sons of Ephraim (Joseph's younger son) took part in a cattle raid against a city in southern Canaan and were slain in the process.

1 Chronicles 7:22. *And Ephraim their father mourned many days, and his brethren came to comfort him.*

It is not clearly stated that this passage refers to the period during which the Israelites were in Egypt and, indeed, it is improbable that it does. Egypt was then in a strong and settled period of its history and it is unlikely that cattle raids within its borders would be permitted. Then, too, the site of the raid is some 150 miles from Goshen and that is a long distance to go chasing cattle.

It may well be that this verse records an early passage in tribal history within Canaan some centuries after the period when Jacob's sons had been alive. Ephraim may here represent the tribe generally rather than the ancestor individually.

Except for this one reference, all else concerning Jacob's sons is extra-Biblical legend. Joseph is supposed to have been the first of the brethren to have died and Levi the last. About 100 B.C., a book entitled "*The Testament of the Twelve Patriarchs*" was written, containing what were purportedly the deathbed statements of each of the twelve sons of Jacob. Each son reviewed his own life, bewailed his shortcomings, and urged his children to avoid his sins and to practice virtue. Whatever moral and ethical values these lectures might have, they are valueless as history.

Pharaoh [of the Oppression]

In any case, Exodus records that after the deaths of Joseph and his brothers, the Israelites prospered, multiplied, and grew numerous. And then:

> Exodus 1:8. . . . *there arose up a new king over Egypt, which knew not Joseph.*

The new Pharaoh, unlike Joseph's kindly patron, had no sympathy for the Israelites but, rather, feared them as a possible source of danger in the land and, therefore, took stern measures against them.

If the Pharaoh of Joseph were, indeed, one of the early Hyksos kings, then it seems fairly clear what happened—

The Hyksos did not, after all, completely control Egypt. Their power was concentrated in the delta and, far to the south, native Egyptian forces held local power and gathered strength.

About 500 miles up the Nile was a city later known to the Greeks as Thebes and it was the most prominent city of upper Egypt. Under the Old Kingdom and the Middle Kingdom, its importance was masked by Memphis and the cities of the delta. In times of political disintegration, however, dynasties at Thebes sometimes ruled over a virtually independent south. The 11th dynasty, for instance, in the years preceding the establishment of the Middle Kingdom, ruled from Thebes.

Once the Hyksos conquered Egypt, Thebes had another chance. Throughout the Hyksos period, it maintained a precarious independence, and gradually learned those military techniques (the horse and chariot, an improved bow, the use of body armor) of which it had been ignorant and with which the Hyksos armies had conquered Egypt.

In 1570 B.C., Ahmose, the first king of a new dynasty, the 18th, came to power in Thebes and launched a firm attack against the Hyksos, now complacent and rather decadent. Ahmose defeated them, broke their power, and made himself Pharaoh over all Egypt— once more under a native dynasty after a century and a half of foreign rule.

Ahmose might well have been the "new king over Egypt, which knew not Joseph." As representative of the resurgent Egyptians, he could have nothing but dislike and suspicion for the Israelites, who had been brought in by the Hyksos and whom he might consider nothing more than a remnant of them. In any renewed invasion from Asia, Ahmose might well consider that the Israelites would join with the invaders, to whom they would be bound by ties of culture and language.

Ahmose's reign, though it may have marked the beginning of this downturn in Israelite fortunes, may not have seen it carried through to completion. This sort of thing feeds on itself. The Israelites, treated as second-class citizens and as objects of suspicion, become disaffected and this disaffection is itself the excuse for intensified oppression. The oppressor, rightly fearing the resentment of the oppressed, finds discrimination escalating into slavery almost automatically.

Exodus 1:13. And the Egyptians made the children of Israel to serve with rigour:

Exodus 1:14. And they made their lives bitter with hard bondage . . .

It is the particular Pharaoh (not necessarily Ahmose; indeed, almost certainly not Ahmose) under whom Israelite enslavement reached its peak who is termed the "Pharaoh of the Oppression."

In deciding, then, who the Pharaoh of the Oppression might be, let us turn to Egyptian history.

After the time of Ahmose, the Egyptians, with the new battle techniques they had learned from the Hyksos, entered the most militarily successful era of their history. This period is known as the "New Kingdom" or, because Egypt spectacularly extended its power over portions of adjoining Asia, the "Empire."

The great military events that attended the establishment and maintenance of the Egyptian Empire took place entirely during the period of Israelite enslavement in Egypt and therefore no whisper of it is retained in the Bible, whose writers concentrated entirely on the fate of the Israelites.

Under Thutmose I (1525-08 B.C.) and Thutmose III (1490-36 B.C.)—particularly the latter, sometimes called "Thutmose the Great" and "the Napoleon of Ancient Egypt"—victorious Egyptian armies scoured the western half of the Fertile Crescent. In 1479 B.C., Thutmose III won a great battle at Megiddo, a city of northern Canaan, about fifty miles north of Jerusalem. With that, Canaan and all the land northward, nearly to the Euphrates, became Egyptian. Under Amenhotep III (1397-70 B.C.) the empire rested upon a plateau of prosperity and success.

With the son of Amenhotep III, Amenhotep IV (1370-53 B.C.), a decline set in. The new king was a religious revolutionary. In a land of numerous gods, he was a monotheist, recognizing a single god, Aton, represented in nature by the sun. Since his own name Amenhotep means "Amen is content" and glorifies the god, Amen, the new Pharaoh rejected the name as idolatrous and called himself Ikhnaton ("Aton is satisfied"). He also established a new capital at a city he named Akhetaton ("the horizon of Aton") located about halfway between Thebes and the delta. On its site now stands the village of Tell el Amarna.

Ikhnaton tried to establish the new monotheism throughout Egypt by force, but the priests of the older gods fought him relentlessly and on their side was the innate conservatism of the Egyptian people. After Ikhnaton's early death and a short reign of only about seventeen years, his new religion fell apart. Under his young son-in-law Tutankhaton (1352-43 B.C.) the old priesthood won a complete victory. Akhetaton was abandoned and Tutankhaton was forced to change his name to Tutankhamon.

While Ikhnaton was absorbed in his religious revolution, the Asian dominions of the empire were under constant attack. In A.D. 1887, the ruins of Akhetaton yielded a large cache of letters from Egyptian viceroys in Asia. It is a melancholy tale of continuous incursions from the north and east and of useless pleas for help to Ikhnaton, who lacked the ability, or perhaps the will, to fight off the marauding bands from the desert.

A more formidable foe was arising in the north. The Hittite Old Kingdom (see page 78) had been weakened and rendered harmless by Thutmose III, but after that conqueror's death, the Hittites hardened once more into their New Kingdom. In Ikhnaton's time, the greatest of the Hittite kings, Shubbiluliu, was on the throne. He conquered Mitanni and beat back the Egyptian boundary to Canaan itself.

After Tutenkhamon's death (and it was his untouched tomb that was discovered in A.D. 1922; see page 63) the 18th dynasty quickly declined and petered out. In its place a new family succeeded to the throne. This was the 19th dynasty, and its first member, Rameses I, became Pharaoh in 1304 B.C. Under him, the Egyptian Empire experienced a new period of vigor.

This dynasty reached its peak under Rameses II ("Rameses the Great"), whose long reign stretched from 1290 to 1223 B.C., and during this time Egypt came into direct conflict with the Hittites. In 1288 B.C., a great battle was fought between the two empires at Kadesh, about eighty miles north of Damascus. The battle was indecisive, as was the entire war, which ended in a compromise peace by which the Hittites retained their conquests of the previous century. The effort to withstand Egypt had, however, fatally weakened the Hittite power and had seriously strained Egypt itself.

Rameses II is the most famous of all the Pharaohs. His long reign gave him ample time to indulge in all his grandiose notions. He beautified Thebes, which was at the height of its splendor during his reign. He covered Egypt with gigantic statues of himself, with self-glorifying inscriptions, and is reported to have had 160 children by numerous wives and concubines.

Rameses II contributed largely to the later legend of "Sesostris." When, eight centuries after Egypt's great days of empire, Herodotus, the Greek historian, visited the ancient land, the priests and antiquarians of Egypt gladly rehearsed the glorious past, with improvements. By Herodotus' time, Egypt was far in decline and had been conquered by two different Asian empires, the Assyrian and the Persian. It suited Egyptian pride therefore to recall a time, now dimly lost in the mists of the far past, when it had been Egypt that was the world empire.

The name Herodotus reports for the conqueror was Sesostris, the actual name of three Pharaohs of the 12th dynasty, the first of whom might conceivably have been Abraham's Pharaoh (see page 64). The Middle Kingdom had first carried Egypt's power beyond its borders into Ethiopia. These deeds were combined with the still greater ones of Thutmose III and Rameses II and the whole escalated to the point where "Sesostris" conquered all of Ethiopia, penetrated Asia far beyond the Euphrates, marched through Asia Minor and into Europe, subduing the plains beyond the Black Sea.

After Rameses II, there were no further grounds for dreaming of a Sesostris. Egypt began to decline and, with only occasional minor rallies, each less successful than the one before, continued to decline throughout Biblical times.

Where, then, in this long history would the Pharaoh of the Oppression be found?

Ikhnaton offers an attractive possibility. He was unique in the long line of Pharaohs; a rebel, a breaker of tradition, a monotheist. Could he have been the kindly Pharaoh, welcoming the monotheistic Jacob and his sons into Egypt? This is quite unlikely, unfortunately, as Ikhnaton's reign is considerably too late for that.

There is another possibility. Could Ikhnaton have been reigning at the close of the period of Israelite enslavement rather than its start? Could he have learned his monotheism from Moses or, as some have suggested, could Moses have learned it from Ikhnaton?

Could it be, in fact, that Ikhnaton's father, Amenhotep III, was the strong Pharaoh of the Oppression, and that under Ikhnaton's feeble and self-absorbed rule, the Israelites broke out of Egypt? In favor of this are the Tell el Amarna reports from Canaan of the onslaught of the desert tribes. Might not these be the Israelites themselves, now out of Egypt and driving hard to conquer Canaan?

This is unlikely on several counts. In the first place, Ikhnaton's reign is too early for the Israelite conquest of Canaan. Such an early conquest will not square with the better-known dates of later events in the Bible.

This is not to deny that Canaan was under assault from the desert under Ikhnaton but it is very likely that the assaulters at that time were the tribes who settled down along the borders of Canaan (having failed to penetrate its interior against Egyptian defenses) as the Edomites, Moabites, and Ammonites. After all, the Biblical story is quite clear on the point that when the Israelites themselves approached

Canaan, the Edomites, Moabites, and Ammonites were already established on the ground and in firm possession of the land to the
east and south of the Dead Sea.*

To be sure, these earlier invaders were closely allied to the Israelites
and it may even be that some of the tribes who were later to
join in the Israelite confederacy were already attacking Canaan and
were to be joined later by tribes emerging from Egypt. There are
some who suggest that only the Joseph tribes, Ephraim and Manasseh,
were enslaved in Egypt; and that after they left Egypt they joined a
federation of tribes who were attacking Canaan directly from the
desert.

Then, too, if the Israelites had emerged from Egypt and conquered
Canaan during and after the reign of Ikhnaton, they would have
been caught up in the gigantic campaigns of Rameses II that followed. The Bible could not very well have failed to capture even an
echo of the mighty battle of Kadesh.

One must look later, then, for the Pharaoh of the Oppression and
speculation inevitably alights on Rameses II himself. Why not?
Rameses II was a vainglorious despot quite capable of making the
most arbitrary use of his powers. He was engaged in a life-and-
death struggle with an Asian power and he was bound to look upon
the Asians within his own realm with the utmost suspicion. It is quite
conceivable that the Hittites would try to make use of an Israelite
insurrection to divert Egyptian power, that at least some Israelites
would look with favor on such a scheme, and that Rameses would
suspect them of complicity even if they did not. Intensified enslavement and even a program of genocide is possible.

Furthermore, the reign of Rameses II is followed by a decline
during which the Israelites could have broken out of Egypt. What's
more, the decline does not reverse itself. Egypt does *not* enter Asia
with renewed power so that the Israelites can conquer and occupy
Canaan without interference from Egypt.

It would seem then that Rameses II would have to be the Pharaoh
of the Oppression, *if* there is any Pharaoh of the Oppression at all.
This last reservation is made necessary by the fact that there is no
record outside the Bible of Israelites in Egypt, of their enslavement,

* The letters at Tell el Amarna refer to the invaders as "Khabiri"; that is, "Hebrews." However, the men of Edom, Moab, and Ammon were as Hebrew as the
men of Israel.

and of their escape. In particular, none of the events in Exodus are to be found anywhere in the Egyptian records uncovered by modern archaeologists.

Pithom and Raamses

One of the pieces of evidence that points to Rameses II as the Pharaoh of the Oppression is contained in the nature of the work done by the Israelite slaves.

> Exodus 1:11. . . . *And they built for Pharaoh treasure cities, Pithom and Raamses.*

(The phrase "treasure cities" is clearly a mistranslation. The Revised Standard Version has "store-cities" in its place; cities, that is, in which provisions were stored for the use of armies advancing into Asia.)

The name Raamses (which in the Hebrew requires a very small change to become Rameses) seems significant. The name Rameses does not occur at all among the Pharaohs of the first eighteen dynasties, but eleven Pharaohs of that name are to be found in the 19th and 20th dynasties. Of them, Rameses II is by far the most famous and successful; also the most self-glorifying and the most apt to name a city for himself.

The ruins of Pithom (*pa-tum* in Egyptian, meaning "house of the setting sun") were discovered in 1882 about twelve miles west of what is now the Suez Canal. It was on a canal which Rameses II had had built from an eastern branch of the Nile to the bodies of water then making up the northernmost reaches of the Red Sea—a kind of primitive Suez Canal. The ruins contain, among other things, a statue of Rameses II, indicating that the city may well have been built in his reign.

Pithom is located in Goshen (see page 114) and Raamses was probably built some miles west of Pithom. Conceivably, a case may be made here. Since Rameses II was planning his large expedition into Asia against the Hittites, he needed good supply depots to his rear. Pithom and Raamses on the northeastern frontier would suit his purpose exactly, and since the Israelites were settled on the spot, it was convenient to make use of their labor.

Although the Bible specifically describes the Israelites as having built cities, many casual readers of the Bible seem to have picked up the notion that the Israelite slaves built the pyramids. This is not so. The pyramids were built a thousand years before Joseph entered Egypt.

This also disposes of the feeling that the pyramids might be the storehouses built under Joseph's direction to store the grain of the seven plentiful years. The pyramids couldn't serve such a purpose anyway, even if they were built in Joseph's time, for they are virtually solid structures with tunnels and cavities only large enough to hold the sarcophagus of a Pharaoh. As a matter of fact, the pyramids— oddly enough—are nowhere mentioned in the Bible.

The Daughter of Pharaoh

Rameses II, according to the Biblical story, commanded all Israelite boy babies to be drowned. As a result, when a son was born to a woman of the tribe of Levi, she tried to save him by placing him in a small boat (or "ark") of bulrushes, daubed with pitch to make it waterproof, and setting that afloat on the Nile. (The bulrushes were papyrus reeds, which the Egyptians used in making light boats and the pith of which they used in making a writing material. Our word "paper" comes from papyrus, even though paper is made from other materials now.)

The small boat containing the baby was discovered:

Exodus 2:5. And the daughter of Pharaoh came down to wash herself at the river . . . and . . . saw the ark among the flags . . .

Who the "daughter of Pharaoh" might be is, of course, not known. She is not named in the Bible and, since Rameses II is supposed to have had something like fifty daughters, there seems no hope of ever identifying the young lady. To be sure, the ancient Jewish historian Josephus, who retells the story of the Bible, filling in the gaps with later legend, gives her name as Thermouthes, but no Egyptian princess of that name and period is known. One of the early Church fathers gave the name as Merris and the name "Meri" does occur in the inscriptions of the time. But that could be mere coincidence.

Moses

The Hebrew name of the child is Mosheh. In the Septuagint, the various Hebrew names of the Bible are changed into Greek equivalents. This involves some nearly inevitable changes. The Greek alphabet doesn't include a letter for the "sh" sound, which does not occur in Greek, so a simple "s" must be substituted. Then, since Greek names almost invariably end in "s," a final "s" must be added. In this way, Mosheh becomes Moses.

The English versions of the New Testament (almost all of which was originally written in Greek) usually contain Hebrew names in the Greek form. For instance, Jesus is the Greek form of the Hebrew "Joshua." English versions of the Old Testament, however, usually restore the Hebrew forms as far as possible. This was not possible at all in the case of Moses, since that particular Greek form had become too well known to the population generally to be altered.

The priestly editors of the Hexateuch saw in the word "Mosheh" a similarity to the Hebrew *mashah*, meaning "to draw out," and therefore gave that as the derivation of the name:

> Exodus 2:10. . . . *Pharaoh's daughter . . . called his name Moses: and she said, Because I drew him out of the water.*

Now an Egyptian princess is scarcely going to turn to the Hebrew language for a name (even if she could be imagined as bothering to learn the slaves' language in the first place). Besides, Moses happens to have a much more straightforward and natural meaning in Egyptian. It means "son." (Thus Thutmose means "son of Thoth" and Rameses means "son of Ra," both Thoth and Ra being Egyptian gods.)

The legend surrounding Moses' infancy seems no more plausible than the Hebrew derivation given his name. Ancient legends are full of tales of children cast away for some reason or other who are miraculously saved and go on to become people of great importance. In the Greek legends, this is the case with Perseus, Oedipus, and Paris, for instance; in the Roman legends, with Romulus; in the Persian legends, with Cyrus.

Most significant of all is a legend told of Sargon of Agade (see page 50) who lived over a thousand years before the time of Moses. The legend of Sargon has been found on Babylonian tablets dating back to several centuries before the Exile. The priests in Babylon who were preparing the Hexateuch in its final form must have heard the legend, and it is very likely that they appropriated it.

Sargon of Agade is described as the illegitimate son of a noblewoman who bore him in shame and secrecy, and then exposed him. She did this by putting him in a small boat of reeds, daubed with pitch, and letting him drift down the river. The baby was rescued by a poor man who raised him as his own son.

The Biblical writers improved the tale, however. Moses was a legitimate son and was raised by a princess.

There are no Biblical details concerning Moses' youth, but the legends of later times fill those years with activity designed to magnify the glory of the future leader of the Israelites. Josephus tells, for instance, how invading Ethiopians had Egypt at their mercy when Moses took over leadership of the Egyptian army and utterly defeated the Ethiopians. There is no evidence in Egyptian annals, however, for the events described by Josephus.

Midian

As a grown man, Moses found himself sympathizing with the Israelite slaves, presumably out of humanity and possibly because he had learned of his own origins. In a fit of anger he killed an Egyptian overseer and, when this was found out, left Egypt hurriedly, to avoid execution at the orders of an angered Pharaoh.

Exodus 2:15. . . . *Moses fled from the face of Pharaoh and dwelt in the land of Midian* . . .

Midian, it seems quite likely, is located in northwestern Arabia, just east of the Red Sea, about two hundred miles southeast of Goshen. It represents the shortest distance Moses could have traveled and placed himself outside the boundaries of Imperial Egypt.

According to later tradition, Moses was forty years old at the time of his flight to Midian. This is too pat, for it divides Moses' Biblically allotted lifetime of 120 years into neat thirds. From birth to 40, he would be an Egyptian prince, from 40 to 80 an exile in Midian, and from 80 to 120 a leader of the Israelites.

Pharaoh [of the Exodus]

While Moses was in Midian, getting married and having a son, a crucial change took place in Egypt:

> Exodus 2:23. And it came to pass in process of time, that the king of Egypt died . . .

and that took place in 1223 B.C., if the Pharaoh of the Oppression was indeed Rameses II.

Succeeding Rameses II was the far weaker Merneptah, who is usually thought of as the Pharaoh of the Exodus, the Pharaoh under whom the dramatic events described in the rest of the Book of Exodus took place.

Since these events represent little less than a complete disaster for Egypt, it is to be expected that the reign of Merneptah might be listed in Egyptian annals as one filled with trouble.

And so it is. To be sure, the exact events described in Exodus are not to be found anywhere in the Egyptian records, but there was plenty of trouble of another sort and Merneptah's reign witnessed a time of troubles for the whole region rimming the eastern Mediterranean Sea.

Every once in a while, in the course of ancient history, there come times when nomad peoples seem to be on the move. One tribe drives against another which in turn pushes against the next and so on like a series of falling dominoes. The settled cities of the civilized areas of the world eventually meet the brunt of the force and since their peoples cannot easily move and yield to the pressure, civilizations often meet with disaster at such times.

The thirteenth century B.C. witnessed one of these troublesome mass migrations of peoples. The pressure of barbarian invasions was beginning to be felt in Greece and southeastern Europe generally. Under that pressure, raiding bands from Greece, Crete, and such areas spread out across the Aegean Sea and plunged their way, west, south, and east. They invaded Asia Minor, and the Trojan War may have been an item in that invasion.

As a result of the disorders that racked Asia Minor then, a native people, the Phrygians, rose to power and dealt the final blow to the Hittite Empire, which had been fatally wounded in its great war against Rameses II. As a result, the Hittites declined to a bare remnant, and appeared to the Israelites, when they finally conquered Canaan, as no more than another small tribe.

Then, too, some tribes leaving Asia Minor under the pressure of invasions may have traveled westward to found the Etruscan civilization in Italy.

The invaders from southeastern Europe landed as well on the coasts of Egypt. To the Egyptians, they were the "Peoples of the Sea." The Egyptians managed to fight them off but only at great cost and the damage done the nation undoubtedly contributed greatly to the decline of its vigor. In the disorders accompanying the invasion, it is not at all unreasonable that the Israelites may have seized the opportunity to depart.

Furthermore, for the first time since the reign of Thutmose I, three centuries before, the Egyptian hold on Canaan was broken. A contingent of the Peoples of the Sea invaded Canaan and established themselves as the Philistines on its southern coast. Egyptian armies were either defeated or, very likely, melted away when they were called home to defend the motherland itself. Egyptian power did not return to Canaan for nine centuries, and the Israelites, in their drive to conquer Canaan, had to face only the native Canaanites and *not* a powerful Egyptian army. Indeed, for centuries their most inveterate enemies were the Philistines who had entered Canaan from the west, while the Israelites had plunged in from the east.

It seems to make sense, therefore, to accept Merneptah as the Pharaoh of the Exodus, whether one accepts the actual details described in the Bible or not.

Horeb

Moses' task of leading the Israelites out of Egypt begins in Midian.

Exodus 3:1. *Now Moses kept the flock of Jethro his father in law . . . and he led the flock . . . to the mountain of God, even to Horeb.*

It is common to consider mountains as particularly sacred to divine beings; one need only consider the Greek gods and their home on Mount Olympus. Apparently, the Bible has reference here to a mountain which was considered in the old Israelite traditions to be sacred to God.

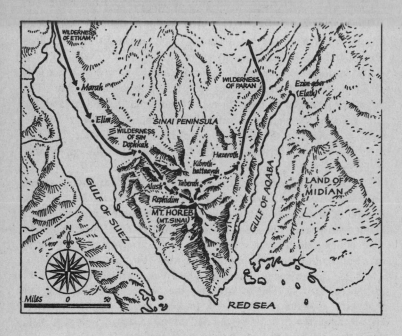

Mount Horeb (Sinai)

The mountain is called Horeb here, but in other places in Exodus it is called Sinai. Both names are accepted as referring to the same mountain but it is the latter name which is much better known. It is not located in Canaan—everyone agrees on that—so it must represent an ancient tradition of holiness indeed, one that preceded the entry of the Israelites into Canaan. It is a holiness, moreover, which is not associated with the patriarchal age, for Sinai is never mentioned in the Book of Genesis.

Indeed, the holiness may trace back to Sumerian mythology for the name Sinai could refer back to the moon-god, Sin, who was an important object of worship both in Ur and in Haran (see page 59). In that case, though, one might wonder why there was no association of Sinai with Abraham, who lived in both Ur and Haran.

Some scholars believe that Mount Sinai is to be found somewhere on the Arabian side of the Red Sea, because that is where Moses was at the time. If Sinai were really connected with Sumerian mythology, that, too, would bespeak a location reasonably close to the Fertile Crescent. Then too, in several poetic passages of the Bible, Sinai is associated with mountains south of Canaan. For example, in a passage of Deuteronomy, commonly called the "Song of Moses," we have:

> Deuteronomy 33:2 . . . *The Lord came from Sinai, and rose up from Seir* . . .

Indeed, considering the parallelism of Hebrew poetry, and its trick of saying the same thing twice with slight variation, one might even be tempted to argue that Mount Sinai *is* Mount Seir (also called Mount Hor).

However, in early Christian times the tradition arose that the mountain was located on the triangular peninsula that lies on the boundary between Africa and Asia and that is now, in consequence, known as Sinai.

The Sinai Peninsula, about 140 miles long, is bounded on the north by the Mediterranean Sea and on the south by the Red Sea. The northern end of the Red Sea divides into two narrow arms, like the eyestalks of a snail, which bound Sinai on the southwest and southeast. The western horn, which is the longer and wider, is the Gulf of Suez; the eastern, the Gulf of Aqaba.

When Egypt was powerful, Sinai was part of its realm, as during the Middle Kingdom and during the Empire. After the invasion of the Peoples of the Sea, the ebbing of Egyptian power left Sinai to its own nomadic inhabitants. (Nowadays, Sinai forms part of modern Egypt but was occupied by Israel after the Six-day War of 1967.)

In southern Sinai is a range of mountains among which Mount Sinai is supposed to be located. By a tradition dating back to the sixth century A.D. it is identified particularly with the tallest peak, which is about 7400 feet, or nearly one and a half miles high. This peak bears the Arabic name of Jebel Musa ("Mount of Moses").

Jehovah

On Mount Horeb, Moses becomes aware of a bush that is burning steadily but is not consumed. He approaches and God, speaking to him out of the bush, commands him to return to Egypt and to lead the Israelites out of slavery.

In the process, God reveals his personal name:

Exodus 3:14. *And God said unto Moses, I AM THAT I AM . . .*

The phrase, capitalized as a gesture of respectful awe, is translated I AM WHO I AM in the Revised Standard Version, with a footnote giving alternate readings of I AM WHAT I AM and I WILL BE WHAT I WILL BE.

Apparently the name of the Lord is here connected with some form of the word "to be," either in the present or future tense, as though the primary nature of God is eternal existence.

Moses returns to Egypt along with his elder brother, Aaron, but his first efforts fail to impress Pharaoh. The Egyptian monarch sharpens the oppression so that the Israelites themselves, who had first hailed Moses, turn against him. God reassures Moses and pronounces his name once more, this time in a briefer version:

Exodus 6:3. . . . *I appeared unto Abraham, unto Isaac, and unto Jacob, by the name of God Almighty, but by my name JEHOVAH was I not known to them.*

The name here given for God is the YHVH I mentioned earlier (see page 20).

In later history, the Jews grew increasingly reluctant to articulate the actual name of God and it became a habitual gesture of respect with them to substitute for the four consonants wherever they occur the respectful title of "the Lord," which in Hebrew is *Adonai.*

In both the King James Version and the Revised Standard Version this procedure is followed and YHVH is consistently translated as "Lord." Exodus 6:3 is the one place where the King James Version abandons caution and actually makes use of the name of God. The Revised Standard Version does not do so but remains consistent and translates the clause in Exodus 6:3 as "but by my name the

Lord I did not make myself known to them." (The translation from the Masoretic text gives the Hebrew consonants themselves, untranslated, with a footnote directing that it be read "the Lord.")

The name Jehovah is almost universally accepted by English-speaking Christians as the manner of pronouncing YHVH, but that arose by mistake.

It seems that as the centuries passed and the Jews of later history spread throughout the east and began to speak Aramaic, Babylonian, and Greek, in preference to Hebrew, there grew up the danger that the proper pronunciation of the Biblical language would be forgotten. The Jewish scholars therefore placed little diacritical marks under the Hebrew consonants, indicating the vowel sounds that went with them in each particular word.

For YHVH, however, they did not produce the proper diacritical marks since the name was not supposed to be pronounced anyway. Instead, they wrote the diacritical marks for *Adonai*, the word that *was* supposed to be pronounced. Sometime during the Middle Ages, a Christian scholar, supposing that the vowels of *Adonai* belonged with the consonants YHVH, wrote out the name in full as Jehovah. (The initial J in Latin is pronounced like an initial Y in English.)

This mistake has persisted and will probably continue to persist. Actually, modern scholars seem to have decided that the correct pronunciation of YHVH is Yahveh.

During the greater portion of Old Testament times it was by no means certain that the worship of Yahveh, according to the ritual set forth in the first five books of the Bible (which, according to long-accepted tradition, both Jewish and Christian, were written by Moses), would win out among the Israelites. I will, in this book, speak of those who believed in the worship of Yahveh (particularly in the exclusive worship of Yahveh as the *only* God) as Yahvists.

Aaron

Moses and his brother Aaron were of the tribe of Levi and in later generations the priesthood was to be confined to the descendants of Aaron, so that the expression "Levite" came to be virtually synonymous with "priest." In view of this, Exodus pauses here to give an account of the genealogy of Aaron.

Levi is described as having had three sons, of whom Kohath was second, while Kohath had four sons of whom the first two were Amram and Izhar. The age at the time of death is given for Levi, Kohath, and Amram as 137, 133, and 137 years respectively, so that there is still the echo, here, of the patriarchal age of moderately extended lifetimes.

> Exodus 6:20. *And Amram took him Jochebed . . . to wife; and she bare him Aaron and Moses . . .*
>
> Exodus 6:21. *And the sons of Izhar; Korah . . .*

Korah, who was later to rebel against Moses and come to a bad end, is here described as Moses' first cousin. He is also the ancestor (despite his rebellion) of one of the guilds of Temple musicians, variously referred to in the Bible as the Korahites, Korhites, or Korathites, and who will be mentioned in connection with the Book of Psalms.

The line of Aaron is taken further:

> Exodus 6:23. *And Aaron took him Elisheba . . . to wife; and she bare him Nadab, and Abihu, Eleazar and Ithamar.*
>
> . . . .
>
> Exodus 6:25. *And Eleazar . . . took him one of the daughters of Putiel to wife; and she bare him Phinehas.*

Nadab and Abihu died in the course of the Exodus but Eleazar and Ithamar survived to become the ancestors of the two chief priestly families of later times. Aaron was the first High Priest and he was succeeded by his son Eleazar and, eventually, by his grandson, Phinehas.

The Magicians of Egypt

After the Levite genealogy, the writers of Exodus return to the main current of its account.

Moses and Aaron approach Pharaoh once more and try to impress him by turning a rod into a serpent. Pharaoh, however, scorns what he considers a parlor trick and calls his own men to duplicate it.

> Exodus 7:11. . . . *the magicians of Egypt . . . did in like manner with their enchantments.*

The names of these magicians are not given. In the New Testament, however, in the second of Paul's Epistles to Timothy, there is the passage:

2 Timothy 3:8. . . . *Jannes and Jambres withstood Moses* . . .

There were a number who withstood Moses in the course of the passage of the Israelites from Egypt to Canaan. None of these had names that were anything like Jannes and Jambres, names which do not occur anywhere else in the Bible, in fact. The usual assumption, therefore, is that Paul was drawing upon some well-known legend which gave the names Jannes and Jambres to the Egyptian magicians who tried to duplicate the works of Moses and to show him up as a mere conjurer before Pharaoh. Indeed, some rabbinical legends have Jannes and Jambres so impressed by Moses that they eventually joined the Israelites, but died in the course of the Exodus.

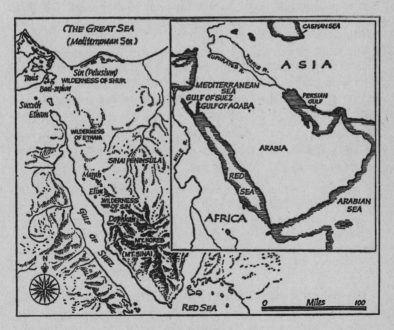

The Red Sea

Passover

With Pharaoh scorning the first demonstration, Moses and Aaron bring, in swift succession, a series of disasters upon Egypt. These, involving visitations of frogs and insects, various pestilences, unusual weather such as hail or darkness, are generally referred to as "the ten plagues of Egypt."

Although these plagues, if they had taken place as described in the Bible, must have loomed large in any contemporary records or in later histories, no reference to them is to be found in any source outside the Bible. In 1950, Immanuel Velikovsky, in his book *Worlds in Collision* attempted to account for the plagues (and for some other events described in the Bible) by supposing that the planet Venus had undergone a near collision with the earth. The book created a moderate sensation among the general public for a while, but the reaction of astronomers varied from amusement to anger, and the Velikovskian theory has never, for one moment, been taken seriously either by scientists or by Biblical scholars.

The tenth plague was the crucial one. In its course, the first-born male of every house in Egypt was slain by divine action. The Israelites were spared. Each family was directed to eat a ceremonial meal and to place the blood of the lamb eaten in the course of that meal on the door of the house:

> Exodus 12:23. . . . *the Lord will pass through to smite the Egyptians; and when he seeth the blood . . . the Lord will pass over the door and will not . . . smite you.*

In commemoration of this awesome event, which marked the beginning of the escape from Egypt and the establishment of the Israelites as a nation, a ceremonial meal is eaten each year. The ceremony is named (according to the Bible) after the promise of God to "pass over" the Israelite houses. The original instructions refer to it thus:

> Exodus 12:11. . . . *it is the Lord's passover.*

The Hebrew word translated here as "passover" is *pesach* and the Biblical writers saw a similarity to the Hebrew word meaning "to pass over" and therefore wrote the passages in such a way as to stress that similarity. The real meaning of *pesach* is unknown.

In all probablity, the Passover was an agricultural festival long ante-dating the time of Moses. Such festivals are common in all agricultural societies. (Americans have even invented one for themselves—Thanks-giving.) Usually such festivals, even among the early Israelites, were thoroughly pagan in inspiration.

The priestly writers of the Hexateuch could not revise the early traditions in too extreme a fashion. The various festivals were too popular and too deeply ingrained in tradition to be done away with. The best that could be done was to associate them firmly with some legendary event in Biblical history and divorce them from idolatry. Passover, the most important of the agricultural festivals, was associated with the most important event in the early legends—the Exodus.

(Such changed associations are common in the development of reli-gions. Thus, in the early history of Christianity, the pagan celebra-tion of the winter solstice—the Saturnalia—was converted into Christ-mas and made into the celebration of the birth of Jesus—something that will be discussed further in the second volume.)

After the Exile, the Passover was one of the three festivals during which all pious Jews attempted to travel to Jerusalem and worship at the Temple. It was in the course of one of these Passovers that Jesus was crucified.

The anniversary of the resurrection of Jesus is still celebrated at the same time of the year as Passover, although never on the same day, for the Christian method of calculating the day differs from the Jew-ish method.

That anniversary is, in English, called "Easter" and this is another example of religious adaptation. The word comes from the name of an old Teutonic goddess of spring. A pagan spring festival was converted into the commemoration of the resurrection but its pagan name was kept to make the transition as easy as possible.

The word "Easter" is sometimes, quite wrongly, applied to Passover. This is done on one occasion in the King James Version. In the Book of Acts, it is described how the Apostle Peter was imprisoned at the time of the Passover, with the intention of bringing him to trial once the festival was over. The ruler is described as

Acts 12:4. . . . *intending after Easter to bring him forth to the people.*

The Revised Standard Version changes Easter to Passover in this case, of course.

Abib

The month in which the Exodus took place, and in which the Passover was celebrated, was Abib.

Exodus 13.4. *This day came ye out in the month Abib.*

Abib is an example of the names of the months used in pre-Exilic times. The word means "kernel of grain" and marks the time of the year when such kernels appeared.

Other such ancient names are mentioned here and there in the Bible. In connection with the building of the Temple under Solomon, for instance, the Bible records:

1 Kings 6:37. *In the fourth year was the foundation of the house of the Lord laid, in the month Zif:*

1 Kings 6:38. *And in the eleventh year, in the month Bul . . . was the house finished . . .*

The temple was then dedicated:

1 Kings 8:2. *And all the men of Israel assembled . . . at the feast in the month Ethanim . . .*

During the Babylonian Exile, however, the Jews made use of the Babylonian calendar and they kept that throughout their later history, down to the present day. The names of the months in the Jewish calendar are Babylonian now and are used in those Biblical books that are clearly post-Exilic, especially the books of Nehemiah and Esther. Thus, the month earlier known as Abib, in which Passover was celebrated, became Nisan:

Nehemiah 2:1. *And it came to pass in the month Nisan . . .*

The Red Sea

After the tenth plague, Pharaoh's resistance broke and he agreed to allow the Israelites to leave the land:

Exodus 12:37. *And the children of Israel journeyed from Rameses to Succoth . . .*

The location of Succoth is not agreed upon, but many people believe it to be located very close to Pithom (see page 126) or even to be identical with it. If so, the Israelites, upon leaving Egypt, headed east.

Had they borne northward, they could have reached and followed the coast, taking the most direct and shortest route into Canaan. That, however, would have led them into trouble.

The Peoples of the Sea were now invading various sections of the Egyptian realm. (This, in fact, may well have been the historical equivalent of the dramatic Biblical story of the plagues.) The Peoples of the Sea were establishing themselves on the very portion of the Canaanite coast that the Israelites would have reached first.

The Israelites, who were liberated slaves unused to war, were in no position to take on the well-armed, war-hardened invaders from the sea, soon to appear importantly in the Biblical story as the Philistines. The Israelites had to travel eastward, therefore, in order to flank the Philistine position and this brought them to the Red Sea.

Exodus 13:17. . . . *God led them not through the way of the land of the Philistines, although that was near; for God said, Lest peradventure the people repent when they see war, and they return to Egypt:*
Exodus 13:18. *But God led the people about, through the way of the wilderness of the Red Sea . . .*

The Red Sea is a long, narrow arm of the Indian Ocean, extending northwest and southeast in an almost straight line for 1450 miles. Its width is only between 150 and 200 miles, and from its shape one can guess that it is part of the Great Rift Valley.

The Red Sea is one of the most unpleasant parts of the ocean. It separates the African desert from the Arabian desert and receives little water in the form of rainfall, while the sun, baking as hotly as anywhere on earth, evaporates much water. For that reason, despite the fact that water constantly pours into the southern end of the sea, which is open to the main body of the Indian Ocean, the Red Sea manages to be saltier than any other part of the ocean. It is up to 4.1 per cent salt at the closed northern end, as compared to 3.5 per cent for the oceans generally.

The name "Red Sea" is of Greek origin and in Roman times, the name spread out into that portion of the Indian Ocean into which the sea opened—what we now call the Gulf of Aden, the Arabian Sea, and the Persian Gulf.

Why "Red"? There are several theories. The waters may turn red through some infestation of microscopic plants; the shells on the shore (or the rocks) may be red; the reflection of the setting sun as seen from Arabia may turn the waters red. You can take your pick. Perhaps none of these is the right reason; or perhaps there is no reason.

Pi-hahiroth

With the Israelites in the process of leaving Egypt, Pharaoh regretted having given permission for their departure. At the head of a detachment of cavalry he set out after them.

> Exodus 14:9. . . . *the Egyptians pursued after them . . . and overtook them encamping by the sea, beside Pi-hahiroth . . .*

The Bible then relates the story of the escape of the Israelites when the waters of the Red Sea miraculously parted for them, and then returned in time to drown the pursuing Egyptians.

Where did this parting take place? Presumably in the neighborhood of Pi-hahiroth, but the one great catch is that no one knows exactly where Pi-hahiroth might have been located.

We can eliminate the main body of the Red Sea at once. To imagine that the Israelites crossed the Red Sea proper, passing over 150 miles or so of emptied sea bottom which, in places, is something like a mile and a half deep, is unnecessary. Had they done so, they would have ended in the main portion of the Arabian peninsula and there is nothing in succeeding events, as described in the Bible, to make one think that happened. The succeeding events take place, rather, in the Sinai Peninsula and that is separated from Egypt by a northwestern extension of the Red Sea now known as the Gulf of Suez.

The Gulf of Suez is a miniature of the Red Sea; something of the same shape, but not as long, not as wide, and not as deep. It is two hundred miles long, nowhere more than thirty miles wide, and, at its northern end, it is only eighteen feet deep.

Even the Gulf of Suez, as it exists today, may not be the site of the Israelite "crossing of the Red Sea." The Hebrew name for the body of water that was crossed is *yam suph*. The phrase is translated as "Red Sea," but its literal meaning is "the sea of reeds."

In Exodus times (it is generally thought) the Gulf of Suez extended somewhat farther northward than it does today. In particular, it included two shallow bodies of brackish water called the Bitter Lakes. (These marshes are no longer on the map because they were filled in at the time the Suez Canal was built.)

If the Gulf of Suez extended up to and including the Bitter Lakes, this extension might have represented a shallow basin of sea water filled with reeds along its shores, and this might have been a Sea of Reeds in literal truth. The site of Pi-hahiroth may have been on the shores of this vanished extension of the Red Sea.

It would seem, from the Biblical account, that every one of the pursuing Egyptians was drowned. If a Pharaoh accompanied them, he was drowned, too. There are no records outside the Bible which indicate Merneptah, or any Pharaoh, to have drowned in the Red Sea. Nevertheless, if Merneptah died in this fashion, then the Exodus took place in 1211 B.C. by the best modern reckoning.

According to the Biblical reckoning:

Exodus 12:40. *Now the sojourning of the children of Israel, who dwelt in Egypt, was four hundred and thirty years.*

If this is accepted, then the entry of Jacob and his sons into Egypt took place in 1641 B.C. This date is neatly within the period of the Hyksos domination of Egypt as would be expected (see page 108).

Omer

The Israelites were fed, miraculously, by a food called manna dropping from the heavens. There have been attempts to advance a non-miraculous explanation. Some suggest the manna to have been the exudate of some particular tree. Others suggest it to have been a species of lichen. Whatever the nub of the account, however, it has been embroidered out of recognition by the Biblical writers.

The tale of the manna is from the P document as can be seen from the careful instructions given for the gathering of the manna and the warnings to observe the Sabbath. (This form of ritualism and meticulousness is characteristic of P.) It is therefore a late elaboration of some early legend, and there is no point in taking it literally.

Part of the instructions are:

Exodus 16:16. . . . *Gather of it . . . an omer for every man . . .*

But how large is an omer? Even the editors of the Hexateuch seem to have been worried by that, for they added a definition:

Exodus 16:36. *Now an omer is the tenth part of an ephah.*

Of course, if one doesn't know how large an ephah is that doesn't help. The trouble is that while strange units of measure are always difficult to put into familiar terms, there is particular confusion among the early Israelites.

Those of pre-Exilic times used Egyptian systems of measurement and those of post-Exilic times used Babylonian systems, and it is not always easy to tell them apart. The best estimate is that the omer is a little less than half a peck in our common units or about four liters in the metric system.

Amalek

After the crossing of the Red Sea, the Israelites headed for Mount Sinai, and the situation now changes radically. A weakened Egypt has been left behind and will not play a role as an adversary of the Israelites for fully three centuries. In its place are new enemies, the Semitic peoples who had, within the past century, settled down in the areas surrounding Canaan, displacing the earlier inhabitants. These, naturally, resisted the later influx of the Israelites.

The first of these mentioned as encountering the Israelites were Amalekites:

Exodus 17:8. *Then came Amalek and fought with Israel in Rephidim.*

The location of Rephidim is unknown. If Mount Sinai is located in its traditional place near the southern apex of the Sinai Peninsula, then Rephidim would have to be located somewhere in the southern portion of the peninsula and it becomes a matter of wonder that the Amalekites were to be found there. References elsewhere in the Bible seem to place the Amalekites chiefly to the immediate south of Canaan and to make them neighbors, or even a branch, of the Edomites. This was recognized by the Biblical writers themselves since the eponym, Amalek, was described as a grandson of Esau/Edom (see page 103).

If the Israelites had reached the region south of Canaan on their way to Mount Sinai that would be a point in favor of those who would identify Mount Sinai with Mount Seir (see page 133). Or perhaps the story is displaced and the battle with Amalek in Rephidim did not take place en route to Mount Sinai but long afterward when the Israelites had left the mountain and were indeed in the region south of Canaan.

Putting such questions to one side, the Israelites maintained a strong tradition of continuing an undying enmity with the Amalekites; more so than with their other enemies. This may be because the Amalekites were the first to make war upon the Israelites, when they were least equipped to fight back, or because they did so in what seemed to the Israelites to be a peculiarly unfair and frustrating manner. Later, in the Book of Deuteronomy, Moses, in summarizing the events following the Exodus, is quoted:

Deuteronomy 25:17. *Remember what Amalek did unto thee by the way, when ye were come forth out of Egypt;*

Deuteronomy 25:18. *How he met thee by the way, and smote the hindmost of thee, even all that were feeble behind thee, when thou wast faint and weary . . .*

The Amalekites seemed strong to the Israelites, and in a prophecy described as having been uttered later in their progress toward Canaan, by Balaam, a non-Israelite prophet, they are described grandiloquently:

Numbers 25:20. . . . *Amalek was the first of the nations . . .*

and this is usually taken to mean that they were the most powerful of the nations of the region.

Perhaps they were, temporarily. Nomadic groups sometimes rise to tremendous local power as a result of sudden raids upon unprepared or decadent enemies and then vanish almost entirely after a comparatively short time. The outstanding example of this in history is the career of the Mongols, who, in the thirteenth century A.D., nearly conquered the world—then faded away.

The Amalekites could have anticipated the Mongolian feat only in the smallest way and over a very restricted area for neither the Egyptian nor the Babylonian records mention any people that can be identified with the Amalekites. The Bible is our only source concerning them.

The first pitched battle between the Amalekites and the Israelites ended in complete victory for the latter. War between them continued, however, until two centuries later, when Saul, Israel's first king, was to end the task, wiping out the Amalekite power and leaving only remnants, about which little further is heard.

Joshua

In this first battle with the Amalekites, a new military leader makes his appearance.

> Exodus 17:9. And Moses said unto Joshua, Choose us out men, and go out, fight with Amalek . . .

The fact that Joshua is introduced without warning or identification is one reason for thinking that this passage concerning the Amalekites is misplaced and actually describes something that took place near the end of the Exodus rather than near the beginning.

Later Joshua is mentioned as Oshea (Hoshea, in the Revised Standard Version) and is identified as the son of Nun and as a member of the tribe of Ephraim. Oshea ("salvation") was apparently his original name and Moses changed it to one more in line with Yahvism:

> Numbers 13:16. . . . And Moses called Oshea the son of Nun Jehoshua.

Jehoshua, of which Joshua is a shortened form, means "Yahveh is salvation."

Joshua remained Moses' military aide throughout the Exodus and eventually succeeded Moses as leader of the Israelites generally. This is the first indication of the military pre-eminence of the tribe of Ephraim, a pre-eminence they were to hold throughout the tribal period.

In later Old Testament times, it became more common to abbreviate Jehoshua as Jeshua. In Greek, the sound "sh" (not present in the Greek alphabet) was replaced by "s" and the usual Greek name-ending of "-s" was added so that Jeshua became Jesus.

Indeed, the New Testament (originally written in Greek) refers to Joshua, Moses' general, as Jesus on two occasions—at least in the King James Version. Thus, in the Book of the Acts of the Apostles, when Stephen summarizes Old Testament history for his audience, he refers to the tabernacle built under Moses' direction in the wilderness:

> Acts 7:45. *Which also our fathers that came after brought in* [to Canaan] *with Jesus* . . .

In the Revised Standard Version, the name in Acts 7:45 is given as Joshua. It is, of course, quite impossible for any version to change the name of Jesus Christ back to the Hebrew Joshua. That name is too fixed in human consciousness in its Greek form.

Cherubim

After the battle with the Amalekites, the Israelites reached Mount Sinai. There Moses ascended the mountain to receive instructions concerning various moral precepts (including the Ten Commandments) as well as the details of the structures to be built for the worship of God, the clothing of the High Priest, various rites, and so on.

Most sacred of the structures described was the "ark of the covenant," a simple chest which was to contain the tablets on which the Ten Commandments were inscribed, and over which the very presence of God was supposed to hover.

The ark was covered by a slab of gold called the mercy seat and—

> Exodus 25:18. *And thou shalt make two cherubims of gold* . . . *in the two ends of the mercy seat.*
>
> . . . .
>
> Exodus 25:20. *And the cherubims shall stretch forth their wings on high, covering the mercy seat with their wings, and their faces shall look one to another* . . .

(Actually, "cherubims" is a false plural. In Hebrew, the singular is *cherub*, the plural *cherubim*. The Revised Standard Version substitutes the simple "cherubim.")

It is not really certain what the cherubim might be. During the Assyrian period, the readers of the Biblical writings seem to have been expected to know what was meant by the word without the necessity of description or explanation. Thus, when Adam and Eve were driven out of Eden, God is described as placing guardians about the garden to prevent any return by man:

> Genesis 3:24. . . . *he placed at the east of the garden of Eden Cherubims, and a flaming sword which turned every way* . . .

The verse simply says "Cherubims" without description or explanation.

In connection with the ark of the covenant, the wings are mentioned, but not in order to explain the appearance of the cherubim for nothing else is described. The verses merely take pains to describe the exact position of the wings, which the readers are otherwise taken to be quite familiar with.

Centuries later, when Solomon built his Temple, he too made use of cherubim in appropriately enlarged scale:

> 1 Kings 6:23. *And* . . . *he made two cherubims of olive tree, each ten cubits high.*
> 1 Kings 6:24. *And five cubits was the one wing of the cherub and five cubits the other* . . .

Again, the mere fact of wingedness is all that is mentioned.

It might be simple to think that cherubim were merely human figures with wings, such as we usually visualize angels to be. Indeed, in later Jewish legends, the cherubim figured as among the higher orders of angels. (Moderns often apply the term to the winged Cupids depicted in sweetly sentimental paintings with the result that the term has come to be applied to children.)

On the other hand, the cherubim were guardians of objects particularly holy and unapproachable, and they might well have been fearsome in shape. The Assyrians, for instance, built at the gateways of their palaces and temples monstrous creatures meant to guard kings and gods. These were large representations of bulls, with the head of a man and wings of an eagle. Other types of composite creatures are also familiar in the various mythologies. For instance, there are the Greek sphinxes, which had the head of a woman, the wings of an eagle, and the body of a lion.

There is nothing in the Bible that would eliminate the possibility that it was winged bulls or winged lions, rather than winged men, that crouched on the mercy seat.

In favor of the cherubim as composite creatures is the initial vision in the Book of Ezekiel. Here, the prophet describes beings (later referred to by him as cherubim) which are clearly composite.

> Ezekiel 1:6. . . . *every one had four faces, and every one had four wings.*
>
> Ezekiel 1:7. . . . *and the sole of their feet was like the sole of a calf's foot . . .*
>
> . . . .
>
> Ezekiel 1:10. . . . *they four had the face of a man, and the face of a lion, on the right side; and they four had the face of an ox on the left side; they four also had the face of an eagle.*

The description, as we now have it, may be mangled and distorted with the passing of the years, and there is much dispute over the vision, but the cherubim as envisioned by the ancient Israelites must have been more than simply a winged human figure.

The Urim and the Thummim

Even more puzzling than the cherubim are objects which enter into the meticulous and detailed description of the garments of the High Priest. The ephod, a kind of linen vest, was partly covered by a breastplate bearing twelve jewels, one for each of the tribes, and carrying upon it some sort of pocket:

> Exodus 28:30. *And thou shalt put in the breastplate of judgment the Urim and the Thummim . . .*

Nobody knows what the Urim and Thummim are. The words are Hebrew, but translating them is of no help, for they mean "lights" and "perfections" respectively.

The most frequent guess is that the Urim and Thummim represent a form of lot used for guidance in determining the will of God. There might be one type of object indicating "yes" and another indicating "no" and if yes-no questions are put, the answers are given by the type of object which pops out of the pouch. It is even possible that a blank object was also included, one which signified neither yes nor no, indicating that divine guidance was refused.

The Bible certainly indicates that in early Israelite history, divine guidance was expected to make itself manifest in some sort of chance event. When King Saul was searching for the individual who had committed a sin, he set the Israelites generally on one side (letting them, perhaps, be represented by one of the lot-objects) and himself and his son Jonathan on the other (letting them be represented by the other lot-objects).

1 Samuel 14:41. *Therefore Saul said unto the Lord God of Israel, Give a perfect lot. And Saul and Jonathan were taken: but the people escaped.*

However, in this and other cases, in the King James Version, where casting lots is used to obtain divine guidance, the Urim and Thummim are not specifically mentioned. And usually when the Urim and Thummim are mentioned, the nature of their use is not described. There is only one place where the two combine and that is in the days before King Saul's final battle, when he sought for guidance and found none:

1 Samuel 28:6. *And when Saul inquired of the Lord, the Lord answered him not, neither by dreams, nor by Urim, nor by prophets.*

The Revised Standard Version, however, accepts a version of 1 Samuel 14:41 which is fuller than that found in the King James and which, indeed, makes matters explicit: "Therefore Saul said, 'O Lord God of Israel, why hast thou not answered thy servant this day? If this guilt is in me or in Jonathan my son, O Lord, God of Israel, give Urim; but if this guilt is in thy people Israel, give Thummim.' And Jonathan and Saul were taken, but the people escaped."

This sort of guidance by lot passed out of use before the end of the Old Testament period.

The Molten Calf

Moses' stay on Mount Sinai continued for so long that the Israelites back in the camp began to fear that he might never return. This encouraged those among them who felt uncomfortable with an invisible God. It is very common to desire some visible manifestation of the deity (nowadays as well as in ancient times) and the pressure increased on Aaron to supply one.

Aaron asked for gold:

> Exodus 32:4. *And he . . . fashioned it with a graving tool, after he had made it a molten calf: and they said, These be thy gods, O Israel . . .*

The choice of image is not as surprising as it might sound to modern ears. Primitive man did not differentiate as carefully between men and animals as we do. Before the rise of modern technology, wild carnivores were a continuing terror and menace and it was by no means certain that some animals, at least, might not be equal or superior to man. Then, too, many peoples believed that the souls of men might be reborn in animal form and that one particular species of creature might have close ties of subtle kindred with their own particular tribe. Others felt that since some animals were a necessary source of food, a representation of these creatures had somehow to be honored and propitiated.

Animal worship has, therefore, in one way or another, attracted man throughout history. Nowadays, it is most common in India, where among the Hindus cattle may not be killed, much less eaten, despite the endemic starvation in the land. This practice gives rise to the well-known phrase "sacred cow" for any belief rigidly held beyond reason.

In ancient times, animal worship was most widespread in Egypt. As an example, the city of Memphis paid special reverence to a sacred bull, Hapi, (known to the Greeks as Apis). The bull was considered a manifestation of the god Osiris and was given divine honors. Everything about it was surrounded with ritual and its every action was supposed to have great significance.

One might suppose that it was the Egyptian example that inspired
the Israelites at the foot of Mount Sinai, but that is not necessarily so.
To people who depend on cattle for meat, milk, and labor, the bull is
bound to be considered an important figure indeed, because on his
fertility all depended. Bulls would therefore play an important part in
the ritual of many groups of people. The early Cretans, during the
time when the Israelites were in Egypt, had long observed religious
rituals in which bulls played a key role. Two thousand years later,
the rites of Mithraism, a religion of Persian origin, also involved bulls.
The Assyrians had their winged bulls and the other peoples of the
Fertile Crescent also held bulls in varying degrees of reverence.

The Israelites, therefore, were not at all likely to see anything
strange in bull worship, and the "calf" Aaron formed was undoubtedly
a young bull. Indeed, if the cherubim were, as I myself suspect, winged
bulls (see page 149), then the transition from an invisible presence
resting between the cherubim on the ark of the covenant, to the
cherubim themselves, could be an easy one. It might not even represent a full retreat from Yahvism since the golden figure might be
taken for Yahveh made manifest.

This section of the Book of Exodus is thought to be based on
legends that arose primarily among the Joseph tribes in northern
Canaan. It may be that in very early tribal history some special association was made between the Joseph tribes and bulls. Thus, Moses,
shortly before his death, is described as blessing each of the tribes
separately, and when it is the turn of Joseph, part of the blessing is:

Deuteronomy 33:17. *His glory is like the firstling of his bullock* . . .

This shows up more specifically when, three centuries after the Exodus, the kingdom of Solomon splits into two halves. Since Jerusalem,
which had been the center of worship under David and Solomon,
remained with the southern half, it seemed politically dangerous to the
king of the northern kingdom to allow such worship to continue.
This king was Jeroboam of the tribe of Ephraim, one of the Joseph
tribes, and he turned naturally, it would appear, to the bull, the ancient
animal symbol of his tribe.

1 Kings 12:28. *Whereupon the king . . . made two calves of gold,
and said unto them, It is too much for you to go up to Jerusalem:
behold thy gods, O Israel* . . .

The use of the bull as a manifestation of God continued in the northern kingdom to the end of its history. However, it never obtained a foothold in the southern kingdom, and it is from the southern kingdom that the history of later Judaism and Christianity descends.

While the Israelites were celebrating the image of the young bull, Moses descended from the mountain. A brief civil war followed, with the Levites ranging themselves on Moses' side. The ringleaders among the bull-worshipers were slaughtered, and Moses' authority was reaffirmed.

With that done, Moses continued with his task of instituting the rituals of Yahvism, and the Book of Exodus ends with a careful accounting of how the ark of the covenant, the clothing of the High Priest, and other items are prepared in exact fulfillment of the instructions earlier given.

3. LEVITICUS

Leviticus

The third book of the Bible begins:

Leviticus 1:1. *And the Lord called unto Moses . . .*

The first word in Hebrew is Vayikrah ("And he called") and that is the Hebrew title of the book.

The book is virtually one long section of the P document, given over to ritualistic detail, so that it is easily the dullest book in the Bible to the casual reader.

Its instructions are of primary interest to the priesthood, who are drawn from among the descendants of Aaron, who was himself of the tribe of Levi. Aaron and his descendants are therefore Levites, and the word became synonymous with "priest."

The translators of the Septuagint, mindful of the book's involvement with the priesthood, called it "Levitikon" ("the Levitical book") and we make use of the Latin equivalent, "Leviticus."

Leaven

One of the instructions concerning the ritual of sacrifice ordains the avoidance of the use of leaven in objects offered to God:

Leviticus 2:11. *No meat offering which ye shall bring unto the Lord, shall be made with leaven . . .*

Originally, the flour used in making bread was simply baked into flat, hard cakes that had the virtue of remaining fit to eat for long periods of time.

Dough which had, however, been left standing, would sometimes pick up microorganisms from the air and begin to ferment. The process of fermentation produced carbon dioxide which formed bubbles in the thick dough and puffed it up. Bread made from such fermented dough was light and fluffy. It would not keep as well as bread made from unfermented dough, but would tend to get dry and moldy, but it was still pleasant to eat when fresh.

A key step in bread manufacture must have taken place (in prehistoric times) when it was discovered that there was no need to wait for dough to ferment spontaneously. A small piece of already fermented dough would hasten the fermentation of large batches of fresh dough. This became proverbial, and the Apostle Paul, for instance, in speaking of the pervasive influence of evil says:

1 Corinthians 5:6. . . . *Know ye not that a little leaven leaveneth the whole lump?*

The word "leaven" (from a Latin word meaning "to raise") is a translation of the Hebrew word *hametz*, meaning "to be sour," something that is often characteristic of fermenting material. Our own equivalent word, "yeast," is traced back to a Sanskrit word meaning "to boil," which is a reference to the bubbles of carbon dioxide formed.

To the Israelites, fermentation seemed a form of corruption, and however pleasant leavened bread might be to eat, there was still the stigma of corruption and impurity about it. Bread to be offered on the altar to God must be pure and uncorrupt and must, therefore, be unleavened.

On Passover, because of the holiness of the season, only unleavened bread might be eaten and no trace of leaven must be found anywhere in the house. Indeed, a synonym for Passover is "the feast of unleavened bread."

Exodus 23:15. *Thou shalt keep the feast of unleavened bread . . . in the time appointed of the month Abib; for in it thou camest out from Egypt . . .*

The Last Supper of Jesus and his disciples took place at the time of Passover. The bread broken by Jesus was therefore unleavened, and the wafer used in the Catholic Mass, in commemoration of that event, is unleavened too.

Undoubtedly the use of unleavened bread in ritual is extremely ancient, dating back to long before the Exodus. The priestly editors of the Hexateuch had to find some circumstance in the flight from Egypt that made the eating of unleavened bread particularly appropriate as a way of commemorating the Exodus. They found this in the haste in which the Israelites left; a haste so great that the relatively slow process of fermentation could not be waited for:

Exodus 12:33. *And the Egyptians were urgent upon the people, that they might send them out of the land in haste . . .*

Unclean

Much of Leviticus deals with the clean and unclean:

Leviticus 5:2. *. . . if a soul touch any unclean thing . . .*

To us, clean and unclean tends to be a hygienic matter. Something is unclean if it is dirty, or has an offensive smell, or is laden with dangerous bacteria. The Biblical use of the term involves religious ritual.

Something is clean if it may be offered as a sacrifice to God, or if it may stand in the presence of God. Something that may not be offered as a sacrifice is unclean. People who, because of some deformity or disease, or because they have touched an unclean thing or performed a forbidden act, are themselves unclean and cannot approach the altar until the uncleanness has been removed.

In Leviticus, the items of food that are clean and may be eaten, and those that are unclean and may not be eaten, are listed in detail. For instance:

Leviticus 11:3. *Whatsoever parteth the hoof, and is clovenfooted, and cheweth the cud, among the beasts, that shall ye eat.*

. . . .

Leviticus 11:7. *And the swine, though he divide the hoof, and be clovenfooted, yet he cheweth not the cud; he is unclean unto you.*

The basis on which animals are divided into clean and unclean is not known. Some say it is a matter of pragmatic rules of hygiene, some bring in primitive notions of totemism, some find in it a desire to forbid practices common to surrounding idolatry. Perhaps the chief thing in the mind of the priesthood that prepared the book of Leviticus was to work out a code of behavior that would serve to keep the Jews distinct and their religion intact from the attractions of surrounding cultures.

If so, the priesthood succeeded, for these sections of Leviticus were the basis of the dietary laws which became so important to the post-Exilic Jews. The dietary laws were so intricate and compulsive as to prevent pious Jews from eating with non-Jews, since the food prepared by non-Jews could never meet the standards of ceremonial cleanness.

And while many different foods were considered unclean, swine somehow represented the epitome of uncleanness—perhaps because it was so common a part of the diet of the surrounding Gentiles that its absence in the Jewish dietary was particularly conspicuous.

The disputes recorded in the New Testament over the matter of cleanness, between Jesus and his followers on the one hand and the orthodox Jews on the other, must be understood only in the ritualistic sense, of course, never in the hygienic.

The Day of Atonement

Leviticus is concerned with how to cancel out the consequences of sin, too, as well as of uncleanness. To sin—that is, to disobey the commandments of God, as Adam and Eve did in eating the fruit of the tree (the "original sin")—involves separation from God. To cancel sin according to a prescribed ritual is to restore one's self to the presence of God, to make one's self once more "at one" with God. The sinner must "atone" therefore, or make "atonement."

The High Priest can atone for the entire nation by means of appropriate rituals, and this is done on a particular day:

> Leviticus 23:27. . . . *on the tenth day of this seventh month there shall be a day of atonement . . . and ye shall afflict your souls . . .*

"Day of atonement" is a translation of the Hebrew *Yom Kippur*. Yom Kippur is now the holiest day of the Jewish calendar and a strict day-long fast is involved ("ye shall afflict your souls"). Nevertheless, there is no record of the holiday having been observed until post-Exilic times.

Azazel

Yet if the Day of Atonement is itself a post-Exilic development, some of the rites associated with it must be old indeed. As part of the ritual two goats must be selected:

> Leviticus 16:8. *And Aaron shall cast lots upon the two goats, one lot for the Lord, and the other lot for the scapegoat.*

The goat upon whom the Lord's lot fell (and here one might expect the Urim and Thummim would be used) would be sacrificed to the Lord as atonement for the sins of the nation. The other would be led off into the wilderness bearing with it all those sins, so that punishment might befall it rather than the nation of Israel and its people. Because the second goat escapes into the wilderness and is not sacrificed, the King James Version refers to it as a "scapegoat" ("escaped goat"). It is for this reason that the word has come to be applied to any person or object who, himself innocent, suffers vicariously for the deeds of another.

However, the Hebrew word that is translated as "scapegoat" in the King James Version is actually *Azazel*. The Revised Standard Version does not translate the word but makes the verse read: "And Aaron shall cast lots upon the two goats, one lot for the Lord and the other lot for Azazel."

Azazel is mentioned nowhere else in the Bible save for this one chapter, but it seems quite likely that it is the name of a demon thought of as dwelling in the wilderness. It might be pictured as an evil spirit that is the source of sin. In sending the second goat into the wilderness, the sins it carries could be viewed as returning to their source.

Later legends elaborated on Azazel. He was supposed to be one of the fallen angels, exiled from Heaven because he would not accept newly created man as superior. An alternative suggestion involves a rather obscure passage in the Book of Genesis:

Genesis 6:2. . . . *the sons of God saw the daughters of men that they were fair; and they took them wives of all which they chose.*

. . . .

Genesis 6:4. . . . *and they bare children to them, the same became mighty men which were of old, men of renown.*

This remnant of primitive mythology, lingering on in the Bible, was interpreted literally by the later Jews. They thought the angels, deliberately rebelling against God, chose to corrupt themselves with mankind out of lust for women and that this act helped bring on the Flood. Some versions of this legend made Azazel the chief of these angels.

Devils

Another relic of the past is contained in the next chapter, which commands centralized worship under the guidance of the priesthood, and forbids older, more independent rites:

Leviticus 17:7. *And they shall no more offer their sacrifice unto devils* . . .

The word "devil" is from the Greek *diabolos,* which means "slanderer." The name applies to evil spirits that slander God in men's ears, urging them on to disobedience and sin. They can also be viewed as slandering human beings to God, as Satan, in the Book of Job, is pictured as slandering Job.

In this particular verse, "devils" is a translation of the Hebrew word *sairrim,* which, literally, means "wild goats." There is a widespread tendency to think of goats as lustful animals personifying the wild, fructifying force of nature. The Greeks visualized the woods to be full of nature spirits in the shape of men with the horns, tail, and hindquarters of goats, always in a state of sexual heat. They called them "satyrs" and the word has entered the modern psychiatric vocabulary to represent men suffering from insatiable sexual desires.

To the Yahvists, with their strait-laced sexual mores, such fertility gods were nothing more than evil spirits.

The Revised Standard Version recognizes the specific similarity of the satyrs to the sairrim and has Leviticus 17:7 read: "So they shall no more slay their sacrifices for satyrs . . ."

The popular conception of Satan today, with his horns, tail, and cloven hoof, shows that he is still pictured as a satyr.

Blood

The eating of blood is strongly forbidden:

> Leviticus 17:10. . . . *I will even set my face against that soul that eateth blood, and will cut him off from among his people.*
> Leviticus 17:11. *For the life of the flesh is in the blood . . .*

Blood is considered to contain the principle of life, as is reasonable, seeing that long-continued bleeding will kill a man who seems otherwise unharmed. Life, as the creation of God, cannot be appropriated by man, and man cannot, therefore, eat blood.

This prohibition was pronounced before the revelation at Sinai, for even Noah, after the Flood, is cited as having received such instructions. God tells Noah what he may eat:

> Genesis 9:3. *Every moving thing that liveth shall be meat for you . . .*
> Genesis 9:4. *But flesh with the life thereof, which is the blood thereof, shall ye not eat.*

This was interpreted by the later Jews as meaning that even those who did not receive the revelation at Sinai were still required to refrain from eating blood.

Thus, when a controversy arose in the early Christian church as to whether Gentile converts were required to accept the dietary regulations of the Mosaic law, the decision was that they were not so required. Nevertheless, their freedom was not absolute, for the conservative leaders of the church at Jerusalem insisted:

> Acts 15:20. . . . *that we write unto them that they abstain from pollutions of idols, and from fornication, and from things strangled, and from blood.*

Familiar Spirits

There are prohibitions of all sorts in the Book of Leviticus. There are lists of foods that one might not eat, and lists of sexual practices that one must not tolerate. Unethical behavior of various sorts are forbidden. In addition, some practices are forbidden by the Mosaic law which seem to be harmless enough. Thus:

Exodus 23:19. . . . *Thou shalt not seethe a kid in his mother's milk.*

and:

Leviticus 19:27. *Ye shall not round the corners of your heads, neither shalt thou mar the corners of thy beard.*

Presumably, this was designed to warn against practices that were particularly associated with heathens and idolatry. The Egyptian priesthood, for instance, shaved the hair from head and face.

Later Jews made elaborate deductions from such verses. The prohibition against boiling meat in milk, for instance, was built up into complicated avoidance of eating meat and dairy dishes at the same meal, or even preparing them or serving them, at different times, in the same utensils.

Another prohibition is:

Leviticus 19:31. *Regard not them that have familiar spirits, neither seek after wizards . . .*

A wizard is a "wise man," presumably one who knows how to bend supernatural forces to his will. He would be one who could govern spirits, and make servants of them. A "familiar spirit" is a "servant-spirit," from the Latin word *famulus*, meaning "servant."

The Bible does not say that such spirits do not exist, or that wizards do not have the power to which they pretend. The objections rests on the fact that the rites practiced by wizards are idolatrous.

The feminine version of the word "wizard" is "witch" and the Bible judges them harshly in one of the shortest and most influential of the Biblical verses:

Exodus 22:18. *Thou shalt not suffer a witch to live.*

Many unnecessary persecutions and cruelties have been visited on women (especially old women) as a result of this verse.

(It must be remembered, however, that ancient pagan practices endured, under cover, throughout the centuries of Christian Europe. Fighting witchcraft was sometimes Christianity's way of fighting an older and competing religion.)

Molech

The Book of Leviticus inveighed particularly against one particular form of idolatry.

To be sure, the Bible denounces all forms of idolatry; all forms of worship in which divine beings were represented in the form of some tangible likeness of a man, an animal, or a composite creature. It is possible to argue that the idol is not the god worshiped but only a visible representation of an invisible, divine essence, but even if this were so, the tendency of the ordinary worshiper would be to consider the visible object as the god.

The Yahvists thought this danger to be so great that increasingly, through Biblical times, they set their face against any image at all and grew more and more firm on that subject. —And one particular idol roused them to enormous rage.

Leviticus 20:2. . . . *Whosoever he be of the children of Israel, or of the strangers that sojourn in Israel, that giveth any of his seed unto Molech; he shall surely be put to death . . .*

Molech is, in this case, almost certainly a version of *melech* ("king"). It is a way of referring to the god of the people, similar to "the lord." The Biblical writers grew increasingly unable, as the centuries passed, to speak of idols as kings or lords and avoided this by pronouncing the word *bosheth* ("shame") whenever they came to such a reference to an idol. When diacritical marks (see page 135) were added to the words, *melech* received the marks for *bosheth*. In that way, *melech* became Molech.

The worship of Molech involved the sacrifice of children. Primitive men felt that the dearer and more loved the object sacrificed to a god, the more impressed the god would be and the more apt to answer the prayer. In times of dire distress, then, children would be sacrificed, even perhaps the child of the king.

In the later days of the Israelite kingdoms, when affairs were frequently desperate, such child sacrifice was performed. One suggestion is that living children were burnt to death in a fire built within the brazen idol, but it may be that the children were slain first and then sacrificed in some more ordinary fashion.

One of the later kings of Judah, Ahaz, sacrificed his son in this fashion:

> 2 Kings 16:3. *But he* [Ahaz] . . . *made his son to pass through the fire, according to the abominations of the heathen* . . .

Undoubtedly, many men of the period applied the word *melech* to Yahveh, and assumed themselves to be sacrificing to God in an approved manner as Abraham was ready to do in sacrificing Isaac. Of course, those who disapproved of human sacrifice must have been quick to point out that the sacrifice of Isaac was prevented. Even so, the prophets had to go to special pains to state, specifically, that Yahveh did not approve. The verses in Leviticus were made firm and strong and Jeremiah, in rehearsing the complaints of God against the Jews, has Him say:

> Jeremiah 7:31. *And they* . . . *burn their sons and their daughters in the fire; which I commanded them not, neither came it into my heart.*

Jubile

A special festival is mentioned in Leviticus, which seems to have been a priestly ideal that was never put thoroughly into practice:

> Leviticus 25:8. *And thou shalt number* . . . *seven times seven years* . . .
> Leviticus 25:9. *Then shalt thou cause the trumpet of the jubile to sound* . . . *in the day of atonement* . . .
> Leviticus 25:10. *And ye shall hallow the fiftieth year* . . .

The land was to remain fallow during the year; land which had been leased out was to be restored to the original owners; slaves were to be freed. In a way, it was a method of starting things fresh every half century so as to prevent the accumulation of economic injustice. It was a beautiful idea, but impractical.

Nevertheless, the word "jubile" (usually spelled "jubilee" and derived from the Hebrew word for trumpet) has come to represent a fiftieth anniversary.

About 100 B.C., a book was written by some unnamed Jew or Jews purporting to detail the primitive history of humanity. It modeled itself on Genesis but added a great many legendary details that had been built up since Genesis had reached its final form some three centuries before. It includes much detail concerning angels, for instance, and traces late customs back to the earliest times. Because it gives the history in a series of chapters, each dealing with a fifty-year period, it is called the "Book of Jubilees."

4. NUMBERS

Numbers

The fourth book of the Bible begins:

Numbers 1:1. *And the Lord spake unto Moses in the wilderness* . . .

The Hebrew name is taken from that first verse for it is "Bemidbar" meaning "in the wilderness."

The translators of the Septuagint were, however, impressed by the fact that the book includes the results of two censuses of the fighting men of the Israelite tribes. They therefore named the book "Arithmoi" ("Numbers"). The name of this book, unlike those of the first three, is translated into English, and is called "Numbers."

The Sum of the Congregation

The first census is recorded at the very start of the book:

Numbers 1:2. *Take ye the sum of all the congregation* . . .
Numbers 1:3. *From twenty years old and upward, all that are able to go forth to war* . . .

The second census was carried out forty years afterward, shortly before the entry into Canaan:

Numbers 26:2. *Take the sum of all the congregation . . . from twenty years old and upward . . . all that are able to go to war* . . .

The figures presented by the Book of Numbers are as follows:

Tribe	First Census	Second Census
Reuben	46,500	43,730
Simeon	59,300	22,200
Gad	45,650	40,500
Judah	74,600	76,500
Issachar	54,400	64,300
Zebulun	57,400	60,500
Ephraim	40,500	32,500
Manasseh	32,200	52,700
Benjamin	35,400	45,600
Dan	62,700	64,400
Asher	41,500	53,400
Naphtali	53,400	45,400
Total	603,550	601,730

These are only the adult males, of course. If one counts in the women and children and the "mixed-multitude" or half-breed hangers-on to whom the Bible occasionally refers, one gets the picture of some two million people wandering about the Sinai Peninsula. This seems implausibly large, considering this is more than the number of Israelites in the Davidic kingdom at its height. One suspects that the numbers represent a later tradition of questionable accuracy.

Regardless of the accuracy of the figures, however, two points can be made which reflect later history. First, the most populous tribes were pictured as Judah and Joseph. (If Ephraim and Manasseh are taken together, the Joseph tribes have 72,700 in the first census, almost the figure for Judah; and 85,200 in the second census, surpassing the figure for Judah.) This seems to reflect the situation four centuries later when the Davidic kingdom had split in two, with the Joseph tribes dominating the northern kingdom and Judah the southern.

Secondly, the most startling change in numbers is that of Simeon, which, between the first and second census, loses more than three fifths of its numbers. No other tribe is pictured as suffering anywhere near such losses and there is nothing in the actual events of Numbers to account for it. This, apparently, is an indication that at the time of the conquest of Canaan, Simeon was already considerably weakened, and this helps account for the fact that it played no great role in later Israelite history. This may be the result of a disastrous early attack on Shechem by Simeon and Levi, described in Genesis (see page 100) and made to appear there as though it were a victory of patriarchal times.

The tribe of Levi was not numbered with the other tribes for they were not to be among the warriors. Their task was to perform the priestly functions. Therefore, all the males were counted and not merely those above twenty years. The figure in the first census came to 22,273 and in the second to 23,000. Levi is thus made to seem smaller than any of the other tribes and this too may be a reflection of the attack on Shechem.

The Ethiopian Woman

The Israelites set out on their march toward Canaan and along the way, Moses had to contend with various types of disaffection. Even within his own family there was dissension, for his sister, Miriam, and his brother, Aaron, entered into an intrigue against him:

Numbers 12:1. *And Miriam and Aaron spake against Moses because of the Ethiopian woman whom he had married* . . .

From this verse one might picture, as many people do, a Negro woman as Moses' wife, since "Ethiopian" is used frequently nowadays as a euphemistic synonym for "Negro." However, there is no reason to think that a Negro woman was involved, or even an Ethiopian woman in the modern sense. The Hebrew word here translated as "Ethiopian" is "Cushi" and in the Revised Standard Version, Moses' wife is described as "the Cushite woman."

As I explained earlier (see page 19), a Cushite might indeed be an Ethiopian. According to legend, Moses served as an Egyptian general in his youth and led his troops in a victorious campaign in Ethiopia and might, conceivably, have picked up a wife or concubine there. However, there is no Biblical evidence of this and the legend of Moses' Ethiopian adventures is probably based on nothing stronger than this single verse.

Against this view is the fact that the Cushites are also Arabian peoples (see page 20).

Only one woman is specifically mentioned in the Bible as being married to Moses. Moses' marriage took place during his flight into Midian, in Arabia, and his stay at the home of a desert priest (see page 129):

Exodus 2:21. *And Moses was content to dwell with the man; and he gave Moses Zipporah his daughter.*

Zipporah may very well have been the Cushite woman referred to in Numbers 12:1. She could be resented by Miriam out of generalized intrafamilial jealousy, or, specifically, because she *was* a "Cushite woman"; that is, a Midianite and a foreigner, and not an Israelite.

In any case, Moses faced down his brother and sister and won out over dissent as he did on numerous other occasions in the course of the Exodus.

Caleb

Having reached the wilderness of Paran (see page 87) south of Canaan, Moses took the cautious step of sending spies into the land in order to observe the situation. Their reports might then serve as a ground for a rational distribution of forces and an efficient plan of campaign.

Twelve spies were selected, one from each tribe, but of these only two were of importance. One was Oshea of Ephraim, whom Moses renamed Jehoshua, or Joshua (see page 146). The other was a Judean:

Numbers 13:6. *Of the tribe of Judah, Caleb the son of Jephunneh.*

The career of Caleb is, in many respects, parallel to that of Joshua. Where Joshua was a hero of legends originating with the northern tribes, Caleb was the analogous hero of the southern ones.

In this verse, Caleb is treated as though he were simply a Judean, but in the Book of Joshua he is referred to more fully:

Joshua 14:6. . . . *Caleb the son of Jephunneh the Kenezite . . .*

A Kenezite or ("Kenizzite," as in the Revised Standard Version) is a descendant of Kenaz, who is listed in Genesis as a son of Eliphaz, the first-born of Esau. The Kenizzites, therefore, are an Edomite clan, who must have been adopted into the Judean tribe. This is not the only indication that the tribe of Judah contained non-Israelite elements. In Chapter 38 of Genesis, Judah is described as making an alien marriage:

Genesis 38:2. *And Judah saw there a daughter of a certain Canaanite . . . and he took her . . .*

This may be an indication that the tribe of Judah, located in southern Canaan, was at least partly Canaanite and Edomite in nature. It is even possible that in the early tribal period, Judah was not felt to be part of Israel, for in certain key portions of the book, Judah is conspicuously ignored. Even in Davidic times, when Judah was not only an integral part of Israel but supplied it with a ruling dynasty, there was a continuing lack of sympathy between it and the northern tribes. This was exacerbated into downright enmity and ended finally in civil war and schism.

Zin

From Paran, the spies traveled northward:

Numbers 13:21. *So they went up, and searched the land from the wilderness of Zin unto Rehob . . .*
Numbers 13:22. *And they . . . came unto Hebron; where . . . the children of Anak were. (Now Hebron was built seven years before Zoan in Egypt.)*
Numbers 13:23. *And they came unto the brook of Eshcol, and cut down from thence a branch with one cluster of grapes, . . . and they brought of the pomegranates and of the figs.*

Verse 21 indicates the thoroughness of the search for "the wilderness of Zin" is taken to be the northern edge of Paran, and therefore the desert area just south of Beersheba, while Rehob (exact location unknown) is a site in the extreme north of Canaan. The effect is that of saying that the United States has been searched "from Maine to California."

This may be hyperbole and the chief attention was concentrated on Hebron, the southernmost of the large, well-fortified cities of Canaan. It was formidable enough to allow the metaphoric description of its inhabitants as giants—a description later accepted literally (see page 73).

The parenthetical phrase makes Hebron's legendary ancientness specific by stating it to be seven years older than Zoan. Zoan is the Semitic name for the town called Tanis by the Greeks. It was the capital of the Hyksos kingdom and is used as a comparison because it was the nearest to Canaan of the notable cities of Egypt and therefore, perhaps, the best known.

The ancientness of Egyptian civilization was the proud boast of Egypt and was acknowledged with awe by its neighbors. There was no better way of testifying to the extreme age of a city than by claiming it to be older than an Egyptian city.

While Canaan would not seem an absolute garden spot to someone from California or the Nile, it would certainly seem so to tribes invading from the desert. Well-watered oases such as that in which Hebron was situated would seem particularly fertile and would justify the well-known description of Canaan used in several places in the early books of the Bible. Thus, in God's first interview with Moses, he promises to bring the Israelites out of Egypt:

> Exodus 3:8. . . . unto a good land and a large, unto a land flowing with milk and honey . . .

The produce of Eshcol, a district of orchards near Hebron, was brought back to the waiting Israelite host as proof that the description was justified.

Kadesh

The report of the spies was brought back to the place where the Israelites had established a semipermanent station:

> Numbers 13:26. And they went and came to . . . the children of Israel, unto the wilderness of Paran to Kadesh . . .

Kadesh means "holy" and probably received its name because it had some sacred associations for the pre-Israelite inhabitants of the

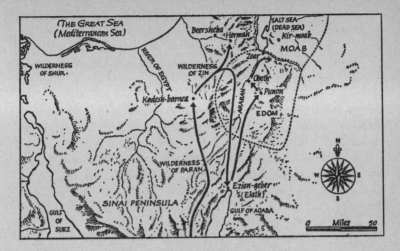

Kadesh-barnea

area. It is identified with a place called Ain Kadis today, located about fifty miles south of Hebron and in the northeastern corner of the Sinai Peninsula.

Despite the fertility of the Hebron area, the spies returned with an utterly pessimistic majority report. They felt the Canaanite cities were entirely too strong to be taken by assault and predicted disaster for any invasion attempt. Only Joshua and Caleb presented a minority report in favor of an immediate assault and they were nearly stoned as a result.

The disheartened Israelites considered a return to Egypt but Moses held them in place and for the next thirty-eight years, Kadesh remained the Israelite capital, while Moses and Joshua organized their forces for the task that lay ahead.

Korah, Dathan, and Abiram

The stay at Kadesh was bound to be a difficult one for Moses. Year after year of inactivity, with Canaan at hand but inaccessible, seemed to make a mockery of the Exodus and to cast doubt upon Moses' capacity as a leader. Serious disaffection appeared:

Numbers 16:1. *Now Korah, the son of Izhar* . . . *and Dathan and Abiram* . . . *sons of Reuben took men:*

. . . .

Numbers 16:3. *And they gathered themselves together against Moses and against Aaron* . . .

Apparently, this chapter combines into one account what were actually two separate rebellions against Moses, one by Korah, and one by the Reubenites.

The rebellion by Korah was specifically a religious schism. Moses and Aaron were the sons of Amram, while Korah was the son of Amram's younger brother, Izhar (see page 136). Since Moses assigned the lion's share of the priestly duties to Aaron and the Amramites, Korah felt unjustly discriminated against.

Korah's rebellion was put down, but perhaps not without a compromise being reached. At least Numbers points out later that, despite the destruction of Korah and his band:

Numbers 26:11. *Notwithstanding the children of Korah died not.*

In fact, the Korahites survived to become a hereditary guild of Temple musicians, a concession they might have received in the case of a Levite civil war, the memory of which forms the basis of the sixteenth chapter of Numbers.

The Reubenite rebellion of Dathan and Abiram seems to have been purely political. At some early point in tribal history, Reuben must have held the leadership because the tradition is firm that Reuben is the oldest son of Israel. In the course of the Exodus, the Reubenites must have witnessed with dismay the shift in the religious leadership to the tribe of Levi (Moses and Aaron) and the military leadership to the tribe of Ephraim (Joshua). The tale of Dathan and Abiram must be based on the memory of some attempt of Reuben to regain its leadership and this attempt may also echo in the cryptic verse in Genesis which describes Reuben as committing incest with his father's concubine (see page 102).

The Reubenite rebellion was also crushed and never again in Israelite history did the tribe of Reuben play a significant role.

The Pit

The particular punishment of the rebellious Reubenites, according to the Biblical description, was that of being swallowed alive by the earth:

Numbers 16:32. *And the earth opened her mouth, and swallowed them up . . .*
Numbers 16:33. *They . . . went down alive into the pit . . .*

The Hebrew word, here translated as "the pit" is *Sheol*, and in the Revised Standard Version, Sheol is left untranslated. Sheol was visualized by the early Israelites as an underground world to which the souls of the dead departed. It was thought of at first as a dim place where there was no particular torture, but where there was an absence of joy. Nor was there any distinction between good and evil; all human beings went there upon death except those few who, like Enoch and Elijah, were taken alive to Heaven.

The picture is like that of other such places imagined by early men. The Greeks had such a world ruled by a god, Hades, and in the early Nordic myths there was such a world ruled by a goddess, Hel. Sheol is therefore replaced by "Hell" in some places in the Bible, and in the New Testament, which was originally written in Greek, it was translated as "Hades."

The moralization of Sheol, its conversion into a place of torture for the wicked, while the good go elsewhere, came later in history, toward the end of Old Testament times.

Mount Hor

The old generation was passing away, and few remained of those who were adults at the time of the Exodus. Miriam, Moses' sister, died at Kadesh, for instance.

The time came when some move had to be made. A direct assault from the south against Hebron seemed to be still out of the question and the alternative was to flank Hebron by traveling northeastward. Canaan could then be attacked from the more vulnerable east.

In order to travel directly northeastward, however, the territory of Edom would have had to be traversed. The Edomites were recognized as a Hebrew people related to the Israelites and the use of force against them was therefore ruled out. Permission was requested by Moses to pass through their territory peacefully, but this was refused. In later years, this refusal was used as a grievance against Edom and as a cause for enmity.

It was therefore necessary to outflank Edom's fortified areas, so the Israelites traveled southeastward:

Numbers 20:22. And the children of Israel . . . journeyed from Kadesh, and came unto Mount Hor.

Mount Hor is often identified with the highest peak in the Seir mountain range (see page 96). Aaron died at this time and was buried on Mount Hor and the peak which is now identified with it is called Jebel Harun ("Mount Aaron") in Arabic.

Some statistics concerning Aaron's death are given later:

Numbers 33:38. And Aaron . . . died there, in the fortieth year after the children of Israel were come out of the land of Egypt.
Numbers 33:39. And Aaron was an hundred and twenty and three years old . . .

If the Exodus took place in 1211 B.C., then the death of Aaron took place in 1171 B.C. That must also have been the year of the death of Moses and of the entry into Canaan, for events now follow quickly although the Bible continues to interrupt those events with long speeches by Moses and others.

If we accept Aaron's age at his death, he must have been born in 1294 B.C., while Moses, who was three years younger, was born in 1291 B.C. (This last is an interesting date for it virtually coincides with the beginning of the reign of Rameses II, the Pharaoh of the Oppression; see page 125.)

The Serpent of Brass

When the period of mourning for Aaron was done, the Israelites continued their outflanking march, by traveling southward to the tip of the Gulf of Aqaba, around Edomite territory and then north again.

Here there occurs an event which was to have continuing traditions later.

A plague of serpents harassed the Israelites, the Bible explains:

Numbers 21:9. *And Moses made a serpent of brass, and put it upon a pole, and it came to pass, that if a serpent had bitten any man, when he beheld the serpent of brass, he lived.*

This is an example of "sympathetic magic," the belief that like effects like, which is common among primitive people. (The most familiar example we have today is the voodoo belief that sticking pins in images will bring pain and sickness to the person represented by the image.) The use of the serpent, as described in this verse, is rather similar to the principles of homeopathic medicine, which follows the "hair of the dog that bit you" sort of reasoning.

The serpent is a particularly important animal in religious ritual, whether for good or evil. The fact that a serpent moves in so quiet and hidden a fashion and strikes so suddenly and so unexpectedly with so poisoned a fang, makes it an obvious representation of cunning and evil. It is such a representation of cunning evil in the story of the garden of Eden, for instance:

Genesis 3:1. *Now the serpent was more subtil than any beast of the field . . .*

Something that is dangerous and evil is to be feared, and something that is feared had better be treated well and propitiated, so that serpents could be worshiped even while dreaded.

Then, too, the serpent is looked upon as symbolizing immortality because of its ability to shed its skin. Any primitive man, observing the process by which a serpent sheds an old, dull skin and emerges in a new, brightly colored one, might be excused if he assumed the serpent had undergone a process of rejuvenation. (We ourselves also shed our skin but we do so continuously, and little by little, here and there, so that the process is quite unnoticeable.)

Thus, in the Gilgamesh legend (see page 40), when the hero finally gains the plant that brought immortality, he has it stolen from him by a serpent, which then becomes immortal. (In the garden of Eden, it is the serpent who steals immortality from Adam and Eve, although it is not itself made immortal as a result, but is punished.)

The immortal serpent, victor over death, can thus be considered the

particular associate of the medical profession, which labors to stave
off, if not to conquer, death. Serpents were sacred to Asklepios, the
Greek god of medicine, and even today the Medical Corps of the
U. S. Army has as its insignia the caduceus, a staff about which two
serpents are encircled.

In later Israelite history, however, as Yahvism grew stronger and
more uncompromising, the serpent of brass, worshiped by the people,
came under sharper and sharper disapproval. The fact of the association with Moses did not save it. The end came in the reign of Hezekiah, king of Judah, some five centuries after the Exodus:

> 2 Kings 18:4. He [Hezekiah] . . . brake in pieces the brasen
> serpent that Moses had made: for unto those days the children of
> Israel did burn incense to it: and he called it Nehushtan.

Nehushtan is usually translated as "a piece of brass." The impression one gets from the final clause of this verse, as given in the King
James Version, is that when Hezekiah destroyed the serpent, he
countered the shock of the populace by contemptuously labeling the
object as of no ritual value at all but as nothing more than a piece
of brass.

However, Nehushtan is related not only to the Hebrew word for
"brass" but also to the word for "serpent." Nehushtan may have been
the name of the object without any connotation of contempt. Indeed,
the Revised Standard Version translates the final clause of 2 Kings 18:4
as "it was called Nehushtan," a matter-of-fact statement of information
without interpretation.

Sihon

Even the circling of Edom did not remove all difficulties. East of
Canaan lay the two kingdoms of Moab and Ammon. Of these two,
Moab was the more southerly, occupying the eastern shores of the
Dead Sea, while Ammon, to the north, lay east of the Jordan River.

Both were recognized by the Israelites to be Hebrew peoples, descendants of Terah by way of Lot and therefore (according to the
interpretation of the Biblical writers), like Edom, immune to attack.
Both Moab and Ammon had, presumably, established themselves at
the borders of Canaan a century and a half before, in the time of
Ikhnaton (see page 124).

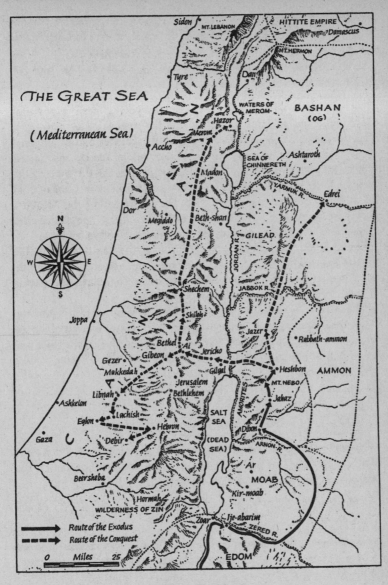

The Great Sea
(Mediterranean Sea)

Sidon
MT. LEBANON
HITTITE EMPIRE
Damascus
Tyre
Dan
MT. HERMON
WATERS OF MEROM
BASHAN (OG)
Hazor
Merom
Accho
Ashtaroth
SEA OF CHINNERETH
Madon
Dor
Megiddo
Beth-shan
YARMUK R.
Edrei
GILEAD
N
W   E
S
Shechem
JABBOK R.
Jazer
Shiloh
Joppa
Bethel
Ai
Jericho
Rabbath-ammon
Gibeon
Gezer
Makkedah
Gilgal
Heshbon
AMMON
Jerusalem
Bethlehem
MT. NEBO
Libnah
Ashkelon
Lachish
Jahaz
Eglon
Hebron
SALT SEA
Dibon
Gaza
Debir
(DEAD SEA)
ARNON R.
Beersheba
Ar
MOAB
Hormah
Kir-moab
WILDERNESS OF ZIN
Zoar
Ije-abarim
ZERED R.
⟶ Route of the Exodus
⟶ Route of the Conquest
0   Miles   25
EDOM

Moab and Ammon

Just before the Israelites had arrived, however, the kingdoms—Moab in particular—had had to withstand the shock of another onslaught.

Numbers 2:26. . . . *Sihon the king of the Amorites . . . had fought against the former king of Moab, and taken all his land out of his hand, even unto Arnon.*

The Amorites had, some seven centuries before, been a powerful people and had ruled most of the Fertile Crescent (see page 50). They had fallen before the onslaughts of the Hittites and of Imperial Egypt and were now either in subjection or, in places, maintained themselves precariously in patchwork principalities. At the time of the Exodus, there were, presumably, Amorite principalities in Canaan, and Sihon may have been the ruler of one. His attack against the Moabites may have represented the last successful action of the Canaanites against the remorseless pressure of the various Hebrew tribes.

Before Sihon's onslaught, Moab controlled the territory up to the Jabbok River. This is described elsewhere in this chapter as the southern boundary of Ammon and Sihon, therefore, conquered the stretch of land from the Jabbok down to the Arnon.

The Arnon, by the way, is a small river, flowing westward into the Dead Sea, reaching that body of water just about midway along its eastern shore. In later Biblical history it remained the northern boundary of Moab. Its modern name is Wadi Mojib, "Mojib" being a clear echo of "Moab."

Chemosh

In connection with the brief account of the victory of Sihon over Moab, a fragment of a victory ode exulting over the defeat of the Moabites is included. In part, it reads:

Numbers 22:29. *Woe to thee, Moab! thou art undone, O people of Chemosh . . .*

Chemosh was the national god of Moab and it was natural to speak of Moab, in those days of wide acceptance of local gods, as the "people of Chemosh."

Only a few thinkers in those primitive times recognized a universal God. Generally, the feeling was that each bit of land had its own god, and that over its own bit of land each god had godlike power. It was even felt that the god was tied to the land; that if one traveled elsewhere it became necessary to worship the god of *that* land unless one carried his own god. Thus, when Rachel left the house of her father Laban, she took Laban's idols with her:

> Genesis 31:19 . . . *and Rachel had stolen the images that were her father's.*

and Laban was more distressed at this than at the loss of his daughters and the goods and cattle that Jacob had carried off:

> Genesis 31:30. . . . *though thou wouldest needs be gone . . . wherefore hast thou stolen my gods?*

The manner in which the Israelites carried the ark of the covenant with them during their travels in the wilderness had a little of the flavor of carrying God with them. Otherwise, one suspects, they might have felt it necessary always to travel back to Sinai to commune with Him.

In the religious thought of that day, there was no necessary feeling of antagonism toward the gods of other tribes, provided no actual war was going on and the enemy was not calling upon his god for help in your destruction (as you were calling upon yours for help in his destruction). The situation might be much the same as in our own feeling for the flags of foreign nations. If we are at peace with a foreign nation, international usage requires that we treat its flag with decent respect even in our own land. It would be even more a matter of elementary courtesy to treat the flag of a foreign nation with respect while inside the borders of that nation.

In later times, however, as a consciousness of the universality of Yahveh grew among the Israelites, and as the feeling deepened that there was only one God, not only for the Israelites but for all the world—that there was one *only* God—the attitude of the Yahvists toward the gods of other tribes hardened. The foreign gods were not only potential enemies; they were no gods at all. At most, they were demons who imposed their worship on the ignorant, unenlightened, or wicked. As a result, when Chemosh was referred to in later books of the Bible, it was as something shameful:

> 1 Kings 11:7. . . . *Chemosh, the abomination of Moab . . .*

Heshbon

The conflict between Sihon and Moab presented a wonderful opportunity for the Israelites. Whereas Moab and Ammon were related tribes, according to the Biblical interpretation of events, and therefore untouchable, Sihon was a non-Hebrew and might be attacked. Or, to put it in less idealistic fashion, Moab and Ammon were settled kingdoms with well-fortified borders that it might be difficult to attack. Thus the chapter states:

> Numbers 21:24. . . . *the border of the children of Ammon was strong.*

(It may be, however, that this verse is mistranslated and that the Hebrew word translated as "strong" refers to the town of Jazer, defining it as the boundary of Ammon.)

It would seem reasonable, though, that the region conquered by Sihon would be in a state of confusion and weakness. The strong points, overthrown and broken down by the Amorites, might not yet have been restored; and although the Amorites had cowed Moab into submission they might be in no condition now to face a new, fresh foe.

This proved, indeed, to be the case. Israel demanded passage through the land, something Sihon could not allow. When passage was refused, the Israelites attacked, and defeated the Amorites,

> Numbers 21:24. . . . *and possessed his land from Arnon unto Jabbok . . .*
> Numbers 21:25. *And Israel . . . dwelt in all the cities of the Amorites, in Heshbon . . .*

Heshbon was the chief city of the region and was located about twenty miles east of the northern tip of the Dead Sea. It is still there as a town in Jordan, with the Arabic name of Hesban.

Bashan

The Israelites had now established themselves firmly on the eastern bank of the Jordan and had a base from which to launch the conquest of Canaan itself. That base, however, had to be broadened as widely as possible. Assuming that Moab and Ammon must remain inviolate, there was still the fertile pastures north of Ammon. These were attractive to the Israelites.

Numbers 21:33. *And they turned and went up by the way of Bashan: and Og the king of Bashan went out against them . . . to the battle at Edrei.*

The exact borders of Bashan are uncertain but it was, in general, located to the east of the Sea of Galilee. It was for a long time a prosperous, fertile region, so much so that the quality of its cattle became proverbial in Biblical times—and through the Bible in our own times, too. In the 22nd Psalm, its cattle are used metaphorically to represent the intensity of woes besetting the psalmist:

Psalm 22:12. *Many bulls have compassed me: strong bulls of Bashan have beset me round.*

And the prophet Amos uses them to represent the prosperous and self-satisfied aristocrats of the nation:

Amos 4:1. *Hear this word, ye kine of Bashan . . .*

Bashan was also famous for its oaks. The prophet Ezekiel, in ironically listing the glories of the merchant city of Tyre before going on to prophesy its utter fall, describes the excellence of its ships by saying, in part,

Ezekiel 27:5. *Of the oaks of Bashan have they made thine oars . . .*

Bashan remained prosperous under shifting tides of political change until it was taken over by the Arabs in the seventh century A.D. After that, decline was rapid. Nowadays, the territory that was once Bashan makes up the southwestern corner of Syria, bordering Jordan to its south and Israel to its west. Edrei, the sight of the battle between Og and the Israelites, exists now as the town of Deraa, right on the Jordanian border, with a population of about four thousand.

The territory is now largely occupied by the Druses, a Mohammedan sect which, since its establishment about A.D. 1000, has managed to maintain its existence even against the far superior power of the Turks before World War I, or the French after it.

The conquest of Bashan was one of the events in early Israelite military history that most impressed the later writers, both Biblical and post-Biblical. Part of the reason is that Og, king of Bashan, was reputed to be a giant. This is based upon a statement in the Book of Deuteronomy, where Moses is pictured as reviewing the events following the Exodus:

> Deuteronomy 3:11 For only Og king of Bashan remained of the remnant of giants; behold, his bedstead was a bedstead of iron . . . nine cubits was the length thereof and four cubits the breadth of it . . .

Judging from measurements made on the ruins of the Temple at Jerusalem (whose measurements in cubits we know), it would seem that a cubit is equal to about seventeen and a half inches. In that case, Og's bed was about thirteen feet long and six feet wide.* A large bed, to be sure, though it need not be taken that Og's body had to fill it top to bottom and side to side.

Later rabbinical writers expanded on Og's size and made him the last of the Nephilim who lived before the Flood (see page 72). To survive the Flood, however, Og would have had to be in Noah's ark, into which he could not fit. The legendmakers have it, then, that he sat astride the ark and was fed by Noah till the waters fell.

This association of Og and the Flood (concerning which there is no Biblical evidence whatever) may have been helped along by the fact that the Greek myths had an ancient King Ogyges who reigned during a great deluge. It might have seemed reasonable (to legendmakers) to suppose that Og and Ogyges were different forms of the same name.

The manner of Og's legendary death is also dramatic. He raised a huge mountain to hurl at the Israelites and tripped and fell in the attempt. Thereupon, Moses himself leaped at him and killed him. It is very likely that this last picture of Og is borrowed from the semicomic Greek myth of the revolt of the giants against Zeus and the Olympians. Those giants hurled mountains (one of the mountains crashed into the sea, according to the tale, and became Sicily) but were slain anyway.

---

* There are large, iron-gray stones of basalt placed over primitive graves in the area east of Jordan, about the size indicated in the verse. If this is considered, metaphorically, as the final resting place or "bed" of a ruler or warrior, that might account for the rise of the legend of Og's gianthood.

Balaam

The fact that the Israelites had conquered Heshbon and Bashan was quite sufficient to alarm Moab. Even though its own territory had not been attacked, it had no assurance it was not next on the list. Besides, Moab could scarcely have failed to consider Heshbon, the recent conquest of Sihon, as its own territory, and the Israelites, having conquered it in turn, were certainly not planning to restore it to Moab.

Balak, the king of Moab, decided to weaken the Israelites by the more subtle means of the supernatural, rather than by outright attack.

Numbers 22:5. *He sent messengers therefore unto Balaam . . . to Pethor . . . saying . . .*

Numbers 22:6. *. . . curse me this people . . . for . . . he whom thou blessest is blessed, and he whom thou cursest is cursed.*

Apparently, Balaam was a well-known sorcerer or magician of his time, one who was believed to know the rites whereby supernatural help or harm could be called down and who had demonstrated his knowledge and skill, at least to the satisfaction of common report.

Balaam's fame in this respect can be regarded as widespread for his town of Pethor is usually accepted as being on the Euphrates, some four hundred miles north of Moab. It is identified with a town called "Pitru" in the Assyrian records and "Pedru" in the Egyptian records. (Some consider this distance too great to be plausible and suggest that the verse has undergone some distortion and that Balaam was really an Ammonite living only a few dozen miles north of Moab.)

Balaam's power was accepted even by the Israelites and nowhere in the Bible is Balaam's power to bless and curse derided. It is rather treated as a fortunate miracle that God chose to make Balaam's curses come to nothing.

Indeed, belief can be sufficient. If the Moabites were convinced of the efficacy of Balaam's curse on the Israelites, they would fight with more confidence and spirit in the battle that followed. And if the Israelites were likewise convinced, they would have been correspondingly disheartened and might well have been defeated and driven away by the Moabites.

According to the later view, Balaam served for hire and bestowed his blessing and curses not necessarily as inspired to do so by God, but in response to the fees he was offered by those who wished to employ him. Thus, in the book of Jude in the New Testament, Jude says:

> Jude 1:11 *Woe unto them! for they . . . ran greedily after the error of Balaam for reward . . .*

For this reason the expression "Balaamite" is used to describe someone who uses religion primarily as a money-making device.

Baal

Balak had to send several times for Balaam, who was reluctant to accept the commission. (The several-times-repeated journey is a point in favor of those who feel that Balaam's home was not very far removed from Moab. The story of the missions is not entirely self-consistent and was probably derived from two separate and somewhat conflicting sources.)

Eventually Balaam did saddle up for the journey to Moab and on that journey occurred the famous incident of his talking ass. An angel blocked the way; an angel that the ass carrying Balaam could see but Balaam himself could not. When the ass balked, Balaam beat him and the ass spoke up in its own defense. This is one of the two incidents in the Bible in which an animal is depicted as speaking. (The serpent in Eden is the other.) The miraculous nature of this incident is such that later legends described the ass's mouth as one of the objects specially created in the initial week of creation for use in later history.

Once Balaam arrived in Moab, Balak hastened to place him where his curses might be most effective; in the mountain heights near Heaven where the gods might best hear him and where the power of his words could best fan out over the Israelites whom he was to curse:

> Numbers 22:41. . . . *Balak took Balaam and brought him up into the high places of Baal, that thence he might see . . . part of the* [Israelite] *people.*

The phrase "high places of Baal" is a translation of the Hebrew *Bamoth-Baal*, which later, in the Book of Joshua, is mentioned as a town in Moab. The town was located in the highlands, however, and was named in honor of Baal because the site was associated with important religious rites. The effect is therefore the same whether one speaks of "Bamoth-Baal" or of "the high places of Baal."

The word *baal* meant, in the various Semitic languages, "master" or "owner," sometimes in a very mundane sense. In the Book of Exodus, one finds:

> Exodus 21:28. . . . *the owner of the ox shall be quit.*

and "owner" is here the translation of the Hebrew word *baal*.

"Baal" was also used as a common title for Semitic deities with the precise connotation of the English "Lord." It was never used as the specific name of any idol. Indeed, the Israelites used the word as a title for Yahveh at least up through the time of David. Thus, one of the sons of King Saul (who was always depicted as a sincere Yahvist) was named Ishbaal or "man of the Lord," and one of his grandsons, Merib-baal or "hero of the Lord."

The word *baal* was so frequently used for idols, however, that the later Biblical writers could not look upon it as simply "Lord" or apply it, under any circumstance, to Yahveh. The term *Adonai* for "Lord" succeeded *baal* and in time, it became even disgraceful to use the earlier term. When the name Ishbaal had to be written, for instance, Ish-bosheth was used instead:

> 2 Samuel 2:8. . . . *Abner . . . took Ish-bosheth the son of Saul, and brought him over to Mahanaim;*

Bosheth meant "shame" and was used to indicate what was considered a shameful word. The effect is the same as our own habit of sometimes using asterisks to fill out an improper word. It is as though we were to write "Ishbaal" as "Ish****."

Pisgah

Unfortunately, for the Moabites, Balaam found himself unable to curse the Israelites. Under the direct inspiration of God, according to the Biblical account, his attempts to curse were converted into blessings. Balak desperately sought other posts which might prove more efficacious:

Numbers 23:14. *And he* [Balak] *brought him* [Balaam] . . . *to the top of Pisgah* . . .

Numbers 23:28. *And Baluk brought Balaam unto the top of Peor* . . .

Mount Pisgah is nowadays identified with a peak only six miles southwest of Heshbon and perhaps twelve miles east of the northern end of the Dead Sea. It is twenty miles north of the Arnon River and if the identification is correct, it makes it obvious that Moabite forces were edging into the territory recently conquered by the Israelites—perhaps while the main force of the latter was occupied in Bashan.

Mount Pisgah is 2644 feet high, or just about half a mile. Mount Peor, which has no certain identification, was probably somewhat north of Pisgah, so that although Peor was not quite as high a peak as Pisgah, it was closer to the enemy. An alternate name of Pisgah is Nebo and under the latter name it is most famous as the place of burial of Moses.

Unicorn

Balaam's inability to curse continued at all stations. From Mount Pisgah, Balaam praised God, saying:

Numbers 23:22. *God brought them out of Egypt; he* [Israel] *hath as it were the strength of an unicorn.*

The Bible mentions the unicorn on several other occasions, notably in the Book of Job:

Job 39:9. *Will the unicorn be willing to serve thee, or abide by thy crib?*

The Hebrew word represented in the King James Version by "unicorn" is *re'em*, which undoubtedly refers to the wild ox (*urus* or *aurochs*) ancestral to the domesticated cattle of today. The *re'em* still flourished in early historical times and a few existed into modern times although it is now extinct. It was a dangerous creature of great strength and was similar in form and temperament to the Asian buffaloes.

The Revised Standard Version translates *re'em* always as "wild ox." The verse in Numbers is translated as "they have as it were the horns of the wild ox," while the one in Job is translated "Is the wild ox willing to serve you?" The Anchor Bible translates the verse in Job as "Will the buffalo deign to serve you?"

The wild ox was a favorite prey of the hunt-loving Assyrian monarchs (the animal was called *rumu* in Assyrian, essentially the same word as *re'em*) and was displayed in their large bas-reliefs. Here the wild ox was invariably shown in profile and only one horn was visible. One can well imagine that the animal represented in this fashion would come to be called "one-horn" as a familar nickname, much as we might refer to "longhorns" in speaking of a certain breed of cattle.

As the animal itself grew less common under the pressure of increasing human population and the depredations of the hunt, it might come to be forgotten that there was a second horn hidden behind the first in the sculptures and "one-horn" might come to be considered a literal description of the animal.

When the first Greek translation of the Bible was prepared about 250 B.C. the animal was already rare in the long-settled areas of the Near East and the Greeks, who had had no direct experience with it, had no word for it. They used a translation of "one-horn" instead and it became *monokeros*. In Latin and in English it became the Latin word for "one-horn"; that is, "unicorn."

The Biblical writers could scarcely have had the intention of implying that the wild ox literally had one horn. There is one Biblical quotation, in fact, that clearly contradicts that notion. In the Book of Deuteronomy, when Moses is giving his final blessing to each tribe, he speaks of the tribe of Joseph (Ephraim and Manasseh) as follows:

Deuteronomy 33:17. *His glory is like the firstling of his bullock, and his horns are like the horns of unicorns . . .*

Here the word unicorn is placed in the plural since the thought of a "one-horn's" single horn seems to make the phrase "horns of a unicorn" self-contradictory. Still, the original Hebrew has the word in the singular so that we must speak of the "horns of a unicorn," which makes it clear that a unicorn has more than one horn. In ad-

dition, the parallelism used in Hebrew poetry makes it natural to
equate "unicorn" and "bullock," showing that the unicorn is something very much resembling a young bull. The Revised Standard
Version has, in this verse, the phrase "the horns of a wild ox."

And yet the fact that the Bible speaks of a unicorn seemed, through
most of history, to place the seal of divine assurance upon the fact that
a one-horned animal existed. The unicorn is therefore commonplace
in legends and stories.

This is especially so since travelers in Greek times spoke of a one-
horned beast that existed in India, and assigned great powers to the
single horn of that animal. For instance, a cup made out of the horn
of such a beast rendered harmless any poisonous liquid that might be
poured into it.

There is, indeed, a one-horned beast in India (as well as in Malaya,
Sumatra, and Africa) and this is the rhinoceros (from Greek words
meaning "nose-horn"). The horn on its snout is not a true horn but
is a concretion of hair; nevertheless, the concretion looks like a horn
and fulfills the purpose of one. It is very likely that the rhinoceros is
the Greek unicorn, although its horn scarcely possesses the magic
qualities attributed to it in legend.

Since the rhinoceros is one of the largest land animals still alive,
and is possessed of enormous strength, it might be thought to fit
the description in the Bible. Some Latin translations of the Bible
therefore convert the Greek *monokeros* into "rhinoceros." But this is
farfetched. It is very unlikely that the Biblical writer knew of the
rhinoceros and they certainly knew of the wild ox.

The unicorn entered European legend without reference to the
rhinoceros, which was as unknown to the medieval Westerner as to the
Biblical Israelite. The shape of the unicorn was, to the European, whatever fancy pleased to make it, and it is most familiar to us now as
a rather horselike creature with a single long horn on its forehead. In
this shape, two unicorns were depicted as supporting the royal arms of
Scotland. When Scotland and England were combined under the
House of Stuart in 1603, the Scottish unicorns joined the English lions
on the coat of arms of what now became Great Britain.

The old enmity between the two nations is reflected in the nursery
rhyme "The lion and the unicorn were fighting for the crown." The
fact that it is an English rhyme and that England usually won the

wars, though never conclusively, is signified by the second line, "The lion beat the unicorn all around the town."

The most distinctive feature of this modern unicorn is its horn, which is long, thin, slowly tapering, and a straight helix. It has precisely the shape and dimensions, in fact, of the single tooth of the male of a species of whale called the narwhal. This tooth takes the shape of a tusk, sometimes twenty feet long.

Undoubtedly, sailors occasionally obtained such tusks and then sold them to landlubbers for great sums by claiming each to be the horn of a unicorn with all the magical virtue of that object.

The Daughters of Moab

Though neither force nor enchantments had removed the Israelite danger from Moab, mere propinquity seemed on the point of becoming sufficient for the purpose. The Israelites, with their years of wandering through wilderness, had not been able to develop elaborate rituals and they found themselves fascinated by the enticing rites of the more sophisticated religions of settled city-dwellers:

> Numbers 25:1. *And Israel . . . began to commit whoredom with the daughters of Moab.*
> Numbers 25:2. *And they* [the Moabite women] *called the people unto the sacrifices of their gods . . .*
> Numbers 25:3 *And Israel joined himself unto Baal-Peor . . .*

where Baal-Peor ("the Lord of Mount Peor") was, presumably, Chemosh.

The apostasy of the Israelites is, according to the Biblical story, punished by a plague, and by firm measures on the part of Moses, who ordered the slaughter of the idolaters. Equating national gods with something of the emotions borne by national flags today, the horror of the Biblical writers at this event might be compared to our own feelings if we discovered a sizable segment of our own population gathering in time of war to salute the enemy flag and to sing the enemy anthem.

Nor was this trespass with respect to Chemosh considered an accident. It was supposed to be a deliberate policy on the part of the Moabites (following the advice of Balaam) to use their women for the purpose of seducing the Israelites to apostasy. Thus, Moses, in a later verse, is described as saying of foreign women:

> Numbers 31:16. *Behold, these caused the children of Israel, through the counsel of Balaam, to commit trespass against the Lord* . . .

The memory of this incident strengthened the position of the more intransigeant Yahvists in later history against intermarriage with foreign women.

Gilead

After the episode of Balaam and the incident of the seduction of the Israelites by Moab, it might be expected that war between Moab and Israel would be described. Instead, it is Midian that is attacked by Israel. The Midianite tribes of the eastern desert are described as having been in alliance with Moab against Israel, as having participated in the call to Balaam, and the Midianite women are also described as seducing Israelites.

This tale of war against the Midianites has its difficulties, however, and it is commonly thought to be unhistorical. It may perhaps be a pious invention of later times to mask an actual war fought inconclusively against Moab. After all, Moab remained in being and in control of the territory east of the Dead Sea for centuries. By failing to mention any war with Moab the Biblical writers could continue to maintain the position that the Israelites did not attack any Hebrew tribe.

Yet even with Moab in existence, the Israelites remained in occupation of most of the area east of the Jordan River and the Sea of Galilee. Part of this was Ammonite territory but the Bible is silent as to the fate of the Ammonites in this period. The Israelites are not described as attacking the Ammonites, a Hebrew people, yet their territory was soon to be settled by Israelite tribes. Indeed, part of the confederacy was eying the territory even in Moses' lifetime while the projected conquest of Canaan proper had not yet begun:

> Numbers 32:1. *Now the children of Reuben and the children of Gad had a very great multitude of cattle: and when they saw* . . . *the land of Gilead* . . . *behold, the place was a place for cattle;*

The boundaries of Gilead are indefinite but at its broadest, it covers the whole of the area east of the Jordan River; the "Trans-Jordan" we might call it.

Gilead had appeared earlier in the Biblical account. When Jacob had left Laban to return to Canaan, Laban pursued him and caught up with him in Gilead for a final interview:

Genesis 31:23. *And he* [Laban] . . . *pursued after him* [Jacob] *seven days journey; and* . . . *overtook him in the mount Gilead.*

Mount Gilead could refer to the range of highlands running down the eastern side of the Jordan, or to a particularly prominent peak in that range just south of the Jabbok River and about twelve miles east of the Jordan. It is some 3600 feet high.

The tribes requesting the land had first to convince Moses that they were not proposing to quit the confederacy. They would participate in the conquest of Canaan and would return to their Trans-Jordanian holdings only after that conquest was assured. Once that was made plain, Moses permitted the allotment.

Gilead was, in consequence, divided among the cattle-owning tribes of Reuben and Gad. Reuben took the area south of Heshbon and north of Moab, while Gad had virtually the entire east bank of the Jordan. Bashan fell to the lot of part of the tribe of Manasseh (another portion of which occupied territory in Canaan proper).

In one sense, the Trans-Jordan was a good location, for the area was described as rich and desirable. It was, however, also exposed. Reuben was under the perpetual shadow of Moab and quickly faded out of Israelite history, probably through absorption into Moabite culture. Gad and Manasseh were exposed to raids from the Ammonites and the Midianites, and later had to bear the first brunt of the more serious assaults of the Syrian and Assyrian armies in the latter days of the Israelite kingdom.

The name Gilead may be a corruption of Gad (which occupied much of it) or vice versa. On the other hand, the Biblical genealogies have Gilead a grandson of Manasseh:

Numbers 26:26. *Of the sons of Manasseh:* . . . *Machir* . . . *and Machir begat Gilead* . . .

There may be some connection between this eponymous ancestor of the body of men known as "Gileadites," the land itself, and the fact that a portion of the tribe of Manasseh occupied part of Gilead.

Just as Bashan was particularly known for its cattle, so Gilead was famous for the resinous products of some of its trees and shrubs; products which could be turned into soothing, fragrant ointments and used as skin softeners, cosmetics, perfumes, and incense.

This balsam, or balm, of Gilead was highly valued. When Joseph's brothers were planning to sell him for a slave it was to a party of traders to whom they sold him and they:

Genesis 37:25. . . . *came from Gilead with their camels bearing spicery and balm and myrrh, going to carry it down to Egypt.*

When the prophet Jeremiah pleads with the people to return to the Lord, pointing out that the remedy to all their evils is in their midst only waiting for them, he makes use of the metaphorical (and rhetorical) question:

Jeremiah 8:22. *Is there no balm in Gilead . . .*

The question is intended to have the obvious answer, yes! So, reasons Jeremiah, is God present for the relief of His people.

5. DEUTERONOMY

Deuteronomy

The fifth book of the Bible begins:

Deuteronomy 1:1. *These be the words which Moses spake . . .*

In Hebrew, the opening phrase is *Elleh haddebarim* and that, or the briefer form "Debarim" ("words") is the Hebrew name of the book.

The book does not advance Israelite history but purports to be the record of a series of addresses given by Moses on the eve of his death and of the Israelite entry into Canaan. These addresses recapitulate the events of the Exodus and restate key portions of the law as it was received from Sinai.

One might suppose that it was for this reason that the Greek-speaking translaters of the Septuagint named the book "Deuteronomion" (which became our own Deuteronomy) or "second law."

Actually, however, the Greek name arose through a misapprehension. In the course of his discourses, Moses enjoins strict obedience to the law on the part of the future kings of Israel:

Deuteronomy 17:18. . . . *when he* [the king] *sitteth upon the throne of his kingdom . . . he shall write him a copy of this law . . .*
Deuteronomy 17:19. *And it shall be with him, and he shall read therein . . . that he may learn . . . to keep all the words of this law . . .*

The phrase in verse 18, "a copy of this law" was incorrectly translated in the Septuagint as *deuteronomion* ("a second law") and it is from this that our name derives.

THE GREAT SEA

(Mediterranean Sea)

MT. LEBANON
HITTITE EMPIRE
Sidon
Zarephath
Damascus
Tyre
MT. HERMON
Laish (Dan)
BASHAN
KINGDOM OF OG
Accho
Hazor
Chinnereth
Karnaim
Ashtaroth
Madon
SEA OF CHINNERETH
Dor
CANAANITES
Edrei
Megiddo
Beth-shan
Pella
Ramoth-gilead
Tirzah
Jabesh-gilead
Shechem
Succoth
Jacob's Well
Penuel
AMORITES
Joppa
HIVITES
Jazer
JABBOK R.
Lod
Bethel
Rabbath-ammon
Ai
Jericho
Gezer Gibam
KINGDOM OF SIHON
Jerusalem
Gilgal
Heshbon
AMMON
(Jebus, Salem)
Ashdod
Bethleham
Medeba
Gath
JEBUSITES
SALT SEA
Ashkelon
Lachish
Mamre
Jahaz
Gaza
Eglon Debir
Kirjath-arba
Dibon
(Azzah)
Gerar
(Hebron)
Aroer
(DEAD SEA)
GERAR R.
ARNON R.
Raphia
Beersheba
AT
Arad
Kir-moab
BESOR R.
Hormah
AMALEKITES
KENITES
MOAB
RIVER OF EGYPT
Rehoboth
Zoar
ZERED R.
Oboth
ARABAH
Kadesh-barnea
Punon
EDOM

0   Miles   25

Canaan Before the Conquest

The bulk of Deuteronomy is neither J, E, nor P, but represents a fourth major source of the Hexateuch. It seems quite likely that Deuteronomy is the one book of the Hexateuch that existed in essentially its present fashion before the Exile.

At least, Deuteronomy, or part of it, is usually identified with "the book of the law" discovered in the Temple in 621 B.C. during the reign of King Josiah:

> 2 Kings 22:8. *And Hilkiah the high priest said unto Shaphan the scribe, I have found the book of the law in the house of the Lord . . .*

This came at a time when there was periodic strife between the temporal and spiritual power in the kingdom and when there had been two recent reigns that were disastrous for the Yahvists. On the other hand, there was now an impressionable young king on the throne, Josiah.

Perhaps it occurred to some among the priesthood to prepare an organized exposition of the laws which, in Yahvist eyes, ought to govern the king and the people, writing into it a clear spiritual supremacy. This writing, as the "book of the law" was then providentially "discovered" in the Temple and brought to the king. The doctrine, placed in the mouth of Moses, treated as of great antiquity, and put forward most eloquently, was bound to impress the king.

It did, and the priestly plan succeeded in full. Until then, Yahvism had been a minority sect, often persecuted, and sometimes in danger of being wiped out altogether. Now, for the first time, it assumed an ascendancy, and, thanks to the enthusiastic co-operation of Josiah, it was made the official religion of the land.

There was backsliding after Josiah's death, but Yahvism had been made powerful enough to meet the challenge of the Exile, which followed soon after. The Yahvistic priests, during the Exile, as they edited the old traditions and codified the laws, incorporated Deuteronomy virtually intact into the Hexateuch.

After the Exile, Yahvism, the minority sect, had become Judaism, the national religion of the people. Through its daughter religions, Christianity and Islam, Yahvism came to dominate the religious life of well over a billion people in the time that has passed since then. If Deuteronomy is dealt with briefly in this book because it is not primarily concerned with history, that does not mean it may not be the most important part of the Bible in some ways; or even the most important piece of writing in the world.

Lebanon

Moses begins his recapitulation of events at Sinai with God's instructions that the Israelites leave for Canaan. The boundaries of Canaan as assigned to them by God are given, and these are the ideal boundaries which, in the north particularly, were only very temporarily achieved at Israel's brief peak of power two centuries after the conquest:

> Deuteronomy 1:7. . . . *unto Lebanon, unto . . . the river Euphrates.*
>
> Deuteronomy 1:8. *Behold, I have set the land before you . . .*

Lebanon referred originally to two mountain ranges north of Canaan running parallel to the Mediterranean coast; one about twenty miles inland and the other about forty miles inland, each about a hundred miles long. These are higher than the highlands of Canaan, and have some peaks up to two miles high. The Lebanese mountains are therefore more notable for their snowy peaks than are any of the heights in Canaan and it is from that, apparently, that the mountain ranges and the land in which they are found get their names. "Lebanon" is from the Hebrew word for "white."

The Greeks distorted the name somewhat and called the mountain range nearer the sea the "Libanus" and the one farther inland the "Anti-Libanus." Between is a valley, about ten miles wide, which the Greeks called "Coele-Syria." Literally, this is "hollow Syria" and means, in freer translation, "the valley of Syria."

In post-Biblical times, the area around the Lebanese ranges was the home of a Christian sect, the Maronites, which persisted (under severe persecution at times) through the long centuries of Mohammedan domination. When the area was freed of Turkish rule, the French (who took over Syria as a mandate under the League of Nations) established Lebanon as a district separate from the rest of Syria, thanks to its difference in religion. In 1944, when independence came to the mandate, the region became a separate and independent state, the Lebanese Republic.

Modern Lebanon is a small nation, about twice as large as Delaware, and has a population of about 2,200,000. It lies directly north of modern Israel and the two are the only non-Moslem powers in a sea of Arabic states.

Just as Bashan was known for its bulls and oaks, and Gilead for its balm, Lebanon was known for its forests of cedar. Cedarwood is fragrant and makes excellent building material. Solomon built much of the Temple and of his palace out of cedar:

> 1 Kings 7:2. *He built also the house* [his palace] *of the forest of Lebanon . . . upon four rows of cedar pillars, with cedar beams upon the pillars.*

The cedar tree was looked upon as a particularly stately and magnificent tree, rivaling the oak as king of the forest.

During the time of the judges, Jotham, the lone survivor of a massacred family, addressed those who had helped conduct the massacre in a fable intended to imply that the worst people were now ruling the land. These he represented by the bramble, and he went on to point out that such a lowly object in its vainglory would not hesitate to attack the highest and best. He has the bramble say:

> Judges 9:15. . . . *and if not, let fire come out of the bramble, and devour the cedars of Lebanon.*

Similarly, Isaiah, in warning the proud and haughty to beware God's judgment (in "the day of the Lord"), uses both the cedars of Lebanon and the oaks of Bashan as metaphors for haughty pride.

> Isaiah 2:12. *For the day of the Lord . . . shall be upon every one that is proud and lofty . . .*
> Isaiah 2:13. *And upon all the cedars of Lebanon . . . and upon all the oaks of Bashan,*

The beauty and fragrance of the cedars and of their wood, and the use of cedar in temples and palaces, lent a glamorous glow to Lebanon generally, and this is made full use of in the Song of Solomon.

> Song of Solomon 4:8. *Come with me . from Lebanon, my spouse . . .*
> Song of Solomon 4:11. . . . *the smell of thy garments is like the smell of Lebanon.*

And the loved one is described as:

> Song of Solomon 4:15. *A fountain of gardens, a well of living waters, and streams from Lebanon.*

The Island of Caphtor

Caphtor

Moses goes on to describe the route followed by the Israelites from Sinai to the Jordan, then pauses to tell something of the prehistory of Canaan. He describes the tribes that were evicted from their territory by the invading Edomites, Moabites, and Ammonites (presumably in the period of Ikhnaton.) The pre-Hebrew tribes are described, in accordance with later legends, as giants (see page 72.)

In the list, however, are the Avim, who were displaced by a non-Hebrew people:

Deuteronomy 2:23. *And the Avims which dwelt in Hazerim, even unto Azzah, the Caphtorims, which came forth out of Caphtor, destroyed them, and dwelt in their stead.*

The district spoken of is the southern portion of the seacoast of Canaan. The town Azzah is taken to be Gaza, for instance, and that is near the southern edge of what, in the next stage of Israelite history, was to be Philistine territory. The Philistines did take the area at the time of the Exodus or shortly before and they ruled there in the centuries afterward. It seems certain then that by Caphtorim are meant the Philistines.

For further Biblical evidence, we find that the prophet Amos makes the identification when he quotes God as saying:

Amos 9:7. . . . . *Have not I brought up . . . the Philistines from Caphtor . . .*

and Jeremiah does the same when he says:

Jeremiah 47:4. . . . . *the Lord will spoil the Philistines the remnant of the country of Caphtor.*

The question then is: Where is Caphtor?

Unlike the other groups who established kingdoms over sections of Canaan and surrounding regions at this time, the Caphtorim (Philistines) established themselves on the seacoast. They, it would seem, invaded from the sea, rather than from Arabia. Indeed, it seems almost inevitable to conclude that they were part of the Peoples of the Sea who, in Merneptah's reign, were raiding the Egyptian coast. This may be an important hint as to the identity of Caphtor, since the Peoples of the Sea were, in part at least, of Greek origin.

This is borne out by the fact that the Israelites always spoke of the Philistines, particularly, as being "uncircumcised." Circumcision was a rite that was by no means confined to the Israelites. It was practiced among the ancient Egyptians and among most of the Semites of the western portion of the Fertile Crescent (the latter, perhaps, through Egyptian cultural influence.)

Abraham is described as not having been circumcised until he was well advanced in years:

Genesis 17:24. *And Abraham was ninety years old and nine, when he was circumcised . . .*

but, according to the Biblical story, Abraham was an east-Semite or a
non-Semite by birth. His circumcision can be viewed as the adoption of
a west-Semitic rite.

The Philistines remained uncircumcised and it is tempting to think
of them, then, as being neither Egyptian nor west-Semitic in culture
and that leaves the strong possibility of their being Greek.

What, then, was the situation of the Greek world at the time of the
Exodus, and before?

About 2000 B.C., in the time of Abraham, the Greeks entered the
peninsula which is now called Greece. They found to the south, on the
island of Crete (about sixty miles off the southeastern tip of Greece),
an already advanced civilization. This was the Minoan civilization,
named for the legendary King Minos of Crete.

The Greeks occupied the Greek peninsula and absorbed the Minoan
culture, building strong cities of their own on that peninsula. These
early Greeks may be referred to as Mycenaeans because one of their
chief cities was Mycenae.

The Mycenaeans expanded vigorously at the expense of the declining
Minoan culture and by 1400 B.C., shortly before the time of Ikhnaton,
the original Minoans no longer formed a separate and distinct people.
Even in Crete itself, the Greek language prevailed.

The Mycenaeans, soon after 1400 B.C., were beginning to feel the
push of new waves of barbarians from the interior, including less
civilized tribes of Greek-speaking peoples, and were themselves in increasing turmoil. Armed bands, seeking new homes after their old
ones were ravaged, or merely seeking to carve out new dominions in
place of a growingly insecure home base, made up strong contingents
of the Peoples of the Sea.

The Mycenaeans of the Greek mainland were close to Asia Minor
and they invaded that peninsula. The tale of the war against Troy
seems to be a distant memory of that invasion. The Trojan War may
have initiated (or been part of) the general turmoil on that peninsula
that led to the final destruction of the Hittite Empire.

Could it be then that armed bands from Crete fanned southward
to Egypt and eastward to Canaan, and that Caphtor refers to the
island of Crete? Most Biblical scholars are content to think so.

Of course, not everything about the Philistines is Greek. In language
and customs they are largely Semitic. The names of their cities, their

kings, and their gods are Semitic words. This may represent a certain assimilation of west-Semitic culture after the invasion, but it may also indicate that the original invasion was at least partly Semitic to begin with.

Is this possible? Yes, it is, even if Caphtor was Crete. Greek myths make the Cretan king, Minos, the son of Europa, a princess from a portion of the Canaanite coast called by the Greeks Phoenicia. The Canaanite princess had been brought to Crete by Zeus in the guise of a bull.

This may be the mythical reminiscence of the days when trade and cultural exchange between the Minoan and Canaanite civilizations was rich and full. The Minoan civilization might even have stemmed in part from the older Canaanite civilization.

Nor was this fusion long-distance only. Both Minoans and Canaanites were in those days a seagoing people. At the height of Minoan power, the Cretan navy dominated the eastern Mediterranean and Cretan ships brought Minoan products and Minoan culture to the island of Cyprus, 350 miles to the east, and to the southern regions of the Asia Minor coast, which in spots is only fifty miles north of Cyprus. Canaanite (Phoenician) colonies were also established on Cyprus and throughout Biblical times, Cyprus remained part Greek and part Canaanite in culture.

Could it be, then, that the Israelites and Greeks, both heir to a kind of fused Minoan-Canaanite culture, are first cousins culturally speaking? Some archaeologists feel themselves attracted to this rather startling possibility.

Can it also be that the Caphtorim who invaded the southern coast of Canaan were not raiders from distant Crete, but from the much closer Cyprus and its environs? In that case Caphtor would be Cyprus and the raiders might have a Minoan-Canaanite culture, fusing Semitic language with a lack of circumcision.

Tiny, uncertain clues come from the fact that in Egyptian inscriptions, the term "Kafto" is used for a region that seems to include the southern coast of Asia Minor. Arguing on the other side, however, is the fact that the name for the inhabitants of Cyprus, as given in the Old Testament, seems to be "Chittim" or "Kittim."

This name seems to be derived from Kition (Citium, in Latin), a city on the southeastern coast of Cyprus and the chief center of

Canaanite (Phoenician) culture on the island. It is possible that a name meant for the chief city eventually spread out to include the entire island, displacing the older name of Caphtor.

Mount Hermon

Moses then describes the manner in which the Israelites conquered the district about Heshbon, and defeated Og of Bashan:

> Deuteronomy 3:8. *And we took . . . the land . . . from the river of Arnon unto Mount Hermon.*

Mount Hermon makes a good landmark for the northern edge of Canaan, so that to say "unto Mount Hermon" is like saying "to the northern limits of Canaan." Mount Hermon, about forty miles north of the Sea of Galilee, is a peak in the Anti-Libanus range; indeed, the highest peak, being 9232 feet high. Its modern name is Jebel esh Sheikh and it is on the border between Lebanon and Syria, about fifteen miles northeast of the northern border of modern Israel.

Rabbath

In telling of the crowning victory over Og, mention is made of Og's giant bedstead (see page 182):

> Deuteronomy 3:11. . . . *his bedstead was a bedstead of iron; is it not in Rabbath of the children of Ammon? . . .*

This city is sometimes referred to as Rabbath-ammon, to differentiate it from other cities of the same name elsewhere (as we would say Portland, Maine, to distinguish it from Portland, Oregon). An alternate spelling is Rabbah.

Rabbath was an important city of the trans-Jordan area, and lay about fifteen miles northeast of Heshbon. It was the chief city of the Ammonites and in that city the memory of the Ammonites survives although the tribe itself has long since vanished. The town, under the name of Amman, survives today as the capital of Jordan and has a population of some 250,000.

Mount Gerizim

After enumerating again the laws delivered from Mount Sinai, Moses warns the Israelites that there is both a blessing and a curse involved; a blessing if they are obedient to the law and a curse if they are not. Once they enter Canaan, they are to accede to this fact by solemn ritual in a specific spot:

Deuteronomy 11:29. . . . *thou shalt put the blessing upon mount Gerizim and the curse upon mount Ebal.*

Gerizim and Ebal were the two mountains that flanked the narrow valley in which Shechem was located (see page 99), Gerizim on the south and Ebal on the north. They are not high mountains, the former being a bit less than 3000 feet high, the latter a bit more than 3000.

Later in Deuteronomy, in the twenty-seventh chapter, Moses describes in detail how, after the conquest of Canaan, the tribes shall distribute themselves on Mount Gerizim and Mount Ebal, one group to pronounce blessings and the other to pronounce curses. No doubt this reflects the religious importance of the area of Shechem in pre-Israelite days and marks the aura of sanctity that lingered over the area even after the Israelite conquest. This was true particularly of Mount Gerizim, which was associated with the blessings.

Among the later Jews, all holy places were gradually subordinated to and eventually swallowed by the Temple at Jerusalem, but Mount Gerizim continued as *the* sacred mountain to the sect of the Samaritans prominent in the region in New Testament times.

Belial

Moses goes on to warn the Israelites against the dangers of false prophets and of those who would worship other gods. He warns against:

Deuteronomy 13:13. . . . *children of Belial . . . saying, Let us go and serve other gods . . .*

The word *belial* means, literally, "not profitable." Something that is *belial* is worthless and empty; "children of Belial" are people whose views and opinions are worthless and empty, and therefore not to be listened to.

It is a short step from considering something worthless to considering it wicked. We have a similar case in English. The word "naughty" originally meant worthless or empty, or something that "contained or was worth naught," but came to mean wicked (although today it has degenerated to the point where it merely describes troublesome children).

The use of *belial* untranslated, especially if it is left capitalized, as in the King James Version, tempts one into thinking of Belial as a spirit of evil, perhaps as the devil himself. This is avoided in the Revised Standard Version, which substitutes "base fellows" for "children of Belial."

Nevertheless, it is not only moderns who come to consider Belial the name of a demon. By New Testament times, the Jews had come to do just this and Belial had become a synonym for Satan. Thus, in the Second Epistle to the Corinthians, the Apostle Paul asks:

> 2 Corinthians 6:15. *And what concord hath Christ with Belial?* . . .

Saints

The last words ascribed to Moses in Deuteronomy make up a poem containing short comments on each of the tribes, praising them, or giving some intimation of the role they were to play in the time of the kingdoms. The poem ("the blessing of Moses") begins with an invocation of God:

> Deuteronomy 33:2. *And he* [Moses] *said, The Lord came from Sinai, and rose up from Seir* . . . *he shined forth from mount Paran, and he came with ten thousands of saints* . . .

The word "saint" is from the Latin *sanctus*, meaning "holy." That which is sanctified or holy is reserved for God and is withdrawn from worldly uses. The word "saints" in the verse just quoted is a translation of the Hebrew word *kadesh* but that can mean either a "holy person" or a "holy place." Thus, the town at which the Israelites camped for many years was Kadesh-barnea ("the holy place of Barnea").

It may be, then, that, with the parallelism of Hebrew poetry, the verse names the place at which God appears (the mountains south of Canaan) in slightly different ways: Sinai, Seir, Paran, and finally Meribath-Kadesh (some region near Kadesh-barnea). This is not in the least farfetched for there is such a place, mentioned only four verses earlier, with a slightly different spelling:

> Deuteronomy 32:51. . . . *ye* [Moses] *trespassed against me* [God] *among the children of Israel at the waters of Meribah-Kadesh.*

The translation of the place name into "ten thousands of saints" thus gives an erroneous picture.

In the Psalms, the expression "saints" usually refers to godly, pious people, very much in the modern manner, and is a translation of *hasid* ("pious"). Thus:

> Psalm 31:23. *O love the Lord, all ye his saints . . .*

In the time of the persecution of the Jews by the Seleucid king Antiochus IV, in 170 B.C. and afterward, the beleaguered Jews began to picture themselves as a people devoted to God and surrounded by hordes of evil idolaters. All believing Jews were *kadesh* and could be referred to in translation as "saints." When Daniel predicts that the Jews will eventually be secure, and glory in an ideal kingdom set up by God, he says:

> Daniel 7:18. *But the saints of the most High shall take the kingdom . . .*

In the New Testament, Paul commonly takes the same view of the beleaguered early Christians. To him, writing in Greek, they are *oi hagioi* ("the holy ones" or "the saints"). Thus:

> Philippians 1:1. *Paul and Timotheus . . . to all the saints . . . which are at Philippi . . .*

The Blessing of Moses

Like the earlier blessing of Jacob (see page 116), the blessing of Moses seems to be a collection of traditional sayings, assigned in ret-

rospect to an early personage. Of the two, the blessing of Moses
seems to be the later, and is appropriately ascribed, therefore, to the
later personage.

For one thing the reference to Joseph in the blessing of Jacob
makes no reference to the separate tribes of Ephraim and Manasseh.
The blessing of Moses does, however, speaking of:

Deuteronomy 33:17. . . . *the ten thousands of Ephraim, and the
thousands of Manasseh.*

The fact that Joseph and Levi receive the longest and most glowing
blessing would indicate that the sayings were collected and put into
final form by priestly hands in the northern kingdom of Israel, which
was dominated by the Joseph tribes and, in particular, by the "ten
thousands" of the more populous Ephraim. In that case, this would
have had to be done before the destruction of the northern kingdom in 722 B.C.

This is further indicated by the fact that the tribe of Judah is given
brief and rather cool notice:

Deuteronomy 33:7. . . . *let his hands be sufficient for him; and be
thou an help to him from his enemies.*

No mention is made of Judah's kingship. This is natural if the sayings were collected in the northern kingdom after it had split away
from Judean domination and would certainly not recognize the validity of the Davidic kingship. In the blessing of Jacob, however, much
is made of the Judean kingship, which would indicate that that collection dated back to the time of the undivided kingdom—about 950 B.C.
perhaps.

The blessing of Moses indicates further the decline of the tribes of
Reuben and Simeon, of which signs are present even in the earlier
blessing of Jacob.

Simeon is not mentioned at all in the blessing of Moses. The tribe
has lost its tribal identity, has been absorbed into Judah, and is
completely dismissed by the northern sources. Of Reuben, all that
can be said is:

Deuteronomy 33:6. *Let Reuben live, and not die; and let not his
men be few.*

But even this palliates the actual situation for the word "not" was added by the pious translators of the King James Version, who would not let Moses say something that sounded like a curse. However, the word "not" is not present in the original Hebrew.

Catholic versions translate the verse: "May Ruben live and not die out, but let his men be few." This represents the actual situation in early tribal times and by the time of the kingdoms, Reuben *did* die out, having been absorbed by Moab.

—With the conclusion of the speeches in the book of Deuteronomy, Moses is taken to the top of Mount Nebo/Mount Pisgah, views Canaan, which he is not to be allowed to enter, dies, and is buried. His eventful life thus comes to its close.

6. JOSHUA

Joshua

To the Jews, the first five books of the Bible ("The Law") make up the first of the three grand divisions of the Old Testament. The second division includes twenty-one books that together make up "the Prophets." Of these, the first six, which are primarily historical, are "the early Prophets" and, the Book of Joshua, named for the general whose actions dominate the events it describes, is the first.

However, Joshua is made up of the same sources as the five books of the Law, was put into final written form at the same time, apparently, by the same priestly groups, and brings the theme of the first five books to a climax. There is thus plenty of justification in treating the first six books (the Hexateuch) as a unit. (The rabbinical tradition that Joshua himself wrote the book can be ignored.)

The Book of Joshua describes an idealized version of the conquest of Canaan—a conquest that brings to a triumphant climax God's promise of Canaan to the descendants of Abraham, as described in Genesis.

The Israelite army, under unified leadership, is pictured as conquering the entire land in a brilliant set of campaigns. Actually, as would appear from other evidence in the Bible itself, the conquest was far more disorganized, gradual, and imperfect than that. Still, the key incidents in Joshua, though made neat and glossy by priestly piety at the time of the Exile (some seven centuries after the events described in Joshua), may well reflect traditions that in turn represent actual events.

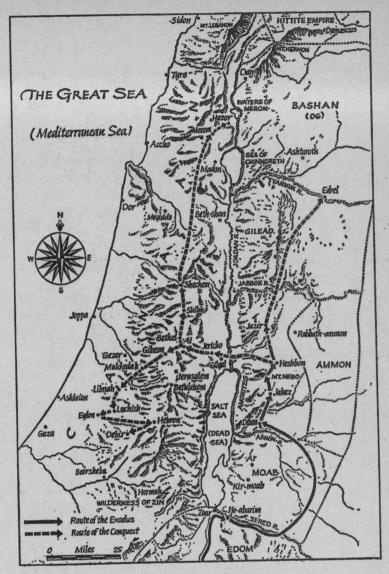

The Conquest of Canaan

Jericho

The Book of Joshua begins at the moment of the death of Moses, with Joshua ben Nun, who, until then, had been Moses' military aide, promoted to commander in chief. It is after Joshua that the book is named, of course.

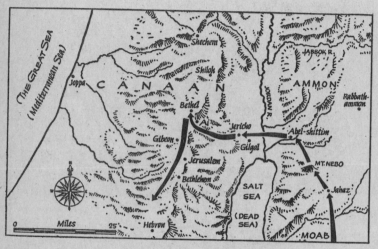

The City of Jericho

At once, Joshua made preparations to launch an offensive into Canaan.

> Joshua 2:1. And Joshua . . . sent out of Shittim two men to spy secretly, saying, Go view the land, even Jericho . . .

Jericho was a fortified town in the Jordan valley, five miles west of the Jordan itself and some fifteen miles northeast of Jerusalem. It is situated 850 feet below sea level and shares the semitropical temperatures of the Jordan valley generally.

Jericho is a very ancient populated site and there are signs of a town having existed there prior to 5000 B.C. The city faced by Joshua may have been the third located on the site; the first two each having in its turn been destroyed.

City-dwelling is one of the key symptoms of what we might call civilization (the very word "civilization" comes from the Latin word for "city-dweller"; that is, "citizen"). To build a city, even a simple one out of dried mud that takes up no more room all told than a modern city block, requires a certain level of technology and social co-operation. It is awesome to think that Canaan had already seen three thousand years of civilization at least at the time that Abraham entered.

It may have been much more than that. Older cities have been found in the Fertile Crescent. In 1966, archaeologists from the University of Toronto reported finding a site in the region of the upper Euphrates containing houses that must have been built as long ago as 8500 B.C. In comparison with such a date, the pyramids are modern structures, and Abraham almost a contemporary.

The Jericho that Joshua faced was well fortified indeed; the ruins believed to be Canaanite Jericho have walls twelve to fourteen feet thick. The spies, however, discovered morale within the town to be disastrously low. They had no trouble finding refuge with a harlot named Rahab who was willing to betray the town in exchange for safety during the inevitable sack. She reported:

> Joshua 2:9. . . . *your terror is fallen upon us, and . . . all the inhabitants of the land faint because of you.*

When this news was brought back to Joshua, he must have felt confident that with the defenders disheartened and with a "fifth column" within the town, he had only to attack. He made ready to do just that.

Gilgal

Joshua ordered the Israelite army out of Shittim, an encampment some five miles east of Jordan. Marching westward, he crossed the Jordan (which parted for him, according to the Biblical story, as the Sea of Reeds did for Moses). Joshua ordered that twelve stones be taken up from the temporarily dry bed of the Jordan.

> Joshua 4:19. *And the people . . . encamped in Gilgal in the east border of Jericho.*
> Joshua 4:20. *And those twelve stones, which they took out of the Jordan, did Joshua pitch in Gilgal.*

The word *gilgal* means "a circle of stones" and there are several places with that name mentioned in the Bible. A circle of large stones had religious significance to the men of the Stone Age, and such circles can be found in many places. The most famous and largest such circle still surviving—at least in part—is at Stonehenge in England. The Stonehenge circle is believed now to have served as a primitive calendar for the dating of such phenomena as lunar eclipses, but such is the close connection between astronomy and religion in primitive cultures that it is easy to believe that it served a religious purpose at the same time.

The best-known Gilgal in Canaan is this one mentioned in Joshua 4:19, and it is usually located a few miles from Jericho in the direction of Jordan. It is quite likely that the circle of stones that gave the area its name dated back to Canaanite times and played a role in Canaanite religion. The aura of sanctity that lingered over it even after the conquest would have been highly repugnant to Yahvism if it had not been somehow assimilated to the priestly view of history. (This ability to assimilate earlier notions is characteristic of successful religions. Islam assimilated the Kaaba and the holiness of Mecca from the pagan past and Christianity assimilated the Christmas celebration from pagan rites centering about the winter solstice.)

In this case, the circle of stones was associated with Joshua's crossing of the Jordan. Nor does the fact that there were twelve stones necessarily reflect the twelve tribes of Israel and therefore point to Israelite origin. Through an astronomic accident, the cycle of seasons is about twelve times as long as the cycle of the moon's phases; i.e., the year is made up of twelve months. For this reason, the number twelve could have enormous significance to an agricultural society. For instance, the twelve signs of the zodiac are arranged to mark off the twelve months as the sun makes its circuit of the sky in the course of a year. Indeed, some try to relate the twelve tribes of Israel (why exactly twelve?) to the twelve signs of the zodiac, but this may be going a bit far. Some leeway must be allowed to coincidence, surely.

The Wall [of Jericho]

The siege of Jericho, as described in the Bible, was accompanied by ritualistic parades about the city by armed men, with priests also circling the city, bearing the ark of the covenant and blowing on trumpets. This was repeated for six days and on the seventh day the city was circled seven times (an indication of the small size of the city by modern standards). When that was done

Joshua 6:20. . . . *the people shouted with a great shout, that the wall fell down flat* . . .

If the Biblical account is taken literally, this is a miracle, but those who seek natural explanations often suggest that it was an earthquake that did the trick. If so, it was a most fortunately timed earthquake.

Actually, it is easy to suppose that the circling of the city had a carefully designed tactical purpose. In the first place, it served to dishearten the city's defenders still further, for the people of Jericho would be nervous indeed at the somber and majestic spinning of a supernatural net about the city. To the religiously devout of those days, the invaders were calling on a perhaps powerful God who might be expected to do almost anything. The rulers of the city must have had much trouble to keep the populace from surrendering on the spot.

Secondly, while the defenders watched in fascination at the slow parading about the city, and listened to the awesome sound of the trumpets, they might not have had time to see and hear the very mundane activity of Joshua's sappers slowly undermining the city's walls.

So Jericho fell. The city was sacked and, it was intended, destroyed for all time.

Joshua 6:26. *And Joshua* [said] . . . *Cursed be the man* . . . *that riseth up and buildeth this city Jericho* . . .

It has happened many times that cities have been destroyed and their sites cursed by inveterate enemies. The best-known case outside the Bible is that of Carthage, the largest and strongest Canaanite town in history (it was a Phoenician colony). Carthage had been engaged in three colossal wars with Rome, spaced out over more than a century, and at one point had come within a hairbreadth of defeating Rome. When Rome finally took Carthage in 146 B.C., it utterly destroyed the town and made provision that it never be rebuilt.

However, towns aren't built for no reason; they are usually placed at the site of a sea harbor or river crossing, or in some position where they control trade routes. The men of a properly positioned city become

prosperous indeed and it is unlikely that such a position can be allowed
to stand empty forever, whatever the curse resting upon it.

Thus, a little over a century after its destruction, Carthage was built
again after all. Roman Carthage flourished for six centuries, almost as
long as the original Canaanite town had existed.

In the same way, the time came when Jericho was rebuilt, almost
upon the cursed site. In the reign of King Ahab, three centuries after
Joshua, a new Israelite Jericho arose and this survived and flourished
through New Testament times. This new Jericho was destroyed in
the course of invasions of Persians and Arabs in the seventh century
A.D. and still another Jericho was built by the Crusaders four centuries
after that.

This last Jericho still exists today, its Arabic name being the
recognizable Eriha. Its present population is about 2000.

Ai

After the fall of Jericho, Joshua continued the advance westward into
the heart of central Canaan.

Joshua 7:2. And Joshua sent men from Jericho to Ai, which is . . .
on the east side of Bethel.

Ai was twelve miles northwest of Jericho and two miles further still
to the northwest was Bethel, the important city associated with Jacob's
dream of a ladder (see page 94). The two cities were either under
common rule or acted in alliance against the Israelites.

The invaders, overconfident at first, attacked with too few numbers
and were beaten off. Joshua therefore placed a contingent of men in
ambush, then made a more careful attack. This time, he pretended defeat and ordered his men to break and run. The men of Ai and Bethel,
overconfident in their turn, incautiously left their defenses to engage in
hot pursuit. At an appropriate moment, the Israelites turned to fight
and when the Canaanites attempted to return to their cities they
found those cities occupied by the Israelites who had been in ambush. Ai was sacked, burned, and destroyed. Unlike Jericho, it was
never rebuilt.

(After this, the Bible recounts how the Israelites ascended Mount
Gerizim and Mount Ebal to perform the rituals of blessings and

curses that Moses had called for before his death. It is not likely that
this could have been done at so early a stage of the conquest but only
after Canaan was under more or less complete control. However, the
Deuteronomist writers were anxious to show the manner in which the
Israelites had obeyed the dictates of Moses to the utmost—as an example to their own times. They inserted the passage, therefore, at the
very earliest opportunity.)

Gibeon

The two victories of the Israelites over Jericho and over Ai put all
of Canaan into a state of urgent alarm. This was particularly true of
the city of Gibeon:

Joshua 9:3. *And when the inhabitants of Gibeon heard what*
Joshua had done unto Jericho and to Ai,
Joshua 9:4. *They did work wilily . . .*

One could scarcely blame Gibeon. The city is located about seventeen miles west of Jericho and five miles south of Ai, so it was very
likely to be the next target of the Israelite army.

(Gibeon was a large city for its time but is now represented only
by a small village, with the recognizable Arabic name of El Jib. The
people of Gibeon were Hivites, one of the tribes routinely mentioned
in the early books of the Bible as destined to conquest by the Israelites.
The Hivites had also controlled Shechem in patriarchal times; see page
100.)

The Gibeonites worked "wilily" by putting on worn clothes and
taking moldy provisions with them. When they appeared before Joshua
at his camp in Gilgal, they represented themselves as ambassadors
from a far country. A treaty of peace was made with them and later,
when the deception was discovered, the treaty was honored and
Gibeon was not destroyed, nor were its people slaughtered. The
Gibeonites are described as having been reduced to slavery but this
may not actually have come to pass until Solomon's time three centuries later.

It is difficult to see how the Gibeonites could have fooled Joshua in
this manner, or to believe that the fierce Israelite invaders would have
honored a treaty secured by deception. However, the writers of the

Book of Joshua, while describing an ideal and complete conquest of
Canaan, had to account for the known fact that some Canaanite
cities maintained a reasonable degree of independence into the time
of David and Solomon. The tale of the trickery of Gibeon was one way
of doing so without detracting from Joshua's military glory.

Ajalon

The defection of Gibeon to the Israelites was another serious blow
to the Canaanites. The petty kingdoms of the south, under the leadership of the large towns of Jerusalem and Hebron, formed a confederacy against the common foe and marched against Gibeon in order to
force it back into the Canaanite ranks.

Joshua and his forces moved quickly to the relief of Gibeon and in a
great battle scattered and destroyed the Canaanites. It was during this
battle that one of the best known of the events described in the Bible
took place:

> Joshua 10:12. *Then spake Joshua . . . Sun, stand thou still upon*
> *Gibeon; and thou, Moon, in the valley of Ajalon.*
> Joshua 10:13. *And the sun stood still, and the moon stayed . . .*
> *So the sun . . . hasted not to go down about a whole day.*
> Joshua 10:14. *And there was no day like that before it or after*
> *it . . .*

Ajalon was a town about ten miles west of Gibeon.

The Bible describes this miraculous lengthening of the day to have
been carried through for the purpose of allowing the Israelites to
complete their victory. Interpreting them literally, men used these
verses twenty-five centuries after the time of Joshua to fight the Coper-
nican theory that the sun stood still and the earth moved about it.
After all, if Joshua has to order the sun "stand thou still" it must
imply that ordinarily the sun is moving. (This difficulty disappears if
one understands the principle of "relative motion," but it is not the
purpose of this book to consider the relationship of the Bible to science
and we will pass on.)

Following that battle, the Bible rapidly describes Joshua's sweep
through southern Canaan, in which he captures a series of cities in
the territory that was later to make up the territory of the tribe of

Judah. Hebron itself was taken but no mention is made of Jerusalem —and no wonder, for Jerusalem remained independent and Canaanite until the days of David.

Merom

It was next the turn of the cities of northern Canaan to form a league against Joshua.

Joshua 11:5. *And when all these kings were met together, they came and pitched together at the waters of Merom, to fight against Israel.*

The Jordan River, in its course, passes through or flows into three enclosed bodies of water. The southernmost and largest is, of course, the Dead Sea (see page 71). Some sixty-five miles north of the Dead Sea is the Sea of Galilee, and about a dozen miles still farther north is Lake Huleh. It is Lake Huleh which is usually taken to be the "waters of Merom." It is the smallest of the three bodies of water associated with the Jordan; it is only four miles long and three and a half miles wide.

Zidon

At Merom, Joshua won another great victory and is described as leading the pursuit far (improbably far, in fact) to the north.

Joshua 11:8. *And the Lord delivered them into the hand of Israel, who smote them, and chased them unto great Zidon . . .*

Zidon, or Sidon, is a city on the Mediterranean shore about 130 miles north of Jerusalem. The area about Zidon (Sidon), which nowadays makes up the coastal region of modern Lebanon, was inhabited by Canaanites who were never conquered by the Israelites. Even at the time of Israel's greatest power, the Canaanite cities of the Lebanese shore, though in alliance with Israel, were not subjected to it.

At the time of the Israelite conquest of Canaan, the largest and most powerful of these north-Canaanite cities was Zidon (Sidon) and the people of the entire region were therefore referred to in the Bible as Zidonians or Sidonians.

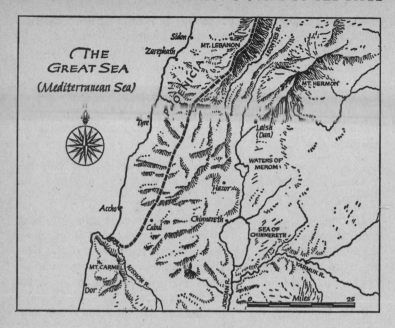

The City of Zidon

The people of the region were famous for their manufacture of a purple-red dye and made use of it in their own clothing to such an extent that the color gave a name to the people and the land. It is sometimes stated that the word "Canaan" is derived from an old Semitic word meaning "purple." That may or may not be so but it is quite clear that the Greek name for the region is derived from the color of the dye. The Greek name is "Phoenicia" from their word meaning "purple-red." It is as Phoenicians that the people are almost invariably known nowadays, though the word is not used in the Bible. Nor should the familiar term "Phoenician" be allowed to obscure the fact that the people we call Phoenicians were racially and culturally indistinguishable from the Canaanites to the south.

At the time of Joshua, the Phoenicians may already have made their greatest single contribution to culture—the invention of the alphabet. Writing itself seems to have been invented in a number of different places independently—in Sumeria, in China, in Central America. In all these cases, however, the symbols used were pictures of objects or abstract markings representing words or concepts.

As far as we know the Phoenicians were the first (at some dim period in their ancient history) to hit upon the idea of taking a few markings and letting each stand for a single consonant. By putting such markings (letters) together any word whatever could be produced; and even an unfamiliar word could then be pronounced by sounding the letters. The Phoenician alphabet was adopted by the various Hebrew tribes, including the Moabites and Israelites.

The Greeks adopted the Phoenician alphabet, too, allowing some of the letters to stand for vowel sounds. (Greek myths clearly state that the letters were introduced by the Phoenician prince, Cadmus, who migrated to Greece and founded the Greek city of Thebes.)

Indeed, it is usually accepted that the alphabet (as distinct from writing in general) was invented only once, and that all modern alphabets, however odd some of them seem, are more or less distorted versions of the original Phoenician alphabet.

In the centuries immediately after the Israelite conquest, the importance of Sidon declined. The greatest days of Phoenicia were still ahead; these, indeed, coinciding with the greatest days of Israel. In those great days, however, leadership would fall to other cities, not Sidon. Yet Sidon exists today as Saida, a Lebanese port with a population of about 25,000. Its once-excellent harbor is half silted up and is almost entirely useless. The town is surrounded by fruit orchards, however, and it is the Mediterranean terminus of an oil pipeline from Saudi Arabia.

The Philistines

Even under the idealized picture of the conquest as presented in the Book of Joshua, there was no denying that sections of Canaan remained unconquered. The chief of these included the section along the southern coast of Canaan:

Joshua 13:2. *This is the land that yet remaineth: all the borders of the Philistines . . .*

Joshua 13:3. *. . . the Gazathites, and the Ashdothites, the Eshkalonites, the Gittites, and the Ekronites . . .*

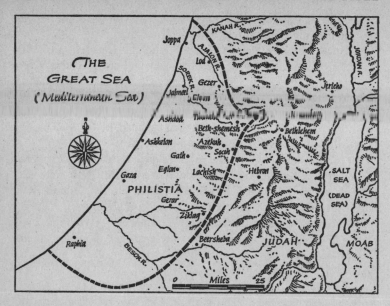

Philistia

The term "Philistine," which replaces the older term "Caphtorim" (see page 199), may be the name the people of the region gave themselves. The Egyptian inscriptions speak of them as the "Pulesati." In Hebrew, this became "Pelishtim" and in Greek "Philistinoi."

In historical records outside the Bible, the Philistines are first heard of in the records of a new Egyptian dynasty, the 20th. After the death of Merneptah in 1211 B.C., the great 19th dynasty of Rameses II petered out with a few feeble Pharaohs of short reigns. The 20th dynasty began with the reign of Setnakht, in 1192 B.C.

In 1190 B.C., Rameses III came to the throne and began a reign of over thirty years. He was the last powerful native monarch of Egypt. Under him the Peoples of the Sea were finally driven off and a certain order and strength came back to Egypt. His influence was strong in Asia but even he could not reverse the flow of history, and events in Canaan continued without actual military interference on the Pharaoh's part. The Israelite conquest of Canaan seems to have taken place in his reign.

Furthermore, his archives refer to the coming of the "Pulesati."

They may have been a final contingent of the Peoples of the Sea, driven out of Egypt proper by Rameses' armies, and forced to turn to the Canaanite coast. Thus, the Philistines conquered the coast even as the Israelites were conquering the interior. The two great adversaries of the next several centuries had entered the land simultaneously.

The center of Philistine power was a sixty-mile stretch of the southern shore of Canaan, a region which can be referred to as "Philistia." The name persisted long after the great days of Philistine power had passed. Herodotus, the Greek historian, writing in the fifth century B.C., referred to the region as "Palaistina" and the name was eventually applied by the Romans to all of Canaan. Even today, "Palestine" has been used in naming the entire region once known as Canaan.

Philistia was composed of the five cities whose inhabitants are listed in Joshua 13:3—Ekron, Ashdod, Ashkelon, Gath, and Gaza. They seem to have been city-states, after the Greek fashion, with considerable independence, but capable of joining on occasion to fight a common enemy.

The northernmost of the cities was Ekron. This was about twenty five miles west of Jerusalem and some nine miles from the sea. It still exists as a village named Akir.

Twelve miles southwest of Ekron, and three miles from the sea, is Ashdod, which was known as Azotos to the Greeks and survives today as the village of Esdud with a population of about 3500. In Philistia's prime, however, Ashdod was probably the most powerful of the five cities.

Another twelve miles southwest is Ashkelon, the only one of the five to be an actual seaport. The greatest event in its history came at the time of the Crusades (when it was known as Askalon to Europeans). In A.D. 1099, it was the site of a great victory of the Crusaders over the Egyptians. In 1270, however, it was destroyed by the Egyptian sultan of the time and it is a desolate site now.

Twelve miles east of Ashkelon is Gath, the most inland of the Philistine cities. Its inhabitants are "Gittites." It is most famous for the fact that it was the home city of the giant Goliath, whom the young David slew in single combat. However, it is the most thoroughly vanished of the Philistine cities and its exact site is uncertain.

Twelve miles south of Ashkelon and three miles from the sea is Gaza, the most southerly of the Philistine cities. Of the five, it has

survived best and has had the most colorful history. It fell to Alexander
the Great (eight centuries after the time of Joshua) after a long and
desperate siege. It was an early Christian center and then a Moslem
center. Battles were fought over it by the Turks and by Napoleon.

It gained contemporary notoriety as a result of the war between
Israel and Egypt that followed the granting of independence to the
former in 1948. Egyptian forces occupied Gaza and have maintained
that occupation ever since. The Palestinian coast from Gaza to Egypt,
about twenty-five miles long and an average of five miles deep, came to
be known as the "Gaza strip." It was filled with Arab refugees from
Israel, who were not resettled but kept in place as a political maneuver
in order that enmity between Israel and the Arab world be exacerbated.
Gaza's normal population is about 80,000 but with the addition of the
refugees, well over 200,000 people filled it. The Gaza strip was taken by
Israel in the course of the Six-day War in 1967.

The Tribes

Despite the admitted incompleteness of the conquest, the Book of
Joshua goes on to describe the allotment of land in Canaan to each
of the tribes, according to the instructions Joshua is recorded as having
received from God.

Joshua 13:7. *Now therefore divide this land for an inheritance
unto the nine tribes, and the half tribe of Manasseh.*

Almost all the rest of the Book of Joshua is given over to a painstaking account of the division of the land. It makes for very dull
reading but it takes the place of a map in modern books and undoubtedly represents the situation as it arose out of the numerous
frictions and settlements between the tribes in the days before the
monarchy when they were in uneasy alliance, or in even uneasier strife.

Two of the tribes, Reuben and Gad, together with part of the
tribe of Manasseh, had already received grants east of the Jordan (see
page 191). West of the Jordan, in Canaan proper, Judah received the
southernmost portion, its territory stretching as far north as Jerusalem.
South of Judah were some desert hamlets that made up the allotment
of the disappearing tribe of Simeon.

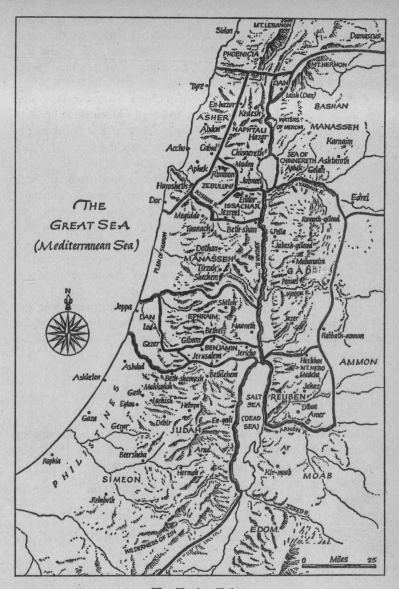

The Twelve Tribes

Across central Canaan, centered in Shechem, was the remainder of Manasseh. Between Manasseh and Judah lay Dan on the coast, and Ephraim and Benjamin inland. Benjamin included Jericho and Gibeon. North of Manasseh was Asher along the coast and, inland, Issachar, Zebulun, and Naphtali, going from south to north.

It is important to realize the small size of the allotments. Benjamin, the smallest of the tribes, occupied a territory of about three hundred square miles. This is about as large as the area of the five boroughs of New York City, and considerably smaller than the area of the city of Los Angeles.

All these tribal boundaries were idealized versions referred back in time from the situation as it existed in the period of the monarchy. They could not have existed in the form given at the time of the conquest. Jerusalem was assigned to Judah, for instance, but that town was not conquered by Israelites until the time of David. Philistia was divided between Judah and Dan, but Philistia was not conquered until David's time, too. The tribe of Asher was awarded much of the Phoenician coast which it never, in actual fact, controlled.

The tribe of Levi received no actual land grant. Its central role was that of serving as a priesthood and for that purpose it was considered enough that its members be granted a number of towns scattered through the various tribal areas.

Mount Ephraim

The Book of Joshua ends with the death of the secular and religious leaders of the Israelites of the period: Joshua and Eleazar (the latter being the son of Aaron and the nephew of Moses).

Joshua 24:30. *And they buried him* [Joshua] *in . . . mount Ephraim . . .*

. . . .

Joshua 24:33. *And Eleazar, the son of Aaron died; and they buried him in a hill . . . in mount Ephraim.*

There is a line of hills running down the length of Canaan between the coastal plain and the plain of the Jordan. That portion which lies in the territory of Ephraim is called Mount Ephraim. The reference does not seem to be to a particular peak but, as we would perhaps say today, to "the Ephraim hills," or "the Ephraim highlands."

With the end of the Book of Joshua, we can consider Canaan as essentially Israelite territory, even if not completely so. Instead of Canaan, the territory will now be referred to as Israel.

7. JUDGES

Judah and Simeon

The Book of Judges, which describes the history of Israel immediately after the conquest, is rather miscellaneous in nature and is apparently a collection of ancient documents, not necessarily very closely related to each other. Although signs of editing are clear, the tale is not smoothed into a unified and pretty whole as in the Book of Joshua. So much is left that is unedifying and unflattering to Israel that one is forced to trust the Book of Judges to be a more accurate reflection of secular history than the Book of Joshua can be.

The first chapter of Judges deals with the conquest from a viewpoint entirely different from that in Joshua. Here there is no single army under unified command sweeping to a quick, complete victory. Rather, there is the picture of disunited tribes, each struggling alone against the enemy and not doing too well at it, in many cases.

Thus, no mention is made of Joshua's strenuous campaign through the south. Instead, the conquest of the area about Hebron is the task of the tribe of Judah in alliance with Simeon:

> Judges 1:3. And Judah said unto Simeon his brother, Come up with me into my lot, that we may fight against the Canaanites; and I likewise will go with thee into thy lot . . .

Although the forces of Judah (the weak tribe of Simeon probably did not make a significant contribution) are described as uniformly

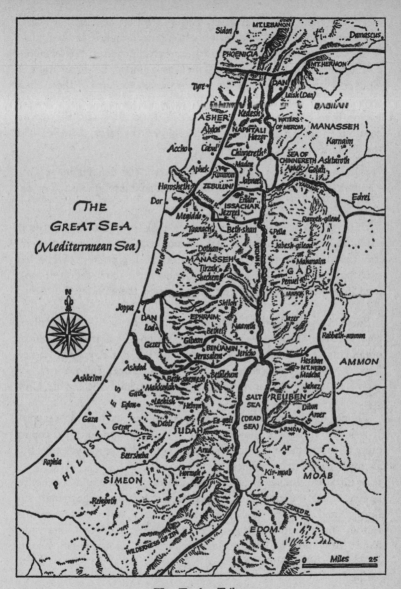

The Twelve Tribes

successful, taking even Jerusalem and the Philistine cities of Gaza, Ashkelon, and Ekron, the victories were nevertheless limited. The highland areas, more sparsely settled, were abandoned to the Israelites. In the sense that these areas were previously under the domination of citics such as Jerusalem and Gaza, territory appertaining to those cities were annexed and the cities might then be glowingly described as having been conquered. The actual cities themselves and the tightly controlled lowland areas about them could not be taken, however, and the Bible makes the reason for that clear:

> Judges 1:19. . . . he [Judah] *drave out the inhabitants of the mountain; but could not drive out the inhabitants of the valley, because they had chariots of iron.*

Until 3500 B.C. mankind used for its tools only those materials it could find at hand; materials that did not require sophisticated chemical treatment—bone, hide, wood, and stone, for instance. Stone has survived best through the ages and we know most about the stone tools used in ancient times. We refer to the period therefore as the "Stone Age."

Small nuggets of metals which occur free in nature (gold, silver, copper, meteoric iron) were occasionally found, and perhaps used as ornaments. It was not till about 3500 B.C. that the Egyptians learned how to smelt appropriate ores and obtain copper in quantity. By 3000 B.C. copper was in widespread use throughout the Fertile Crescent.

Copper itself is not hard enough to serve well as tools or weapons. It was soon discovered, however, that if tin ores were added to copper ores, a copper-tin alloy called bronze could be produced and this is much harder than copper.

By 2500 B.C. bronze weapons were coming into use and the Fertile Crescent was entering the "Bronze Age." A bronze spearpoint was sharper and tougher than one made of flint and could penetrate leather shields with no trouble. Bronze shields could, on the other hand, easily turn and blunt stone weapons. A bronze-armored army could, without difficulty, defeat a larger army fighting with stone and leather.

By 2000 B.C. the Bronze Age was penetrating Europe, and the battles of the Trojan War, as carefully described by Homer, were fought by warriors with bronze armor, bronze shields, and bronze weapons.

Bronze was an expensive material, however. Copper ores were rare, though sufficient quantities could at first be obtained from the Sinai Peninsula and from Cyprus. (Indeed, the word "copper" is supposed to be derived from "Cyprus.") Tin ores were even rarer. Phoenician trading vessels ventured long distances for the tin ores needed to manufacture bronze and reached the "Tin Islands." This is usually supposed to be the peninsula of Cornwall in southwestern England, together with some islands off its coast. It is interesting to think that Canaanites were in England thousands of years before the Romans.

Iron is much more common than either copper or tin and, under the proper treatment, is much harder than bronze. Iron, in other words, is at once cheaper and better than bronze. Why was it not used? The answer to that is that iron ores are not as easily smelted as are copper and tin ores; iron ores require hotter fires and more complicated metallurgical processes.

The first successful method for smelting iron ore was developed somewhere in or near Hittite territory about 1400 B.C. (while the Israelites were in Egyptian slavery). The new technique, which gave birth to the "Iron Age," did not come in time to save the Hittites but it survived the destruction of the Hittite Empire. It spread slowly through the Fertile Crescent and into Europe.

At the time of the Israelite conquest of Canaan, the use of iron in restricted quantities had come to the more sophisticated towns, but desert tribes were still innocent of its use. The Israelites, therefore, entered Canaan at the dividing line between the Bronze Age and the Iron Age, and had to fight iron with bronze. What they could do by sheer numbers and energy, they did. But anyone fighting iron with bronze reaches a quick limit to conquest. The men of Judah found this out the hard way.

So, apparently, did the men of the other Israelite tribes. Through the rest of the chapter, the failure of each tribe to complete the conquest by capturing the larger cities in their regions is carefully detailed. The tribe of Benjamin did not take Jerusalem; the tribe of Manasseh did not take Bethshea; the tribe of Ephraim did not take Gezer; the tribe of Zebulun did not take Kitron; the tribe of Asher did not take Zidon; and so on.

The Judges

Under the circumstances, the Israelite occupation of Canaan could scarcely have served as the opening of an immediate period of prosperity. Clinging precariously to the highlands, disunited, technologically backward, it was inevitable that the Israelites remain in subjection to one foreign power after another.

Only occasionally could one tribe or another gain a degree of freedom through the action of some competent military leader.

Judges 2:16. *Nevertheless the Lord raised up judges, which delivered them out of the hand of those that spoiled them.*

The word "judge" is here used in the sense of a "ruler" since in early cultures, the chief function of a tribal ruler in peacetime was that of judging disputes and reaching, it was to be hoped, some just decision. This had the crucial purpose of preventing internal feuds and disputes that would weaken the entire population in the face of some always waiting outer enemy.

Twelve judges are considered to have held sway over the tribes between the conquest of Canaan and the establishment of the monarchy. This number is arrived at rather shakily, but it has the significance of matching the number of Israelite tribes so that later tradition clung to it.

It was often customary in the past to suppose that each judge held sway over all Israel and that the periods of their power followed one another. If we assume this and carefully follow the references to periods of time (usually expressed in round numbers that are clearly not intended to be exact), the period of time covered by the Book of Judges works out to be 410 years.

The period ends with the accession of Saul to the throne and that event can be dated with fair confidence at 1028 B.C. The 410-year period for the Book of Judges would then place the conquest of Canaan around 1440 B.C. and the Exodus about 1480 B.C.

This is quite impossible. The Exodus and conquest could not conceivably have taken place in the fifteenth century B.C.

Instead, we must place the most likely date for the Exodus at about 1200 B.C. and the death of Joshua at about 1150 B.C. This means that the period of time covered by the Book of Judges cannot be more than 125 to 150 years.

To account for this short period, one need only assume that the judges did not rule all Israel and did not serve consecutively. The Book of Judges is a collection of sagas produced by each tribe separately with some editor or editors weaving them together into a single tale without bothering to detail the chronology. Under such circumstances, it would seem reasonable that the various judges ruled over single tribes or small groups of tribes and that two or three might flourish simultaneously.

At this low point in Israelite history—from 1150 to 1028 B.C.—it was all the Israelites could do to fight off the petty powers of the western half of the Fertile Crescent. They were fortunate indeed in that they had to face no great empires. Against a man like Thutmose III or Hammurabi, their judges would not have saved them.

In Egypt, Rameses III, the last of the strong native Pharaohs, died in 1158 B.C., almost simultaneously with Joshua. His successors were eight Pharaohs, all named Rameses, who were weak and of little importance. In 1075 B.C., the 21st dynasty began to rule and these consisted of the high priests in the distant city of Thebes. During the entire period of the judges, Egypt might as well have been on another planet.

In the east, the nation of Assyria was slowly gathering strength. The region of Assyria, on the upper Tigris, had developed a civilization in the earliest times. It had been part of the empire of Sargon of Agade (see page 50) but in later times, when the Tigris-Euphrates region was fragmented into city-states and Sumeria was dying, it went through a period of prosperity and strength. In the patriarchal period, Assyria was a land of wealthy merchants.

It fell under the domination of Hammurabi, but recovered its independence and by 1500 B.C. formed one of the group of states contending for control of the Fertile Crescent. These rivals were the Egyptian Empire, the Hittite Empire, the Mitannian Empire, and the Assyrian Empire. The Hittites badly weakened Mitanni and were in turn badly weakened by Egypt. When Egyptian power in Asia began to decay under Ikhnaton, Assyria became the strongest nation in the area.

In 1235 B.C., Tukulti-Ninurta I became king of Assyria and he was still reigning at the time of the Exodus. Under cover of the havoc being

created by the barbarian migrations of the time, Assyria absorbed what
was left of Mitanni and then conquered Babylonia, extending its power
to the Persian Gulf. Tukulti-Ninurta became extolled in legend as
the first conquering Assyrian king and serves as the model for the
Biblical Nimrod (see page 52) and the Greek Ninus in consequence.

However, Assyria was not yet ready for the domination of the entire
Fertile Crescent. Tukulti-Ninurta was followed by weak successors
under whom Babylonia regained its independence. The Assyrian king
Tiglath-Pileser I, who reigned from 1116 to 1093 B.C., again pushed
the land toward a period of power, but he too was followed by weak
successors who had to contend with the onslaughts of a new group of
nomads, the Aramaeans, from the north.

In other words, during the period of the judges, the day of Egypt
was over, and the day of Assyria had not yet quite come. In the
gap of time between the two, the Israelites were able to develop against
the opposition of only such enemies as they could (just barely) handle.

Ashtaroth

The later editor of the Book of Judges must have found it hard to
account for sufferings and defeats of the Israelites in view of the
tradition of divine providence that surrounded the tales of the Exodus
and conquest under Moses and Joshua.

His pious explanation of the later events was that defeat and enslavement were punishments visited upon the Israelites for succumbing to the lure of Canaanite religious rites.

> Judges 2:11. *And the children of Israel did evil . . . and served*
> *Baalim.*
>
> . . . .
>
> Judges 2:13. . . . *and Ashtaroth.*

The "-im" suffix is the regular Hebrew plural so that "Baalim"
should be translated "Baals" (and *is* so translated in the Revised
Standard Version). Ashtaroth, like Baalim, is also a plural. The singular
form in this case is Ashtoreth and this is the feminine equivalent of a
Baal. Just as Baal ("Lord") is the general title for a male Semitic deity,
so Ashtoreth ("Lady") is the general title for a female Semitic deity.

Ashtoreth is, actually, a distortion of the correct name, Ashtarte. The distortion is caused by pious editors who later substituted the vowel sounds of *bosheth* ("shame") into the name; doing as they had done in converting "Melech" to "Molech" (see page 162).

The most famous Ashtarte was the one worshiped in Tyre, the chief Phoenician city in the time of the monarchy. Her worship was to have an important influence on the kingdom of Israel. The version of her name used in Greek mythology is Astarte. The chief of the Babylonian goddesses bore another version of the name—Ishtar.

Othniel

Over and over again, the refrain of the Book of Judges is sounded. The Israelites serve other gods and are punished by subjection to a foreign tyrant. They repent and a judge arises to free them.

The first case arises almost immediately after the conquest.

Judges 3:7. *And the children of Israel did evil . . . and served Baalim and the groves.*

Judges 3:8. . . . [and] *the Lord . . . sold them into the hand of Chushan-rishathaim king of Mesopotamia . . .*

Judges 3:9. *And when the children of Israel cried unto the Lord, the Lord raised up a deliverer . . . Othniel the son of Kenaz, Caleb's younger brother.*

The Hebrew word translated in Judges 3:7 as "groves" is *asheroth*, the plural form of the word *asherah*. The term is left untranslated in the various modern versions of the Bible, for Asheroth is another term used to refer to female Canaanite deities. The confusion arises from the fact that the word is also used to indicate a pole or wooden pillar—a relic of ancient tree worship, perhaps—which was considered sacred to the goddess. From a pole to a tree to a grove is not a difficult progression. It may be that Asherah originated as still another form of Ashtarte.

"Mesopotamia" is the translation of "Aram-Naharaim," the district where Haran is located, so that the invasion may be viewed as coming from the north. There is no chance of locating the region specifically for Chushan-rishathaim (or Cushan-rishathaim) means, in Hebrew, "the Cushite of double wickedness." This was undoubtedly not the true name of the individual, but rather a scornful title given him by the Biblical writers. Who he might really be is therefore impossible to tell.

If the invasion came from the north, one must wonder why it is Othniel who leads the reaction to it. Othniel is a folk hero of Judah and the conqueror of Hebron according to Judges 1:13, and therefore a dweller in the extreme south. Either Canaan-Ephraim conquered all of Canaan down to Judah, or else Othniel acted as commander in chief of the united tribes. Neither seems very likely. Possibly the confusion is the result of a telescoping of two traditions, a northern and a southern.

Ehud

The next invasion, after the Israelites had again fallen prey to strange gods, is less puzzling.

> Judges 3:12. . . . *Eglon the king of Moab* . . .
> Judges 3:13. . . . *gathered unto him the children of Ammon and Amalek, and went and smote Israel, and possessed the city of palm trees.*

The picture is that of a federation of Trans-Jordanian Hebrew tribes formed under the leadership of Moab. These then repeated Joshua's tactic of striking across the Jordan River in the direction of Jericho ("the city of palm trees"). Jericho itself no longer existed but the confederacy occupied the surrounding area, which now formed the territory of the tribe of Benjamin.

The tide was turned when Ehud, a left-handed Benjamite, sent to Eglon with tribute, managed to stab him to death. (Presumably the left-handed use of a dagger hidden on the right side, rather than on the customary left, caught the king by surprise.) In the confusion that followed, an Israelite attack succeeded in driving the Moabites back across the Jordan.

Hazor

Othniel and Ehud are the first and second judges, and following the tale of Ehud is the barest mention of a third judge, Shamgar, who apparently won a victory over the Philistines. Following that comes a circumstantial tale of a major danger.

Judges 4:2. *And the Lord sold them* [the Israelites] *into the hand of Jabin . . . that reigned in Hazor; the captain of whose host was Sisera, which dwelt in Harosheth . . .*

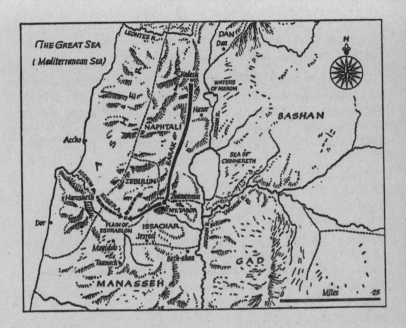

Hazor

Judges 4:3. *. . . . he had nine hundred chariots of iron; and twenty years he mightily oppressed the children of Israel.*

Hazor is located in far northern Canaan, in the territory assigned to the tribe of Naphtali. It is about four miles southwest of Lake Huleh. Harosheth is some forty miles southwest, near the sea, in the territory of Zebulun.

One gets the picture of a league of northern Canaanite cities, unconquered thanks to their iron-equipped armies, laying tribute on the northern Israelite tribes.

This situation clearly indicates the manner in which the account given in the Book of Joshua is a heavily idealized version of the conquest. It had been a King Jabin of Hazor who, according to the Book of Joshua, had led the northern coalition against the Israelites, and had been disastrously defeated by the waters of Merom (see page 217). Joshua followed up that victory energetically:

Joshua 11:10 . . . . Joshua . . . took Hazor, and smote the king thereof with the sword . . .

Joshua 11:11. *And they smote all the souls that were therein, utterly destroying them . . . and he burnt Hazor with fire.*

Could Joshua have actually won so great a victory? If so, how account for the phenomenal comeback of Hazor, which within a few decades was back in existence under another King Jabin and strong enough to control northern Israel. Or was the Canaanite defeat, to be described a bit later, anachronistically pushed back into Joshua's time?

Deborah

For a period of time after the conquest, Ephraim maintained its position as the leading tribe. Even if the over-all leadership of Joshua of Ephraim was a later idealization, it can nevertheless be taken that he won important victories even if he only led the Ephraimites. The glamour of Joshua's victories would extend forward over the generations and give Ephraim a jealously guarded claim to military pre-eminence.

In any united action of the tribes it would be taken for granted that Ephraim would supply the initiative and leadership; and failure on the part of other tribes to recognize this would result in civil war, as actually happened on at least one important occasion. (This is rather similar to the experience in Greece five or six centuries later, when any united action by the Greek city-states was almost automatically undertaken only under the leadership of Sparta.)

Ephraimite hegemony must have been most marked over the neighboring tribes of Benjamin to the south and Manasseh to the north. This may be reflected in the tradition that all three were descended from those sons of Jacob who had Rachel for a mother (Joseph and Benjamin). Ephraim, in other words, headed the close alliance of the

"Rachel tribes," and exerted its influence more informally beyond that central nucleus.

The term "Mount Ephraim" can be applied specifically to the hill country of Ephraim, but it can, in view of this, also be applied more loosely to the extension of the highland area north and south of Ephraim's immediate territory. This is all the more reasonable since the Book of Judges was put into final form after the time of the existence of the northern kingdom of Israel, which was so dominated by the tribe of Ephraim that Ephraim was used, poetically, as the name of the kingdom. "Mount Ephraim" would therefore naturally be used sometimes for the highlands of the north tribal area generally.

Thus, after Ehud the Benjamite had assassinated Eglon of Moab, he retired to the Israelite strongholds in the hills:

Judges 3:27. . . . he blew a trumpet in the mountain of Ephraim, and the children of Israel went down with him from the mount . . .

It is not necessary to conclude that Ehud had to move into the territory of Ephraim proper in order to send out messages to rally troops. He could have done so from the western section of Benjamin. Nevertheless, it is natural to suppose that the Ephraimites must have joined him.

As is often the case when one member of a loose confederation is the recognized military leader, aggression is allowed to continue as long as the territory of that leader is not directly threatened. Thus, in Greece, it was often difficult to get Sparta to take action as long as the Peloponnesus was not invaded. Similarly, Ephraim was slow to act against the Moabites as long as it was only Benjamite territory that was occupied, and they were equally slow to act as long as Jabin of Hazor and his general Sisera confined their activity to placing the northern tribes of Naphtali and Zebulun under tribute.

There may at this time have been some sort of internal difficulties in Ephraim that we have no knowledge of, for the Rachel tribes seem to be led by a woman—a most unusual situation.

Judges 4:4. And Deborah, a prophetess . . . judged Israel at that time.
Judges 4:5. And she dwelt . . . between Ramah and Bethel in mount Ephraim . . .

The area between Ramah and Bethel was Benjamite territory and here is an example of the broader use of the term "mount Ephraim."

Mount Tabor

But as Canaanite hegemony in the north grew more menacing (or as the political situation within Ephraim became more settled), Deborah prepared to take action:

> Judges 4:6. And she sent and called Barak . . . of Kedesh-naphtali and said unto him . . . Go and draw toward mount Tabor, and take with thee ten thousand men of . . . Naphtali and . . . Zebulun
>
> Judges 4:7. And I will draw unto thee to the river Kishon Sisera, the captain of Jabin's army . . .

Kedesh, seven miles northwest of Hazor, was the most important Israelite town in Naphtali (and was called Kedesh-naphtali to differentiate it from other towns of the name). Presumably, it was the center of Israelite resistance and Barak was a guerrilla leader keeping the hopes of Israel alive. Now Deborah was urging him to combine the forces available to him and risk it in a pitched battle on Mount Tabor.

Mount Tabor is located at the southern border of Naphtali, where it meets the borders of Zebulun and Issachar. It is about twenty-five miles southwest of Hazor, forming a convenient rallying point for troops from several tribes, and an easily defensible area where they might gather and prepare. (Mount Tabor is only about five miles southeast of Nazareth, which over a thousand years later was to be the home of Jesus.)

The Kishon River, about fifty miles long, flows northwestward through northern Palestine, through the territory of Issachar and Zebulun, into what is now called the Bay of Acre. A northern tributary has its origin just west of Mount Tabor.

Barak was reluctant to risk his forces in the uncertainty of a pitched battle without assurance of firm Ephraimite support (just as the Greek city-states in later centuries were reluctant to oppose some foreign enemy without assurance of Spartan help).

Judges 4:8. *And Barak said unto her, If thou wilt go with me,
then I will go; but if thou wilt not go with me, then I will not go.*

Deborah gave the necessary assurance and at the head of the largest
alliance and the strongest Israelite army since the time of Joshua,
Barak defeated Sisera. Sisera was killed in flight by a woman to whom
he turned for help, and the Israelite army continued the war against
Jabin until Hazor was taken and destroyed, this time for good.

The Song of Deborah

The fifth chapter of the Book of Judges is notable for the "Song
of Deborah," considered one of the most ancient portions of the
Bible:

Judges 5:1. *Then sang Deborah and Barak . . . on that day . . .*

It was a paean of triumph at the victory over Sisera and in it
Deborah lists the tribes of the coalition that took part in the victory.
Ephraim and its satellites, Benjamin and Manasseh, are, of course,
listed first:

Judges 5:14. *Out of Ephraim was there a root of them . . . ;
after thee, Benjamin, among thy people; out of Machir came down
governors, and out of Zebulun they that handle the pen of the
writer.*
Judges 5:15. *And the princes of Issachar were with Deborah . . .*
. . . .
Judges 5:18. *Zebulun and Naphtali were a people that jeoparded
their lives . . .*

Machir is, apparently, an alternate name for Manasseh. Perhaps
the tribe of Manasseh is actually the union of two tribes, one of
which was called Machir (a term more often used for that portion of
the tribe that held territory east of the Jordan). The Bible solves the
problem by making Machir a son of Manasseh.

Genesis 50:23. . . . *the children also of Machir, the son of
Manasseh were brought up upon Joseph's knees.*

Here the implication is that Machir was the only son of Manasseh, so that both Manasseh and Machir could serve as eponymous ancestors for the entire tribe.

Six of the tribes, then, took part in the battle: Ephraim, Benjamin, Manasseh, Zebulun, Issachar, and Naphtali, forming a solid bloc along the interior of northern Canaan.

Four of the tribes are singled out for mutiongh of not having joined:

Judges 5:15. . . . *For the divisions of Reuben, there were great thoughts of heart.*

Judges 5:16. *Why abodest thou among the sheepfolds, to hear the bleatings of the flocks? . . .*

Judges 5:17. *Gilead [Gad] abode beyond Jordan: and why did Dan remain in ships? Asher continued on the sea shore . . .*

The abstentions were reasonable after all. Asher on the northern shore facing the Phoenicians, and Dan on the southern shore facing the Philistines may well have had ample troubles at home without looking for enemies elsewhere. Reuben, which stood irresolute and finally decided to remain at home, was having similar trouble with Moab. Indeed, this chapter is the last in the Bible to mention Reuben as a tribe, so it had not long to endure. Gad was the only strong tribe that might have joined but didn't, and it may have felt secure behind the river and saw no need to risk lives.

Notice that the tribe of Judah, and its satellite Simeon, are not mentioned. It is quite possible that during the period of the judges, Judah was not part of the Israelite coalition and may not even have been recognized as part of Israel.

Indeed, it was only for a century, under the kings Saul, David, and Solomon, that Judah was united with Israel. Under Saul (an Israelite), Judah was in rebellion; and under David and Solomon (Judeans), Israel was restive. After Solomon, the two portions of the land fell apart and remained apart for the rest of their history.

Jezreel

In addition to the Canaanite enemy within the land, the Israelites were subjected to periodic raids by the nomads from beyond the Jordan—the Midianites and Amalekites. The tribe of Manasseh, which bordered on the central Jordan, suffered particularly from these raids into Israel, and the defense against the nomads was undertaken by Gideon, a member of that tribe. His opportunity came with the next raid:

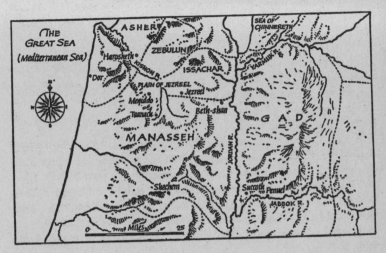

Jezreel

Judges 6:33. Then all the Midianites and the Amalekites . . . gathered together, and went over, and pitched in the valley of Jezreel.

A river flows into the Jordan from the west about fifteen miles south of Lake Galilee and cuts through the line of hills that runs down the center of Israel. That is the valley of Jezreel and it represents a natural opening into the heart of northern Israel for raiders from the east.

The valley of Jezreel is in the territory of Issachar but Gideon did not intend to let Issachar fight alone:

Judges 6:35. And he sent messengers throughout all Manasseh . . . and . . . unto Asher, and unto Zebulun, and unto Naphtali; and they came up to meet them.

It was almost the same confederacy that fought the Hazorites under Sisera, but with the vital omission of Ephraim.

We can only guess why Gideon omitted Ephraim, but perhaps it was something like this. If Ephraim joined the coalition it would only be as the leader and they, in their military pride, would insist on a direct frontal attack. Gideon had what he thought was a better plan and to carry it through he needed to retain control in his own hands—which meant omitting Ephraim. His plan, he felt, would work against a nomad host stronger in numbers than in discipline and organization.

He led a small band by night to the heights overlooking the Midianite encampment and attacked suddenly, with noise and lights, rather than with arms. Roused, shaken, not knowing what was going on, convinced that a formidable host had surrounded them, the Midianites fled in panic back to the Jordan, where the main army was waiting to destroy them at the fords.

Ephraim, having been notified with deliberate tardiness by Gideon and directed to the fords, participated in the battle at the Jordan, but it was plain to them that the successful strategy was Gideon's.

They were humiliated and angered. Not only had Gideon deliberately failed to recognize Ephraim's leadership, but he had then gone on to head a coalition and win a victory without them. Civil war was threatened between those who followed Gideon and an annoyed and jealous Ephraim:

Judges 8:1. And the men of Ephraim said unto him [Gideon], Why hast thou served us thus, that thou calledst us not, when thou wentest out to fight with the Midianites? And they did chide with him sharply.

Smoothly, Gideon suggested that the crucial point of the battle came at the fords of the Jordan, where Ephraim had captured a number of the Midianite leaders. His own role, a mere raid, he dismissed as quite minor. The offended Ephraimites allowed themselves to be soothed and civil war was averted.

Succoth

Gideon pursued the remnant of the Midianite army east of the Jordan, in order to complete the victory. Partly, too, the pursuit of the enemy was a matter of private vengeance, for Zebah and Zalmunna, two Midianite leaders still at large, had been responsible (as it turned out) for the death of Gideon's brothers.

In the course of the pursuit, Gideon passed through the territory of the tribe of Gad, which was continuing its policy of isolation. It had not joined the coalition against Jabin and Sisera and it had not joined the coalition against the Midianites. (Since the Midianites would have had to pass through Gadite territory to reach the Jordan on their way into Israel, there is a strong possibility that Gad was worse than neutral; that it did not oppose the Midianites and paid them tribute in order that they might remain in peace while devastation fell on the land west of the Jordan.)

Even after Gideon's victory, they temporized and sought the safety of neutrality. When Gideon entered Succoth, on the Jabbok River perhaps four miles east of the Jordan, and asked for supplies, he was refused:

> Judges 8:6. . . . the princes of Succoth said, Are the hands of Zebah and Zalmunna now in thine hand, that we should give bread unto thine army?

In other words, Gideon might yet be defeated and Succoth was not going to risk retaliation by the Midianites. The nearby town of Penuel (where Jacob had once wrestled with an angel) took the same attitude.

Gideon could do nothing about this at the time; the Midianites came first. He caught up with the nomads at Karkor, the exact site of which is unknown, but which may be some thirty miles east of the Jordan (a deep eastward penetration for an Israelite army of the time). Again Gideon won a complete victory, capturing the Midianite leaders and eventually executing them.

He then took reprisal against the Gadites, destroying the fortifications of Penuel, and executing the leading men of Succoth.

Gideon and Abimelech

The victories of Gideon had been sufficiently dramatic to give him the prestige required for kingship; that is, for hereditary rule.

> Judges 8:22. Then the men of Israel said unto Gideon, Rule thou over us, both thou, and thy son, and thy son's son also . . .

Judges 8:23. *And Gideon said unto them, I will not rule over you . . . The Lord shall rule over you.*

This response was in accord with the views of the time at which the Book of Judges reached its final form; that is, after the time of the monarchy. The kings of Israel (and, to a lesser extent, of Judah) were all too often strongly anti-Yahvist. The Yahvists were, in turn, anti-monarchic, and this shows up in several places in the Bible.

Nevertheless, the chances are that Gideon *did* accept the kingship, if not "of Israel" then at least of Manasseh. He certainly ruled as judge in his lifetime and, after his death, the crucial test is whether his power was hereditary. Apparently it was, for his sons succeeded him to power. Again the power was just over Manasseh for only places in Manasseh are mentioned in this portion of the Book of Judges.

The advantage of hereditary rule lies in the fact that the succession can be made automatic, that it will pass from father to son (or to some other close relative) according to some fixed rule. The land is therefore not plunged into broils and civil war with the death of each ruler.

For this to work well, those relatives who do not inherit the kingdom should stand aside with good grace, but this did not always happen in ancient monarchies. With royal polygamy practiced, there would be large numbers of sons born of different mothers. The wives of the harem would intrigue for the succession of their own sons and the sons themselves would seek factions within the kingdom. The result would often be broils and civil wars anyway.

This was to be most clearly shown in Biblical history in the case of Israel's greatest king, David, but a little foretaste is given now. Gideon was a polygamist, and a fruitful one:

Judges 8:30. *And Gideon had threescore and ten sons of his body begotten; for he had many wives.*

Judges 8:31. *And his concubine that was in Shechem, she also bare him a son whose name he called Abimelech.*

It is interesting that "Abimelech" means "my father is king." The "king" might be a reference to a god rather than to Gideon, so perhaps it should not be taken too literally.

The question was which of Gideon's sons was to succeed him. In this connection, Abimelech may have felt like an outsider. Shechem was still essentially a Canaanite city, worshiping a Canaanite god, Baal-berith ("Lord of the covenant") and Abimelech as the son of a Canaanite woman may have been scorned and rejected by his brothers.

In any case, he made a virtue of necessity and intrigued with his mother's clan in Shechem, pointing out that they would fare better under one of their own as king. They saw the point and financed his next step, which was to hire a private army and use it to attack and slaughter the other sons. Left in power, Abimelech assumed the kingship but retained it for only a short while before trouble started:

> Judges 9:22. *When Abimelech had reigned three years over Israel,*
>
> Judges 9:23. . . . *an evil spirit* [arose] *between Abimelech and the men of Shechem . . .*

The Shechemites, disenchanted with Abimelech for some reason, rebelled against him. Abimelech bloodily suppressed the Shechemite rebellion and then went on to subdue other disaffected cities of Manasseh. He marched against Thebez (which is thought to be represented nowadays by a village named Tubas), about twelve miles northeast of Shechem. He took the city but was killed in the process.

Thus ended the house of Gideon and the first brief attempt at establishing a monarchy in Israel.

Mizpeh

Deborah and Gideon may be counted as the fourth and fifth of the judges, respectively. Two more, Tola and Jair (the sixth and seventh), are briefly mentioned in a verse apiece and soon thereafter the scene shifts to the Trans-Jordan.

While the tribe of Gad (Gilead) remained aloof from the troubles of Israel proper, it did not dwell in complete peace, even if the momentary irruption of Gideon's Manassite army is discounted.

When the tribe of Gad had settled in its territory, it had displaced the Ammonites, pushing them away from the Jordan valley and toward the east. This was not accomplished peacefully, of course, and there was continuing war between the Gadites and the Ammonites. The climax of that war is described:

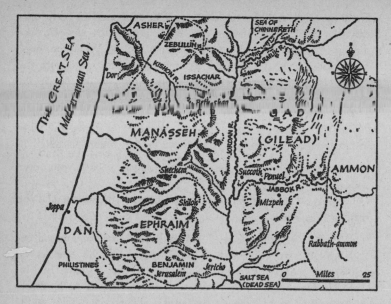

Mizpeh

Judges 10:17. *Then the children of Ammon were gathered to-gether, and encamped in Gilead. And the children of Israel assem-bled themselves together, and encamped in Mizpeh.*

The exact site of Mizpeh is uncertain but it may have been some twenty miles southeast of the town of Succoth, earlier mentioned in connection with Gideon's raid across the Jordan. It was near the east-ern border of Gadite territory.

At the head of the Gadite army was Jephthah, who, in his eagerness to win, vows, in case of victory, to sacrifice to God the first living thing that emerges from his house upon his return home. Jephthah wins a complete victory over the Ammonites and, on his return home, it is his daughter and only child who emerges to greet him. Jephthah is forced, in agony, to sacrifice her.

This tale of human sacrifice is so at odds with the rituals of Yahvism that it is a matter of surprise that the later editors of the Book of Judges allowed it to remain without some sign of disapproval. It is often suggested that the tale is left unvarnished in an attempt to assimilate into Yahvism the ritual of a pagan festival. The story concludes:

> Judges 11:39. . . . *And it was a custom in Israel,*
> Judges 11:40. *That the daughters of Israel went yearly to lament the daughter of Jephthah the Gileadite four days in a year.*

There were well-known rites all over the ancient world celebrating the death and subsequent rebirth of a god. This represented the annual agricultural cycle: the death of crops in the winter and their rebirth in the spring. It would be customary for women to bewail the death of the god with great ceremony each year, and then to rejoice at the news of the rebirth.

To deprive the women of their long-established custom would have been difficult; to transfer it from a heathen god to the daughter of an Israelite hero might have been easier.

Shibboleth

The victory of Jephthah displeased the Ephraimites, as Gideon's victory had displeased them. The tribe of Gad, it seemed to Ephraim, was attempting to take over the headship of Israel. Jephthah did not succeed, as Gideon had, in mollifying the Ephraimites and this time there was civil war.

The Ephraimite forces, with the self-confidence of a tribe considering itself militarily supreme among the Israelites, promptly invaded Gad, crossing the Jordan to do so.

Jephthah, in all probability, faded away before them, luring them deeper into the country and farther from their bases, while he sent contingents to occupy the fords of the Jordan and cut off their retreat. In a sharp battle, he then defeated the Ephraimites and when the beaten army fled, they found their way across the Jordan barred:

> Judges 12:5. . . . *when those Ephraimites which were escaped said, Let me go over; . . . the men of Gilead said unto him, Art thou an Ephraimite? If he said, Nay;*
> Judges 12:6. *Then said they unto him, Say now Shibboleth: and he said Sibboleth: for he could not frame to pronounce it right. Then they took him, and slew him . . .*

The word *shibboleth* meant "stream" but it had no significance in itself; it merely supplied the "sh" sound that was missing in the Ephraimite dialect. As a result of this passage, the word "shibboleth" is used in English to represent any catchword that serves to distinguish one group of men from another.

Forty-two thousand Ephraimites are recorded as having died in this ▓▓▓▓ ▓▓▓▓ ▓▓▓▓ ▓▓▓▓▓ ▓▓ ▓▓▓▓▓▓▓▓▓▓▓ ▓▓▓▓▓▓▓▓▓ ▓▓▓ ▓▓▓ ▓▓▓▓▓▓ ▓▓▓▓ serious enough to end the Ephraimite hegemony over Israel. When the day came that a king finally arose over Israel, it was not from the tribe of Ephraim that he was taken.

Nazarite

Jephthah may be counted as the eighth judge and, after the conclusion of his story, three more are briefly mentioned in a verse or two apiece. These are Ibzan, Elon, and Abdon, the ninth, tenth, and eleventh judges respectively.

And now again there is a shift in scene; this time westward, to the southern coast, where the great enemy was the Philistines. The tribe that suffered most seriously from them was Dan, whose territory lay in the northern section of Philistia, which was dominated by the Philistines throughout the period of the judges.

Around the struggles between Danites and their Philistine overlords there arose tales of a folk hero, Samson. Samson is not a leader of an army, like Barak, Gideon, or Jephthah. He is, instead, a kind of Robin Hood or Superman, conducting a one-man campaign against the enemy and winning his way by brute strength, rather than by skill or intelligence.

It is uncertain how much of a nubbin of historical truth lies behind the undoubtedly exaggerated stories concerning him, for much of the Samson story can be made to fit into the type of solar myths common in ancient times: in which the life of a hero reflects the course of the sun through the heavens.

Samson's life is miraculous from the start, for his birth is announced to his mother beforehand by an angel:

> Judges 13:5. *For, lo, thou shalt conceive, and bear a son; and no rasor shall come on his head; for the child shall be a Nazarite unto God from the womb* . . .

The word "Nazarite" means "one who is separate"; that is, one who marks himself off from ordinary human beings and devotes himself to the spiritual life. The Nazarite in ancient Israel has some of the flavor of the monk in Christendom.

Nazarites must have been fairly common in the later monarchy and the rules for becoming one were written into the Book of Numbers and thus made part of the law of Moses:

> Numbers 6:2. . . . *When either man or woman shall . . . vow a vow of a Nazarite, to separate themselves unto the Lord:*
> Numbers 6:3. *He shall separate himself from wine and strong drink . . .*
>   . . . .
> Numbers 6:6. . . . *he shall come at no dead body.*

Samson is the first person in the Bible to be recorded as a Nazarite, but he certainly was not an edifying one. Nothing about his life indicated any spiritual uplift, or even any moral sense. Nor did he fulfill the barest minimum of the Nazarite vows since he did come into contact with dead bodies and he participated at feasts where there must have been much drinking.

Only his unshaven head and long hair remain of the Nazarite way of life, and this is an essential part of a solar myth since long hair represents the rays of the sun. It may well be that it is merely to account for the long hair in a non-idolatrous fashion that the later editors of the Book of Judges made him a Nazarite and put him in a role he fit so poorly.

Zorah

Samson was born:

> Judges 13:24. *And the woman bare a son, and called his name Samson: and the child grew . . .*
> Judges 13:25. . . . *in the camp of Dan between Zorah and Esh-taol.*

Zorah, the home of Manoah, Samson's father, is located in the eastern section of Danite territory, about fifteen miles west of Jerusalem. Eshtaol is a couple of miles to its east.

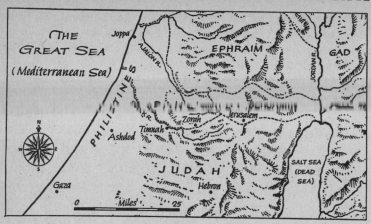

Zorah

The very name Samson ("Shimshon" in Hebrew) bears a striking resemblance to the word *shemesh*, meaning "sun." Only two miles south of Zorah was the town of Beth-shemesh ("house of the sun") believed to be a center of sun-worship.

Delilah

From the beginning, Samson displayed a penchant for Philistine girls:

> Judges 14:1. And Samson . . . *saw a woman in Timnath of the daughters of the Philistines.*
> Judges 14:2. And he . . . *told his father and his mother, and said . . . get her for me to wife.*

(Timnath was a town about six miles west of Zorah.)

Samson did not marry her in the end but in the course of the courtship and engagement, he performed typical feats. He killed a lion with his bare hands; he killed thirty Philistines in anger over having lost a wager; he tied torches to the tails of foxes and turned them loose in Philistine grainfields.

Later, he breaks loose from binding ropes and singlehandedly slaughters large numbers of Philistines; he escapes from a city which has locked its gates on him, by lifting the gates bodily and carrying them away, and so on. None of these feats do Israel any good or the Philistines any serious harm, and many of them can be shown to fit solar myths commonly told in ancient times.

But then Samson meets his match in the form of another Philistine girl:

> Judges 16:4. And it came to pass afterward, that he loved a woman in the valley of Sorek, whose name was Delilah.

The Sorek River flows westward from the neighborhood of Jerusalem to the sea. It forms the southern boundary of Danite territory and cuts through Philistia south of Ekron and north of Ashdod. It is a natural route for eastward invasion of Philistine armies into central Israel.

Delilah is bribed by her Philistine compatriots to find out from Samson the secret of his strength. After several evasions, he tells her:

> Judges 16:17. . . . There hath not come a rasor upon mine head . . . if I be shaven, then my strength will go from me, and I shall become weak, and be like any other man.

> . . . .

> Judges 16:19. And she [Delilah] made him [Samson] sleep upon her knees; and she called for a man, and she caused him to shave off the seven locks of his head; . . . and his strength went from him.

There is nothing in the Nazarite ritual that implies that it is the purpose of the long hair to give unusual strength to a man. This is clearly mythological and fits in with the sun motif.

Delilah's name is closely akin to the Hebrew lilah ("night") so apparently the tale tells of night overcoming the sun and depriving it of its rays as it sets toward the horizon and becomes ruddy and dim.

Dagon

Now at last the Philistines could take Samson. They blinded him (the sun, which may be viewed as the eye of the heavens, is removed and vanishes from the sky with the coming of night) and put him to hard labor in prison. Then, in celebration

> Judges 16:23. . . . the lords of the Philistines gathered them together for to offer a great sacrifice unto Dagon their god . . .

Very little is known about the nature of Dagon for the rites to this god of the Philistines of Gaza and Ashdod died out after Old Testament times. Because the word "Dagon" resembles *dag*, the Hebrew word for "fish," the idol has often been supposed to represent a fish-god and even to be in the form of a merman, man above the waist and fish below. This is the view he which Milton mentions Dagon in *Paradise Lost* when he calls the roll of the fallen angels.

Since the Philistines were a coastal people, to whom fish and fishing could have been important, this seemed reasonable. However, the name of the god is even closer to *dagan*, the Hebrew word for "grain," and it is therefore even more reasonable to suppose that Dagon was an agricultural god, a very common type of deity.

The one other important mention of Dagon in the Bible gives some hint of the appearance of the idol. In later years, the Philistines capture the ark of the covenant and take it into the temple of Dagon with drastic results for their idol:

> 1 Samuel 5:4. *And when they arose early on the morrow, behold, Dagon was fallen upon his face . . . and the head of Dagon and both . . . hands were cut off . . . ; only the stump of Dagon was left to him.*

In the Revised Standard Version, the final phrase is given as "only the trunk of Dagon was left to him."

If the bottom half of the idol had been that of a fish, it seems very difficult to believe that the Biblical writers would not have said "only the tail of Dagon was left to him." The weight of the evidence would seem to lie, then, despite Milton, in favor of Dagon as a grain-god.

In any case, the name Dagon is clearly Semitic and is a good example of how Philistine culture was Semitized after their arrival in Canaan (if not before).

The feast to celebrate the capture of Samson did not end well for the Philistines. They brought out the blinded Samson in order to make their enjoyment of the occasion the keener.

> Judges 16:22. *Howbeit the hair of his head began to grow again after he was shaven.*

Again the sun myth can be seen here, for although the eye of the day is blinded and the sun disappears, it invariably appears again. It rises once more in the east, with its rays weak and dim, yes, but growing brighter and stronger as it climbs in the sky.

In a last display of strength, Samson pushes apart the pillars supporting the roof of the large house in which they feasted. He himself, and many Philistines, died in the collapse that followed. In this way, a story which had many of the aspects of farce ended with a touch of tragic dignity. Samson is the twelfth judge, the last in the Book of Judges.

Dan

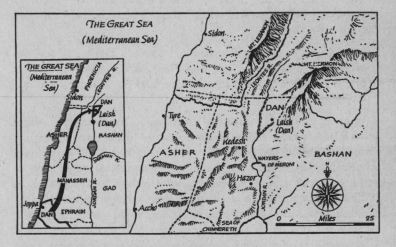

Dan and the Danite Migration

The Book of Judges does not end with the twelfth judge. The last five chapters add two supplementary narratives which are placed in this book because they belong in its particular historical period. The writer specifies this:

Judges 18:1. *In those days there was no king in Israel . . .*

Unlike the earlier accounts in this book, however, these final incidents are not associated with the feats of any specific judge.

The first account deals with the tribe of Dan, which found itself unbearably oppressed by the overpowering might of the Philistines, who occupied most of the region theoretically assigned to Dan at the conquest and dominated the rest.

Judges 18:2. . . . *in those days the tribe of the Danites sought them an inheritance to dwell in; for unto that day all their inheritance had not fallen unto them . . .*

"In those days" merely specifies the period of the judges; it does not tell us certainly whether it comes before or after the feats of Samson. If it is assumed that because the incident follows the tales of Samson, it therefore occurs later in time and is good evidence that Samson's activities did not seriously weaken the Philistines or help the Danites.

The Danites decided, therefore, to seek for an area far away from the powerful Philistines, and sent a group of five men to reconnoiter the far north. Eventually

Judges 18:7. . . . *the five men . . . came to Laish, and saw the people that were therein, how they dwelt careless, after the manner of the Zidonians . . . and they were far from the Zidonians and had no business with any man.*

In other words, they found a Phoenician (Canaanite) city, thirty miles inland, which could not easily be rescued by the main Phoenician power centers on the coast. Furthermore, it had lived in peaceful isolation, without having formed military alliances that might serve to make an assault against the city expensive and subject to retaliation.

The scouts reported this on returning home, whereupon a body of six hundred men were sent northward to secure the place. In passing through the territory of the bordering tribe of Ephraim, they calmly appropriated an idol built by Micah, an unoffending Ephraimite who had been hospitable to the spies on their earlier trip. They also took with them the Levite who had served as private chaplain to the Ephraimite. When Micah objected, the Danites threatened to kill him into the bargain.

Judges 18:26. *And the children of Dan went their way: and when Micah saw that they were too strong for him, he turned and went back unto his house.*

This is an example of the anarchy of the times and the disunity of the tribes. Danites felt no compunction, presumably, in stealing from

Ephraimites. (From the fact that no Ephraimite force advanced to oppose the marauding Danites, it might be supposed that this happened after Ephraim's catastrophic defeat at the hands of Jephthah.)

Nor were the Danites the only offenders in this respect. They were offended against as well. When Samson, a Danite, was conducting his harassment of the Philistines, a band of men of Judah (neighboring Danite territory to the south and southeast), fearing general Philistine reprisals, acted to remove the troublemaking Samson:

Judges 15:12. . . . *they said unto him, We are come down to bind thee, that we may deliver thee into the hand of the Philistines . . .*

They fulfilled their threat, too (though Samson later escaped the Philistines by means of his superstrength). Apparently, the men of Judah did not hesitate to sacrifice a Danite to what we would consider the common enemy.

As it is put in the final verse of the Book of Judges:

Judges 21:25. *In those days there was no king in Israel: every man did that which was right in his own eyes.*

This lack of law and order, this feeling that might was the only right, goes far to explain the eventual Israelite clamor for a king and is something even the general anti-monarchic attitude of the final editors of the Book of Judges cannot hide.

But to return to the migrating Danite band—

They reached Laish and attacked it as consciencelessly as they had robbed the Ephraimite and with as great a success. They destroyed Laish and built a new city in its place.

Judges 18:29. *And they called the name of the city Dan . . .*

The site of Dan is usually identified with the Arab town Tell el Kady, located on the upper Jordan, nearly thirty miles north of the Sea of Galilee. ("Dan" and "Kady" both mean "judge.")

Dan represented the farthest northern reach of any purely Israelite territory (although Israelite dominion in the greatest days of the monarchy extended much farther north over areas occupied by non-Israelites). The phrase "from Dan to Beersheba" can therefore be taken to mean "all Israel" since Beersheba was the southernmost Israelite town of any consequence. The distance from Dan to Beersheba is about

150 miles, which is equal to the distance from Albany to New York, a respectable distance in Old Testament times.

The site of Dan still stands at the northernmost edge of modern Israel, though Beersheba is far from the southern edge. Modern Israel controls a 120-mile stretch of desert (the Negev) south of Beersheba. Israel now extends over an extreme length of 270 miles.

Dan's position made it as isolated and exposed in its new role as an Israelite city as it had been in its earlier role as a Phoenician city. Not long after the death of Solomon, it was taken by a Syrian army from the north and that was the end of it. Its span of existence was two centuries.

Gibeah

The next account, the one with which the Book of Judges ends, is an even more distressing story, one which even more clearly indicates the state of anarchy and lawlessness that prevailed in Israel before the kingship was established.

It concerns a man of Ephraim who was traveling northward from Judah with his concubine, intending to cross the intervening territory

Gibeah

of Benjamin. The day was drawing to a close when he and his party reached Jerusalem, which lies on the boundary dividing the territory of

Judah from Benjamin. He might have stayed there for the night, but Jerusalem was then under the control of the non-Israelite Jebusites and the man of Ephraim preferred to find a nearby Israelite city in which to stay.

Judges 19:12. . . . *We will not turn aside hither into the city of a stranger . . . ; we will pass over to Gibeah.*

(Gibeah lay five miles north of Jerusalem and was an important Benjamite center.) There he managed to find a night's lodging with an old man, who happened to be a fellow Ephraimite. That night, however, a gang of Benjamite toughs besieged the old man's house, and seizing the concubine, abused and eventually killed her.

Again, it would seem, tribal disunity exacerbated the situation. One cannot help thinking that the Benjamites would not have acted with such disregard of humanity if they had not been dealing with Ephraimites, members of another tribe, and therefore strangers.

The irony of it is that if the Ephraimite and his concubine had slept over in Jerusalem, the "city of a stranger" which he would not enter, he would probably have been safe.

The "outrage at Gibeah" is the city's only claim to a very dubious fame, and it was held up in later centuries as the very epitome of sinfulness, a standard against which to measure disgrace. Thus, the prophet Hosea, writing some four centuries later of his own generation, said:

Hosea 9:9. *They have deeply corrupted themselves as in the days of Gibeah . . .*

Mizpeh [Benjamin]

The account of the events following the outrage of Gibeah is a puzzling one, for in several ways it seems inconsistent with other parts of Biblical history. When news of the outrage was spread among the tribes:

Judges 20:1. . . . *all the children of Israel went out, and the congregation was gathered together as one man, from Dan even to Beersheba, with the land of Gilead, unto the Lord in Mizpeh.*

The Mizpeh here is not the one in Gadite territory where Jephthah's troops gathered before the battle with the Ammonites. Rather it was a town in Benjamin, near its border with Ephraim. In the period of the judges, this was used as a tribal meeting place on several occasions.

We need not literally suppose, of course, that "all the children of Israel" assembled there; but rather that representatives of all the tribes were there, including even those from beyond the Jordan.

The gathering is pictured as being horrified at the event and unanimously deciding on united action against Gibeah.

Judges 20:11. *So all the men of Israel were gathered against the city, knit together as one man.*

And yet this seems so unlikely. Throughout the period of the judges, the tribes of Israel did not unite even under the most pressing of dangers. They did not all unite against Sisera or against the Midianites or against the Ammonites. Indeed, Manasseh's fight against the Midianites nearly provoked civil war with Ephraim, and Gad's fight against the Ammonites did provoke such a civil war. Therefore it seems quite unbelievable that a united front could be set up on this occasion.

Perhaps the later editors idealized the situation. Could it be that what actually happened was that all Ephraim, rather than all Israel, united against Benjamin in defense of the manhandled Ephraimites?

If one were to search for historic justification, however, one might suppose that the Book of Joshua was accurate and that at the time of the conquest and perhaps immediately afterward the Israelite tribes *were* taking common action. Might then the outrage at Gibeah have happened right at the start of the period of the judges, despite its position at the end of the book?

After all, when in the war that followed, Israel suffered initial defeats, they turned to the ark of the covenant for advice and the Bible pauses in its account to say:

Judges 20:28. *And Phinehas, the son of Eleazar, the son of Aaron, stood before it in those days . . .*

But Eleazar was contemporary with Joshua, so that events occurring in the lifetime of Eleazar's son must be taking place immediately after the conquest, and while united action was still, presumably, part of the Israelite tradition.

The war finally turned against Benjamin. The Israelites were victorious, Gibeah was sacked, and the entire Benjamite territory devastated. Indeed, the Benjamite population was almost wiped out.

Judges 20:47. *But six hundred men turned and fled . . . unto the rock Rimmon.*

The "rock Rimmon" is sometimes identified with a wild, hilly region five miles north of Gibeah.

Only these six hundred men, the Biblical story indicates, remained of the Benjamites. Even if we assume an exaggeration, the story, if it has a foundation of historical truth at all, must indicate a serious and even devastating defeat of Benjamin. If so, it could not have happened toward the end of the period of the judges, for Benjamin was prosperous then. It was from Benjamin, in fact, that a king of Israel was soon to be drawn. On the other hand, the picture of a greatly weakened Benjamin early in the period of the judges might be considered consistent with the Moabite invasion that put Benjamin under enemy occupation and provoked the counteraction of Ehud (see page 234).

Jabesh-gilead

The story goes on to say that Israel repented the destruction of Benjamin and was unwilling to see a tribe disappear. The six hundred survivors might serve as a nucleus for repopulation but the Israelites had sworn to give them no wives. They looked therefore for some city or group that had not been represented in the war against Benjamin and that had therefore not participated in the oath.

Judges 21:8. *. . . And behold, there came none to the camp from Jabesh-gilead . . .*

Jabesh-gilead was a Gadite city, located east of the Jordan River about fifteen miles north of Succoth.

The Israelites proceeded to sack Jabesh-gilead and obtain a supply of wives for the Benjamites. In this way, Benjamin survived. Again, if this happened at all it could not have happened late in the period

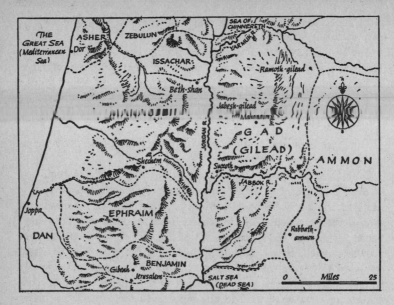

Jabesh-gilead

of judges for in the time of King Saul, which followed hard after, Jabesh-gilead was a flourishing town.

(I can't resist the personal speculation that some Israelite writer in the early period of the monarchy decided to write what we would today call a historical romance centering about the affair at Gibeah. He filled it with violence and action and did not hesitate to adjust history to the dramatic needs of the story. And then, somehow, the tale was taken seriously by the priestly editors who later drew together the various tribal traditions into the Book of Judges. It was therefore included, but was placed at the end because it seemed to fit nowhere. Now, there it is, a puzzle for Biblical scholars to try to decipher.)

8. RUTH

THE BOOK OF RUTH * BETHLEHEM-JUDAH * MAHLON AND CHILION * RUTH * DAVID

The Book of Ruth

Following the Book of Judges, in the various versions of the Bible used by Christians, is a short book of four chapters, titled Ruth after its heroine. It is set in the time of the judges:

Ruth 1:1. *Now it came to pass in the days when the judges ruled . . .*

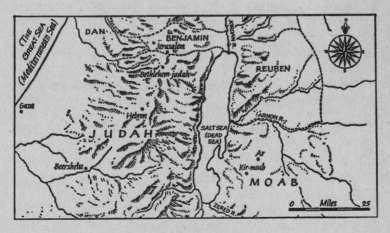

Judah and Moab

One might almost think it was another of the tales of the time. Something to add to the accounts of the wars of Gideon and Jephthah, the exploits of Samson, the migration of the Danites, the outrage at Gibeah. Why then is it not made a part of the Book of Judges?

The answer is that it is not just another of the tales of the time. The material in the Book of Judges is uniformly bloody, primitive, and at times even repulsive, as is to be expected of stories based on the contemporary chronicles of a crude, barbaric era. The story of Ruth, on the other hand, is a charming pastoral idyl, written as though by someone looking back at a period from a long distance, and seeing it in the light of the "good old days," a time of simplicity and peace and good will—which the time certainly was not.

In short, the Book of Ruth was composed in the fifth century B.C. in all likelihood, after the return of the Jews from exile and some seven centuries after the time it purports to describe. And even though its central thesis is based on historic tradition, perhaps the details surrounding it are fictional.

The Jews recognized this by including the book only in the third division of the Bible—"The Writings." The books in this section were considered by them to be literature, rather than history.

Nevertheless, the historic point it makes is so important to the Christian scheme of things, that it has been drawn forward into the historic section of the Bible and placed in its appropriate position in the story—immediately after the Book of Judges.

Bethlehem-judah

The tale begins with a famine that drives a family of Israelites out of their home in Judah:

> Ruth 1:1. . . . And a certain man of Bethlehem-judah went to sojourn in the country of Moab, he, and his wife, and his two sons.

Bethlehem-judah is so called to distinguish it from Bethlehem-zebulun, about seventy-five miles northward. Bethlehem-judah is so much the more famous for reasons that will soon be made plain that any reference simply to Bethlehem may be taken to mean Bethlehem-judah.

In fact, the only mention of Bethlehem-zebulun in the Bible is thought to be in connection with Ibzan, one of the minor judges (the ninth in order) glancingly mentioned in the Book of Judges:

Judges 12:8. *And after him* [Jephthah] *Ibzan of Bethlehem judged Israel.*

Bethlehem-judah, located about six miles south of Jerusalem, apparently bore an earlier name of Ephrath (see page 102). Even in the time of David, the men of Bethlehem could be called Ephrathites:

1 Samuel 17:12. *Now David was the son of that Ephrathite of Bethlehem-judah, whose name was Jesse . . .*

and the writer of Ruth follows that custom in connection with the family entering Moab:

Ruth 1:2. *And the name of the man was Elimelech, and the name of his wife Naomi, and the name of his two sons Mahlon and Chilion, Ephrathites of Bethlehem-judah . . .*

Bethlehem had until now been mentioned in the Bible only in unhappy connections. Rachel had died near it, giving birth to Benjamin. The Danites migrating northward to consummate a bloody aggression took with them a Levite who was from Bethlehem-judah. The concubine who was brutally outraged and killed in Gibeah was of Bethlehem-judah.

Now, however, Bethlehem begins to take on a new and unique importance through its association with this family and what is to follow.

Mahlon and Chilion

In Moab, Elimelech dies, but his sons marry Moabite girls:

Ruth 1:4. *And they took them wives of the women of Moab; the name of the one was Orpah, and the name of the other Ruth: and they dwelled there about ten years.*

Ruth 1:5. *And Mahlon and Chilion died also both of them . . .*

Since "Mahlon" means "sickness" and "Chilion" means "wasting," they don't seem to be the type of names anyone would give children. Further, from the early death of the two sons, the names appear

entirely too appropriate. The use of such appropriate names is, however, often characteristic of fiction.

Ruth

Naomi, bereft of her husband and sons, decides to return to
Bethlehem and assumes that her daughters-in-law will not wish to go
with her into a strange land. Orpah does indeed part from her, but
the other daughter-in-law, Ruth, refuses flatly:

> Ruth 1:16. *And Ruth said, Intreat me not to leave thee . . .
> for whither thou goest, I will go; and where thou lodgest, I will
> lodge; thy people shall be my people, and thy God my God;*

and the two go to Bethlehem.

In Bethlehem, Ruth meets Boaz, a rich relative of Naomi's, who is
attracted to the girl despite the fact that she is a foreigner, and is
grateful to her for the love and care she is showing Naomi. Naomi
shrewdly arranges matters so that Boaz ends by offering to marry
Ruth in full, traditional style.

The marriage is made and eventually a son is born, which comforts
Naomi and consoles her for her own losses. Ruth, her loyal daughter-
in-law, although a Moabitess, is now considered a fully assimilated
member of the community and the Israelite women praise her:

> Ruth 4:14. *And the women said unto Naomi . . .*
> Ruth 4:15. *. . . thy daughter in law, which loveth thee, . . .
> is better to thee than seven sons . . .*

She has remained ever since, to all men, one of the most attractive
women in the Bible.

David

But now comes the real point of the story:

> Ruth 4:17. *And the women . . . gave it* [Ruth's son] *a name . . .
> Obed: he is the father of Jesse, the father of David.*

Ruth, in other words, was the great-grandmother of Israel's hero-king David.

The purpose of the book seems clear. It was written at the time when the Jews, like Naomi, were returning from exile. The exiles were bitterly anxious to purify the land from the strangers who had been settled on it during the Exile. Their leaders established a rigid and narrow racial policy by which all intermarriage with foreigners was forbidden and all who had already married foreign wives must put them away.

But there must have been many among the Jews who were appalled at the pettiness of such a policy and at the heartlessness with which it would have to be enforced. One of them wrote the Book of Ruth as a clarion call for universality and for the recognition of the essential brotherhood of man.

In writing the tale, the author might have been inspired by the existence of an actual tradition to the effect that David was part Moabite in ancestry. Certainly, at one period in his life when he was in peril and it seemed to him that not only he but his entire family was in danger of slaughter, David brought his parents to Moab for safety:

1 Samuel 22:3. *And David . . . said unto the king of Moab, Let my father and my mother . . . be with you, till I know what God will do for me.*

At the time, it may have been good policy for Moab's king to support David, who was then rebelling against Saul, since in that way Israel could be weakened. Nevertheless, David's confidence in Moab at this juncture may also have arisen from a realization of kinship.

If there was such a tradition, the writer of the Book of Ruth made superb use of it, and whether the details he added are fictional or not is of little moment as far as the book's deeper meaning is concerned.

By making the heroine a Moabitess, the writer sharpened the point of the story, for Moabite women were the traditional corrupters of Israelite men, thanks to the well-known story told in the Book of Numbers (see page 189). And yet this foreign woman was the ancestress of David.

The point could not have been made stronger. Not only could a foreigner be assimilated into Judaism and prove a worthy addition to it, but the foreigner might be the source of the highest good. Ought one to forbid foreign marriages as was done after the return from exile? Why, if Boaz's foreign marriage had been forbidden, there would have been no David.

To Christians, the importance went even further. Through David, Ruth was an ancestress of Jesus, and therefore the tale tends to reinforce the Christian view of the Messiah; that he is for all mankind and not for the Jews alone.

9. 1 SAMUEL

Shiloh

We now move into a period of increasingly reliable history. The next group of books tells of the establishment of the monarchy, and of its progress, first as a single kingdom of Israel, then as two smaller kingdoms, until the final destruction of one and the temporary destruction of the other.

Originally this history was detailed in two books. The former was called "Samuel" because it dealt with the prophet and judge of that name, and with the first two kings of Israel, both of whom were anointed by that prophet. The second was called "Kings" for obvious reasons.

Since both books were rather long, and therefore inconvenient to handle in the days when books were printed on long rolls, the Jewish scholars in Egypt, who prepared the first Greek translation of the Bible about 250 B.C., divided each book into two parts. Thus, we now have 1 Samuel, 2 Samuel, 1 Kings and 2 Kings. Since all four books deal with the monarchy it would also be reasonable to call them 1 Kings, 2 Kings, 3 Kings, and 4 Kings. This, in fact, is what is done in the Catholic versions of the Bible. Nevertheless, I will follow the convention of the King James Version.

The book of 1 Samuel begins with Samuel's parents:

1 Samuel 1:1. *Now there was a certain man of Ramathaim-zophim, of mount Ephraim, and his name was Elkanah . . .*

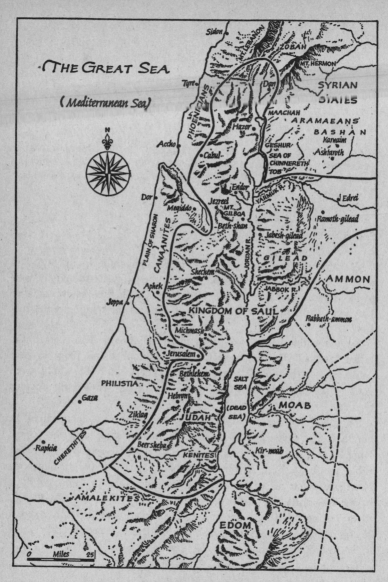

The Kingdom of Saul

Ramathaim-zophim is also referred to as Ramathaim, or even as Ramah (but is then to be distinguished from the better-known Ramah in Benjamin). The site is not certain but the consensus seems to place it in western Ephraim about ten miles east of the modern

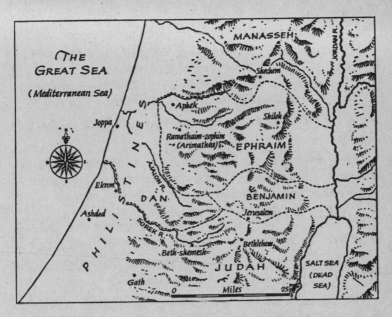

Shiloh

city of Tel Aviv. In New Testament times, it is to appear once again, but under the Greek version of the name—Arimathea.

Elkanah was an Ephraimite. His genealogy is traced back to his great-great-grandfather, who is identified as

1 Samuel 1:1. . . . *Zuph, an Ephrathite.*

This, however, is an error. The Revised Standard Version, as well as the New Catholic Edition and the Masoretic Edition all identify Zuph as "an Ephraimite." It is a small point, but if Samuel is viewed as having been descended from an Ephrathite, that is, from a man of Bethlehem-judah, his later relationship to David of Bethlehem may be misconstrued.

On the other hand, although Elkanah and his son Samuel are Ephraimites in the sense that they live in Ephraim, they are described in later records as being Levites by descent.

> 1 Chronicles 6:33. . . . *Of the sons of the Kohathites:* . . . *Shemuel,*
>
> 1 Chronicles 6.34. *The son of Elkanah* . . ,

The Kohathites are the descendants of Kohath, second son of Levi. (Shemuel is but the Hebrew form of the name we call Samuel, and it is given as Samuel in this verse in the Revised Standard Version.) The tale continues, with reference to Elkanah:

> 1 Samuel 1:3. *And this man went* . . . *yearly to worship* . . . *in Shiloh* . . .

Shiloh, located in the hill country in the center of Ephraim, was the spiritual nucleus of the region. To it, Israelites traveled to sacrifice at appropriate times of the year, as, over a century later, they were to travel to the Temple at Jerusalem.

The history of Shiloh as the site of a religious shrine sacred to Israel dates back, according to tradition, to the time of Joshua:

> Joshua 18:1. *And* . . . *Israel assembled together at Shiloh, and set up the tabernacle of the congregation there.*

This tabernacle had been constructed at Mount Sinai, as described in the final third of the Book of Exodus, and it included the ark of the covenant, which was considered the resting place of God Himself. Eli, serving as High Priest at Shiloh at this time, was also an Ephraimite, who according to later tradition was a Levite, and a descendant of Ithamar, fourth and youngest son of Aaron.

Elkanah's wife, Hannah, had no children, and at Shiloh, she vowed that if she were granted a child, he would be raised as a Nazarite and devoted to the Lord. She later had a child, named him Samuel, and eventually sent him to Eli to serve at the temple.

The story is rather similar to that told of Samson and it may be that the story here has been, rather unaptly, cast back into the Book of Judges in order to explain Samson's long hair in a non-mythological fashion.

Aphek

In the interval since the Israelites had entered Canaan, matters had settled down in some ways. The Canaanites in the north had been crushed in the battle against Sisera. The various competing peoples across the Jordan—the Moabites, Ammonites, Midianites, and Amalekites—had been held off and beaten back through the activity of men such as Ehud, Gideon, and Jephthah.

But that left the Philistines, the most technologically advanced, best organized, and hence most dangerous of the early enemies of Israel. They were strong in the north, controlled the coastal area completely, and were dominant over the territory of Judah in the southern portion of Israel. This is indicated by the statement of the men of Judah who came to bind Samson and deliver him to the Philistines:

Judges 15:11. . . . [The] *men of Judah . . . said to Samson, Knowest thou not that the Philistines are rulers over us?*

The core of Israelite resistance to the Philistines was the centrally located Rachel tribes, headed by Ephraim. These had been weakened in the war against the Trans-Jordanian tribes under Jephthah, so it was a good time for the Philistines to make their advance, and the scene was set for a great, perhaps a climactic battle:

1 Samuel 4:1. . . . *Now Israel went out against the Philistines to battle, . . . and the Philistines pitched in Aphek.*

The site of Aphek is not certain, but there seems reason to think that the later town of Antipatris (mentioned in the New Testament) was built on its site. Aphek was, in that case, at the western edge of Ephraimite territory (perhaps five miles north of Samuel's home town of Ramathaim) and at the northern edge of Philistine territory (about twenty miles north of Ekron, the most northerly member of the Philistine federation).

After a preliminary defeat, the Israelites thought to alter matters by bringing the ark of the covenant into the camp, in the belief that the physical presence of God would ensure victory. The Philistines

themselves accepted the validity of this view and are pictured as in
deep consternation over the effect of the presence of the God of the
Israelites. They nerved themselves to a desperate fight.

In a great battle, the Israelites were totally defeated; the two sons
of Eli, who were with the army, were slain, and the ark of the covenant was taken. At hearing the news, the old High Priest, Eli, died
of shock.

This battle, which may have taken place about 1080 B.C., marks
the end of Shiloh as a religious center, less than a century after
Joshua had established it as such by moving his headquarters there.
Its actual fate is not described in the Bible. Because of the eventual
overriding concern with Jerusalem as *the* religious center of the nation,
references to earlier shrines are reduced to a minimum.

Still there are hints, as when the prophet Jeremiah threatens the
king of Judah with destruction, quoting God's words as:

> Jeremiah 26:6. *Then will I make this house like Shiloh . . .*

It seems very likely that in the aftermath of the battle, the Philistines plundered deep into Israelite territory, destroying Shiloh. For
a period of about half a century thereafter, Philistine domination extended, more or less loosely, over all of Canaan. The period from 1080
to 1030 B.C. may be taken as the peak of Philistine power.

Kirjath-jearim

Although Shiloh was gone, the ark of the covenant remained, al-
beit in enemy hands. The Biblical writers could not allow themselves
to lose sight of the ark (which was eventually to grace the Temple
at Jerusalem) and they devote two chapters to tracing its progress
through Philistine territory.

The Philistines, who thoroughly accepted the ark as representing
the physical presence of an enemy God, were in awe of it, and quite
ready to see in any misfortune that befell themselves the angry work
of that God. Ashdod, where the ark was first placed, experienced
misfortunes, passed it on to Gath, which suffered equally, and passed
it on to Ekron. The Ekronites indignantly refused it.

It was decided, therefore, after the ark had remained among the

Kirjath-jearim

Philistine cities for some seven months, to send the dangerous object into the interior so that distance might lend security. The ark left Philistia proper and passed into the land of Judah, which was then under tight Philistine control.

The first stopping place was Beth-shemesh (see page 250), which also suffered misfortunes, and the ark was sent still further on to a place where it was to remain for several decades:

> 1 Samuel 7:1. *And the men of Kirjath-jearim came, and fetched up the ark of the Lord . . .*
>
> 1 Samuel 7:2. *And . . . while the ark abode in Kirjath-jearim . . . the time was long . . . and . . . Israel lamented after the Lord.*

Kirjath-jearim is usually identified with a site about ten miles northwest of Jerusalem. It was at the extreme edge of the area directly controlled by the Philistines. In other words, it was as far distant as they could manage from their own population centers and yet not so far distant that the Ephraimites could repossess it. In point of fact, the Ephraimites never did. When the ark once more became the object of a centralized worship, it was the men of Judah who obtained it.

Mizpeh

What resistance the Rachel tribes could offer after the disaster at Aphek centered about the person of Samuel. His association, as a child, with the destroyed shrine at Shiloh gave him standing in later years as a priest, and he did not flinch in the emergency:

1 Samuel 7:5. *And Samuel said, Gather all Israel to Mizpeh.*

This is the Mizpeh referred to in connection with the aftermath of the outrage of Gibeah (see page 257). Its use in the Book of Judges, in what may have been a fictional account, was probably drawn from the more historic association with Samuel and its use as a rallying point for what forces could be gathered from among the shattered Israelites. The modern site of Mizpeh is occupied by a village known to the Arabs as Nebi Samwel ("the prophet Samuel"), and it is there that the traditional site of his grave is located.

The Bible goes on to make it appear that the Philistines were massively defeated under Samuel, but this is doubtful. If it were so, the desperate battle of Saul against the Philistines in succeeding years would be difficult to explain. More likely, the anti-monarchic bias of some of the priestly records incorporated into 1 Samuel (as in Judges) is evident here and the feats of Saul and David are pushed backward in time and given to Samuel the priest. Samuel's position is perhaps more accurately presented in the picture of the geographical extent of Samuel's power:

1 Samuel 7:16. *And he* [Samuel] *went from year to year in circuit to Bethel, and Gilgal, and Mizpeh, and judged Israel in all those places.*

Gilgal is not the town mentioned earlier in connection with the advance of Joshua across the Jordan (see page 211) but is thought to be another of the same name located about midway between Samuel's home town Ramah (Ramathaim-zophim) and the destroyed Shiloh. Bethel is ten miles south of Gilgal and Mizpeh is about eight miles southwest of Bethel.

The picture one gets, then, is that of a twenty-mile strip of hill country in Ephraim and Benjamin, resolutely maintaining the apparently lost cause of Israel, and engaged in a more or less successful guerrilla war against the Philistines.

Saul

Whatever successes Samuel was able to achieve served only to keep in being a rather unsatisfactory state of affairs. Samuel kept matters from growing worse, but there seemed to be no signs that they would grow better. The Philistines had to be beaten and not merely held off. For this reason, particularly after Samuel had grown old, the clamor grew among the Israelites for a king. A half century had passed since the disaster at Aphek and it was time.

Samuel is pictured as warning the people against a monarchy, describing the burdens that would be placed upon them by a king. Here, once again, the anti-monarchism of the priestly historian shows itself. But whether Samuel objected or not, he set about searching for a suitable candidate for the kingship. This he found in the form of a young Benjamite:

1 Samuel 9:1. *Now there was a man of Benjamin, whose name was Kish . . .*
1 Samuel 9:2. *And he had a son, whose name was Saul, a choice young man, and a goodly . . .*

Saul, apparently, had been kept aloof from the problems of the day, and was not involved in the guerrilla fighting against the Philistines for, as it turned out, he did not even know of Samuel. (This seems puzzling, but perhaps the matter is not as strange as it appears. A guerrilla leader can scarcely find it safe to publicize himself too much. He is most secure and his operations most successful if he remains out of the limelight.)

Saul's encounter with Samuel came when he was trekking through the hills in search of three asses his father had lost. They passed near Samuel's station of the moment and Saul's servant, who had heard of Samuel, but only as a kind of magician, urged that they avail themselves of his services. For a piece of silver, Samuel might consent to do the equivalent of looking into a crystal ball and locating the asses.

Samuel, however, had his mind on something far more important. On seeing Saul he had the inspiration of making him king. Saul is described as extremely tall and good-looking and it might have occurred to Samuel that such a man would look every inch the king and by his appearance alone rally the people about him. Samuel may have thought further that it would not be difficult to dominate the young man and remain at his side as the all-powerful prime minister. He therefore anointed Saul as king:

> 1 Samuel 10:1. *Then Samuel took a vial of oil, and poured it upon his* [Saul's] *head, and kissed him, and said* . . . *the Lord hath anointed thee* . . .

The act of anointing probably originated as an act of cleansing. In the days before soap, scented oils would serve to remove grime and leave a pleasant fragrance behind. One would naturally anoint one's self when about to go before a superior; how much more so when about to go before God.

Therefore, when something was to be dedicated to God or presented before Him, the act of anointing was usually involved and it became symbolic of a divine grace being conferred upon the object or person anointed.

Thus, when Jacob dreamed of the ladder in Bethel, he took the stone he had rested his head upon, set it up as a pillar:

> Genesis 28:18. . . . *and poured oil upon the top of it.*

Again, when Aaron was formally made High Priest by Moses:

> Leviticus 8:12. *And he* [Moses] *poured of the anointing oil upon Aaron's head, and anointed him, to sanctify him.*

Now the device was used by Samuel to imply the special spiritual character of the kingship. Indeed, it came to be accepted that no one was really a king until he had gone through the careful ritual of anointing, so that the phrase "the anointed one" came to be synonymous with "the king."

Samuel next called a council at Mizpeh and carefully arranged matters so that Saul was chosen by lot, making use, presumably, of the Urim and Thummim (see page 150). Saul, who had already been secretly anointed, was now proclaimed king openly by the shouts of the representatives gathered at the council. This is believed to have taken place in 1028 B.C.

Jabesh-gilead

It was one thing to demand a king and quite another to rally round a particular individual chosen as king. To take up arms against

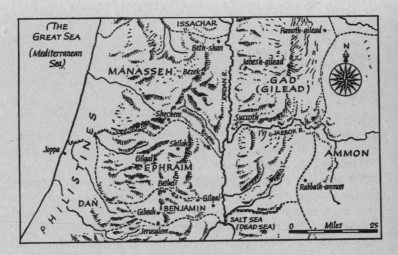

Jabesh-gilead

the Philistines was a serious thing and it required an experienced and able general. Saul was not yet tested in this respect.

1 Samuel 10:27. *But the children of Belial said, How shall this man save us? And they despised him* . . .

The test came soon enough:

1 Samuel 11:1. *Then Nahash the Ammonite came up and encamped against Jabesh-gilead* . . .

Jabesh-gilead, six miles east of the central Jordan, was, like all the Trans-Jordan, subjected to periodic Ammonite raids from the east. The greatest crisis had come in the time of Jephthah, but the great Ammonite defeat then had merely abated the danger. It had not ended it.

Jabesh-gilead, expecting no help from an Israel which was treading softly in the shadow of the Philistine power, made ready to surrender, but the terms of Nahash were brutal and sadistic—he insisted that the population of the city submit to having each their right eye put out. The people of Jabesh-gilead asked for a seven-day period of grace before submitting even to this and sent, in desperation, for a help they still dared not expect.

1 Samuel 11:4. *Then came the messengers to Gibeah of Saul, and told the tidings . . .*

Saul, however, rose to the occasion, sounding the call to arms and rallying an army behind him.

1 Samuel 11:7. *. . . And . . . the people . . . came out with one consent.*

1 Samuel 11:8. *And . . . he numbered them in Bezek . . .*

Bezek is in the hills of Manasseh, five miles north of Thebez, where Abimelech died (see page 245). It was due west of where Jabesh-gilead lay on the other side of the Jordan.

The numbers given of the troops that gathered on that occasion represent a late tradition and are impossibly high (300,000 men of Israel and 30,000 men of Judah) and anachronistically assume a divided kingdom, something that lay a century in the future. In actuality, Saul probably was able to gather merely the men from the areas of the Rachel tribes, and obtained a much smaller number—but enough to do the job. He marched across the Jordan and defeated the Ammonites. Jabesh-gilead was saved.

The enthusiasm of Israel for Saul was now great indeed. A general to lead Israel against the Philistines had been found. Saul was crowned king a second time at Gilgal, amid wild celebration.

(Of course, this double crowning of Saul may well represent the imperfect fusion of two traditions. The first would be a priestly anti-monarchic tradition in which the great judge of Israel, Samuel, anoints and crowns an unknown, bashful youth. The second would be a Benjamite tradition in which a tribal hero, Saul, accomplishes a great feat of arms and is acclaimed king in a triumph with which Samuel had nothing to do. The story of Samuel himself may represent a similar fusion of two traditions; one in which he is the warlike judge who rules all Israel and one in which he is an obscure seer with no more than a local reputation.)

Notice that Saul established his capital at Gibeah in Benjamin: the town of the "outrage." The Bible has occasion to tell later of the gratitude of the people of Jabesh-gilead to Saul. The Jabeshites remained loyal, in fact, when Saul and his house had sunk low in defeat.

Now the spirit of loyalty between two regions—in disaster as well as in prosperity—always strikes a romantic note in history if only because such disinterest on a regional scale is hard to find. In Greek history there is the friendship of Plataea and Athens, a friendship in which Plataea persevered to the death, for instance.

It was perhaps this well-known and romantic relationship between Gibeah of Saul and Jabesh-gilead that was in the mind of the writer of the possibly fictional tale of the consequences of the outrage at Gibeah. In that tale, Jabesh-gilead is pictured as the one Israelite town refusing to fight against Gibeah and as being destroyed in consequence.

Jonathan

With the Rachel tribes under a war hero, intensified conflict with the Philistines is inevitable; and at this point, Saul's son Jonathan is suddenly introduced:

1 Samuel 13:1. *Saul reigned one year; and when he had reigned two years over Israel,*

1 Samuel 13:2. *Saul chose him three thousand men of Israel, whereof two thousand were with Saul . . . and a thousand were with Jonathan . . .*

When Saul was introduced in the tale of his search for his father's asses, he was described as a young man, and yet he might even so have been a father of little children. To suppose, however, that two years after his anointing he is the father of a grown man capable of conducting men in war is difficult. The problem here rests with 1 Samuel 13:1, which is not actually a translation of the Hebrew but merely an attempt to make sense out of the original words. Literally translated, the Hebrew clause that begins the verse reads: "Saul was one year old when he began to reign."

It seems that something has been lost and the Revised Standard

Version has the verse read "Saul was . . . years old when he began to reign; and he reigned . . . and two years over Israel." It explains in a footnote that the gaps represent missing material.

It may well be that 1 Samuel 13:1 is actually a summarizing chronological verse that might say, for instance, "Saul was twenty-five years old when he began to reign; and he reigned twenty-two years over Israel." Saul himself probably didn't reign that long but the house of Saul, that is, he himself and one of his sons, reigned together that long.

In that case, we needn't suppose that the introduction of Jonathan comes two years after the start of Saul's reign. It might have come at any time; well toward the end of it, perhaps. Jonathan might therefore have been a boy at the time his father became king and a warlike young man at the time of the events in this chapter and the next.

As to what happened in the interval after the victory at Jabesh-gilead had settled Saul on the throne, we can easily suppose that the time was filled with a slow strengthening of Saul's kingdom. Quite obviously, Saul was starting from scratch:

> 1 Samuel 13:19. *Now there was no smith found throughout all the land of Israel: for the Philistines said, Lest the Hebrews make them swords or spears:*

The ill-armed Israelites might skulk in their fastnesses and emerge for hit-and-run raids but if Saul was to lead them into pitched battle they would simply have to be well armed. Undoubtedly, it took time to get the arms, capture them, buy them, or, perhaps, develop the skills necessary to make them. This dull interval of slow strengthening is slurred over in the Bible.

Michmash

Jonathan launched an attack:

> 1 Samuel 13:3. *And Jonathan smote the garrison of the Philistines that was in Geba . . .*
>
> . . . .
>
> 1 Samuel 13:5. *And the Philistines gathered themselves together to fight with Israel . . . and pitched in Michmash . . .*

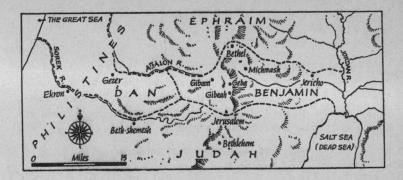

Michmash

The Philistine outpost of Geba may really refer to the much larger and more important town of Gibeon, five miles west of Saul's capital, Gibeah. (Gibeon is the town that once deceived Joshua at the time of the conquest—see page 215.)

The Philistines, reacting to this provocation, advanced on Geba at once and reached Michmash, two miles northeast of Geba. (The town still exists and is known to the Arabs as Mukhmas.) The Israelite population scattered and hid before the advancing Philistines and Saul held back his small army and refused to give battle. Jonathan, however, conducted another raiding party against the Philistines, guiding his men over the hills to attack the Philistine camp from an unexpected quarter. The Philistines, keyed up for an Israelite onslaught, mistook the relatively small attacking party for the main force of the enemy, and in a moment of panic, fled.

Jonathan had acted without orders and, indeed, probably against orders. Saul was angered, therefore, and undoubtedly jealous at the vast acclaim that greeted his son, and ordered Jonathan's execution. (The Bible advances a ritualistic explanation for the order.) The army refused to permit the execution, however, and a certain coldness must have remained thereafter between father and son. (It is not uncommon in monarchies, down to modern times, for rivalry and even hatred to exist between the king and the heir apparent.)

The Philistine defeat at Michmash was important. The Philistines temporarily fell back to their coastal and southern strongholds and Saul was given greater room for maneuver.

Agag

With the respite from the Philistine menace, Saul was able to turn southward to secure the desert border and lay the groundwork for a possible outflanking maneuver against the Philistine coast. The chosen target was the Amalekites, with whom the Israelites are described as having a traditional enmity dating back to the time of Moses.

> 1 Samuel 15:7. *And Saul smote the Amalekites* . . .
> 1 Samuel 15:8. *And he took Agag the king of the Amalekites alive* . . .

Agag, the ruler of a petty Amalekite tribe, cannot have been particularly powerful or renowned, and would not be considered so were it not for a remark in one of Balaam's blessings (see page 186). Speaking of Israel's future, Balaam says:

> Numbers 24:7. . . . *his king shall be higher than Agag* . . .

as though Agag were a standard symbol of great power.

Most scholars agree that the mention of Agag in this verse is a copyist's error. The name may originally have been Og. This would make sense, for the story of Balaam is placed at a time when Og of Bashan had been the mightiest monarch yet faced by the Israelites (see page 182). To say that the future king of Israel would be greater than Og would have been appropriate to the occasion, and the accidental change of Og to Agag is not a difficult one to imagine.

The Prophets

And yet while Saul was establishing and securing his kingdom, there were internal frictions. Saul the king and Samuel the kingmaker were at odds.

From the start, Samuel had kept his hand on the wheel of state for at the very time of Saul's anointing we hear for the first time of bands of prophets. When Saul was returning home from his encounter with Samuel:

> 1 Samuel 10:10. . . . *behold, a company of prophets met him* . . .

These prophets were groups of men who devoted themselves to ecstatic devotions. They would play instruments, sing, dance, put themselves into wild trances, and fall down in frenzy. They rather resembled certain orders of dervishes of later Islamic times, and if the word were here given as "dervishes" rather than "prophets," the picture would be clearer.

In their trances and ecstasies, these prophets or dervishes were believed to be divinely possessed, to have access to more than human knowledge, to be able to pronounce oracles, and so on. The very word "prophet" is from Greek words meaning "to speak forth"; that is, to relate and interpret the will of God as made manifest to the prophet during his trance or ecstasy.

In the time of Saul, the companies of prophets were by no means completely edifying. They may, indeed, have been hang-overs of paganism. Samuel, as the spiritual leader of the time, seems to have attempted to guide their energies into the path of Yahvism, but it is difficult to say how much success he might have had.

Yet the prophets were an excellent tool. They had the capacity to stir and influence the people and they tended to be strongly nationalistic, ready always to serve as the backbone of resistance against foreign oppression. Samuel, as their head, could direct them to meet and join Saul. It was the support of the bands of prophets that was Samuel's practical contribution to the establishment of Saul's kingship:

> 1 Samuel 10:26. *And Saul . . . went home to Gibeah; and there went with him a band of men, whose hearts God had touched . . .*

Undoubtedly, Samuel maintained his grip on Saul through the prophetic bands and yet Saul, after his victory at Jabesh-gilead, must have been increasingly irked at prophetic interference in his policies and must have attempted on several occasions to establish his independence.

The crisis came over the battle with the Amalekites. In rousing the people against the tribesmen, Samuel demanded that the Amalekites be exterminated entirely; a kind of "destroy the infidel" outlook. Saul, more humane or more practical, took Agag alive and kept the herds and other spoil from useless destruction. Samuel was enraged at this, executed Agag with his own hands, and told Saul:

1 Samuel 15:23. . . . *Because thou hast rejected the word of the Lord, he hath also rejected thee from being king.*

Bethlehem

Samuel, having moved into the opposition, needed someone to put up against Saul, and turned to the tribe of Judah:

1 Samuel 16:4. *And Samuel . . . came to Bethlehem . . .*

Prior to the time of Saul, the tribe of Judah is almost ignored in the Bible; so much so that there is strong suspicion that Judah was not considered part of Israel up to that time.

In the Book of Judges, Caleb and Othniel appear early as conquerors of southern Canaan, where later the tribe of Judah was to be. They are not Israelites, however, but members of Edomite clans. The tribe is not mentioned in the Song of Deborah, or in the course of the warlike deeds of Gideon or Jephthah.

In connection with the adventures of Samson, Judah's role is a completely inglorious one. Judah is subject to the Philistines and makes no move to throw off the yoke. Instead, to avoid trouble, the men of Judah hand Samson over to the Philistines.

Judah is mentioned in connection with Saul's battle at Jabesh-gilead, and is said to have supplied 10 per cent of the army. This, however, may be a later and non-historical addition, intended to show Judah as being involved in the national revival.

However, Saul in fighting the Amalekites, who inhabited the desert south of Judah, would have had to pass through Judah. It may be, then, that one of the consequences of the Philistine defeat at Michmash was the revolt of parts of Judah against the Philistines and their formation of an alliance with Saul.

And yet Judah's allegiance to Saul would have to be relatively weak. To the men of Judah, Saul would be a foreigner, and a Judean would therefore be more likely to be a suitable instrument for Samuel than would a member of the northern tribes who were becoming increasingly loyal to their hard-working, if not quite brilliant, king.

Then, too, Judah throughout its history was more strongly Yahvistic than the remainder of Israel was. The populous cities of the Canaanites had been in central and northern Canaan and it was there that the religious influence of the Canaanites had more successfully diluted the simpler desert rituals of Yahvism. Judah, closer always to the desert, might be more influenced by Samuel's Yahvistic point of view.

(It is interesting to compare Judah with Macedon. In ancient Greece, Macedon was a border area, Greek in culture and language but rather more primitive, and looked upon as semibarbaric by the Greeks themselves. At the time the Greeks were fighting their national war against Persia, Macedon remained under Persian domination, but the time was to come when Macedon defeated Persia more thoroughly than Greece ever did, and was to rule, briefly, over all of Greece.

In the same way, Judah was a border area of Israel, Israelite in culture and language but rather more primitive and looked upon, in all probability, as semi-Canaanite by the Israelites themselves. At the time the Israelites were fighting their national war against the great Philistine enemy, Judah remained under Philistine domination, but the time was to come when Judah defeated the Philistines more thoroughly than Israel ever did, and was to rule, briefly, over all of Israel.)

David

In Bethlehem, Samuel visited Jesse, the grandson of Boaz and Ruth (see page 264) and a man of wealth and substance. An appropriate member of his family would command widespread support throughout Judah. Jesse had eight sons and Samuel was most impressed with the youngest, David:

> 1 Samuel 16:12. . . . *he was ruddy, . . . and goodly to look to* . . .

> 1 Samuel 16:13: *The Samuel took the horn of oil and anointed him in the midst of his brethren* . . .

Once again, Samuel had chosen a handsome young man to make into a king.

Meanwhile, Saul, knowing that Samuel and the prophets had turned against him, and suspecting they would rouse rebellion, had grown, rather understandably, moody and suspicious. The courtiers suggested music as therapy and one of them (it is very tempting to suspect he was in Samuel's pay) suggested that a certain David, whom he praised as a skilled harpist, be brought to court.

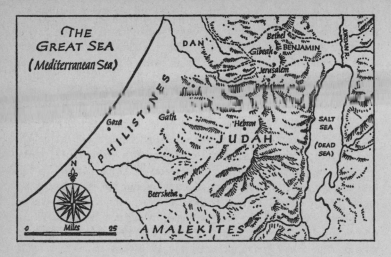

Judah in David's Time

1 Samuel 16:21. *And David came to Saul, . . . and he became his armourbearer.*

. . . .

1 Samuel 16:23. *And . . . when the evil spirit . . . was upon Saul, . . . David took an harp, and played . . . so Saul was refreshed and was well . . .*

With David at court, gaining the confidence of Saul, and serving his apprenticeship in war under him, Samuel's plan was working well.

Goliath

There follows a second tale describing the introduction of David to Saul's court, one that is inconsistent with the first. Both are included, without any attempt to enforce consistency, as though the Biblical writers were saying, "On the other hand, some say this . . ."

The second tale begins with a confrontation between the Philistines and the Israelites:

1 Samuel 17:1. *Now the Philistines gathered together their armies to battle . . . at Shocoh . . .*

Shocoh is a town in Judah, about thirteen miles west of Bethlehem. If it is correct to assume that Saul's battle against the Amalekites was made possible by his alliance with a Judah that was rebelling against the Philistines, then it is reasonable to suppose that the Philistines would strive to restore Judah to the yoke by force, and that Saul's troops would be sent south to support the new ally.

At Shocoh, the armies faced each other in stalemate, each waiting for some favorable moment or condition to attack and, during the wait, a man of Gath challenged any member of the Israelite army to single combat, suggesting that victory for the entire army rest with the winner of the duel. He is described as a giant:

> 1 Samuel 17:4. . . . *Goliath of Gath, whose height was six cubits and a span.*

Accepting the cubit as roughly seventeen inches, and the span as nine inches, that would make his height just over nine feet. (The dramatic nature of this story, by the way, has so impressed later generations that "Goliath" has entered the English language as a term used for anything of monstrous size.)

Jesse's three oldest sons were serving with the army, and Jesse sent his youngest son, David, with supplies for his soldier brothers. The youngster heard the challenge and was indignant that it remained unaccepted. David offered to fight Goliath and faced him, unarmored, bearing only a sling. With a smooth stone, whirled speedily from the sling and aimed unerringly, he killed the giant and the Philistines fled.

This is one of the most famous stories in the Bible, so much so that any unequally matched contest is considered a "David-and-Goliath battle."

But the very drama of the story makes it suspect. In any real battle, would either army risk the outcome on a single combat? The circumstances surrounding the fight seem to be the deliberate creation of a skilled writer, intended to produce a profound emotional effect. Goliath's height and armor are stressed and exaggerated, as is David's youth and unarmed courage.

Then, after the battle, it turns out that neither Saul nor his general know the lad, and that it is only through his great fame as the slayer of Goliath that David gains entry into the court. This is a direct contradiction to the more believable story in the previous chapter.

Actually, the Bible contains a hint as to how the story of David and Goliath may have come to be written. Later, when the Bible lists some of the important warriors fighting in David's armies and tells of their feats of arms, we find:

> 2 Samuel 21:19. . . . *Elhanan . . . a Bethlehemite, slew the brother of Goliath the Gittite . . .*

Since "Gittite" means "a man of Gath" the verse seems clear. Goliath had a brother and he, too, was killed by a native of Bethlehem. But the phrase "the brother of" was added by the translators of the King James Version, who followed a similar verse in another book of the Bible.

In the Book of 1 Chronicles, which retells the history given in the Books of 1 Samuel and 2 Samuel, but which was written some centuries later, we have:

> 1 Chronicles 20:5. . . . *and Elhanan . . . slew Lahmi the brother of Goliath the Gittite . . .*

Lahmi is not mentioned elsewhere in the Bible and it is at least possible that it is an accidental spelling of "Bethlehemite." The writer of this verse may have assumed that to leave out the phrase "the brother of" would make the verse inconsistent with the well-known story that David killed Goliath, so he put it in. The translators of the King James Version followed suit in the original verse in 2 Samuel.

Nevertheless, there is no certainty that anything dropped out of the verse in 2 Samuel, and the Revised Standard Version gives 2 Samuel 21:19 as simply: ". . . Elhanan . . . the Bethlehemite, slew Goliath the Gittite . . ."

It might be, then, that the otherwise unknown Elhanan killed Goliath in the course of some battle and that a panegyricist in later years wrote a little historical tale filled with romantic and edifying detail, in which he ascribed the feat to Israel's great hero-king. Like the story of George Washington and the cherry tree, it caught on and came to be accepted as history. The telltale verse in 2 Samuel remained, however, and had to be patched up in 1 Chronicles—and in the King James translation.

David and Jonathan

In whatever fashion David came to court, whether as a harpist or as a war hero, he met Jonathan the heir apparent there:

1 Samuel 18:1. . . . *the soul of Jonathan was knit with the soul of David, and Jonathan loved him as his own soul.*

The intensity and disinterest of this friendship is such that the phrase "David and Jonathan" has become a byword for deep friendship, like the equivalent "Damon and Pythias" drawn from Greek history.

The Bible takes pains to show David innocent of all wrongdoing with respect to Saul, but even accepting the Biblical account, one wonders if the innocence was complete. David had been anointed by Samuel and therefore knew he was king, in the eyes of the priestly faction at least. How innocent toward Saul could he be?

Saul himself could eye David only with deep suspicion as time went on and as David's charm and his skill in war gained popularity for him. Even leaving the anointing episode to one side, we must remember that a popular general is always dangerous to a king.

Furthermore, Saul was probably suspicious of his own son as an aftermath of the battle of Michmash. To watch the popular heir apparent join forces with the popular general could lead to only one thought in the mind of any prudent king—they were plotting a coup.

1 Samuel 18:9. *And Saul eyed David from that day and forward.*

Nob

David could not remain unaware of the gathering coldness of the suspicious Saul and when Jonathan warned him of the danger to his life, David left court and joined those he felt to be sympathetic toward him:

1 Samuel 19:18. *So David fled, and escaped and came to Samuel to Ramah . . .*

If anything was needed to convict David in Saul's eyes, this was it, of course. Saul sent an armed contingent to take David, who eventually eluded them.

1 Samuel 21:1. *Then came David to Nob to Ahimelech the priest . . .*

The actual location of Nob is uncertain. The best Biblical evidence for that location comes from the Book of Isaiah. The prophet is describing the advance of the Assyrian army against Jerusalem and the climax comes:

Isaiah 10:32. *As yet shall he* [Assyria] *remain at Nob that day: he shall shake his hand against . . . Jerusalem.*

Since the Assyrian is advancing from the north that would make it seem as though Nob were on a height not far from Jerusalem in that direction, and in fact its site is traditionally identified with a hill in Benjamite territory two miles north of that city.

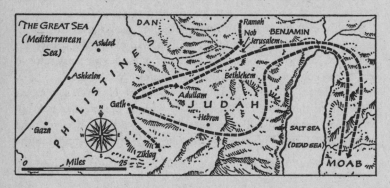

The City of Nob: Dashed line indicates David's flight

David must logically have been striving to reach the safety of Judah where his fellow tribesmen might rally round him. Saul must, equally logically, have foreseen this and kept men watching the routes toward Judah. David's doubling back into Benjamite territory and getting help under the nose of the king succeeded through its unexpectedness.

Nob seems to have represented the remnant of the old Shiloh-worship. Ahimelech is described as the son of a man who is elsewhere described as the grandson of Eli, the last High Priest at Shiloh, and it may have been to Nob that the survivors of the Philistine sack of the earlier holy city had fled.

Saul, angered at David's having eluded him, breaks out into reproaches against his courtiers, accusing all of them of conspiracy and making it quite clear he considers David merely a tool of Jonathan:

> 1 Samuel 22:8. . . . *my son hath made a league with the son of Jesse . . . my son hath stirred up my servant . . .*

One of the men about him, Doeg (identified as an Edomite), had seen David in Nob and so informed Saul. The furious king jumped at once to the conclusion that the priests were conspiring with David (although the Biblical version shows Ahimelech to have helped David under the impression that David was on state business for the king). Saul had felt it impolitic to move directly against the influential Samuel, but the relatively weak contingent of prophets and priests under Ahimelech seemed fair game.

Saul marched against Nob, took and destroyed the city, then ordered the eighty-five priests slaughtered. No Israelite dared perform the task, but Doeg the Edomite did it. One son of Ahimelech, Abiathar, escaped, however, and eventually joined David. He was the last survivor of the old line of Shiloh, the great-great-grandson of Eli.

Adullam

Meanwhile, David had finally made his way to Judah and was joined by members of his tribe:

> 1 Samuel 22:1. *David . . . escaped to the cave Adullam: and . . . all his father's house . . . went down thither to him.*
>
> 1 Samuel 22:2. *And every one that was in distress . . . in debt . . . discontented, gathered themselves unto him; . . . there were with him about four hundred men.*

Adullam is in the Judean hill country about fifteen miles from Bethlehem and only two miles southeast of the place where David is described as having killed Goliath. In that stronghold he fortified himself and became the leader of a guerrilla band. What followed was virtually war between David and Israel.

In this war, Israel was much the stronger and David survived only by skillful evasion tactics, moving from place to place and remaining always one step ahead of the vengeful and remorseless Saul. David fully realized that war as conducted in those days (and sometimes in our own) extended death to the families of the enemy, so he took his parents for safekeeping to Moab. (This tends to reflect the possibility that David was part Moabite by ancestry; see page 205.)

Ziklag

A number of tales are told of the futile hunt of Saul after David, and the Biblical writer takes obvious delight in the cleverness of David in eluding the pursuit.

Nevertheless, it seemed clear to David that he could not count on his luck holding forever. Sooner or later, a misstep would leave him surrounded by overwhelming forces. He decided, under this pressure, to join the Philistines as the only way of securing adequate protection:

> 1 Samuel 27:2. *And David . . . passed over with . . . six hundred men . . . unto Achish . . . king of Gath.*

Achish could only be pleased to take into his service a tried captain with a desperate band of men who could be viewed as deadly enemies of Saul. In a sense, Judah, having allied itself with Saul against the Philistines, was now allying itself with the Philistines against Saul.

Achish as part of the bargain gave David what would, in medieval times, have been called a fief of his own:

> 1 Samuel 27:6. *Then Achish gave him Ziklag that day . . .*

Ziklag was a city at the southern border of Judah, in what had once been counted as Simeonite territory, but which was now still under Philistine domination. Its exact site is unknown, but the best guess seems to be that it was about twenty miles southwest of Gath and a dozen miles from the sea.

David's role as a mercenary leader in the service of the Philistines was acutely embarrassing to the Biblical writers. They take pains to assure the reader that while Achish thought David was raiding Israelite outposts in Judah, David was *really* raiding the Amalekites and other nomad tribes of the desert. It seems unlikely that Achish could possibly have been fooled in this manner. It is reasonable to suppose, rather, that if David was serving as a mercenary, he did what he was hired to do.

It is interesting that in the course of his Philistine service, David is nowhere referred to by the Philistines as the slayer of Goliath. This is rather suggestive of the non-historical nature of that famous duel.

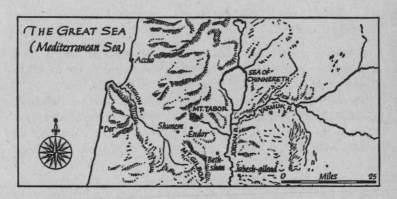

Mount Gilboa

Gilboa

The Philistines saw their chance now. Judah was alienated from Saul over the matter of David, and the priestly party had been offended past repair, thanks to the slaughter at Nob. The time was ideal for a renewed attack on Israel.

1 Samuel 28:4. *And the Philistines gathered themselves together, and came and pitched in Shunem; and Saul gathered all Israel together, and they pitched in Gilboa.*

Mount Gilboa, a mountain ridge about ten miles long, with its highest point about 1700 feet above sea level, is in northern Israel about seven miles west of the Jordan River, and some forty miles north of Gibeah.

Shunem, where the Philistines were encamped, lay some ten miles
to the northwest. It is only five miles south of Mount Tabor, where
Barak had once gathered the forces of northern Israel against Sisera.

Saul feared the worst and turned for advice to the priests. They
would not help him and Samuel, who might in this time of national
emergency have had the greatness to be reconciled, was recently dead
Saul, in desperation, sought out a practitioner of the older Canaanite
cults. Upon inquiring, he was told:

> 1 Samuel 28:7. . . . *Behold, there is a woman that hath a familiar
> spirit at En-dor.*

A familiar spirit is one who serves the human being calling upon
it (the Latin *famulus* means "servant"). Saul sought to obtain advice
from Samuel by having this spirit bring him from the dead.

This woman with the familiar spirit is the well-known "witch of
Endor." The town of Endor is about two miles from Shunem, midway
between the latter town and Mount Tabor. Its only importance in
history or in the Bible is its connection with the witch in this one
chapter.

To get to the witch of Endor, Saul had to disguise himself and
pass through the enemy lines. It served him nothing, however. The
witch's magical rites resulted in a prophecy of disaster (as was logical,
considering the obvious desperation and despair of Saul) and that
prophecy further intensified the despair. Saul and the Israelite army
was broken in morale before ever the fight began.

The Biblical narrator pauses here to explain in considerable detail
that David (Israel's national hero) did not take part in the disastrous
battle that followed. David offered to fight with the Philistine armies,
but the Philistine leaders would not have it. They feared that in the
heat of the battle, David might attempt to improve his own situation
by defecting to Saul. David was forced to return to Ziklag and there
he was soon fully engaged in reversing a temporary victory of the
Amalekites.

The Philistines then attacked the Israelite encampment on Gilboa
and won a complete victory. Jonathan was killed and Saul committed
suicide. The battle of Gilboa and the death of Saul are thought to
have taken place in 1013 B.C. Saul, therefore, had reigned fifteen
years.

Beth-shan

At one blow, all the hard-won gains of Saul were destroyed. The Philistines were again in control of virtually all Israelite territory west of the Jordan. The Rachel tribes, which had been the core of the national revival, were prostrate.

The extent of the Philistine victory is symbolized by the manner in which the victors displayed Saul's corpse as a means of expressing their contempt for the beaten king and destroying what remained of Israelite morale:

> 1 Samuel 31:10. . . . *and they* [the Philistines] *fastened his body to the wall of Beth-shan.*

Beth-shan was an important Canaanite center about six miles northeast of Mount Gilboa. It had been a Philistine outpost ever since the battle of Aphek and was probably the center of Philistine power in the regions to the north of the Rachel tribes; a power Saul had never been able to break. (It is very probable that Saul was never really king over more than the Rachel tribes of Benjamin, Ephraim, and Manasseh, at the most. To the north and west lay the Philistines, to the south Judah.)

But there was the east, too. The Trans-Jordanian tribes had been allied with Saul since the battle against the Ammonites at Jabesh-gilead. Jabesh-gilead, which lay about a dozen miles southeast of Beth-shan, remembered Saul's service to them particularly, and now repaid it in the only way they could. They mounted an attack against Beth-shan, rescued Saul's body, and buried it with all due honor.

And thus, with the death of Saul and with honor, at least, saved, though all else seemed lost, the Book of 1 Samuel comes to an end.

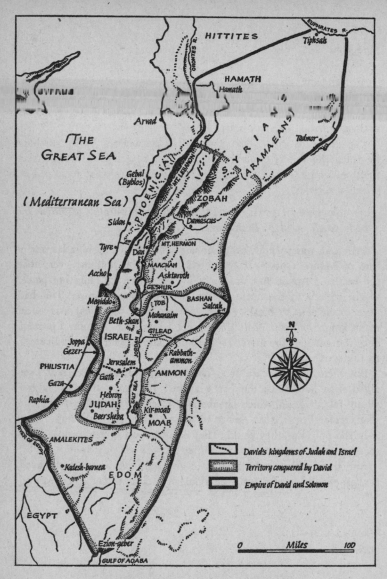

The following labels appear on the map:

HITTITES

EUPHRATES R.

Tiphsah

ORONTES R.

HAMATH
Hamath

Arvad

Tadmor

THE
GREAT SEA

S Y R I A N
(ARAMAEANS)

MT. LEBANON

Gebal
(Byblos)

PHOENICIA

ZOBAH

(Mediterranean Sea)

Sidon

Damascus

Tyre

Dan

MT. HERMON

Accho

MAACHAH

Ashtaroth

GESHUR

Megiddo

TOB

BASHAN
Salcah

Beth-shan

Mahanaim

JORDAN R.

ISRAEL

GILEAD

Joppa
Gezer

Rabbath-
ammon

PHILISTIA

Jerusalem

Gath

AMMON

Gaza

SALT SEA

Raphia

Hebron

JUDAH

Beersheba

Kir-moab

MOAB

RIVER OF EGYPT

AMALEKITES

Kadesh-barnea

EDOM

EGYPT

Ezion-geber

GULF OF AQABA

N

0   Miles   100

Legend:
David's kingdoms of Judah and Israel
Territory conquered by David
Empire of David and Solomon

The Empire of David and Solomon

10. 2 SAMUEL

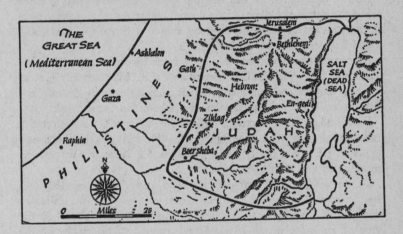

Hebron

Hebron

With the death of Saul and the smashing defeat of Israel, the
Philistines controlled all of Canaan west of the Jordan. There wasn't
even, for the moment, a nucleus of resistance in the hill country
of the Rachel tribes where, for so many years before the coming
of the monarchy, Samuel had kept alive the hopes of Israel.

There was David, to be sure, but he was a man of Judah who
had been leading a guerrilla war against Saul and the kingdom of

Israel, and was therefore not a man to whom patriotic Israelites could easily turn. Besides, at the moment of Saul's death, David was actually a Philistine vassal.

Yet it was not as a mere Philistine vassal that David viewed himself. His first step was to establish his clear leadership over Judah at least:

2 Samuel 2:3. And his men that were with him did David bring up . . . and they dwelt in the cities of Hebron.

2 Samuel 2:4. And the men of Judah came, and there they anointed David king over the house of Judah . . .

David reigned as king of Judah in Hebron from 1013 to 1006 B.C.

David's assumption of the kingship would not have been possible before the battle of Gilboa, for Saul would quite naturally have viewed an independent Judah under a strong king as a threat to himself and would have taken steps to crush David.

As it was, David was free not only from Israelite interference but even from Philistine hostility. Presumably the Philistines felt him to be a safe puppet and considered his kingship a device to distract and further divide the subject peoples over whom they now ruled.

David, however, in choosing Hebron for his capital had selected a well-fortified town in a thoroughly defensible hill area in the center of Judah. He would not be easily dislodged if it came to war between himself and the Philistines.

To prepare for that war—which David knew to be inevitable, if the Philistines did not—David set about winning over the followers of the dead Saul and the remnant of those who still cherished the hope of an independent Israel. David aspired to leadership of the Hebrew tribes generally.

Mahanaim

Yet the Israelite kingdom was not quite wiped out, either. Saul had had four sons. The three oldest had died at Gilboa:

1 Samuel 31:2. . . . and the Philistines slew Jonathan, and Abinadab, and Malchishua, Saul's sons.

but there remained the fourth son, Ish-bosheth. Abner, Saul's general in chief, who had survived the battle of Gilboa, fled with Ish-bosheth to safety across the Jordan:

THE
GREAT SEA
(Mediterranean Sea)

Tyre
Dan
PHOENICIA
MAACHAH
Accho
SEA OF
CHINNERETH
GESHUR
YARMUK R.
KISHON R.
TOB.
Edrei
Megiddo
Ramoth-gilead
BASHAN
Jabesh-gilead
Mahanaim
ISRAEL
Shechem
PHILISTINES
JABBOK R.
Joppa
Shiloh
AMMON
JORDAN R.
Jerusalem
Rabbath-
ammon
JUDAH
SALT SEA
(DEAD SEA)
0   Miles   25

Mahanaim

2 Samuel 2:8. . . . Abner . . . took Ish-bosheth the son of Saul, and brought him over to Mahanaim;
2 Samuel 2:9. And made him king . . .

The Trans-Jordanians might be expected to be fiercely loyal to the house of Saul in memory of that king's vigorous rescue of Jabesh-gilead. Since the Philistines apparently saw no profit to be gained by extending their lines of communication in a perilous advance across the Jordan (something that had once served to destroy Ephraim; see page 247), Ish-bosheth and Abner were momentarily safe.

The exact location of Mahanaim in the Trans-Jordan is not known. Some place it south of the Jabbok River and others north. One guess is that it was located at a point some four miles east of Jabesh-gilead.

Michal

David, the new king of Judah, began a course of difficult negotiation with Abner in an attempt to establish a united kingdom. Unfortunately, David's general in chief, Joab, was a war hawk who felt that only outright conquest was the course to pursue. He forced a war in which the Israelite army was defeated.

The weakening kingdom of Ish-bosheth held out, however, and David's purposes were blunted. He did not want to rule by right of conquest, with the certainty of rebellion afterward. He hoped, rather, for a legal accession to power in the hope of founding a permanently united kingdom.

Fortunately for David, Abner quarreled with Ish-bosheth and began to dicker with David behind his own monarch's back. David, sensing the coming of victory, set his price. In return for peace and, presumably, for a high post for Abner in the united kingdom, David said:

> 2 Samuel 3:13. . . . Thou shalt not see my face, except thou first bring Michal Saul's daughter . . .
> 2 Samuel 3:14. . . . which I espoused . . .

Michal had married David in the days when Saul was firm on his throne and David had served as a successful military leader under him. After David's flight from court, Michal had been given in marriage to someone else.

David's intent here is clear. As husband to Michal and son-in-law to the dead Saul, he would gain a kind of legal right to the succession to the throne of Israel. If, in particular, he were to have a son by Michal, that son would represent the fusion of the houses of Saul and of David and he could eventually be expected to reign over both kingdoms in peace and legality.

Michal was delivered to David by an Ish-bosheth too weak to dare refuse and Abner proceeded to make his alliance with David. The implacable Joab, however, sought out Abner and killed him. This threatened to upset the apple cart for Abner was highly regarded by the Israelites. David avoided disaster only by a public act of contrition.

Some at Ish-bosheth's court could now see the inevitable and two of the army leaders assassinated the king and brought his head to David. David quickly disassociated himself from this crime, too, executing the assassins.

But no grown son of Saul remained and the despairing Israelites could see that their only safety lay now in the hands of the shrewd king of Judah:

> 2 Samuel 5:3. *So all the elders of Israel came to the king to Hebron; and king David made a league with them . . . and they anointed David king over Israel.*

The united kingdom over which David thus came to rule in 1006 B.C. is called Israel in the Bible, but the kingdom was never really single. The two halves of the nation were never truly amalgamated. Israel remained conscious of its greater sophistication and wealth as compared to the rustic Judah and resented being governed by a dynasty of Judah. It might be best to consider David, and his son after him, to be kings of a dual monarchy, Israel-Judah.

Zion

Having achieved legal rule over Israel as well as Judah, David wanted to cement that rule in the will of the people generally. To gain that, David realized he would have to give up Hebron as his capital, for that city was far too closely identified with Judah. David could not afford to have himself considered nothing more than a man of Judah. Nor could he transfer his government into Israel itself, for if that gained the approval of the Israelites, it might lose him Judah, and Judah was the core of his strength.

But between the territory of Judah and Israel, and belonging to neither, was the city of Jerusalem. If that were David's capital it could satisfy both parts of the dual monarchy since it would represent a kind of neutral territory.

Furthermore, it was still occupied by a Canaanite tribe, the Jebusites, so that its existence represented an inconvenient barrier between the two halves of the kingdom, while its conquest would be a national victory hailed by both halves alike.

Finally, Jerusalem held an extremely strong position, as was evidenced by the fact that the Jebusites had kept their ground steadily

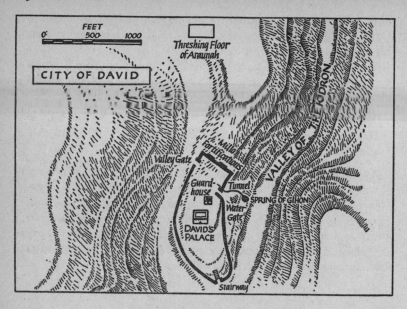

Zion and the City of David

against all efforts on the part of the Israelites to dislodge them. If David could take it, it would prove an equally sure stronghold for him.

For all these excellent reasons of state, Jerusalem was therefore placed under siege:

> 2 Samuel 5:6. *And the king and his men went to Jerusalem unto the Jebusites, the inhabitants of the land* . . .

The course of the siege is not clearly given in the following verses, but the outcome is certain. David won, and the magnitude of his victory raised his stature as a military leader in Israel as well as Judah, ensuring his kingship on a wave of national pride.

> 2 Samuel 5:7. . . . *David took the strong hold of Zion: the same is the city of David.*

Zion was the fortified height (about 2440 feet high) within the town—the place where the defenders could hold out longest. It was the equivalent of the Athenian Acropolis, for instance. When Zion was taken, Jerusalem was taken. Since it was upon Zion that David built his palace, it became the "city of David." Later, David's son, Solomon, was to build the Temple on Zion, so that the hill became the military, political, and religious center of Israel.

As such, it came to symbolize (especially in poetic language) all of Jerusalem, or even all of Israel. In the last century, the movement to restore a Jewish homeland in Palestine has been called "Zionism" as a result.

There seems no doubt that Zion in located in the southeastern portion of what is now called the "Old City" of Jerusalem. In Christian times, the tradition arose that Zion lay on a ridge about half a mile to the west, but this is no longer taken seriously.

The modern city of Jerusalem was divided between Jordan and Israel in 1948. All of the "Old City," which is on the site of ancient Jerusalem, including Zion, became part of Jordan then.

The "New City" built to the west of the "Old City" was begun in 1860 thanks to the money and drive of the British-Jewish philanthropist Sir Moses Haim Montefiore. It is now much larger than the "Old City," with a population three times as numerous. The "New City" serves as the capital of modern Israel, but it is the "Old City" that contains the holy relics of the past.

As a result of the Six-day War of 1967, Israel took all of Jerusalem and declared its determination never to yield any part of it again.

Tyre

The Israelites under David were still largely a pastoral and agricultural people. If David wanted to build an elaborate palace for himself on his new stronghold of Zion, he had to seek help among the relatively sophisticated inhabitants of the Canaanite cities.

2 Samuel 5:11. *And Hiram king of Tyre sent messengers to David, and cedar trees, and carpenters, and masons: and they built David an house.*

Tyre is a Phoenician city situated on the Mediterranean coast about twenty miles south of Zidon (Sidon). According to Herodotus, the Tyrians maintained that their city had been founded as far back as 2750 B.C., but undoubtedly local pride was imposing itself on the eager

Greek tourist. From mention (or lack of mention) in the old Egyptian records it would seem that Tyre was not founded until 1450 B.C. and in the beginning was a colony of the still older Zidon.

Originally, Tyre may have been located on the mainland, but its greatness came when it shifted to a rocky island offshore, making itself almost immune from conquest and, while its fleet remained in being, from enforced starvation. Indeed, its name ("Zor" in Hebrew) means "rock." Nowadays, the old rock upon which Tyre built its greatness has joined the mainland, thanks to the silting up of the sea between. The site is now a peninsula on the coast of modern Lebanon, and is occupied by a town, Souro, with a population of about eight thousand.

Tyre's merchants penetrated the western Mediterranean and even passed outward into the Atlantic Ocean. As a result of gaining a monopoly on trade with what was then the far west, Tyre grew rich and powerful. During the time of the judges, it had been Zidon that had been the most important of the Phoenician cities (see page 217), but sometime during the reign of Saul, Tyre began to move ahead. From then on, till the end of Phoenician history, Tyre remained the leading city of the region.

The first king of Tyre of whom there is a reliable record is Abibaal, who came to the throne about 1020 B.C., when Saul reigned in Israel. He remained on the throne through David's reign. His son, Hiram, was, in turn, a contemporary of David's son, Solomon. It was Hiram whose artisans built Solomon's Temple. The importance of Hiram's role in connection with this supremely important structure sent its shadow backward in time so that his artisans are reported as having built David's palace, too, though that was certainly built during the reign of Hiram's father.

Valley of Rephaim

By now it must have become clear to the Philistines that David had grown too strong to serve as a safe puppet. His accession to the kingship of Israel, over and above that of Judah, had undoubtedly taken place without Philistine permission and must automatically have meant a break with them:

2 Samuel 5:17. . . . *when the Philistines heard that they had anointed David king over Israel, all the Philistines came up to seek David . . .*

2 Samuel 5:18. . . . *and spread themselves in the valley of Rephaim.*

It would have been wise for the Philistines to have struck at once, but perhaps the various cities, never firmly united, could not bring themselves to act until David had captured Jerusalem and by then it was really too late.

The valley of Rephaim lies between Jerusalem and Bethlehem and very likely the Philistines placed Jerusalem under siege. That this is so appears from the further statement:

2 Samuel 5:16. . . . *David . . . went down to the hold.*

The hold (stronghold) is almost certainly Jerusalem and within that nearly impregnable fortress, David could allow the Philistines to blunt their armor uselessly while armies gathered elsewhere in Israel and he planned his counterattack.

In two separate battles, he defeated them handily. The erstwhile puppet had become a conqueror and the Philistines fell back upon their coastal cities. They were never again to control the interior and David had become undisputed master of the territory of the twelve tribes of Israel and Judah.

Baale

David realized that it was insufficient to have Jerusalem as the political center only of the dual monarchy. Among the differences separating Israel and Judah were variations in religious customs and traditions. It would be wise, therefore, to take measures to centralize and unify the religion of the new nation, focus it on Jerusalem, and build a bridge between the north and south in the form of a common ritual.

A marvelous opportunity presented itself in connection with the ark of the covenant, the central object of worship of the Rachel tribes in the days of the judges. It had been taken from Israel by the Philistines (see page 272) and ever since had been kept at the city of Kirjath-jearim on the northern boundaries of Judah, about ten miles west of Jerusalem. Why not bring it to Jerusalem, and establish it as a center of worship? The object was Israelite, the place was Judean, and both parts of the nation would be satisfied.

2 Samuel 6:2. *And David arose, and went with all the people . . . from Baale of Judah to bring up from thence the ark of God*

Baale (or Baale-judah) is used here as an alternate name for Kirjath-jearim.

Moab

Master in his own land, David's next step was to cast his eyes abroad for imperial conquests—the common attitude of rulers of the time (and of our time as well).

The conquest began with Moab, which he reduced to a tributary nation. Considering David's earlier friendly relations with the Moabites and his traditional descent from a Moabite woman (see page 265), we would be curious to know what caused the war, but the Bible gives no clue:

2 Samuel 8:2. *And he [David] smote Moab, and . . . the Moabites became David's servants and brought gifts.*

This event bears a relation to one of the oracles traditionally assigned to Balaam (see page 186). He had been hired by the king of Moab to curse Israel and it seemed ironically just to the Biblical writers that he was forced, in his trance, to curse Moab instead:

Numbers 24:17. *. . . there shall come a Star out of Jacob, and a Sceptre shall rise out of Israel, and shall smite the corners of Moab . . .*

This verse has been taken by many Christians to represent a Messianic prophecy, and to forecast the coming of Jesus and the defeat by him of idolatry and evil. It is for this reason that the words "Star" and "Sceptre" are capitalized in the King James Version (but not in the Revised Standard Version).

A more prosaic possibility is that the oracle (reduced to writing only in the time of the kingdoms) is a triumphantly nationalistic reference to David and his Moabite conquest.

Ammon

One by one the neighboring principalities fell before David, whose foreign wars were uniformly successful.

When a new king acceded to the throne of Ammon, David sent messages of congratulations as a routine courtesy. The new king, suspecting the messengers of intended espionage, treated them with scornful disrespect, shaving half their beards and cutting off parts of their garments. This amounted to a declaration of war.

David treated it as such and the Ammonites formed an alliance with the Aramaean (Syrian) cities to the north, who also viewed with alarm the sudden rise of the new kingdom of Israel-Judah.

2 Samuel 10:6. . . . *the children of Ammon sent and hired the Syrians of Beth-rehob, and the Syrians of Zoba . . .*

The Aramaeans had entered the area north of Israel (an area called Syria by the Greeks and retaining that name to this day) after the fall of the Hittite Empire, mingling, as they did so, with the remnants of the Hittite people. Their coming was part of the same restless movement that had brought the Philistines and the Hebrew tribes into Canaan.

The united forces were defeated by David and his general, Joab. The Ammonites and Syrians were both conquered, and the Edomites in the south as well, and by 980 B.C., David ruled an empire that stretched from the Red Sea to the upper Euphrates. It took up all the eastern border of the Mediterranean, except for part of the actual shore which remained in the possession of the Phoenician cities. These retained their independence but were careful to remain on friendly terms with David.

David's realm was not large as empires go, covering, at its peak, an area of only thirty thousand square miles—about the size of the state of Maine. It was feeble and small compared to the Egyptian and Hittite Empires that preceded it, or the Assyrian, Babylonian, and Persian Empires that were to succeed it. Indeed, it existed at all only because of the accident of history that placed David in the midst of a short and rare period when there happened to be no great empires in Asia.

Nevertheless, David's empire remained a period of glory for Israel, when compared with the centuries before and after, and was looked back upon with pride and nostalgia by all the later generations that followed David.

Mephibosheth

If David was extending his sway externally, he had to be at least equally careful and vigorous in establishing his power internally. He must have been perfectly aware that Israel was bound to remain restive under a Judean dynasty and that this restiveness might find a rallying point about someone of the old Israelite dynasty of Saul.

It was customary in ancient monarchies (and in some comparatively modern ones, too) to remove all remaining members of displaced dynasties for the sake of the security of the reigning king, or, if one wanted to express matters more idealistically, for the peace and good order of the realm.

To murder Saul's descendants in cold blood would have been bad politically, possibly provoking the civil war David was trying to prevent. The opportunity to do so safely eventually came, however:

2 Samuel 21:1. *Then there was a famine in the days of David three years, year after year . . .*

That was David's chance. In the general anxiety to end the famine, people would assent to actions that might otherwise be strongly disapproved—if those actions were taken as being designed to propitiate an angry Deity. The blame for the famine was therefore carefully placed by the priesthood:

2 Samuel 21:1. . . . . *It is for Saul, and for his bloody house, because he slew the Gibeonites.*

The occasion upon which Saul slew the Gibeonites is not specifically mentioned in the Bible. Such an action on the part of Saul was a serious violation of the treaty of peace between the Israelites and the Gibeonites, a peace which, according to tradition, had been made in the days of Joshua (see page 215). To the Gibeonites, such a violation would seem to have well deserved the anger of God.

It is also just barely possible that this is a reference to Saul's slaughter of the priests at Nob (see page 290). Abiathar had been the sole survivor of the massacre and now served as a high priestly official under David. His own rather understandable animus against the house of Saul would, in that case, have made him more than willing to co-operate with David in this respect.

For the official purpose of appeasing the Gibeonites, then, David hanged seven of the male descendants of Saul, including two sons (by a concubine) and five grandsons. The rains, of course, eventually came (they always do) and that seemed to justify the act. To inhibit the chance of second thoughts on the part of the Israelites once the famine was over, David labored to keep their good will by paying somber respects to those who had been executed, burying them with honor in their ancestral tomb, and transferring the bodies of Saul and Jonathan to that tomb also.

The male members of the house of Saul seemed done with, but David was not entirely certain:

2 Samuel 9:1. *And David said, Is there yet any that is left of the house of Saul, that I may shew him kindness . . .*

This verse appears in the Bible a dozen chapters before the execution of the seven descendants of Saul, so that the irony is lost. This event, however, must have come after the executions or David would not have been forced to search so hard for "any that is left of the house of Saul."

One member of that house remained. This was Mephibosheth, the son of Jonathan. He had been five years old at the time of Saul's final and fatal battle on Mount Gilboa. At the news that Saul and Jonathan were dead and the army lost, there was wild confusion in the palace at Gibeah. A nurse fled with Jonathan's youngster and dropped him. His legs were damaged and he was crippled for the rest of his life.

Mephibosheth was in hiding during David's reign (a course of action rendered prudent by the executions) but his whereabouts were betrayed to David, who found that he could not, in this case, readily solve matters by another execution. First, Mephibosheth was a son of Jonathan, with whom he had once sworn a compact of friendship. Then, to consider matters more practically, the young man was a cripple and not likely to attract the loyalty of a rebel force, seeing that he was in no position to lead an army.

And yet, David did not abandon caution entirely. He allowed Mephibosheth to live, but he kept him at court and under his eye:

2 Samuel 9:13. *So Mephibosheth dwelt in Jerusalem; for he did eat continually at the king's table* . . .

Uriah the Hittite

Another domestic affair related in detail was the manner in which David came to make an addition to his harem. The importance of this lay in the fact that it was a son of David by this new woman who eventually succeeded to the throne of Israel.

David first saw her bathing on the roof of her house. Much taken by her appearance, he sent to find out her identity and was told:

2 Samuel 11:3. . . . *Is not this Bathsheba, the daughter of Eliam, the wife of Uriah the Hittite?*

It had been two centuries, now, since the Hittite Empire had disappeared, but their culture lingered. They had been driven out of Asia Minor, a region in which the Phrygians were now dominant, but Hittite principalities had been established southward in what is now Syria. There, mingled with the Aramaeans, the Hittites maintained themselves for two more centuries until the entire region—Hittites, Aramaeans, Israelites together—went under the heel of the Assyrian Empire.

But we are still in David's reign. David, in his northward drive of conquest, had absorbed these Hittite city-states and it is not surprising that a number of their soldiers, including Uriah, had entered his service. From the fact that Uriah is a Hebrew name ("the Lord is light") it may well be that Uriah had sought preferment by adjusting his religious beliefs to those of the king and had changed his name to suit.

In any case, he received a poor reward. David appropriated Uriah's wife and then sent him out to battle (the war against the Ammonites was proceeding at the time) with instructions to Joab to arrange for Uriah's death. This was done.

Although the Biblical writers praise David all they can, they cannot praise this. David is blamed and denounced by Nathan, a religious leader of the time. The courage of the reproof and the manner in which David accepted that reproof is one of the more moving passages in the Bible. There are few enough occasions in history, both before David and since, when an absolute monarch bowed before someone who clearly set forth the difference between good and evil.

Absalom

David's cautious eye on the house of Saul kept matters safe in that direction, but when trouble came, it came from an unexpected quarter, the royal family itself.

Unfortunately, civil wars based on family rivalries were all too common in the ancient monarchies, and the reasons are not hard to find. Chiefly, they stemmed from the institution of polygamy, which was quite widespread at the time, even among the Israelites.

A harem served the king's pleasure and it was also a matter of status, for the power and glory of the king, and therefore of the people he ruled, was held to be reflected by the luxury and richness of his way of life. But polygamy also ensured a large supply of sons and in an age of high infant mortality, a large supply was required in order to make it likely that at least one or two might grow to healthy manhood and lead the nation after the death of the old king.

The value of this was largely negated, however, by the fact that there was usually no rigorous rule of descent. Of the royal house, the strongest, most decisive, or most unscrupulous might seize the throne by rapid action at the time of the king's death.

To prevent this, and the civil war that often took place thereafter, the old king might choose a successor, a choice that would carry great weight with the officialdom of the realm and with the people. To attain such a royal seal of approval, the different women of the harem would intrigue endlessly.

Sometimes an overeager son, either not certain of the father's blessing, or overcertain of his backing, would try to settle matters by striking *before* the death of the old king. It was this which happened in David's reign.

David's oldest son was Amnon, born while David was still merely king of Judah and reigning in Hebron. Under ordinary circumstances, he might be expected to have been the heir. David's second son was

Chileab, who is not mentioned after the verse recording his birth and may, therefore, have died young. His third son was Absalom.

Both Amnon and Absalom were full-grown men in the latter part of David's reign; both in the prime of life; and both, undoubtedly, with their eye on the succession. They were half brothers only, being the sons of different mothers. Under harem conditions, this meant there was bound to be no feeling of brotherhood between them.

The open break came in connection with Tamar, the full sister of Absalom and the half sister of Amnon. Amnon brutally raped Tamar, who fled in shame to the house of Absalom. Absalom, feeling now he would have popular opinion on his side, waited his chance to catch Amnon off guard.

Two years passed, during which, no doubt, Amnon felt the danger had passed, the memory of his crime dimmed. Absalom arranged a festival to which Amnon and the other princes were invited. Amnon was deliberately allowed to get drunk and when merriment was at its height, Absalom had his men strike and Amnon was killed.

That broke up the party, of course, and Absalom, uncertain of his father's reaction, quickly left the country.

2 Samuel 13:37. *But Absalom fled, and went to Talmai . . . king of Geshur.*

Talmai was his mother's father, and Geshur was one of the city-states to the north. It is usually placed just east of the Sea of Galilee.

Absalom was, however, the oldest surviving son of David and it was dangerous to leave him in exile. Enemies of Israel could easily invade the country on the pretext of placing Absalom on the throne and many in Israel might side with him. The country would then be divided against an essentially foreign invasion. This may have been in the mind of Joab, the realistic commander in chief of David's army. He maneuvered Absalom's return after three years, and his formal reconciliation with David after two more years.

Absalom was not satisfied, however. He was now David's logical heir, but could he count on David's blessing? Would not David, mindful of the killing of Amnon, choose another of his sons for the kingship?

Absalom determined to take no chance, but to prepare for action on his own. He was popular with the people, because he was good-looking and because of the natural sympathy he must have gained as the aggrieved party in the affair with Amnon. More than that, Absalom initiated a careful and deliberate campaign to ingratiate himself with the people by display of affability and graciousness and by a studied appearance of concern for their problems.

2 Samuel 15:6. . . . *so Absalom stole the hearts of the men of Israel.*

After four years (the King James Version says "forty" but this is widely considered a mistake and the Revised Standard Version says "four") he felt the time had come. He received permission to visit Hebron on what seemed a harmless pretext and once there, he had himself declared king and raised the standards of rebellion.

Undoubtedly, he had paved the way in Hebron and many were prepared, in advance, to back him. It is interesting that it was in Hebron, the Judean center, that Absalom made his first open move. Apparently, Absalom had strong Judean backing. Why this should be so the Bible does not specifically say. One might guess, however, that David throughout his reign had been concerned to win over the good will of the Israelites and had leaned over backward to avoid favoring his own Judeans. And there might well have been a strong Judean party which resented this and which would have preferred a king under whom a straightforward Judean hegemony over the empire might have been arranged.

Amasa, a Judean and, in fact, a cousin of Joab and a somewhat more distant relative of David himself, served as Absalom's general. Ahithophel, a native of the Judean city of Giloh, also defected to Absalom. He had been a member of David's council and had a formidable reputation for wisdom.

Later in the book, when the more eminent of David's soldiers are listed, mention is made of:

2 Samuel 23:34. . . . *Eliam the son of Ahithophel the Gilonite.*

This Eliam might conceivably be the same Eliam earlier mentioned as the father of Bathsheba. It might therefore be that Ahithophel was the grandfather of the woman who turned out to be David's favorite wife, and the great-grandfather of the man who turned out to be David's successor. It doesn't seem likely that in that case, he would defect to a son of David who was no relative of his own. On the other hand, he might have had no expectation that his own descendant

would someday be king and he might have experienced humiliation
at the highhanded manner in which David had brought his granddaughter into the royal harem. There is no way of deciding this.

Kidron

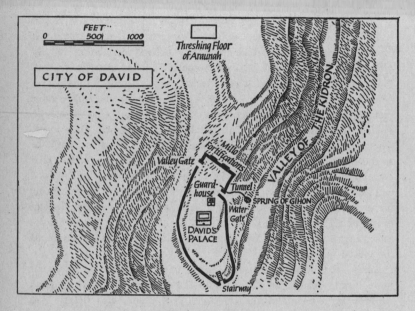

Valley of the Kidron

David reacted at once. Absalom had prepared his net carefully and
Jerusalem was unsafe. The old king's one chance was to get out into
the open and across the Jordan where he might gather an army. Time
could be on his side if he could snatch time. The people might grow
disenchanted with Absalom; they might quail at the thought of attacking David if David did not at once succumb; they might even
remember that the old king had found Israel and Judah in the grip of
the Philistines and had raised them to empire, and might grow
ashamed of their rebellion.

With his household, then, his staff and his armed bodyguard, he
left the city:

2 Samuel 15:23. . . . *and all the people passed over: the king also himself passed over the brook Kidron . . . toward the way of the wilderness.*

Jerusalem is bounded on the east by the Kidron valley, which is now dry but which, in Biblical times, was the bed of a small stream, the brook Kidron, which flowed south into the Dead Sea.

Having crossed the Kidron, David and his retinue mounted the line of hills to the east.

2 Samuel 15:30. *And David went up by the ascent of Mount Olivet . . .*

Mount Olivet, or, as it is better known, the Mount of Olives, is a ridge about two and a half miles long, running north and south about half a mile east of Jerusalem and separated from that city by the Kidron valley. The highest part of Mount Olivet, due east of Zion, is about half a mile high.

Shimei

Dangers multiplied, for it was not merely a question of David's replacement by Absalom, but of the disintegration of the barely established empire. On Mount Olivet, David was overtaken by the servant of Mephibosheth, the son of Jonathan and only living direct descendant of Saul. According to the servant, Mephibosheth was remaining in Jerusalem in the hope of being called to the throne. After all, if, with Judean support, Absalom gained the throne, it might be the throne of Judah only, and Israel, regaining its independence, might turn to its older dynasty.

The extent of this danger was made plainer in Bahurim (a town whose exact site is unknown but which lay somewhere between Jerusalem and the Jordan). Shimei lived there, a Benjamite, a collateral relative of Saul, and presumably a man of influence in the area:

2 Samuel 16:5. . . . *Shimei . . . came forth, and cursed still as he came.*

2 Samuel 16:6. *And he cast stones at David . . .*

2 Samuel 16:7. *And thus said Shimei . . .*

2 Samuel 16:8. *The Lord hath returned upon thee all the blood*

of the house of Saul, in whose stead thou hast reigned; and the Lord hath delivered the kingdom into the hand of Absalom thy son: and behold thou art taken in thy mischief, because thou art a bloody man.

It sounds very much as though Shimei is referring to the execution of Saul's descendants (not described till several chapters later). The soldiers with David offered to kill Shimei, but David did not allow that. Shimei's curses were doing him little harm but what Shimei now had the courage to say in David's adversity, others might be thinking, and an unnecessary outrage against Shimei might simply serve to swell Absalom's army with Benjamites.

Hushai

What strength David possessed now lay in the fact that the core of his army, his elite troops, remained faithful and were with him. They were few in number but they could be counted on to give a good account of themselves.

Ahithophel, however, advised Absalom to attack David at once, even while the king was retiring in disorder toward the Jordan and before he could cross the river and begin organizing an army. Move now, while David is off balance, he urged in effect; strike while the iron is hot.

Now Absalom made his fatal mistake.

2 Samuel 17:5. *Then said Absalom, Call now Hushai . . . and let us hear likewise what he saith.*

Hushai was another of David's counselors, but was not a Judean. He was of the city of Archi, which was included in the territory of Ephraim. Unlike Ahithophel, he had not defected to Absalom but had been directed by David to remain in Jerusalem as what we would today call a "double agent."

Hushai gave the advice calculated to give David the one thing he needed—time. Hushai warned Absalom that a hasty attack on David might lead to a preliminary defeat by David's hardened warriors. The defeat might be minor and of no military significance but to the people it would prove that David was still the invincible conqueror and they would lose heart and melt away from Absalom. Therefore, said Hushai, do not attack till you have built up a large army.

Absalom took Hushai's advice and waited to build up his large army and that was his end. David got safely over the Jordan, where the Trans-Jordan tribes rallied round him as they had rallied round Ishbosheth, the son of Saul, a generation earlier. Ahithophel, deciding that victory for Absalom was now impossible, killed himself.

David's newly organized army, under his veteran officers, then struck back across the Jordan, meeting Absalom's hastily raised and poorly led levies, and utterly defeated them. Absalom was taken, and although David had ordered that he be unharmed, the practical Joab thought otherwise. A rebel left alive was one who would rebel again someday, and so he had Absalom killed.

David now returned to Jerusalem and resumed the undisputed kingship. Shimei, the Benjamite who had cursed David, came quickly to make his submission, while Mephibosheth came also, maintaining that he had been slandered, and that no thought of assuming the kingship had ever occurred to him.

David, aware that the victory did not necessarily wipe out the sources of disaffection, was careful to take no revenge. Shimei was allowed to live; Mephibosheth was taken back into favor. This was intended to appease the Israelite nationalists. As a measure of reconciliation with the Judean nationalists, he accepted Amasa, who had served as Absalom's general, as commander in chief in place of Joab. (Presumably, David did not forget Joab's action in killing Absalom against orders.)

Sheba

David's mildness was of no help. Certain factions among the Israelites, disappointed at the re-establishment of the Judean dynasty over the united kingdom, revolted. Their leader was Sheba, a Benjamite and therefore of the tribe of Saul. He rallied Israel about him on a purely nationalistic slogan:

> 2 Samuel 20:1. . . . *and he blew a trumpet, and said, We have no part in David, neither have we inheritance in the son of Jesse: every man to his tents, O Israel.*

Once again David's army had to take the field. The resourceful and unscrupulous Joab found, in this renewed war, an opportunity to gain his generalship once more. He assassinated Amasa and took over the army, leading it northward. Sheba retreated hastily but was caught and trapped in Abel of Beth-maacah, a city in the north, just across the Jordan River from Dan. The inhabitants of the city killed Sheba in order to prevent the otherwise inevitable sack, and the rebellion came to an end.

Araunah

The tale of David's reign is now essentially over. The Book of 2 Samuel concludes with a summarizing list of David's heroes and of some of their exploits, with a couple of psalms attributed to David, and with one final tale included in the last chapter of 2 Samuel because of its connection with the chief accomplishment of David's successor. This last tale begins with a census:

2 Samuel 24:1. *And again the anger of the Lord was kindled against Israel, and he moved David against them to say, Go, number Israel and Judah.*

Why a census is treated, in this chapter, as a sin, is uncertain. Twice, a census was supposed to have taken place in the wilderness before the entry into Canaan (see page 165) and neither time was this described as a sin. Moses himself had, according to the Biblical story, instituted it.

Of course, in ancient times, a census was not a regular procedure designed to provide the statistical data necessary to help guide the destinies of a nation. It was rather a course of procedure taken at irregular periods for one of two specific reasons: a reorganization of the military draft, or a reorganization of the system of taxation.

The former purpose is indicated by the fact that in the census described at the end of the Book of 2 Samuel only men of military age were counted:

2 Samuel 24:9. . . . *and there were in Israel eight hundred thousand valiant men that drew the sword; and the men of Judah were five hundred thousand.*

This estimate (a very rough one, for methods of enumeration in ancient times are by no means to be compared with those of today) may be rather exaggerated for it indicates a total population of about four million, or very nearly the combined population of Israel and Jordan today.

That a census might also be used for taxation is best indicated in the famous chapter in the Gospel of St. Luke which begins:

> Luke 2:1. And . . . there went out a decree from Caesar Augustus that all the world should be taxed.

and this involved first of all an enrollment of individuals, or what amounts to a census. The verse in the Revised Standard Version is given as "a decree went out from Caesar Augustus that all the world should be enrolled," while the New Catholic Edition translates the verse as "a decree went forth from Caesar Augustus that a census of the whole world should be taken."

In either case, whether for a military draft or for taxation, a census was bound to be unpopular and, if any natural disaster followed, those who opposed it would be sure to point to that as evidence of divine displeasure.

In this case the disaster was a pestilence that is recorded as killing seventy thousand men. The Biblical writers describe the occasion dramatically by having God stop the angel of death when Jerusalem was on the point of being destroyed. The exact position of the angel at the time of the order to halt is given:

> 2 Samuel 24:16. . . . And the angel of the Lord was by the threshingplace of Araunah the Jebusite.
>
> 2 Samuel 24:17. And David . . . saw the angel that smote the people . . .

David therefore purchased that threshing place and built an altar upon it. His son Solomon was later to build the Temple upon this same site, and it is tempting to think that the story of David and the census was embroidered with supernatural detail by the later writers in order to supply additional sanctification of the ground upon which the Temple stood.

11. 1 KINGS

ADONIJAH * THE PHARAOH [OF SOLOMON] * TIPHSAH * THE HOUSE OF THE
LORD * OPHIR * SHEBA * TARSHISH * HADAD THE EDOMITE * REZON * AHIJAH *
SHISHAK * REHOBOAM * JEROBOAM * BEN-HADAD * SAMARIA * JEZEBEL *
ELIJAH * ZAREPHATH * MOUNT CARMEL * JEZREEL * BEN-HADAD II * APHEK *
NABOTH * RAMOTH-GILEAD

Adonijah

The First Book of Kings opens in the year 973 B.C., the fortieth
and last year of the reign of David. The old king had clearly only a
short time to live and the matter of the succession came up again.
Now that the three oldest sons of David were dead, the fourth,
Adonijah, seemed (to himself, certainly) the natural successor.

1 Kings 1:5. *Then Adonijah . . . exalted himself, saying, I will
be king . . .*

To be sure, David had not indicated him as successor, but then
neither had he indicated anyone else—at least not openly. Adonijah
made sure of the support of the army and of the priesthood by en-
listing on his side Joab, the commander in chief, and Abiathar, the
survivor of the slaughter at Nob and the last priest of the house of
Eli.

Both Joab and Abiathar were now old men, however, and their
power was on the decline. In opposition to Joab was the younger
soldier Benaiah, captain of the king's bodyguard, and in opposition to
Abiathar was the younger priest Zadok.

The younger men had their own candidate, Solomon, the son of
Bathsheba, who had retained her influence over David and who was
willing to take the chance of facing the old king concerning this matter.
On their side, also, was Nathan, head of the prophetic party.

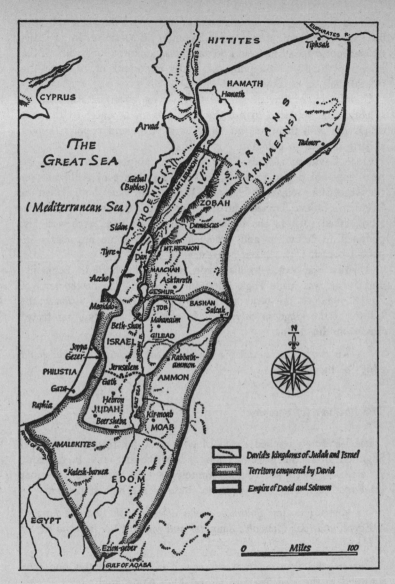

The Empire of David and Solomon

David was not proof against such pressures and it might well have been his own intention to appoint Solomon his successor. In any case, he was forced to act now, and Solomon was anointed king with all the necessary ritual and trapping and, most important of all, with the official blessing of David.

Upon news of this event, the feast being given by Adonijah to celebrate his accession to the throne broke up at once. In the face of David's will, there was no further argument, and popular support shifted at once to Solomon.

Once David actually died and Solomon sat upon the throne, the new king took action to make sure that no chance of civil war over the succession remained. Adonijah and Joab were both killed at Solomon's orders. Shimei, who still represented the remnant of those who harked back to the dynasty of Saul (see page 315) was first confined to Jerusalem and, when he left on some apparently innocent occasion, was taken and executed.

Abiathar was exiled to his home city of Anathoth in Benjamin, and Zadok was made High Priest in his place. The descendants of Zadok remained the head of the Jerusalem priesthood through the history of the kingdom thereafter. In this way, Solomon was seated firmly on the throne.

> 1 Kings 2:46. . . . *And the kingdom was established in the hand of Solomon.*

The Pharaoh [of Solomon]

Israel had now reached a peak of power and prestige which enabled Solomon to take his place as a monarch of the first rank. In gathering a harem, he need not confine himself to local girls and to minor princesses only, but could aspire to those of the highest prestige.

> 1 Kings 3:1. *And Solomon made affinity with Pharaoh king of Egypt, and took Pharaoh's daughter and brought her into the city of David . . .*

This is the first mention of any Pharaoh since the one who drowned in the Red Sea and as usual no name is given.

The social prestige of marriage into the family of Pharaoh is great and at the time it must have made a triumphant impression. The

slaves who had fled Egypt centuries before now had grown so powerful that their king was worthy of a marriage alliance with Pharaoh.

The show was much more than the actuality, however, for Egypt
was by no means the Egypt it had been. The 20th dynasty, which had
vegetated along under its line of Rameses (see page 220) while the
judges dominated Canaan, came to an end about 1075 B.C. in the lifetime of Samuel and a hundred years before the accession of Solomon.

Since then, Egypt had disintegrated. The Pharaohs of the 21st
dynasty ruled only the Nile delta, while upper Egypt was under the
domination of the priests of Ammon, who ruled as virtual monarchs
from Thebes, the capital of the conquering monarchs of the great
18th dynasty.

The Egyptian capital under the 21st dynasty was Tanis or Zoan,
the city which, seven centuries earlier, had served as the capital of the
Hyksos. About the time of David's death, Psusennes II ascended
the Egyptian throne. His position as Pharaoh of the delta was not
enviable. He had to face the constant hostility of the Theban priests
and, in addition, there was a growing pressure from the desert tribes
to the west.

No doubt he felt that an alliance with Solomon, via the usual route
of a dynastic marriage, might secure his eastern flank and give him some
dependable military help if this was needed. He was willing to pay for
it, too, for he sent an expedition to capture a Canaanite city, Gezer,
in Philistine territory and gave it to Solomon as a dowry with his
daughter. It is the single recorded territorial annexation of Solomon's
reign.

Solomon's army was not, in actual fact, called upon, but the then
high prestige of Israel might have helped, for Psusennes retained his
shaky throne for well over thirty years, almost to the end of Solomon's
reign.

Tiphsah

The two Books of Kings reached their final form four centuries after
the great days of Solomon, at a time when Jerusalem had been ruling
over sharply restricted territory for a long time and when its very life
seemed at the mercy of powerful empires to the east. The reign of
Solomon, at the time in which Jerusalem's sway over surrounding

territory was at its maximum, is looked back upon
delight. The extent of Solomon's kingdom is given:

> 1 Kings 4:24. . . . *he had dominion over all the*
> *side the river, from Tiphsah even to Azzah [Gaz*
> *kings on this side the river: and he had peace on*
> *about him.*

The river is clearly the Euphrates; no one doubts
(meaning "ford") is commonly identified as the city
Greeks as Thapsacus, which is some three hundred mi
Jerusalem. There is indeed a ford at that spot and sin
the most convenient place for crossing the middle Eu
ished and was, in Greek times, a sizable and prospe

No doubt, Solomon's hold that far north was quite t
resented nothing more than the fact that the cities of
tribute and were otherwise undisturbed in their local

Nevertheless, the boundaries of Solomon's kingdom
to Gaza, remained the ideal boundary in the ey
historians. (Each nation seems to consider its "righ
those it happened to hold at the peak of its power
is overlapping in every direction with the "rightful
every neighboring power.)

In a way, the reign of Solomon is the climax
history. The promise of Canaan is fulfilled. The esca
Egypt have made their way to Canaan, conquered it
into an empire and now finally, under Solomon:

> 1 Kings 4:25. . . . *Judah and Israel dwelt safely,*
> *his vine and under his fig tree, from Dan even t*

One might almost be tempted to heave a sigh
happiness after so many tribulations and to let it
lived happily ever after" ending, except that there a
history. Life goes on and a plateau of power will r

The House of the Lord

If Solomon's reign was the climax of early Isra
building of the Temple was the climax of Solom

slaves who had fled Egypt centuries before now had grown so powerful that their king was worthy of a marriage alliance with Pharaoh.

The show was much more than the actuality, however, for Egypt
was by no means the Egypt it had been. The 20th dynasty, which had
vegetated along under its line of Rameses (see page 220) while the
judges dominated Canaan, came to an end about 1075 B.C. in the lifetime of Samuel and a hundred years before the accession of Solomon.

Since then, Egypt had disintegrated. The Pharaohs of the 21st
dynasty ruled only the Nile delta, while upper Egypt was under the
domination of the priests of Ammon, who ruled as virtual monarchs
from Thebes, the capital of the conquering monarchs of the great
18th dynasty.

The Egyptian capital under the 21st dynasty was Tanis or Zoan,
the city which, seven centuries earlier, had served as the capital of the
Hyksos. About the time of David's death, Psusennes II ascended
the Egyptian throne. His position as Pharaoh of the delta was not
enviable. He had to face the constant hostility of the Theban priests
and, in addition, there was a growing pressure from the desert tribes
to the west.

No doubt he felt that an alliance with Solomon, via the usual route
of a dynastic marriage, might secure his eastern flank and give him some
dependable military help if this was needed. He was willing to pay for
it, too, for he sent an expedition to capture a Canaanite city, Gezer,
in Philistine territory and gave it to Solomon as a dowry with his
daughter. It is the single recorded territorial annexation of Solomon's
reign.

Solomon's army was not, in actual fact, called upon, but the then
high prestige of Israel might have helped, for Psusennes retained his
shaky throne for well over thirty years, almost to the end of Solomon's
reign.

Tiphsah

The two Books of Kings reached their final form four centuries after
the great days of Solomon, at a time when Jerusalem had been ruling
over sharply restricted territory for a long time and when its very life
seemed at the mercy of powerful empires to the east. The reign of
Solomon, at the time in which Jerusalem's sway over surrounding

territory was at its maximum, is looked back upon with rhapsodic delight. The extent of Solomon's kingdom is given:

> 1 Kings 4:24. . . . *he had dominion over all the region on this side the river, from Tiphsah even to Azzah [Gaza], over all the kings on this side the river: and he had peace on all sides round about him.*

The river is clearly the Euphrates; no one doubts that. Tiphsah (meaning "ford") is commonly identified as the city known to the Greeks as Thapsacus, which is some three hundred miles northeast of Jerusalem. There is indeed a ford at that spot and since it controlled the most convenient place for crossing the middle Euphrates, it flourished and was, in Greek times, a sizable and prosperous city.

No doubt, Solomon's hold that far north was quite tenuous, and represented nothing more than the fact that the cities of Syria paid him tribute and were otherwise undisturbed in their local rule.

Nevertheless, the boundaries of Solomon's kingdom, from Tiphsah to Gaza, remained the ideal boundary in the eyes of the later historians. (Each nation seems to consider its "rightful boundaries" those it happened to hold at the peak of its power. Naturally, there is overlapping in every direction with the "rightful boundaries" of every neighboring power.)

In a way, the reign of Solomon is the climax of early Biblical history. The promise of Canaan is fulfilled. The escaping slaves from Egypt have made their way to Canaan, conquered it, held it, built it into an empire and now finally, under Solomon:

> 1 Kings 4:25. . . . *Judah and Israel dwelt safely, every man under his vine and under his fig tree, from Dan even to Beersheba . . .*

One might almost be tempted to heave a sigh of relief at such happiness after so many tribulations and to let it stand as a "they lived happily ever after" ending, except that there are no endings in history. Life goes on and a plateau of power will recede.

The House of the Lord

If Solomon's reign was the climax of early Israelite history, the building of the Temple was the climax of Solomon's reign in the

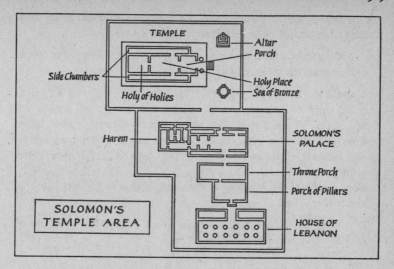

The House of the Lord

eyes of the Biblical writers. David had planned a Temple but his reign had been too stormy to give him the required years of peace it would have taken to build it. Solomon had those years of peace.

What Solomon needed were the necessary raw materials and skilled artisans and for both of these he could turn to Phoenicia. Hiram had just become king of Tyre in 969 B.C., four years after Solomon had ascended the throne and he, too, was ready for a large project. (Hiram was so famous to the Biblical writers in connection with the Temple that he was anachronistically placed on the throne of Tyre in David's time—see page 304.)

1 Kings 5:2. *And Solomon sent to Hiram, saying . . .*

. . . .

1 Kings 5:5. *. . . behold, I purpose to build an house unto the name of the Lord my God . . .*

. . . .

1 Kings 6:1. *And it came to pass . . . in the fourth year of Solomon's reign . . . that he began to build the house of the Lord.*

Undoubtedly, Hiram, a shrewd businessman, was well aware that his neighbor's ambitious plans would redound to the profit of Tyre, for he would supply the necessary timber and workmen at his own price and it would be a high one:

> 1 Kings 5:7. *And it came to pass, when Hiram heard the words of Solomon, that he rejoiced greatly* . . .

There is nothing wrong, in itself, in a building program. Fitted to the economy of a nation, it supplies employment and builds national pride. Unfortunately, the temptation is always present to go too far and Solomon (like many other monarchs before and after— as, for example, Rameses II of Egypt and Louis XIV of France) went too far.

For one thing, the building of the Temple meant the lavish use of forced labor:

> 1 Kings 5:13. *And king Solomon raised a levy out of all Israel; and the levy was thirty thousand men.*
> 1 Kings 5:14. *And he sent them to Lebanon* . . .

The Revised Standard Version translates the verse, "King Solomon raised a levy of forced labor out of all Israel."

Later it is stated that it was the remaining Canaanites only who were thus enslaved in fulfillment of the curse recorded as having been pronounced on Ham (see page 45).

> 1 Kings 9:22. *But of the children of Israel did Solomon make no bondmen* . . .

This last, however, sounds like a defense against the list of grievances presented by the Israelites who broke away from the Davidic dynasty. It seems much more likely that the labor gangs were formed from all available sources, from Israelites as well as Canaanites. The same might be said for taxes, which, Solomon saw to it, were collected efficiently.

The amount by which Solomon overextended his resources in his building program is indicated by the fact that he could not pay Hiram all the accumulated debt in either cash or goods but had to cede land as well. Once the building program was complete:

> 1 Kings 9:11. . . . *king Solomon gave Hiram twenty cities* . . .

The cities thus ceded were part of the tribal holdings of Naphtali in Israel. This could not help but be offensive to Israelite pride and was another item in the gathering score against the Davidic dynasty.

The building of the Temple is such a key fact to the Biblical writers that they give its date not only in terms of Solomon's reign but in terms of the greater sweep of Israelite history as well:

> 1 Kings 6:1. *And it came to pass in the four hundred and eightieth year after the children of Israel were come out of the land of Egypt . . . that he* [Solomon] *began to build the house of the Lord.*

This cannot be right. Four hundred eighty years before the beginning of the building of the Temple was 1449 B.C. and that was in the midst of the conquering reign of Thutmose III, Egypt's most victorious monarch. To have the Exodus take place then is unthinkable.

The Biblical writers frequently show themselves to be very number conscious and, indeed, in Greek and Roman times an almost mystical number lore grew up among them. This was called "gematria" (a corruption of the Greek, *geometria*) and it was by no means unique to the Jews. Numbers have a fascination for all peoples and mystical associations and combinations of numbers are to be found in all cultures. Even the rational Greeks were not immune and the great philosopher Pythagoras founded a school that simultaneously did great work in mathematics and foolishly wandered astray after number mysticism.

The 480-year period may in part have been suggested by counting the various judges as having ruled consecutively (see page 230) instead of, in part, concurrently, and the exact figure may have been suggested by the fact that 480 is equal to 12 multiplied by 40. After all, forty years can be considered the length of a full generation, and twelve has the mystical value of being the number of tribes (or, for that matter, the numbers of signs of the zodiac). What the writers are saying then is that the Temple was built a dozen generations after the Exodus.

Actually, 480 years is just about double the most likely figure. Counting from 1211 B.C., the death of Merneptah (see page 143), the beginning of the building of the Temple turns out to be 242 years after the Exodus.

Seven years were spent in building the Temple, which was therefore finished and dedicated in 962 B.C. and into which the ark of the covenant was then placed. Solomon also built a palace for himself and one for his Egyptian queen as well as fortifications for various towns.

Before leaving the subject, one item in the description of the Temple furnishings has attached to it an odd bit of mathematical curiosa. This involves one of the items described as having been made by a Tyrian metalworker:

> 1 Kings 7:23. *And he made a molten sea, ten cubits from the one brim to the other . . . and a line of thirty cubits did compass it round about.*

The exact function of the "molten sea" is not stated, though it seems most likely that it was a container for water used in the various rituals. The interesting point is that its upper rim seems to be circular in shape with a diameter of ten cubits and a circumference of thirty cubits. This is impossible, for the ratio of the circumference to the diameter (a ratio called "pi" by mathematicians) is given here as 30/10 or 3, whereas the real value of pi is an unending decimal which begins 3.14159 . . . If the molten sea were really ten cubits in diameter it would have to be just under thirty-one and a half cubits in circumference.

The explanation is, of course, that the Biblical writers were not mathematicians or even interested in mathematics and were merely giving approximate figures. Still, to those who are obsessed with the notion that every word in the Bible is infallible (and who know a little mathematics) it is bound to come as a shock to be told that the Bible says that the value of pi is 3.

Ophir

Solomon used Hiram's help also in building a navy for Israel and in supplying it with Tyrian sailors, then the best in the world. With it, Solomon was able to engage in sea trade:

> 1 Kings 9:28. *And they came to Ophir, and fetched from thence gold . . . and brought it to king Solomon.*

Ophir and Tarshish

Where Ophir might be is completely unknown but the puzzle of its whereabouts has never ceased to fascinate Biblical scholars, partly because of the aura of wealth that lay about it. There are not many places that serve as sources of gold, after all, and the gold of Ophir was accounted so fine and high in quality that the proverbial association became inevitable, like the cedars of Lebanon, the balm of Gilead, and the bulls of Bashan.

Thus, Job, in praising wisdom above all else and speaking of how impossible it is to find a price for it, says:

Job 28:16. *It cannot be valued with the gold of Ophir . . .*

The one clear hint as to the location of Ophir is given two verses before this first mention in connection with Solomon's sea trade.

1 Kings 9:26. *And king Solomon made a navy of ships in Ezion-geber, which is beside Eloth, on the shore of the Red sea, in the land of Edom.*

Ezion-geber and Eloth (or Elath) stood at the northern tip of the Gulf of Aqaba (see page 133). Since the independence of modern Israel, Elath has been built up again and is once more the nation's Red Sea port.

We might argue then that Ophir was located somewhere that could be reached by way of the Red Sea. This still leaves the matter rather wide open. India can be reached by way of the Red Sea and in after-times, Ophir was located still farther afield, in places which became famous for riches and wealth—the Far East, even Peru.

And yet the ships of the tenth century B.C. were not fit for long ocean voyages. The closer Ophir can be located to Israel, the more likely the location.

The one other place which the Biblical writers pause to describe as a source of fine gold is Havilah (see page 28). The location of Havilah is also uncertain but some scholars place it somewhere in southern Arabia and it seems reasonable to suppose that Ophir is also to be located there, perhaps on the site of what is now the kingdom of Yemen. This is the more probable because the mention of Ophir is followed by the mention of another kingdom (almost by reflex association, as it were) which is more surely located in that area.

Sheba

The penetration of Israel southward brought a return visit from a monarch of the south:

1 Kings 10:1. *And when the queen of Sheba heard of the fame of Solomon . . . she came to prove him with hard questions.*

The location of Sheba is by no means mysterious. In southwestern Arabia, on the site of what is now Yemen, there was a kingdom known to the Arabs as Saba and to the Greeks and Romans as Sabaea. There seems little doubt that this is the Biblical Sheba. And it might be that Ophir represents a district of Sheba, for the queen is pictured as wealthy:

1 Kings 10:2. *And she came to Jerusalem with a very great train, with camels that bare spices, and very much gold, and precious stones . . .*

(Sabaea was so prosperous that Romans called the area Arabia Felix —"fortunate Arabia"—in comparison with other parts of the peninsula, which contained one of the most unpleasant deserts in the world.)

However prosaically definite we may be about Sheba itself, there is little to be said about the queen. There is no record of any particular queen of Sheba, or of any such visit to Jerusalem, outside the Bible. Nor is the queen as much as given a name in the Bible. The later Arabs evolved the myth that her name was Balkis, and she is mentioned by that name in the Koran.

The modern Ethiopians have a tradition that queen Balkis was actually the queen of their own nation. This is not as completely odd as it might sound. Modern Ethiopia is just across the Red Sea from Sheba (or Yemen) at a point where that sea narrows down to a width of twenty miles or so. There is rather easy communication between the two nations and there have been times when Ethiopia dominated sections of southwestern Arabia. To be sure, this was some twelve centuries after Solomon but the connection is there to be remembered with the usual distortion.

The Ethiopians maintain that queen Balkis had a son by Solomon, and name that son Menelik. From Menelik is supposed to be descended the present ruling line of the emperors of Ethiopia. One of the traditional titles of the Ethiopian emperor, even today, is "Lion of Judah" in reference to this supposed Judean ancestry.

Tarshish

Solomon's commerce stretched out in another direction as well:

> 1 Kings 10:22. . . . *the king had at sea a navy of Tharshish with the navy of Hiram: once in three years came the navy of Tharshish, bringing gold, and silver, ivory, and apes and peacocks.*

Tharshish, more commonly referred to in the Bible as Tarshish, is sometimes considered as synonymous with Ophir. It is then suggested that Ophir must be three years journey from Israel and must thus be someplace distant like the Far East. However, it seems clear that two different fleets are here being described. There is the "navy of Hiram" and the "navy of Tharshish"; Solomon has one "with" (together with, or in addition to) another. The men of Hiram bring goods from Ophir, and the men of Tarshish bring goods from elsewhere.

Actually, the whereabouts of Tarshish is almost as mysterious as that of Ophir. There is no hint in the Bible of its location. It is very frequently equated with the district known to the Greeks and Romans as Tartessus. The chief evidence for this is the similarity in names and the fact that it is sufficiently far from Jerusalem to make the three-year term for the round trip and the period of trading seem reasonable.

Tartessus was the name given by the Greeks to that portion of Spain west of Gibraltar. Its capital city (of the same name) was at the mouth of the Guadalquivir River, about seventy-five miles northwest of Gibraltar. It was founded by the Phoenicians about 1200 B.C.; that is, at the time of the Exodus. It was at the height of its commercial prosperity in Solomon's reign. (Eventually, though, all of the commerce of the western Mediterranean was brought under the control of Carthage, the most successful of the Phoenician colonies. About 480 B.C., Carthage, then at the height of its power, destroyed Tartessus.)

There might be some question as to whether "ivory, and apes and peacocks" might be found in Spain, but why not? The Barbary ape (not a true ape) is still to be found in Gibraltar and in ancient times it must have been more widely spread. As for ivory, there were elephants in north Africa in ancient times.

Hadad the Edomite

The strength of the land (which Solomon poured freely into his building projects and his efforts at imperial luxury) declined and this made it more difficult to retain the hold over the increasingly restless subject peoples.

Solomon did possess a certain imperial responsibility and attempted to retain popularity with these peoples through an enlightened religious policy. He not only allowed them freedom of worship but tried to demonstrate himself to be king over all his subjects and not over the Judeans and Israelites alone. He added women of the subject nations to his harem (intended, and accepted, as an honor) and allowed temples to be built to their gods for their convenience.

This was undoubtedly good policy (it fits in with our modern notions of religious freedom) but it was viewed with dislike and hostility by the prophetic party. That hostility grew in the course of the later centuries and the Biblical writers expressed their opinion of Solomon's course of action unmistakably:

> 1 Kings 11:5. *For Solomon went after . . . Milcom the abomination of the Ammonites.*
>
> . . . .
>
> 1 Kings 11:7. *Then did Solomon build an high place for Chemosh, the abomination of Moab . . .*

That Solomon's attempts at placating the peoples of the realm were not unnecessary is shown by the fact that there were rebellions here and there, marring the idyllic picture of the reign which was drawn in the earlier chapters. Edom gave trouble from the beginning of Solomon's reign:

> 1 Kings 11:14. *And the Lord stirred up an adversary unto Solomon, Hadad the Edomite . . .*

Hadad was a member of the old Edomite royal house, who had survived the slaughter following Joab's conquest of Edom during David's reign. He had found sanctuary in Egypt but once David was dead, he made his way back to Edom. Exactly how he played his part as "adversary" against Solomon we are not told, but it seems quite reasonable to suppose he declared himself king of Edom and carried on a continuing guerrilla war with the royal army.

Rezon

There were similar troubles in the north:

1 Kings 11:23. *And God stirred him* [Solomon] *up another adversary, Rezon the son of Eliadah . . .*
1 Kings 11:24. *And he gathered men unto him . . . and they went to Damascus, and dwelt therein . . .*

The Syrian city-states had been placed under tribute by David, but Solomon's less warlike hand did not suffice to keep them in subjection. Rezon, gathering a guerrilla band about him, seized Damascus, and established himself there as an independent power.

Ahijah

Israel's greatest danger, however, was from within. The hostility between Judah and Israel had never died but was merely sleeping—with one eye open. That open eye consisted of the prophetic party.

Even in the days of Saul, Israel's first king, there had been the clash between the royal power and that of the prophets under the leadership of Samuel (see page 283).

Under David and Solomon, with the power, prestige, and glory of the monarchy at an all-time high, the role of the prophets sank accordingly and they made comparatively little impingement upon history. Nathan the prophet, however, did not hesitate to beard David and denounce him to his face in the matter of Uriah the Hittite (see page 310)—and was able to survive the encounter, too, and force the mighty king to do penance. It was the support of Nathan and the prophetic party that might have swung the balance to Solomon and against Adonijah when David lay dying.

Solomon's policy of religious toleration alienated the prophetic party, particularly those who were of Israelite (rather than Judean) origin. The prophets of Israel may not even have entirely approved the centralization of worship at Jerusalem and the consequent lessening of importance of the various Israelite shrines. For them, religious feelings went hand in hand with nationalism.

Ahijah, an Israelite prophet of Shiloh in Ephraim (which, in Eli's time a century before, had been the home of the most important shrine in Israel), must have been one of these prophet-nationalists. He had his eye on Jeroboam, also an Ephraimite, one who held high office under Solomon and who seemed to have the qualities of leadership.

> 1 Kings 11:29. . . . *when Jeroboam went out of Jerusalem . . . the prophet Ahijah the Shilonite found him . . .*
>
> 1 Kings 11:30. *And Ahijah caught the new garment that was on him, and rent it . . .*
>
> 1 Kings 11:31. *And he said to Jeroboam . . . thus saith the Lord . . . Behold I will rend the kingdom out of the hand of Solomon . . .*

With the backing of the prophetic party and of many disgruntled Israelites, Jeroboam rose in rebellion.

Shishak

The rebellion failed—for the while—and Jeroboam had to flee, but he had made himself an Israelite hero and Israel did not forget him.

> 1 Kings 11:40. . . . *And Jeroboam arose and fled into Egypt, unto Shishak king of Egypt, and was in Egypt until the death of Solomon.*

Egypt had had its own increasing troubles. The 21st dynasty which ruled the delta came to an end with the death of Solomon's father-in-law in 940 B.C. Anarchy increased further then, as rival generals seized at power. One of these was Sheshonk (the Biblical Shishak), who was a member of a tribe occupying the regions west of the Nile valley.

The whole northern coast of Africa west of Egypt was called Libya by the Greeks (a name of unknown origin). To the Greek writers on Egyptian history, therefore, Shishak was a Libyan, and the 22nd dynasty, which he founded, was the "Libyan dynasty."

Shishak's power extended only over the delta; upper Egypt continued under the rule of the priests of Thebes. Shishak was the only member of the dynasty who displayed any vigor at all. After him came a series of rulers who lorded it over separate sections of the delta and quarreled among themselves.

Even Shishak could not have been very impressive, for the Bible nowhere refers to him as "Pharaoh," but merely as "king." The impression is that he was not considered a legitimate Egyptian monarch, but merely a usurping general. He is the first ruler of Egypt, by the way, to whom the Biblical writers give an actual name.

Shishak was shrewd enough to recognize that Jeroboam might be a useful tool in combating or even destroying the power of his neighbor to the northeast and he offered him ready asylum, as a predecessor had once offered asylum to Hadad the Edomite.

Rehoboam

Solomon, like his father, reigned forty years, dying in 933 B.C. (These forty-year reigns of David and Solomon are suspiciously even. Each king reigned a full "generation." Still, the acceptance of Biblical chronology in this instance gives rise to no inconsistencies and there is no good reason to suggest any alternative.)

Solomon must have had many sons but there is no talk of any problems of succession. Only one son is mentioned and he becomes the third king of the Davidic dynasty.

> 1 Kings 11:43. . . . *and Rehoboam his* [Solomon's] *son reigned in his stead.*

His crowning made him king of Judah only. To become king of Israel as well, he had to undergo a similar rite at the old holy Ephraimite city of Shechem:

> 1 Kings 12:1. *And Rehoboam went to Shechem: for all Israel were come to Shechem to make him king.*

(Perhaps David and Solomon had to do the same but that is not mentioned in the Bible. It is mentioned in Rehoboam's case because of the events that now transpired.)

The Israelites did not come to the crowning in any compliant mood. It was not their intention to crown Rehoboam and make him legitimate

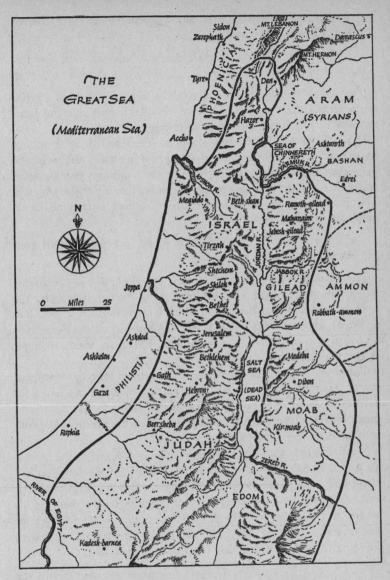

Israel and Judah During Rehoboam's Time

king of Israel unless he would in turn guarantee some relief from repression. They said to him:

1 Kings 12:4. *Thy father made our yoke grievous: now therefore make thou the grievous service . . . lighter, and we will serve thee.*

The young Rehoboam, with deplorable lack of judgment, scorned gentle speech. He threatened to make the yoke heavier still, and Israel revolted in an explosion of nationalist fury.

It was Rehoboam's intention to subdue the rebellion by force, but its strength and violence was surprising. Furthermore, the prophetic party even in Judah was apparently not entirely unhappy over the split. A weakening of the royal power meant a strengthening of the prophets. The Judean prophet Shemaiah counseled against attempting to reunite the kingdom by force:

1 Kings 12:24. . . . *Ye shall not go up, nor fight against your brethren the children of Israel . . .*

The rebellion was successful, therefore, and the split was permanent. Rehoboam was left the king of Judah only, though, ironically, the territory of the tribe of Benjamin (which had given the first royal line to Israel) remained with Judah, since the prosperity of the Benjamites now depended on Judah's one metropolis, Jerusalem, which lay right at the Benjamite borders.

The united kingdom of Israel-Judah had endured for only three quarters of a century, from 1006 B.C. to 933 B.C., and under two monarchs only. Now there were two sister kingdoms, Israel to the north and Judah to the south. (They are sometimes called the northern kingdom and southern kingdom respectively)

Nor did Rehoboam's troubles end once he had bowed to the inevitable and accepted the secession of Israel. Aside from the fact that bad blood and border warfare remained between the two kingdoms, Shishak of Egypt seized the opportunity offered him by the chaos on his borders to attack the divided and weakened nation in the fifth year of Rehoboam's reign (928 B.C.). He laid siege to Jerusalem, or perhaps occupied it, and in either case carried off much loot.

1 Kings 14:26. *And he* [Shishak] *took away the treasures of the house of the Lord, and the treasures of the king's house; he . . . took away all . . .*

Not only had Solomon's kingdom broken in two but Solomon's material glory was gone. The Temple in its original golden splendor (if we accept the description given by the Bible) lasted just forty years.

Jeroboam

Jeroboam had returned from exile as soon as word of Solomon's death reached him. It was he who led the Israelite party that demanded concessions of Rehoboam; it was he who led the rebellion that followed Rehoboam's refusal; and it was he who was made the first king of the re-established kingdom of Israel:

> 1 Kings 12:20. . . . when . . . Israel heard that Jeroboam was come again . . . they . . . made him king over all Israel . . .

Israel thus regained its independence, which it had lost after the death of Ish-bosheth. Jeroboam established his capital at Shechem at first, then at the more centrally located Tirzah, twelve miles to the northeast.

Having regained political independence for Israel, Jeroboam felt it necessary to regain religious independence as well for he reasoned:

> 1 Kings 12:27. If this people go up to do sacrifice in the house of the Lord at Jerusalem, then shall the heart of this people turn again . . . unto Rehoboam.

Jeroboam therefore set up sanctuaries at the northern and southern limits of his new kingdom, at Dan and Bethel, and there all Israelites were to sacrifice. The schism was complete.

Undoubtedly, this action of Jeroboam's was popular with the Israelites, who might well have looked upon the Temple at Jerusalem as a radical (and therefore irreligious) innovation, built on foreign soil by a foreign dynasty through forced labor.

Nevertheless, the new policy did not suit the prophetic party. Probably they would have preferred a closer adherence to ancient tradition, a reactivation of the shrines at places like Shechem and Shiloh, and a High Priesthood like that of Eli re-established. And this, precisely, was what Jeroboam probably didn't want; he wanted a ritual tied in with the new monarchy that would strengthen his dynasty. Then, too, Jeroboam had compromised with the desires of those people less capable of worshiping an abstract deity by placing the images of bulls in his sanctuary, symbolizing the fructifying element in nature.

Ahijah, the prophet, quickly disenchanted with the king he had helped to the throne, inveighed against him and delivered what he proclaimed to be God's word of doom:

> 1 Kings 14:9. . . . thou hast . . . made thee other gods, and molten images . . .
>
> 1 Kings 14:10. Therefore, behold, I will bring evil upon the house of Jeroboam . . .

Indeed, Jeroboam's dynasty was not to endure long, but the new kingdom of Israel was to persevere under several different dynasties for over two centuries. The kingdom of Judah, while always less prosperous and powerful than its northern sister, remained under the Davidic dynasty throughout and endured for three and a half centuries.

It is very common to speak of Israel as consisting of ten tribes, since there were traditionally twelve tribes in Israel and only Judah and Benjamin remained under Rehoboam. However, the tribal system had faded under David and Solomon, and in any case Reuben and Simeon had disappeared by the time of the schism. At best, then, the kingdom of Israel consisted of eight tribes.

Rehoboam died in 917 B.C. after having reigned sixteen years. Jeroboam died in 912 B.C., having reigned twenty-one years.

Ben-hadad

The division of the kingdom of David and Solomon made a continuation of any policy of imperial conquest virtually impossible. Neither half by itself had the strength to be a conquering nation, particularly since the energies of each were absorbed by a smolderingly continuous hostility between them. Each nation, furthermore, sought allies among the neighbors and enemies of the other and each labored to enfeeble the other by any means.

In Judah, Abijam, the son of Rehoboam, began his reign in 917 B.C., and he was succeeded by his son Asa in 915 B.C. They were the fourth and fifth kings of the Davidic dynasty.

In Israel, Jeroboam's son Nadab began his rule in 912 B.C. A rebellion against him by one of his generals, Baasha, succeeded. Nadab was slain and Baasha ascended the throne in 911 B.C. As a measure of prudence, to prevent a counter-revolt, he did as was often customary in these cases and had all the male members of Jeroboam's family executed. Jeroboam's dynasty thus survived Jeroboam's death by just one year.

Both Asa of Judah and Baasha of Israel had long reigns, the former reigning for forty years to 875 B.C. and the latter twenty-three years to 888 B.C. War between Israel and Judah continued in those years, and Asa, getting the worst of it, sought help abroad:

> 1 Kings 15:18. *Then Asa took . . . silver and . . . gold . . . and sent them to Ben-hadad . . . king of Syria, that dwelt at Damascus, saying,*
>
> 1 Kings 15:19. *There is a league between me and thee . . .*

Ben-hadad was the third member of the dynasty founded by Rezon (see page 334). In less than half a century, Damascus, from a small principality precariously maintaining its independence against Solomon, had grown to take over the leadership of the other Aramaean regions so that one could speak of Ben-hadad as a "king of Syria." And where David had crushed the Syrian towns and extorted tribute from them, the great-great-grandson of David paid tribute to them in order to gain their help.

Syria was now at least the equal of Israel in strength. It accepted the alliance of Judah and attacked Israel's northern frontier, sacking the city of Dan, for instance, and apparently destroying it permanently, for it is not further mentioned in the Bible. Baasha was forced to make peace and for the next century and a half, Syria, rather than Judah, was Israel's chief enemy.

Samaria

The history of Israel continued to be troubled with dynastic problems. Baasha's son Elah succeeded in 888 B.C. and then history repeated itself. In a palace revolution, Zimri, a leader among Elah's bodyguard, killed Elah and all the family of Baasha. He did not, however, survive to establish a new dynasty.

The general of Israel's armed forces, Omri, was then engaged in

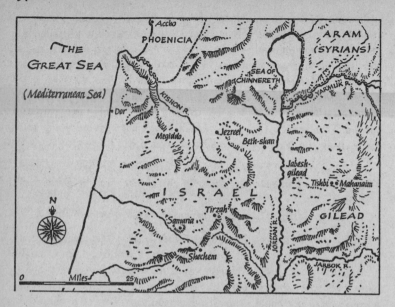

Samaria

besieging a Philistine city. He was acclaimed king of Israel by his troops and marched on Tirzah. Zimri died in the fiery ruins of his palace; another contender for the throne, Tibni, was also defeated and killed; and by 887 B.C. Omri held the throne firmly, the first member of Israel's third dynasty.

The capital city of Tirzah had now seen two dynasties brutally wiped out; the first having endured only twenty-two years, the second twenty-four years. That in itself was enough to make it an uncomfortable place for the new king. He cast about for a suitable site for a new capital, one that could be firmly identified with the new dynasty.

1 Kings 16:24. *And he bought the hill Samaria of Shemer . . . and built on the hill . . . the city . . . Samaria.*

The Hebrew name of the city, Shomron, is derived from Shemer, the name of the clan, or the individual, who owned the land before Omri's purchase. Samaria is, of course, the Greek version of the name.

Samaria lay about six miles northwest of Shechem, about midway between the Jordan River and the Mediterranean. It was centrally located in the kingdom and had considerable potentiality for defense
since it was located on an isolated hill. It remained the capital of Israel
through the remaining history of the kingdom (though its kings had
favorite residences elsewhere on occasion, notably at Jezreel) and
was sufficiently important to make Samaria a frequently used synonym
for the entire kingdom.

The energetic Omri reigned for only a dozen years but in that time,
secure in his new capital, he made Israel respected among her neighbors. To counter the danger of Syria, he made an alliance with the
Phoenician cities and so stabilized the kingdom that his son could reign
in peace after him—the first time that had happened in Israel's troubled history since the schism.

Such was the reputation of the king that in Assyrian inscriptions,
Israel is referred to as the "land of Omri."

Jezebel

Omri was succeeded by his son Ahab in 875 B.C. with the royal power
strengthened by the Phoenician alliance. At about the time that Omri
had come to the throne, the dynasty of Hiram (see page 325) had been
wiped out by Ithobaal (the Biblical "Ethbaal"), a priest of Ashtoreth,
who then succeeded to the throne. By Ahab's time. Ithobaal's seat on
the throne was clearly secure and Ahab felt safe in committing himself
not only to an alliance but to the reinforcing cement of a dynastic
marriage.

1 Kings 16:31. . . . *he* [Ahab] *took to wife Jezebel the daughter
of Ethbaal king of the Zidonians* . . .

It was customary for kings in that time of religious inclusiveness to
allow foreign queens their own religious rites, as Solomon had done
for his own numerous wives.

Jezebel, however, was a dominating woman who wanted not merely
to pursue the worship of her own particular "baal" (Melkart, a specific
name which does not appear in the Bible) but labored to establish
its worship throughout Israel generally. This may have been more than

religious fervor; it may have been a device on her part to tie Israel more firmly to the Phoenician cities for the benefit of both.

It apparently suited Ahab's purposes to encourage her in this, for the prophetic party with its attempts to limit royal power and to dictate foreign policy along supernationalist lines could, in his eyes, well stand being weakened.

1 Kings 16:30. *And he [Ahab] reared up an altar for Baal in the house of Baal which he had built in Samaria.*

Elijah

It was the good fortune of the prophetic party that it now found itself in the hands of a strong leader, Elijah, the most dominating prophetic figure since Samuel. In the face of persecution, Elijah and his followers hardened their own stand and became increasingly intolerant of other worship.

Because of the deadly battle that followed, which was, in the long run, won by the Yahvists, Jezebel has become the very byword of a wicked, idolatrous woman, whereas Elijah was remembered by later generations with a veneration second only to Moses'.

Elijah enters the Biblical story as the forecaster of a drought that was to take place as punishment for the policies of Jezebel.

1 Kings 17:1. *And Elijah the Tishbite, who was of the inhabitants of Gilead, said unto Ahab . . . there shall not be dew nor rain these years . . .*

Elijah was from Tishbi, a town in Gilead, east of the Jordan. Its site is uncertain but it has been identified with a small village just west of Mahanaim.

Zarephath

Elijah's bearding of Ahab made it necessary for the prophet to remain in hiding thereafter, first in the Jordan valley and then far north in Phoenicia itself (the very home of the religious enemy where, perhaps, it was least likely that the royalist forces would look for him).

1 Kings 17:10. . . . *he arose and went to Zarephath . . .*

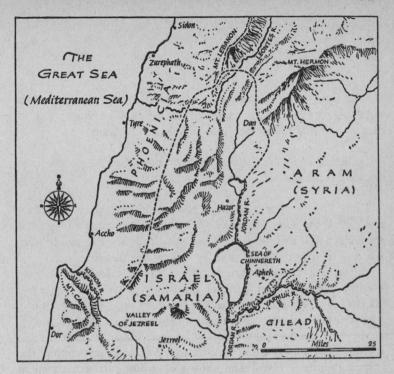

Zarephath and Mount Carmel

Zarephath is on the Phoenician seacoast, nearly twenty miles north of Tyre (Jezebel's home city) and eight miles south of Sidon. The modern Arabic town of Sarafand stands near the place. Among the ruins of the ancient town there stands a church on the traditional site of the house in which Elijah lodged during his stay there.

Back in Israel, the state of the prophetic party worsened. Only those remained alive who escaped Jezebel's harsh hand by flight or by going into hiding. Thus, Obadiah, a high official of Ahab's court and a secret Yahvist, helped some to live:

> 1 Kings 18:4. . . . *when Jezebel cut off the prophets of the Lord . . . Obadiah took an hundred prophets, and hid them . . . and fed them . . .*

Mount Carmel

After three years, however, Elijah took the chance of facing Ahab once more to foretell the imminent ending of the drought and to propose a direct contest between Yahveh and Melkart.

1 Kings 18:19. *Now therefore send, and gather to me all Israel unto Mount Carmel . . .*

There, Elijah proposed, eight hundred and fifty worshipers of Melkart and other Phoenician deities were to gather and attempt to light the fire under a sacrifice by means of their rites, while he alone and by himself was to try to do the same by calling on Yahveh.

Carmel is a mountainous ridge, about fifteen miles long, running northwest-southeast, just south of the Kishon River (see page 238). Its Hebrew name means "garden" or "vineyard" and, in ancient times particularly, it was well wooded and attractive. The maximum height, at about the middle of the ridge, is 1732 feet. Where it meets the sea, it forms a promontory called Cape Carmel. At the sea, just north of the ridge is the city of Haifa. The whole area is now part of the modern nation of Israel and Haifa is its second largest city. In ancient times, however, the site of Haifa carried no town of any importance.

The most important event in the history of Mount Carmel was the competition between Elijah and the worshipers of Melkart. Partly because of this and partly because it made for a pleasant retreat, it was a haunt for anchorites in early Christian times. When Palestine was temporarily in the hands of the Crusaders in the twelfth century A.D., a monastery was built there and an order of Carmelites was founded, an order which still flourishes.

The competition at Mount Carmel, which the Bible relates with loving detail, ended in a complete victory for Elijah. The wood caught fire at Elijah's word, after all the hundreds of competing priests found themselves unable to do a thing.

Ahab, witnessing the feat, was awed and impressed and allowed Elijah to order the massacre of the Baalists at the Kishon River.

Jezreel

For the moment, the towering figure of Elijah dominated King Ahab, all the more so as the drought ended at this time. Together, king and prophet left Mount Carmel:

> 1 Kings 18:45. . . . *And Ahab rode, and went to Jezreel.*
> 1 Kings 18:46. *And* . . . *Elijah* . . . *ran before Ahab to the entrance of Jezreel.*

The city of Jezreel was located in the valley of Jezreel (see page 241) about twenty-five miles southeast of Carmel and an equal distance north of Samaria. It was a favorite residence of Ahab and Jezebel.

Ahab must have told Jezebel of Elijah's deed with great enthusiasm but Jezebel was not impressed. She undoubtedly knew how the priests of Melkart arranged miracles when they wished to impress the populace, and she must have been certain that Elijah had merely managed to outsmart her own group in chicanery, nothing more.

We can well imagine that under her withering scorn, Ahab's newfound enthusiasm for the prophets faded. He allowed Jezebel to take over the reins of the religious policy once more and again Elijah was forced into exile, traveling southward this time through Judah to Mount Sinai, the traditional home of Yahveh.

It seemed to him that only the complete overthrow of the house of Omri would save Yahvism and he began long-range plans in this direction. Aware that the consummation of those plans might outlast his own time, he selected a successor to himself, one strong enough, in his estimation, to carry on the fight:

> 1 Kings 19:19. *So he departed thence, and found Elisha* . . . *who was plowing* . . . *and Elijah passed by him, and cast his mantle upon him.*

Ben-hadad II

Meanwhile Ahab had his hands full with the Syrian problem. Ben-hadad, who had defeated Israel badly in Baasha's time several

decades before had been succeeded by his son Hadad-ezer, who is
referred to in the Bible as another Ben-hadad, and who can therefore
be called Ben-hadad II. (Hadad was a storm-god, well known over
southwestern Asia and particularly popular at Damascus. He served as
the national god of the Syrians and his name was therefore commonly incorporated into the royal name. Ben-hadad means the "son
of Hadad.")

Ben-hadad II continued the firm, anti-Israel policy of his father:

> 1 Kings 20:1. *And Ben-hadad the king of Syria gathered all his*
> *host together . . . and he went up and besieged Samaria . . .*

Samaria held out but was hard pressed indeed and, for a while,
was minded to surrender even under harsh terms. At this sign of
weakness, however, Ben-hadad raised the price for surrender and
Ahab was forced into continued warfare. He decided to risk everything on a pitched battle and retorted to a threat of destruction sent
him by Ben-hadad with an aphorism that, in one form or another, is
famous:

> 1 Kings 20:11. *And the king of Israel answered and said, Tell*
> *him, Let not him that girdeth on his harness boast himself as he*
> *that putteth it off.*

In other words, "Don't boast at the start of a battle as you would
at the end of a victorious one." Or, in its most common form to
us: "Don't count your chickens before they are hatched."

And Ahab proved his meaning well, for the Israelites fought with the
fury of despair and the overconfident Syrian army was forced to
flee after many casualties. —

Aphek

A second battle was fought the next year.

> 1 Kings 20:26. *And it came to pass at the return of the year,*
> *that Ben-hadad numbered the Syrians and went up to Aphek, to*
> *fight against Israel.*

This is not the Aphek that figured in the wars against the
Philistines two centuries earlier (see page 271), but is rather a town

that is identified with the modern village of Fik, about three miles east of the Sea of Galilee, and roughly midway between Samaria and Damascus.

It was a measure of the size of the victory of the previous year that Ahab, who had then been besieged in his capital, could now meet the foe at the frontier.

This time the victory was again Israel's to an extent even greater than the first. Ben-hadad was forced to surrender, relinquish his father's conquests, and allow Israel commercial privileges in Damascus. Israel was stronger now than at any time since the schism with Judah.

In Ahab's wars against Syria, the prophetic party was on his side. Whatever the quarrels between prophets and monarch within the land, they closed ranks against the foreigner. Thus, it was a prophet who encouraged Ahab before the relief of Samaria:

> 1 Kings 20:13. And . . . there came a prophet unto Ahab . . . saying, Thus saith the Lord, Hast thou seen all this great multitude? behold, I will deliver it into thine hand this day . . .

But Ahab's relatively mild peace with the Syrians bitterly displeased the ultranationalist prophetic party and intensified their opposition to the throne.

Yet Ahab seems to have been statesmanlike in this respect. A living Syria, allied with Israel, and unembittered by unnecessary destruction and harsh oppression, could be a useful friend, particularly since a new enemy to both loomed to the north.

Assyria, of which much more will be said later, was under a strong king, Shalmaneser III, and was spreading its domination over the Fertile Crescent. According to Assyrian documents a battle was fought in 854 B.C. at Karkar (or Qarqar), a city located about a hundred miles north of Damascus, between Shalmaneser and an allied army led by Ben-hadad and Ahab in alliance. The Assyrians claim a victory but that is routine in the chronicles of the time. The fact is that the Assyrians annexed no territory and were therefore held to a draw at the least.

This stand against Assyria saved both Syria and Israel and gave each over a century of additional life and that certainly vindicated Ahab's policy of not fighting Syria to exhaustion so that both might fall helplessly into the Assyrian throat.

Oddly enough, there is no mention of the battle of Karkar in the

Bible. It may be that the Biblical writers were not willing to report
so clear an indication that the prophetic party was wrong and Ahab
right.

Naboth

Indeed, the Bible passes directly from the Syrian victory to the
darkest deed of Ahab's reign as though to neutralize his military
prowess by reference to his moral shortcomings.

Near Ahab's palace in Jezreel, there was a vineyard owned by
a man named Naboth, which Ahab would have liked to have for his
own.

> 1 Kings 21:2. *And Ahab spake unto Naboth saying, Give me
> thy vineyard . . . and I will give thee for it a better vineyard . . .
> or . . . the worth of it in money.*

Naboth refused to sell his ancestral holdings, however, and Ahab
was helpless. Jezebel, however, was not. She bribed two men to swear
that Naboth had committed treason and blasphemy and Naboth, thus
framed, was executed. His vineyard, naturally, was confiscated by the
throne, as was routine for the property of traitors.

The deed was very much like that in which David had arranged
the death of Uriah and the "confiscation" of Uriah's wife. As Nathan
had then denounced David to his face, so now Elijah appeared to denounce Ahab. Once more, the prophetic party placed itself on record
as favoring the liberties of the people against royal oppression.

Ramoth-gilead

Israel was strong enough now, in the last years of Ahab's reign,
to exert a clear domination over Judah, as well as over Syria. In
875 B.C., the same year in which Ahab had succeeded to the throne of
Israel, Asa of Judah had died and his son Jehoshaphat (the sixth king
of the Davidic dynasty) had succeeded. The continuing war with
Israel had brought little good to Judah, and Jehoshaphat discontinued
it and sought instead alliance and friendship with Ahab. He turned
his eyes southward for expansion, maintaining the old grip on Edom

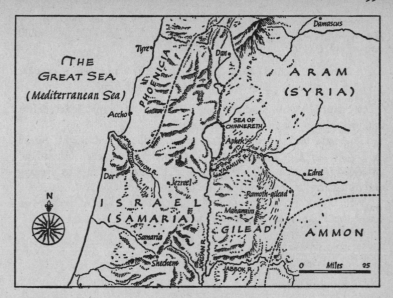

Ramoth-gilead

and trying to reinstate Solomon's old trade on the Red Sea, Judah's only gateway to the wide world outside. Here he was unsuccessful as Judah lacked the necessary experience with seagoing. An offer of help by Ahab was refused, for Jehoshaphat, though willing to be friends with Ahab, was not willing to give Ahab too much power in Judah.

The war with Syria had not been brought to a completely successful conclusion in Ahab's eyes, however, for one important piece of Israelite territory remained in Syrian hands. Ahab proposed to Jehoshaphat a united campaign against Syria for the recovery of the territory:

1 Kings 22:4. *And he* [Ahab] *said unto Jehoshaphat, Wilt thou go with me to battle to Ramoth-gilead?* . . .

Ramoth-gilead is another of the Trans-Jordan cities. Its exact location is unknown but it is usually considered to be somewhere north of Mahanaim.

There is an indication here that Yahvism was stronger in Judah than in Israel. Before the battle, Ahab consulted the prophets (at

Jehoshaphat's suggestion) but chose four hundred prophets of the Phoenician deities. They predicted victory, but Jehoshaphat would not accept that:

> 1 Kings 22:7. And Jehoshaphat said, Is there not here a prophet of the Lord besides, that we might inquire of him?

Reluctantly, Ahab produced one, who promptly predicted defeat and was placed in prison for his pains.

The battle took place. It was long and bloody and might indeed have gone to the Israelites, but a chance arrow struck Ahab and wounded him seriously. Though he fought on, death came by evening and the Israelites broke off the battle.

With the death, in 853 B.C., of Ahab, after a reign of twenty-two years, the First Book of Kings comes to an end.

12. 2 KINGS

MOAB • BAALZEBUB • ELISHA • MESHA • NAAMAN • JEHORAM OF JUDAH • HAZAEL • JEHU • JEHOASH • BEN-HADAD III • AMAZIAH • JEROBOAM II • PUL • REZIN • SHALMANESER V • SO • HABOR • SAMARITANS • SENNACHERIB • TIRHAKAH • ESARHADDON • BERODACH-BALADAN • MANASSEH • JOSIAH • PHARAOH-NECHOH • NEBUCHADNEZZAR • GEDALIAH • EVIL-MERODACH

Moab

The death of a strong king is bound to be followed by disorders, as subject peoples seize the chance to rebel, and as surrounding independent nations take the opportunity to attack. Moab struck as soon as news reached it of Ahab's death:

> 2 Kings 1:1. *Then Moab rebelled against Israel after the death of Ahab.*

The schism between Israel and Judah had made it almost impossible for either nation to do much more than hold its own territory. Judah maintained a precarious hold on Edom, and Israel held the Trans-Jordan. Syria in the north of Israel was permanently independent and when it was strong, its power tended to stretch out over the Trans-Jordan.

Similarly, when Israel was strong, its armies pressed south from Gilead and controlled Moab. This happened in the reign of Omri when that capable monarch (much underrated in the Bible) took Moab about 880 B.C. Ahab held it through his own stormy reign, but with his death Moab rose.

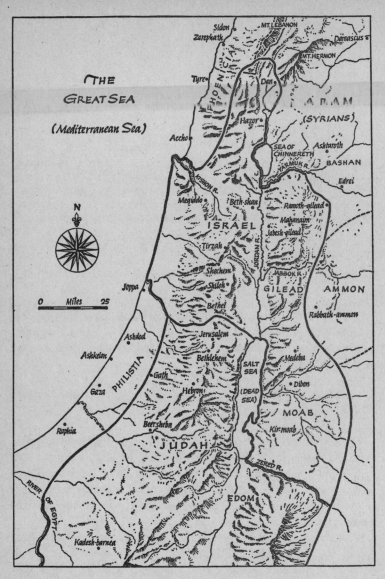

The following labels appear on the map:

Sidon
Zarephath
MT. LEBANON
Damascus

Tyre
Dan
MT. HERMON

THE
GREAT SEA

(Mediterranean Sea)

PHOENICIA

ARAM
(SYRIANS)

Hazor

SEA OF
CHINNERETH
Ashtaroth
BASHAN

Accho

KISHON R.
YARMUK R.
Edrei

N

Megiddo
Beth-shan
Ramoth-gilead

ISRAEL
Mahanaim
Jabesh-gilead

Tirzah

JORDAN R.

0   Miles   25

Shechem
JABBOK R.

Joppa
Shiloh
GILEAD
AMMON

Bethel
Rabbath-ammon

Jerusalem

Ashdod
Bethlehem
Medeba

Ashkelon
PHILISTIA
SALT
SEA

Gath
Dibon

Gaza
Hebron
(DEAD
SEA)

Beersheba
Kir-moab

Raphia
MOAB

JUDAH
ZERED R.

RIVER OF EGYPT
EDOM

Kadesh-barnea

Israel and Judah

Baalzebub

Ahab's son Ahaziah succeeded to the throne (the first time an Israelite dynasty survived to be represented by a third member) and found himself faced with the Moabite insurrection. Unfortunately, he sustained a bad fall, lay seriously ill, and was unable to lead the army.

2 Kings 1:2. . . . *and he [Ahaziah] sent messengers and said unto them, Go, inquire of Baalzebub the god of Ekron whether I shall recover of this disease.*

Baalzebub (more familiar in the New Testament version of the spelling, Beelzebub) means "Lord of the Flies."

This sounds odd at first and there are at least two explanations of its meaning. One is that the actual name was Baalzebul, meaning "Lord of the House," that is, "Lord of the Temple," a natural title for people to give their chief god. It would then seem that the Biblical writers, unable to bring themselves to give an idol a title which seemed to them to belong only to Yahveh, converted it to Baalzebub by the change of a letter.

A second explanation is that Baalzebub really did mean "Lord of the Flies" and that this was a legitimate title of the chief god of the Philistine city of Ekron, for it meant he had the power to bring or prevent insect plagues, which were great and fearful realities in the ancient world. It is not unlikely that the ancients noticed the rise in disease incidence where flies were plentiful and a "Lord of the Flies" might be, in general, a god with special powers in the field of health and medicine. This would explain why Ahaziah in his extremity should seek out Baalzebub in particular even though (as he must have known) this would enrage the prophetic party in Israel. And this it did, for Elijah arrived at once to denounce the action.

For some reason, Baalzebub grew to receive particular attention from the later Jews as the idolatrous god par excellence. Thus, when the reports of Jesus' ability to heal men spread, some said skeptically:

Matthew 12:24. . . . *This fellow doth not cast out devils, but by Beelzebub the prince of the devils.*

By "prince" we mean leader or chief so that Beelzebub (the New Testament spelling) was considered the chief devil, the being more familiarly known to us as Satan. In *Paradise Lost*, John Milton makes use of a whole hierarchy of fallen angels and therefore has Satan and Beelzebub as separate beings, but he makes Beelzebub second only to Satan.

To return to Ahaziah— His appeal to Baalzebub was of no help to him. He died after reigning two years and his younger brother, Jehoram, also referred to as Joram, fourth member of the dynasty of Omri, ascended the throne in 852 B.C.

Elisha

Elijah, the great leader of the prophetic party, did not long survive Ahaziah. The Bible recounts the legend that he was taken up alive into heaven:

> 2 Kings 2:11. . . . *there appeared a chariot of fire, and horses of fire, . . . and Elijah went up by a whirlwind into heaven.*

His lieutenant, Elisha, remained behind to inherit his position and his aims. This is indicated by a physical action that has entered into the language as a metaphor:

> 2 Kings 2:13. *He* [Elisha] *took up . . . the mantle of Elijah that fell upon him, and went back . . .*

From this point on, to his death a half century or more later, Elisha headed the prophetic party and kept it in vigorous life.

Elijah lived on, however, in the awed memory of later generations. His bold stand against a powerful king and queen in favor of Yahvism, his courageous denunciation of tyranny and absolutism, was infinitely impressive and must have led to the feeling that nothing less than a living translation into heaven could do for so holy a man. This, in turn, encouraged the thought that someone taken alive into heaven might someday return alive from heaven.

In later generations when the kingdom of Israel and Judah had both been destroyed and when the surviving Jews looked forward with mingled hope and dread to the day when the Lord would set up a new order on earth, it was felt that Elijah would then play a key role. Thus, the prophet Malachi, writing four centuries after Elijah, states God's promise as:

> Malachi 4:5. *Behold, I will send you Elijah the prophet before the coming of the great and dreadful day of the Lord.*

In the New Testament, in which the view is taken that the new order on earth has been brought by Jesus, the forecoming of Elijah is accepted. Jesus is quoted as saying:

> Matthew 17:12. *But I say unto you, That Elias* [Elijah] *is come already . . .*
> Matthew 17:13. *Then the disciples understood that he spake unto them of John the Baptist.*

Mesha

Moab was still in successful rebellion at the time of Jehoram's accession to the throne of Israel, and the fact is noted once more, this time with the name of the Moabite ruler:

> 2 Kings 3:4. *And Mesha king of Moab . . .*
> 2 Kings 3:5. . . . *rebelled against the king of Israel.*

Israel under Jehoram was still allied with Jehoshaphat of Judah and this fact offered the Israelite monarch a strategic opportunity. Rather than attack Moab from the north in a straight head-to-head clash, a combined Israelite-Judean army could move southward through Edom (a Judean dependency) and around the southern edge of the Dead Sea. Moab could then be attacked along her unprepared southern frontier. The march, however, was a difficult one. The heat and lack of water must have badly damaged soldier morale and led Jehoram to fear either an ignominious retreat or a disastrous defeat.

Jehoshaphat at this point (as several years before with Ahab) suggested that a prophet be consulted. (This is good policy since if the prophet predicts victory, soldier morale shoots upward and this may indeed suffice to produce victory.) This time it was Elisha that stood before the monarchs and again it is clear that the prophetic party

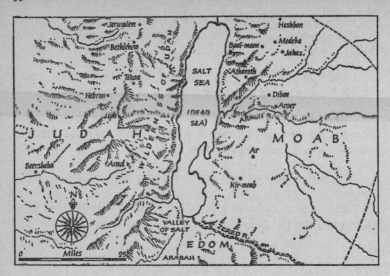

Mesha's Kingdom

was closer at heart to rustic Judah than to citified Israel, for Elisha says contemptuously to Jehoram:

2 Kings 3:14. . . . *were it not that I regard the presence of Jehoshaphat . . . I would not look toward thee, nor see thee.*

Elisha predicts victory and, indeed, victories of the combined kings over the Moabites are recorded. But then, in one cryptic verse, the whole is nullified and Moab is left free and independent.

2 Kings 3:27. *Then he* [Mesha of Moab] *took his eldest son . . . and offered him for a burnt offering upon the wall. And there was great indignation against Israel: and they* [the allied forces] *departed from him, and returned to their own land.*

To understand this, we must remember that Moab's cultural and religious level was much like that of Israel and Judah. In 1869, a German missionary, F. A. Klein, discovered a memorial inscription on a piece of black basalt, three and a half feet high and two feet wide. It was found in the ruins of Dibon, a Moabite city about twelve miles east of the Dead Sea and some four miles north of the Arnon River.

It turned out to be an inscription in ancient Hebrew (the oldest lengthy inscription in that writing now extant) and it had been set up by Mesha to commemorate the events of his reign. It is called the "stone of Mesha" or the "Moabite stone."

The language used has a Biblical sound except that the Moabite god, Chemosh, replaces the Israelite God, Yahveh. Thus, the stone says: "Omri, King of Israel, afflicted Moab for many days, because Chemosh was angry with his land." Also, "Chemosh said unto me, Go, take Nebo against Israel" and "Chemosh drave him out from before me," and so on.

To many at this time it must have seemed that there was a rough kind of democracy among gods, each having its own territory within which it might ordinarily be supreme, until such time as one god might develop greater strength than another so that the human agents of one would then be able to invade the land and defeat the human agents of the other. This view, "henotheism," was that of the vast majority of ancient peoples.

It is very likely that even the Yahvists were at this time henotheists, though this is hard to tell from the Bible, for the later writers, whose views of Yahveh were considerably more exalted, would have been embarrassed by such evidence as they might find in the traditional legends and chronicles and would have modified them. Verse 3:27 in 2 Kings is a case in point.

If a god is angry with his people, he may be propitiated by a sacrifice; the more valued the object sacrificed the more certain the propitiation. The sacrifice of a human would be better than that of any animal and the sacrifice of the heir to the throne would be best of all. The Biblical writers are firm in their insistence that Yahveh was not like the gods of other nations and abhorred human sacrifice, but Abraham's near sacrifice of Isaac, and Jephthah's actual sacrifice of his daughter are traces of a more primitive view.

Certainly Chemosh did not disapprove of human sacrifice and Mesha, driven to despair by the victorious advance of the allied army, sacrificed his son. This could well be a useful act in a henotheistic society. The Moabite army, aware of the sacrifice, would be certain that Chemosh would now be fighting on their side. Since the battle was on Moabite territory and Chemosh was supreme in Moab, they could fight with the assurance of victory.

The allied army, equally aware of the sacrifice, would feel Yahveh to be weak on alien soil and would fight in equal expectation of defeat. With the Moabites sure of winning and the Israelites sure of losing there could only be one outcome.

The phrase "there was great indignation against Israel" is given in the Revised Standard Version as "there came great wrath upon Israel," and it seems very likely that the indignation or wrath here spoken of was that of Chemosh. It is possible that the earliest form of the verse was "there came the great wrath of Chemosh upon Israel," and the Biblical writers, unwilling to make it appear that Chemosh was a real god who could display effective wrath, or was anything more than a false idol, eliminated the mention of his name.

Naaman

The early chapters of 2 Kings include a number of wonder tales concerning Elisha, and the best developed of these involves a Syrian general who, according to Jewish legend (but *not* according to anything in the Bible) had been the one whose arrow had slain Ahab:

> 2 Kings 5:1. *Now Naaman, captain of the host of the king of Syria, was . . . a mighty man in valour, but he was a leper.*

A young Israelite maidservant, taken captive in the wars with Israel, suggested that Naaman consult the wonder-working Elisha in Israel. Naaman followed this advice and was instructed to wash himself seven times in the Jordan River. Despite Naaman's initial nationalistic indignation at the suggestion that the Jordan had greater curative powers than the rivers of Syria, he did as he was told and was cured.

This, naturally, convinced Naaman of the power of Yahveh:

> 2 Kings 5:17. *And Naaman said, Shall there not . . . be given to thy servant two mules' burden of earth? for thy servant will henceforth offer neither burnt offering nor sacrifice unto other gods, but unto the Lord.*

Henotheistically, he required the earth, for in sacrificing to Yahveh, he would have to stand on the soil of Israel, or it would do no good. By bringing some Israelite soil to Damascus he would create for himself a little island over which Yahveh would have power.

Israel and Syria (Aram)

Naaman also recognized that he could not carry his private worship too far or make it too exclusive, and he said to Elisha:

> 2 Kings 5:18. *In this thing the Lord pardon thy servant, that when my master goeth into the house of Rimmon to worship there, and he leaneth on my hand, and I bow myself in the house of Rimmon . . .*

Elisha's answer was a simple:

> 2 Kings 5:19. . . . *Go in peace . . .*

which was the equivalent of consent. Perhaps the earliest versions of the story gave the consent more explicitly, for Elisha (who is not recorded as objecting to Naaman's assumption that only on Israelite soil could Yahveh be worshiped) might have been more of a henotheist himself than the later Biblical writers were willing to allow.

Rimmon, by the way, seems to be an alternate name for Hadad, the national god of Damascus. Hadad was a storm-god and "Rimmon" seems to mean "the Thunderer." (This was precisely the epithet often given to the Greek storm-god, Zeus.)

As a result of verse 5:18, the expression "to bow to Rimmon" has come to mean the act of conforming to a social custom one knows to be wrong merely in order to avoid trouble.

Jehoram of Judah

Judah continued her policy of careful subservience to Israel. When, in 851 B.C., Jehoshaphat of Judah died, after having reigned for twenty-four years:

> 2 Kings 8:16. . . . *Jehoram the son of Jehoshaphat . . . began to reign.*

Jehoram (or Joram) of Judah, the seventh king of the Davidic dynasty, happened to have the same name as that of the contemporary king of Israel. Another link was in the form of a dynastic marriage, for Jehoram of Judah was married to Athaliah, the daughter of Ahab and Jezebel, and was therefore brother-in-law, as well as namesake, to Jehoram of Israel.

While Jehoshaphat had been alive, Yahvism was in the ascendant in Judah at least, but Jehoram of Judah was, apparently, as much under the influence of Athaliah as Ahab of Israel had been under the influence of Jezebel:

> 2 Kings 8:18. *And he* [Jehoram of Judah] *walked in the way of . . . the house of Ahab: for the daughter of Ahab was his wife.*

Then, too, just as after the death of Ahab, Moab had revolted against Israel, so now after the death of Jehoshaphat, Edom revolted against Judah.

Jehoram died in 844 B.C. and his son Ahaziah, the eighth king of the Davidic dynasty, came to the throne. (To add further to the confusion of those trying to keep these names straight, Ahaziah, the son of Jehoram of Judah, was the namesake of Ahaziah, the elder brother of Jehoram of Israel.)

Ahaziah of Judah was a young man of twenty-two, completely under the thumb of his mother Athaliah. Judah seemed doomed to be absorbed by Israel.

Hazael

That this did not happen was due, partly, to Israel's continuing troubles with Syria.

About the time that Ahaziah became king of a shrunken and tottering Judah, a palace revolution took place in Damascus. When Ben-hadad II of Syria fell sick, one of his courtiers, Hazael, hastened the death of the old king:

> 2 Kings 8:15. . . . he [Hazael] *took a thick cloth, and dipped it in water, and spread it on his* [Ben-hadad's] *face so that he died: and Hazael reigned in his stead.*

Hazael turned out to be a vigorous ruler and under him, in fact, Syria rose to the peak of its power.

The war over Ramoth-gilead, where Ahab had received his fatal wound a dozen years before, was renewed now. In the course of the war, Jehoram of Israel was wounded and forced to retire to Jezreel, leaving the army under the command of his general, Jehu.

While Jehoram remained in Jezreel, recuperating, his ally (and nephew) Ahaziah of Judah came to Jezreel, as an assurance, presumably, of his loyalty. Jezebel was still alive, and in Jezreel, and it might well have been a source of pride to her to see the two kings together; one her son and the other her grandson. Disaster, however, was close at hand.

Jehu

Jehoram's wound gave the prophetic party its opportunity. A disabled king was useless in time of war and the people might welcome the opportunity to place a vigorous general on the throne instead. Such a general was Jehu, who was either a Yahvist or was willing to become one to gain the throne.

Elisha sent to assure him of the support of the prophetic party and urged him to assume the kingship. His fellow officers were enthusiastically willing:

> 2 Kings 9:13. . . . *they hasted . . . and blew with trumpets, saying, Jehu is king.*

Jehu marched instantly on Jezreel with the intention of laying it under siege and establishing his kingship by executing Jehoram. Jehoram and Ahaziah, the two kings, came out to meet Jehu's army and did so, according to the Biblical writer, in the very vineyard that had once belonged to Naboth (see page 350). There Jehu killed Jehoram and when Ahaziah attempted to escape, had him pursued and killed likewise.

Jezebel, her son and grandson dead, retained her pride and courage to the end.

> 2 Kings 9:30. *And when Jehu was come to Jezreel, Jezebel heard of it; and she painted her face, and tired her head, and looked out at a window.*

That is, she put on eye make-up (the Revised Standard Version renders the phrase "she painted her eyes and adorned her head") to hide any signs of grief and to show herself even at this last moment a queen. Posterity, unwilling to give the old queen credit for any virtue, even that of courage, uses the term "painted Jezebel" to signify not bravery in the face of disaster, but merely to signify wickedness—usually sexual wickedness, of which there is no Biblical ground for accusing Jezebel.

From the window, Jezebel taunted Jehu with being another Zimri, who had killed a king but who had lived to rule only seven days before giving way to Omri, the founder of the house which Jehu was now destroying (see page 342).

Jehu did not allow himself to be disturbed by the comparison. He had Jezebel thrown from the window and killed. Having done that, he proceeded to take the usual dynastic precautions:

> 2 Kings 10:11. *So Jehu slew all that remained of the house of Ahab in Jezreel, and all his great men, and his kinsfolks, and his priests, until he left him none remaining.*

The house of Omri, Israel's third dynasty, had thus lasted forty-four years, and had seen four kings: Omri, Ahab, Ahaziah, and Jehoram. Now, in 843 B.C., the line was at an end and Jehu founded the fourth dynasty of Israel.

The worship of the Phoenician god, Melkart, was so intimately entwined with the house of Omri that it was good policy for Jehu to destroy the cult. He killed its priests and desecrated its temples and restored Yahvism to its wonted supremacy. However, it was Yahvism after the fashion of Jeroboam, with its bull-worshiping sanctuaries. To the more advanced of the prophetic party, this was insufficient.

Moreover, the civil war in Israel was Hazael's opportunity. The army in Ramoth-gilead could scarcely stand before him while Israel itself was convulsed in political and religious revolution.

> 2 Kings 10:32. *In those days . . . Hazael smote them in all the coasts of Israel;*
>
> 2 Kings 10:33. *From Jordan eastward, all the land of Gilead . . .*

Israel, its Trans-Jordanian territories lost, was penned between the Jordan and the sea.

Jehu had to find help. None could be received from Phoenicia after Jehu's actions against the Tyrian princess Jezebel and all that she had represented. Nor could any be expected from Judah, which was, temporarily, in the grip of Jezebel's vengeful daughter, Athaliah.

Jehu therefore turned to the one remaining source of help—Assyria. That powerful nation was still under the rule of Shalmaneser III, who, nearly fifteen years before, had been withstood by the united forces of Syria and Israel. Now the new king of Israel paid tribute to Assyria in 841 B.C. and acknowledged Assyrian overlordship in return for Assyrian help against Syria, thus helping to hasten the day when Syria and Israel alike would fall prey to the Assyrian power.

The fact of Jehu's tribute to Assyria is known from Assyrian inscriptions; it is not mentioned in the Bible. The Assyrian records call Jehu by the then usual title used by them for the kings of Israel—the "son of Omri." This, despite the fact that Jehu, far from being a descendant of Omri, had just killed every such descendant he could find. Jehu reigned for twenty-eight years, dying in 816 B.C.

Jehoash

The house of Omri still remained in Judah in the person of Ahaziah's mother, Athaliah, the daughter of Ahab and Jezebel. She

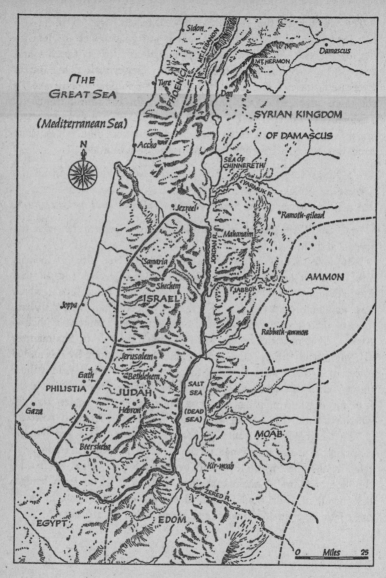

Syria at Its Height

seized power at the news of the slaying of her son Ahaziah by the usurper, Jehu. To keep herself in power, she destroyed all the males of the house of David she could find.

2 Kings 11:2. *But Jehosheba, the daughter of king Joram* [Jehoram of Judah], *sister of Ahaziah, took Joash the son of Ahaziah, and stole him from among the king's sons which were slain; and they hid him . . . from Athaliah, so that he was not slain.*

2 Kings 11:3. *And he was with her hid in the house of the Lord six years. And Athaliah did reign over the land.*

If Jehosheba was the daughter of king Jehoram and the sister of Ahaziah, she must also have been the daughter of Athaliah, unless she was the daughter of Jehoram by a concubine. The Bible does not make that clear. It seems difficult to believe that Athaliah would kill her own grandsons and it may be that the "king's sons" referred to are the various male members of the house of David, the sons and grandsons of Jehoram by various concubines.

The hiding of Jehoash (or Joash) might conceivably have been intended not so much to save him from death, but to save him from an upbringing according to Athaliah's religious views.

In 837 B.C., Jehoiada the High Priest (and husband of Jehosheba) felt the time was right. He displayed the person of the boy-king to the Judean generals and allowed the mystic aura of descent from David to do its work.

The army was won over and Athaliah was killed. The cult of Melkart which she had established in Jerusalem was wiped out, and Jehoash reigned as the ninth king of the Davidic dynasty.

It is interesting to note, though, that Jehoash was the grandson of Athaliah and the great-grandson of Ahab and Jezebel. Through all future kings of Judah ran the blood not only of David but also of Jezebel.

The reign of Jehoash had its share of disasters. Hazael of Syria, having swept up the Trans-Jordan, circled the Dead Sea, laid siege to and conquered the Philistine city of Gath, and was then ready to march against Jerusalem itself. The city was saved only when Jehoash used the treasures of the Temple as tribute to Hazael, bribing him, in effect, to leave Jerusalem in peace.

This humiliated the army leaders, of course, and enraged the priest-hood. In 797 B.C., Jehoash, having so narrowly escaped one palace revolution when a baby, fell prey to another, and was assassinated by disaffected conspirators. He had reigned thirty-nine years—forty-five, if the period of Athaliah's usurpation is added to the toll.

Ben-hadad III

After Jehu's death in 816 B.C., his son Jehoahaz succeeded to the throne and continued to wage a losing fight against the formidable Hazael of Syria. Jehoahaz, after a sixteen-year reign, died in 800 B.C. and was succeeded by his son Jehoash. (Again the reigning monarchs of Israel and Judah were, for a few years, namesakes.)

The Syrian tide was beginning to ebb, however. In 810 B.C., the Syrian conqueror had died:

> 2 Kings 13:24. . . . *Hazael king of Syria died: and Ben-hadad his son, reigned in his stead.*

This was Ben-hadad III, whose proper name, apparently, before he adopted the royal cognomen, was Mari. Israel's temporary salvation lay not so much in its own efforts as in the fact that Syria was at this time being pounded hard by Assyria.

Assyrian power was in a period of rapid decline after the death of Shalmaneser III in 824 B.C. (while Jehu was still king of Israel) but in a brief flash of effort under Adadnirari III, it managed to besiege Damascus in 805 B.C. and inflict serious punishment.

Assyria's weakness prevented her from completing the conquest of Syria, but the hand of Ben-hadad III had been permanently en-feebled and Israel in three campaigns under Jehoash was able to re-cover the territories lost to Hazael.

The Israelite monarch was supported in these campaigns by the ultranationalist prophetic party, of course. In the course of these campaigns, Elisha died and a sorrowing Jehoash was at his bedside.

Elisha was not succeeded by anyone of similar force, and the prophetic party in Israel declined and was not an important factor in the final three quarters of a century of Israel's existence.

Amaziah

The fortunes of Judah also seemed to take a temporary upturn. In the reign of Amaziah, Edom, which had retained its independence for fifty years since the death of Jehoshaphat, was retaken:

> 2 Kings 14:7. *He* [Amaziah] *slew of Edom . . . ten thousand . . .*

Amaziah, heartened by this victory, attempted then to break the subservient alliance that the kings of Judah had maintained with the kings of Israel for eighty years. Unfortunately, he was not that strong. He might beat Edom but in battle with Israel he lost. Jerusalem was taken by Jehoash of Israel, part of its fortifications were destroyed, and the Temple was sacked.

Amaziah, as a result of this military humiliation, met the same fate as his father. In 780 B.C., after a seventeen-year reign, Amaziah was assassinated and his son Azariah sat on the throne as the eleventh king of the Davidic dynasty.

Jeroboam II

In 785 B.C. Jehoash of Israel died and was succeeded by his son Jeroboam II, the fourth monarch of the line of Jehu. He reigned for forty years till 744 B.C. and under him Israel reached the height of prosperity and power.

Syria's desperate wounding by Assyria combined with the Assyrian period of weakness that intensified afterward and left a power vacuum to the north. Jeroboam II filled it:

> 2 Kings 14:25. *He restored the coast of Israel from the entering of Hamath unto the sea of the plain.*

Hamath is a town in northern Syria and the sea of the plain is the Dead Sea. By this verse is meant then that Israel was in control of all of Syria, probably in the sense that the cities of Syria were forced to pay tribute to Jeroboam. (Syrian home rule continued, however, and there was still a ruler in Damascus who might be called the king of

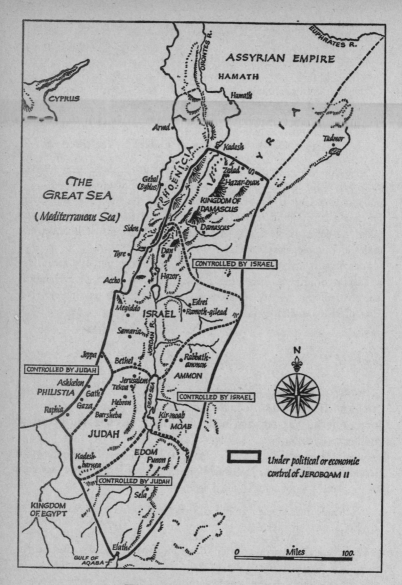

The Kingdom of Jeroboam II

Syria.) Judah, as a result of its defeat during the previous reign, was probably also a tributary, so that for the space of a few decades at least, the empire of David and Solomon seemed restored.

It was but a brief bit of Indian summer, however, that could endure only until giant Assyria was on its feet again. It lasted the time of Jeroboam II, but scarcely any more.

When Zachariah, the son of Jeroboam II, ascended the throne of Israel in 744 B.C., he represented the fifth generation of the line of Jehu, whose great-great-grandson he was. The dynasty had endured an unprecedented (for Israel) hundred years—but the end was at hand. Zachariah had been reigning only six months when he was unseated and murdered by a palace conspiracy, and after a month of confusion, an army officer named Menahem forced his own acceptance as the new king.

Pul

Menahem's hold on the throne was insecure and, as is not uncommon in such cases, he sought foreign help:

> 2 Kings 15:19. And Pul the king of Assyria came against the land: and Menahem gave Pul a thousand talents of silver, that his hand might be with him to confirm the kingdom in his hand.

Assyria had had prior contacts with Israel (see pages 349 and 365) but until now it had been Syria that was the prime danger. Now it was Assyria itself and so although the Biblical writers had ignored Assyria before, they can do so no longer. In this verse, contact between Assyria and Israel is mentioned for the first time, and it might be well here to review Assyria's history.

Assyria had been a wealthy and prosperous merchant realm in Abraham's time and this period of its history is sometimes referred to as the "Old Assyrian Empire." In the next few centuries, however, Assyria was hard put to it to survive under the pressures of the great powers of the age: Egypt, the Hittites, and the Mitanni.

It was only after the destruction and anarchy that followed upon the coming of the Peoples of the Sea that Assyria was to have its chance again. With the Hittite and Mitanni realms virtually destroyed and with Egypt weakened and driven out of Asia, Assyria stepped forward.

About 1200 B.C., while the Israelites were making their way toward Canaan, the Assyrian king Tukulti-Ninurta (the Biblical Nimrod— see page 53) conquered Babylonia, introducing a period sometimes called the "Middle Assyrian Empire." The Middle Empire reached the height of its power under Tiglath-Pileser I, who ruled from 1116 to 1078 B.C., during the period of the judges in Israel.

Tiglath-Pileser I carried his conquests westward and was the first Assyrian monarch to reach the Mediterranean, doing so in the region north of Canaan.

The Assyrian hold at that distance was still light and after the death of Tiglath-Pileser there was a decline. The Aramaean tribes, advancing southward and eastward from Asia Minor, threw back the Assyrians and put an end to their Middle Empire. It was as a result of the gap that followed in Assyrian power that David was able to establish his own empire over the western half of the Fertile Crescent.

The Aramaeans occupied Syria and were themselves subjected by David, but in Solomon's time they established the kingdom of Damascus that was to cost Israel so much in the days of Ahab and his successors.

Once again, Assyria revived. In 883 B.C., when Omri was king of Israel, a strong Assyrian monarch, Ashurnasirpal, came to the throne, and founded the "Late Assyrian Empire." He reorganized the Assyrian army and made maximum use of iron weapons and armor. These were much cheaper than bronze weapons and made it possible for the Assyrians to equip a mass army of infantry that could smash through the lighter and more specialized chariot-led armies of their foes.

Ashurnasirpal also introduced a policy of extreme cruelty. The inhabitants of captured cities were fiendishly tortured to death. This may have resulted from the king's innate sadism or as part of a deliberate policy for weakening the will of the enemy through terror. If the latter was the case, it succeeded, and Ashurnasirpal re-established the empire of Tiglath-Pileser I, which again reached the Mediterranean.

His son Shalmaneser III succeeded to the throne in 859 B.C. during the reign of Ahab, and Assyrian force, firmly established to the north, turned southward against Syria and Israel. The battle of Karkar in 854 B.C. (see page 349) blunted that drive for the while.

Nevertheless, Assyria's giant strength hovered remorselessly over the two kingdoms and both, at various times, were forced to pay tribute to her. The case of Jehu has been mentioned (see page 365).

Shalmaneser died in 824 B.C. and once again, Assyria was governed by incompetent rulers and the threat of her armies receded, as she found herself fighting for her life against the growing might of the new kingdom of Urartu to the northwest (see page 41). It was in this interval that first Hazael of Syria and then Jeroboam II of Israel were able to enjoy brief periods of illusory power.

In 745 B.C., just before the death of Jeroboam II, an Assyrian general deposed the feeble Assyrian monarch of the moment and placed himself on the throne as the first of a new dynasty of Assyrian kings. For a final period of a century and a half Assyria grew great again—greater than it had ever been before.

The new king is the Biblical "Pul," and this may be a form of his real name, "Pulu," by which he is listed in the Babylonian annals. A usurper needs to pile about himself all the emotional values he can manage and so Pul adopted the glorious name (to Assyrians) of Tiglath-Pileser and became the third to be so called.

It was Pul, or Tiglath-Pileser III, who checked the career of the kingdom of Urartu, defeating it in 743 B.C. And it was to Tiglath-Pileser III that Menahem paid tribute.

Rezin

Worse was to follow. In 738 B.C., Menahem's son Pekahiah, the second king of Israel's fifth dynasty, succeeded to the throne and carried on his father's pro-Assyrian policy (actually the only safe and logical one for the times). This did not suit the more rabid war hawks, however, and the general in chief, Pekah, initiated a conspiracy and killed him, becoming king in 737 B.C. The fifth dynasty had lasted only seven years.

Pekah then set about forming an anti-Assyrian alliance like that which had been at least reasonably successful a little over a century before at Karkar. He allied himself with Rezin of Damascus for that purpose and they endeavored to bring in Judah as a third member.

Judah had just come through a comparatively prosperous period in her history. In 780 B.C., Azariah, the eleventh king of the Davidic line, had succeeded his father Amaziah. In a forty-year reign he led a Judah which remained quietly in the shadow of Jeroboam II, and experienced a reasonable peace and prosperity.

In later life, Azariah developed leprosy and his son Jotham became regent about 750 B.C., succeeding to the throne as twelfth king of the Davidic line in 740 B.C.

Jotham was not ready to join the anti-Assyrian alliance, suspecting, and quite rightly, that the alliance would not succeed and would merely hasten the day it was intended to stave off. The kings of Syria and Israel attempted to change Jotham's mind by force.

> 2 Kings 15:37. *In those days the Lord began to send against Judah, Rezin the king of Syria, and Pekah* [of Israel] . . .

Judah resisted and the war was still continuing when Jotham died and was succeeded by his son Ahaz, thirteenth king of the Davidic line, in 736 B.C.

The Syrian forces occupied Edom and besieged Jerusalem. In this connection, the King James Version first makes use of the word "Jew" as an alternate form of "Judean" or "man of Judah."

> 2 Kings 16:6. . . . *Rezin . . . recovered Elath . . . and drave the Jews from Elath* . . .

although the Revised Standard Version translates the phrase "and drove the men of Judah from Elath."

Ahaz, seeing the inevitable defeat before him, took the truly desperate expedient of sending tribute to Tiglath-Pileser III as a token of submission, and appealing to him for help.

The Assyrian monarch responded at once and with a strong hand:

> 2 Kings 15:29. *In the days of Pekah . . . came Tiglath-Pileser . . . and took . . . Gilead, and . . . all the land of Naphtali.*

Nor was Syria to be neglected:

> 2 Kings 16:9. . . . *the king of Assyria went up against Damascus and took it . . . and slew Rezin.*

In 732 B.C. the Syrian kingdom came to an end after an existence of two and a half centuries. Damascus has remained an important and flourishing city ever since but it came under foreign rule in 732 B.C.

and remained under foreign rule in unbroken fashion for over twenty-six hundred years. Not until A.D. 1941 did Damascus again become the capital of a native Syrian nation (although it has in times past become the capital of a large empire under a foreign dynasty).

Thus only thirteen years after the death of Jeroboam II, Israel was virtually confined to the district surrounding Samaria.

Shalmaneser V

With Syria crushed and Israel chastened, all attempts at resistance in the western end of the Fertile Crescent came, at least temporarily, to an end. Tiglath-Pileser III could turn to the eastern end and crush a rebellion in Babylonia. (Babylonia was in a state of perennial revolt against Assyria but all the revolts were crushed—except the last one.)

Meanwhile, another palace revolution—the last one—had upset the throne of Israel. Pekah, whose reign had been unsuccessful and who had led his kingdom into disaster against the Assyrians, was assassinated as a result of a conspiracy led by a man named Hoshea. Hoshea became king in 732 B.C. According to the Assyrian records, Hoshea was appointed by Tiglath-Pileser III or, at least, did not become king until he had received Assyrian approval.

While Tiglath-Pileser lived, Hoshea remained submissive to Assyria. When Tiglath-Pileser died, in 726 B.C., there was an instant stirring. As stated earlier, the death of a strong king calls forth prompt rebellions on the chance that his successor will be a weakling and that the confusion of an interregnum will last long enough to make the rebellion successful.

Tiglath's son and successor, Shalmaneser V, took quick action, however. Hoshea was one of those who placed himself in rebellion on the death of the old king and Shalmaneser turned on him.

2 Kings 17:3. *Against him* [Hoshea] *came up Shalmaneser king of Assyria; and Hoshea became his servant, and gave him presents.*

In other words, Hoshea acknowledged Assyrian domination and Israel became a tributary kingdom. Even so, Hoshea would not have gotten off so lightly, in all probability, if Shalmaneser had not had pressing problems elsewhere.

So

At the first opportunity after the departure of Shalmaneser's army, Hoshea judged that various complications would keep the Assyrian busy indefinitely, and rebelled again. He sought further assurance by sending for help from abroad:

> 2 Kings 17:4. . . . *he . . . sent messengers to So king of Egypt, and brought no present to the king of Assyria . . .*

Again Egypt makes a shadowy appearance in the Bible. The Libyan dynasty of Sheshonk (the Biblical Shishak) was petering out into the usual final whimper at about this time. In the delta, a pair of native kings (the 24th dynasty) ruled briefly, and a line of kings from Ethiopia in the south also seized power, forming the 25th dynasty.

This is the first impingement of Ethiopia upon Israel, if one eliminates the highly dubious case of the queen of Sheba (see page 331).

The main core of ancient Ethiopia was located northwest of the modern kingdom of that name. It was to be found just south of Egypt in the territory now occupied by the Sudan. Under the conquering Pharaohs of the 18th dynasty, Ethiopia was conquered by Egypt and remained a subject province for four centuries.

About 1100 B.C., toward the end of Egypt's 20th dynasty and well after the death of her last powerful Pharaoh, Rameses III, Ethiopia gained her independence and formed an increasingly powerful state centered about the city of Napata. This was located on the upper Nile, near the fourth cataract, quite close to the modern city of Merowe in northern Sudan.

This kingdom, consistently called Ethiopia in the English version of the Bible (and Cush in the Hebrew original) is sometimes called Nubia to distinguish it from the modern Ethiopia.

By 736 B.C. Ethiopia was beginning to turn the tables on Egypt and while Assyria was destroying Syria and Israel, the Ethiopians took over parts of the Nile delta.

It was to the aggressors of the south that Hoshea turned for salvation from the aggressors of the north. So, king of Egypt, is referred to as Shab'i in the Assyrian records and it is just possible he may represent Shabaka of the 25th dynasty.

Egypt's motivation is clear. She could not help but view the continuing growth of Assyrian strength with alarm and she did everything she could to encourage rebellions among the Assyrian vassal states. Unfortunately, she had virtually no power of her own, and although she could subsidize and bribe, she could not support. Those nations which listened to Egyptian blandishments and accepted Egyptian gold invariably found that at the crucial moment, when they faced the Assyrian army, Egyptian help was nowhere to be found or was, at best, inadequate.

In the end it was disaster for everybody—including Egypt.

Habor

Shalmaneser reacted vigorously again at the news of the renewed rebellion. He marched against Israel, laid it waste, captured and deposed Hoshea, and then, in 725 B.C., laid siege to Samaria.

With the courage of despair, Samaria, isolated and hopeless, managed to continue its resistance for three years. Perhaps this resistance exasperated the Assyrians generally and Shalmaneser was made the scapegoat. In any case, Shalmaneser died in 722 B.C., possibly through assassination, since a usurper (possibly the conspirator who arranged the assassination) came to the throne and served as the first monarch of Assyria's last and most spectacular dynasty.

The usurper again chose a glorious name intended to shed a glow of honored tradition about himself. He went far, far back to the days of Sargon of Agade (see page 50) seventeen centuries before, for the purpose. Since there was an earlier Sargon in the list of Assyrian kings, this new one is known as Sargon II.

It was Sargon II who completed Shalmaneser's work and brought the siege of Samaria to a quick and successful conclusion, even though the Bible does not take note of the change in monarch but refers to him only as "the king of Assyria."

2 Kings 17:6. *In the ninth year of Hoshea, the king of Assyria* [Sargon] *took Samaria and carried Israel away into Assyria, and placed them in Halah and in Habor by the river of Gozan, and in the cities of the Medes.*

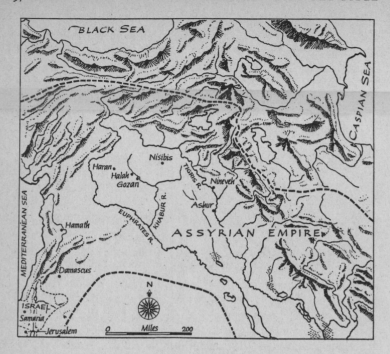

Habor (Khabur), the River of Gozan

Thus, in 722 B.C., there came to a permanent end the kingdom of Israel, which had existed for a little over two hundred years since the successful rebellion led by Jeroboam. To those interested in coincidences, it might be noted that Israel entered Canaan four and a half centuries before under a Hoshea (Joshua) and now left under another Hoshea.

Sargon adopted a procedure introduced by Tiglath-Pileser III. Instead of pacifying a territory by wholesale murder and destruction, which made it less profitable thereafter to its Assyrian masters, the same end was attained by deporting the leading citizens of a nation to another portion of the empire, while new colonists were brought in. In this way, the ties and tradition that bound peoples to the land were broken—an important matter to a henotheistic people who felt themselves deserted by their god—and the will to resist and rebel atrophied.

In this case, some twenty-seven thousand Israelites were deported. This obviously did not represent the entire population of Israel but it probably included virtually all the ruling classes: the landowners and leaders.

They were never heard of again, and they have long been known to tradition as the "Ten Lost Tribes" of Israel.

Later generations found it difficult to believe that the tribes to whom God had made so many promises could really be wiped out even though the Bible ascribes the destruction of those tribes to the fact that they had abandoned Yahvism and worshiped idols.

Many people believed legends to the effect that the Ten Tribes still existed in some remote fastness of Asia or Africa, that they had established a powerful kingdom, and that they would someday emerge, glowing with true religion, to rescue the downtrodden Jews (or Christians, depending on who was devising the legends) from their oppressors.

The Jewish historian Josephus, writing eight centuries after the destruction of Israel, reported that the Ten Tribes still existed beyond the Euphrates and were a powerful nation. After that the stories grew wilder and wilder. The Ten Tribes were supposed to form a powerful kingdom in Ethiopia, or in Mongolia, or even in America.

Some even believed that existing modern nations might be the descendants of the Ten Tribes. In the nineteenth century, the notion grew in some circles that the Ten Tribes somehow became the Scythians, living north of the Black Sea in Greek times, that these became the Saxons ("Isaac's sons"), and, since these invaded Britain, that the English people are therefore the descendants of the Ten Tribes. Surely it is hard to imagine anything more silly than these beliefs of the so-called "British-Israelite" cult.

What really happened to the Ten Tribes? The apparent truth is completely unromantic. The Second Book of Kings says, in a slightly garbled verse, that they were deported to "Halah and in Habor by the river of Gozan, and in the cities of the Medes."

Habor is almost certainly the river now known as Khabur, which is a tributary of the Euphrates, flowing into it from the north. The Khabur River rises in southeastern Turkey and flows generally southward for about two hundred miles through what is now northeastern Syria. It enters the Euphrates about thirty miles south of the Syrian provincial town of Deir ez Zor. Gozan and Halah are cities on the

Khabur. They are referred to as the "cities of the Medes" not because they were in Median territory at the time, but because they had come under Median domination a century and a half later when the material in the Second Book of Kings reached its final form.

What it amounts to, then, is that the Israelites were moved about 450 miles northeastward to the top of the Fertile Crescent. They were indeed only about sixty miles east of the city of Haran where Abraham had sojourned on his way to Canaan (see page 59).

And what happened to the Ten Tribes on the Khabur River? Nothing very startling. They undoubtedly intermarried with the people of the region, adopted the gods and customs of the region, and "vanished" by assimilation.

This is what usually happens to tribes who come to be isolated from "home base." What happened to the Vandals who had once invaded and conquered North Africa? To the Alans, who had once conquered Hungary? To the Khazars, who once controlled the Ukraine?

To be sure, two centuries later, the inhabitants of Judah were deported and did *not* assimilate themselves into the new surroundings. Because the Jews survived (and there were reasons for it), one wonders why the Israelites did not. That, however, is the reverse of the real problem. One should accept the fact that the Israelites did not survive, and wonder why the Jews did!

Samaritans

To eke out the depleted population of Israel, Sargon brought in colonists from other parts of the Assyrian Empire.

> 2 Kings 17:24. *And the king of Assyria brought men from Babylon . . . and placed them in the cities of Samaria instead of the children of Israel . . .*

It is these colonists and their descendants that in later books of the Bible are referred to as "Samaritans."

At first the immigrants tried to maintain their own religious traditions, but henotheistic feelings were strong and when natural disaster struck the blame was placed on the fact that:

Samaria and Surrounding Lands

2 Kings 17:26. . . . *they know not the manner of the God of the land.*

One of the deported priests was therefore returned.

2 Kings 17:28. . . . *one of the priests . . . dwelt in Bethel, and taught them how they should fear the Lord.*

This did not, however, bring about friendly relations with the people of Judah. The Yahvism they were taught was admixed with what seemed to the Judeans to be all sorts of error.

2 Kings 17:33. *They feared the Lord, and served their own gods, after the manner of the nations* [from which they came] . . .

2 Kings 17:34. *Unto this day they do after their former manners* . . .

The Samaritan religion became, in effect, a kind of Yahvistic heresy, and the orthodox of Judah would by no means accept that and seemed more hostile at times to the heretics than to the outright pagan. (This kind of attitude also existed among Christians of later centuries, so it is not as puzzling as it might be.) Much of later Biblical history involves a running and irreconcilable feud between the Judeans and the Samaritans, an odd shadow of the original feud with a similar territorial basis between David and Saul and between Rehoboam and Jeroboam.

Sennacherib

Only Judah was left now. In 720 B.C., two years after the end of Israel, Ahaz died, and his son Hezekiah (the fourteenth king of the Davidic dynasty) came to the throne.

Under him for some years there was a period of peace and even of relative prosperity as he was careful to do nothing to offend Assyria. Under him also, the prophetic party achieved full domination. Isaiah, an important and influential spokesman of Yahvism, flourished in his reign, and no doubt the Judeans were impressed by the continual insistence on the part of the Yahvists that the reason Israel had come to a bad end was its addiction to idol worship.

Sargon meanwhile continued his victorious career, defeating Urartu

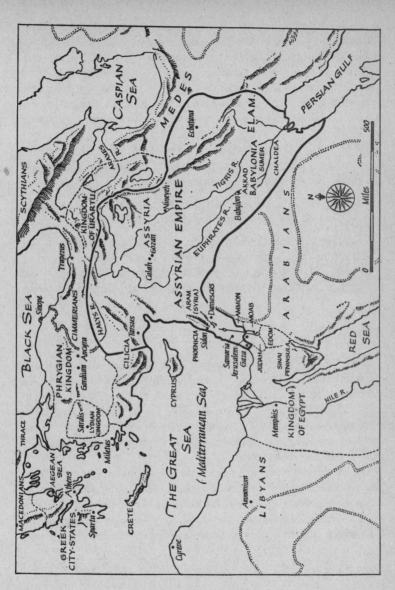

The Assyrian Empire under Sennacherib

to the north so badly that it entered a period of decline and played
no significant part in history thereafter. He also managed to keep the
turbulent Chaldean tribes, which now controlled Babylonia, under control, though they were a continual source of trouble for him.

However, in 705 B.C. Sargon died, and this was the signal for con-
spiracies and rebellions against Assyria. Hezekiah, encouraged by the
nationalist prophetic party, was among those who stopped payment of
tribute.

Sargon's son, however, had succeeded to the throne and was not to
be trifled with. He had to tend to serious rebellions in Babylonia but
eventually, in 701 B.C., he turned his attention to Judah:

> 2 Kings 18:13. Now . . . did Sennacherib king of Assyria come
> up against all the fenced cities of Judah, and took them.

Sennacherib is the Biblical version of the name of Sargon's son,
which might, more accurately, be given as Sinakhe-erba.

Hezekiah at once gave in and offered tribute but Sennacherib was
not to be so mollified. His army advanced and laid siege to Jerusalem.

Tirhakah

It would seem that if the Assyrian army had been allowed to concentrate its full efforts upon Jerusalem, the city must have fallen.
However, that was not to be. Assyria's cruelties in establishing its empire brought its own nemesis in its wake for its subjects revolted at
every possible chance and the last century of Assyria's existence was
one long battle against rebellion with her monarchs scarcely able to
draw a free breath between.

The Bible, unfortunately, is not entirely clear as to exactly what
happened in this particular case, since attention is concentrated on the
propaganda exchanges between the besiegers and besieged, rather than
upon military events beyond Jerusalem. However, one can deduce that
Sennacherib had to detach forces to take care of trouble farther west.

> 2 Kings 19:9. . . . he heard say of Tirhakah king of Ethiopia,
> Behold he is come out to fight against thee . . .

By the king of Ethiopia is meant one of the Ethiopian rulers of the
Nile delta. The one in question may be Taharqa.

Tirhakah, or Taharqa, was badly defeated, but even the defeat distracted the Assyrians and helped Jerusalem, and in the end Sennacherib was forced to leave Judah without taking the capital.

The reasons for this are varied. The Bible attributes it to a plague which suddenly struck and killed 185,000 Assyrians in the army in one night.

The Greek historian Herodotus doesn't mention the siege of Jerusalem, but he does speak of Sennacherib's campaign against Egypt and he describes a sudden retreat of the Assyrians, too, explaining that it took place because a plague of mice had gnawed their arrows and quivers and the leatherwork of their shields.

As for the records of Sennacherib, they speak only of victories, of a besieged Jerusalem, of tribute sent him by Hezekiah.

The indisputable fact, however, is that while Jerusalem was besieged as Samaria had been besieged a quarter century earlier, Jerusalem survived, where Samaria did not. Judah retained its national identity where Israel had not.

On the other hand, the fact is just as indisputable that Judah sustained severe damage, that its land had been laid waste, that its capital had barely escaped destruction, and that the end was merely that Judah was still a tributary of Assyria.

Undoubtedly, although the Bible treats the episode as a great victory redounding to the credit of Isaiah and the prophetic party, the prophetic party lost much prestige. It was a victory that was hard to distinguish from a disaster.

Esarhaddon

Sennacherib came to a bad end, for he was assassinated while supervising at religious rites in 681 B.C. Two of his own sons were the assassins, but a third son defeated the parricides and drove them into exile, assuming the throne himself:

2 Kings 19:37. . . . *And Esarhaddon his son reigned in his stead.*

The Bible tells us nothing more of Esarhaddon (Assur-ah-iddin), but he was the third capable member of the line of Sargon II.

Esarhaddon recognized the fact that Assyria would never have rest until the rebellions that cropped up constantly here and there in the

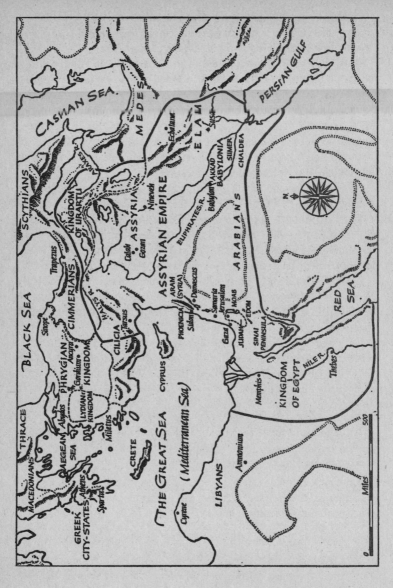

The Assyrian Empire under Esarhaddon

realm ceased. He did not see that it was Assyrian policy itself that was responsible, but placed the blame on Egyptian gold.

He therefore decided to strike the poison at the source. He marched an army into the Nile delta, defeated the Egyptians in 671 B.C., and took over control of Egypt. For the space of a generation, the northern half of the kingdom was more or less under Assyrian control, though it remained restless and the native leaders still waited their chance in the south.

Berodach-baladan

There is no question but that one of the reasons for the survival of Judah lay in the fact that the Assyrian kings had always to concentrate on, first and foremost, Babylonia.

For three centuries, Babylonia had been more or less under the domination of Assyria. Conscious of a past history of over two thousand years and of great empires of their own, the Babylonians never entirely submitted but rose time and again.

In the last few decades, the rough Chaldean tribes that had emerged from the Arabian deserts south of Babylonia had been encroaching on Babylonia and by Sargon's time, they were in control of Babylon itself.

Sargon and Sennacherib were forced into chronic warfare with the Chaldean leader Marduk-apal-iddin, a name which, in the Bible, is distorted into Merodach-baladan and, in the Second Book of Kings, through a misprint which has been piously retained across the centuries, into Berodach-baladan.

The Chaldean sought for allies everywhere among the enemies outside the Assyrian Empire and the rebels within the empire. Among the latter was Hezekiah.

2 Kings 20:12. *At that time Berodach-baladan . . . king of Babylon, sent letters and a present to Hezekiah.*

It is not certain when this embassy took place. It may have occurred in the early days of Sennacherib's reign and may have been a direct cause of the campaign of that monarch against Jerusalem. Perhaps, too, it was action by Merodach-baladan that forced Sennacherib to lift the siege of Jerusalem.

Merodach-baladan was eventually defeated by Sennacherib, but while he occupied Assyrian energies, so much the less remained to be expended on Judah.

The prophetic party disapproved of dealings of this sort, for they were isolationists as well as nationalists. To the monarchs of the time, the combination of isolationism and nationalism seemed suicide. One either submitted to the ruling empire, or one sought and found allies before rebelling.

Manasseh

Hezekiah died in 693 B.C., and his twelve-year-old son Manasseh, the fifteenth king of the Davidic line, ascended the throne and ruled for fifty-five years.

Now the disastrous rebellion against Sennacherib came back to plague the prophetic party. Assyria continued strong and was simply not to be withstood. Undoubtedly, the prophets continued to preach singlehanded rebellion and trust in God, but Manasseh and his advisers would not have any of that.

The prophetic party was therefore suppressed with violence:

> 2 Kings 21:16. *Moreover Manasseh shed innocent blood very much . . .*

and tradition has it that Isaiah himself found a martyr's death in the course of this reign.

And yet, Manasseh's reward was that he secured for Judah peace and prosperity during a long fifty-five-year reign—the longest in Biblical annals. It might seem on the face of it that Manasseh and Judah were being rewarded by a pleased Deity but when the Yahvists gained control later on, Manasseh's memory was vilified. If he had statesmanlike motives for his actions, they were suppressed and forgotten.

Manasseh's system continued in the short reign of his son Amon, who ruled from 639 to 638 B.C. as the sixteenth king of the Davidic line.

Josiah

In 638 B.C., Amon's son Josiah, the seventeenth king of the Davidic line, ascended the throne as an eight-year-old boy, and now there came a mighty change.

For one thing, Assyria was suddenly, and quite unexpectedly, falling upon evil days. She was suppressing rebellions with clearly greater effort. The hopes of all the subject nations, including Judah, were rising. The vision of freedom was before their eyes and nationalist movements were gaining strength everywhere. In Judah, that nationalist movement was embodied in the prophetic party.

As the young Josiah matured, he proved to be susceptible to the regenerating nationalism and was sympathetic to Yahvism. The last strong Assyrian king died in 625 B.C. when Josiah was twenty-one and the Assyrian Empire began to fall apart almost at once. By 620 B.C., things had matured to the point where the priesthood could safely suggest the appropriation of funds for the repair of the Temple. The Temple had, naturally, undergone considerable deterioration during the long period under which the anti-Yahvist kings Manasseh and Amon had been on the throne.

In the course of these repairs, a discovery was made:

2 Kings 22:8. And Hilkiah the high priest said unto Shaphan the scribe, I have found the book of the law in the house of the Lord.

The "book of the law" is usually identified by Biblical scholars as part of the Book of Deuteronomy. This may actually have been reduced to writing in 650 B.C. during the long and, for the Yahvists, horrible reign of Manasseh. The Yahvist tradition may well have seemed in danger of perishing and the secret commitment of that tradition to writing may have seemed the only way out. The book would then have been hidden in the Temple and been brought forth only when a new king, sympathetic to Yahvism, was on the throne.

Josiah, greatly impressed by the words of Deuteronomy, led Judah into a complete and thoroughgoing revival. Every scrap of idolatry was removed from the land. For instance:

2 Kings 23:10. And he defiled Topheth, which is in the valley of the children of Hinnom, that no man might make his son or his daughter to pass through the fire to Molech.

Manasseh had, according to the Bible, himself sacrificed his son to Molech (see page 163) and Topheth was the name given to the furnaces at which this was done.

The furnace used for the rites in Judah was located in the "valley of the children of Hinnom." The phrase "of Hinnom" is "Ge-Hinnom" in Hebrew. This valley curves past the southern end of Jerusalem and joins the valley of Kidron.

Such was the horror felt by the later Jews at the sort of religious rites that went on at the Topheth in Ge-Hinnom, and such the strong association with a kind of destructive fire, that both words (Tophet and Gehenna in English) became synonymous with Hell.

Josiah's reformation was complete and was climaxed by a celebration of the Passover:

> 2 Kings 23:22. *Surely there was not holden such a passover from the days of the judges that judged Israel, nor in all the days of the kings of Israel, nor of the kings of Judah.*

This was the final victory of Yahvism among the Judeans. Succeeding kings might backslide but the people did not. Military disaster seemed but to strengthen their beliefs. From this point on, then, Yahvism, which had earlier been merely one of the sects competing for a hold on the people of Israel and Judah, begins its transition to Judaism, the religion of the Jewish people.

Pharaoh-nechoh

But Josiah's fate was bound up with the great events taking place in the world beyond the narrow confines of Judah.

Esarhaddon's conquest of Egypt did not end rebellions in Assyria. Rather, it meant that Assyria had a new area of rebellion to worry about, for Egypt was itself seething with continual unrest. Indeed, when Esarhaddon died in 668 B.C., it was while he was marching toward Egypt to put down a rebellion.

He was succeeded by his son Asshurbanipal, the fourth king of the line of Sargon II and the last great king of Assyria, but one who is not mentioned in the Bible at all. Asshurbanipal was not a great conquering king, though he managed to put down rebellions and defend the empire against barbarian incursions. He is best known as a patron of culture and he collected the greatest library the world had yet seen.

Ever since the reign of Sargon II, the Cimmerians, barbarians from the north of the Black Sea (see page 46), had been pouring southward into Asia Minor and into Assyrian territory. Assyria had been able to defeat them only with great effort and at great cost. Asshurbanipal

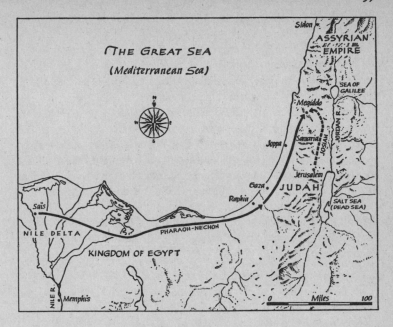

Necho's Expedition

had to lead two expeditions into rebellious Egypt and fight two bitter campaigns against the Chaldeans in Babylonia. He had also to fight against the barbarian Medes to the east of Babylonia.

By main force, Assyria was held together, but more and more its strength was a matter of outer show only. The Assyrian Empire was like a hollow structure with the walls growing thinner and thinner. It looked well but one good, hard knock—

The subject nations sensed this and waited eagerly and, as mentioned earlier, nationalist movements grew stronger.

Asshurbanipal died in 625 B.C., five years before Josiah's reformation, and that was the signal for the final rebellion. The Chaldeans of Babylonia joined forces with the Medes and together they attacked the Assyrian homeland. The Assyrian army, finally stretched beyond endurance, broke. Nineveh, the Assyrian capital, was taken in 612 B.C. and the Assyrian Empire came to an end and the conquerors divided the spoil among themselves.

For a few years, however, a remnant of the Assyrian Empire, centered about Haran (see page 59), held out under a general named Ashur-uballit.

Meanwhile, important events were transpiring in Egypt, too. The rebellion that had been in progress there at the time of Esarhaddon's death was never properly repressed by Asshurbanipal, who found himself intensely busy elsewhere. Egypt could not be quieted.

Psamtik, an Egyptian general who ruled the delta as a viceroy for the Assyrians, took over in his own name and by 652 B.C. he controlled the country. He became Psamtik I, first Pharaoh of the 26th dynasty, and established his capital at Saïs, a city on a western branch of the Nile, near the Mediterranean, about 175 miles northwest of Memphis. For this reason, the period during which the 26th dynasty ruled is known as the Saitic period.

In 610 B.C., two years after the destruction of Nineveh, Psamtik I died and was succeeded by his son Necho, known in the Bible as Pharaoh-nechoh.

2 Kings 23:29. *In his* [Josiah's] *days Pharaoh-nechoh king of Egypt went up against the king of Assyria to the river Euphrates: and king Josiah went against him; and he* [Pharaoh-nechoh] *slew him* [Josiah] *at Megiddo, . . .*

The king of Assyria here referred to can only have been Ashur-uballit at Haran. Necho wanted his share of the Assyrian spoils, and keep Chaldea from becoming too powerful, while Josiah was anxious to keep Necho out of Asia in order that he himself might control Syria as in the time of Solomon.

The armies met at Megiddo in Samaritan territory about fifty-five miles north of Jerusalem in 608 B.C. It was a spot where, over six centuries before, Thutmose III had fought a gigantic battle against the Canaanites (see page 122). Almost as though the days of the Egyptian Empire had returned, Necho won a victory, Josiah was killed, and Egyptian power was established in the southwest corner of Asia.

Josiah had reigned for thirty years and now he was succeeded by his son Jehoahaz, the eighteenth king of the Davidic line, but the choice did not please Necho. He carried off Jehoahaz to life imprisonment in Egypt and established Jehoiakim, another son of Josiah (and the nineteenth king of the Davidic line) in his place.

For a while Jehoiakim remained an Egyptian puppet, faithfully paying tribute to Necho. To do that, he had to recede from the Yahvist position of his father. He could not listen to the nationalist prophetic party which had brought death to Josiah when he fought Egypt without allies, in the approved prophetic fashion.

2 Kings 23:37. *And he* [Jehoiakim] *did that which was evil in the sight of the Lord* . . .

Nebuchadnezzar

Necho's adventure in imperialism did not last long.

The Chaldean leader who had mounted the successful campaign against the Assyrian Empire and who had taken the Assyrian capital at Nineveh was Nabopolassar, who, under Asshurbanipal, had served as viceroy of Babylonia.

Having accomplished that task of taking Nineveh, and spending some years in consolidating his victory, he then sent his forces westward against Necho, placing those forces under his son. The son's name was Nabu-kudurri-usur ("Nebo defend the boundary"), which comes out in the Bible as Nebuchadnezzar. The father died in 605 B.C. before the campaign was finished and the son ascended the throne as Nebuchadnezzar II (Nebuchadnezzar I had reigned five hundred years earlier over Babylonia).

The empire of Nabopolassar and Nebuchadnezzar is variously known as the "New Babylonian Empire," the "Neo-Babylonian Empire," and the "Chaldean Empire."

In the first year of his reign, Nebuchadnezzar met Necho at Carchemish. Carchemish had once been an important city of the Mitanni and, later, of the Hittites. It had been captured by Thutmose III for the Egyptian Empire, and by Sargon II for the Assyrian Empire. It was located on the upper Euphrates River on what is now the boundary between Syria and Turkey, about sixty miles west of Haran and nearly five hundred miles north of Jerusalem.

Nebuchadnezzar was completely victorious at Carchemish and Necho, his dreams of Asian glory forever gone, scuttled back to Egypt and remained there till his death in 593 B.C.

Meanwhile Nebuchadnezzar cleaned up the last pockets of Assyrian resistance at Haran by 601 B.C. He could then turn his attention in 600 B.C. to minor problems such as Judah.

The Sixth Century B.C.

2 Kings 24:1. . . . *Nebuchadnezzar king of Babylon came up, and Jehoiakim became his servant three years: then he turned and rebelled against him.*

Judah switched from being an Egyptian tributary to being a Babylonian one. Its rebellion in 597 B.C. was, of course, worse than useless. Jehoiakim died at its beginning after an eleven-year reign and his son Jehoiachin ascended the throne as the twentieth king of the Davidic line.

Jehoiachin only reigned for three months, for Nebuchadnezzar laid siege to the rebellious Jerusalem in 597 B.C., taking the city, stripping it of whatever he could find, and carrying off the king and the principal men to the number of ten thousand.

Jerusalem and Judah remained in being, however, and Nebuchadnezzar appointed Jehoiachin's uncle (the brother of Jehoiakim and the third son of Josiah to sit on the throne) to the throne. The new king, taking the name of Zedekiah, was the twenty-first king of the Davidic line—and the last.

He began as a docile puppet of the Chaldean monarch, but as once Hoshea had been lured into fatal revolt by promised help from So of Egypt that never materialized, so now Zedekiah was lured into a revolt just as fatal by an Egyptian promise just as false.

In 587 B.C. Zedekiah rose and the Babylonian army returned to the siege. After a year and a half, the city was taken. Zedekiah and a remnant of the army tried to flee but were smashed near Jericho.

Zedekiah was imprisoned and blinded, his sons were executed, and further deportations depopulated the land. The kingdom of Judah came to an end 427 years after the accession of David to the throne, and the Temple itself was destroyed.

Gedaliah

There remained Judeans in Judah, of course, even after the deportations, and Nebuchadnezzar appointed a governor to rule them.

2 Kings 25:22. . . . *Nebuchadnezzar . . . over them . . . made Gedaliah the son of Ahikam, the son of Shaphan, ruler.*

Gedaliah was the grandson of the scribe who, in the reign of Josiah, had received the news of the discovery of the Book of Deuteronomy and who had carried that news to Josiah. Now, thirty-four years after that discovery and the great Passover that had climaxed it, Judah was half empty and the scribe's grandson ruled over the remnant.

Gedaliah tried to build anew but the people, fearing further punishment from Nebuchadnezzar, assassinated him and many fled to Egypt. Judah was more desolate than ever.

Evil-merodach

The Jews in Babylonia might well have been assimilated and might have "disappeared" as the Israelites in Assyria had a century and a half before. As it turned out (with important consequences in world history) they did not. They survived to return to Judah and to carry on their traditions and their culture.

It is rather fitting, therefore, that the Second Book of Kings does not end with the destruction of Jerusalem and the Temple, the end of Judah, and the emptying of the land. Rather, it goes a little past that to show something that reads like the faint promise of a beginning of better days.

> 2 Kings 25:27. . . . *in the seven and thirtieth year of the captivity of Jehoiachin king of Judah . . . Evil-merodach . . . did lift up the head of Jehoiachin . . . out of prison.*

Nebuchadnezzar had died in 562 B.C. and was succeeded by his son Amel-Marduk ("man of Marduk"), which, in the Bible, becomes "Evil-merodach."

He apparently took a kindlier attitude toward the captive Jews, freeing Jehoiachin, who had been briefly king of Judah at the time of Nebuchadnezzar's first siege of the city.

He may have thought of re-establishing the Jews in their homeland but he did not reign long enough to carry that thought through, if he had it at all. In 560 B.C., he was killed in a palace conspiracy, and the Jews remained captive for another generation.

It is on this moment of renewed optimism, however, that the Second Book of Kings ends.

13. 1 CHRONICLES

ADAM · JUDAH · BOAZ · ZERUIAH · SOLOMON · JOSIAH · JOHANAN ·
JECONIAH · LEVI · MERIB-BAAL · DAVID · SATAN

Adam

Following the Book of 2 Kings is a pair of books (1 Chronicles and 2 Chronicles) that, in a sense, recapitulate the whole of the Bible from the beginning to the fall of Jerusalem.

These books were written after the return from exile in Babylon. It was usual to suppose, earlier, that they were written as late as 300 or even 250 B.C., but more recent thinking on the subject seems to favor a date as early as 400 B.C.

The Hebrew title of the books is "Dibre Hayyamim" meaning "records of the times," for which "chronicles" is certainly an adequate translation. When the Bible was translated into the Greek, however, the translators found the books most significant in the sense that they supplied fuller information concerning the history of Judah than was contained in the Books of 1 and 2 Kings. For that reason they referred to the books as "Paraleipomenon" ("concerning things omitted"). This name is retained (in Latin spelling) in the Catholic translations of the Bible, where one can find 1 and 2 Paralipomenon in place of 1 and 2 Chronicles.

In the Hebrew Bible, the Books of 1 and 2 Chronicles are placed in the third and least esteemed division, "The Writings," because of their late composition. What's more, they are placed at the very end of the section, which makes them the last of all the books in the Hebrew canon.

In the Latin translation and in the various English versions that

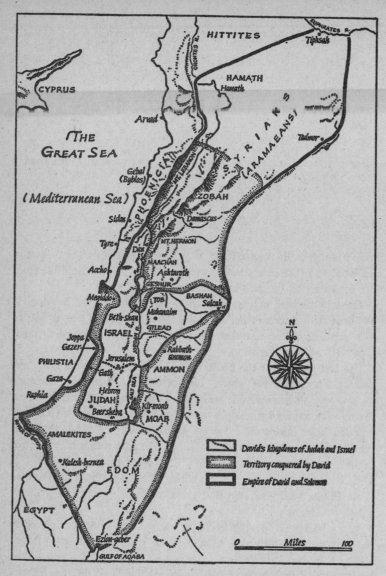

The Empire of David and Solomon

stem from it, the Books of 1 and 2 Chronicles follow (more logically, perhaps) immediately after 1 and 2 Kings, so much of which they repeat.

The situation at the time the "Chronicler" was writing was one that was completely different from that prevailing while the kingdom of Judah existed. It was then only patriotic to believe that the kingdom and the Davidic line that ruled it would continue forever, and this belief is reflected in the Bible. Thus, Nathan the Prophet quotes the words of the Lord to David:

2 Samuel 7:16. *And thine house and thy kingdom shall be established for ever before thee . . .*

But the Chronicler and his generation knew well that the kingdom of Judah had come to an end in 586 B.C. and that no king of the line of David had reigned for nearly two centuries and that, moreover, there was no immediate prospect of the re-establishment of the kingdom under a Davidic monarch.

It became necessary to interpret history in another fashion, then, and to understand the words of God, as given in tradition, in another way. The Chronicler therefore set about writing a history that would yield that interpretation.

For his purposes, it was necessary to get through the very earliest ages in only the briefest possible way and this could be done through a list of genealogies. Not only would genealogies be the most economical way of reaching the essential moment at which he wanted to begin his history proper, but it would also be of devouring interest to the Jews.

The Exile had broken the chain of tradition that had marched down the centuries during the time of the kingdoms, and had wiped out many records. Family relationships may have become fuzzy and national pride had bitten the dust in the decades of imprisonment. Through an adequate listing of authentic genealogies, each returning Jew could place himself accurately in the tribal system and society could renew itself properly.

And so it comes about that the first word of 1 Chronicles is Adam:

1 Chronicles 1:1. *Adam, Sheth, Enosh,*

Judah

The first chapter suffices for the hasty recital of names that serves to take care of all the Biblical genealogies but those of Jacob (Israel). Beginning with Chapter 2, the genealogy of the twelve tribes of Israel can be given.

In the earlier books of the Bible, the tribes are treated in the traditional order of their seniority. Reuben comes first, then Simeon, then Levi, and only then Judah—the fourth-born. The Chronicler was aware of this:

> 1 Chronicles 5:1. . . . *the sons of Reuben the firstborn of Israel* . . .

Nevertheless, from the vantage point of 400 B.C., it is clear that *the* important tribe is Judah:

> 1 Chronicles 5:2. *For Judah prevailed above his brethren, and of him came the chief ruler* . . .

and therefore the genealogy of Judah was taken up first in defiance of birthright. It was, moreover, taken up in greater detail than that of any of the other tribes. In fact, the four tribes that made up the kingdom of Judah (Judah itself; Simeon, which had been amalgamated into Judah's tribal system before David; Benjamin; and Levi) are treated in a total of 258 verses, while the remaining tribes of the forever-vanished kingdom of Israel receive a total of fifty verses. And Judah itself has the lion's share—one hundred verses.

Boaz

As quickly as he can, the Chronicler proceeds to the ancestry of David and this goes in part:

> 1 Chronicles 6:11. . . . *and Salma begat Boaz,*
> 1 Chronicles 6:12. *And Boaz begat Obed* . . .

No mention is made of Boaz having begotten Obed by Ruth (see page 265). This is not because the Chronicler ignores women completely, for in listing the sons of Judah, he says:

> 1 Chronicles 2:4. *And Tamar his daughter in law bare him Pharez and Zerah* . . .

The Book of Ruth may have been written at about the time that the Chronicler was working on his own writings and it is not at all hard to believe that he was aware of its contents (for it had to be popular or it would not have gotten into the Hebrew canon).

Two possibilities suggest themselves, each with a certain plausibility. The Book of Ruth may, indeed, have been a piece of historical fiction and no such woman as Ruth may have appeared in the early records which the Chronicler used as his source material.

Or else, if the writer of the Book of Ruth made use of an authentic tradition then it may be that the Chronicler deliberately refused to use it. The Chronicler was on the side of those who favored a rigid exclusivism among the returning Jews, a putting away of foreign wives, and the Book of Ruth was written to present the other side (see page 265). The Chronicler might have preferred to ignore, therefore, the part-Moabite ancestry of David.

Zeruiah

When Jesse is reached, his children are listed, including David (his youngest son) and two sisters:

> 1 Chronicles 2:15. . . . *David* . . .
> 1 Chronicles 2:16. *Whose sisters were Zeruiah and Abigail* . . .

If the Chronicler is correct, then some of David's heroes are close relatives. Thus, Zeruiah had three sons: Abishai, Joab, and Asahel, who were all David's lieutenants in his early days as an outlaw. In particular, Joab rose to be commander in chief. All three were David's nephews. Again, Abigail was the mother of Amasa, who was Absalom's general (see page 313) and who briefly replaced Joab as commander in chief. He, too, was a nephew of David, which may help account for David's leniency after the crushing of Absalom's rebellion.

Solomon

The third chapter begins with a listing of David's sons. Nineteen of them are listed and the list is by no means exhaustive.

1 Chronicles 3:9. *These were all the sons of David, beside the sons of the concubines . . .*

Of these Solomon is the tenth listed so that there might possibly have been at least nine sons ahead of him in line for the throne. The deaths of the first and third (Amnon and Absalom) in the lifetime of David are described in 2 Samuel, and the fourth (Adonijah) lived to dispute the succession. Of the rest nothing is known.

There follows immediately the line of descent of Solomon, which includes only those who were kings of Judah:

1 Chronicles 3:10. *And Solomon's son was Rehoboam, Abia [Abijam] his son, Asa his son, Jehoshaphat his son,*
1 Chronicles 3:11. *Joram his son . . .*

Starting with David, son succeeded father as king of Judah down to Josiah, a list of seventeen generations, quite a remarkable record for any dynasty.

Josiah

With Josiah, there is for the first time more than one son listed:

1 Chronicles 3:15. *And the sons of Josiah were . . . Johanan . . . Jehoiakim . . . Zedekiah . . . Shallum.*
1 Chronicles 3:16. *And the sons of Jehoiakim: Jeconiah . . .*

Upon Josiah's death in the battle of Megiddo, one of his sons succeeded to the throne, Jehoahaz, and this one is not listed by that name in verse 3:15. In the Book of Jeremiah, however, that prophet (who lived at the time and witnessed the events) speaks of the matter:

Jeremiah 22:11. . . . *Shallum the son of Josiah . . . reigned instead of Josiah . . .*

Jeremiah 22:12. . . . *he shall die in the place whither they have led him captive.*

Jehoahaz was indeed taken captive by Pharaoh-nechoh and kept in captivity to his death (see page 392). It would seem, then, that Shallum was the personal name of the prince and Jehoahaz was his "throne name," assumed when he became king. It is not at all an uncommon practice for a person to change his name upon becoming king. Sometimes the name is changed in order to choose one that has associations with the throne, so that Mari of Syria became Ben-hadad upon becoming king (see page 368) and Pulu of Assyria became Tiglath-Pileser (see page 373). In modern times, the best-known case of systematic name-changing upon achieving high position is the case of the Popes at Rome: Achille Ratti became Pius XI in 1922; Eugenio Pacelli succeeded him as Pius XII in 1939; Angelo Roncalli succeeded him as John XXIII in 1958; and Giovanni Montini succeeded him as Paul VI in 1963.

Apparently Shallum/Jehoahaz was appointed king by popular acclaim despite the fact that he was the youngest of Josiah's sons:

2 Kings 23:30. . . . *And the people of the land took Jehoahaz . . . and made him king . . .*

It might be conjectured that this was because he was the most anti-Egyptian of Josiah's sons and therefore most popular. This may be why Necho had him removed at once and replaced with Jehoiakim, whom he may have considered more tractable and who was, in any case, the oldest surviving son of Josiah and therefore the one with the best claim to the throne anyway. (The eldest son, Johanan, of whom nothing more is heard, may have died in Josiah's lifetime.)

Jehoiakim is the first king of Judah to replace a brother rather than a father. In his case, the name by which he is listed in 1 Chronicles is already his throne name:

2 Kings 23:34. *And Pharaoh-nechoh made Eliakim . . . king . . . and turned his name to Jehoiakim.*

Jehoiakim was succeeded by his son Jehoiachin, whose name is given in 1 Chronicles as Jeconiah.

Jehoiachin (Jeconiah) was on the throne only a short while before being taken and carried off into lifelong captivity by Nebuchadnezzar (sharing the fate, if not the captor, of his uncle Jehoahaz).

In his place, Nebuchadnezzar put on the throne the one remaining son of Josiah; the prince whose name is given as Zedekiah in 3:15. This, too, is a throne name:

> 2 Kings 24:17. *And the king of Babylon made Mattaniah . . . king . . . and changed his name to Zedekiah.*

Zedekiah was the last reigning king of Judah.

Johanan

In a way, though, it is Johanan, Josiah's first-born (who probably died young) who bears the most interesting name. Johanan is a shortened version of Jehohanan, meaning "Yahveh is gracious."

The name "Johanan" appears only once in the Biblical books coming before 1 Chronicles and that once is at the very end of the book immediately preceding—2 Kings. The name was that of an army officer of the time of Gedaliah:

> 2 Kings 25:23. . . . *there came to Gedaliah . . . Johanan the son of Careah, . . .*

In the later books of the Bible, the name is mentioned more often.

Remember, now, that the initial "J" in English versions of Biblical names is equivalent to the Hebrew letter "yodh," which represents the sound "y." The Greeks would start such a name with their letter "iota," which we write "I," and which also sounds like a "y" at the beginning of a word. It is natural, then, that the Greek version of "Johanan" would be "Ioannes" if we allow further for the absence of the "h" in the Greek alphabet and for the Greek habit of placing an "s" at the end of almost all names. This is easily seen to be equivalent to the German "Johannes," and this, in turn, is easily shortened to the English "John."

In other words, however strange the name "Johanan" may appear to us when we come across it in the Old Testament, it is the same name that we find as "John" in English versions of the New Testament, and is the name that in one form or another is most common of all among Europeans and men of European ancestry.

Jeconiah

The last part of the third chapter traces the line of David through the Exile. It begins with Jeconiah (Jehoiachin), the grandson of Josiah, who was briefly king of Judah in 597 B.C. and who was carried off to exile by Nebuchadnezzar. He remained alive and even survived to be well treated by Amel-Marduk (Evil-merodach) after Nebuchadnezzar's death (see page 396).

1 Chronicles 3:17. *And the sons of Jeconiah; Assir, Salathiel . . .*

Eight sons are listed, but the first, Assir, is not really a son. It means "captive" and the Revised Standard Version translates verse 3:17 (using an alternate version of Salathiel's name): "and the sons of Jeconiah, the captive: Shealtiel."

The sons of Pediah, Jeconiah's third son, are given, and then those of Zerubbabel the oldest son of Pediah, and so on.

In the volume of the Anchor Bible which deals with 1 Chronicles, the following approximate birth years are given:

Pedaiah	595 B.C.
Zerubbabel	570 B.C.
Hananiah	545 B.C.
Shechaniah	520 B.C.
Shemaiah	495 B.C.
Neariah	470 B.C.
Elioenai	445 B.C.
Hodaviah	420 B.C.

Hodaviah, according to the genealogy, is the eighth generation after Jeconiah and the twenty-sixth generation after David.

Hodaviah was the eldest son of Elioenai and he had six younger brothers, of whom Anani was the youngest. The Anchor Bible estimates that the birth date of the youngest son was about 405 B.C.

Thus, the line of David is followed through for nearly two centuries after the end of the kingdom and the fact that the record ends with Anani is one indication that the Chronicler might have been writing about 400 B.C.

The careful manner in which the Chronicler details the genealogy might be taken as a reasonable indication of the fact that the Chronicler does not consider the kingdom of Judah or the Davidic line to have come to an irrevocable end.

Nevertheless, one gets the distinct impression that the Chronicler is not sanguine about the Davidic line. As the history he is about to write will demonstrate, there is something he considers an alternate to the kingdom and its monarch—and that is the Temple and its High Priest. The Temple had, indeed, been restored in the Chronicler's day and as the supremacy among the tribes passed from Reuben to Judah, so it might conceivably be that the promise of external existence would pass from kingdom to Temple.

Levi

Thus, when the Chronicler reaches the tribe of Levi, he gives it a detailed genealogy second only to that of Judah, for it is from that tribe that the priesthood is drawn:

1 Chronicles 6:1. *The sons of Levi . . .*

The list of High Priests is given during the time of the kingdom, ending with:

1 Chronicles 6:15. *And Jehozadak went into captivity . . . by the hand of Nebuchadnezzar.*

Jehozadak was the twelfth in descent from Zadok, who had become High Priest at the beginning of the reign of Solomon (see page 322). Zadok himself is the ninth in descent from Eleazar, the son of Aaron.

Merib-baal

The genealogies of the remaining tribes are then run through, more or less quickly, until the last—Benjamin—is reached. Benjamin is, of course, the youngest son of Jacob according to tradition, but there are other possible excuses for its position. Saul, whom David replaced as king, was a Benjamite, and if David's tribe Judah is considered first, it is rather neat to consider Saul's tribe Benjamin last. Besides, it is through Benjamin that one approaches the genealogy of Saul and it is with the death of Saul that the Chronicler intends to begin his history proper.

1 Chronicles 8:33. . . . *Saul begat Jonathan . . .*
1 Chronicles 8:34. *And the son of Jonathan was Merib-baal; and Merib-baal begat Micah.*

Merib-baal is an alternate name of Mephibosheth (see page 309) and through Micah, Saul's descendants are continued many generations, presumably to the time of exile. Apparently, the line of Saul (though reduced by David's policy to Mephibosheth alone) managed to flourish. Referring to the later members of the line:

1 Chronicles 8:40. *And the sons of Ulam . . . had many sons, and sons' sons, an hundred and fifty.*

It is interesting to note, though, that at no time past David's reign is there a record of any attempt to restore the line of Saul.

David

David, the human hero of the Chronicler's history, is not a hero in his capacity as a human being, but rather as an ideal founder of Temple-worship. Of his life story only the central "Temple-core" is kept; that plus lists of names of genealogical interest. His youth, his adventures with Saul and Jonathan, the personal sins and problems of later life—all are eliminated. Even his conquests, when mentioned, are important only because the loot gained makes it possible for the Temple to be built, furnished, and ornamented.

Thus, Saul's death is described and then:

1 Chronicles 11:3. . . . *came all the elders of Israel . . . to Hebron . . . and they anointed David king over Israel . . .*

There is no mention of the seven years in which Ish-bosheth was king of Israel in the Trans-Jordan, of Abner's defection and of the political intrigues that followed (see page 300). One would suppose that in a single moment of exaltation, David was unanimously raised to the kingship.

Once David is king, the Chronicler moves on to the capture of

Jerusalem, so that we now have the man who initiates Temple-worship, and the place where it is initiated. The bringing of the ark of the covenant to Jerusalem is told in great detail, as is David's thwarted intention to build the actual Temple himself, and the preparation he makes to have his successor do so. Then we pass on to his death and the succession of Solomon to the throne. There is no mention of the dynastic dispute between Solomon and Adonijah (see page 320).

This picture of David's reign is, in our modern view, so limited and partial as to amount to a falsification of history. There was, however, undoubtedly no conscious attempt at falsification as such on the part of the Chronicler, who did not have our view of history. Rather, he was trying, according to his lights, to "truthify" history, so to speak. That is, he saw in the history of the Davidic monarchy a central thread which he wished to expose more clearly to all men. He therefore cut away what were to him obscuring irrelevancies and painted that central thread in brighter colors to make it more visible. The result is history which we might call "impressionistic" and its purpose, as with impressionistic art, is to make apparent what realism might hide.

Satan

Only once in the Chronicler's history does David appear less than ideal and that is in connection with his sin in taking a census. This item, however, must be included, for it is central to the theme. It was on the threshing floor where David, according to the legend, had seen the angel (see page 319) that the Temple was to be built. Yet, even so, the tale is told with an important difference.

In the pre-Exilic version of the story, it is stated:

> 2 Samuel 24:1. . . . *the anger of the Lord was kindled against Israel, and he moved David against them to say, Go, number Israel and Judah.*

God alone is here viewed as the source of all things and it is God who inspires David's evil impulse. By the time of the Chronicler, however, there had come to seem to be a flavor of blasphemy in supposing that God would punish Israel by first inspiring an evil act that he could then use as an excuse for the punishment. As the Chronicler tells the story, then:

1 Chronicles 21:1. *And Satan stood up against Israel, and provoked David to number Israel.*

The Hebrew word *satan* means "adversary"; that is, one who opposes. It does not necessarily have to have a supernatural sense, and is occasionally used in the Bible to represent an ordinary human adversary. The Hebrew word is then translated as simply "adversary." A case of this kind is in the Book of 1 Kings, where Rezon of Syria rebels against Solomon:

1 Kings 11:24. *And he was an adversary to Israel all the days of Solomon* . . .

Sometime after the Babylonian captivity, however, the notion arose that there was a supernatural Adversary; a being whose official duty it was to work for man's evil as God worked for man's good. This capital-S Satan was without power to force men to do evil, but he could tempt men to sin and turn against God, and it was by succumbing to such temptation that man brought evil into the world.

Such a concept was useful in that it helped explain the source of evil, for it is always difficult to explain the existence of evil and misery in the world and the frequent apparent triumph of bad over good in the face of the existence of an all-powerful, all-good God. Even if one explained that evil came as a punishment to sinning mankind, where came the evil within man that caused him to sin in the first place? Thus, the notion of a supernatural Satan pushing man toward sin was convenient.

And the concept came, very likely, by way of the Persians.

By 400 B.C., when the Chronicler was writing, the Persians had become the dominant nation in Asia, and Persian thought would be expected to be very influential among all nations which, like Judah, were under Persian rule. This was particularly so since Persian religion had just been systematized by a great prophet, Zarathustra (Zoroaster, in the Latinized form of the name), at about the time of the return from Babylonian captivity, and the earth rang, so to speak, with the new doctrine.

Zoroastrianism offered a dualistic view of the universe. There was a principle of good, Ahura-Mazda (or Ormuzd), and a principle of evil, Ahriman, which were viewed as virtually independent of each other and very nearly equal. The creation of the world, its develop-

ment and history, were all incidents in the unending celestial warfare
between these two principles, each at the head of a separate army of
innumerable spirits.

There is a certain exciting drama to such a view of the universe,
and Judaism was penetrated by it to a limited extent. A principle of
evil, Satan, was conceived of, but never viewed as independent of
God or equal to Him. Instead, Satan is considered to be as surely a
creation of God as man himself is.

In later times, he was described as having been an angel originally,
even the chief of the angels. Through pride, however, he refused to
obey God and bow down to man at the time of the creation of Adam.
He was therefore, with numerous followers, ejected from heaven. Once
fallen, he became twisted with envy and infinite malice and took on
the task of tempting mankind to fall from grace as he himself had.

Satan is not mentioned, as such, in any of the books of the Bible
before 1 Chronicles, but the workings of evil found here and there
could be reinterpreted in the new light. Most importantly, Satan was
equated with the serpent who tempted Eve in the garden of Eden.

The tale of Satan, of his rebellion against God, and of his fall
from heaven, forms the central framework of Milton's great epic
poem *Paradise Lost*, which is based on the first chapters of Genesis.

Furthermore, Satan does not perform his evil task without remaining
under the firm control of God. It is even possible to view Satan as
fulfilling the necessary function of tempting mankind and of improv-
ing the nature of the soul by exercising it, so to speak; keeping it
muscular by giving it temptations to overcome. Satan might then, too,
act as a sieve separating the better souls from the worse.

It was part of Satan's function to carry an evil report of man to
God, to slander them. (This shows itself best in the Book of Job.)
The Greek word for "slanderer" is *diabolos* (literally "to throw across,"
since slanderous words are like obstacles thrown across the path to
block progress) and from this comes our word "devil" and the adjective
"diabolical." The word "devil" is used in places in the King James
Version to refer to woodland fertility spirits, which are called "satyrs" in
the Revised Standard Version (see page 159), but the capital-D Devil
is Satan. Satan, the Adversary, is also the Devil, the Slanderer. The
Mohammedans call the Adversary Eblis, also from *diabolos*.

In Zoroastrianism, the powers of evil who fight under the banner of
Ahriman are the "devas," but this has nothing to do with "devil."

Quite the contrary! The same word occurs in Sanskrit and is given to the gods and the spirits of good in India.

This is not really surprising for the gods of one people are the demons of their neighbors. Undoubtedly, Indian religious thought was penetrating Persia in Zarathustra's time and in beating it back, the Persians stigmatized the alien gods as demons—as the Jews considered Canaanite gods to be abominations, and as the Christians later converted the Greek and Roman gods into evil spirits.

The word "deva" reaches us not through Persian but through Sanskrit and therefore retains its godlike aspect. From it we get the Greek *dios*, the Latin *deus*, and the French *dieu*, all meaning "God," as well as our English adjective "divine."

14. 2 CHRONICLES

Joppa

What interests the Chronicler concerning the reign of Solomon is his building of the Temple and his wealth. Since, to the Chronicler, material benefits accompany righteous action, and since no righteous action is greater than the building of the Temple, Solomon's wealth is described in terms of unbridled exaggeration.

Solomon arranges with Hiram of Tyre (here called Huram) for the supplies needed for the Temple. Hiram agrees:

> 2 Chronicles 2:16. *And we will cut wood . . . and . . . bring it to thee in floats by sea to Joppa; and thou shalt carry it up to Jerusalem.*

Joppa (the modern Jaffa) is a port on the Mediterranean about thirty-five miles northwest of Jerusalem. It was the nearest sizable harbor (though not a very good one) to the capital city and was the natural seaport to which to send material bound for Jerusalem.

It first enters history as one of the towns captured by Thutmose III when that Egyptian conqueror established his empire in Asia. After the decline of Egypt, Joppa came under Phoenician control. It is mentioned in the Book of Joshua as part of the idealized territory of the tribe of Dan, but it never came under Israelite control at any time before David (none of the coastal strip did—that remained Philistine to the south and Phoenician to the north). It is only now, therefore, except for the mention in Joshua, that Joppa appears in the Bible.

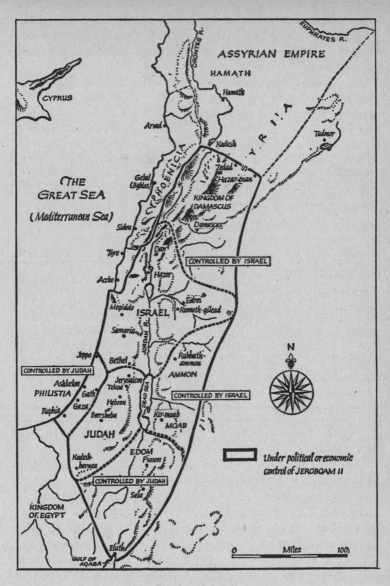

Israel and Judah

As the seaport of Jerusalem, Joppa was of considerable importance at the time of the Crusades, changing hands between the Christians and Moslems several times, but eventually settling down to a long Turkish control.

In 1909, when Palestine was still part of the Ottoman Empire and when Joppa or Jaffa was a strongly Arabic town, the Jews of the city established a suburb of their own, three miles to the north, which they called Tel Aviv. After World War I, when Palestine became a British mandate, the Jewish town, thanks to immigration and financial help from abroad, quickly grew into a modern city designed along Western lines.

After Israel won its independence in 1948, Tel Aviv served as the interim capital until 1950, when the new city of Jerusalem took its place. In 1950, Tel Aviv was combined with Jaffa (from which most of the Arabs had departed) into a single municipality. Tel Aviv/Jaffa is now the largest city in Israel, with a population of about four hundred thousand.

Joppa bears the rather odd distinction of being one of the few Canaanite cities to play a role in a Greek myth. The hero Perseus had killed the monstrous Medusa in the far-off land of the Hyperboreans and was hurrying home when he spied a naked woman chained to a rock on a cliff outside the city of Joppa. This was Andromeda, being sacrificed to a sea monster by her father Cepheus and her mother Cassiopeia, who were the Ethiopian king and queen of Joppa. He rescued her, of course.

But why should the rulers of Joppa be described as Ethiopians? If it is not to be dismissed as merely the ignorance of geography on the part of the Greek mythmakers, we can speculate, perhaps, as follows—

While the Greek legends may have reached their later, relatively sophisticated, forms at the hands of Greek poets of the Golden Age, they were undoubtedly based on hoary old tales stretching back into the dim past. The legends are placed in Mycenaean times before the Trojan War—a time when Egypt was the greatest power in the world and the Pharaohs of the 18th and 19th dynasties controlled adjacent portions of Asia, including Canaan. Therefore, it was fair enough to speak of an Egyptian king of Joppa, meaning the governor who ruled under Pharaoh.

In the eighth century B.C., however, when Greece was becoming a colonizing land and when her ships were pushing out over the Mediterranean for the first time since the fall of the great kingdoms of Trojan times, she became aware of an Egypt that was then under an Ethiopian dynasty. It was easy to read this backward into time and replace the Egyptian "king" at Joppa by an Ethiopian one.

Mount Moriah

The building of the Temple is begun:

2 Chronicles 3:1. *Then Solomon began to build the house of the Lord at Jerusalem in Mount Moriah . . . in the place that David had prepared in the threshingfloor of Ornan the Jebusite.*

Thus, the place of the Temple is here tied in with two awesome episodes of the past, something that the description in 1 Kings did not do. At the threshingfloor of Ornan (called Araunah in 2 Samuel; see page 319) David had seen an angel, and in the land of Moriah, Abraham had nearly sacrificed Isaac (see page 87).

(The Samaritans, on the other hand, maintained that Abraham had nearly sacrificed Isaac on Mount Gerizim, since that was *their* sacred mountain.)

Arabia

Once the Temple is completed, the Chronicler tells of the visit of the queen of Sheba and continues to describe the wealth and glory of Solomon:

2 Chronicles 9:14. *. . . And all the kings of Arabia . . . brought gold and silver to Solomon.*

In the earlier books of the Bible, the tribes in the arid regions south and east of Canaan were named separately, so that there is mention of Ammonites, Moabites, Edomites, Amalekites, Midianites, and so on.

Only now is the general geographic term "Arabia" used. "Arabia" is the Latinized version of "Arab," which is the general Semitic term for the people of the desert beyond Canaan. The meaning of "Arab" is not certain. It might simply mean "nomad" for the word resembles the Hebrew *arabah*, meaning "steppe." It might also mean something self-glorifying like "man of the master race."

In any case, Arabia is now the name given to the large, mostly desert peninsula south of the Fertile Crescent, which is about one million square miles in area and has a population, nowadays, of about ten million.

Many people think of it as the original home of the peoples speaking Semitic languages. Since it is not a fertile territory, its population easily multiplies past the point where the land will support it and tribes will therefore wander northward into one portion or another of the Fertile Crescent. This tendency may well have been most marked in prehistoric times, when the trend to aridity was first making itself felt, but it has continued well into historic times, the most recent and, in some respects, greatest eruption coming in the seventh century A.D., when Arabs spread Mohammedanism across vast tracts in Asia and Africa.

The Akkadians may have emerged from Arabia to invade Sumeria at the dawn of history and give the area its conquering hero, Sargon. The various Canaanite groups may have come from Arabia, as may the later Aramaeans and Chaldeans, to say nothing of the Hebrew tribes themselves.

Rehoboam

For the period after Solomon's death, the Chronicler follows the history of Judah, and of Judah only. The history of Israel, except where it impinges on Judah, is ignored, for in the Chronicler's time it was clear that Israel had been a dead end and was gone. Even Elijah and Elisha are ignored. It was through Judah and Judah alone, the Chronicler was certain, that the eternal nature of God's promises were to be fulfilled.

The history of Judah is a history of the Temple and of the monarchy. The Temple is a great constant; the ideal place of worship and the true hero of the history. The monarchy, on the other hand, is a swinging pendulum. There are good kings who reform worship and bring it in line with the Temple ideal; there are bad kings who pervert worship and encourage idolatry. There are kings who are at times good and at times bad.

The Chronicler's thesis is that true religion and worldly prosperity go hand in hand; good kings prosper and bad kings suffer. To make that thesis clear, both prosperity and suffering are enormously exaggerated. Good kings win over vast hordes of enemies and are wealthy indeed; bad kings lose enormous battles. Repentance converts bad to good at once; apostasy as quickly converts good to bad, and at every stage of the game there is some prophet or priest to encourage the good and denounce the bad.

In the Book of 1 Kings, for instance, Rehoboam, the successor of Solomon, is briefly dealt with and is described as uniformly unfortunate. He brings about the schism between Israel and Judah through nothing less than criminal folly, and he suffers the invasion of Shishak of Egypt.

In the Book of 2 Chronicles, however, there is a pendulum swing. Immediately after the schism, the Levites in Israel are described as flocking to Judah:

2 Chronicles 11:13. *And the priests and the Levites that were in all Israel resorted to him* [Rehoboam] *out of all their coasts.*

The Book of 1 Kings does say that Jeroboam is setting up his shrines in Bethel and Dan appointed non-Levites as priests—

1 Kings 12:31. . . . *he . . . made priests of the lowest of the people, which were not of the sons of Levi.*

—so that it seems reasonable that Levites should emigrate to Judah where the Temple-worship and priestly honor would be open to them. This is not specified in 1 Kings, but it suits the Chronicler's purpose to emphasize this and possibly exaggerate it since it shows that only in Judah did true religion continue and that what religion remained in Israel was totally false.

Rehoboam and the Levites at first behaved themselves:

2 Chronicles 11:17. . . . *for three years they walked in the way of David and Solomon.*

and therefore Rehoboam prospered:

> 2 Chronicles 11:21. . . . *he took eighteen wives, and threescore concubines; and begat twenty and eight sons, and threescore daughters.*

But then he backslid:

> 2 Chronicles 12:1. . . . *Rehoboam . . . forsook the law . . . and all Israel with him.*
> 2 Chronicles 12:2. *And . . . Shishak king of Egypt came up against Jerusalem, because they had transgressed . . .*
> 2 Chronicles 12:3. *With twelve hundred chariots, and threescore thousand horsemen: and . . . people . . . without number . . . the Lubims, the Sukkiims, and the Ethiopians.*

The Chronicler exaggerates the size of the army, but the details are otherwise plausible. Shishak is the first of the Libyan dynasty and the "Lubims" are, without much question, the Libyan cohorts that served under him. The Ethiopians are mercenaries from the south. The Sukkiims are less easily identifiable but it may be a reference to Succoth (or Sukkoth), a town in the eastern portion of the Nile delta (see page 141). The Sukkiims may therefore be the native Egyptians of the delta.

As a result of the invasion, Rehoboam and the nation swung back in response to a warning by Shemaiah the prophet:

> 2 Chronicles 12:6. *Whereupon the princes of Israel and the king humbled themselves . . .*

In consequence of that, while Jerusalem and the Temple were looted, king and nation were not entirely destroyed.

Abijah

Succeeding Rehoboam was his son Abijah, which may be the throne name, where Abijam (the name used in 1 Kings) was the proper name.

The Chronicler usually gives the name of the king's mother at the time his accession is noted, since this is of genealogical interest. In the case of Abijam there seems to be some confusion in this respect.

1 Kings 15:2. . . . *his* [Abijam's] *mother's name was Maachah, the daughter of Abishalom.*

2 Chronicles 11:20. . . . *he* [Rehoboam] *took Maachah the daughter of Absalom, which bare him Abijah . . .*

2 Chronicles 13:2. . . . *His* [Abijah's] *mother's name . . . was Michaiah the daughter of Uriel of Gibeah . . .*

Absalom, David's rebel son, did have a mother named Maachah, and may have had a daughter (or granddaughter) of the same name, although she is never mentioned in the chapters dealing with Absalom. And who Uriel might be is unknown. There is no likelihood that the confusion can ever be straightened out but it is interesting that if Absalom is really Abijah's grandfather (or great-grandfather) then for all that his bid for the throne was lost, his blood flows in all the kings of the Davidic line after Rehoboam.

In 1 Kings, it is simply stated that Abijah (Abijam) of Judah and Jeroboam of Israel were at war, and no details are given. However, the stronger Israel did not manage to beat down the weaker Judah and the Chronicler uses that as a way of demonstrating his thesis. He describes a battle in which eight hundred thousand men of Israel fought four hundred thousand men of Judah. Abijah made a rousing pro-Temple speech to the enemy before the battle and even though the Israelites outnumbered the Judeans and surrounded them besides, the Judeans won a great victory and

2 Chronicles 13:17. . . . *there fell down slain of Israel five hundred thousand men*

so that Jeroboam was permanently enfeebled and soon died:

2 Chronicles 13:21. *But Abijah waxed mighty, and married fourteen wives . . .*

Asa

Asa, the son of Abijah, is described as a reforming king. Consequently, one can be confident that he has nothing to fear in the face of a new invasion—one that is not mentioned in 1 Kings:

2 Chronicles 14:9. *And there came out against them* [Judah] *Zerah the Ethiopian with an host of a thousand thousand and three hundred chariots and came unto Mareshah.*

The thought of a million-man army swarming into Judah (Mareshah is about twenty-five miles southwest of Jerusalem) in the ninth century B.C. rather staggers the imagination. The Chronicler, however, is just emphasizing the glory of Asa's eventual victory and the figure need not be taken seriously.

2 Chronicles 14:11. *And Asa cried unto the Lord* . . .
2 Chronicles 14:12. *So the Lord smote the Ethiopians before Asa* . . .
2 Chronicles 14:13. *And Asa* . . . *pursued them unto Gerar* . . .
2 Chronicles 14:14. *And they smote all the cities round about Gerar* . . .

The Chronicler may exaggerate and moralize but he does not, apparently, manufacture stories outright. Zerah and his invasion are not mentioned in 1 Kings, which, however, concentrates to a large extent on Israel, and it may well be that Zerah's attack was actually only a minor raid by a border chieftain.

Shishak, after his own successful raid, may have placed an army detachment at Gerar, south of Judah, and in Asa's time, an Ethiopian mercenary may have been in charge of that detachment. It would be his raid that was beaten off.

Asa reigned from 915 to 875 B.C. and in this period the second Pharaoh of the Libyan dynasty reigned. He was Osorkon I, who reigned from 919 to 883 B.C. It is not beyond the realm of the possible that Zerah was Osorkon.

In Asa's case, however, the pendulum swings back. He is pressed hard by Baasha of Israel and therefore makes an alliance with Syria. Such trust in worldly alliances rather than in the Lord offends the prophetic party, and the Chronicler hastens from that to an account of Asa's death through a disease of the feet. He puts in a further touch of disapproval in a pair of verses that are sometimes used in modern times as a jibe at the medical profession:

2 Chronicles 16:12. . . . *yet in his disease he sought not to the Lord but to the physicians.*
2 Chronicles 16:13. *And Asa slept with his fathers* . . .

Jehoshaphat

The next king, Jehoshaphat, is described by the Chronicler as a great reforming monarch, and his reign is therefore a time of peace and power:

> 2 Chronicles 17:12. *And Jehoshaphat waxed great exceedingly* . . .

The fact that Jehoshaphat was a loyal and even subservient ally of Ahab of Israel (the worldly reason for Judah's peace and prosperity at this time) is mentioned in connection with their combined war at Ramoth-gilead, during the course of which Ahab died (see page 352). Jehoshaphat is only mildly denounced for this, however.

His continuing reform policy leads to a great victory over the Moabites and Ammonites, but his continuing alliance with Israel is blamed for the failure of his trading fleet (see page 351).

Jehoiada

With Jehoram, the husband of Athaliah and therefore the son-in-law of Ahab and Jezebel (see page 362), and his son Ahaziah (the son also of Athaliah) there is a serious reaction. Under the influence of Athaliah, Phoenician cults are brought into Judah. Both monarchs came to a bad end, therefore. Under Jehoram, Jerusalem was taken and sacked by Philistines and Arabs and the king died soon after of an incurable disease of the intestines. As for Ahaziah, he was slain in Israel, in the course of the revolution of Jehu (see page 364).

Athaliah's usurpation and the saving of Joash is then taken up (see page 367) and here the hero is Jehoiada the High Priest and the husband of Jehoshabeath (Jehosheba), the royal infant's aunt.

Jehoiada organizes the conspiracy that kills Athaliah and places Joash on the throne, but does so with meticulous care that the Temple ritual be observed in all its details. He reinstates reform and as long as he lives all goes well. His death is recorded in a way that is reminiscent of Genesis:

> 2 Chronicles 24:15. *But Jehoiada waxed old, and was full of days when he died; an hundred and thirty years old was he when he died.*

Thereafter Joash backslid and when he is reproved for this by
Zechariah, the son of Jehoiada, the king has Zechariah stoned to death
in the court of the Temple:

2 Chronicles 24:22. *Thus Joash the king remembered not the
kindness which Jehoiada . . . had done to him, but slew his son . . .*

As a result a small Syrian army invaded the land and defeated a
larger Judean defending force; Joash was afflicted with disease and,
finally, was assassinated by men of his court.

Amaziah

The next king, Amaziah, began his reign quite well. Having decided to reconquer Edom, which had rebelled after Jehoshaphat's death,
he hired a hundred thousand Israelite mercenaries. When the prophetic
party objected to this dependence on worldly help, Amaziah released
them and forfeited the money with which he had hired them. As a
result:

2 Chronicles 25:11. *And Amaziah . . . smote of the children of
Seir ten thousand.*

Amaziah's victory led him into trouble, however, for he was attracted by the Edomite gods.

2 Chronicles 25:14. . . . *Amaziah . . . brought the gods of the
children of Seir, and . . . bowed down . . . before them . . .*

It is this which the Chronicler finds to be the cause of Amaziah's
subsequent defeat by Joash of Israel (see page 369) and his final assassination at the hands of conspirators.

Uzziah

Amaziah was succeeded by his son:

2 Chronicles 26:1. *Then all the people of Judah took Uzziah . . .
and made him king . . .*

Uzziah is, apparently, the throne name of the king, while his proper name (used in 2 Kings) is Azariah. Uzziah was a reforming king and this accounted to the Chronicler for the fact that he defeated the Philistines and Ammonites, that he successfully reorganized the Judean army and strongly fortified Jerusalem.

2 Chronicles 26:15. . . . *And his name spread far abroad; for he was marvellously helped, till he was strong.*

In a worldly sense, Uzziah's prosperity was probably due to his careful subservience to the successful Jeroboam II of Israel. The prosperous Uzziah, however, overstepped the bounds and trespassed on the prerogatives of the priesthood. (David and Solomon had successfully done so, but the position of the priests had hardened since those days.)

2 Chronicles 26:16. . . . *when he* [Uzziah] *was strong, his heart was lifted up . . . and* [he] *went into the temple of the Lord to burn incense . . .*

He was promptly stricken with leprosy and remained a leper till he died.

Ahaz

The Chronicler's pendulum continues to swing. Jotham succeeds his father Uzziah and continues the reform policy. In consequence, he defeats the Ammonites.

Under Ahaz, the next king, there is a reaction and Judah is promptly defeated by the Syrians. And as Ahaz's idolatry is particularly heinous, the punishment described is extravagantly high:

2 Chronicles 28:6. *For Pekah* [of Israel] *. . . slew in Judah an hundred and twenty thousand in one day . . . because they had forsaken the Lord . . .*

Hezekiah

Ahaz's son Hezekiah is, however, the greatest reformer of all, in the Chronicler's view. Hezekiah is, indeed, exalted by him to a point of equality with the later king, Josiah. This makes sense from the

Chronicler's standpoint, since Hezekiah was victorious in battle and
Josiah was defeated, so that the reforming deeds of the former must
at least equal, if not surpass, those of the latter.

Hezekiah began by reopening and rededicating the Temple, which
apparently had been closed during the disastrous reign of Ahaz. He
then prepared and kept an extremely elaborate Passover and followed
that by the destruction of all idolatrous altars in the kingdom.

Following all this righteous behavior, Sennacherib invaded Judah
and laid siege to Jerusalem (see page 384), and to the Chronicler
it seems perfectly natural that the Assyrian should retreat without being able to take the city.

> 2 Chronicles 32:27. *And Hezekiah had exceeding much riches
> and honour* . . .
>
> . . . .
>
> 2 Chronicles 32:30. . . . *And Hezekiah prospered in all his
> works.*

Manasseh

But following what to the Chronicler was the best of the kings of
Judah in the days after Solomon, came his son Manasseh, who was
the worst. He restored all the ways of his grandfather, Ahaz:

> 2 Chronicles 33:9. *So Manasseh made Judah and the inhabitants
> of Jerusalem to err, and to do worse than the heathen* . . .

Now the Chronicler is in a dilemma, for Manasseh reigned for fifty-
five years and, as far as we can tell from 2 Kings, that reign was one
of peace and quiet.

The Chronicler therefore brings disaster upon him; a disaster not
mentioned in 2 Kings:

> 2 Chronicles 33:11. *Wherefore the Lord brought upon him the cap-
> tains of the host of the king of Assyria, which took Manasseh* . . .
> *and bound him* . . . *and carried him to Babylon.*

Now the Chronicler may color heavily, but he does not, apparently,
attempt outright invention. We may assume then that something happened in the reign of Manasseh which the Chronicler was able to
interpret as captivity.

It is certain that Judah was an Assyrian tributary in the days of Manasseh and tributary kings were not uncommonly forced to visit the capital as an expression of loyalty or to engage in some administrative function or other. Assyrian records speak of two occasions on which Manasseh was present in the capital. One of these occasions was in 672 B.C. after Manasseh had been reigning for twenty years. Esarhaddon was then king of Assyria and was anxious to assure his son and heir, Asshurbanipal, a quiet succession. He therefore ordered the various vassal kings, including Manasseh, to Assyria to swear allegiance and vow loyalty.

Manasseh was not actually taken to Assyria by a conquering army but it is quite possible that he left in the company of an Assyrian military guard and the people (and even Manasseh himself) could not be quite sure that the dread Esarhaddon might not decide to keep him captive and replace him on the throne with someone else. Out of this, it was easy for the Chronicler to devise Manasseh's captivity and point the moral.

However, Manasseh returned from Assyria and ruled for another generation. That could not be denied and it had to be explained according to the Chronicler's system. The only way was to have Manasseh repent and then return to Jerusalem as a reforming king (something that is not mentioned in 2 Kings, nor in the words of the contemporary prophet Jeremiah).

2 Chronicles 33:12. *And when he* [Manasseh] *was in affliction, he besought the Lord . . . and humbled himself greatly . . .*

2 Chronicles 33:13. *And prayed unto him; and he* [the Lord] *. . . heard his supplication, and brought him again to Jerusalem . . .*

The Prayer of Manasses

Particular interest would naturally be centered about the prayer of Manasseh. Because Manasseh was so consummate and notorious a sinner, his redemption by prayer was a clear indication that all men might find forgiveness if properly penitent and this was a matter of great theological interest. Naturally, there was curiosity as to the nature of the prayer, particularly since the Chronicler says the prayer exists in the records, even though he does not give it himself.

2 Chronicles 33:18. Now the rest of the acts of Manasseh, and his prayer unto his God . . . are written in the book of the kings of Israel.

2 Chronicles 33:19. His prayer also, and how God was intreated of him, . . . are written among the sayings of the seers.

If, by "the book of the kings of Israel," the Biblical Book of a Kings is meant, the Chronicler errs, for the prayer is not to be found there (or is no longer to be found there, at any rate). As for the "sayings of the seers" in which the prayer is to be found, this is lost.

In later years, however, perhaps about 100 B.C., a prayer was written by an unnamed poet, a prayer designed for the use of sinners who craved mercy. It was a short prayer, only fifteen verses long, but was so beautiful that it became easy to believe that it was indeed the prayer that had been uttered by Manassch in his Assyrian dungeon. It therefore came to be included in some editions of the Bible as that prayer.

In particular, it was included in the Greek translation of the Bible that circulated among the Greek-speaking Jews of the city of Alexandria, in Egypt.

This translation is called the Septuagint, from the Latin word for "seventy." According to legend, Ptolemy II, king of Egypt, was on good terms with his subjects, the Alexandrian Jews, and agreed to help them prepare a translation of their holy books. He brought in seventy-two scholars (altered by later legends to an even seventy) from Jerusalem at his own expense and had them translate the first five books of the Bible (the Pentateuch) into Greek. It was the first translation of any of the Biblical books into a foreign language. Over the next two centuries, additional books were translated and these eventually included the supposed prayer of Manasseh (which may, to be sure, have been written in Greek to begin with).

About 90 A.D., Jewish scholars gathered in a Judean town named Jamnia, about thirty miles west of Jerusalem. Twenty years before, the Romans had sacked Jerusalem and destroyed the Temple and the Jews were scattered abroad. Only the Bible and the tenets of Judaism which it contained could be counted on to hold them together. There had therefore to be one standard Bible for all Jews and the scholars had to decide of what books this Bible would consist.

The books they accepted now make up the Jewish Bible. In general, though, they did not accept those books, however edifying, that were written after about 150 B.C. Those were too clearly the work of men rather than of God. One of the books *not* accepted by the Jewish scholars was the prayer of Manasseh.

Some of the eliminated books nevertheless remained in the Septuagint. Christian scholars made use of the Septuagint, and when Latin translations were made, the books eliminated by the Jewish scholars were translated and kept. Some are still to be found in English-language Bibles used by Catholics today.

Jerome, who about A.D. 400 prepared the Vulgate, or the official Latin Bible now used by the Catholic Church, worked in Palestine, learned Hebrew, used the assistance of rabbis, and consulted Hebrew versions of the Bible as well as the Septuagint. He knew of the difference in the books they contained.

For those books contained in the Greek version and not in the Hebrew, Jerome used the word "Apocrypha." This word means "hidden" and, after all, some of the books in the Greek Bible had been withdrawn and, therefore, "hidden" from the reader who studied the Hebrew Bible. Thus, the prayer of Manasseh becomes one of the apocryphal books, or, to put the phrase in a slightly different form, part of the Apocrypha.

The Protestant versions of the Bible (including the King James) follow the Hebrew system and do not include the Apocrypha. For that reason, the prayer of Manasseh, is not to be found in the King James version of the Bible. Nevertheless, the apocryphal books were put into English by the translators of the King James Version and exist also in the Revised Standard Version. Since the translation was from the Greek, the Greek form of Manasseh is used and the final "-s" used in Greek names makes the book "The Prayer of Manasses." In the Revised Standard Version, however, it is "The Prayer of Manasseh."

Josiah

Amon, who follows Manasseh, is another backslider and is assassinated—but then comes Josiah.

Although the Chronicler has placed as much of the reforming credit as possible upon Hezekiah, there is no question but that after the reigns of Manasseh and Amon, reform is once again needed, and the tradition of Josiah's work is, in any case, too strong to be ignored. The tale is therefore repeated, complete with the discovery of the Book of Deuteronomy and the celebration of the great Passover.

Yet Josiah died in battle and the Chronicler had to explain that. Of course, the death was, in one sense, a blessing, for it meant that Josiah would not survive to see the destruction of the Temple and of the kingdom.

This is not, however, enough for the Chronicler, who needs a positive cause. Therefore, on the occasion of Josiah's fatal war against Necho of Egypt, the Chronicler adds something not present in 2 Kings. As the battle of Megiddo approaches, the Egyptian monarch sends ambassadors to the Judean, with the message:

> 2 Chronicles 36:21. . . . *I come not against thee this day . . . God commanded me to make haste: forbear thee from meddling with God, who is with me . . .*
> 2 Chronicles 36:22. *Nevertheless Josiah . . . hearkened not unto the words of Necho from the mouth of God . . .*

In other words, Josiah died because in this case he was disobedient to God.

King of the Chaldees

The reigns of the sons and grandson of Josiah, ending with Zedekiah, are hastened through briefly. All backslid as did the people and the priests:

> 2 Chronicles 36:14. *Moreover all the chief of the priests, and the people, transgressed very much . . .*

They were warned by prophets but that did no good:

> 2 Chronicles 36:16. *But they* [the people] *mocked the messengers of God, and despised his words, and misused his prophets, until the wrath of the Lord arose against his people, till there was no remedy.*
> 2 Chronicles 36:17. *Therefore he brought upon them the king of the Chaldees* [Nebuchadnezzar] *. . .*

So, ironically, history comes full circle. One wonders if the Chronicler, in using the phrase "king of the Chaldees" rather than the more natural "king of Babylon," does not deliberately stress the irony. After all, Abraham, to whom Canaan was first promised, reached that land from Ur of the Chaldees (see page 56) and now the Jews are carried out of that land by the king of the Chaldees.

15. EZRA

The Chronicler

The Chronicler did not complete his story with the downfall of Zedekiah and the destruction of the Temple in 586 B.C. He was writing, after all, about 400 B.C. at the earliest estimate and much remained to be told.

The actual period of exile was of little interest to him, for the Temple, the non-human hero of his history, did not then exist. He therefore fills in that period with nothing more than genealogies like that of the line of descent of Jeconiah in the third chapter of 1 Chronicles (see page 405).

A half century after Zedekiah's death, however, there begins a period in which the project of the rebuilding of the Temple comes under discussion and now the Chronicler's interest is aroused once more. Immediately after his account of the end of the kingdom of Judah, therefore, the Chronicler passes on to an account of a royal proclamation by the new king of a new nation; a proclamation which led to the construction of a new Temple.

Because of this gap in time and the radically sudden change in atmosphere from an established kingdom and a centuries-old Temple to a band of impoverished returnees trying desperately to build a house of worship, there was a tendency to divide the Chronicler's history at this point. The earlier portion makes up 1 Chronicles and 2 Chron-

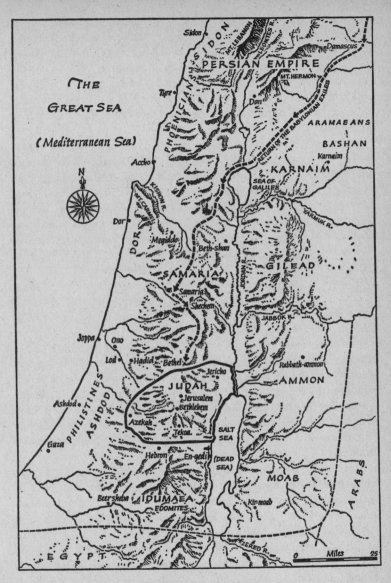

Jerusalem Restored

icles.* The later portion might be called the Book of Ezra, or perhaps the Book of Ezra and Nehemiah, because these two men, Ezra the scribe and Nehemiah the governor, played important roles in the re-establishment of the Temple and of the community.

In Jewish tradition, it was Ezra the scribe who wrote these books; who was the man I have been referring to as the Chronicler. There is no certainty about this, but, on the other hand, there is nothing implausible about it either.

The Jewish scholars who placed the Bible in its final form toward the end of the first century A.D. recognized that the Book of Ezra and Nehemiah, like 1 and 2 Chronicles, could appear only in "the Writings" because of its comparatively late date of composition. However, whereas 1 and 2 Chronicles duplicated, to a very large extent, the early historical books of the Bible, Ezra and Nehemiah added new material not present elsewhere. For that reason Ezra and Nehemiah was more useful and was placed ahead of 1 and 2 Chronicles, even though from the historical viewpoint it came afterward.

In order to make the historical connection clear despite this reversal of chronology, the verses at the dividing line are duplicated. The first three verses of Ezra are quoted virtually verbatim at the very end of the last chapter of 2 Chronicles.

In the various versions of the Bible used by Christians, 1 and 2 Chronicles are placed not at the end of the Old Testament but immediately after 1 and 2 Kings. Then, as an additional piece of logical arrangement, the Book of Ezra appears not before but *after* 1 and 2 Chronicles, so that the Chronicler's history can be read as a unit, with the only jog coming at the point where the verses ending 2 Chronicles are repeated at the beginning of Ezra. (The repetition is retained.)

It eventually became customary to divide the final part of the Chronicler's history into two parts, the Book of Ezra, and the Book of Nehemiah. In view of the belief that Ezra was the Chronicler and wrote both books, and since he appears in both books, it is also possible to call the books 1 Ezra and 2 Ezra. This is adhered to in Catholic versions of the Bible, which, however, make use of the Greek form of the name so that the books become 1 Esdras and 2 Esdras.

* These are handled as two separate books only for convenience sake, as in the case of 1 and 2 Samuel and 1 and 2 Kings, with full recognition that actually they form a single work.

The Sixth Century B.C.

Cyrus, king of Persia

The Book of Ezra begins with the event that first initiated the rebuilding of the Temple and dates it in the fashion of ancient times:

Ezra 1:1. *Now in the first year of Cyrus king of Persia* . . .

In this way, the Chronicler skips lightly over a vast change that had come over the political complexion of western Asia.

The Chaldeans, in defeating the Assyrians and taking Nineveh, had been in alliance with the Medes, a people living to the north of Assyria and south of the Caspian Sea—a region known as Media. After the fall of Nineveh, the Chaldeans, ruling from Babylon, had taken control of the entire Fertile Crescent, while the Medes extended their rule over a vast stretch of land to the north and east.

The Median Empire was much the larger in area but it stretched over barbaric areas of nomad tribes. The Chaldeans, on the other hand, ruled the very cradle of civilization, a land of intensely irrigated, agriculturally rich land, full of large and luxurious cities. Under Nebuchadnezzar, who came to the throne of Chaldea in 605 B.C., Babylon was the largest, wealthiest, and most powerful city in the world and was capital of its mightiest empire.

Nebuchadnezzar died in 561 B.C. after a most successful rule of forty-four years, having survived the capture of Jerusalem by a full quarter century. The monarchs who followed him were, however, much weaker than he. His son Amel-Marduk (the Evil-merodach of the Bible; see page 396) succeeded him but was dethroned by a conspiracy in 560 B.C. After several years of instability, Nabonidus, who was not of the line of Nebuchadnezzar, ascended the throne in 556 B.C. He was a scholar rather than a soldier and left the rule of Babylon to others while he involved himself in antiquarian studies.

Media, the one great power which might have taken advantage of the weakness of the Babylonian kings, was not particularly warlike either. In 593 B.C., while Nebuchadnezzar was still comparatively new on the throne, Astyages became king of the Medes. He was still king when Nebuchadnezzar died and his long reign was peaceful. It happened, however, that within a decade of Nebuchadnezzar's death, the

Median Empire was shaken by war and a new tribe became dominant.

This tribe had been living under Median rule in a district now called Fars, which lies along the northern shores of the Persian Gulf. To the ancient inhabitants of the land, it was Parsa, and to the Greeks, Persis. It is from the last that we get our present words "Persia" and "Persian."

The Persians were closely akin to the Medes, with similar language and similar traditions, so that there was much confusion concerning the two among foreigners. Sometimes they were spoken of as "the Medes and the Persians." Sometimes, Jews and Greeks alike spoke of "Medes" when they really meant "Persians."

About 600 B.C., there was born to one of the leading Persian families a child they named Kurush. In Hebrew, this name became Koresh, and in Greek, Kuros. The last, in Latin spelling, is Cyrus, and it is by that name that we know him. Later, legends arose which made Cyrus the grandson of Astyages, and stated that the Median king had exposed the baby to certain death because an oracle had foretold that he would be killed and replaced on the throne by the infant once he had grown to manhood. Cyrus was suckled and kept alive by a dog and then taken care of by a shepherd till he was grown.

This legend can be dismissed. Similar stories are told of the founders of other nations—of Romulus, the legendary founder of Rome, for instance. Such a story has the ulterior purpose of serving to cast a mantle of legitimacy over a usurper and making him seem the lawful successor to the king he has replaced by force.

It is much more likely that Cyrus was exactly what he seemed: a Persian leader who was no member of the royal line at all. He rebelled against Astyages, and about 550 B.C. succeeded in placing himself upon the throne. What had been the Median Empire was now the Persian Empire.

Cyrus now entered upon a career of conquest. He took all of Asia Minor and extended the borders of his kingdom to the shores of the Aegean Sea. In 538 B.C. he took Babylon from its disorganized rulers and all the Fertile Crescent was in his hands. To the Jews in Babylon, this was the "first year of Cyrus king of Persia."

The Persian Empire, as put together by Cyrus, was the greatest realm that western Asia had yet seen. It encompassed all the Asian territory of Assyria, plus Asia Minor and large tracts to the east.

Jeremiah

Cyrus was completely unlike the conquerors who had flourished before him. He did not engage in wholesale killings and deportations. Rather he chose to treat the conquered peoples gently, allowing them their self-respect and even considerable home rule. The result was that the Persian Empire was an administrative success as well as a territorial one. It experienced revolts, to be sure, but it also enjoyed periods of peace over wide areas. The moral, for conquerors, would seem to be plain. The lighter the grip, the firmer the hold.

The Jews were one of the groups that benefited from Cyrus's policy. The Persian king found a group of them making up a rather prosperous colony in Babylon and he offered to allow them to return:

> Ezra 1:3. *Who is there among you of all his* [God's] *people? . . . let him go up to Jerusalem . . . and build the house of the Lord . . .*

The Chronicler points out that thus was fulfilled a prophecy of Jeremiah, something that is mentioned briefly here but more fully at the end of 2 Chronicles:

> 2 Chronicles 36:20. . . . *they* [the Jewish exiles] *were servants to him* [Nebuchadnezzar] *and his sons until the reign of Persia:*
> 2 Chronicles 36:21. *To fulfill the word of the Lord by . . . Jeremiah, until the land . . . lay desolate . . . threescore and ten years.*

The prophecy is recorded in the Book of Jeremiah, thus:

> Jeremiah 29:10. *For thus saith the Lord, That after seventy years be accomplished at Babylon I will visit you . . . causing you to return to this place.*

And yet the period of exile was not seventy years. From the destruction of the Temple in 586 B.C. to Cyrus's proclamation in 538 B.C. was a lapse of time of only forty-eight years.

Of course, Jeremiah and the Chronicler may not have thought of seventy years as representing a precise length of time. (Ancient historians were much less time conscious than we are.) Seventy years may merely have meant the "lifetime of a man" to them.

On the other hand, the seventy years that were accomplished at Babylon may refer to the duration of the Chaldean Empire, which from the accession of Nebuchadnezzar to that of Cyrus lasted sixty-seven years.

And again, the reference may be to the Temple itself rather than to the people, as I shall explain later in the chapter.

Sheshbazzar

There was a quick response to Cyrus's edict:

Ezra 1:5. *Then rose up the chief of the fathers of Judah and Benjamin, and the ... Levites ... to go up to build the house of the Lord ...*

Ezra 1:6. *And all they that were about them strengthened their hands with ... silver ... gold ... goods ... beasts ...*

The specific mention of the tribes of Judah, Benjamin, and Levi makes it clear that only the exiles of the kingdom of Judah are involved. The descendants of earlier exiles from the kingdom of Israel, carried off by Sargon of Assyria, would still be somewhere in the dominions of Cyrus and might conceivably have been included in the edict. However, it was now nearly two centuries since the Israelites had been carried off. By now, apparently, they had been absorbed and had lost all consciousness of being Israelites.

Even the Jews in Babylon had assimilated themselves to an extent. Not all went rushing back to Jerusalem. Some remained behind. The fact that they donated objects of value to help those who were planning to make the trip indicates that they were reasonably well-to-do and might have seen no point in leaving a place where they were prosperous and secure and where by now they felt at home. (This is precisely the situation in which modern American Jews find themselves. Many are prosperous and secure and see no reason to leave their homes and flock to Israel—though they are willing to make financial contributions.)

Cyrus is described as also contributing to the returnees, ordering that the various Temple furnishings, which had been carried off by Nebuchadnezzar, be returned:

Ezra 1:7. . . . *Cyrus . . . brought forth the vessels of the house of the Lord . . .*

Ezra 1:8. *Even those did Cyrus . . . bring forth by the hand of Mithredath . . . and numbered them unto Sheshbazzar, the prince of Judah.*

Mithredath is an interesting name. It means "given by Mithra," one of the important Persian deities on the side of Ormuzd and the forces of good (see page 409). A later version of the Persian religion, built about Mithra as a sun symbol, was known as Mithraism and, in the time of the Roman Empire, it vied with Christianity for supremacy. The Greek version of the name Mithredath is Mithridates. Rulers by this name reigned over the kingdoms of Parthia and of Pontus in Roman times. In particular, Mithridates VI of Pontus (sometimes known as Mithradates the Great) fought Rome nearly to a standstill in the first century B.C.

The name "Sheshbazzar" is a puzzle. Its meaning is unclear but it is certainly a Babylonian name and not a Hebrew one. Yet it is borne by someone who is "the prince of Judah." Presumably the Jews exiled in Babylon tended to adopt Babylonian names just as American Jews tend to adopt American names.

Since Sheshbazzar is "the prince of Judah," it is natural to look for him among those of the Davidic line listed earlier by the Chronicler. The sons of Jeconiah, the exiled king of Judah, are there given:

1 Chronicles 3:17. . . . *Salathiel his [Jeconiah's] son,*
1 Chronicles 3:18. *Malchiram also, and Pediah, and Shenazar . . .*

It is very tempting to identify Shenazar (itself apparently a Babylonian name) with Sheshbazzar. If so, Sheshbazzar would be the fourth son of Jeconiah. If the three older sons were dead or incapacitated, Sheshbazzar would be literally the prince of Judah, the legal king of the land. It is even conceivable that the difference between Shenazar and Sheshbazzar arises because the son of Jeconiah adopted the latter as a throne name once his leadership of Judah was thus officially recognized.

To be sure, Cyrus had no intention of restoring Judah as a political kingdom, whether independent or tributary, but merely wished to restore Jerusalem as the center of what seemed to him to be an unimportant cult.

Zerubbabel

Sheshbazzar led a party to Jerusalem and under him, apparently, the work began:

> Ezra 5:16. . . . *Sheshbazzar . . . laid the foundation of the house of God . . .*

However, if so, he was apparently only a titular head, cast in the role as (perhaps) the oldest living scion of the house of David and therefore lending an air of sanctity and legitimacy to the project. As the son of Jeconiah he must have been an old man at the time of this first return, and a younger man would have taken over after Sheshbazzar's ceremonial laying of the cornerstone, so to speak. Later on, it is only this younger man who is mentioned:

> Ezra 2:1. *Now these are the children . . . that went up out of the captivity . . .*
> Ezra 2:2. *Which came with Zerubbabel . . .*

Some suggest that Zerubbabel (also a Babylonian name, meaning "child of Babylon") is simply another name for Sheshbazzar, but nothing forces this assumption. Zerubbabel is a distinct individual also mentioned among the descendants of Jeconiah:

> 1 Chronicles 3:19. *And the sons of Pedaiah were, Zerubbabel, and Shimei.*

Elsewhere, to be sure, he is listed as the son of another:

> Ezra 5:2. *Then rose up Zerubbabel the son of Shealtiel . . .*

However, Shealtiel is commonly equated with Salathiel, listed in 1 Chronicles as Jeconiah's oldest son. In either case, Zerubbabel is the nephew of Sheshbazzar, the grandson of Jeconiah, and therefore the great-great-grandson of Josiah and the descendant, in the twentieth generation, of David.

Jeshua

Eventually, an altar was built upon which sacrifices might be performed:

> Ezra 3:2. *Then stood up Jeshua the son of Jozadak . . . and Zerubbabel . . . and builded the altar . . .*

The name Jeshua is a form of the earlier Joshua, which is itself a shortened form of Jehoshua. This form appears commonly in the Chronicler's history, and it has special interest because it is this name which, in the Greek form, is Jesus.

Jeshua is the son of Jozadak (Jehozadak), who is listed in the sixth chapter of 1 Chronicles as the High Priest at the time of the fall of the kingdom, the High Priest who went into Babylonian captivity (see page 406).

Now his son had returned to officiate at the altar. Thus, not only is the secular power unbroken in the line from Jeconiah to Sheshbazzar to Zerubbabel; but the priestly power is unbroken, too, from Jehozadak to Jeshua.

The Adversaries of Judah

But the returnees were not building the Temple in a vacuum. There were people living in what had once been the kingdoms of Israel and Judah. These included those who had never been exiled in the first place. Sargon of Assyria carried off only a small portion of the Israelites, and Nebuchadnezzar of Babylon only a small portion of the Judeans. In both cases, though, the exiles had been taken from the upper classes—the administrators, landowners, artisans, scholars, and intellectuals generally. Those who remained behind were the peasants and the unlettered.

Then, too, the Assyrian kings had resettled Israel with outsiders and these had undoubtedly intermarried with the remaining natives to form the Samaritans (see page 380). After the exile from Judah, these Samaritans had spread southward to take over parts of what had once

been northern Judah, while the Edomites moved northward from
their desert fastnesses into what had once been southern Judah.

The Jewish exiles in Babylon, on the other hand, had prospered
and had further developed Judaism. As compensation for the loss of
their land and freedom, they turned to that which alone distinguished
them clearly from their neighbors—their sacred writings. The various
traditions and law codes may have hardened and fused and the early
books of the Bible may have approached their final form during the
Exile. (It may be for this reason that so much of the first few chapters
of Genesis has a marked tinge of Babylonic myth about it—see page
40.)

Then, too, important prophets helped develop the ideas of Judaism
further, so that the Jews of Babylon had a religion advanced and
etherealized in many respects beyond that which was held traditionally
by the remaining inhabitants of Judah.

For these reasons the rebuilding of the Temple was bound to bring
trouble. To the people living in the land about Jerusalem, the returnees
were foreigners who came flooding into the land in a highhanded
fashion, with strange religious ways and haughty speech. To the returnees, on the other hand, the people living on the land were strangers
and foreigners, occupying usurped space, and practicing a debased religion only superficially resembling Judaism.

The situation was precisely the same as that in the twentieth century
when Jews from Europe and America returned to an Israel they considered their ancestral home and found themselves face to face with
Arab dwellers who considered them strangers and intruders. The apparently irreconcilable hostility of Israel and its Arab neighbors mirrors
the hostility of the Jews and Samaritans in Persian times and later.

> Ezra 4:1. . . . *the adversaries of Judah and Benjamin* [the Sa-
> maritans] . . .
> Ezra 4:2. . . . *came to Zerubbabel . . . and said . . . let us build*
> *with you* . . .
> Ezra 4:3 *But Zerubbabel . . . said unto them, You have nothing*
> *to do with us.*

There is nothing at this point to indicate that the offer of the
Samaritans was insincere. Zerubbabel might have been more diplomatic,
but, like Rehoboam four centuries before (see page 338), he was

harsh and insulting, and the result was the same, enmity in place of possible co-operation.

Darius I

The Samaritans could not oppose the Jews directly since both alike were under the firm eye of the Persian kings. The Samaritans could, however, try to influence those kings by pointing out the possible dangers of allowing an exclusivistic religious group to come to power in a place as strategically situated as Jerusalem.

> Ezra 4:4. *Then the people of the land weakened the hands of the people of Judah, and troubled them in building.*
> Ezra 4:5. *And hired counsellors against them to frustrate, their purpose all the days of Cyrus king of Persia, even until the reign of Darius king of Persia.*

Cyrus died in 530 B.C., eight years after his edict allowing the Jews to return to Jerusalem. Succeeding him was his son Cambyses, (Kambujiya, in Persian) who had been ruling Babylon while his father was off on his campaigns. In order to ensure his place on the throne, Cambyses had his brother Smerdis executed. He then set out to conquer Egypt, the one portion of the Assyrian Empire which had not yet been taken over by the conquering Persians.

In Egypt the 26th dynasty was still in power. Seventy years had passed since Necho (against whom Josiah of Judah had fought) had died and now the Pharaoh was Psamtik III. In 525 B.C. Cambyses marched against him and won an easy victory. Psamtik III was overthrown and later executed, so that Saitic Egypt came to an end. For over a century afterward, Persian kings were to rule as the 27th dynasty.

Cambyses attempted to extend his African dominions even more, with plans to attack Ethiopia to the south, or Carthage to the west, but the deserts were too hostile and his line of communications too long. Furthermore, a Zoroastrian priest, pretending to be Cambyses' dead brother Smerdis, was proclaiming himself king back in Persia and Cambyses had to hurry home. On the way back, in 521 B.C., he died, whether through natural causes, or as a result of assassination or suicide.

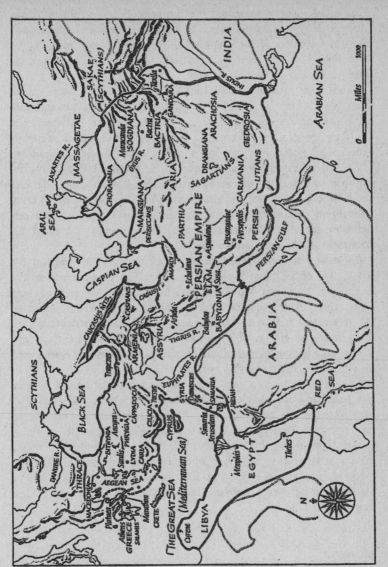

The Persian Empire

For some months thereafter, the usurper was in control of Persia, but opposition to him centered about Darius (Darayavaush, in Persian) who was a member of the younger branch of the Persian royal family. Gathering other noblemen about himself, he attacked the usurper, defeated him, and made himself king.

Darius faced rebellions in his turn almost at once, but he put them down with a sure hand and with great skill He then proceeded to reorganize the kingdom, dividing it up into provinces (satrapies), establishing good roads and canals, arranging for a sound monetary system, and generally overseeing a strong and efficient government.

He also continued Persian conquests. He extended Persian control eastward over sections of northwestern India (the modern Pakistan) and, about 512 B.C., led an army across the Hellespont into Thrace (the region making up modern Bulgaria). It was the first time any Asian monarch had led an army into Europe and he brought his dominions up to the Danube River.

Darius is best remembered among Westerners for the events of the last decade of his thirty-five-year-long reign. The Greek cities on the Aegean coast of Asia Minor revolted in 500 B.C. and received help from Athens. The revolt was crushed and Darius set about punishing the Athenians. A Persian expeditionary force landed on Athenian territory near the village of Marathon in 490 B.C. and there, in one of the most famous battles of ancient times, was defeated. Darius died in 486 B.C. with Athens still unpunished.

This last defeat was a very minor one as far as the Persian Empire was concerned and should not be allowed to obscure the fact that Darius's reign was essentially one of great achievements both abroad and at home. Under him, Persia reached the peak of its power.

The short reign of Cambyses tends to be overshadowed by the greater achievements of Cyrus who preceded him and Darius who followed him, and the Book of Ezra moves straight from Cyrus to Darius, slurring over Cambyses. Indeed, Cambyses is nowhere mentioned in the Bible.

Ahasuerus

Before going into details concerning the results of the intrigues carried on by the Samaritans at the courts of Cyrus and Darius, the

Book of Ezra rounds off those intrigues by describing their continuation into the following reigns:

Ezra 4:6. *And in the reign of Ahasuerus . . . wrote they unto him an accusation against the inhabitants of Judah and Jerusalem.*

After the death of Darius I in 486 B.C., his son Xerxes succeeded to the throne. Xerxes continued his father's plan of punishing the Greeks. He had to pause first, though, to suppress a serious revolt in Egypt and took several years; time used by the Greeks in desperate preparation for the coming Persian assault.

Finally, a mighty Persian army invaded Greece and an equally mighty Persian fleet (manned by Phoenicians, for the most part) swept the Aegean. Xerxes' navy was defeated in 480 B.C. in the battle of Salamis and his army was defeated on land the next year at Plataea. Xerxes gave up the plan to conquer Greece and retired to a life of ease with his harem.

The "Persian War" makes up the main body of the history of Herodotus, the first great history of Western tradition, and its events have made up a drama almost without parallel in all the twenty-five hundred years that have since elapsed. Those mighty events, however, cast no ripple in Biblical affairs for they did not affect the Jews, and no mention is made of them in the Bible.

It is generally accepted that Xerxes is the Ahasuerus referred to in Ezra 4:6. The names do not seem similar but "Xerxes" is, after all, only the Greek version of the king's name. To the Persians, Xerxes was Khshayarsha. Place an "A" in front and the change to Ahasuerus is not a difficult one to see.

Artaxerxes

The tale of Samaritan intrigues continues:

Ezra 4:7. *And in the days of Artaxerxes . . .*

In 465 B.C., Xerxes was assassinated in a court intrigue and his son Artaxerxes I (Artakhshatra) succeeded. During Artaxerxes' forty-year reign, the Persian Empire held its own. It kept off the Greeks, not so much with armies as with money, encouraging them to fight among themselves. Rebellions flared here and there in the vast Persian dominions but they were easily put down and in the end Artaxerxes died in peace in 424 B.C.

Aramaic

To be sure, by the time of Xerxes and Artaxerxes, it was not the Temple that was in question; that had been completed in Darius's reign, as will be explained later, and was a dead issue. Rather, it was the fact that the Jews were also attempting to build walls about Jerusalem that was now in question.

This could easily be interpreted as a rebellious act, since the Jews might be planning to protect themselves by these walls against the Persian army. The Samaritans therefore wrote to Artaxerxes, pointing out that the Jews had once controlled large sections of the Fertile Crescent from Jerusalem and had a bad record as rebels against the Assyrians and Babylonians who had preceded the Persians. And, as the Bible says,

Ezra 4:7. . . . *the letter was written in the Syrian tongue* . . .

In fact, in the original version of the Book of Ezra, this letter is quoted in Aramaic (Syrian).

Aramaic is a Semitic dialect, closely related to Hebrew but sufficiently different so that a person understanding one would have trouble understanding the other. The relationship is perhaps like that of German to Dutch, or French to Spanish.

Aramaic was more widely spread than Hebrew. At the time of the Exodus, the Aramaean tribes had drifted not only into Syria (Aram) but into many of the regions of the Fertile Crescent, including Babylonia. It followed that knowledge of Aramaic came to be widespread through the area. The Aramaeans prospered as merchants, traveled widely, and their language became a kind of lingua franca, a language in which most educated people could manage to make themselves understood, even though one might not understand the native language of the other.

Thus, at the time the Assyrians under Sennacherib were besieging Jerusalem, Assyrian emissaries shouted propaganda messages in Hebrew from outside the walls in order to dishearten the defenders. The Judean emissaries, hoping to stop this, asked humbly:

2 Kings 18:26. . . . *Speak, I pray thee . . . in the Syrian language; for we understand it . . .*

Both Assyrians and Judeans could meet on the common ground of the Aramaic tongue.

Presumably, the Jews in Babylon found it easy to get along with Aramaic until they learned Babylonian, so that Hebrew began to be almost foreign to them (as it is to most Jews outside Israel today). Furthermore, the mixed population in what had once been Israel and Judah probably found themselves drifting to Aramaic.

For that reason certain books written late in Biblical times, sections of the Book of Daniel in particular, were written in Aramaic. And in New Testament times, Aramaic was the language of the Jewish people generally. Thus, Jesus spoke in Aramaic rather than in Hebrew.

Asnapper

In the course of this letter in Aramaic, the original petitioners describe themselves by the cities they had inhabited before the Assyrian resettlement of peoples. The list concludes:

Ezra 4:10. *And the rest of the nations whom the great and noble Asnapper brought over, and set in the cities of Samaria . . .*

Clearly, Asnapper must refer to some important Assyrian monarch who ruled after the destruction of the kingdom of Israel. There were four of these and the first three—Sargon, Sennacherib, and Esarhaddon—are mentioned by name in the Bible so that Asnapper is not likely to be one of them. That leaves the fourth—Asshurbanipal (see page 390)—and it is generally accepted that this is who is meant by Asnapper.

Achmetha

With the record of Samaritan obstructionism through the century following Cyrus's decree made clear, the story goes back to the first decades of work. Apparently Samaritan hostility at the start had interrupted work on the Temple itself:

> Ezra 4:24. *Then ceased the work of the house of God . . . unto the second year of the reign of Darius . . .*

The work was still in a state of suspended animation in 520 B.C., in other words, eighteen years after Cyrus's original edict. Under the verbal lash of enthusiasts such as Haggai and Zechariah, work started again:

> Ezra 5:2. *Then rose up Zerubbabel . . . and Jeshua . . . and began to build the house of God . . .*

But now there were new Persian governors over the area and some question arose as to what structure was being erected and by what right. The Jews referred to the edict under Cyrus, but Cyrus was dead, as was his successor, and the confusion of a civil war had just taken place. The matter had to be referred to Darius himself, and the records were successfully searched:

> Ezra 6:2. *And there was found at Achmetha, in the palace that is in the province of the Medes, a roll, and therein was a record . . .*

Achmetha is about 280 miles northeast of Babylon. Its name in the language of its ancient inhabitants was Hangmatana, which became Ecbatana to the Greeks and Hamadan to the modern inhabitants. Hamadan is now part of modern Iran, 180 miles west of the Iranian capital, Teheran, and possessing a population of over one hundred thousand.

Ecbatana, to use its most familiar ancient name, had its greatest political importance in the half century following the fall of Nineveh, for it was then the capital of the Median Empire. Cyrus took it in 550 B.C. and it lost its status as capital in favor of cities in Persia itself. However, its location among the mountains made it a good place for a summer residence so that it continued to serve as a kind of subsidiary royal center.

Darius, having located the decree, confirmed it, and ordered his local officials in Judea to hasten and encourage the building.

> Ezra 6:15. *And this house* [the Temple] *was finished . . . in the sixth year of the reign of Darius the king.*

Since Darius became king in 521 B.C. and that year counts as his first, the Temple was completed in 516 B.C. just twenty-two years after Cyrus's decree and just seventy years after the Temple had been destroyed by Nebuchadnezzar. It is certainly tempting to feel that the seventy years of exile referred to by Jeremiah can be interpreted as applying not to the physical exile of the Jews in Babylon so much as to their spiritual exile from the Temple.

Sometimes the rebuilt Temple is called the "second Temple." The first had endured from 923 to 586 B.C.—a stretch of 337 years. The second Temple was to do better. It was to endure 586 years until its destruction by the Romans in A.D. 70.

Ezra

There is now a lapse of at least half a century and Ezra appears on the scene. The name is a shortened form of Azariah, a common name carried by some two dozen people mentioned in the Bible, including that king of Judah who is also known by the throne name of Uzziah.

Ezra 7:6. . . . Ezra went up from Babylon . . .
Ezra 7:7. . . . in the seventh year of Artaxerxes the king.

If we assume that it is Artaxerxes I who is meant, he came to the throne in 465 B.C. and his seventh year would be 459–58 B.C. That would be the year, then, of Ezra's visit to Jerusalem.

If Ezra is considered the Chronicler, a point in favor is the fact that on introducing himself he proudly gives his pedigree, tracing it back to Aaron (but skipping a number of generations in doing so). He also describes his function:

Ezra 7:6. . . . he [Ezra] was a ready scribe in the law of Moses . . .

A scribe is "one who writes," a secretary; and it was precisely during the Exile that scribes became particularly important. The legal, theological, and historical traditions of the Jews had to be reduced to writing and prepared in many copies now that the people were scattered; otherwise isolated groups would forget.

Ezra was one of the group who copied and studied the books

and since these books contained the Jewish ritual law, he (and other scribes, too) was the equivalent of what we might today call a lawyer.

There is an important difference between a prophet and a scribe. A prophet speaks from inspiration and not only can, but often does, break new ground. A scribe is bound to the letter and, in fact, has a vested interest in the preservation of the letter since only by its exact knowledge does he fulfill his function. There is for that reason a certain aridity about scribes, a certain lack of flexibility which, in periods of stress and emergency, keeps them from moving with the times and forces them into what may prove unpopular and even untenable positions. In the New Testament, scribes are usually mentioned with disapproval.

One difficulty arises concerning the date 458 B.C. given above as the year of Ezra's arrival in Jerusalem. If Ezra is indeed the Chronicler then it might seem he would have to be alive at least as late as 400 B.C. since some of the genealogies in 1 Chronicles stretch that far. Yet Ezra had already obtained a reputation by the time of his visit to Jerusalem and could not have been a young man. If mature in in 458 B.C., could he still be alive in 400 B.C.?

It is possible, of course, that he might have written the history before 400 B.C. and that a disciple added the verses required to bring it up to date, so to speak. On the other hand, Ezra may have come to Jerusalem considerably later than 458 B.C.

Artaxerxes I was not the only king of his name to rule over Persia. After the death of Artaxerxes I in 424 B.C., one of his sons ruled under the name of Xerxes II and then another as Darius II. In 404 B.C., Darius II died, and his son, Artaxerxes II, came to the throne. If it is this second Artaxerxes to whom Ezra refers in 7:7, then Ezra came to Jerusalem in 398 B.C.

Unfortunately, there is no easy way of determining from the Biblical account which Artaxerxes is meant and of deciding whether Ezra arrived in 458 or 398 B.C.

Hattush

One possible hint lies with one of the heads of the families that are described as coming to Jerusalem with Ezra:

Ezra 8:2. . . . *of the sons of David; Hattush.*

Hattush is listed in the Davidic genealogy in the third chapter of 1 Chronicles:

> 1 Chronicles 3:19. . . . *and the sons of Zerubbabel; Meshullam and Hananiah* . . .
>
> . . . .
>
> 1 Chronicles 3:21. *And the sons of Hananiah* . . . *Shechaniah.*
> 1 Chronicles 3:22. *And the sons of Shechaniah; Shemaiah; and the sons of Shemaiah; Hattush* . . .

Hattush was thus the great-great-grandson of Zerubbabel, and a member of the twenty-fourth generation after David.

According to the Anchor Bible, Hattush's younger brother Neariah has an estimated birth year of 470 B.C. (see page 405). We might suppose then that Hattush was born in 475 B.C. If, then, Ezra had come to Jerusalem in 458 B.C., Hattush would have been seventeen years old; a fine age for the trip, but would he then be considered among those described by Ezra as:

> Ezra 8:1. *These are now the chief of their fathers* . . .

or, to use the phraseology of the Revised Standard Version, "These are the heads of their fathers' houses . . ."?

Surely a seventeen-year-old boy would scarcely be the head of the house of David. There would very likely be older members to serve that function.

Yet if Ezra had come to Jerusalem in 398 B.C., Hattush would be seventy-seven years old and would make a good patriarchal head of the royal house, but is it likely that a man of that age would decide to make the arduous trip to Jerusalem?

So one still stands irresolute as to which of the two dates to choose.

Regardless of the date, though, the line of David had lost its political significance. Even the nominal sovereignty of a Sheshbazzar or a Zerubbabel was gone. The Jewish community was become a theocracy and when Ezra arrived it was he, the scribe, and not Hattush, the prince, who was in charge.

He found that in the time that had elapsed since the rebuilding of the Temple, there had been much intermarrying between the returnees and those who had been in the land all along. Horrified, Ezra demanded and enforced the end of such marriages and the ejection of foreign wives and their children from the community.

This was thought of at the time as the only sure way in which Judaism could be preserved in pure form. Intermarriage was bound to be followed by a dilution of social custom and a distortion of ritual, it seemed. This may be so, in fact, but to those of us who now live in a pluralistic society and try to measure up to its ideals, Ezra's policy seems inhumane, narrow, and wrong. That there were those among the Jews themselves who also thought so, is evidenced by the fact that at about this time the beautiful little Book of Ruth was written (see page 265) and proved so popular that it was included in the Hebrew Bible despite the fact that its heroine was a Moabitess.

16. NEHEMIAH

SHUSHAN • SANBALLAT THE HORONITE • ELIASHIB • ASHDODITES • EZRA • 1 ESDRAS

Shushan

The events of the next book also deal with the period of the restoration of the Temple and it begins at once with the identity of the chief character:

Nehemiah 1:1. *The words of Nehemiah . . .*

from which the name of the book is derived. Much of the book consists of the memoirs of Nehemiah, presumably quoted and edited into a larger whole by the Chronicler (or Ezra, if that be he).

The date of the beginning of the events of the book is also given; twice, in fact:

Nehemiah 1:2. . . . *in the twentieth year, as I was in Shushan the palace . . .*

and, again:

Nehemiah 2:1. . . . *in the twentieth year of Artaxerxes the king . . .*

If the king is Artaxerxes I, then his twentieth year is 446–45 B.C.; if Artaxerxes II, it is 385–84 B.C. The second date is too late if we are to accept the fact that the Chronicler was writing in 400 B.C. Therefore we can place ourselves in the year 445 B.C., some seventy years after the completion of the second Temple.

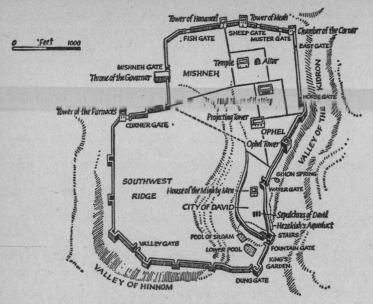

Jerusalem at the Time of Nehemiah

Nehemiah held an honorable post as cupbearer to the Persian king, which gave him the chance to talk to him personally:

Nehemiah 2:1. . . . *I took up the wine, and gave it unto the king* . . .

and such conversations could, apparently, take place in the presence of the queen:

Nehemiah 2:6. *And the king said unto me,* (*the queen also sitting by him*) . . .

Personal service in the presence of the queen would seem to mean, in an eastern court of the time, that Nehemiah was a eunuch. The Bible does not, however, make that clear.

Shushan, the scene in which we first find Nehemiah, is better known to us by the Greek version of its name, Susa. Susa is far more ancient than the Persian kingdom, since it was in its earliest history the capital of the kingdom of Elam, which lay northeast of Babylonia and northwest of Fars, the Persian homeland.

Elam was a rival of Babylonia even before the time of Abraham. It was conquered by Sargon of Agade (see page 50) and by Hammurabi (see page 69). When Babylon was weak, however, Elam had occasional periods of domination. Chedorlaomer (see page 68) was a king of Elam, for instance.

The most dramatic period of Elam's history, however, came in the time of Assyrian domination. Just as Egypt sought to save itself from Assyria by encouraging revolts against that land in Judah, Israel, and Syria, so Elam encouraged revolts in Babylon. Merodach-baladan (see page 387) managed to maintain himself against Assyria only with Elamite support. It was probably only because Assyria had its hands continually full with Elam that Judah managed to hang on to a nominal independence and survive to see Assyria destroyed.

Elam did not have Judah's good fortune, however. It did not survive. It fought Assyria in campaign after campaign for a century, coming back after defeat, always resolute, always defiant. It is a great epic of its sort, but because there is no Elamite literature that survives today that can compare with the historical books of the Bible, or with the writings of the Greeks, the Elamite struggle is carried on in soundless darkness and is all but vanished from modern consciousness. Finally, in 640 B.C., after several campaigns by Asshurbanipal, Elam was utterly destroyed and devastated and Susa was razed to the ground.

The best of what remained of the Elamite population was deported and some of them must have been added to the Samaritans for among the people represented by the letter to Artaxerxes (see page 446) are:

Ezra 4:9. . . . *the Susanchites . . . and the Elamites,*
Ezra 4:10. . . . *whom . . . Asnapper brought over, and set in the cities of Samaria . . .*

Here is the additional reason for considering Asnapper to be Asshurbanipal.

Elam played no further role in history but it had its posthumous revenge. The effort to crush Elam cost the last bit of strength Assyria could muster. It was exhausted and within a generation it fell before the combined might of the Chaldeans and the Medes, and was wiped out every bit as thoroughly as Elam had been.

Meanwhile, the Persians were able to expand northwestward from Fars into Elam, thereafter generally called Susiana, and make it an

integral part of Persia. Susa was rebuilt by Darius I and made into
the winter capital of the empire. Its site (in what is now southwestern
Iran) is marked only by ruins and by a little village named Shush.

Sanballat the Horonite

At the time that the Book of Nehemiah opens, a party of Jews
had arrived in Susa. Their business is not described but one can
reasonably speculate that it might have been in connection with the
letter to Artaxerxes sent by the Samaritans. The Jews of Jerusalem
feared its consequences and might well have sent a deputation to
Artaxerxes to present their own case. In doing so, they would have
approached Nehemiah, as a Jew who had access to the ear of the king.

They informed Nehemiah that conditions in Jerusalem were bad and
that the walls about the city had been destroyed, presumably by
Samaritan enemies supported by the local Persian officials.

After several months, Nehemiah succeeded in approaching Artaxerxes
and in persuading him to grant permission for the walls to be built
and for Nehemiah to travel to Jerusalem to oversee the matter. According to the later Jewish historian Josephus, Nehemiah did not arrive in Jerusalem till 440 B.C.

In Jerusalem, Nehemiah faced opposition from the local governors.
After he had surveyed the state of the walls, he proposed an immediate
drive to rebuild them:

> Nehemiah 2:19. But when Sanballat the Horonite, and Tobiah
> . . . the Ammonite, and Geshem the Arabian, heard it, they . . .
> said . . . will ye rebel against the king?

Sanballat bears a Babylonian name (Sin-uballit, which means "Sin
[the moon-goddess] has given life"). This does not necessarily mean
that he was a moon-goddess worshiper, since he may just have been
using a popular name of the period, just as a modern American might
have Hannibal as a first name without any intention of showing himself to be a worshiper of the Carthaginian Baal. As a Horonite,
Sanballat was a native of Beth-horon, a town ten miles northwest
of Jerusalem. Presumably he was a Samaritan and perhaps even the
local governor of Samaria.

Tobiah has a Hebrew name and is described, later in the book, as being connected to various Jews by marriage. He is called an Ammonite probably because he was the local governor of districts in the Trans-Jordan. It is quite likely that he was a Yahvist but was certainly not an orthodox Jew as orthodoxy was then viewed. Either he was a Samaritan, or a Jew who was in sympathy with the Samaritans.

Geshem the Arabian apparently was a Nabataean, a member of an Arabic tribe that now appears on the Biblical horizon. After the destruction of the kingdom of Judah, the Edomites moved northward into Judah and behind them came the Nabataeans, who occupied what had previously been Edom. Their capital was established at Petra, a city which had elaborate house and temple fronts carved out of the pink cliffside. It attained prosperity because it was an important crossing point for various trade routes. Its site is often equated with the Edomite city of Selah, which is mentioned in the Bible in connection with Amaziah's reconquest of Edom (see page 369):

2 Kings 14:7. *He* [Amaziah] . . . *took Selah by war* . . .

In the third century B.C. the Nabataeans were to form a prosperous kingdom. At the time the Romans were crushing the Jewish rebellion in A.D. 68, they also annexed the Nabataean kingdom. It became the province of Arabia Petraea. Nearly two centuries later, the province even gave an emperor to Rome, Philip "the Arabian."

Eliashib

The building of the walls began, with the High Priest initiating the proceedings:

Nehemiah 3:1. *Then Eliashib the high priest rose up with his . . . priests, and they builded the sheep gate* . . .

Eliashib continues the line of priests descending from Zadok, the High Priest under Solomon, for he is the grandson of Jeshua who returned with Zerubbabel (see page 440):

Nehemiah 12:10. *And Jeshua begat Joiakim, Joiakim also begat Eliashib* . . .

The walls as built enclosed a tiny city indeed; the "city of David" in the south (that is, the rocky heights of Zion on which David had built his palace six centuries before) and the Temple and its environs to the north. The entire enclosure may have been seven modern city blocks long and an average of two city blocks wide.

Ashdodites

The Samaritans and other surrounding nations, annoyed at the progress of the wall, were prepared to take mob action against it.

In a very real sense, the little Judean enclave at Jerusalem was surrounded. There were Samaritans under Sanballat to the north; the Trans-Jordanian tribes under Tobiah to the east, and the Nabataeans under Geshem to the south. To complete the circle there was also an enemy to the west:

> Nehemiah 4:7. . . . the Arabians, and the Ammonites, and the Ashdodites . . . were very wroth.

The Ashdodites refer, in a narrow sense, to the inhabitants of the Philistine city of Ashdod (see page 221). The phrase has come to mean more than that in post-Exilic times.

The Philistines had been subdued by David and had formed part of the united kingdom first and then, later, of the kingdom of Judah, but they had continued to maintain their cultural identity. At various times they rebelled but under Uzziah they were reduced to submission again:

> 2 Chronicles 26:6. And he [Uzziah] . . . warred against the Philistines, and brake down the wall of Gath . . . and the wall of Ashdod . . .

However, the Philistines suffered with Judah in the days of Assyrian ascendance, for in 711 B.C.:

> Isaiah 20:1. . . . Sargon the king of Assyria . . . fought against Ashdod and took it.

The Assyrian governor who thenceforth ruled Philistine territory had his seat at Ashdod. The term "Ashdodite" came, therefore, to mean the Philistines generally, so that Nehemiah was facing the Philistines as seven centuries before Samson had faced them.

Nehemiah's answer was a resolute defense. Half the Jews built the walls and half patrolled the environs of the city, armed and ready for war. The builders themselves wore swords and the atmosphere was very much like that in the frontier villages of modern Israel, where farmers plow their fields with rifles strapped to their backs.

Presumably, the Samaritans were not ready to make actual war. That would get them in trouble with Persia since Nehemiah had the royal permission for the work. Since Nehemiah refused to be thwarted by the mere war of nerves involved in continuing threats and menacing scowls, the raising of the walls continued and, according to Josephus, they were completed in 437 B.C.

Nehemiah also labored to solve the economic difficulties of the tiny community and mentions a date still later, for at one point he says:

> Nehemiah 6:14. . . . *from the time that I was appointed . . . governor . . . from the twentieth year even unto the two and thirtieth year of Artaxerxes . . .*

You might think that this ought to settle which of the Artaxerxes Nehemiah worked under since surely both would not have reigned for the comparatively long time of thirty-two years. However, through a coincidence, Artaxerxes I reigned forty-one years and Artaxerxes II reigned forty-six years. If, however, we still consider the king to have been Artaxerxes I, the year that Nehemiah now mentions as the thirty-second of the king is 433 B.C.

Ezra

Chapters 8, 9, and 10 of Nehemiah suddenly return to Ezra, who is described as reading to the population of Jerusalem out of the sacred writings:

> Nehemiah 8:1. *And all the people gathered themselves together . . . and they spake unto Ezra the scribe to bring the book of the law of Moses . . .*
> Nehemiah 8:2. *And Ezra . . . brought the law before the congregation . . .*
> Nehemiah 8:3. *And he read therein . . . before the men and the women . . .*

Ezra then led a religious reform which was different from all those that had preceded. Now there was no longer merely the spoken word of a prophet, or even just the book found in the Temple in Josiah's time (which may have possessed only dubious authority in the eyes of many of the men of the time). There was now the whole body of the Torah, the first five books of the Bible, written, expounded, and interpreted by the scribes so that all men might now study, understand, and observe the very letter of the law.

The presence of the written law (to which the prophetic books and the "Writings" were later added to form the Bible) made it impossible for the Jews ever again to waver from Judaism. The Jews kept the faith thereafter, through exiles far more widespread, prolonged, and inhumanly cruel than that visited upon them by Nebuchadnezzar.

This episode of the reading of the law brings up once again the problem of the chronology of Ezra. Ezra appears in two places; first at the end of the Book of Ezra, where he breaks up the mixed marriages, and second at the end of the Book of Nehemiah, where he leads the religious reform. It would seem that these two sections belong together; that the breakup of the mixed marriages ought to be followed at once by the religious reform and that the interposition of the Nehemiah chapters is artificial.

The question then is whether the Ezra story, as a whole, comes before Nehemiah or after Nehemiah, and this again depends on which Artaxerxes is referred to in Ezra 7:7 (see page 449). If Nehemiah's work in Jerusalem took place from 445 to 433 B.C., then Ezra's work comes first if he really came to Jerusalem in 458 B.C. in the seventh year of Artaxerxes I. It comes afterward, on the other hand, if he came to Jerusalem in 398 B.C. in the seventh year of Artaxerxes II.

One additional verse can now be called upon to help make the decision. When Ezra arrived in Jerusalem and was shocked to discover the prevalence of mixed marriages:

> Ezra 10:6. *Then Ezra rose up . . . and went into the chamber of Johanan the son of Eliashib: and . . . did eat no bread, nor drink water: for he mourned . . .*

Is it possible that the Eliashib mentioned here is the Eliashib who was High Priest in Nehemiah's time (see pag 457)? Eliashib did have a son or grandson named Johanan:

Nehemiah 12:22. *The Levites in the days of Eliashib, Joiada, and Johanan . . .*

What's more, Johanan did serve as High Priest. The Jewish colony in Elephantine, a city in upper Egypt, addressed letters to him dated 408 B.C. and he is further mentioned in Josephus.

If the Johanan of Ezra 10:6 is this Johanan, it would be very strong evidence in favor of Ezra's arrival in Jerusalem in 398 B.C. in the seventh year of Artaxerxes II.

And yet not all doubt is removed. Neither Johanan nor Eliashib is described here as a High Priest or even as a priest and it is possible (though perhaps not likely) that Ezra's host for the night was just an ordinary individual with the increasingly common name of Johanan.

1 Esdras

The tale told by the Chronicler concerning the destruction and rebuilding of the Temple is told over again in another book, also attributed to Ezra. This one is considered apocryphal, however, and to distinguish it from the canonical Book of Ezra, use is made of the Greek equivalent of the name and it is called 1 Esdras (for there is another apocryphal book called 2 Esdras). To those who adhere to the Catholic system of referring to the Books of Ezra and Nehemiah as 1 Esdras and 2 Esdras, the apocryphal books are 3 Esdras and 4 Esdras.

Both 1 and 2 Esdras were included in some Greek versions of the Bible. At the Council of Trent in 1546, however, the Catholic Church decided officially which books it would consider canonical and these did not include the Prayer of Manasses (see page 425) or either of the Esdras books. These are apocryphal to Catholics as well as to Jews and Protestants.

1 Esdras was written no earlier than 150 B.C. and perhaps considerably later (though not later than A.D. 50 since Josephus refers to it). In general, 1 Esdras deviates from Ezra-Nehemiah only in unimportant details and its chief point of interest lies in the retelling of an old fable.

The fable is told as taking place in the reign of Darius, who, after a feast, retired to sleep. Three of his bodyguard pass the time by each stating what he thinks is the strongest. The first chooses wine, the second the king, and the third, women.

(In the original tale, it would have made more sense if the first chose the king—the obvious choice—the second wine, and the third women. The second can then point out that even the king succumbs to wine, and the third that even the king respects his mother and loves his wife. Both second and third are correct but since the third would undoubtedly please the women of the court he would be the sure winner.)

In 1 Esdras, the story is modified to suit the writer's purposes. The third guardsman chooses more than merely women:

1 Esdras 3:12. *The third wrote, Women are strongest: but above all things Truth beareth away the victory.*

Darius is told of the contest, is amused, and demands that each guardsman defend his point of view before the open court. The first and second speak in favor of wine and the king. Then the third guardsman is, for the first time, identified:

1 Esdras 4:13. *Then the third, who had spoken of women, and of the truth, (this was Zorobabel) began to speak.*

(Since the apocryphal books appear in the Greek and not in the Hebrew, proper names are given closer to the Greek than the Hebrew forms in the King James Version—unlike the situation in connection with the canonical books. Hence we have Zorobabel rather than Zerubbabel.)

Zerubbabel speaks of women, as in the old fable, but then launches into an impressive encomium on truth, ending:

1 Esdras 4:40. . . . *Blessed be the God of truth.*
1 Esdras 4:41. . . . *And all the people then shouted, and said, Great is Truth, and mighty above all things.*

Since Zerubbabel had won, Darius offered to grant him whatever he might wish, and Zerubbabel immediately asked him to confirm Cyrus's decree that the Temple be rebuilt. Thus, this fable is tied in with Jewish history.

It is unlikely in the extreme that anything like this ever happened, but it is a pretty story.

17. ESTHER

AHASUERUS • INDIA • VASHTI • MORDECAI • HAMAN • PUR • ZERESH • THE
REST OF ESTHER

Ahasuerus

Following the historical books comes what can only be described
as a piece of historical fiction, the Book of Esther.

Esther does not have the gentle charm of the Book of Ruth, the
earlier book that seems to have fictional elements. It is, instead, a savage
book. The Book of Esther is, in fact, the one book of the Bible in which
the word "God" does not occur.

Esther may have been written as late as 130 B.C. and it breathes the
air of nationalism one would expect of that period in which the Jews
were finally living in an independent kingdom again after having undergone a period of savage persecution. It is probably the chauvinistic
nationalism of the book that made it so popular among Jews as to force
its inclusion in the Biblical canon.

The book begins by placing itself in time.

Esther 1:1. *Now it came to pass in the days of Ahasuerus* . . .

Ahasuerus is usually identified with Xerxes I (see page 445), who
reigned from 486 to 465 B.C. At this period the Persian Empire was
still apparently at the peak of its power, as it had been under Darius,
but the downhill slide was already beginning. Xerxes is best known to
history in connection with his great expedition against Greece, which
failed so miserably.

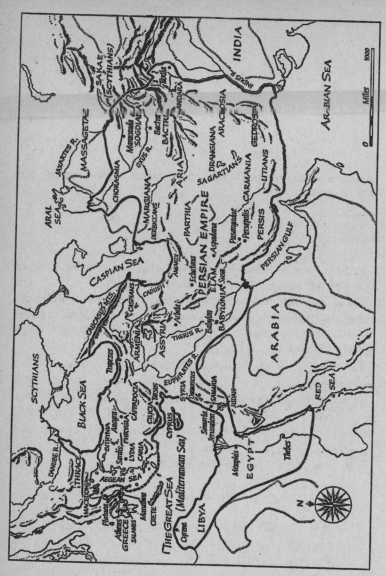

The Persian Empire

India

A good indication of the late date of publication of the book is the fact that it is not enough to mention Ahasuerus. The monarch must be identified:

> Esther 1:1. . . . *(this is Ahasuerus which reigned, from India even unto Ethiopia, over an hundred and seven and twenty provinces:)*

This describes, accurately enough, the wide extent of the territory of the Persian Empire at its height. The verse is also remarkable for being the one place (except for a similar expression in another verse later in this same book) where India is mentioned in the Bible.

Nor can there be any doubt that the Hebrew word used in this place, "Hoddu," can mean anything but India. Not only did Ahasuerus (Xerxes) actually rule from Ethiopia to India, but the words "Hoddu" and "India" come from the same source.

Indian civilization dates far back indeed; farther back than modern archaeologists suspected early in this century. Since 1920, ruins along the Indus River have been excavated, yielding traces of unexpectedly large and well-planned cities near the sites of villages now known as Harappa and Mohenjo-Daro; cities that might date as far back as 3300 B.C. This Indus civilization was one of the three ancient ones of the dawn of city building, for it was contemporaneous with the Sumerian culture (see page 30) and with the Egyptian Old Kingdom (see page 63).

About 1200 B.C., the Indus valley was invaded by people whom we call "Aryans." They spoke an early form of the Indo-European group of languages, Sanskrit, so that one sometimes speaks of that group as the "Aryan languages." They came from what is now called Iran, the nation which lies to the west of the Indus valley. Indeed, Iran (and Iraq, too) are forms of the word "Aryan."

Aryan invasion came in the era in which there were vast movements of peoples everywhere, and it was part of the same unsettlement that brought the Philistines and Hebrews into Canaan.

What the name of the Indus River was before the Aryans came, we don't know. The Aryans, however, called it "Sindhu," which, in Sanskrit, simply means "river." The name was applied to the region

traversed by the river and the area about the mouth o...
called "Sind."

Persia invaded the region of the Indus about 500 ...
of Darius I. In Persian, Sind became "Hind" or "Hi...
gradually spread from the Indus valley through all th...
nent, which became "Hindustan" ("the land of H...
speak of the natives as "Hindus," their religion as...
their chief language as "Hindi."

The Jews adopted the Persian word with a littl...
"Hindu" became "Hoddu."

The Greeks also adopted the Persian word with a...
distortion and "Hindu" became "Indos." From this co...
version of "Indus" for the river and "India" for the su...
being the Latin forms.

Ironically enough, in 1947, when the Indian subco...
independence, it was broken into two nations, and th...
Indus River, the *original* India, lost the name and is...
stan. It is the rest of the region that is called India...

Only from the time of Darius, to shortly after the...
der the Great—500 to 300 B.C.—were the Indus valley...
valley under the control of a single political system. B...
India was beyond the Biblical horizon and after that...
again (though never completely) until A.D. 1500,...
civilization again impinged upon it, this time perm...

Vashti

The tale of the Book of Esther begins in the third...
of Ahasuerus (484 B.C.) with a tremendously elaborate...
a feast lasting half a year. (This was at a time when th...
just crushed a rebellion in Egypt and another in B...
preparing a tremendous army for the ill-fated invasio...
the end of the great feast, a more intimate, week-lo...
officials of the kingdom was initiated.

Esther 1:9. *Also Vashti the queen made a feast f...
the royal house . . .*

Vashti is unknown to history and, indeed, goes unmentioned in the Bible outside the Book of Esther. Xerxes' real wife during the early portion of his reign was Amestris, the daughter of a Persian general, if we go by Herodotus.

Yet Vashti is not a purely made-up name. It has a definite source, the same source from which the names of all the chief characters of the book (aside from Ahasuerus) are drawn. This source is simply Babylonian mythology. Vashti is the name of an Elamite goddess.

Mordecai

Toward the end of this final feast, when Ahasuerus was quite drunk, he ordered Vashti to come to him in order that he might display her beauty. Vashti refused this indignity and Ahasuerus, in a fit of anger, had her deposed as queen. He then ordered that beautiful women be gathered together in order that out of them he might pick another queen.

> Esther 2:5. *Now in Shushan the palace there was a certain Jew, whose name was Mordecai . . .*
>
> Esther 2:6. *Who had been carried away from Jerusalem . . . with Jeconiah . . . whom Nebuchadnezzar . . . had carried away.*
>
> Esther 2:7. *And he brought up Hadassah, that is, Esther, his uncle's daughter . . .*

Mordecai is here described as having been carried off with Jeconiah (Jehoiachin; see page 395), an event that took place in 597 B.C., and as still being alive in 484 B.C. This would imply that Mordecai, and Esther too, were centenarians at the time of this tale. This indicates the author of the book, who is living three and a half centuries after the events he describes, is *not* following ancient records but is inventing things and is uncertain of his chronology.

The name Mordecai is not Hebrew and, instead, seems to be suspiciously like that of the chief god of the Babylonians, Marduk, which, in its Hebrew form, is Merodach. As for Esther (the official throne name that came to be carried by Mordecai's cousin), that is even more clearly a form of Ishtar, the chief Babylonian goddess. Indeed, the Aramaic version of that goddess's name is indeed Esther. The name Hadassah, by which Esther was originally known within the family, is closely related to a Babylonian word for "bride," which is used as a title for Ishtar. And in Babylonian mythology Marduk and Ishtar are cousins, as are Mordecai and Esther in the Book of Esther.

It is very tempting to suppose that the writer of Esther is adapting Babylonian mythology into a supposedly historical tale designed to please the ears of his readers.

Be that as it may, the tale goes on to relate that Esther was included among the maidens brought to Ahasuerus and that he preferred her to the others and made her his queen.

> Esther 2:16. So Esther was taken unto king Ahasuerus . . . in the seventh year of his reign.
> Esther 2:17. And the king . . . made her queen instead of Vashti.

According to this tale, then, Esther became queen in 480 B.C., the year of the battle of Salamis (see page 445). To be sure, the name Esther is rather like the name of Xerxes' queen, Amestris, but there is nothing about the known facts concerning Amestris that in any way resembles what is told in this book concerning Esther.

At the advice of her cousin Mordecai, Esther does not tell the king that she is Jewish, but Mordecai remains in clandestine touch with her. This turns out to be useful for when Mordecai learns of a palace intrigue against Ahasuerus, he informs Esther, who, in turn, warns the king. The intriguers are hanged and Mordecai is officially commended in the records.

Haman

Now the chief villain appears:

> Esther 3:1. After these things did king Ahasuerus promote Haman the son of Hammedatha the Agagite, and advanced him . . . above all the princes . . .

Haman is made the equivalent of prime minister, in other words. As prime minister of Ahasuerus (Xerxes), one would expect that the Greeks would have heard of him. He is not to be found in Herodotus, however, or in any of the other Greek historians, nor is anyone to be found with any similar name.

On the other hand, the chief male deity of the Elamites was named Hamman.

This introduces an interesting speculation. In the centuries before the establishment of the Persian Empire, Elam was at intermittent war with whichever nation ruled the Tigris-Euphrates region to the northwest. The final round in the struggle came under Asshurbanipal, when the Assyrians once and for all destroyed Elam (see page 455).

In a sense then, Babylonia replaced Elam in the city of Susa during the final decades of the Assyrian Empire; and according to the thinking of the time, the Babylonian gods replaced the Elamite gods. The chief Babylonian god, Marduk, replaced the chief Elamite god, Hamman, and the chief Babylonian goddess, Ishtar, replaced the Elamite goddess, Vashti. This is similar to the events in the Book of Esther, in which Esther replaces Vashti as queen in Shushan (Susa), and, as is recounted later in the book, Mordecai replaces Haman as prime minister.

Haman is identified as the son of an "Agagite." There is no mention of this tribe in secular history or, indeed, anywhere in the Bible outside this book. However, Agag is the name given in the Bible to the king of the Amalekites who was captured by Saul and killed by Samuel.

> 1 Samuel 15:32. *Then said Samuel, Bring ye hither to me Agag the king of the Amalekites . . .*
>
> 1 Samuel 15:33. *. . . And Samuel hewed Agag in pieces . . .*

It is to be assumed, then, that Haman is being described as an Amalekite.

This would have special significance to the readers of the book for the Amalekites were considered prototypes of the enemies of Israel; and with the Amalekites the Bible predicted nothing but unrelenting war. It seemed reasonable that a remaining individual of that anti-Jewish tribe would now set himself about destroying the Jews.

Furthermore, Mordecai's ancestry was described upon his introduction:

> Esther 2:5. *. . . Mordecai, the son of Jair, the son of Shimei, the son of Kish, a Benjamite.*

He was of the tribe of Saul then, and possibly even a descendant of Saul, who had once defeated and captured the ancestor of Haman. Thus, the conflict in the Book of Esther would echo the conflict in the First Book of Samuel.

Pur

Haman's hatred of the Jews is goaded on by the fact that Mordecai refused to bow before him when all others showed him the respect due a prime minister. The reason for Mordecai's refusal is not given but the usual explanation is that he was unwilling to give to a mere human the kind of reverence due only to God.

Haman is then depicted as turning to some ritualistic device for determining a fortunate day for the forthcoming massacre of the Jews.

Esther 3:7. . . . *in the twelfth year of king Ahasuerus, they cast Pur, that is, the lot . . .*

In other words, the writer of the Book of Esther equates "Pur" ("Purim" in the plural) with lots, possibly like the Urim and Thummim (see page 150) used in ancient Yahvistic rituals. Later on, the events recounted in this book are made the occasion for a commemorative feast which the author names Purim because of this. This feast is still celebrated by Jews to this day.

Actually, it is quite uncertain that Purim really means "lots," or what the origin of the festival might be.

There are suggestions that Purim might actually be a Babylonian spring festival which involved some mythic tale of the seasons involving Marduk and Ishtar. This festival was adopted by the Jews in Babylon, just as Jews in America are unable to resist the gigantic social pressure of the season and adopt the secular aspects of the Christmas celebrations. It may have been one of the purposes of the writer of the Book of Esther to revise the Babylonian myth into Jewish history and convert a pagan festival into a patriotic Jewish observance.

Having established the day of reckoning (which turns out to be nearly a year in the future), Haman persuades Ahasuerus to give him carte blanche to destroy the Jews, who, Haman assures the king, do not consider themselves bound by the king's laws and are therefore rebels. Ahasuerus allows Haman his way.

Zeresh

Mordecai at once appeals to Esther to use her influence with the king to nullify the decree. Esther begins by requesting that Ahasuerus and Haman attend a banquet she will give. They agree and Haman in particular is in high spirits at this mark of royal favor.

Yet on seeing Mordecai, who still refuses to bow to him, he is enraged and frustrated. When he returns home, he recounts all his good fortune to his wife and family but admits that it all means nothing as long as Mordecai lives.

> Esther 5:14. *Then said Zeresh his wife . . . Let a gallows be made . . . that Mordecai may be hanged thereon: then go thou . . . unto the banquet . . .*

Now in Elamite mythology, the chief god, Hamman, has as his wife the goddess Kirisha. This is suspiciously similar to Zeresh and is another point in favor of the mythological inspiration of this book.

The night before the banquet, the king, sleepless, has the records read to him and learns of Mordecai's part in frustrating the palace plot. He therefore calls in Haman to ask his advice on the method of honoring a man who deserved great gratitude from the king. Haman, feeling it is himself who is in question, describes an elaborate ceremony which is then, to Haman's infinite disgust, applied to Mordecai.

Then, at the banquet, Esther reveals herself to be Jewish and demands the life of Haman. Ahasuerus grants her request and Haman is hanged on the very gallows he had designed for Mordecai. Mordecai is made prime minister in Haman's place.

The decree that the Jews be slaughtered could not be rescinded for, as the book relates, the laws of the Medes and Persians cannot be altered. However, the Jews are allowed to defend themselves and there is a kind of civil war in which the Jews are victorious. (These last events are completely implausible and there is no record of such a civil war anywhere outside this book.)

The Rest of Esther

The Book of Esther, as it stands, however pleasing it might be to nationalistic Jews, was troublesome to others, if only because it made no reference to God. For that reason, a number of additions were made to supply the lack, together with circumstantial quotes from supposed documents (quotations that are so unrealistic as to detract still further from the possible historicity of the book).

The Jewish scholars did not accept these additions but they appear in the Septuagint. These additions, called "The Rest of Esther" by the translators of the King James Version, therefore make up part of the Apocrypha.

Jerome, in translating the Bible into Latin, recognized the apocryphal nature of the additions but did not eliminate them. Instead, he removed them from their proper place in the book and put them at the end as a series of supplements. This arrangement is to be found in Catholic versions of English Bibles.

The Rest of Esther contains a verse which seems to give the name of the translator of part (or perhaps all) of the Book of Esther into Greek:

> Esther 11:1. *In the fourth year of the reign of Ptolemeus and Cleopatra, Dositheus . . . brought this epistle . . . which they said . . . Lysimachus the son of Ptolemeus, that was in Jerusalem, had interpreted . . .*

All the kings of Egypt from 305 to 44 B.C. (Macedonian in extraction) were named Ptolemaios, or Ptolemy in the English version. A very common name for the Egyptian queens at this time was Cleopatra. In 116 B.C. Ptolemy VIII came to the throne and ruled in conjunction with his mother, Cleopatra III. If this is the Ptolemy and Cleopatra intended, then the fourth year of their reign would be 113 B.C.

As for Lysimachus, he must be an Alexandrian Jew living in Jerusalem. The Alexandrian Jews at the time would frequently have Greek names as American Jews today frequently have American names. That his father's name was Ptolemy would not make him a prince, either. No doubt many men carried the name who were by no means part of the royal family.

The Rest of Esther goes on to talk of Mordecai's dreams, and of the details of the plot against the king which he foils. Mordecai's prayers, and Esther's, are quoted. (In his prayer, Mordecai explains that it is not out of pride that he refuses to bow to Haman, but in order that he might not give to man what ought only to be given to God.) In addition, two letters are quoted which purport to be official orders from Ahasuerus, the first ordering that the Jews be exterminated and the second permitting the Jews to defend themselves and to live under their own laws.

One oddity in the last letter is a strange accusation against Haman:

> Esther 16:10. *For Aman* [Haman], *a Macedonian . . . a stranger from the Persian blood . . .*

For Ahasuerus (Xerxes) to denounce Haman as a Macedonian is a clear anachronism. The time was to come, a century and a half after the incidents in Esther were supposed to have happened, when the Macedonian conqueror Alexander the Great was to destroy the Persian Empire and make it his own, but in Xerxes' time, Macedon was a kingdom under Persian domination, not dangerous to anybody.

Still, at the time Esther was written it was the Macedonian kings of the Seleucid Empire, and not the ancient and nearly forgotten Amalekites, who were the great enemies of the Jews, and this verse can be considered a thrust at them.

10. JOB

Job

The Book of Job, which follows Esther, is a philosophic drama dealing with the problem of good and evil. It is so little concerned with secular history that the question of whether it describes events that really happened does not really arise. Its religious and ethical message would be the same even if it is the fiction it seems to be.

No one can say exactly when the book might have been written. Most scholars seem to conclude that the book as we now have it is post-Exilic, and was composed sometime during the Persian period. It begins:

Job 1:1. *There was a man . . . whose name was Job . . .*

No genealogy is given for Job, and no connection with Biblical history is attempted. Perhaps none was needed at the time of writing, for Job seems to have been the hero of a well-known legend; a legend describing a good man of superhuman patience who bore up under great misfortune without ever losing his faith in God.

The original legend must be ancient (there is even a form of it existing in Babylonian literature) and the writer of the Biblical Book of Job includes it as a prose introduction and a prose ending to the book. In between that beginning and ending, however, he inserts his own deep poetic probing of the relationship between God and man, allowing it to be carried like rich cargo within the simple and sturdy vessel of the well-known Job legend.

Canaan Before the Conquest

There is one Biblical reference that seems to deal with the original Job legend. This is to be found in the writings of the prophet Ezekiel, who lived during the Exile and therefore, very likely, before the Book of Job was written. When Ezekiel quotes God's warning that He will destroy idolators, it is specified that evildoers will not escape because of the merits of the pious among them.

Ezekiel 14:13. . . . *when the land sinneth against me . . . then will I . . . cut off man and beast from it:*
Ezekiel 14:14. *Though these three men, Noah, Daniel, and Job were in it, they should deliver but their own souls . . .*

Uz

Job's genealogy may not be given, but his home is.

Job 1:1. *There was a man in the land of Uz, whose name was Job . . .*
. . . .
Job 1:3. . . . *this man was the greatest of all the men of the east.*

At once the question arises: Where was Uz? As far as the essential point of the book is concerned, the question need not be asked, for the great problem dealt with in the Book of Job transcends time and space. But here we are devoting ourselves to the secular side of the Bible and the "land of Uz" must have had some significance to the original readers of the book. What was that significance?

The fact that Job is characterized as "the greatest of all the men of the east" would seem to imply that he was a wealthy sheik, dwelling to the east of Canaan on the border of the desert.

If, however, we turn back to the genealogical lists of Genesis, we find:

Genesis 10:22. *The children of Shem; . . . Aram.*
Genesis 10:23. *And the children of Aram; Uz . . .*

The names in these early genealogies stand for eponymous ancestors, and individuals are said to be related when the areas or tribes they represent are neighboring. If the individual Uz is said to be a son of

Aram, it is reasonable to suppose that the land of Uz is a district in Aram (that is, Syria) and that Uz is therefore north of Canaan. Indeed, Assyrian inscriptions speak of a district called "Ussai" in Syria.

Yet, on the other hand, the prophet Jeremiah at one point lists the kingdoms slated to meet God's wrath and works his way up the Mediterranean coast from Egypt to Phoenicia:

> Jeremiah 25:19. *Pharaoh king of Egypt* . . .
> Jeremiah 25:20. . . . *and all the kings of the land of Uz, and all the kings of the land of the Philistines* . . .

This would seem to place Uz between Egypt and Philistia and, therefore, to the south of Canaan.

An even clearer indication of this is to be found in a verse in the Book of Lamentations. In that book, the writer, bewailing the fate of Jerusalem after its destruction by Nebuchadnezzar, bursts out into a sarcastically bitter denunciation of Edom, which he pictures as rejoicing over Jerusalem's fall:

> Lamentations 4:21. *Rejoice and be glad, O daughter of Edom, that dwellest in the land of Uz* . . .

There are thus Biblical reasons for supposing Uz to be either east, north, or south of Canaan, and this is certainly an unsatisfactory state of affairs.

Still, when the descendants of Esau are given in Genesis, Uz crops up again among them:

> Genesis 36:28. *The children of Dishan are these; Uz* . . .

A few verses later on the rulers of Edom are listed:

> Genesis 36:31. *And these are the kings that reigned in the land of Edom before there reigned any king over* . . . *Israel.*
> Genesis 36:32. . . . *Bela the son of Beor reigned in Edom* . . .
> Genesis 36:33. *And Bela died and Jobab* . . . *reigned in his stead.*

Could Jobab have been Job? Could the writer of the book have viewed Job as a king in Edom while the Israelites were still struggling to establish themselves in Canaan? Certainly, the later rabbis seemed to think that Uz was in Edom and that Job was a wealthy Edomite who lived during the time when the Israelites were enslaved in Egypt.

(Because the story was placed at this time, rabbinic tradition had it that the Book of Job was written by Moses, something modern scholars do not accept, of course.)

Satan

With Job introduced, the scene switches to heaven:

> Job 1:6. . . . *there was a day when the sons of God came to present themselves before the Lord, and Satan came also among them.*

This mention of Satan, whose name is not to be found in any of the books based on pre-Exilic records, is one of the reasons for supposing the book to be post-Exilic.

The Persian influence is shown in the picture of God as the head of a numerous court of assisting spirits. The difference from the Persian view rests in the fact that Satan is not the coequal head of a band of evil spirits but is merely a single spirit, as much subject to God as are the others. Satan has, apparently, the important and useful role of testing human beings to see whether their faith in God is staunch, or merely superficial. In this role, he acts only with God's permission and only as far as God permits.

Teman

God praises Job's piety to Satan, who at once points out that it is easy for a wealthy and fortunate man to be grateful for the rewards he receives. God therefore gives Satan permission to visit Job with misfortune in order to demonstrate that Job will remain pious.

Job's flocks and goods are destroyed; his sons and daughters are killed; he himself is afflicted with boils. At no time, however, does Job allow any blasphemous expression to cross his lips. He remains pious and continues to praise God.

Three friends then come to Job:

> Job 2:11. . . . *Eliphaz the Temanite and Bildad the Shuhite and Zophar the Naamathite: . . . to mourn with him and to comfort him.*

Eliphaz the Temanite is certainly intended to be considered an Edomite:

Genesis 36:4. *And Adah bare to Esau Eliphaz . . .*

. . . .

Genesis 36:11. *And the sons of Eliphaz were Teman . . .*

Teman (a word meaning "south" in Hebrew) seems to have been the name of a district in Edom (an alternate name for Esau; see page 93). In several places in the Bible, Teman is used as a poetic synonym for all of Edom. Thus, in the Book of Jeremiah, the prophet says:

Jeremiah 49:7. *Concerning Edom, thus saith the Lord of hosts; Is wisdom no more in Teman? . . .*

If we say then "Eliphaz the Temanite," we might as well say "Eliphaz the southerner" or "Eliphaz the Edomite." Perhaps the writer even meant Eliphaz the son of Esau. In all likelihood, the original readers of the book took him to be either this Eliphaz or a near descendant of him.

Bildad the Shuhite is, apparently, a descendant of Shuah:

Genesis 25:2. *And she* [Keturah] *bare him* [Abraham] *. . . Shuah.*

Abraham's sons by Keturah apparently serve as the eponymous ancestors for the various Arabian tribes, Midian being the best known. The Shuhites, Bildad among them, would be Arabians then, living to the south or southeast of Edom.

Zophar the Naamathite was an inhabitant of the town of Naamah. There was a town in Judah by that name but no one thinks that town was meant. Presumably, it was another town of that name farther to the south.

Even if the case of Zophar is omitted, the probable locations of Eliphaz and Bildad make it seem all the more likely that the writer viewed Job as dwelling south of Canaan and that he was probably considered an Edomite.

In the original story, the constancy of Job was rewarded by a return of his prosperity and a growth of new happiness—as is, indeed, recorded at the end of the book. Between the beginning just described and that ending, however, the writer has put in a series of speeches by Job and answers by his friends (plus a final answer by God) that hold the meat of the book. In these speeches, Job is anything but patient and uncomplaining, and seriously questions the justice of God. Nevertheless, this has not, for some reason, altered the common conception of Job as a patient, uncomplaining man.

Orion

Most of the brilliantly poetical give-and-take of the Book of Job involves ethical and theological questions not the concern of this volume. Yet amid the flow of metaphor some interesting material objects are mentioned. Most of the few specific astronomical references to be found in the Bible, for instance, are here in Job.

Job reasons that misfortunes have fallen upon him undeservedly and that God is acting as a capricious tyrant. He lists the great accomplishments of God, accomplishments which prove Him to be far beyond the reach of mere man and make His presumed tyranny impossible to challenge. Job includes among God's accomplishments:

Job 9:9. . . . [God] *maketh Arcturus, Orion, and Pleiades, and the chambers of the south.*

The Hebrew word translated here as Orion is *kesil* which means "fool." How do we go from "fool" to "Orion"? Let's begin with Orion.

By all odds, the most spectacular constellation of the heavens, particularly in the winter when nights are longest and casual observation of the sky most likely, is Orion. No other constellation contains so many bright stars.

The seven brightest stars are arranged in a particularly suggestive manner. Two are on top, two on bottom, while the remaining three form a closely spaced line between. It is not very difficult to see in this arrangement a large man. The two upper stars represent the shoulders, the two lower stars the legs, and the three middle stars the waistline or belt. If fainter stars are added there are three stars in a vertical line suspended from the belt, making a kind of sword, and there are stars above one shoulder which can be pictured as representing an arm and a club. There are even stars beyond the other shoulder that can, without stretching matters too badly, represent some sort of shield.

It is almost inevitable, then, that the constellation be interpreted as representing either a giant warrior or a giant hunter. In the Greek myths, Orion was a giant hunter whose deeds are reminiscent of the better-known Hercules. According to one version, he was beloved by Artemis, the goddess of the hunt (naturally, a great hunter would be). His boasting and conceit offended the other gods, however, and Apollo paid him back by playing on Artemis' vanity. He dared her to shoot at a target she could barely see, expressing doubt of her ability to hit it. In vainglorious display, she shot at it accurately and when she raced for the target to retrieve her kill she found it had been Orion and she had slain him. In grief, she placed him in the sky.

However, the early Greeks borrowed most or all of their astronomy from the Babylonians; and among them this concept of a giant in the sky. The Babylonians pictured the constellation as a bound giant; bound presumably for some act of rebellion against the gods. The Jews in the course of the Exile would naturally pick up Babylonian astronomy. They might easily have viewed the bound giant as Nimrod, punished for his presumption in attempting to erect the Tower of Babel (itself a Babylon-inspired legend; see page 55). Clearly, any man who tried to defy God was a fool and to the Jews it would be natural, then, to refer to the constellation we call Orion as "The Fool."

The chains binding Orion are mentioned later in the Book of Job, when God challenges man to match the divine powers:

Job 38:31. *Canst thou . . . loose the bands of Orion?*

The Pleiades

A second constellation mentioned in Job 9:9 is *kimah*. This is taken to mean a closely bound group of stars, and the best known of all closely bound groups is a small cluster of medium-bright stars called the Pleiades. The notion of a close-bound cluster arises from the later verse just mentioned, of which the first part is:

Job 38:31. *Canst thou bind the sweet influences of Pleiades . . .*

The "sweet influences" are the forces of attraction holding the stars of the Pleiades together and the Revised Standard Version has the verse read, "Can you bind the chains of the Pleiades . . ."

In Greek mythology, the Pleiades were seven sisters whom, in life, Orion the hunter chased. They were rescued by the gods, who changed them into doves, then placed them in the heavens. However, they are not far to one side of the constellation Orion, who seems still to be pursuing them across the skies.

Arcturus

The third constellation mentioned in Job 9:9 is *ash*. It is translated as "Arcturus" in the King James Version but this is the least certain of the three translations. Arcturus is not a constellation (that is, a group of apparently connected stars) but a single star; one of the brightest in the heavens, to be sure.

It is referred to again in God's speech questioning man's powers:

Job 38:32. *Canst thou . . . guide Arcturus with his sons?*

The reference to "sons" makes little sense in connection with Arcturus. However, if we search for another constellation in the skies as notable as Orion or as unusual as the Pleiades, we must consider Ursa Major, the Great Bear. Its most noticeable feature is the group of seven stars we know as the "Big Dipper." Not only are these stars quite bright and eye-catching, but they are so near the north celestial pole that they never set in North Temperate latitudes at any time of night or year. Even today, people who know nothing else about the night sky will point out the Big Dipper without trouble.

If one considers *ash* to signify the Great Bear, then the "sons" might refer to the three stars in the handle of the Big Dipper (often pictured as an incongruously long tail to the bear). The cup of the Dipper would be part of the constellation proper, and the three stars of the handle would be the sons tagging along in polite single file.

The Revised Standard Version therefore translates Job 9:9 as "Who made the Bear and Orion, the Pleaides, and the chambers of the south" and translates Job 38:32 as "Can you . . . guide the Bear with its children?"

As for the fourth object mentioned in Job 9:9—*khadre teman*—its significance is completely lost. It is translated literally as "chambers of the south" in the King James Version, in the Revised Standard Version and in the Anchor Bible. Further than that no one can go.

Buz

Eventually, Job's eloquence in his own defense confounds his three friends and Job's accusations against God, which have been mounting in intensity and fervor, demand a divine answer. This is delayed six chapters, however, when a fourth friend is suddenly introduced. He is described as being angry that Job's view of God as a tyrant had seemingly prevailed.

Job 32:2. *Then was kindled the wrath of Elihu the son of Barachel the Buzite, of the kindred of Ram . . .*

Here, too, arises the question of a Syrian versus an Edomite scene for the story. As a Buzite, Elihu may be considered a descendant of someone named Buz, or as an inhabitant of a land named Buz. Buz appears in Genesis among the descendants of Nahor, the brother of Abraham. These are listed as:

Genesis 22:21. *Huz his firstborn, and Buz his brother . . .*

Since Nahor was living in Haran at the time, well north of Canaan, a northern or Syrian locale for Buz might be indicated. This is particularly interesting since "Huz" might more accurately be rendered "Uz" and is so rendered in the Revised Standard Version and in the Anchor Bible. Both Uz, the home of Job, and Buz, the home of Elihu's father, are indicated to be in the north. This is made more pointed by the statement that Elihu was "of the kindred of Ram" for some feel that Ram is a misprint for "Aram" or Syria.

Against all this is the fact that Jeremiah, in listing the nations being warned by God (see page 477), mentions Buz as follows:

Jeremiah 25:23. *Dedan and Tema, and Buz . . .*

Now in the Book of Genesis, Dedan is listed as a grandson of Abraham by Keturah:

Genesis 25:1. . . . *Abraham took a wife, and her name was Keturah.*
Genesis 25:2. *And she bare him . . . Jokshan . . .*
Genesis 25:3. *And Jokshan begat . . . Dedan . . .*

while Tema is a son of Ishmael:

> Genesis 25:13. . . . *these are the names of the sons of Ishmael* . . .
> . . . .
> Genesis 25:15. *Hadar, and Tema.* . . .

Since Dedan and Tema are thus shown to be Arabic clans, Jeremiah's grouping of Dun with those two would mean that Duz also was an Arabic clan, and the southern scene for Job is again indicated.

The long speech of Elihu that follows his introduction seems to be a late interpolation. At least, Elihu adds nothing particularly new to previous arguments, he is not answered by Job, nor is he mentioned later in the book.

Mazzaroth

At the conclusion of Elihu's speech, God is suddenly introduced, and personally answers Job, contrasting divine omnipotence with human limitations. He points out, for instance, that man is unable to order the heavens. He introduces one astronomical object not mentioned earlier in the book:

> Job 38:32. *Canst thou bring forth Mazzaroth in his season?*

Mazzaroth occurs only in this one verse of the Bible and is a transliteration of the Hebrew word. The connection of Mazzaroth with seasonal progression (it is brought forth "in his season") rouses some speculation that it might mean the zodiacal constellations as a group. Each of these reaches the zenith at a different month of the year so that the whole acts as a primitive calendar of the year's seasons. There is also the possibility that Mazzaroth means "the planets," whose paths follow a much more complicated pattern against the sky and which therefore require much greater virtuosity to govern and regulate.

Behemoth

God goes on to describe further the wonders of nature which have been divinely created, guided, and regulated and which mankind is incompetent to cope with.

Job 40:15. *Behold now behemoth, which I made with thee; he eateth grass as an ox.*

The Hebrew word *behemoth* is the plural of *behemah*, meaning "beast." The word is placed in the plural to imply, apparently, that the behemoth is many beasts in size and strength; it is the greatest of beasts.

We have here a description of a huge herbivorous creature of powerful strength, and it would be natural to equate behemoth with the elephant, which is the largest land animal alive today and which "eateth grass as an ox."

Further verses, however, rather spoil this notion:

Job 40:21. *He lieth . . . in the covert of the reed, and fens.*
Job 40:22. . . . *the willows of the brook compass him about.*

This gives the impression of a river animal and turns the attention to the hippopotamus, the second largest land animal. It, too, is herbivorous.

In ancient times, the hippopotamus was quite common along the Nile and it is to be expected that the writer of the Book of Job was familiar with it. (Indeed, might not the writer have lived in Egypt and been a little hazy about Palestinian geography, thus giving rise to some of the uncertainties concerning the geographic setting of the book?)

Nevertheless, as the Anchor Bible points out, the behemoth seems to be larger and stronger than even a hippopotamus or elephant. Instead, it bears a mythological character, especially in the later rabbinical tales, and in some of the Apocrypha, where the behemoth is pictured as unimaginably colossal and as designed to be killed in the Messianic age to feed all the righteous at once. The Anchor Bible suggests that it might be a hang-over from a Mesopotamian myth of the great bull killed by Gilgamesh.

Leviathan

God, having described behemoth at some length, goes on at even greater length to describe another creature.

Job 41:1. *Canst thou draw out leviathan with an hook?*

The leviathan is obviously a sea creature and is described as the largest and most fearsome of them. Most Biblical commentators consider Leviathan, at least in this passage, to represent the deadly man-eating crocodile of the Nile, a fit companion piece for the hippopotamus of the Nile.

Very commonly, in poetic imagery, the term is applied to a sea creature which far surpasses the crocodile in size—the whale. The largest whale, the blue whale of Antarctic waters, is up to a hundred feet long and weighs as much as 150 tons. It is not only the largest animal now alive, but the largest animal that *ever* lived, the dinosaurs and other extinct animals of aeons past included.

But again there seem to be strong mythological components to Leviathan, as to behemoth. In many mythologies, the supreme god, shortly after his birth, or his coming into being, is described as defeating some huge monster. Often, he creates the universe out of the remnants of that monster. This can be taken as symbolizing the victory of order over disorder; of cosmos over chaos.

In Babylonian mythology, Marduk, the chief god, destroys the monster Tiamat and creates the universe out of it. Tiamat is supposed to be the symbolic representation of the sea, and Marduk's creation of the universe thus parallels the creation of civilization by the Sumerians. To create a settled agricultural society, the Sumerians had to tame the rivers in order that floods might be prevented and orderly irrigation ensured.

This Babylonian myth representing the origin of civilization can be traced very shadowily into the Bible. At the very start of Genesis, the creation is described:

> Genesis 1:2. *And the earth was without form and void; and darkness was upon the face of the deep . . .*

"The deep"—that is, the chaotic and unorganized sea—is a translation of the Hebrew *tehom*, which is rather similar to Tiamat.

God does not fight the deep or kill it, but by the sheer force of divine command creates the world. Nevertheless, this version may be a late one, superimposed by a more sophisticated priesthood upon an earlier and more primitive version of the creation that hewed closer to the common mythological notions.

For instance, in the 74th Psalm, the power of God is described as follows:

Psalms 74:13. *Thou didst divide the sea by thy strength: thou brakest the heads of the dragons in the waters.*

Psalms 74:14. *Thou brakest the heads of leviathan in pieces . . .*

This is often taken as a symbolic description of God's punishment of the Egyptians (represented as "leviathan" and as a "dragon") prior to the Exodus, and of his feat in parting the Red Sea. This is a reasonable interpretation, since it could easily be considered poetically appropriate to represent Egypt as a crocodile, just as today we represent the United States by an eagle and the Soviet Union by a bear. But it is also possible that this is a reference to a primitive myth in which God is pictured as bringing about the creation by destroying the monster representing the chaotic sea.

Leviathan can also represent the forces of evil in the world, to be slain (symbolically) by God at the end of days in order to create a new world of righteousness and good, just as it was slain at the beginning of days to create the world that now exists. Thus, in the words of the prophet Isaiah:

Isaiah 27:1. *In that day the Lord . . . shall punish leviathan the piercing serpent . . . and he shall slay the dragon that is in the sea.*

At the end of God's speech, Job realizes divine omnipotence and understands the folly of trying to penetrate God's plans and purposes with the limited mind of a human being. He repents and is then restored to more wealth than he originally had. He has a new set of sons and daughters and dies in happiness after a long life.

19. PSALMS

David

The Book of Psalms consists of 150 devotional poems, intended to be chanted. The Hebrew name of the book is "Tehillim," meaning "praises," since a great many of them praise God. The expression "psalm" is from a Greek word meaning "to pluck at strings," a clear indication of the musical instruments intended to accompany the chanting. *Psalterion* is the Greek word for a stringed instrument and the collection of psalms is called the "Psalter."

Traditionally, the authorship of most of the psalms is attributed to king David, so that the book is sometimes referred to as "The Psalms of David." Fully 101 of the psalms have captions that state the name of the author and in seventy-three cases he is given as David, sometimes with details as to the circumstances under which the psalm was written.

Nevertheless, there is no way of proving the authorship of any individual psalm. The Psalter is a collection of five separate anthologies of psalms and may not have reached its present form till 150 B.C. Some of the psalms clearly indicate their post-Exilic origin, although it is quite possible that others may date back to quite early times, even to David's.

The temptation to attribute psalms to David is a natural one. He is stated in the historical books to be a skilled harpist. When Saul was troubled with melancholia, the monarch sought surcease in music:

1 Samuel 16:17. *And Saul said . . . Provide me now a man that can play well, and bring him to me.*

1 Samuel 16:18. *Then answered one of the servants and said, Behold, I have seen a son of Jesse . . . that is cunning in playing . . .*

And when David was brought to court:

1 Samuel 16:23. *. . . David took an harp, and played with his hand: so Saul was refreshed . . .*

Furthermore, poetic works are introduced into the Second Book of Samuel and attributed to David. The most notable is the dirge over Saul and Jonathan, supposed to have been composed by David after the disastrous battle of Gilboa; a dirge that begins:

2 Samuel 1:19. *The beauty of Israel is slain upon thy high places: how are the mighty fallen!*

Outright psalms are attributed to him, too:

2 Samuel 23:1. *Now these be the last words of David. David . . . the sweet psalmist of Israel, said,*

It might be natural, then, to attribute any particularly good, or particularly popular, psalm to the sweet psalmist of Israel.

The Son

Psalm 2 is an example of one that sounds as though it could be pre-Exilic. It is clearly written in celebration of the coronation of a new king, and from the archaic nature of the language, it is generally placed in the time of the monarchy.

The psalm visualizes subject peoples planning rebellion and enemies planning to attack (as was but too often customary in the unsettled times when a new king was ascending the throne). Then the new king himself speaks and pictures God as standing behind him and as promising him dominion and power:

Psalm 2:7. *. . . the Lord hath said unto me, Thou art my Son; this day have I begotten thee.*

The kings of the ancient monarchies of the Middle East customarily considered themselves to be the adopted sons of the national god, and the day of the coronation was the day on which they were "begotten" as such sons. The Jews were not entirely free of this view.

Thus, when the prophet Nathan informs David that God does not wish him, as a man of war, to build the Temple, he nevertheless adds that God will establish David's line upon the throne and take particular care of the dynasty:

> 2 Samuel 7:13. . . . *I will stablish the throne of his* [David's] *kingdom for ever.*
>
> 2 Samuel 7:14. *I will be his father, and he shall be my son . . .*

Later Christian thought saw more to it than this, however. Jesus, as the Messiah, was considered as bearing a special relationship to God; a relationship that was most easily expressed in the word "son." This psalm was therefore considered to have Messianic significance, and even if it were written with a particular earthly king in mind, it nevertheless had a further, deeper meaning, and applied to the Messiah. It is for this reason that the King James Version capitalizes the word "Son" in the twelfth verse of the psalm. The Revised Standard Version, which is less concerned with Messianic prophecies, puts the word in the lower case.

Selah

The 3rd Psalm is the first to have a title:

> Psalm 3: *A Psalm of David, when he fled from Absalom his son.*

The Hebrew could mean either "A Psalm Written by David" or "A Psalm Concerning David" and it is to be noted that the phrase "A Psalm of David" can also have either of these two meanings in English. However, the traditional assumption is that it means "written by."

The psalm contains an odd word at the end of three of the verses:

> Psalm 3:2. *Many there be which say of my soul, There is no help for him in God. Selah.*

The expression "Selah" occurs seventy-one times altogether in the Book of Psalms, almost always at the end of a verse, and usually at the end of a natural pause in the thought. Presumably, it gives some direction to those chanting the psalm, but what that direction might be, nobody knows.

Neginoth

Other directions involving the musical accompaniment of the psalms are sometimes given in the titles.

Psalm 4. *To the chief Musician on Neginoth* . . .
Psalm 5. *To the chief Musician upon Nehiloth* . . .

Neginoth means "stringed instruments," while *nehiloth* means "pipes" or "wind instruments." In the Revised Standard Version, the title to Psalm 4 is given as "To the choirmaster, with stringed instruments," while that to Psalm 5 is given as ". . . for the flutes . . ."
The title of Psalm 6 is less easily interpreted:

Psalm 6. *To the chief Musician on Neginoth upon Sheminith* . . .

Sheminith means "the eighth" and this could mean an eight-stringed instrument. It could also refer to an octave, and means perhaps that the psalm is to be sung in two voices an octave apart.
The title of Psalm 7 is more puzzling still:

Psalm 7. *Shiggaion of David, which he sang unto the Lord, concerning the words of Cush the Benjamite.*

The meaning of *shiggaion* is unknown and, out of desperation, it is usually considered as simply meaning "psalm." And if that were not puzzle enough, the reference to Cush the Benjamite is likewise mysterious, for no reference to this incident occurs elsewhere in the Bible.
It also seems useless to attempt to interpret the titles of the next two psalms:

Psalm 8. *To the chief Musician upon Gittith* . . .
Psalm 9. *To the chief Musician upon Muthlabben* . . .

Gittith is, presumably, some sort of musical instrument, but no one can say what. *Muthlabben* might be dismissed in similar fashion but it seems to mean "death of" and that cannot be right. Either it also means something else, or it is the result of a copyist's error, and the original meaning can no longer be salvaged.

Psalm 9 contains still another mysterious word:

> Psalm 9:16. . . . *the wicked is snared in the work of his own hands. Higgaion. Selah.*

Higgaion means "meditation" and perhaps it directs a pause during which the singers may meditate on what has been chanted.

The title of Psalm 16 is:

> Psalm 16. *Michtam of David.*

Michtam has been connected with the Hebrew word for gold, and it is conceivable that the 16th Psalm is estimated by the anthologists who gathered this group as a particularly good one; a "golden psalm," in other words.

Sheol

The 18th Psalm, one of the longer ones, has a title to suit:

> Psalm 18. . . . *A Psalm of David . . . in the day that the Lord delivered him from the hand of all his enemies, and from the hand of Saul . . .*

This particular psalm is quoted in the twenty-second chapter of 2 Samuel after the description of the rebellions of Absalom and of Sheba are done with (see page 318). David has indeed been delivered from the hand of all his enemies but it is puzzling why Saul, the enemy disposed of a generation earlier, should be singled out for mention.

One possibility (accepted by the Anchor Bible) is that "Saul" is a copyist's error for Sheol, the afterworld (see page 173). The psalm would then be one of gratitude for the psalmist's escape from death. This seems to fit in with the subject matter of the psalm:

> Psalm 18:4. *The sorrows of death compassed me . . .*
> Psalm 18:5. *The sorrows of hell* [Sheol] *compassed me about . . .*

Even in the immediate post-Exilic period, the picture of Sheol is still that of a shadowy existence, like that of the Greek Hades rather

Al-taschith means "do not destroy." Can this, too, be the first words of a well-known melody of the times? Or did some copyist make a hasty note to ensure the safety of a copy he had just prepared and did the little notation then get frozen into the Biblical canon?

Acrostics

The 25th Psalm has a structure that is completely lost in English translation. Each line begins with a different letter of the Hebrew alphabet, in order. The first line begins with *aleph*, the second with *beth*, the third with *gimmel*, and so on.

Such an arrangement, in which the initial letters of successive verses (or final letters, or both) give the alphabet in order, or spell out words, are called "acrostics," from a Greek expression meaning "the ends of verses."

The 25th Psalm is by no means the only acrostic psalm. The 34th is another example. The 119th Psalm is a particularly complicated one for it consists of twenty-two parts, each of which contains eight lines. Each part is headed by a successive letter of the alphabet, and each of the eight lines of that part begins with that letter.

Biblical acrostics are found outside the Book of Psalms, too. The last section of the last chapter of Proverbs is an anacrostic poem praising the virtuous woman. Again, each of the first four chapters of Lamentations is an acrostic poem.

Acrostics have their uses. By starting each line with a letter in alphabetic order, an aid to memory is granted the reciter. Then, too, it is pleasant for a poet to display his virtuosity by writing an attractive poem within the limits of an artificial convention. On the other hand, the limits so set often force a writer to settle for less than the best, and acrostic poems in the Bible tend to display a certain illogicality in sequence. A line has to be written to fit the new initial rather than to carry on the previous thought.

Sirion

The 29th Psalm describes the might of God in terms of nature images:

Psalm 29:5. *The voice of the Lord breaketh the cedars* . . .

Psalm 29:6. *He maketh them also to skip like a calf; Lebanon and Sirion like a young unicorn.*

Sirion, here, is the Phoenician term for Mount Hermon (see page 202) in Lebanon. This is stated specifically in Deuteronomy:

Deuteronomy 3.9. (*Which Hermon the Sidonians call Sirion; and the Amorites call it Shenir;*)

The use of a Phoenician name is no accident. Apparently, this psalm is a Yahvistic adaptation of an older Canaanite hymn to the storm-god. The parallelism in verse 6 between "calf" and "young unicorn" again shows the unicorn to be a wild ox (see page 186). The Revised Standard Version has the verse read, "He makes Lebanon to skip like a calf, and Sirion like a young wild ox."

Maschil

The 32nd Psalm has the title:

Psalm 32. *A Psalm of David. Maschil.*

The word *Maschil* is left untranslated in both the Revised Standard Version and the Anchor Bible, here and in the title of several other psalms, but seems to carry the connotation of "instruction." Perhaps the psalms so denoted were supposed to carry special occult meanings apparent only to the initiated, but this is just a guess.

Abimelech

The 34th Psalm has a circumstantial title:

Psalm 34. *A Psalm of David, when he changed his behaviour before Abimelech* . . .

This must surely refer to the episode in David's life when, as a fugitive from Saul, he sought refuge in the court of Achish, king of Gath. Fearing that the Philistines would kill him or give him up to Saul, he feigned madness in order to ensure his release:

1 Samuel 21:13. *And he* [David] *changed his behaviour before them* [the Philistines], *and feigned himself mad . . .*

It is usual to suppose that the reference to Abimelech in the title of the 34th Psalm is a copyist's mistake for Achish. However, it is just possible that Abimelech was a general title for Philistine kings. In Genesis, Abimelech, king of Gerar, is mentioned in two different tales. The Genesis tales refer to a time before the coming of the Philistines, to be sure, but the title may have lingered on, as Egyptian kings were called Pharaoh regardless of their name or dynasty.

Jeduthun

The 39th Psalm seems to be dedicated to an individual:

Psalm 39. *To the chief Musician, even to Jeduthun . . .*

There were, apparently, three chief clans devoted to the musical service of the Temple. The Chronicler traced back the ancestry of these clans to the time of David:

1 Chronicles 25:1. *Moreover David . . . separated to the service of the sons of Asaph, and of Heman, and of Jeduthun, who should prophesy with harps, with psalteries, and with cymbals.*

What the title may really mean is that the psalm is "after the manner of Jeduthun"; that is, in the style made use of by the clan. Or perhaps it had been composed by members of the clan, despite the routine ascription of the psalm to David.

One psalm is ascribed to Heman:

Psalm 88. . . . *Maschil of Heman the Ezrahite.*

(where Ezrahite should really be Zerahite; see page 107).

Quite a number are ascribed to Asaph:

Psalm 50. *A Psalm of Asaph.*

The eleven psalms from 73 to 83 inclusive are all attributed to Asaph and they may represent a collection used by the Asaphic clan.

The Sons of Korah

The 41st Psalm ends with a verse praising God:

Psalm 41:13. *Blessed be the Lord God of Israel from everlasting, and to everlasting. Amen, and Amen.*

This is not considered part of the psalm but is, rather, a ritualistic formula of praise which serves to end a collection of psalms. Such praise of God is called a "doxology," from a Greek word meaning "giving praise."

Psalms 1 to 41 inclusive are considered to be the first of the five collections making up our Book of Psalms. All of the psalms of this first collection are ascribed to David, or in a few cases are left unascribed. The 42nd Psalm, however, which is the first of the second collection, has a title, but does not include David's name.

Psalm 42. *To the chief Musician, Maschil, for the sons of Korah.*

Although Korah is pictured as a rebellious Levite during the time of the Exodus (see page 172), and as one who was destroyed by Moses, his family remained and survived to form an important group in the Temple ritual:

1 Chronicles 9:19. . . . *the Korahites, were over the work of the service, keepers of the gates of the tabernacle* . . .

The Daughter of Tyre

The 45th Psalm is rather secular. Its title includes a significant phrase:

Psalm 45. . . . *A song of loves.*

It is written, apparently, in honor of a royal marriage and is what the Greeks would call an *epithalamion* ("at the bridal chamber"). The bride is a foreign princess:

Psalm 45:12. *And the daughter of Tyre shall be there with a gift* . . .

The natural assumption might be that the wedding being described is that between Ahab of Israel and Jezebel of Tyre, or between Jehoram of Judah and Athaliah, the daughter of Jezebel (see page 362). It has also been suggested, with perhaps less likelihood, that it celebrates the wedding of Solomon and the Egyptian princess, or of Jeroboam II (see page 369) and some foreign princess.

Solomon

Psalm 72 is one of two in the Book of Psalms that mention Solomon in the title. (The other is the 127th Psalm.)

Psalm 72. *A Psalm for Solomon.*

It is a prayer that the reigning king, probably newly come to the throne, reign long and justly; that he be rich and powerful. The notion that Solomon in particular is concerned arises naturally out of the mention of nations that were traditionally involved with his trading ventures (see page 332).

Psalm 72:10. *The kings of Tarshish and of the isles shall bring presents: the kings of Sheba and Seba shall offer gifts.*

Sheba and Seba are intended to describe two different sections of Arabia. Thus, in the listing of the nations in the tenth chapter of Genesis, both are mentioned in a related fashion:

Genesis 10:7. *And the sons of Cush; Seba . . . and Raamah: and the sons of Raamah; Sheba . . .*

Psalm 72 is the last psalm of the second book. It ends with a doxology and then with a final verse:

Psalm 72:20. *The prayers of David the son of Jesse are ended.*

And so they are as far as this second collection is concerned.

The first two collections of psalms are not entirely independent. As might be expected of different anthologies, there are some duplications. Thus, the 14th Psalm in the first collection is virtually identical with the 53rd Psalm in the second book. Then again, the 70th Psalm in the second book is virtually a repeat of the last five verses of the 40th Psalm in the first book.

Synagogues

The 74th Psalm pictures a land in ruins, with the enemy triumphant. Unless one pictures David speaking in allegories or in prophetic vision, it becomes impossible to ascribe it to him or, in fact, to any period in the history of the kingdoms. At the earliest it must be after the destruction of the Temple by Nebuchadnezzar:

> Psalm 74:7. *They have cast fire into thy sanctuary, they have defiled by casting down the dwelling place of thy name to the ground.*

Indeed, the psalm might possibly be dated later still, for the very next verse goes on to say:

> Psalm 74:8. *They said in their hearts, Let us destroy them together: they have burned up all the synagogues of God in the land.*

The word "synagogue" is from the Greek expression meaning "an assembling together" and is precisely analogous to the Latin-derived "congregation" or the Anglo-Saxon-derived "meeting place." The Revised Standard Version uses the Anglo-Saxon equivalent and translates the verse: "they burned all the meeting places of God in the land."

The synagogue did not become prominent until the time of the Exile. With the Temple destroyed and the ritualistic paraphernalia of a centralized worship gone, something had to be improvised if Judaism were to survive. Worship came to be centered about the written books being produced by the scribes. Groups of Jews gathered at meeting places, or synagogues, to study the books, read them aloud, sing the hymns, and so on.

Even after the return and the rebuilding of the Temple, the new habit persisted. Not all Jews had returned, after all, and even those who were back in the land had become used to the relatively informal gatherings and continued them. By Greek times, the synagogue had grown important indeed, and it was only then, during the Seleucid persecution, that one might say "they have burned up all the synagogues." It is for this reason that suggestions are made that the 74th

Psalm, or at least the version we now possess, may be among the latest ones and may have been composed in 165 B.C.

Rahab

The 87th Psalm lists the heathen nations surrounding Judea, and predicts that all will turn to God and Jerusalem eventually. (Or perhaps the reference is to the Jews who were scattered abroad among the surrounding nations even after the rebuilding of the Temple, with the psalm containing the hope that all would eventually return.) The list of nations contains one strange name, however:

Psalm 87:4. *I will make mention of Rahab and Babylon . . . behold Philistia, and Tyre, with Ethiopia . . .*

Rahab seems to be another name for the mythical monster destroyed by God at the beginning of time to create the world:

Psalm 89:10. *Thou hast broken Rahab in pieces, as one that is slain . . .*

or:

Isaiah 51:9. *Awake, awake, put on strength, O arm of the Lord . . . Art thou not it that has cut Rahab, and wounded the dragon?*

Rahab, like Leviathan (also used as the name for the primitive monster; see page 487), seems to make reference to a nature myth. Where Leviathan is the chaotic sea tamed by the forces of order, so Rahab (meaning "storm") would seem to be the howling of the elements; elements that had to be subdued by the forces of order before they subverted the universe.

But Rahab, like Leviathan, could be used as a symbolic representation of Egypt; and talk of breaking or cutting or wounding could then be equated with God's punishment of Egypt at the time of the Exodus.

The representation of Egypt as a monstrous dragon is a rather appropriate one. Egypt is, essentially, the banks of the Nile River, the ever-fertile ribbon through the desert that saw the growth of a mighty civilization and was the richest portion of the world for thousands of years. The river wound like a great snake or dragon across the land, and Ezekiel uses this metaphor very effectively when he quotes God as saying to Egypt:

> Ezekiel 29:3. . . . *Behold, I am against thee, Pharaoh king of Egypt, the great dragon that lieth in the midst of his rivers* . . .
> Ezekiel 29:4. . . . *I will put hooks in thy jaws . . . and I will bring thee up out of the midst of thy rivers* . . .

Here the language that might be appropriate for the battle between the God of order and the monster of chaos is made into a metaphoric description of a battle between God and Egypt.

Ezekiel wrote during the Exile, and by post-Exilic times, Rahab had apparently become an accepted synonym for Egypt. In the 87th Psalm, it seems clearly to be used in this manner.

Moses

The 89th Psalm, a sad one apparently composed during the Exile, ends the third collection and closes with a doxology. The 90th Psalm, the first of the fourth collection, is the only one in the Book of Psalms that is attributed to none other than Moses:

> Psalm 90. *A Prayer of Moses the man of God.*

This may be because it speaks of the creation—the peculiar province of Genesis, a book traditionally written by Moses.

> Psalm 90:1. *Lord, thou hast been our dwelling place* . . .
> Psalm 90:2. *Before . . . ever thou hadst formed the earth* . . .

Hallelujah

The 104th Psalm ends:

> Psalm 104:35. . . . *Bless thou the Lord, O my soul. Praise ye the Lord.*

The 105th Psalm, immediately afterward, ends also with "Praise ye the Lord." In fact, "Praise ye the Lord" occurs at the beginning or end (or both beginning and end) of fifteen different psalms in the last two collections of the Book of Psalms. In Hebrew, the expression is "Hallelujah" ("praise Yah").

The Greek form of the word is "Alleluia" and that occurs in Revelation:

> Revelation 19:1. . . . *I heard a great voice of much people in heaven, saying, Alleluia . . .*

Mine Anointed

The 105th Psalm has a curiously influential verse. The care of God for those who follow him is detailed; as in the Patriarchal Age, when he cared for Abraham and his few descendants, precariously existing in a hostile land:

> Psalm 105:14. *He suffered no man to do them wrong: yea, he reproved kings for their sakes;*
> Psalm 105:15. *Saying, Touch not mine anointed, and do my prophets no harm.*

The reference seems to be to the passage in Genesis when God reproves Abimelech, king of Gerar, in a dream, after Abimelech has taken Abraham's wife, Sarah, into his harem. God says:

> Genesis 20:7. *Now therefore restore the man his wife; for he is a prophet . . . and if thou restore her not, know thou that thou shalt surely die . . .*

This passage in the 105th Psalm served as a kind of shield for the priesthood against the secular power. In the middle ages, it was used to protect priests from being tried by secular courts, since the king must do God's prophets (a term extended, liberally, over the clergy generally) no harm. This was valuable for the clergy, since the clerical courts did not pronounce the death sentence, and this was called "benefit of clergy."

This was eventually extended to all who could read (since literacy was virtually confined to the clergy in the middle ages). If a person convicted of murder could read a passage from the Bible, he was exempt from execution but was merely branded on the hand. A second murder, however, would mean execution. Literacy meant one murder free, so to speak, but no more. Soon after 1800, this practice was ended. Perhaps too many people were learning to read.

Ham

The 105th Psalm recalls the days of Egyptian slavery, too, and the Exodus that followed:

> Psalm 105:23. *Israel also came into Egypt; and Jacob sojourned in the land of Ham.*

The parallelism of Hebrew poetry shows that "land of Ham" is a name for Egypt. Ham is that son of Noah from whom the nations of northeastern Africa are descended, according to the genealogical lists in Genesis:

> Genesis 10:6. *And the sons of Ham; Cush, and Mizraim . . .*

Mizraim is the Hebrew word for Egypt, so that what is really being said is that Egypt is the son of Ham, and Ham can therefore be used poetically to represent Egypt as well as Mizraim can.

Indeed, Ham is the better name of the two, since the ancient Egyptians' name for their own land was a word very like Ham. The word was usually taken to mean "black" as a reference to the black fertile land bordering the Nile, in contrast to the arid yellow sands of the desert on either side.

Melchizedek

The 106th Psalm ends with a doxology and the 107th begins the fifth and last collection incorporated into the Book of Psalms. The 110th Psalm is another one of those which praises a king, perhaps on the occasion of his coronation, promising him greatness and power. More than that, he is promised priesthood:

> Psalm 110:4. *The Lord hath sworn, and will not repent, Thou art a priest for ever after the order of Melchizedek.*

This might well be a reference to the struggle between king and High Priest for control of the Temple ritual. This struggle appears most prominently in the Bible in connection with the tradition that Uzziah was struck with leprosy as punishment for attempting to lead the Temple rites (see page 423). The priestly position was that only Levites of the line of Zadok could properly conduct them. The king, a member of the tribe of Judah and a descendant of David, could have nothing to do with them.

The Psalm recalls, however, that there was a king of Jerusalem named Melchizedek (see page 73). This was a priest so acceptable to God that Abraham himself did him reverence. The capacity for priesthood might therefore be viewed as adhering to the king in Jerusalem from earliest times, well before the birth of Levi himself. If the king were considered as inheriting that priesthood by virtue of his office, he was a priest "after the order of Melchizedek."

Song of Degrees

Psalms 120 to 134 inclusive bear titles such as:

Psalm 120. A *Song of degrees.*

"Degrees" means "steps." One might picture such psalms being sung as a priestly procession moves up one of the stairways associated with the Temple. For that reason, the title is given as "A Song of Ascents" in the Revised Standard Version.

On the other hand, these psalms might have been used by pilgrims going to the Temple for one of the great festivals. They would "go up" to Jerusalem in stages—or "ascend by degrees." The possibility of pilgrim usage is strengthened by the fact that the writer of the 120th Psalm bemoans the fact that he lives among the heathen:

Psalm 120:5. *Woe is me, that I sojourn in Mesech, that I dwell in the tents of Kedar.*

Mesech, or Meshech, is described in the genealogies of Genesis as being a son of Japheth.

Genesis 10:2. *The sons of Japheth; . . . Tubal, and Meshech, and Tiras.*

while Kedar is a son of Ishmael:

> Genesis 25:13. . . . *The sons of Ishmael . . . Nabajoth; and Kedar, and Adbeel . . .*

These two terms, Mesech and Kedar, are used poetically here to signify non-Jewish societies in general.

The Rivers of Babylon

The 137th Psalm is clearly of Exilic origin:

> Psalm 137:1. *By the rivers of Babylon, there we sat down, yea, we wept, when we remembered Zion.*

Babylon is, of course, on the Euphrates River and the Tigris River is about forty miles to the east. The exiled Jews, spread over the region, might, conceivably, have been referring to these two as the rivers of Babylon.

However, Babylonia was an irrigated land and the reference is much more likely to be to the numerous intersecting canals. We would get a truer picture if we were to read the phrase, "By the canals of Babylon . . ." Indeed, the Revised Standard Version avoids making use of the misleading "rivers" and translates the phrase, "By the waters of Babylon . . ."

20. PROVERBS

SOLOMON • HEZEKIAH • SPARE THE ROD • AGUR • LEMUEL

Solomon

The Book of Proverbs gets its name from its first phrase:

Proverbs 1:1. *The proverbs of . . .*

This phrase, in Hebrew, is "Mishli," which is the title of the book in Hebrew. The word *mishli* might more accurately be translated as "the wise sayings of," as is done in the Anchor Bible.

"Proverb" is a narrow term, for it is not only a "wise saying," but it is also a "folk saying," a pithy one, usually, that has arisen out of the experience of people generally. It is usually of unknown origin and frequently used in everyday speech.

The Book of Proverbs is a heterogeneous collection that includes proverbs in this narrow sense, and more elaborate "wise sayings" as well. It is an example of the "wisdom literature" that was gathered by writers of many ancient nations: the teachings of experience, usually with a strong moralistic or religious bent.

In the case of the Jews, most wisdom literature was ascribed to Solomon almost as a matter of course, for he was, traditionally, the wisest of men:

1 Kings 4:30. *And Solomon's wisdom excelled the wisdom of all the children of the east country, and all the wisdom of Egypt.*

1 Kings 4:31. *For he was wiser than all men . . .*

1 Kings 4:32. *And he spake three thousand proverbs . . .*

Two sections of the Book of Proverbs are indeed made up of a group of short aphorisms which are specifically ascribed to Solomon.

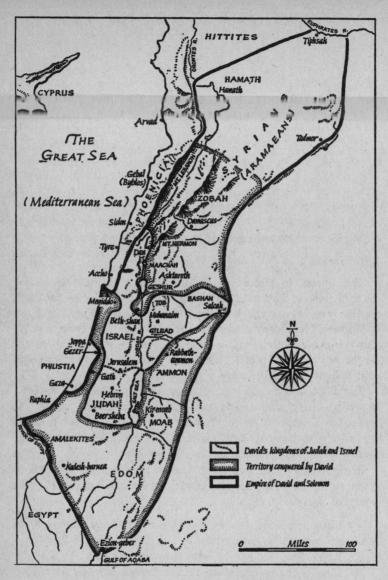

The Empire of David and Solomon

The first extends from Chapter 10 through the first half of Chapter 22 and begins:

Proverbs 10:1. *The proverbs of Solomon* . . .

The second collection covers chapters 25 through 29 and begins:

Proverbs 25:1. *These are also proverbs of Solomon* . . .

There is no doubt but that many of the proverbs are ancient indeed and could have reached back to Solomon's time and even earlier. There is nothing impossible in Solomon having collected a group of proverbs or even having put them into literary form. Still, much of the atmosphere of the book seems to make it almost certainly belong to a period considerably later than Solomon's time, and the final form of the collection, including the two lists of proverbs assigned to Solomon, may not have reached its present form till post-Exilic times, say about 300 B.C. At that time, the general ascription must have been placed at the beginning to cover the entire book:

Proverbs 1:1. *The proverbs of Solomon the son of David, king of Israel.*

Hezekiah

The Book of Proverbs itself implies that at least some of the material in it underwent editing well after the time of Solomon. Thus, in introducing the second collection of Solomonic proverbs:

Proverbs 25:1. *These are also proverbs of Solomon, which the men of Hezekiah king of Judah copied out.*

Hezekiah ruled two centuries after Solomon and was a firm Yahvist. Apparently, he patronized a school of scribes, one of whose tasks was the collection and organization of the Yahvist literature of the past.

Spare the Rod

Some of the Solomonic proverbs are indeed household expressions, in one form or another, even today:

Proverbs 13:24. *He that spareth his rod hateth his son: but he that loveth him chasteneth him betimes.*

This is almost invariably cited as "Spare the rod and spoil the child." More apt to be correctly quoted is:

Proverbs 15:1. A soft answer turneth away wrath . . .

Then there is:

Proverbs 16:18. *Pride goeth before destruction, and an haughty spirit before a fall.*

which is almost universally condensed to "Pride goes before a fall."

Agur

The thirtieth chapter of the book begins with a completely obscure line; at least in the King James Version:

Proverbs 30:1. *The words of Agur the son of Jakeh, even the prophecy: the man spake unto Ithiel, even unto Ithiel and Ucal.*

The phrase "even the prophecy" seems to be the translation of the Hebrew word *massa* and, apparently, this should not be translated, for it is meant here as the name of a locality. The first line should speak of "Agur the son of Jakeh of Massa."

In the Book of Genesis, Massa is mentioned in the genealogical tables:

Genesis 25:13. . . . *the sons of Ishmael . . .*
Genesis 25:14. *And Mishma, and Dumah, and Massa,*

Massa might therefore be assumed to be found in Ishmaelite territory in northern Arabia.

The reference to Ithiel and Ucal makes no sense as such, for these do not seem to be proper names. The Anchor Bible translates the verse as: "The words of Agur ben Jakeh of Massa. The man solemnly affirmed, 'There is no God! There is no God, and I can[not know anything].'"

It would seem, then, that the verse in question describes the statement of an agnostic, which the chapter then goes on to counter.

Lemuel

The first half of the last chapter of Proverbs is assigned to a king other than Solomon; or at least, it appears to be:

Proverbs 31:1. *The words of king Lemuel, the prophecy that his mother taught him.*

Here again "prophecy" might be an unnecessary translation of a place name, and the Revised Standard Version has it: "The words of Lemuel, king of Massa."

There has been some tendency in the past to assume that Lemuel was another name for Solomon, but this is not at all likely. In fact, the Anchor Bible wipes out Lemuel altogether by supposing it to be a copyist's error for a very similar Hebrew word which, when translated, would make the first verse, "Words [of advice] to a king acting foolishly, A solemn injunction which his mother lays on him:"

The last half of this last chapter consists of an acrostic poem in praise of the industrious housewife that begins with the well-known:

Proverbs 31:10. *Who can find a virtuous woman? for her price is far above rubies.*

THE PREACHER * VANITY * THE WISDOM OF SOLOMON

The Preacher

Following the Book of Proverbs is a second item
heading of "wisdom literature." This begins:

Ecclesiastes 1:1. *The words of the Preacher*

"Preacher" is a translation of the Hebrew word *ko*
uncertain meaning. Usually, it is associated with
meaning "an open assembly," so that *koheleth* m
convenes such an assembly or addresses it. If the as
together for the purpose of religious instruction,
would be a preacher.

The Greek word for an assembly is *ekklesia* and
it would be *ekklesiastes*. In Latin spelling that is *eccl*
the title to the book.

The Preacher announces his identity as:

Ecclesiastes 1:1. *The words of the Preacher, the*
in Jerusalem.

This seems to be a clear indication that it is Sol
has often been taken as such. However, this is m
ascription of almost any piece of wisdom literature
ally, the book seems to be post-Exilic and to have b
best guess, between 300 and 200 B.C.

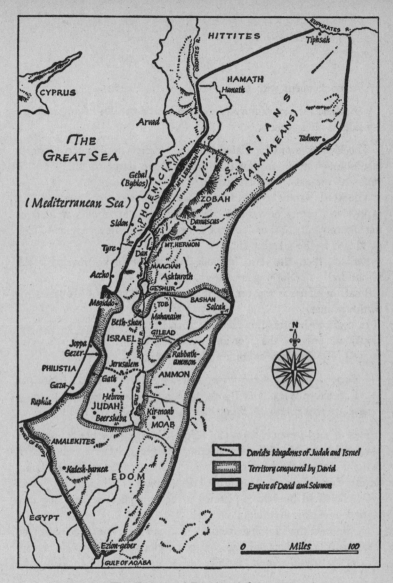

The Empire of David and Solomon

Vanity

The book opens with the author's general thesis:

Ecclesiastes 1:2. *Vanity of vanities, saith the Preacher, vanity of vanities; all is vanity.*

The Hebrew word translated here as "vanity" implies something as insubstantial as air, so that the Anchor Bible translates the verse "A vapor of vapors! . . . All is vapor."

The word "vanity" comes from a Latin term meaning "empty." The expression "vanity of vanities" in Hebrew idiom implies a kind of maximum vanity, just as "song of songs" is the greatest song and "king of kings" is the greatest king.

Perhaps, then, the verse, in modern terms, could be translated "All is nothing . . . Nothing means anything."

That, in effect, is the central thesis of the book—the emptiness of earthly things.

In order to impress this fact, the Preacher maintained that life was empty not only for the poor and weak, but for the rich and powerful as well. He therefore continues his role as king.

Ecclesiastes 1:12. *I the Preacher was king over Israel in Jerusalem.*
Ecclesiastes 1:13. *And I gave my heart to seek and search out by wisdom concerning all things that are done under heaven . . .*

Here it seems even clearer than before that the Preacher is impersonating Solomon. Yet this impersonation continues only through the first two chapters of the book and it would appear to be merely a literary device. Even the most magnificent and happiest of all kings (in Jewish eyes), Solomon himself, is pictured as being unable, in the long run, to find anything meaningful in life.

In the end the Preacher feels all that can be done is to seize the temporary and ephemeral joys that come along and to remain unconcerned for anything more lasting:

Ecclesiastes 8:15. . . . *a man hath no better thing under the sun, than to eat, and to drink, and to be merry . . .*

And in the end he returns to his original thesis:

Ecclesiastes 12:8. *Vanity of vanities, saith the preacher, all is vanity.*

Another writer, apparently appalled at the pessimism of the Preacher, added an addendum to the book; an addendum which came to be included in the canon. Its nub is:

Ecclesiastes 12:13. . . . *Fear God, and keep his commandments* . . .

The Wisdom of Solomon

Not all wisdom literature succeeded in being admitted to the Jewish canon, even though ascribed to Solomon. This happened when the books supposedly written by Solomon were actually composed after the approximate cutoff date of 150 B.C. A case in point is that of a book apparently written by an Alexandrian Jew sometime between 100 and 50 B.C.

The writer, himself unknown, assumes the personality of Solomon in order to dramatize his praise of a personified Wisdom. For this reason the book is known as "The Wisdom of Solomon."

The author's personification of Solomon is clearest in the seventh chapter:

Wisdom of Solomon 7:7. *Wherefore I prayed, and understanding was given me: I called upon God, and the spirit of wisdom came to me.*

This clearly refers back to the passage in the First Book of Kings in which Solomon is described as seeing God in a dream and being offered anything he wishes. Solomon, in the dream, replies:

1 Kings 3:9. *Give . . . thy servant an understanding heart to judge thy people, that I may discern between good and bad . . .*

Since Solomon is, however, certainly *not* the author, this apocryphal book is often called more appropriately "The Book of Wisdom" and it is by that name that it appears in the Catholic versions of the Bible.

Ecclesiasticus

Another piece of wisdom literature is notable for bearing within it the name of the author, speaking in his own right and making no attempt to ascribe his words to an ancient worthy.

> Ecclesiasticus 50:27. *Jesus the son of Sirach of Jerusalem hath written in this book the instruction of understanding and knowledge.*

For this reason, the title of the book is given as "Wisdom of Jesus, Son of Sirach." The name is here presented in Greek form. In Hebrew it would be "Joshua ben Sira." This book was composed too late to qualify for the Jewish canon and was consigned to the Apocrypha. It is, however, to be found in the Catholic version of the Bible.

Because of the high caliber of its ethical teachings, the book was much used as a source of texts for sermons and was closely associated with churchly preaching from quite early times. Cyprian, the bishop of Carthage, took to calling this book "Ecclesiasticus" ("the church book") as early as A.D. 250 and the custom has continued ever since.

Something about the date at which the book was written may be deduced from a reference toward the end of the book. The writer begins

> Ecclesiasticus 44:1. *Let us now praise famous men, and our fathers that begat us.*

He goes on to call the list of notables from Biblical history: Enoch, Noah, Abraham, Isaac, Jacob, Moses, Aaron, Phinehas, Joshua, Caleb, Samuel, Nathan, David, Solomon, Elijah, Elisha, Hezekiah, Isaiah, Josiah, Jeremiah, Ezekiel, Zerubbabel, and Nehemiah.

Having gone through the list, he then proceeds to reach a natural climax by praising a recent spiritual leader of the people—carrying his brief review of history to what was then the contemporary era:

> Ecclesiasticus 50:1. *Simon the high priest, the son of Onias, who in his life repaired the house again, and in his days fortified the temple:*

The trouble is that there were two High Priests by the name of Simon in the early Greek era. The first, whom we might call Simon I, was High Priest about 300 B.C., while the second, Simon II, was High

Priest about 200 B.C. What's more, both had fathers who were named Onias. It is much more likely, though, that Simon II is the one being referred to, for if the book had been written in 300 B.C. or shortly thereafter it would, very likely, have entered the canon.

Backing this view is a reference in the preface to the book—

Ecclesiasticus was originally written in Hebrew. This Hebrew version was lost and, throughout Christian times, the book was known only in Greek and Aramaic, and in translations from manuscripts in those languages. The fact that the Hebrew version did exist, however, was assumed from the statement of a grandson of the writer. He came to Egypt, where the Jews spoke Greek, and in a preface that is usually included with the book, he explains (with becoming modesty) that he labored to prepare a Greek translation from the Hebrew. As for his time of arrival in Egypt, that was "in the eight and thirtieth year . . . when Euergetes was king."

The thirteen Macedonian kings of Egypt, who ruled from 305 to 44 B.C., each took the name Ptolemy, but each added a second name (or had it added by sycophantic courtiers), usually of self-praise. The name "Euergetes" means "benefactor," for instance. There were two Ptolemies so named. One was Ptolemy III, who reigned from 246 to 221 B.C., and the other was Ptolemy VII, who reigned from 145 to 116 B.C. The former reigned twenty-five years and the latter reigned twenty-nine years, so that neither could be said to have an "eight and thirtieth year."

In the case of Ptolemy VII, however, the 145 to 116 B.C. stretch covers only the period in which he was sole ruler. His older brother had begun to rule in 181 B.C. as Ptolemy VI but his record was wretched. In 170 B.C., he had shown himself so incompetent a war leader that public opinion forced him to associate his younger brother with him on the throne. Ptolemy VII might therefore be said to have begun to reign in 170 B.C. and his "eight and thirtieth year" would then be about 132 B.C.

If we assume the translator's grandfather to have written the book half a century before, that would make the date of Ecclesiasticus about 180 B.C.

The existence of a Hebrew version of Ecclesiasticus was confirmed in 1896 when portions of Hebrew manuscripts were found which contained about two thirds of the book. Still older scraps of Ecclesiasticus were found among the Dead Sea Scrolls.

SOLOMON * EN-GEDI * SHARON * THE VOICE OF THE TURTLE * TIRZAH * SHULAMITE

Solomon

The third of the canonical books to be attributed to Solomon is The Song of Solomon. Its first verse is its title:

> Song of Solomon 1:1. *The song of songs, which is Solomon's.*

By "song of songs" the Hebrew idiom expresses a maximum. It is the best or most beautiful song to have been written by Solomon. In the Catholic version of the Bible, the book is known as "The Canticle of Canticles," from the Latin title "Canticum Canticorum" ("Song of Songs"). The Hebrew title is "Shir Ha-shirim," also meaning "Song of Songs."

As in the case of Ecclesiastes, the author of this book is surely not Solomon. The book is post-Exilic and seems to have been written about 300 B.C. or even later. It is attributed to Solomon because of the latter's traditional literary ability:

> 1 Kings 4:32. *And he [Solomon] spake three thousand proverbs: and his songs were a thousand and five.*

The Song of Solomon is a love poem, frankly erotic, apparently composed to celebrate a wedding. This, too, is appropriate, for Solomon had numerous wives and was, presumably, an experienced lover:

> 1 Kings 11:3. . . . *he had seven hundred wives . . . and three hundred concubines . . .*

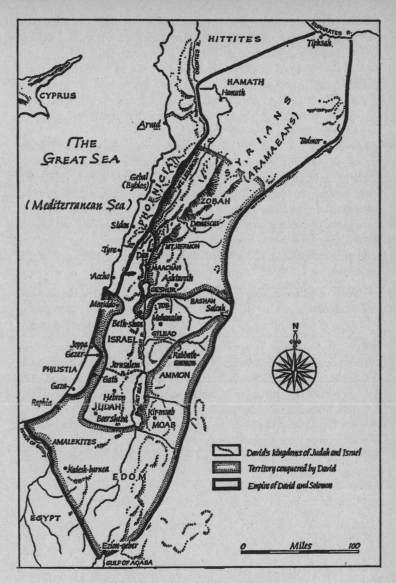

The Empire of David and Solomon

Because of the erotic nature of the book, it has been customary to find allegorical values in it that would make more of it than a description of bodily passion. In the guise of the portrayal of the love of a man and a woman, Jews would have it speak of the love between Yahveh and Israel; Catholics of the love between Christ and the Church; Protestants of the love between God and man's soul.

However, if we simply accept the words as they stand, the book is a human love poem and a very beautiful one.

Interpreting the book literally, it would seem to be a kind of poetic drama, in which a number of different characters speak: the bridegroom, the bride, a chorus of women, and perhaps others. Since the book, as it appears in the Bible, gives no hint as to when one character stops speaking and another starts, or which character says what, the sorting out of the speeches presents a difficult problem but one which, fortunately, need not concern us.

Some speeches are, of course, transparent enough. Surely, it is the bride who says:

> Song of Solomon 1:5. *I am black, but comely . . . as the curtains of Solomon.*
> Song of Solomon 1:6. . . . *I am black, because the sun has looked upon me . . .*

The adjective "black" does not mean that the bride is a Negress for the blackness is the result of exposure to the sun. She is tanned. The Revised Standard Version has the fifth verse read "I am very dark," and the sixth verse, "I am swarthy."

There might be a tendency to think of her as the Egyptian princess who married Solomon, since she might be expected to be dark in coloring. Or else it might be the queen of Sheba; a swarthy Arabian woman. Yet that is only forced upon us if we imagine the poem to be written literally by or about Solomon. Viewed simply as a love poem in the tradition of Solomon, the bride is probably a peasant girl:

> Song of Solomon 1:6. . . . *my mother's children . . . made me the keeper of the vineyards . . .*

En-gedi

The bride speaks of her lover:

Song of Solomon 1:14. *My beloved is unto me as a cluster of camphire in the vineyards of En-gedi.*

En-gedi is a site midway along the western shores of the Dead Sea. It would seem an unlikely place for anything but desolation, yet it is an oasis, thanks to the presence of natural spring water. The name "En-gedi" means "spring of the kid." The site was famous in Jewish history as one of the places in which David found refuge from the pursuing Saul:

1 Samuel 23:29. *And David . . . dwelt in strongholds at En-gedi.*

The expression "camphire," by the way, is a transliteration of the Hebrew *kopher.* By it is meant henna, a shrub with fragrant white flowers. The Revised Standard Version translates it "My beloved is to me a cluster of henna blossoms."

Sharon

The bride describes herself again:

Song of Solomon 2:1. *I am the rose of Sharon, and the lily of the valleys.*

Sharon is a coastal plain lying between Jaffa and Mount Carmel, about fifty miles long and six to twelve miles wide. It doesn't figure often in the Bible for through much of Biblical history it was occupied by the Phoenician and Philistine power.

It passed into Israelite hands under David. He owned flocks of cattle that grazed there under a native herdsman:

1 Chronicles 27:29. *And over the herds that fed in Sharon was Shitrai the Sharonite . . .*

The Voice of the Turtle

The Song of Solomon is full of beautiful nature imagery but one image rings false in modern ears through no fault of its own. The bride describes her beloved as pleading with her to come with him for it is springtime:

Song of Solomon 2:12. *The flowers appear on the earth; the time of the singing of birds is come, and the voice of the turtle is heard in our land.*

The phrase "voice of the turtle" seems odd, for to us the turtle is an ugly, slow-moving, shelled reptile that is voiceless, that is not associated with spring and that certainly doesn't bear association with the beauties of flowers and birds.

It is we, however, who are wrong, and not the verse. There is a type of bird we call a dove, deriving that name from an old Teutonic word that may make reference to its dull, rather dark plumage. It makes a cooing sound which to some ears may sound like tur-tur-tur-tur. The Hebrew word for it, imitating this sound, is *tur*, and the Latin word is *turtur*. By substituting "l" for "r" at the end, this becomes "turtle." The "voice of the turtle" refers to the cooing of this migratory dove which reaches Jerusalem in the springtime.

However, there is also the shelled reptile earlier mentioned. This is called a tortoise, perhaps (but not certainly) from a Latin word meaning "crooked" because of its curved legs. To the ears of English-speaking sailors, "tortoise" seemed an odd-sounding word and they substituted for it the more familiar "turtle," thus giving the ugly reptile the name of a pleasant bird.

In order to distinguish the bird from the reptile, it became necessary to call the bird a "turtledove." It is so spoken of elsewhere in the King James Version, but not here in the Song of Solomon. The Revised Standard Version removes the apparent anomaly by having the clause read "and the voice of the turtledove is heard in our land."

Tirzah

The pangs of love temporarily lost and the thrills of love regained are described and at one point the bridegroom says to the bride:

Song of Solomon 6:4. *Thou art beautiful, O my love, as Tirzah, comely as Jerusalem . . .*

The parallelism of Hebrew poetry forces the writer to seek a synonym or analogy for Jerusalem. He might have used Zion, but was searching for something less routine, perhaps, and chose Tirzah. As Jerusalem was the capital of the southern kingdom, so Tirzah was the capital of the northern kingdom from the time of Jeroboam I to Omri, about 900 to 880 B.C. (see page 339). This is an indication that the poem had to be written after the time of Solomon, for Tirzah was in no way analogous to Jerusalem in the reign of a king ruling over a united kingdom.

On the other hand, we cannot use this verse as evidence that the poem was necessarily written before the time of Omri, when Samaria displaced Tirzah as the capital of Israel. To have made use of Samaria as an analogue of Jerusalem in post-Exilic times would have seemed blasphemous for by then Samaria was the center of the hated and heretical Samaritans. The writer was thus forced to reach back beyond Samaria to Tirzah, which had no impossible associations.

Shulamite

The bride is addressed by her native town, either by the bridegroom or by a chorus:

Song of Solomon 6:13. *Return, return, O Shulamite . . .*

It is usually supposed that Shulamite is a copyist's error for Shunammite, a woman of the town of Shunam, which is about three miles north of Jezreel.

Finally the book reaches its climax in a passionate declaration of the strength of true love:

Song of Solomon 8:7. *Many waters cannot quench love, neither can the floods drown it: if a man would give all the substance of his house for love, it would utterly be contemned.*

In other words, love cannot be destroyed if present; but cannot be bought if absent.

23. ISAIAH

ISAIAH * AMOZ * SERAPHIM * SHEAR-JASHUB * IMMANUEL * THE BRANCH *
COCKATRICE * LUCIFER * APOCALYPSE OF ISAIAH * ARIEL * LILITH * THE
MARTYRDOM OF ISAIAH * SECOND ISAIAH * CYRUS * THE SERVANT OF THE
LORD * BEL * BEULAH

Isaiah

The Old Testament books that follow the Song of Solomon in the Christian versions of the Bible record the work of sixteen named prophets who were supposed to have flourished during the three-century period from 750 to 450 B.C.

These books are not placed entirely in chronological order. They are divided into two sections on the basis of length. Fully two thirds of the material in these prophetic books is to be found in the first three, dealing with the prophets Isaiah, Jeremiah, and Ezekiel. These are the "major prophets" and they, at least, are placed in chronological order. The Book of Isaiah, dealing with the period of Assyrian ascendancy, comes first.

From a strictly historical and secular viewpoint the Book of Isaiah presents many confusions. Isaiah is not likely to have systematically written down his utterances. Rather, his sayings were, presumably, written down by his disciples and followers, with what changes and additions we can only guess. These made up separate collections which some later editor put together, not necessarily in chronological order but rather in that order which he thought would produce the greatest effect.

What's more, as time passed, additional material was added to the book and made to seem the product of Isaiah. The later portions of the book are certainly not Isaiah's work but are the product of a man (possibly two men) living centuries later. The Book of Isaiah may not

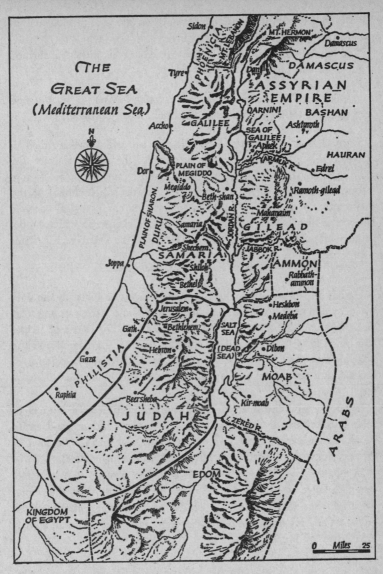

Judah in the Time of Hezekiah

have been put into its present form until as late as 350 B.C., or well over three centuries after Isaiah's death.

The general period in which Isaiah carried out his prophetic mission is given in the first verse of the book:

> Isaiah 1:1. *The vision of Isaiah . . . which he saw . . . in the days of Uzziah, Jotham, Ahaz, and Hezekiah, kings of Judah.*

Since Uzziah came to the throne in 780 B.C. and Hezekiah died in 692 B.C., this at once makes Isaiah a man of the eighth century B.C.

For the actual year of the beginning of his mission, there is more information later in the sixth chapter, a chapter which should, if the final editors of the book had been following a chronological scheme, have come first. Isaiah recounts the miraculous manner in which he became a prophet, and begins his description of the event with a date:

> Isaiah 6:1. *In the year that king Uzziah died . . .*

Uzziah died in 740 B.C. and that, therefore, can be taken as the date when Isaiah began his work. Presumably, he was a relatively young man at the time, for he was still active during Sennacherib's siege of Jerusalem nearly forty years later. If we consider Isaiah to have been a young man of twenty when he saw his vision, he would have been born in 760 B.C. at a time when the fortunes of Israel and Judah were flourishing.

In 760 B.C. Jeroboam II of Israel had extended Israel's borders to their broadest extent since the time of Solomon, and under Uzziah, Judah, too, was prosperous and content (see page 423). The men of the kingdoms must have been contented, foreseeing no evil.

In 745 B.C., however, Jeroboam II died and almost at once Israel began to fall prey to dynastic disorders. In that same year, the strong Tiglath-Pileser III became king of Assyria, and that nation entered on its last and mightiest period of aggression. Israel had less than a quarter century of life left it.

Apparently, Isaiah could clearly see, by 740 B.C., that the good days were gone and the evil times had come and he said so in the manner made necessary by the way of thought of the time. He announced the judgment of Yahveh upon a sinful people.

Amoz

The name of Isaiah's father is given:

Isaiah 1:1 *The vision of Isaiah the son of Amoz* . . .

Absolutely nothing is known concerning Amoz, for he is not mentioned in the Bible except as the father of Isaiah in this verse and in a few others like it. He is to be carefully distinguished from Amos, a prophet who was an older contemporary of Isaiah. (The two names, Amoz and Amos, are less similar in Hebrew than in English.)

There is a rabbinic tradition (based on no more, perhaps, than a similarity in names) that Amoz was a brother of king Amaziah, who was Uzziah's father. If this were so, Isaiah would be a member of the royal family and a first cousin to king Uzziah. He and Uzziah would both be grandsons of Joash, who had been saved as an infant in Athaliah's time (see page 367).

If so, Isaiah is rather unusual, for it would seem natural for prophets of his sort to have been drawn from among the poor, since the prophets were spokesmen of protest. The prophets were, generally, the radicals of their day, frequently standing in opposition to the formal priesthood, which (as long as their prerogatives were preserved) acted in coalition with the monarchy.

The priesthood then, as always, was primarily interested in the minutiae of ritual. This was something that could easily be followed by anyone and generally presented no difficulties. It might be a tedious way of gaining God's favor, but it was not really painful.

The prophets, however, were likely to disdain ritual and to insist, instead, on a high ethical code of behavior, something that could present serious difficulties. After all, it is not only often difficult to perform the ethical good; it is sometimes puzzling to determine what the ethical good might be.

Isaiah, himself, put it this way:

Isaiah 1:11. *To what purpose is the multitude of your sacrifices unto me? saith the Lord* . . .

. . . .

Isaiah 1:13. *Bring no more vain oblations; incense is an abomination to me . . .*

Isaiah 1:14. *Your new moons and your appointed feasts my soul hateth . . .*

. . . .

Isaiah 1:16. *Wash you, make you clean; put away the evil of your doings . . .*

Isaiah 1:17. *Learn to do well; seek judgement, relieve the oppressed, judge the fatherless, plead for the widow.*

Furthermore, there was a tendency for the prophets to denounce the rich and powerful, for these were apt to be the most worldly, most satisfied to let ritual (if anything) serve as religion. Isaiah speaks against the tendency of these rich to squeeze out the poor farmer and to multiply their own holdings, polarizing society into a few large land-owners and many tenant farmers or slaves. (This is a development that tends to affect societies generally, and not ancient Judah alone.) Isaiah says:

Isaiah 5:8. *Woe unto them that join house to house, that lay field to field, till there be no place, that they may be placed alone in the midst of the earth.*

And yet scholars judge from Isaiah's style of writing that he did indeed belong to the upper classes and certainly there are cases in history where aristocrats have lived and fought on behalf of the dispossessed of the world and against, as the saying has it, their own class. The example of the Russian novelist Count Leo Tolstoy springs to mind, for instance.

Seraphim

Isaiah describes his call in terms of a vision of God experienced by him within the Temple:

Isaiah 6:1. *In the year that king Uzziah died I saw also the Lord sitting upon a throne, high and lifted up, and his train filled the temple.*

Isaiah 6:2. *Above it stood the seraphims: each one had six wings;*

with twain he covered his face, and with twain he covered his feet, and with twain he did fly.

Isaiah 6:3. *And one cried unto another and said, Holy, holy, holy, is the Lord of hosts: the whole earth is full of his glory.*

"Seraphim" is the Hebrew plural of *seraph,* so that the word "seraphims" in the King James Version is a double plural, the English form grafted on to the Hebrew. In the Revised Standard Version, the final "s" is dropped.

The seraphim are mentioned only here in the Bible, and they are taken to be winged manlike creatures rather similar to the cherubs described in connection with other visions of God.

In later times, the seraphim were included among the complicated celestial hierarchy worked out by mystical writers. The best-known such hierarchy was produced about A.D. 450, perhaps, by an unknown writer whose work was ascribed to an earlier worthy named Dionysius the Areopagite, and who is himself referred to, in consequence, as the "pseudo-Dionysius."

According to the system of the pseudo-Dionysius there were nine classifications of beings between man and God and of these the angels were lowest and archangels next to the lowest. Above these, in order, came principalities, powers, virtues, dominations, thrones, cherubim, and seraphim. Because the cherubim and seraphim were described in prophetic visions as being in immediate attendance upon God, they naturally rated highest.

In our present age, less wedded to such speculation, a seraph has become merely another word for an angel.

The word "seraph" is related to the Hebrew word *saraph,* meaning "to burn." The seraphim may therefore be spoken of in English as "the Burning Ones." This may refer to the gleaming radiance issuing from them, or the burning ardor with which they serve God.

On the other hand, the word is used elsewhere in the Bible, where it refers not to angelic beings but to "fiery serpents" (as the word is then translated), the adjective presumably referring to the agonizing burning of their poisonous bite.

Numbers 21:6. *And the Lord sent fiery serpents among the people . . .*

If the image of a "fiery serpent" is taken literally, one can scarcely avoid thinking of the lightning. If the earliest view of Yahveh was that of a storm-god, as one would suspect from the Song of Deborah (see page 239) and some of the Psalms (see page 494) then it is thoroughly natural that His manifestation be accompanied by a fearsome display of lightning and by the scudding of the dark storm blast.

By the time of the prophets, however, the lightning had apparently been personified into the winged seraphim, as the storm blast had become the cherubim (see page 494).

Shear-jashub

Already, as Isaiah had received his call, the times were growing manifestly turbulent. Israel and Syria were attempting to organize a coalition against the power of Assyria. When Jotham, who had succeeded Uzziah to the throne of Judah, preferred to remain outside the coalition (judging, rightly, that it was doomed to disastrous failure), the allied forces of Israel and Syria invaded Judah (see page 374). The war continued through 735 B.C., when Jotham died and his son Ahaz succeeded to the throne.

The new king, young and irresolute, required strengthening:

Isaiah 7:3. *Then said the Lord unto Isaiah, Go forth now to meet Ahaz, thou, and Shear-jashub thy son . . .*

The fact that Isaiah could, on a moment's notice, approach the king is usually taken as another indication of his position in the royal family.

Shear-jashub, the name of Isaiah's son, was chosen deliberately by the father for its meaning in connection with the prophetic message. Isaiah says as much:

Isaiah 8:18. *. . . the children whom the Lord hath given me are for signs . . . from the Lord . . .*

The meaning of "Shear-jashub" is "a remnant shall return." This reflects the feeling, common to Isaiah and the prophets generally, that an evil time at hand was to be succeeded eventually by better times. If the nation is left desolate and the population carried off into exile, nevertheless "a remnant shall return" and the nation shall live again.

Perhaps Isaiah's son was born shortly after the prophet's call and was four or five years old at the time of the meeting with Ahaz.

Immanuel

Isaiah assures Ahaz that he need not fear Israel or Syria, for destruction is almost upon them. All Judah need do is to hold out resolutely.

Viewed secularly, we can see reason behind Isaiah's point of view. The energetic Tiglath-Pileser of Assyria must have known that Israel and Syria were attempting to establish a coalition against him and it was certain that he would attack the coalition before they could complete their plans. It was also certain that Assyria would smash the small western nations. Judah, for its safety, need only remain neutral and wait.

Ahaz, however, did not feel it safe to do nothing but hold on. Neutrality in times of great conflict laid one open to the enmity of both sides and Tiglath-Pileser, even if victorious, might consider Judah's neutrality to be a sign of secret enmity. Ahaz felt it politically wise to declare himself on the Assyrian side and accept Assyrian overlordship.

This Isaiah opposed vehemently. He may well have felt that Assyrian overlordship would mean the ascendancy of Assyrian religious practices and the persecution of the nationalistic Yahvists (as in fact came to pass a half century later in the reign of Manasseh) and he argued hard for a go-it-alone policy, promising God's help.

> Isaiah 7:11. *Ask thee a sign of the Lord . . .*
> Isaiah 7:12. *But Ahaz said, I will not ask, neither will I tempt the Lord.*

The word "tempt" is translated as "test" in the Revised Standard Version. Ahaz, in refusing to ask God to meet some test, is technically correct since the Bible on more than one occasion makes it plain that it is not for man to imagine he can make God jump through hoops on demand. Besides, Ahaz has undoubtedly made up his mind and is anxious to end the interview.

Isaiah is annoyed, however, and proceeds to advance a sign anyway:

> Isaiah 7:14. . . . *Behold, a virgin shall conceive, and bear a son, and shall call his name Immanuel.*
>
> . . . .
>
> Isaiah 7:16. . . . *before the child shall know to refuse the evil, and choose the good, the land thou abhorrest shall be forsaken of both her kings.*

In other words, in two or three years, before the time when a child, born in the near future, becomes old enough to exert even the simplest judgment, the attacking kings shall be defeated. And if this happens, Ahaz will be forced to realize that Isaiah sees clearly and speaks truly. (And, indeed, three years later, in 732 B.C., Tiglath-Pileser III took Damascus, executed the Syrian king and permanently destroyed the Syrian kingdom, while Israel, rendered powerless, was allowed a limping life for ten more years; see page 375.)

The most interesting part of Isaiah's "sign," however, is the identity of the child who was to be called Immanuel.

To Christians generally, this is a reference to the virgin birth of Jesus, but that rests, of course, upon the word translated in the King James Version as "virgin." In the Hebrew, the word so translated is *almah* and this is actually used to refer to a young woman who might or might not be a virgin. The Hebrew language has a specific word (*bethulah*) for "virgin" but that is not used here. The Revised Standard Version therefore translates Isaiah 7:14 as "Behold, a young woman shall conceive and bear a son . . ."

But let us leave the Messianic aspect of the verse to one side. Whatever the merits or demerits of the traditional Christian interpretation of the verse, it must have a more immediate meaning. Isaiah could scarcely offer to Ahaz, as a sign for the present predicament, the birth of a child more than seven centuries later.

But what child of his own time can Isaiah be referring to? The name Immanuel means "God is with us" and this has symbolic meaning in connection with Isaiah's message of the moment. God is with Judah and will not allow it to be destroyed by Syria and Israel. No child named Immanuel is, however, recorded as having been born in that period of history, or anywhere in the Bible, for that matter. Still, if the name is symbolic, any other name of equal symbolism might do.

Sometimes it is suggested that the reference may be to Ahaz's own son, Hezekiah, who was to come to the throne eventually. Since he was to be one of the three great Yahvistic kings of Judah (the other two being Jehoshaphat and Josiah) later interpreters tended to apply flattering verses to him. However, Hezekiah became king in 720 B.C. and was already an adult at that time:

2 Kings 18:1. . . . *Hezekiah the son of Ahaz . . . began to reign.*
2 Kings 18:2. *Twenty and five years old was he when he began to reign . . .*

This means he was born in 745 B.C. and at the time of the interview between Ahaz and Isaiah must have been ten years old and had already reached an age at which he was capable of making judgments. Hezekiah is not, therefore, a reasonable choice for Immanuel.

Indeed, if we seek for the simplest and most straightforward solution to the problem, what seems more likely than that Isaiah's reference to a young woman is a reference to his own wife. (Isaiah was only twenty-five at the time and his wife may well have been little more than twenty.) In fact, immediately after the description of the meeting with Ahaz, Isaiah records the birth of a second son:

Isaiah 8:3. . . . *Then said the Lord to me, Call his name Maher-shalal-hash-baz.*
Isaiah 8:4. *For before the child shall have knowledge to cry, My father, and my mother, the riches of Damascus and the spoil of Samaria shall be taken away before the king of Assyria.*

The name "Maher-shalal-hash-baz" means "haste-spoil, speed-booty." The reference is to Syria and Israel, which are hastening onward to become spoil and booty for the Assyrians. And before the child is old enough to say "mama," the end will come for the northern kingdoms.

Thus, Isaiah says precisely the same things for the predicted child Immanuel and for the actual child Maher-shalal-hash-baz. The names are the obverse sides of the coin for Immanuel refers to Judah's good fortune and Maher-shalal-hash-baz to Syria's and to Israel's bad fortune. The names are different but the symbolism is the same and that is what counts.

It seems perfectly reasonable, then, to suppose Isaiah's own son is the predicted Immanuel.

Nevertheless, Ahaz followed his own judgment as to the proper course and became tributary to Assyria. Isaiah had failed to swing the king to the Yahvist way of thinking, and nothing is heard of the prophet in connection with specific political events until the Assyrian siege of Jerusalem a generation later.

The Branch

Some of the writings in the Book of Isaiah expand the prophet's notion that after some disaster of the future, a remnant of the faithful would return and build anew. This remnant, purged of the sins that brought about the disaster, would be ruled by an ideal king:

> Isaiah 9:6. *For unto us a child is born, unto us a son is given; and the government shall be upon his shoulder: and his name shall be called Wonderful, Counseller, The mighty God, The everlasting Father, The Prince of Peace.*
> Isaiah 9:7. *Of the increase of his government and peace there shall be no end . . .*

It may be that such rhapsodic praises of an ideal king might have grown out of odes written in honor of a coronation. In Isaiah's time, such praises might have been sung in honor of Hezekiah's coming to the throne in 720 B.C. The phrase "unto us a child is born, unto us a son is given" would refer to the coronation process by which a king becomes an adopted son of the national god (see page 490). The flattering names given the king and the promise of a reign of perfect happiness would be the lavish poetic license usually taken on such an occasion.

Or, alternatively, the ode might have been written in honor of Josiah, who ascended the throne nearly a century later, in 638 B.C. The ode might then, because of its poetic beauty, have been placed within the Isaianic collection.

However, even if the verses originally referred to a specific king such as Hezekiah or Josiah, the later Jews could not have been satisfied to read no further meaning into them. Neither Hezekiah nor Josiah had had truly successful reigns. Hezekiah had survived the siege of Jerusalem but only just barely and Judah had been devastated. Josiah died in battle and a generation after his death, the Jewish kingdom was destroyed.

More and more, therefore, the references were taken to stand for some ideal king who had not yet arisen, who was to come at some vague time in the future.

The king, of course, would be of the Davidic dynasty; nothing else seemed possible for only the line of David had ever ruled over Judah, and it had been promised eternal kingship in the Bible:

> Isaiah 11:1. *And there shall come forth a rod out of the stem of Jesse, and a Branch shall grow out of his roots:*
> Isaiah 11:2. *And the spirit of the Lord shall rest upon him . . .*

Again this might be the routine flattery applied to a new king such as Hezekiah or Josiah. The new king is always a flourishing new growth; the old king always a decayed old one. If, however, the reference is shifted to an ideal king of the future, the Davidic dynasty might be viewed as cut down (a stem, or more properly translated, a stump, is all that is left) and a new and flourishing growth arises out of it.

In the reign of the ideal king all of creation is restored to the kind of absolute peace one might envision as having originally been found in the garden of Eden:

> Isaiah 11:6. *The wolf also shall dwell with the lamb, and the leopard shall lie down with the kid; and the calf and the young lion and the fatling together; and a little child shall lead them.*

Another such glowing picture of an ideal future, and one even more frequently quoted, occurs near the beginning of the Book of Isaiah:

> Isaiah 2:2. *And it shall come to pass in the last days, that the mountain of the Lord's house shall be . . . exalted . . . and all nations shall flow into it.*
>
> . . . .
>
> Isaiah 2:4. *. . . and they shall beat their swords into plowshares and their spears into pruninghooks: nation shall not lift up sword against nation, neither shall they learn war any more.*

This vision of an ideal future may have begun to grow before the eyes of Jews despondent over the reality of a triumphant Assyria in Isaiah's time. It grew stronger as the disasters of the Babylonian Exile, the disappointments of the return from exile, and the horrors of the

Seleucid persecution overtook the Jews. By New Testament times, this orientation to the future had become the dominant note in Judaism and was, indeed, responsible for the events of the New Testament and for the great turning point in human history heralded by those events.

The ideal future centered about the king of David's line who was to arise. Kings are anointed with oil as part of the religious ceremony that makes them king. Therefore kings can be referred to as "the anointed" and are indeed so referred to in the Bible. Thus, when David had come upon Saul sleeping and had cut off a portion of Saul's robe, his conscience forbade him to do more, although self-interest alone might have counseled a quick assassination:

> 1 Samuel 24:6. . . . the Lord forbid that I should . . . stretch forth mine hand against him, seeing he is the anointed of the Lord.

Nor need the term be restricted to kings anointed according to Yahvistic ritual. Cyrus of Persia is referred to in this manner in the later portions of the Book of Isaiah:

> Isaiah 45:1. Thus saith the Lord to his anointed, to Cyrus . . .

The Hebrew word for "anointed" is mashiakh, which is given in transliterated English as "messiah." More and more, as time passed, and as the Jewish vision was fixed with increasing fervor on the ideal king of the future, the term was confined to him. We can therefore speak of the ideal king as (with a capital) the Messiah.

According to Christian thought, of course, the Messiah is Jesus, and the word "Branch" in Isaiah 11:1 is taken as a reference to Jesus and is therefore capitalized in the King James Version. In the Revised Standard Version, the word is not capitalized.

Cockatrice

In the description of the ideal Messianic kingdom, several ways of indicating the total absence of danger or harm are to be found. In each, the trick is to combine the utterly helpless with the completely harmful. The climax is reached when infants are mingled with serpents.

> Isaiah 11:8. And the sucking child shall play on the hole of the asp, and the weaned child shall put his hand on the cockatrice' den.

The two parts of the verse contain the parallelism that is the essence of Hebrew poetry, and it may be taken that the Hebrew words translated as "asp" and as "cockatrice" both signify some venomous serpent. The asp is, indeed, a small poisonous snake found in Egypt. (Cleopatra was supposed to have committed suicide by allowing an asp to bite her.)

The cockatrice, however, is something else again. The word may have originated in medieval times as a form of "crocodile." The crocodile, like the serpent, is a deadly reptile. It might almost be viewed as a gigantic, thick snake, with stubby legs. To Europeans, unfamiliar with the crocodile except by distant report, the snaky aspects of the creature could easily become dominant.

Moreover, once "cockatrice" is formed from "crocodile," the first syllable is suggestive, and the fevered imagination develops the thought that the monster originates in a cock's egg. This is itself a monstrous perversion of nature for, of course, cocks are male birds that do not lay eggs. The egg, thus perversely laid, must, moreover, be hatched by a serpent, and the product, then, is a creature with a snake's body and a cock's head.

The cockatrice is pictured as the ultimate snake. It kills not by a bite but merely by a look. Not merely its venom, but its very breath is fatal. Because the cockatrice is the most deadly snake and therefore the king of snakes, or because of the cock's comb which may be pictured as a crown, the cockatrice is also called a "basilisk" (from Greek words meaning "little king").

Of course, the Biblical passage in Isaiah (and there are a couple of other verses in this book and in that of Jeremiah which mention the cockatrice) cannot be used as evidence in favor of the reality of this completely imaginary creature. The Hebrew word, translated as "cockatrice" in the King James Version, signified no cock-headed serpent that can kill with a look; it signifies merely a poisonous snake.

In the Revised Standard Version, the word is translated as "adder," which is the name of a common European poisonous snake and, it should perhaps be noted, the only venomous snake to be found in the British Isles. "Adder" is a much less misleading translation of the Hebrew term than "cockatrice" is, but in actuality the adder is not likely to be the specific creature meant by Isaiah. Instead, the horned viper, a poisonous snake found in the Near East, is the most likely candidate.

Lucifer

It is not only Jerusalem and Judah that are warned in the Book of Isaiah concerning the wrath of God. The surrounding heathen nations are also warned of doom, and first in line is Babylon.

It is easy to suspect that chapters 13 and 14, in which the doom of Babylon is foretold with savage imagery, is not really Isaianic. In Isaiah's time, it was Assyria that was the conquering nation and Babylon lay under its thumb in more devastating fashion than Judah did. The paean of hatred and scorn should, it would be expected, be turned against Assyria and the new capital that Sennacherib had built at Nineveh.

On the other hand, a century after Isaiah's time, it was Babylon under Nebuchadnezzar that was the oppressor. It is reasonably likely, then, that this passage is of later origin and was possibly composed during the Exile at a time when Babylon seemed doomed to fall before the conquering armies of Cyrus the Persian.

Picturing Babylon as already fallen, the writer recites a taunting poem of sarcastic contempt for the mighty Babylonian monarch now brought low. In part, it goes:

> Isaiah 14:12. *How art thou fallen from heaven, O Lucifer, son of the morning! . . .*
> Isaiah 14:13. *For thou hast said in thine heart, I will ascend into heaven . . .*
> Isaiah 14:14. . . . *I will be like the most High.*
> Isaiah 14:15. *Yet thou shalt be brought down to hell . . .*

The Hebrew word here translated as "Lucifer" is *helel*. Literally, it means "The Shining One," and is thought to refer to the planetary body we call Venus.

Venus is the brightest of the planets in our sky and, next to the sun and the moon, the brightest object in the heavens. Because of the position of its orbit between the earth's orbit and the sun, it is always seen (from earth) to be fairly close to the sun. When it is in that part of its orbit that puts it to the east of the sun, it shines out most clearly after sunset, and sets never more than three hours afterward. It is then visible only in the evening and is called the evening star.

On the other side of its orbit, when Venus is to the west of the sun, the planet rises first and for a short period of time (never more than three hours), it shines in the eastern sky as dawn gradually breaks. It is then the morning star.

It is only natural that cultures unlearned in astronomy and not particularly observant of the heavens would consider the evening star and the morning star to be two separate bodies. In Isaiah's time, even the clever Greeks were of this opinion. It was not until two centuries after Isaiah's time that the Greek philosopher Pythagoras discovered the two to be the single body that the Greeks then came to call Aphrodite and the Romans (and ourselves) Venus. It is very likely that Pythagoras discovered this in the course of his travels in the East (tradition says he visited Babylonia and it was the Babylonians who were the great astronomers of ancient times).

Venus, in its morning star aspect, could be called the "daystar" for its rising heralds the coming of day. It is also the "son of the morning" for it is only as morning approaches that it is possible to see it. Thus, the Revised Standard Version translates verse 14:12 as "How art thou fallen from heaven, O day-star, son of the morning."

The Greeks, in the period when they thought Venus to be two bodies, called the evening star "Hesperos" and the morning star "Phosphoros." *Hesperos* means "west" and it is always in the west that the evening star appears. *Phosphoros* means "light-bringer" and it is therefore the essential equivalent of "daystar." By the Romans, the Greek terms were translated directly into Latin. The evening star became "Vesper" ("west") and the morning star became "Lucifer" ("light-bringer").

The Hebrew *helel* is therefore translated as Phosphoros in Greek versions of the Bible; and as Lucifer in Latin versions.

The use of the term "Lucifer" in connection with the overweening pride of the Babylonian king is an ironic thrust at the habit of applying fulsome metaphors for royalty. Flattering courtiers would think nothing of naming their king the Morning Star, as though to imply that the sight of him was as welcome as that of the morning star heralding the dawn after a long, cold winter's night. This habit of flattery is confined neither to the East nor to ancient times. Louis XIV of France, two and a half centuries ago, was well known as the Sun King.

The writer of the verses concerning Lucifer ironically described his fall from absolute power to captivity and death as the fall of the morning star from the heavens to Hell.

With time, however, these verses came to gain a more esoteric meaning. By New Testament times, the Jews had developed, in full detail, the legend that Satan had been the leader of the "fallen angels." These were angels who rebelled against God by refusing to bow down before Adam when that first man was created, using as their argument that they were made of light and man only of clay. Satan, the leader of the rebels, thought, in his pride, to supplant God. The rebelling angels were, however, hurled out of Heaven and into Hell. By the time this legend was developed the Jews had come under Greek influence and they may have perhaps been swayed by Greek myths concerning the attempts of the Titans, and later the Giants, to defeat Zeus and assume mastery of the universe. Both Titans and Giants were defeated and imprisoned underground.

But whether Greek-inspired or not, the legend came to be firmly fixed in Jewish consciousness. Jesus refers to it at one point in the Gospel of St. Luke:

> Luke 10:18. And he [Jesus] said . . . I beheld Satan as lightning fall from heaven.

It seemed natural to associate the legend with the Isaianic statement; indeed, that statement about Lucifer may even have helped give rise to the legend. In any case, the early Church fathers considered Isaiah's statement to be a reference to the eviction of the devil from Heaven, and supposed Lucifer to be the angelic name of the creature who, after his fall, came to be known as Satan. It is from this line of argument that our common simile "proud as Lucifer" arose.

Apocalypse of Isaiah

After oracles predicting disaster for a number of individual nations (Moab, Egypt, Tyre, etc.) are presented, there comes a four-chapter sequence (chapters 24 to 27 inclusive) in which extreme disaster for the earth generally is forecast.

These chapters are an example of what is called "apocalyptic" literature, from Greek terms meaning "to uncover"; that is, "to reveal."

Apocalyptic literature purported, in other words, to describe matters that could not be known to man except by inspired revelation. Subjects included in such revelation might be the machinery that controlled the movements of heavenly bodies; the details of the manner in which the universe was created; or, most commonly of all, the details of the fate to befall the earth in the future, particularly the story of the end of earthly history.

The study of the end of days is called "eschatology," from a Greek word meaning "last things." Much apocalyptic writing is eschatological in nature.

After 200 B.C. apocalyptic writing became very common among Jews. The situation seemed to call for it.

Before that time, there had been a tendency to consider the return from the Exile a sort of happy ending of the Biblical story. The Old Testament, as we have it, almost makes it seem so for the latest of the authentic historical books in the Jewish canon is Nehemiah, featuring the restoration of the walls of Jerusalem.

And yet the happy ending seemed to dissolve into nothing; into worse than nothing, for persecution under the Seleucid Empire rose to a high pitch after 200 B.C. and the condition of the Jews was suddenly more miserable than it had been even in the days of Nebuchadnezzar. The frustration was the greater since the new miseries seemed to be without cause.

In the time of the old kingdoms of Israel and Judah, the kings and the people had been periodic idolaters and had been constantly backsliding and were therefore viewed as having been properly punished. After the Exile, however, the Jews had been faithful monotheists, and had not sinned in the same fashion as the generations before the Exile had sinned. Why, then, did matters go so poorly and why was the Seleucid Empire (and, in later centuries, the Roman Empire) so triumphant in its pagan cruelty?

The theory developed that the earth as a whole had grown so wicked that, as in the days just before Noah's Flood, it was past saving, and that it was part of God's scheme to bring all the earth to a destruction from which only a few of the faithful would be saved.

The writers of such literature found a kind of recompense for present injustice in the view of a future in which the mighty tyrants of the earth would be properly punished while the oppressed faithful would be

liberated and brought to joy. God would judge between the good and
the evil in that final day of destruction; even the dead would come
back to life if they were worthy; and there would be the final glorious
rule of God.

In other words, if all were not right now, all would be made right in
the future.

The writers of apocalyptic literature generally ascribed their writings
to some ancient whose name would carry weight and who, for his
holiness, would be considered to have had the whole scheme of history
revealed to him by God. A number were ascribed to Enoch; others were
ascribed to Moses, to Ezra, to Noah, and so on.

At least one rather early apocalypse must have been ascribed to
Isaiah, and successfully so, for it appears in the Book of Isaiah, even
though scholars agree it cannot have been written by him, but must
have been composed some centuries after his death. Chapters 24 to 27
of the Book of Isaiah are commonly referred to as "The Apocalypse of
Isaiah" and that is a good name if it is remembered that it refers to the
book in which it is found rather than the person who uttered it.

The Apocalypse of Isaiah begins with a picture of destruction:

> Isaiah 24:1. *Behold, the Lord maketh the earth empty, and maketh
> it waste, and turneth it upside down.*

It makes veiled allusions, as is common in apocalyptic literature.
After all, since such writings are describing the fall of empires that
are then in secure power, to be too plain in the description would
be to invite an accusation of treason and the inevitable punishment that
would follow. The veiled allusions would be clear enough to the initiated readers. Thus:

> Isaiah 24:10. *The city of confusion is broken down . . .*
> Isaiah 24:11. . . . *all joy is darkened . . .*
> Isaiah 24:12. *In the city is left desolation . . .*

Which is the city of confusion? Clearly, whichever city was acting
the part of tyrant at the time the passage was written. If it were written
in the time of the Exile, it could only mean Babylon and all the readers
would see that at once. Later on, it could be reinterpreted to mean
Antioch, capital of the Seleucid kings, and still later, to mean Rome.

At every period the oppressed Jews of the time would have no doubt as to which was "the city of confusion" (or "city of chaos" as the Revised Standard Version has it), while the authorities, if made aware of the verse, would find it difficult to prove treason in it.

Another example of circumspect allusion is to be found in a reference to Moab:

Isaiah 25:10. . . . *Moab shall be trodden down . . . even as straw is trodden down for the dunghill.*

Moab is the traditional enemy of Israel from the time of Moses (see page 183) but it rarely had its independence, or served as a real danger, after the time of David. Nevertheless, it remained as a person-ification of all the enemies of the Jews and the readers of Isaiah would clearly see Moab as standing for Babylon, Antioch, or Rome, depending on the period in which the verse was read.

At the end of time, the powerful are punished:

Isaiah 24:21. . . . *in that day . . . the Lord shall punish . . . the kings of the earth . . .*
Isaiah 24:22. *And they shall be gathered together as prisoners . . . and shall be shut up . . .*

The oppressed faithful are uplifted:

Isaiah 25:8. . . . *the Lord God will wipe away tears . . . and the rebuke of his people shall he take away . . .*

The dead faithful shall be resurrected:

Isaiah 26:19. *Thy dead men shall live . . . and the earth shall cast out the dead.*

This verse is good evidence for the lateness of the apocalypse, for the doctrine of resurrection of the dead reaches its development in the post-Exilic period, certainly not as early as the lifetime of Isaiah.

God will then put an end to all evil and establish a new order:

Isaiah 27:1. *In that day the Lord . . . shall punish leviathan . . . and he shall slay the dragon that is in the sea.*

Jews will then return from exile (another sign that the passage is to be dated long after the time of Isaiah) to worship God:

Isaiah 27:12. . . . *in that day . . . ye shall be gathered one by one,* O *ye children of Israel.*

Isaiah 27:13. . . . *and shall worship the Lord in the holy mount of Jerusalem.*

Ariel

After the apocalyptic chapters there is a return to clearly Isaianic prophecies concerning the immediate problems of his time. Judah had remained a loyal Assyrian tributary since 735 B.C. and had remained secure while Sargon destroyed Israel and carried its leaders off into an exile from which they never returned (see page 378).

But in 705 B.C., Sargon had died and his son Sennacherib had succeeded to the throne. The various provinces of the Assyrian Empire, taking advantage of possible confusion, of the possible weakness of the new king, rebelled at once. Hezekiah, the son of Ahaz, who was now king of Israel, joined in this rebellion by refusing his tribute. For a while, Judah could do this with impunity for Sennacherib was busy with other, more important, portions of the Assyrian realm. Judah might gamble further that Sennacherib might be defeated resoundingly and that the Assyrian realm might be sufficiently weakened to secure Judah against all retaliation. Such a thing had happened before.

Isaiah, however, did not think it would happen this time.

Isaiah 29:1. Woe *to Ariel, to Ariel, the city where David dwelt!* . . .

Ariel is variously translated as "the lion of God," "the hearth of God," or "the fireplace of God," but by whatever translation it is called it is clearly Jerusalem. Since Jerusalem is the site of the Temple, upon whose altar sacrifices are burnt (hence "hearth" or "fireplace"), Ariel might perhaps be most fairly translated as the "altar of God."

Judah's rebellion was carried through partly at the instigation of Egypt, which was still independent of Assyria, but which feared the inevitable day when Assyria would attack and, probably, conquer. Only by keeping the Assyrian realm in periodic turmoil could she hope to stave off the evil day, and for that purpose, Egypt's wealth was always ready to be handed out to those who determined policy among the

ruin upon the nation (so Manasseh would be convinced) with their inflammatory calls for reliance upon God alone, were suppressed. No doubt many of the more intransigent were executed:

2 Kings 21:16. . . . *Manasseh shed innocent blood very much, till he had filled Jerusalem from one end to another* . . .

It is not specified that Isaiah was killed and it is rather unlikely that he would have been, without its being specifically mentioned. Besides, Manasseh was only twelve when he came to the throne and it might not have been till well on into his reign that his anti-Yahvist policies reached their extreme. Isaiah would have had to be quite old by that time.

But the tradition arose in later times that Isaiah was executed in Manasseh's time. The legend even goes into the gory detail that Isaiah, in trying to escape Manasseh's malignant wrath, hid in a hollow tree and that Manasseh ordered the tree, with Isaiah inside, to be sawed in two.

About A.D. 100 this legend was incorporated into a tale of Jewish origin called "The Martyrdom of Isaiah."

The legend was sufficiently well known even before its commitment to writing (at that there may have been earlier written versions that have not survived) to cast a reflection of itself into the New Testament.

Thus, in the Epistle to the Hebrews, the writer is listing the great deeds of Jewish history, and having reached the time of Joshua, merely summarizes the rest. In hastily listing the hard fates unflinchingly faced by the prophets, he says:

Hebrews 11:37. *They were stoned, they were sawn asunder, were tempted, were slain by the sword* . . .

The phrase "sawn asunder" is thought to be a reference to Isaiah.

Second Isaiah

The Book of Isaiah continues after the end of the Sennacherib chapters—but with a marked and sudden change. The language, style, and background all shift.

In the earlier chapters, Judah is a kingdom facing destruction and

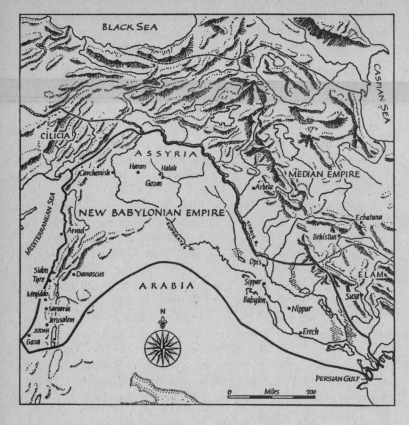

The New Babylonian (Chaldean) Empire

it is castigated unsparingly by the harsh prophetic tongue. In the later chapters, Judah is in exile and despair and it is uplifted with lyric enthusiasm by a prophet promising rescue.

It begins at once:

> Isaiah 40:1. *Comfort ye, comfort ye my people, saith your God.*
> Isaiah 40:2. *Speak ye comfortably to Jerusalem* . . .

Furthermore, Isaiah speaks now not of Ahaz, Hezekiah, and Sennacherib, but of Cyrus of Persia, who ruled a century and a half after Sennacherib:

Isaiah 45:1. *Thus saith the Lord . . . to Cyrus, whose right hand I have holden, to subdue nations before him . . .*

It is possible to argue, if one is wedded to the literal word of the Bible, that the Isaiah of Hezekiah's time foresaw the period of the Exile in great detail, down to the name and deeds of the monarch who was to establish the Persian Empire and liberate the Jews, and that he spoke his vision in a style that was altered from what it had been.

This point of view, however, has no important advocates today. It is assumed instead that a prophet of the period of the Exile wrote under the honored name of Isaiah and that, since he was every bit as great a poet as Isaiah, if not actually greater, his work was included with that of the earlier prophet in the present Book of Isaiah.

So it comes to pass that the great prophet of the Exile, certainly one of the great influential voices of history, is doomed to complete anonymity forever (as far as we can now tell). He can be referred to only as the "Second Isaiah," or, using the Greek term for "second," as the "Deutero-Isaiah."

Cyrus

The Second Isaiah is convinced that the Exile is soon to be broken and he even sees the one whose worldly hands will be used by God to break that exile. Cyrus of Persia has, apparently, just taken Ecbatana, destroyed the Median Empire, and replaced it with the still more powerful Persian Empire. This is considered by the Second Isaiah to be the work of God:

Isaiah 41:2. . . . [God] *raised up the righteous man from the east, called him to his foot, gave the nations before him, and made him rule over kings?*

Cyrus's home province is Persia, which lies east of Babylonia. To the Jews in Babylonian Exile, he is therefore the "man from the east." Now that Cyrus has established himself in the royal seat of Ecbatana, he hovers to the north of Babylonia like a thundercloud and the Second Isaiah gladly waits his coming:

Isaiah 41:25. *I [God] have raised up one from the north, and he shall come . . .*

Cyrus conquered Media in 549 B.C. but it was not until 538 B.C. that he took Babylon. The writings of Second Isaiah seem to fall between these two dates and can be placed about 540 B.C., or just two centuries after the call of the First Isaiah.

We have in the views of the Second Isaiah a clear departure from henotheism (see page 359). The Second Isaiah seems to be certain that Yahveh is as powerful outside Judah as ever He was inside it. Nor does he imagine for a moment that the Babylonian gods are stronger than Yahveh just because the Babylonians had defeated and scattered Yahveh's people. Instead, he pictures a universal God. He thinks of Yahveh as not merely the supreme and only God of Israel, but the supreme and only God of the universe. If Judah was defeated and destroyed and the Jews were driven into exile that was the action of none other than God and served the divine purpose. And if the great heathen conqueror Cyrus appeared on the scene, he too was but another tool in the hand of Yahveh.

The Second Isaiah was even confident that the universality of the only God was something that eventually all people would acknowledge:

Isaiah 45:14. *Thus saith the Lord, the labour of Egypt and merchandise of Ethiopia and of the Sabeans . . . shall come after thee . . . and . . . they shall make supplication unto thee, saying, Surely God is in thee; and there is none else, there is no God.*

The Servant of the Lord

The anonymity of the Second Isaiah might be considered broken by certain passages in which, just conceivably, he may be speaking of himself. The Second Isaiah pictures Israel as particularly serving God's purposes for all the world. He quotes God as saying:

Isaiah 41:9. *But thou Israel art my servant . . .*

The servant may be meek and passive, but he will hold to God's law faithfully until all the world comes to accept it:

Isaiah 42:4. *He shall not fail nor be discouraged, till he have set judgement in the earth: and the isles shall wait for his law.*

But then, at the beginning of the forty-ninth chapter, the Servant is personified. The Second Isaiah speaks in the first person as though he himself represents the idealized Israel serving its God. He is discouraged at the fruitlessness of his efforts:

Isaiah 49:4. *Then I said, I have laboured in vain, I have spent my strength for nought, and in vain . . .*

God encourages him, informing him (in line with the Second Isaiah's views as to the universality of Yahveh) that his mission is not for Jews only:

Isaiah 49:6. . . . *I will also give thee for a light to the Gentiles, that thou mayest be my salvation unto the end of the earth.*

The Second Isaiah describes the Servant of the Lord as suffering for his labors; and if he is talking about himself (in an access of self-pity) it is easy to see that his advanced views on the nature of God might have been found unacceptable not only by the heathen but by most of the Jews of the time and that he would therefore have reason to feel rejected:

Isaiah 53:3. *He* [the Servant] *is despised and rejected of men; a man of sorrows, and acquainted with grief: . . . he was despised, and we esteemed him not.*

According to the later Christian view, the picture drawn by the Second Isaiah is a prophetic foretelling of the career of Jesus. This would be, by that interpretation, a new kind of Messianic prophecy. The Messiah is not pictured as the ideal king of the First Isaiah, who establishes his power with force and who reigns in glory; but rather as a prophet, beaten, bruised, and killed, who even in this fashion was, through apparent total defeat, fulfilling the will of God.

Bel

The Second Isaiah foresees the inevitable destruction of Babylon by Cyrus and rejoices at the downfall of its idols:

Isaiah 46:1. *Bel boweth down, Nebo stoopeth . . .*

Bel is the Babylonian word for "lord," the equivalent of the Phoenician "Baal." Originally, Bel was the name given particularly to the important Sumerian god En-lil, who was a god of the air and sky; a storm-god originally, like the Greek Zeus or the most primitive conceptions of Yahveh. The seat of En-lil's worship was in the Sumerian city of Nippur on the Euphrates, about fifty miles downstream from Babylon.

When Babylon became powerful and grew to dominate the land under Hammurabi (see page 69) its local god, Marduk (Merodach to the Jews) naturally grew, henotheistically, in importance. Marduk assimilated the attributes of En-lil and became the new Bel. (Nippur, however, remained an important center of worship long after it had lost its political importance. Religious ritual is just about the most conservative aspect of human culture.)

The importance of Marduk was emphasized by the creation myth that originated in Babylon. When Tiamat (the chaotic force of the sea) threatened the old Sumerian gods, they dared not battle the monster. It was Marduk, a second-generation god, the son of Ea (a Sumerian god worshiped particularly at Eridu, near what was then the mouth of the Euphrates), who dared venture forth into battle. He destroyed Tiamat and formed the universe out of its remains. With that deed, Marduk was promoted to supremacy over the older Sumerian pantheon, a reflection in heaven of the supremacy on earth of Babylon over the older Sumerian cities.

Of course, when Assyria dominated Babylon, they considered their own national god, Asshur, to have been the hero of the Tiamat story; but under Nebuchadnezzar, with Babylon again supreme, Marduk was also the great god once more. He was Bel-Marduk ("Lord Marduk") or just Bel.

This was understood by the Jews, for the prophet Jeremiah, in predicting the fall of Babylon, uses the two names of the god in poetic parallelism:

Jeremiah 50:2. . . . *Babylon is taken, Bel is confounded, Merodach is broken in pieces . . .*

Nebo (Nabu in Babylonian) was originally a Sumerian god, worshiped at Borsippa, just a couple of miles south of Babylon. He was viewed as a god of wisdom, who had, for instance, invented writing. When Babylon became supreme over Sumeria, Nebo was accepted into the Babylonian system of gods. Because of Borsippa's closeness to Babylon, Nebo may have been familiar to them and have been accepted as a near neighbor of Marduk, so to speak. He was therefore given an honored place in the pantheon, made the son of Marduk in the Babylonian mythology, and placed second in power to him. Nebo's name occurs in that of Nebuchadnezzar.

Beulah

The final eleven chapters of Isaiah seem to strike a lower note than those that went before and many suggest that the Second Isaiah ends with the fifty-fifth chapter. Those that follow, then, are thought to have been written by another and still later hand, the Third Isaiah, or the Trito-Isaiah.

In these final chapters the return from exile is no longer imminent, as it is with the Second Isaiah, but seems actually to have taken place. Where in the Second Isaiah the return is anticipated with jubilation and seen as the coming of an ideal state, there is disillusion with the actuality in the Third Isaiah. Idolatry is denounced; and the reference appears to be to the Samaritans, or to the Jews who had returned and who were falling in with the practices of those who inhabited the land. The leaders of the new community are denounced.

However, as is almost always the case in the prophetic books, there is hope for the future; there is always the idealized state on the horizon. A new and glorified Jerusalem is envisaged:

Isaiah 60:10. *And the sons of strangers shall build up thy walls . . .*

If this verse is taken literally then the walls of Jerusalem had not yet been rebuilt and the Third Isaiah must be writing about 450 B.C., before the coming of Nehemiah. His words would fall about a century after the Second Isaiah and nearly three centuries after the First.

The new, ideal land is described glowingly and, speaking to the personified Jerusalem, the writer says:

Isaiah 62:4. *Thou shalt no more be termed Forsaken; neither shall thy land any more be termed Desolate: but thou shalt be called Hephzi-bah, and thy land Beulah . . .*

Hephzibah means "My delight is in her" and Beulah means "Married." The picture is of God loving and marrying the land. God and His people will be united and inseparable. The Revised Standard Version translates the terms so that the end of the verse reads: ". . . your land . . . shall be called My delight is in her, and your land Married."

Because of this verse, the "land of Beulah" has come to mean something very close to heaven and in Bunyan's *The Pilgrim's Progress* it represents a kind of pleasant anteroom in which the pilgrims rest till they are invited into the Celestial City.

24. JEREMIAH

JEREMIAH * TAHAPANES * RAMAH * SHILOH * AHIKAM * SHESHACH * BARUCH *
JEHOIAKIM * ZEDEKIAH * HANANIAH * THE LETTER OF JEREMIAH *
ZEDEKIAH * NEBUZARADAN * GEDALIAH * ISHMAEL * JOHANAN *
PHARAOH-HOPHRA

Jeremiah

The second of the major prophets, chronologically as well as in his
position in the Bible, is Jeremiah ("Yahveh is exalted"). The book
announces its authorship at once:

> Jeremiah 1:1. *The words of Jeremiah the son of Hilkiah, of the*
> *priests that were in Anathoth in the land of Benjamin.*
> Jeremiah 1:2. *To whom the word of the Lord came in the days*
> *of Josiah . . . in the thirteenth year of his reign.*
> Jeremiah 1:3. . . . *unto the carrying away of Jerusalem cap-*
> *tive . . .*

Since Josiah came to the throne in 638 B.C., the thirteenth year of his
reign would be 626 B.C. and in that year, Jeremiah began a prophetic
mission that was to carry him through more than forty years of tragedy,
to the final fall of Jerusalem and a little beyond. It was a time of
gathering doom, reaching a climax of total disaster, and this is reflected in Jeremiah's writings.

There was in Josiah's time a Hilkiah of importance. Indeed, he was
no less than the High Priest whose discovery of the Book of Deuteronomy in the Temple crystallized the reforms of Josiah:

> 2 Kings 22:8. *And Hilkiah the high priest said unto Shaphan the*
> *scribe, I have found the book of the law in the house of the Lord . . .*

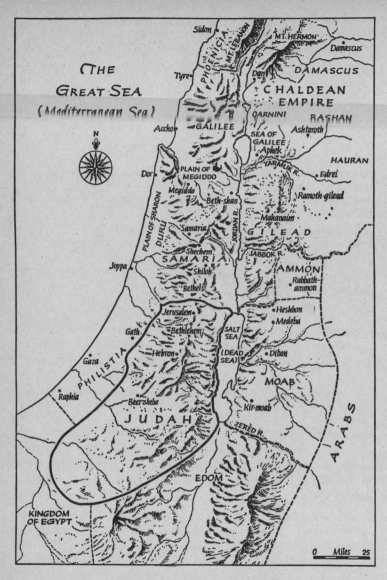

Judah and the Chaldean Empire

There might be an impulse to think of Jeremiah as the son of this High Priest, but this is completely unlikely. If he were, he would be high in the priestly hierarchy. Instead, the first verse makes it plain he is of provincial origin, a member of a priestly clan of the Benjamite town of Anathoth, some four miles northeast of Jerusalem.

As it happens, the Bible speaks earlier of a priest who had his holdings in Anathoth. This was Abiathar, the only survivor of the slaughter at Nob (see page 291) and the last representative of the house of Eli to hold an official position in the priesthood. After David's death, Abiathar had supported Adonijah for the succession (see page 320). When Solomon outmaneuvered Adonijah and established himself on the throne, Abiathar suffered the penalty for having guessed wrong:

1 Kings 2:26. *And unto Abiathar the priest said the king* [Solomon], *Get thee to Anathoth, unto thine own fields . . .*

1 Kings 2:27. *So Solomon thrust out Abiathar from being priest unto the Lord . . .*

Zadok, who had earlier been associated with Abiathar in the highest rank of the priesthood under David, now became sole High Priest, and from him the entire line of High Priests descended, down to the Exile and even beyond.

Far from being of the High Priestly Zadokite line, then, Jeremiah is very likely to have been a descendant of Abiathar and, through him, of Eli, a member of the line that had been displaced by Zadok and his descendants and that had lived in obscurity at Anathoth for three centuries as a result.

Jeremiah, like Isaiah, was presumably quite young when he first received his call. He implies this himself for in describing the call, he quotes himself as answering:

Jeremiah 1:6. . . . *Ah, Lord God! behold, I cannot speak: for I am a child.*

This might be metaphorical; a modest claim to be only a child in understanding. However, if he remained an active prophet for forty years, he must have been a young man at the beginning. If he were twenty at the time, then he was born in 646 B.C., when idolatrous king Manasseh (see page 424) had been on the throne nearly half a century. It would make Jeremiah just about the same age as king Josiah, during whose reign the call had come.

The call came to Jeremiah at a crisis in history, as it had come to Isaiah. To Isaiah it came when the Assyrian menace suddenly rose and overshadowed all else. Now it came to Jeremiah at the time when the Assyrian Empire was beginning its astonishingly rapid collapse and all the Fertile Crescent was thrown into confusion.

In 626 B.C., the very year of Jeremiah's call, Asshurbanipal, the last strong Assyrian king, had died. Rebellions arose everywhere and the strength of the Assyrian army was no longer sufficient to cope with them. Invasions of the Cimmerian nomads from the north had kept Asia Minor in turmoil during Asshurbanipal's reign. They had finally been very largely destroyed but the effort had stretched Assyrian strength past its limits.

Now, with Asshurbanipal's death, the Cimmerians, in what proved to be a last gasp, were raiding southward again, and the distraught Assyrians, busied with revolts in Babylonia and elsewhere, could do nothing about it. It may have been to these Cimmerian raids that an early verse in Jeremiah refers:

> Jeremiah 1:14. *Out of the north an evil shall break forth upon all the inhabitants of the land.*

However, the Cimmerians could not take fortified towns and their relatively undisciplined hordes were most suited to hit-and-run. Their threat was soon done. Other, far more dangerous threats were to follow.

Tahapanes

The chronology of the Book of Jeremiah is incredibly tangled. The Anchor Bible, in order to achieve a kind of chronological order, is forced to shuffle the chapters of Jeremiah, but even so, some passages which are not dated and which do not refer to events that can be dated remain puzzling as far as chronology is concerned.

In the second chapter, Jeremiah complains bitterly of Judah's apostasy: of its following after strange gods and its acceptance of idolatrous customs. This section may therefore come at the beginning of his ministry, before the reforms of Josiah. (The Book of Deuteronomy was found in the Temple five years after Jeremiah's call.)

At one point, in describing the misfortunes that befell Judah as a result of its apostasy, he says:

Jeremiah 2:16. *Also the children of Noph and Tahapanes have broken the crown of thy head.*

Egypt had regained its independence from Assyria in 664 B.C., a generation before Jeremiah's call, and as Assyria declined rapidly, Egypt's relative power increased. For the first time in five centuries it was to play an effective role in international affairs.

The 26th dynasty, which then ruled Egypt, had its power centered in the delta, in the city of Saïs, so that the nation in this period is spoken of as "Saitic Egypt." Noph is Memphis, the ancient capital of the delta (see page 63), so that "the children of Noph" makes a logical metaphorical representation of Egypt.

Tahapanes (spelled Tahpanhes later in Jeremiah, and Tehaphnehes in the Book of Ezekiel) was a frontier town in the northeast of Egypt, near the Mediterranean coast and just about at the site of what is now the Suez Canal. When Saitic Egypt began to face eastward and to dream of expansion into Asia, Tahapanes was fortified and converted into a strong base for military operations. It would be the nearest important Egyptian city to Judah, and the people in Jeremiah's time would be conscious of it as a representation of Egyptian might.

The verse is interpreted by some as referring to the defeat of Judah by Egypt in 608 B.C. when Josiah was killed. Surely the king of Judah might be referred to as "the crown of thy head" by someone addressing the men of Judah. If so, however, Jeremiah's strictures against apostasy would be out of place, for Josiah's reform was approved of, in general, by Jeremiah. Thus, Jeremiah, in addressing the son of Josiah rhetorically:

Jeremiah 22:15. . . . *did not thy father . . . do judgment and justice . . .*

Jeremiah 22:16. *He judged the cause of the poor and needy . . .*

If, then, the second chapter relates to a time before Josiah's reform, 2:16 cannot refer to Josiah's death and may merely have the general meaning of "even the Egyptians are now stronger than you," a scornful reference to the Egypt that had been weak for so long.

The Greeks called Tahapanes Daphne, and the Anchor Bible uses the Greek terms for both cities. "The men of Memphis and Daphne, They too have cracked your skull." Tahapanes is in ruins now but the mound under which it is buried is called Tel Defenneh, so that the name lives.

Ramah

Jeremiah might well have been conscious of his descent from the house of Eli, who had been High Priest at an Ephraimite shrine, for the northern kingdom of Israel seemed often to come to his mind. In fact, there is a sympathy for the lost and scattered Israel which would have been unusual in a Judean, for Judah and Israel were at war through much of their history. Could it be that some of Jeremiah's bitterness arose out of a sense of alienation, a feeling that he was a northerner lost among Judean strangers?

Thus, in his bitter denunciation of Judah (so bitter that such denunciatory speeches are referred to in the English language as "jeremiads") the prophet compares the land unfavorably to the northern kingdom. He defends Israel against the standard Judean argument that the northern kingdom had gone down to Assyrian destruction because it had drifted away from the Davidic line and the true worship at Jerusalem, and sacrificed instead at idolatrous altars in Dan and Bethel. Jeremiah says flatly:

Jeremiah 3:11. *And the Lord said unto me, The backsliding Israel hath justified herself more than treacherous Judah.*

Again, in another passage he weeps over fallen Israel with moving sorrow:

Jeremiah 31:15. . . . *A voice was heard in Ramah, lamentation and bitter weeping; Rahel* [Rachel] *weeping for her children refused to be comforted for her children, because they were not.*

Rachel was the ancestress of the three tribes of Ephraim, Manasseh, and Benjamin. Whether Jeremiah considered himself an Ephraimite through his descent from Eli, or a Benjamite through the site of his family's holdings, he would, in either case, have felt himself a descendant of Rachel.

There were two traditions as to the site of Rachel's grave. One had her buried in Judah, north of Bethlehem:

Genesis 35:19. *And Rachel died, and was buried in the way to Ephrath, which is Bethlehem.*

Another had her buried in Benjamin. Thus, the prophet Samuel speaks of:

> 1 Samuel 10:2. . . . *Rachel's sepulchre in the border of Benjamin at Zelzah . . .*

The location of Zelzah is unknown, but Jeremiah clearly accepts the Benjamite tradition and Zelzah may be an alternative name for Ramah. Ramah is four miles northwest of Jeremiah's home town of Anathoth and it is there he places the tomb of his ancestress. He pictures her ghost as haunting the place and weeping constantly for the tribes carried off into permanent exile a century before.

Then, when Jeremiah begs the men of Judah to return to God and establish an ideal state, he describes such a state as including the returned exiles of Israel:

> Jeremiah 3:18. *In those days the house of Judah shall walk with the house of Israel, and they shall come together out of the land of the north . . .*

Shiloh

Jeremiah's consciousness of his northern origin makes him less apt to accept certain aspects of Josiah's reform. By wiping out all local religious altars and practices as heathen and idolatrous, Josiah had centered all worship at the Temple at Jerusalem and there were many who must have thought that this Temple had magic powers to protect the city and its people. To Jeremiah the Temple was an institution from which his own family had been barred, and in his mind was the memory of an older temple which, in its time, had been just as holy.

Jeremiah denounced the overimportance attached to Jerusalem in his so-called "Temple Sermon," which he delivered within the Temple itself. The Temple Sermon is given early in Jeremiah but is dated in a passage that is found considerably later in the book:

> Jeremiah 26:1. *In the beginning of the reign of Jehoiakim the son of Josiah . . . came this word from the Lord, saying . . .*
> Jeremiah 26:2. . . . *Stand in the court of the Lord's house, and speak unto all the cities of Judah . . .*

The sermon is then given, shortly after the death of Josiah in battle with Egypt in 608 B.C. The Egyptian armies controlled the land for the moment but they made no attempt to lay siege to Jerusalem and take it. It was sufficient for Egypt to rely on their puppet, Jehoiakim, whom their influence had placed on the throne. (Egypt was far more concerned with the gathering strength of the Chaldeans under Nabopolassar and his son Nebuchadnezzar. They had recently taken Nineveh and had established themselves as master of the Tigris-Euphrates.)

Undoubtedly, the nationalist element in Judah, ignoring the realities of the situation, felt that Jerusalem was safe under all circumstances and against all comers simply because of the existence of the Temple and of the purification of Temple-worship by the elimination of all competing cults.

Jeremiah, less impressed by the sanctity of the Temple, said:

> Jeremiah 7:4. *Trust ye not in lying words, saying, The temple of the Lord, The temple of the Lord, The temple of the Lord . . .*

He points out that it is not ritualistic worship and reform that will save Judah, but ethical reform, and quotes God as saying:

> Jeremiah 7:9. *Will ye steal, murder, and commit adultery, and swear falsely . . .*
> Jeremiah 7:10. *And come and stand before me in this house . . . and say, We are delivered . . .*

Then, out of his own background he recalls the case of an earlier temple, the sanctity of which did not keep it from destruction. Jeremiah quotes God as saying:

> Jeremiah 7:12. *But go ye now unto my place which was in Shiloh, where I set my name at the first, and see what I did to it for the wickedness of my people Israel.*

Ahikam

The Temple Sermon got Jeremiah into trouble. As a matter of fact, he was in continual trouble throughout his life. A prophet could not, like Jeremiah, constantly predict the most disastrous evils in the most violent language without making himself unpopular to a populace that wanted (like all populaces) comfort and reassurance. Jeremiah was an annoyance, a gadfly, and there must have been many who would have been willing to see his mouth shut by force. Unfortunately, the Book of Jeremiah gives us no detailed chronological account of the opposition, but there are occasional references in passing. At one point, Jeremiah quotes his enemies:

> Jeremiah 18:18. *Then said they, Come and let us devise devices against Jeremiah . . . let us smite him . . . and let us not give heed to any of his words.*

Jeremiah naturally incurred the wrath of the High Priestly officials, who, at times, did not hesitate to lay violent hands upon him:

> Jeremiah 20:1. *Now Pashur . . . who was . . . chief governor in the house of the Lord, heard that Jeremiah prophesied these things.*
> Jeremiah 20:2. *Then Pashur smote Jeremiah . . . and put him in the stocks . . .*

Jeremiah was as unpopular in his home town as in Jerusalem. The reason is not given but perhaps those at Anathoth were afraid that Jeremiah's unpopularity might spread to the people of his home town. They might have felt that by getting rid of him they would remove themselves from an unpleasant and dangerous spotlight. Jeremiah quotes God, warning the enemies of his own town:

> Jeremiah 11:21. . . . *thus saith the Lord of the men of Anathoth, that seek thy life, saying, Prophesy not in the name of the Lord, that thou die not by our hand:*
> Jeremiah 11:22. . . . *thus saith the Lord of hosts, Behold I will punish them . . .*

Jeremiah underwent a particularly dangerous moment, however, after his Temple Sermon, when in the very Temple itself he had warned Jerusalem of suffering the fate of Shiloh. This naturally outraged the worshipers, who viewed it as outright blasphemy. The people demanded he be executed at once. There was recent precedent for such an action:

> Jeremiah 26:20. . . . *there was . . . a man that prophesied in the name of the Lord, Urijah . . . who prophesied against this city . . .*
> Jeremiah 26:21. *And when Jehoiakim the king . . . sought to put him to death . . . Urijah . . . fled . . . into Egypt.*

Jeremiah 26:22. *And Jehoiakim . . . sent men into Egypt . . .*
Jeremiah 26:23. *And they fetched forth Urijah out of Egypt and brought him unto Jehoiakim . . . who slew him . . .*

Nevertheless, there were people of importance who, either because they agreed with Jeremiah, or feared the consequences of killing a prophet, pleaded against the execution. They cited the case of the prophet Micah, who had spoken much as Jeremiah had spoken back in the reign of Hezekiah a century earlier and who had been left completely unharmed. One man of influence in particular protected Jeremiah and kept him from harm:

Jeremiah 26:24. *. . . the hand of Ahikam the son of Shaphan was with Jeremiah, that they should not give him into the hand of the people to put him to death.*

Ahikam had been a high official under Josiah and had been one of those involved in the reforms under that king:

2 Kings 22:12. *And the king [Josiah] commanded Hilkiah the priest and Ahikam the son of Shaphan . . .*
2 Kings 22:13. *Go ye, inquire of the Lord . . . concerning the words of this book that is found . . .*

Sheshach

One can well imagine that Jeremiah is frustrated and in despair at the fact that his denunciations produce enmity and anger, rather than repentance.

Jeremiah 25:1. *. . . in the fourth year of Jehoiakim . . .*
Jeremiah 25:2. *. . . Jeremiah spake . . . saying*
Jeremiah 25:3. *From the thirteenth year of Josiah . . . even unto this day, that is the three and twentieth year . . . I have spoken unto you, . . . but ye have not hearkened.*

It is now 605 or 604 B.C. and a new crisis is upon Judah. The fall of Assyria is now complete, and the period of confusion that followed is almost over. The Chaldeans, ruling from Babylon, have emerged the winners. In 605 B.C. Nebuchadnezzar, son of Nabopolassar (who had taken Nineveh) defeated Pharaoh-nechoh at Carchemish. The Egyptian conqueror of Josiah was driven back to the Nile and Egypt's short foray into Asia was over. Egypt was not to become a conquering power for three more centuries. Then, in 604 B.C., Nabopolassar died and the victorious Nebuchadnezzar came to the throne.

Jeremiah judged that under Nebuchadnezzar's forceful leadership the Chaldeans would drive on toward the re-establishment of empire over the entire Fertile Crescent, under Babylon now rather than under Nineveh. Sinful Judah would be given over to the Babylonian conqueror by God.

> Jeremiah 25:8. *Thus saith the Lord of hosts; Because ye have not heard my words,*
>
> Jeremiah 25:9. *Behold, I will send . . . Nebuchadrezzar . . . against this land, and against the inhabitants thereof . . . and will utterly destroy them . . .*

(Nebuchadrezzar, as the Babylonian king is called here, is also referred to as Nebuchadnezzar in books written later and even in other parts of the Book of Jeremiah; as, for instance, in the reference:

> Jeremiah 29:1. . . . *all the people whom Nebuchadnezzar had carried away captive . . .*

It is the latter version, with the "n," that is more familiar to the average man, perhaps because it is to be found in the popular Book of Daniel, and which I am therefore routinely using myself. Nevertheless, it is the version with the "r" that is closer to the Babylonian original. The "n" undoubtedly arose through a copyist's error.)

Having predicted Nebuchadnezzar's conquest of Judah, Jeremiah goes on to predict that the people of Judah will go into exile for seventy years (see page 436), and to describe all the nations that are to fall to the conquering Babylonians. In this list, the climax comes with:

> Jeremiah 25:26. . . . *and the king of Sheshach shall drink after them.*

Sheshach does not refer literally to any kingdom or region; it is rather an example of a simple code called "athbash" by which some dangerous reference is made which is clear to the initiated but which does not involve the writer in quite as much danger of execution for treason.

In this code, the letters of the Hebrew alphabet are reversed. The first letter of the alphabet is replaced by the last, the second letter by the next to the last, the third letter by the third from the last, and so on.

In Hebrew, the word "Sheshach" is spelled "shin-shin-caph," where "shin" is the second letter from the end and "caph" is the twelfth letter from the end. If we reverse this and take the second and twelfth letter from the beginning, we have "beth-beth-lamed," which is "Babel," or "Babylon." In short, Sheshach is the code word for Babylon and the prediction is that after Babylon conquers a long list of nations it is Babylon herself who will then be conquered in the end.

That this is so is all the more certain since in a later chapter, in describing the coming fall of Babylon, "Sheshach" is used as a synonym in poetic parallelism:

> Jeremiah 51:41. *How is Sheshach taken!* . . . *how is Babylon become an astonishment among the nations!*

Baruch

Jeremiah felt it necessary, however, to make a final attempt to persuade Judah to change its course from one that promised certain disaster. In the fourth year of Jehoiakim, therefore, he states that he was commanded by God to commit his various utterances to writing:

> Jeremiah 36:4. *Then Jeremiah called Baruch the son of Neriah: and Baruch wrote from the mouth of Jeremiah all the words of the Lord . . . upon a roll of a book.*

Baruch, Jeremiah's trusted secretary in the later part of the prophet's life, remained with Jeremiah till the fall of Jerusalem and after the fall traveled to Egypt with the prophet. According to one tradition, however, Baruch did not remain in Egypt but left it after Jeremiah's death and went to Babylon, where he died in 574 B.C. There is no Biblical evidence in favor of this, but there is nothing impossible about it, either.

Based on this tradition, there is an apocryphal book (accepted as canonical by the Catholics) entitled "The Book of Baruch" and purportedly written by him in Babylon:

Baruch 1:1. *And these are the words . . . which Baruch . . . wrote in Babylon.*

Baruch 1:2. *In the fifth year . . . what time as the Chaldeans took Jerusalem, and burnt it with fire.*

Since Jerusalem was sacked by the Babylonians in 586 B.C., the book is thus dated 582/581 B.C.

The first half of the book is in prose and consists of a confession of national sin, making the destruction of Jerusalem and the exile of the people a just punishment for that sin and now pleading for forgiveness. The second part of the book consists of two poems, one praising wisdom after the fashion of the Wisdom of Solomon (see page 515), and the second promising the consolation of return from exile after the fashion of the Second Isaiah (see page 548). It seems quite certain that the book was not written by Baruch but was written long after his time and is a composite work by different hands, reaching its final form as late as A.D. 100 perhaps.

Two apocalyptic books ascribed to Baruch were discovered in the nineteenth century. These are called the Syriac Apocalypse of Baruch and the Greek Apocalypse of Baruch, after the languages in which the manuscripts were written. They seem to be even later than the apocryphal Book of Baruch.

Jehoiakim

Once his words were committed to writing, Jeremiah was anxious to have them reach the king. Apparently, he did not have the easy entry into the royal presence that Isaiah had, so that he had to work his way through Temple officials who did have such entry. Unfortunately, after his Temple Sermon, Jeremiah was forbidden to enter the Temple grounds and he had to send Baruch.

Jeremiah 36:5. *And Jeremiah commanded Baruch saying . . . I cannot go into the house of the Lord:*

Jeremiah 36:6. *Therefore go thou, and read in the roll . . .*

The scroll was read to Temple functionaries, who anxiously told the king of the matter. The king sent an official for the scroll and had it read to him.

The men of the Temple seem to have been surprisingly anxious to forward Jeremiah's words to the king and there may be good secular reasons for this. The political situation at the moment was particularly ticklish and for once Jeremiah and the Temple may have been pulling in the same direction.

Ever since Necho of Egypt had slain Josiah at Megiddo, Judah had been tributary to Egypt, but now with Babylon in its turn triumphant over Egypt, there was a question as to whether Judah ought to remain faithful to Egypt, or to change sides and go over to Babylonia. Each alternative had its advocates and there was an Egyptian and a Babylonian party in the land. The Temple functionaries, approached by Baruch, may well have been convinced that Egypt was done, and could see that as a practical matter the only safe course was to submit to Nebuchadnezzar. Since Jeremiah was saying the same thing, his writings were eagerly forwarded to the king.

Jehoiakim, however, was apparently of the Egyptian party, and there seem to have been strong personal reasons for that.

After Josiah had been killed at Megiddo, the people of Judah acclaimed his youngest son, Shallum (throne name, Jehoahaz), as king:

> 2 Kings 23:30. . . . And the people of the land took Jehoahaz the son of Josiah, and anointed him, and made him king . . .

But Necho, who now controlled Judah, would not have this. He preferred his own candidate, one whom he could rely on, and who was perhaps bound to him by oaths, sworn in return for the kingship. The Egyptian monarch therefore deposed Shallum and put his older brother on the throne:

> 2 Kings 23:34. And Pharaoh-nechoh made Eliakim the son of Josiah king . . . and turned his name to Jehoiakim, and took Jehoahaz away: and he [Jehoahaz] came to Egypt, and died there.

Jehoiakim was thus beholden to the Egyptian Pharaoh for his throne. Even if he felt no compunctions at violating any oath of loyalty he had given, he would very likely have felt that if Nebuchadnezzar were to take over Judah, even through Judah's peaceful submission, the Babylonian king would be bound to consider Jehoiakim an Egyptian puppet and therefore untrustworthy. He would do as Necho had done and place his own man on the throne. Out of pure self-interest, then, and quite against the national good, Jehoiakim was of the Egyptian party.

Furthermore, Jehoiakim could not very well have felt kindly toward Jeremiah, since the prophet had inveighed against the king personally and in no polite terms, either. Among the prophet's utterances (which, presumably, were not included in the scroll to be handed the king, but which Jehoiakim must have known about) were:

Jeremiah 22:18. . . . *thus saith the Lord concerning Jehoiakim . . . They* [the people] *shall not lament for him . . .*
Jeremiah 22:19. *He shall be buried with the burial of an ass, drawn and cast forth beyond the gates of Jerusalem.*

Therefore, when a courtier named Jehudi read to Jehoiakim the fearful predictions of doom uttered by Jeremiah, Jehoiakim reacted at once with gloomy wrath.

Jeremiah 36:23. . . . *when Jehudi had read three or four leaves, he* [Jehoiakim] *cut it with the penknife, and cast it into the fire . . . until all the roll was consumed . . .*

Jeremiah had Baruch rewrite the scroll, but clearly the pro-Egyptian course was fixed as far as Jehoiakim was concerned. Even when he was finally forced to pay cautious lip service to Nebuchadnezzar he felt unsafe upon the throne and watched for the first opportunity to rebel.

Zedekiah

The opportunity came in 601 B.C. when Nebuchadnezzar suffered a local defeat at the hands of the Egyptians. At once Jehoiakim refused tribute. It took some time for Nebuchadnezzar's hands to be sufficiently free to deal with the situation in force, but by 597 B.C., the Babylonian army was besieging Jerusalem. Jehoiakim died in the course of the siege and his son Jehoiachin (also referred to in the Bible as Jeconiah and Coniah) reigned in his place.

Jerusalem was forced to capitulate, however, and then Nebuchadnezzar did to Jehoiakim's son what he would have done to Jehoiakim if that king had survived (and what Jehoiakim would have expected him to do). Nebuchadnezzar deposed the king and placed his own candidate on the throne. Jehoiachin was carried off into Babylonian captivity after a reign of only three months and with him was carried off much of the aristocracy and elite of the nation. What was left behind was placed under the rule of still another of Josiah's sons:

> 2 Kings 24:17. And the king of Babylon made Mattaniah . . .
> king . . . and changed his name to Zedekiah.

It is conceivable that Jeremiah might have indulged in the hope, in the early days of Zedekiah's accession to the throne, that now all would be well.

The nation, made aware of Babylon's overwhelming power, might settle down to a quiet subservience and experience peace and prosperity in the shadow of Nebuchadnezzar, as a century before, under Manasseh, they had experienced peace and prosperity in the shadow of Esarhaddon of Assyria. In Manasseh's time, however, king and nation had plunged deeply into idolatry. Now (so it might have seemed to Jeremiah), with the experience of Babylonian devastation, the nation would turn to God and cleanse itself. Then a mollified Yahveh would forgive His people, destroy Babylon, and establish an ideal state in Judah.

All this (just possibly) may have been in Jeremiah's mind in connection with the following verses:

> Jeremiah 23:5. Behold, the days come . . . that . . . a King shall
> reign and prosper . . .
> Jeremiah 23:6. In his days Judah shall be saved . . . and this is
> his name whereby he shall be called, the Lord Our Righteousness.

The Lord Our Righteousness is, in Hebrew, Yahveh-tsidkenu, whereas Zedekiah is, in Hebrew, "Tsidkiahu" and means "Righteous is Yahveh." One name is the inverse of the other.

These verses in Jeremiah are usually taken to be Messianic in nature and to speak of an ideal king in the indefinite future. Nevertheless, it is at least conceivable that the reference is to the new king, who had taken the throne name of "Righteous is Yahveh."

Hananiah

If Jeremiah had hopes of peace and recovery, they were quickly blasted. The Egyptian party in Jerusalem remained strong. At every word of disorder anywhere in the Babylonian dominions, their hopes rose and Zedekiah let himself be swayed by the public feeling against Babylon. Judah tried, foolishly, to form a coalition of neighboring states against Babylon, when all of them together were no match for Nebuchadnezzar. They further attempted to get promises of help from Egypt, a nation which always promised, but somehow never delivered.

In Egypt, Necho had died in 593 B.C. and had been succeeded by Psamtik II. Psamtik welcomed into the land various Jewish exiles who, in the unsettled times, felt it safer to flee westward. He even formed a contingent of Jewish soldiers to fight in his armies. Naturally he could not trust such a contingent on the northeastern front where they might have to fight other Jews and might therefore change sides.

Instead, he placed them on the southern frontier, notably on Elephantine, an island in the Nile River, just south of the first cataract (near the southern border of modern Egypt). There they would serve to guard against raiders striking northward from Ethiopia.

In 588 B.C. Psamtik II died and was succeeded by Pharaoh-hophra, whom the Greeks called Apries. It was this Pharaoh who intrigued with the Egyptian party in Judah and encouraged Zedekiah to make a stand against Nebuchadnezzar.

Jeremiah, to dramatize the absolutely suicidal nature of this policy, made a yoke for himself and wore it, telling everyone who would hear that Judah should patiently wear the Babylonian yoke as the only means of survival. Naturally, this seemed an unpatriotic and defeatist attitude and was not popular with the people, who persisted in their belief that Jerusalem and its Temple were inviolable, a belief supported by the announcements of many who claimed to be prophets of God. (The case of Sennacherib's failure actually to take Jerusalem over a century earlier and the failure of Nebuchadnezzar to sack the city after his first siege must undoubtedly have encouraged the prophets in this view.)

Jeremiah 28:1. . . . *in the beginning of the reign of Zedekiah . . . in the fourth year . . . Hananiah . . . spake . . . in the house of the Lord . . . saying,*

Jeremiah 28:2. *Thus speaketh the Lord . . . I have broken the yoke of the king of Babylon.*

Jeremiah 28:3. *Within two full years will I bring again into this place all the vessels of the Lord's house that Nebuchadnezzar . . . took away . . .*

> Jeremiah 28:4. *And I will bring again to this place Jeconiah . . . with all the captives of Judah . . .*

And to dramatize this statement Hananiah broke Jeremiah's yoke to indicate how God would break the yoke of Babylon.

Undoubtedly, this speech, given in Zedekiah's fourth year (594 B.C.), must have been met with the wild approval of the populace. Even Jeremiah did not quite dare stand against it at that moment, for he would undoubtedly have been torn in pieces if he had. Instead, he went along with the jubilant crowd:

> Jeremiah 28:6. *Even the prophet Jeremiah said, Amen: the Lord do so: the Lord perform thy words . . .*

It was only afterward, when the mob had dispersed, that Jeremiah could safely announce that Hananiah was a false prophet, pandering to the nationalist hopes of the people.

The Bible records that he predicted Hananiah's death for false prophecy and that Hananiah died within two months. Nevertheless, it is plain that the people of Judah preferred to believe the flattering, hopeful words of Hananiah rather than the doleful, hopeless words of Jeremiah.

The Letter of Jeremiah

The nationalist agitation within Judah had an echo in Babylon. Undoubtedly, numbers of the exiles believed that God was about to destroy Babylon, as some prophets were predicting, and were ready to rise in revolt. News of this agitated Jeremiah.

The exile of 597 B.C. had drawn off the leaders of Judah, its craftsmen, its intellectuals. Bitterly, Jeremiah had referred to this in a parable of figs:

> Jeremiah 24:1. *The Lord shewed me . . . two baskets of figs . . . after . . . Nebuchadrezzar . . . had carried away captive Jeconiah . . . and the princes of Judah, with the carpenters and smiths . . .*
> Jeremiah 24:2. *One basket had very good figs . . . and the other basket had very naughty figs, which could not be eaten, they were so bad.*

Jeremiah then likened the captives to the good figs and those that remained in Jerusalem to the bad. It is clear that he considered it would be fatal to have the Babylonian exiles rise in rebellion. They would only be slaughtered. To Jeremiah, they seemed the hope of the future. Even if Jerusalem were destroyed, the exiles, he felt, would someday return to start the nation anew.

Jeremiah therefore took the occasion of a mission to Nebuchadnezzar sent by Zedekiah (perhaps protesting his loyalty to Babylon) to send a message to the exiles:

> Jeremiah 29:1. *Now these are the words of the letter that Jeremiah . . . sent from Jerusalem unto . . . all the people whom Nebuchadnezzar had carried away captive . . .*
>
> . . . .
>
> Jeremiah 29:5. *Build ye houses . . . and plant gardens . . .* Jeremiah 29:6. *Take ye wives, and beget sons and daughters . . . that ye may be increased there, and not diminished.* Jeremiah 29:7. *And seek the peace of the city . . .*

In Babylon, at least, Jeremiah's views won out. The exiles in Babylon did make new lives for themselves without abandoning Judaism. They were allowed to live in peace and in due time (actually less than the seventy years predicted by Jeremiah) those who wished to do so were allowed to return to Judah. What's more, those who remained in Babylon were sufficiently prosperous to lend considerable financial help to those who returned (see page 437).

Centuries later, in 100 B.C., a short tract was written which purported to be a copy of the letter that was sent by Jeremiah to the exiles. It is devoted largely to an argument against idol worship, trying to demonstrate by a variety of arguments that idols are useless, helpless, the mere work of men's hands, and so on. It was not accepted as canonical by the Jews but appears in some Greek and Syriac versions of the Bible as a sixth and final chapter to the Book of Baruch. It appears, in this fashion, in the Catholic versions of the Bible, and in the King James Version of the Apocrypha, where it is titled "The Epistle of Jeremy." In the Revised Standard Version of the Apocrypha it is presented as a separate book, made up of a single chapter and called "The Letter of Jeremiah."

Zedekiah

If the exiles in Babylon were kept in quiet and peace, not so the Jews in the homeland. By 589 B.C., the pressure of public opinion had forced Zedekiah into outright rebellion against Nebuchadnezzar and in 588 B.C., Jerusalem was placed under siege by the Chaldean armies, while the rest of the nation, with the exception of one or two strong points, was occupied.

Bitterly, Jeremiah predicted that the city would be destroyed if resistance continued and that the only safety lay in surrender. He actually urged individuals to surrender if the city as a whole did not do so:

> Jeremiah 21:9. *He that abideth in this city shall die by the sword, and by the famine, and by the pestilence: but he that goeth out, and falleth to the Chaldeans . . . shall live . . .*

Such a statement was naturally viewed by the patriots of Judah as treason. An advance by the Egyptian army forced Nebuchadnezzar to lift the siege temporarily and hurry westward to face the Egyptians, and Jeremiah's forebodings seemed to have been turned to nothing. Sennacherib, in his time, had had a similar problem (see page 384) and the siege of Jerusalem at that time had been permanently lifted. Surely this would happen again. Jeremiah warned the people that this would not be so. Nebuchadnezzar would return.

Yet Jeremiah seized the brief respite to attempt to make a trip to Benjamin to attend to his property. He was at once seized by men of the army and accused of trying to desert to the Chaldeans. He denied it vigorously but he was not listened to, and was put in prison.

Zedekiah, however, was by no means certain that Jeremiah was the false prophet he seemed at the moment when the Chaldean siege had been lifted. He apparently had a sneaking belief in Jeremiah's worth and consulted him even while he was in prison (but secretly, to avoid having the nationalists find out).

> Jeremiah 37:17. *Then Zedekiah the king sent, and took him [Jeremiah] out [of prison]; and the king asked him secretly . . . Is there any word from the Lord . . .*

But Jeremiah was obdurate. He predicted only disaster and he was put back into prison. According to one story, he was put into a dungeon without food or water, and would have died if Zedekiah had not been persuaded to take him out at the last minute. One way or another, however, Jeremiah remained in prison for the duration of the siege and never stopped predicting disaster and urging surrender.

Still, he held out a long-range hope, for while in prison, he ostentatiously arranged for the purchase of land in his home town as an indication that the day would yet come when Judah would be Jewish again, despite the Chaldean devastation; a day when such purchases as he now made would hold good.

> Jeremiah 32:15. *For thus saith the Lord . . . Houses and fields and vineyards shall be possessed again in this land.*

Nebuzaradan

The Chaldeans did return to the siege and in 587 B.C., the city was taken, sacked, and burned. The walls were broken down, and the Temple was destroyed. Zedekiah attempted flight but was taken. His children were executed and he himself was blinded. A second deportation of Jews was then ordered by Nebuzaradan, captain of Nebuchadnezzar's elite troops:

> Jeremiah 39:9. *Then Nebuzaradan . . . carried away captive into Babylon the remnant of the people that remained in the city . . .*
> Jeremiah 39:10. *But . . . left of the poor of the people, which had nothing . . . and gave them vineyards and fields.*

Thus, as a result of two successive deportations, one at the beginning of the reign of Zedekiah in 597 B.C. and one at the end in 586 B.C., the elite of the nation were carried off. In Babylon, the exiles retained the essence of Judaism and developed it further. The first five books of the Bible (the Pentateuch or Torah) were put into written form, and apparently the Book of Joshua as well.

Back in Judah, however, the poor who remained, lacking religious sophistication, kept up a form of Yahvism of a more primitive sort.

When, a half century later, Jews from Babylon began to return to Judah, they considered their own developed version of Yahvism to be the only true form, and despised and antagonized those already on the land. It was only with difficulty, therefore, that they managed to rebuild the Temple against local hostilities (see page 441).

The Jews never really returned from Babylon en masse. Even after the rebuilding of the Temple and the walls of Jerusalem, important communities of Jews remained in the cities of Babylonia. These persisted throughout Biblical times and well beyond. After the destruction of the second Temple by the Romans in A.D. 70, Babylonia became the center of Jewish intellectual life for a thousand years.

The Jewish community in Babylonia remained important through the period of renewed Persian domination which followed after the decline of the Seleucid Empire; and for additional centuries after the conquest of the area by the Mohammedan Arabs. Only in A.D. 1100, when the area was falling prey to continuing civil wars and to the dominating power of the comparatively uncivilized Turkish tribes, did the Babylonian centers of Jewish learning fade, while new centers appeared in Moslem Spain.

One must not, therefore, think of the Babylonian Exile as merely a hiatus and a temporary stage in Jewish history. It was of vital importance to the development of Judaism (and of the two religions that arose out of it, Christianity and Mohammedanism) and it was, in some respects, a permanent exile and the beginning of the Diaspora (a Greek word meaning "dispersion"). The Diaspora, a name given collectively to the Jewish communities dwelling outside Judah, continues to this day, twenty-five hundred years after Nebuchadnezzar's time, even despite the re-establishment in 1948 of a Jewish nation in the land that had once been Canaan.

Gedaliah

After the destruction of Jerusalem, Judah was reorganized into a Chaldean province and a native governor was put over what remained of its population:

> 2 Kings 25:22. And as for the people that remained in the land of Judah . . . over them he [Nebuchadnezzar] made Gedaliah the son of Ahikam, the son of Shaphan, ruler.

Gedaliah was the son of the same Ahikam who had on an earlier occasion saved Jeremiah's life (see page 564). A brother of Ahikam and his son (the uncle and cousin of Gedaliah) had been among those who had tried to bring Jeremiah's scroll to the attention of Jehoiakim (see page 567).

Jeremiah 36:10. Then read Baruch . . . the words of Jeremiah in the house of the Lord, in the chamber of Gemariah the son of Shaphan . . .

Jeremiah 36:11. When Michaiah the son of Gemariah . . . had heard . . . all the words of the Lord,

Jeremiah 36:12. Then he went down into the king's house . . .

Apparently, the entire family of Shaphan was strongly pro-Babylonian and of Jeremiah's mind that only through submission to Nebuchadnezzar could Judah find safety. Gedaliah was therefore a natural choice as governor.

After the fall of Jerusalem, Jeremiah, as a well-known spokesman of the pro-Babylonian point of view, was to be taken care of:

Jeremiah 39:11. Now Nebuchadrezzar . . . gave charge concerning Jeremiah to Nebuzaradan . . . saying,

Jeremiah 39:12. Take him, and look well to him, and do him no harm.

. . . .

Jeremiah 39:14. . . . they . . . took Jeremiah out of . . . prison, and committed him unto Gedaliah . . . that he should carry him home.

Ishmael

Gedaliah attempted to re-establish order and to assure the inhabitants of Judah that they might live peaceably under Nebuchadnezzar. Unfortunately, there were elements in opposition to this:

Jeremiah 40:13. . . . Johanan the son of Kareah . . . came to Gedaliah . . .

Jeremiah 40:14. And said unto him, Dost thou . . . know that Baalis the king of the Ammonites hath sent Ishmael the son of Nethaniah to slay thee? . . .

The motives of the Ammonite king are uncertain. Perhaps it was merely the chance of completing the destruction of the Jewish kingdom in memory of the centuries of long hostility. Perhaps he was acting on behalf of Egypt. The fall of Jerusalem could only have doubled and redoubled the desperate intrigues of the Egyptians to keep the area in turmoil and the Chaldeans occupied.

As for Ishmael, he perhaps required no great urging. He is described as:

> Jeremiah 41:1. . . . Ishmael the son of Nethaniah the son of Elishama, of the seed royal . . .

As a member of the royal family, he might have envisaged the re-establishment of the kingdom, with Egyptian help, and his own anointment as king.

Gedaliah was apparently one of those high-minded men who can believe no evil, and he refused to credit the report. In consequence, he was assassinated after having remained in office only three months (or possibly one year and three months).

It was the last straw and after that there was no chance of any sort of Jewish community in the land.

Johanan

The assassination of Gedaliah had been accompanied by a general massacre of those faithful to him, and those Jews who escaped must have been certain that the criminal act of Ishmael would bring down the final installment of Chaldean vengeance.

This time, it seemed very likely, Nebuchadnezzar would not stop to distinguish guilty from innocent but would slaughter all alike, and there seemed no alternative but to flee to the one neighboring land where the Chaldean arm could not yet reach:

> Jeremiah 41:16. Then Johanan the son of Kareah . . . and the remnant of the people . . .
> Jeremiah 41:17. . . . departed . . . to go to enter into Egypt,
> Jeremiah 41:18. Because of the Chaldeans, for they were afraid of them . . .

On the way to Egypt, they passed the home of Jeremiah and asked his advice. Jeremiah did not depart from his pro-Babylonian policy. He felt that in Egypt there would be no more safety than in Judah, and he may even have thought that a flight into Egypt would be a provocation to Nebuchadnezzar; that it would look very much like what we would today call setting up a government-in-exile.

Against Jeremiah's advice, however, the group of Jews traveled on into Egypt. In fact, they forced Jeremiah and Baruch to accompany them.

This new departure of Jews into Egypt (like the legendary one under Jacob and Joseph twelve centuries earlier) had important consequences. The Elephantine colony (see page 571) was probably reinforced and a form of Yahvism was built up there, complete with a temple. The Jews of the colony worshiped Yahveh under the name of Yahu, and picked up elements of Egyptian religion as well. They apparently were not conscious of the manner in which their religious customs departed from those that were being developed in Babylon.

In 1903, papyri were discovered on the island and these revealed that at the time the Temple was being rebuilt in Jerusalem, Elephantine had fallen on bad days. Its temple had been destroyed by the Egyptians and in 407 B.C., they were asking permission of Persian authorities (who now controlled Egypt) to rebuild that temple. They had previously applied for help to the newly built Temple at Jerusalem but had received no answer, since to the Jews at Jerusalem there could be only one Temple. To them, the Jews at Elephantine were heretics and no more to be regarded than the Samaritans.

In Greek times, the entry of Jews into Egypt assumed floodlike proportions. By New Testament times, there were nearly a quarter of a million Jews along the Nile, and something like one third of Egypt's capital city, Alexandria, was Jewish.

In New Testament times, the Jews of Egypt were largely Greek in language and culture. The comparison between the Hellenized Jews of Egypt and those of Judea must have been something like the comparison today between the Americanized Jews of the United States and those of Israel.

Pharaoh-hophra

In Egypt, Jeremiah fought against the dilution of Yahvism by Egyptian practices. His denunciation ended with a thunderous:

Jeremiah 44:30. *Thus saith the Lord; Behold, I will give Pharaoh-hophra king of Egypt into the hand of his enemies and into the hand of them that seek his life* . . .

Pharaoh-hophra, who ruled Egypt at the time of the destruction of Jerusalem, managed to avoid destruction at the hands of Nebuchadnezzar, but Jeremiah's prophecy came to pass just the same.

In 569 B.C., seventeen years after the fall of Jerusalem, Pharaoh-hophra tried to bring under his control a Greek colony established at Cyrene, on the north African coast, about five hundred miles west of the Nile. His troops revolted and acclaimed an officer named Aahmes (Amasis, to the Greeks) as Pharaoh. Troops loyal to Hophra were defeated by the rebels and Hophra was executed while Aahmes reigned in his place.

One wonders if Jeremiah was still alive to see the end of Pharaoh-hophra. He would have been seventy-seven years old then, a not-impossible age. However, there is no way of telling. His denunciation of the Egyptian monarch is his last recorded utterance and there is no Biblical account of his death.

25. LAMENTATIONS

Jeremiah

The Book of Lamentations consists of five separate poems, each making up a separate chapter and all dealing with the central theme of the destruction of Jerusalem and its desolation thereafter. In the Jewish canon, it is considered part of the third division of the Bible, the Writings, and it is not included among the prophetic books. The Hebrew title is taken from the first word. The book begins:

> Lamentations 1:1. *How doth the city sit solitary, that was full of people* . . .

and the Hebrew name is therefore "Ekhah" ("how").

The tradition arose quite early, however, that Jeremiah was the author of Lamentations and for that reason, the book was placed immediately after the Book of Jeremiah in the Septuagint and in the various Christian versions that descended from that. The title of the book in the English versions is, in full, "The Lamentations of Jeremiah."

The case for authorship by Jeremiah rests, generally, in the fact that Jeremiah was the most prominent Biblical character to be in Jerusalem through the period of its great disaster. Then, too, Jeremiah is mentioned in the Bible in connection with the composition of lamentations, that form of poetry which bewails a tragedy. When the reforming king Josiah was brought back dead from the battle of Megiddo:

> 2 Chronicles 35:25. . . . *Jeremiah lamented for Josiah* . . .

This particular lamentation cannot be represented by the Book of Lamentations, of course. For one thing, Jerusalem was not destroyed until twenty-two years after Josiah's death. For another, Lamentations does not mention Josiah. The only reference in it to any king is:

> Lamentations 4:20. *The breath of our nostrils, the anointed of the Lord, was taken* . . .

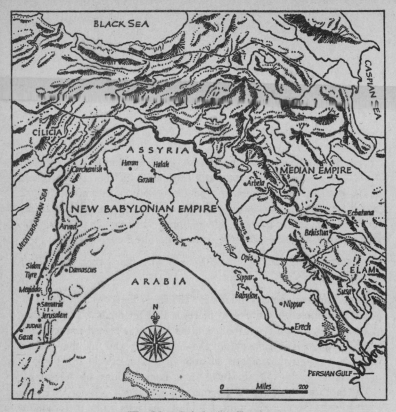

The New Babylonian Empire

and it makes much more sense in the context of the book to suppose
that this is a poetic reference to Zedekiah, Judah's last king.

But it is extremely unlikely that Jeremiah can have been the author
of the book. The mere fact that it is not included in the prophetic
canon in the Hebrew Bible would indicate it was composed rather late.

The five poems do not seem to be by the same hand, the third
chapter in particular seeming different from the rest, and later. Furthermore, the first four poems are acrostics (see page 495), a highly
artificial form, and it doesn't seem likely, somehow, that Jeremiah in his
grief over Jerusalem would sit down to work out, slowly and painfully,
a set of acrostic poems. That rather bears witness to a literary effort
taken on later and in retrospect.

26. EZEKIEL

Ezekiel

Ezekiel ("God strengthens") was, apparently, a younger contemporary of Jeremiah, and it is therefore chronologically fitting that his
utterances should follow those of Jeremiah.

> Ezekiel 1:1. *Now it came to pass in the thirtieth year . . . as I was*
> *among the captives . . . that . . . I saw visions of God.*
> Ezekiel 1:2. *In . . . the fifth year of king Jehoiachin's captivity.*

Ezekiel, then, had been carried off with Jehoiachin after Nebuchadnezzar's first siege of Jerusalem in 597 B.C. The book begins in the
fifth year of that captivity; that is, in 593 B.C. At that time, the kingdom
of Judah still existed, with Zedekiah as its king and with Jeremiah the
prophet warning it, unheeded, of its coming fate.

If by "the thirtieth year" Ezekiel means that he is in the thirtieth
year of his life (something that is not at all certain) then he was
carried off to Babylon in his twenty-fifth year and he was born in
627 B.C., during the reign of Josiah. This would make him some
twenty years younger than Jeremiah and, in fact, he would have been
born the year before Jeremiah received his call. It is possible that, as
some traditions have it, he may even have been a disciple of Jeremiah.

Ezekiel was a priest, presumably of the line of Zadok, since he shows
himself greatly interested in the minutiae of the Temple service.

> Ezekiel 1:3. *The word of the Lord came . . . unto Ezekiel the*
> *priest . . . by the river Chebar . . .*

The New Babylonian Empire

The "river Chebar" is one of the larger canals that interlaced the Babylonian plains. Its name in the original Akkadian was "nar Kabari" ("Grand Canal") and it led from Babylon southeastward to Uruk (Erech). Somewhere on its shores there was the settlement of Jews of whom Ezekiel was a prominent and respected leader.

Tammuz

Ezekiel's call is attended by a mystical vision of God, something like that of Isaiah but attended by greater detail. The prophet is instructed to denounce the wickedness of Jerusalem and to proclaim the imminence of its siege and destruction. A year later, Ezekiel does so by describing visions of the idolatrous practices he claims are being practiced in the very Temple itself:

Ezekiel 8:14. *Then he* [God] *brought me to the door of the gate of the Lord's house which was toward the north; and behold, there sat women weeping for Tammuz.*

In ancient agricultural societies, it was common to personify the phenomenon of the death of vegetation in the winter (or in the acme of summer heat) and its rebirth in the spring (or with the coming of the rains). The personification took the form of a deity who died and was taken into the underworld, from which he was later rescued by another deity. It was customary for women to bewail the death of the deity at fixed times of the year and then to rejoice loudly over the rebirth and resurrection.

To modern Westerners, the most familiar form of this sort of tale is found among the Greek myths. This tale tells of Demeter, the Greek goddess of agriculture, and her daughter Persephone. Persephone is stolen by Hades, the god of the underworld, and Demeter seeks her all over the world. While she seeks, all vegetation dies and winter comes over the world. Eventually, Demeter finds Persephone and a compromise is reached. Persephone may stay with Demeter part of the year and with Hades the rest, and this explains the recurring cycle of growth and death and growth again.

The Babylonians have a myth of this sort, too; one that long antedates the Greek version, of course, and goes back, in fact, to Sumerian days before the time of Abraham. In the Sumerian myth, Dumu-zi (the name which later became Tammuz) is the brother and lover of Ishtar, the goddess of earth and sky. Tammuz is killed by a boar while hunting, or, perhaps, through some thoughtless act of Ishtar, and must descend into the underworld. Ishtar follows and ransoms him only with the greatest difficulty. It is for this Tammuz that the women first wail and then rejoice.

(The Babylonians called the month of the summer solstice Tammuz in honor of the god and the Jews borrowed the name. This heathen god, despite Ezekiel, is still honored in the Jewish calendar today, just as Western calendars contain the month of March, a name used freely by Jews and Christians alike though it honors the pagan god Mars.)

The Tammuz myth spread along with agriculture and always it was to the women that its rites particularly appealed. After all, in primitive societies it is the women who are most concerned with agriculture. In the western half of the Fertile Crescent Tammuz was called "Lord" (*Adonai*). This was "Adonis" in the Greek version of the name and Greek mythology adopted the tale of Tammuz when they told of Adonis, the young lover of Aphrodite, who was killed by a boar to the goddess's infinite distress. (And gave us the word "Adonis" to represent any extremely handsome young man.)

The Israelites undoubtedly worshiped Tammuz and these rites were popular with the women among them. Indeed, the writers of the final version of the Book of Judges probably tried to mask the idolatrous practices of the women by referring to their weeping for Tammuz as weeping for Jephthah's daughter (see page 246).

Nor has the practice died out completely even today, for the emotions surrounding the religious ritual in connection with the death and resurrection of Jesus—Good Friday followed by Easter—owes something to the millennia in which the god of vegetation died and was reborn every year.

Tyrus

The first half of the Book of Ezekiel is given over entirely to the denunciation of Judah and the prediction of disaster for it; all this, presumably, having been uttered in the near-decade period between the time of Ezekiel's call and the final destruction of Jerusalem.

Thereafter, Ezekiel turns upon those nations surrounding Judah who were to share in its destruction at the hands of the conquering Chaldeans:

> Ezekiel 26:1. . . . *in the eleventh year . . . the word of the Lord came unto me saying . . .*
>
> . . . .
>
> Ezekiel 26:7. . . . *Behold, I will bring upon Tyrus Nebuchadnezzar . . .*

Tyrus is the Greek form of the town we call Tyre (and the word appears as Tyre throughout in the Revised Standard Version).

Tyre shared in the troubles suffered by the peoples of the western half of the Fertile Crescent in the face of the advance of first the Assyrians and then the Chaldeans. Fortunately for itself, however, Tyre was on the coast, her citadel being on a rocky island offshore. As long as her ships controlled the sea she could not be starved out. For that reason, she could withstand longer sieges than cities like Damascus, Samaria, and Jerusalem, which could be completely invested. For that same reason, sieges of Tyre were likely to end in a compromise settlement, with Tyre retaining her integrity.

Thus, at the time Shalmaneser V was laying siege to Samaria (see page 375), he was also besieging Tyre. The city resisted firmly through a five-year siege, defeating the ships which the Assyrians used in an attempt to break her life line. In the end, Tyre agreed to pay tribute to Sargon, but it retained its self-government.

It continued to pay tribute to the nations which came to power after the fall of Assyria, but more reluctantly. They shared in the Egyptian-encouraged intrigues against Babylonia that led to Judah's destruction and it was quite obvious that Nebuchadnezzar intended to punish Tyre when he was done with Jerusalem.

Ezekiel's prophecy "in the eleventh year" took place in 587 B.C., when Jerusalem's fate was sealed and when the forthcoming siege of Tyre was a sure thing. Ezekiel goes on to predict Tyre's destruction as a result of this siege and in great detail describes the manner of its sacking. Indeed, throughout the passage Ezekiel glorifies the Chaldean armies as though he were a Babylonian patriot. Perhaps he had been "assimilated" into Babylonian life in this sense for there are no oracles among his utterances that are against Babylon, only against Babylon's enemies (including Judah).

This is not so strange a thought, really. As far as we can tell, the Jewish colonies in Babylonia were well treated; they were allowed the full practice of their religion; they were allowed to enter into the economic life of the nation and grow well-to-do. The proof of this is that when they were finally allowed to return to Judah and rebuild their Temple, many of them preferred to remain in Babylonia. It is not at all impossible to imagine a Jew retaining a profound loyalty to Judaism while feeling a secular patriotism toward a religiously alien but otherwise benevolent power. American Jews are precisely in that sort of position today.

Nevertheless, as it turned out, Ezekiel was overenthusiastic in his pro-Babylonian pride, for Nebuchadnezzar failed after all to sack Tyre. He maintained his siege for thirteen years, till 573 B.C. (three years longer than the renowned siege of Troy) and in the end had to come to a compromise arrangement.

Ezekiel himself had to recognize this hard fact:

> Ezekiel 29:17. *And it came to pass in the seven and twentieth year . . . the word of the Lord came unto me, saying,*
> Ezekiel 29:18. *. . . Nebuchadrezzar . . . caused his army to serve a great service against Tyrus . . . yet had he no wages, nor his army . . .*

This statement is dated 571 B.C., the twenty-seventh year of Ezekiel's captivity, and two years after the siege of Tyre had been lifted. It is the latest dated statement of the prophet and since his call came in the fifth year of his captivity, he was active over a period of at least twenty-two years. If he was thirty years old at the time of his call, he was fifty-two at the time of this statement.

Elishah

Yet before the passage of time enlightens Ezekiel to the true outcome of the siege, he composes a long dirge for supposed-fallen, or going-to-fall Tyre, and in it he recites those places that contribute to the merchant city's wealth and prosperity in a veritable orgy of geographical terms, some of which we can no longer surely identify. Thus:

> Ezekiel 27:7. *. . . blue and purple from the isles of Elishah was that which covered thee.*

There is the possibility that Elishah was a district in Cyprus, an island in the eastern Mediterranean which had been colonized by the Phoenicians. Another possibility, however, involves a farther Phoenician colony, on the northern coast of Africa.

Tradition has it that in 814 B.C., when Joash was on the throne of Judah, a party of Tyrians established a colony near the site of modern Tunis. Through the centuries, this colony, which came to be known as Carthage, from words originally meaning "new town," flourished. By

Ezekiel's time, it dominated north Africa and had established itself in Sicily.

The traditional leader of the original colonizing party had been a Tyrian princess named Dido in the Greek and Roman histories, but that seems to have been her throne name. Her earlier name, according to those same histories, was Elissa. Could it have been that this name actually reflects one of the names by which Carthage was known in the civilized centers of the Fertile Crescent? Is the "Elishah" referred to in this verse Carthage? If so, it is the only reference to Carthage in the Bible.

Again:

Ezekiel 27:8. *The inhabitants of Zidon and Arvad were thy mariners . . .*

Zidon is, of course, Sidon (see page 217). Arvad is an island about two miles off the Syrian coast, some hundred miles north of Sidon. It was quite prosperous in Biblical times.

Gebal

Ezekiel goes on:

Ezekiel 27:9. *The ancients of Gebal . . . were in thee thy calkers.*

Gebal (the modern town of Jubyl in Lebanon) is on the Phoenician seacoast about forty miles north of Sidon. In very ancient times, in the days when the pyramids were being built, Gebal may have been the most important of the Phoenician cities, but it was eventually eclipsed, first by Sidon and later by Tyre.

An inscription in the Phoenicians' alphabet (from which all other alphabets are believed to have descended) has been found in diggings in that city and has been dated back to before the time of the Exodus. It may conceivably have been in Gebal that the alphabet was invented.

In later centuries, Gebal was the center of trade in Egyptian papyrus, which was much valued for book production in Greek and Roman times. Rolls of papyrus came, therefore, to be called *biblia* from the Greek name of the city, which was Byblos. And since in

Christian times the rolls of papyrus on which the Scriptures were written came to be *the* books, they were the "Biblia" par excellence and to this day we call the holy writings of the Jews and Christians the "Bible."

And still more:

> Ezekiel 27:14. They of the house of Togarmah traded in thy fairs with horses . . . *and mules.*

Togarmah is equated with the "Tilgirimmu" mentioned in Assyrian inscriptions. These are taken to be in horse-breeding country in east-central Asia Minor.

The Prince of Tyrus

Ezekiel also inveighed against Tyre's ruler and here, at least, his prophecy did not entirely miss fire:

> Ezekiel 28:2. *Son of man, say unto the prince of Tyrus, Thus saith the Lord God* . . .
> . . . .
> Ezekiel 28:7. . . . *I will bring strangers upon thee* . . .
> Ezekiel 28:8. *They shall bring thee down to the pit and thou shalt die* . . .

The king of Tyre at the time of Nebuchadnezzar's siege was Ithobaal II. (Ithobaal I, ruling three centuries earlier, had been the father of Jezebel.)

Ithobaal II did suffer a personal defeat, for by the terms of the final agreement between Tyre and Nebuchadnezzar, Ithobaal was forced to abdicate and he and his family were taken off to exile in Babylon (but not killed, thus falsifying that part of Ezekiel's prediction). In Ithobaal's place, Baal II ruled an essentially independent Tyre that was nevertheless careful not to offend Babylon needlessly.

Tyre continued to exist in peace and prosperity under the Persians, who conquered and supplanted the Chaldeans. Indeed, it was not until two and a half centuries after Nebuchadnezzar's siege, when a far greater conqueror, Alexander the Great, laid siege to the city, actually took it, and sacked it, that Tyre's pride was finally broken. Never again would it be able to dispute with empires.

Syene

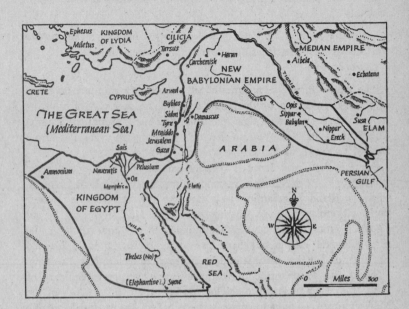

The New Babylonian Empire and Egypt

But it was Egypt which was the real enemy of Nebuchadnezzar. It had been the force behind the little nations that had tried to withstand the Chaldean might. Its gold, its encouragement, even on occasion its armies, had strengthened them. Now, it alone of the ancient centers of civilization remained outside the Chaldean Empire. Somehow, it continued to maintain its independence and Chaldean frustration seems to be mirrored in the lengthy invectives hurled against Egypt by Ezekiel:

> Ezekiel 29:1. *In the tenth year . . . the word of the Lord came to me, saying,*
> Ezekiel 29:2. *. . . set thy face against Pharaoh . . . and prophesy against him and against all Egypt:*

The prophecy is dated 588 B.C., while Jerusalem was still holding out, and while Egypt's interference was delaying the fall of that city. (Ezekiel was certainly no nationalist or he would have been praising Egypt rather than denouncing it at this time.) Ezekiel's denunciation is savage:

Ezekiel again . . . I [God] will make the land of Egypt utterly *waste and desolate, from the tower of Syene even unto the border of Ethiopia.*

The word "tower" is apparently an unnecessary translation of the word *Migdol*. Various fortified posts might be termed Migdol from the stone fortresses or towers that would be their most prominent feature. The Revised Standard Version therefore translates the clause as "from Migdol to Syene, as far as the border of Ethiopia."

Syene is the Greek name of the place called "Seveneh" in Hebrew. It is located on the Nile at just about the position of the First Cataract, with the island Elephantine (see page 571) in the river itself near there. Ethiopian invaders floating down the Nile in order to raid Egyptian cities would have difficulties negotiating the rapids at the First Cataract and might have to bypass it overland. A fortified Egyptian city at that point would be necessary to ensure Egypt's safety.

Syene and Elephantine mark the effective southern boundary of Egypt proper in ancient times. They are about 550 miles south of the Mediterranean. In modern times, Syene is called Aswan, and is notable for being the site of a huge dam that will back up the waters of the Nile into a long lake, serving to irrigate millions of acres of desert and produce much electric power as well. The southern boundary of modern Egypt lies about 150 miles south of Aswan.

Since Ezekiel's threat is that Egypt will be devastated from end to end, and since Syene represents its southern frontier, Migdol must be located on its northern frontier. One guess is that it refers to a town twelve miles south of the Mediterranean and a few miles east of what is now the Suez Canal, which the Greeks called Magadalos.

Pathros

Ezekiel predicts that the Egyptians will be scattered and dispersed through the nations but will experience a kind of partial restoration after forty years.

Ezekiel 29:14. *And I will . . . cause them* [the Egyptians] *to return into the land of Pathros . . . and they shall be there a base kingdom.*

Pathros is the name given to "upper Egypt," the portion of the land south of the delta. The implication is that a portion of Egypt will regain independence to form a weak nation, one that is no longer a great power.

To be sure, this had happened previously in Egyptian history. When the Hyksos controlled the delta, for instance, native Egyptian rulers maintained themselves in Thebes and controlled "Pathros" until they finally took over all of Egypt.

This did not, however, happen on this occasion. Nebuchadnezzar did not conquer Egypt; the Egyptians were not scattered and dispersed; there was no need for any restoration.

To be sure, in 568 B.C., shortly after the death of Pharaoh-hophra (see page 580) and the accession of the usurper Aahmes, Nebuchadnezzar tried to take advantage of the confusion in Egypt by invading the land. We know little of that episode but it could not have been the resounding Babylonian success that Ezekiel had confidently predicted. Egypt survived with no apparent damage.

Indeed, Aahmes survived to rule for another generation over a prosperous Egypt. He witnessed the death of Nebuchadnezzar, the decay of the Chaldean Empire under Nebuchadnezzar's successors, and the final fall of that empire to Cyrus the Persian. He did not die till 525 B.C., just before Egypt itself was to fall to Cambyses, the son of Cyrus.

Ezekiel's prophecies might almost be made to fit (if their virulence is softened) what did befall Egypt at the hands of Cambyses.

Ezekiel 30:15. *And I* [God] *will pour fury upon Sin, the strength of Egypt . . .*

Sin is usually identified with Pelusium, the Greek name for a city on the Mediterranean coast about seventy-five miles east of the Nile delta. It served as an Egyptian stronghold guarding against invasions from the east. When Cambyses marched against Egypt in 525 B.C., he defeated the Egyptian army at Pelusium and there was little resistance to him thereafter. The Revised Standard Version has the verse read "And I will pour my wrath upon Pelusium, the stronghold of Egypt."

But of course, Egypt was not destroyed even when the Persians did conquer it at last some half century after Ezekiel's threatenings, nor were the Egyptians carried off into exile.

Gog

The last third of the Book of Ezekiel is apocalyptic in nature, foretelling first a future invasion of Israel by the hordes of a mysterious ruler from the north; and of their complete defeat:

> Ezekiel 38:1. *And the word of the Lord came unto me, saying,*
> Ezekiel 38:2. *Son of man, set thy face against Gog, the land of Magog . . . and prophesy against him.*

The phrase "the land of Magog" may be an attempt of some later editor to identify the nation led by Gog. In the genealogical tables of Genesis, Magog is listed as the second son of Japheth and may simply mean "the land of Gog" (see page 46). It would make much more sense to say "set thy face against Magog, the land of Gog" and the reversal may be a copyist's error.

In either case, the question is: Who is Gog? It is often suggested that Gog represents Gyges, the founder of the Lydian monarchy, about a century before Ezekiel's time.

Gyges fell in battle against the hordes of nomad Cimmerians coming down from north of the Black Sea and devastating Asia Minor in the reign of Asshurbanipal of Assyria. For decades the nomads remained the terror of the Fertile Crescent and no doubt, for generations afterward, the thought of hordes from the north remained nightmarishly in the minds of men. Perhaps Gyges, the fighter against the Cimmerians, was confused with his foe, and Gog came to mean the nomadic invaders in general.

Eventually, "Gog, the land of Magog" was further distorted into the belief that there were two enemies, Gog and Magog, and that these would afflict the earth in the final days. They are mentioned in just this connection in the New Testament in the Book of Revelation:

> Revelation 20:7. . . . *Satan shall be loosed out of his prison,*
> Revelation 20:8. *And shall go out to deceive the nations . . . Gog and Magog, to gather them together to battle . . .*

In the Book of Ezekiel, written before the effect of Persian dualism on Jewish religious thought, only God is mentioned in connection with Gog. In Revelation, written long after Persian dualism had permeated Judaism, it is Satan who inspires them.

The euphony, perhaps, of the names Gog and Magog has caused them to live on in British legend as a pair of giants born of daughters of the Roman Emperor Diocletian (who reigned about nine hundred years after the time of Ezekiel). Greater-than-life statues called Gog and Magog have been kept in London. The latest of these, fourteen feet high, were constructed in 1708, and were destroyed in 1940 during the bombing of London by the Nazi Luftwaffe.

Following the defeat of Gog, the ideal Israel is established and in his description of this, Ezekiel launches into a meticulous description of the structure of the Temple and of the nature of its ritual. This has served almost as a constitution for the re-established Jewish community under the Persians, so that Ezekiel is sometimes called "the father of Judaism."

Ezekiel did not himself survive, in all probability, to witness the fall of Babylon (he would have had to live to be almost ninety to have done that), but men such as Ezra carried with them the new spirit of Ezekiel, and the second Temple was organized in Ezekiel's image.

27. DANIEL

DANIEL • JEHOIAKIM • BELTESHAZZAR • CHALDEANS • FEET OF CLAY • SHADRACH, MESHACH, AND ABEDNEGO • NEBUCHADNEZZAR • BELSHAZZAR • MENE, MENE, TEKEL, UPHARSIN • DARIUS THE MEDIAN • THE LITTLE HORN • THE ANCIENT OF DAYS • GABRIEL • SEVENTY WEEKS • MESSIAH THE PRINCE • MICHAEL • GRECIA • THE KING OF THE SOUTH • THE SHIPS OF CHITTIM • SUSANNA • BEL AND THE DRAGON

Daniel

In the various Christian versions of the Bible, Daniel is found after Ezekiel as a fourth major prophet. Since the events related in the book supposedly take place during the Babylonian Exile, in the reigns of Nebuchadnezzar and his successors, it comes, in chronological fitness, after the Books of Isaiah, Jeremiah, and Ezekiel.

In the Jewish canon, however, Daniel is not to be found among the prophets at all, but among the Writings. From this, it might be presumed that at the time that Daniel was written the collection of prophetic books had reached their final form and been closed. Since at least one of the prophetic books (Jonah) had been written as late as 300 B.C., it would seem to follow that Daniel was written after 300 B.C. and could not have been written by the individual who gave the book its name and who is the hero of its tales.

In fact, the Book of Daniel is probably among the last written of the Jewish canon and may date from as late as 165 B.C. A few decades later, and it might not have been allowed into the canon at all, but would have had to remain in the Apocrypha (where some might argue it really belongs anyway).

The evidence for this late authorship is manifold. Parts of the book are written in Aramaic, which seems to place it in a time when Aramaic had become so much the common speech of the people that Hebrew

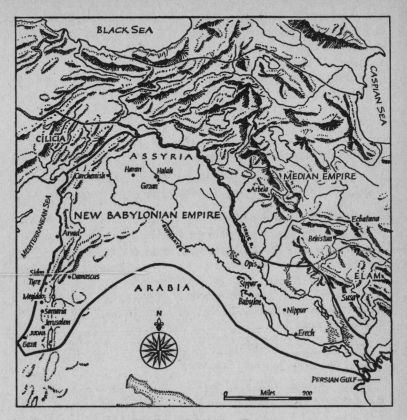

The New Babylonian Empire

was understood only by the educated. Other subtle facets of the language used bespeak the Greek period rather than the time of the Exile.

Where Isaiah, Jeremiah, and Ezekiel make no anachronistic mistakes concerning the times supposed to be theirs, the Book of Daniel is replete with anachronisms as far as it deals with the period of the Exile. It treats, however, of the Greek period with easy correctness and while this might be explained by those dedicated to the literal acceptance of the Bible as a case of prophetic insight, it is odd that Daniel should be so correct in his view of what was to him the "future" and so hazy about his view of what was to him the "present." It is easier to believe that

the writer was a man of Greek times, to whom the Exile was an event
that had taken place four centuries earlier and concerning the fine
details of which he was a bit uncertain.

There is nothing we can say about the Daniel on whom the book of
that name is based except that he must have been a folk hero known
for his wisdom and arcane knowledge. Ezekiel mentions him three
times, in a way which seems to make him an ancient worthy.

Thus, in stressing the fact that God would save only the righteous
out of a sinful city and that not one sinner would be saved for the sake
of those righteous he has God say:

> Ezekiel 14:14. Though . . . Noah, Daniel, and Job, were in it,
> they should deliver but their own souls by their righteousness . . .

Daniel is here equated with Noah, who lived at the time of the
Flood, and Job, who lived before the Exodus. Surely Daniel must be
also ancient. It is always the ancient who are reverenced and it
somehow seems implausible that Ezekiel should pass over such names
as Isaiah and Jeremiah and even Elijah in order to mention a contemporary, and a younger contemporary at that.

Again, when denouncing Ithobaal of Tyre (see page 590), Ezekiel
says sarcastically:

> Ezekiel 28:3. Behold, thou art wiser than Daniel; there is no
> secret that they can hide from thee:

Clearly, the legendary Daniel was renowned for his wisdom and can
be used as a standard in that respect. Surely, he is not a younger
contemporary of Ezekiel. He is an ancient, borrowed by the writer of the
Book of Daniel, who needed someone who was of both exemplary piety
and of unparalleled wisdom. He therefore took this Daniel and placed
him in the period of the Exile.

We can even see why he was placed in that period. It was going to
be the writer's purpose to denounce the Seleucid Empire, which in the
second century B.C. was persecuting Judaism ferociously. To avoid
charges of rebellion and treason, the writer had to refrain from attacking
the Seleucids directly. By putting the book into a period of past
disaster, he could attack them indirectly. He could make Babylon and
Nebuchadnezzar surrogate villains for Syria and the Seleucids and his
readers would know what he meant while the overlords might have
trouble proving it.

Jehoiakim

The anachronisms of Daniel begin with the first verse:

Daniel 1:1. *In the third year of the reign of Jehoiakim . . . came Nebuchadnezzar . . . unto Jerusalem, and besieged it.*
Daniel 1:2. *And the Lord gave Jehoiakim . . . into his* [Nebuchadnezzar's] *hand, with part of the vessels of the house of God: which he carried into the land of Shinar . . .*

The third year of the reign of Jehoiakim would be 606 B.C., at which time Nebuchadnezzar was not yet king of Babylon. It was in 597 that Nebuchadnezzar took Jerusalem the first time (without actually destroying it). Jehoiakim had died by then and it was his son Jehoiachin who was given into the hand of the conqueror.

Then, too, "Shinar" is an archaism that no contemporary of Nebuchadnezzar would have used. That name (the equivalent of "Sumer") was used of the land in Abraham's time (see page 48). To the Hebrews of the Exile, it was Chaldea and the temptation was to push Chaldea into the past (and speak of Ur of the Chaldees, for instance; see page 56) rather than pull Shinar forward.

Finally, Nebuchadnezzar is always spelled with the incorrect "n" in Daniel; and never, as in Jeremiah and Ezekiel, which were really composed in the Exilic period, with an at least occasional "r" to make it the more nearly correct "Nebuchadrezzar."

Belteshazzar

From among the Jews carried away in this first exile (the same in which Ezekiel had been carried away; see page 595) a number of the young men were taken to be brought up with a Chaldean education in order that they might be given positions at court:

Daniel 1:6. *Now among these were . . . Daniel, Hananiah, Mishael, and Azariah:*
Daniel 1:7. *Unto whom the prince of the eunuchs gave names:*

for he gave unto Daniel the name of Belteshazzar; and to Hananiah, of Shadrach; and to Mishael, of Meshach; and to Azariah, of Abednego.

The Yahvistic names, in other words, were changed to those involving the names of Babylonian deities. For instance, Daniel ("God is the judge") becomes Belteshazzar ("Bel protect his life"), where Bel is the great Babylonian god, Marduk (see page 552). Similarly, Azariah ("Yahveh helps") becomes Abednego, or, in proper spelling, Abednebo ("servant of Nebo").

Similarly, Hananiah ("Yahveh is gracious") becomes Shadrach ("Aku commands"), where Aku is, presumably, some lesser deity. Mishael ("who is what God is") becomes Meshach, a word of doubtful meaning, arising, perhaps, through the conversion by the writer of the Hebrew name into one that sounds Babylonian to his ears.

The four Jews did well at court, were accepted into royal favor:

Daniel 1:21. *And Daniel continued even unto the first year of Cyrus.*

Daniel, in other words, remained in favor till 538 B.C., some sixty years after he went into exile. If Daniel were eighteen at the time of the Exile, he would be seventy-eight years old at the fall of Babylon to Cyrus—a not impossible situation. At least we do not have in this book the impossibly condensed chronologies we find in Esther (see page 467).

Chaldeans

Nebuchadnezzar, like Pharaoh in the time of Joseph over a thousand years earlier, had a dream:

Daniel 2:2. *Then the king commanded to call the magicians, and the astrologers, and the sorcerers, and the Chaldeans, for to shew the king his dreams . . .*

. . . .

Daniel 2:4. *Then spake the Chaldeans to the king in Syriack, O king . . . tell thy servants the dream, and we will shew the interpretation.*

The Babylonians, like the Egyptians, were renowned for their magical powers. Actually, civilization and technology were most highly developed in those two areas in pre-Greek times and to peoples less highly developed, the ability to build the pyramids or foretell lunar eclipses would naturally be taken as a sign of magical adeptness. Undoubtedly, the learned among the Egyptians and Babylonians were not in the least averse to allowing the reputation of magic to spread. It enhanced their own value.

In aftertimes, the very word "Chaldean" (or, as we would say today, "Babylonian") came to be synonymous with magician, sorcerer, wise man, or astrologer. Here in verse 2:2, four types of the learned in magical arts are named, with no feeling that one of them refers to a nationality rather than a pursuit.

The very use of the word in this sense is another anachronism. In the time of the Exile, a Chaldean was a mighty and dreaded warrior and the word is used in this sense in the Book of Jeremiah, for instance.

A later editor of the Book of Daniel may have inserted the phrase "in Syriack" (that is, "in Aramaic") to account for the fact that a large section of the book (from this verse on, in fact, to the end of Chapter 7) is in Aramaic. Actually, there is no reason why the court officials should speak Aramaic to the king rather than his native Babylonian; and if they did, there is no real reason why the writer needs to specify it. Then, too, even if he wanted to quote the wise men in Aramaic for greater authenticity, there would be no reason to go on for a number of chapters in that language. Actually, as I said earlier, the Aramaic is an indication of the late composition of the book and the inserted phrase is a completely ineffectual attempt to mask that.

Feet of Clay

Unfortunately for the wise men, Nebuchadnezzar could not recall the dream, and yet he demanded a quick interpretation on pain of death. Daniel, like a new Joseph, offered to first reconstruct the dream and then interpret it, and thus save the lives of the magicians. He said to Nebuchadnezzar:

> Daniel 2:31. *Thou, O king, sawest, and behold a great image* . . .
> Daniel 2:32. *This image's head was of fine gold, his breast and his arms of silver, his belly and his thighs of brass,*

Daniel 2:33. *His legs of iron, his feet part of iron and part of clay.*

Daniel 2:34. *Thou sawest . . . that a stone . . . smote the image upon his feet that were of iron and clay, and brake them to pieces.*

Daniel 2:35. *Then was the iron, the clay, the brass, the silver, and the gold, broken to pieces . . . and the stone . . . became a great mountain, and filled the whole earth.*

It is from the description of this dream that the common expression "feet of clay," meaning a weak point in an otherwise strong object, came into use.

Daniel's interpretation is that Nebuchadnezzar and the Chaldean Empire which he rules is the head of gold.

Daniel 2:39. *And after thee shall arise another kingdom inferior to thee, and another third kingdom of brass, which shall bear rule over all the earth.*

Daniel 2:40. *And the fourth kingdom shall be strong as iron . . .*

Daniel 2:41. *And whereas thou sawest the feet and toes, part of potters' clay, and part of iron, the kingdom shall be divided . . .*

Daniel 2:42. *. . . the kingdom shall be partly strong, and partly broken.*

Daniel 2:44. *And in the days of these kings shall the God of heaven set up a kingdom, which shall never be destroyed . . .*

If this were really said in the time of Nebuchadnezzar, it would be an example of divine prescience indeed; but since it was very likely said four centuries after the time of Nebuchadnezzar it represents a schematic description of known history.

The second kingdom "inferior to thee" was, presumably, the Median Empire, which the writer of Daniel assumes (as can be deduced from a later passage) to have followed the Chaldean Empire. Actually, it existed concurrently with the Chaldean, but, though larger in area, the Median Empire was smaller in wealth, civilization, and military power and was hence inferior.

The third kingdom "which shall bear rule over all the earth" was undoubtedly the Persian Empire, which conquered first the Medes and then the Chaldeans and eventually ruled a vast territory that included almost all the territories known to the Jews of the time.

Finally, the fourth kingdom "strong as iron" is the Macedonian

Empire established by Alexander the Great two and a half centuries after Nebuchadnezzar's time. The two legs of iron symbolize the fact that after Alexander's death his empire was broken up and that two of its large fragments particularly interested the Jews. These were Egypt under the Ptolemies, and western Asia under the Seleucids. The Ptolemaic and Seleucid Empires were at more or less constant war with each other and Judah was torn between them. From 300 to 200 B.C. Judah was mostly under the tolerant sway of the Ptolemies, but after 200 B.C. it came under the intolerant rule of the Seleucids.

It was in the time of terror and agony under the Seleucids that the Book of Daniel was written and the stone, a re-established ideal Judah, that would destroy the Seleucid Empire, consisting as it did of weak monarchs as well as strong ones (clay mixed with iron), was a reference to the Jewish revolt against the Seleucids that began in 168 B.C.

Shadrach, Meshach, and Abednego

The third chapter of Daniel tells another legend about Nebuchadnezzar. He had a huge statue built of himself to which all his subjects were to grant divine honors. Those who refused were to be burned alive and, of course, the loyal Jews, Shadrach, Meshach, and Abednego (Daniel is not mentioned in this chapter for some reason), refused. The indicated punishment was visited upon them:

Daniel 3:23. *And these three men, Shadrach, Meshach and Abednego, fell down bound into the midst of the burning fiery furnace.*

The results were not as expected, however. Nebuchadnezzar, on surveying the situation, said:

Daniel 3:25. . . . *Lo, I see four men loose, walking in the midst of the fire, and they have no hurt; and the form of the fourth is like the Son of God.*

As it stands in the King James Version, the final phrase, capitalized as it is, might seem a clear reference to Jesus, but the phrase is not quite correct. As given in the Revised Standard Version, it reads "the fourth is like a son of the gods," in other words, like an angel.

To explain this more clearly, perhaps, some later hand composed an additional section intended to be placed immediately after verse 3:23. It contained a prayer supposedly recited by Azariah (Abednego) within the furnace and a psalm of praise to God, chanted by the three. This additional section does not appear in the Jewish canon, but only in the Apocrypha. It is accepted as canonical in the Catholic Bible.

The section bears the title of "The Song of the Three Holy Children" in the King James Version, and "The Prayer of Azariah and the Song of the Three Young Men" in the Revised Standard Version.

A few prose verses are also included in the section;

> Three Holy Children 1:26. *But the angel of the Lord came down into the oven . . . and smote the flame of the fire out of the oven;*
> Three Holy Children 1:27. . . . *so that the fire touched them not at all, neither hurt nor troubled them.*

And it was this angel of the Lord, apparently, that the later writer introduced to make it quite plain that it was an angel that Nebuchadnezzar saw, an angel that had performed a miracle.

Clearly, this legend was meant to apply to the time of writing. It was the Seleucid monarchs, not Nebuchadnezzar, who claimed divine honors; and it was the Seleucid monarchs, not Nebuchadnezzar, who threatened the Jews with death for practicing their religion. The writer was assuring the readers of the ever-present and watchful eye of God.

Nebuchadnezzar

The fourth chapter deals with still another legend of Nebuchadnezzar. Again he has a dream and again Daniel interprets it. This time, the interpretation is that Nebuchadnezzar, unless he forswears his sins and reforms, is going to be condemned to lose his mind and eat grass like an ox.

At the end of a year, Nebuchadnezzar in a moment of pride is suddenly stricken:

> Daniel 4:33. *The same hour was the thing fulfilled upon Nebuchadnezzar: and he was driven from men, and did eat grass as oxen, and his body was wet with the dew of heaven, till his hairs were grown like eagles' feathers, and his nails like birds' claws.*

And he remained so until he repented.

Of course, there is no record in secular history of Nebuchadnezzar suffering from any such strange malady, and it is in the highest degree unlikely that he did. It remains only to decide where the writer got the idea that the great Chaldean conqueror browsed on grass.

One guess is particularly attractive. The Assyrians built statues in the shape of bulls with human heads and birds' wings to represent good-luck deities. They are the inspiration of the Biblical cherubim (see page 148). These were built in front of Sargon's palace and are as characteristic of Assyria as the pyramids are of Egypt and the pillared temples of the Greeks. Such figures, or tales of them, must have remained after the Assyrian Empire itself had been destroyed and in Greek times all kinds of fanciful tales must have been made up to account for these composite representations. The tale of a Chaldean monarch who was forced to eat grass like an ox till his hair grew like eagles' feathers is transparently based on such statues.

Belshazzar

The next incident described in Daniel takes place after the death of Nebuchadnezzar and, apparently, shortly before the fall of Babylon to the Persians:

Daniel 5:1. *Belshazzar the king made a great feast . . . and . . .*
Daniel 5:2. *. . . commanded to bring the golden and silver vessels which his father Nebuchadnezzar had taken out of the temple which was in Jerusalem . . .*

Apparently, the writer of Daniel knew of only two kings of Babylon during the period of the Exile: Nebuchadnezzar the first and Belshazzar, supposedly his son, the second and last. A writer actually living in the Exilic period or shortly afterward could not have made that mistake.

Nebuchadnezzar died in 562 B.C., twenty-four years after the destruction of Jerusalem, and was succeeded by his son, Amel-Marduk (not Belshazzar). Amel-Marduk is referred to in the Bible as the "Evil-merodach" who lightened the captivity of Jehoiachin (see page 396).

In 560 B.C., Amel-Marduk was assassinated by his brother-in-law, Nergal-ashur-usur (whose name is slurred into Neriglissar by the

classical historians). For four years this son-in-law of Nebuchadnezzar sat on the throne and it is just barely possible that he is mentioned
in the Bible. Thus, in Jeremiah's description of the fall of Jerusalem,
a list of Nebuchadnezzar's generals is given:

> Jeremiah 39:2. . . . *the city was broken up.*
> Jeremiah 39:3. *And all the princes of the king of Babylon came in*
> . . . *even Nergal-sha-rezer, Samgar-nebo, Sarsechim . . .*

Is it possible that Nergal-sha-rezer is a misspelling of Nergal-ashur-
usur? Can it further be that Nebuchadnezzar bestowed one of his
daughters upon this general, who then, in later years, seized the throne
from his old ruler's weaker son?

Nergal-ashur-usur died in 556 B.C. and was succeeded by his son,
Labashi-Marduk, a grandson of Nebuchadnezzar, but there was opposition to him. The opposition proclaimed Nabu-naido ("Nabu is glorious"), who was no relative at all of Nebuchadnezzar. They won out
and Nabu-naido, better known to us as Nabonidus, the Greek version
of the name, sat on the throne as the last king of the Chaldean Empire.
He was to reign seventeen years.

Where, then, is Belshazzar?

Well, Nabonidus was the son of a priest and, apparently, had had a
scholarly upbringing. His chief interest was in religion and in antiquarian research. He restored old temples and built new ones. He
searched for old cylinders and inscriptions, dug them up carefully and
reproduced them (performing invaluable services for modern historians).

He was not at all interested in war and neglected the defenses of the
nation.

He therefore associated his oldest son with himself and made him a
kind of viceroy. The burdens of the defense of the empire sat upon that
son's shoulders. His name was Bel-shar-utsur ("Bel, protect the king")
and it is he who, in the Book of Daniel, is known as Belshazzar. He is
not the king but the crown prince, and he is not the son, or any other
relation, of Nebuchadnezzar.

The times were growing dark for Chaldea in the time of Nabonidus
and Belshazzar. It had been in 559 B.C., soon after the assassination of
Amel-Marduk, that Cyrus had inherited rule over the Persian tribes. In
550 B.C., after Nabonidus had been on the throne five or six years, Cyrus
defeated and absorbed the Median Empire and became a world power.

The Chaldean Empire faced an overwhelming danger only a dozen years after the death of Nebuchadnezzar.

The empire formed an alliance with Saitic Egypt and with the nation of Lydia in Asia Minor, but that didn't help. In 546 B.C., Lydia was crushed by Persia and all of Asia Minor passed over to Cyrus.

Chaldea was next.

Mene, Mene, Tekel, Upharsin

In the middle of Belshazzar's feast, at which the holy vessels of the Temple were being profaned:

Daniel 5:5. . . . *came forth fingers of a man's hand, and wrote . . . upon . . . the wall of the king's palace . . .*

The words were unintelligible to the onlookers, so Daniel, the now aged interpreter of Nebuchadnezzar's dreams, was sent for. This was his interpretation:

Daniel 5:25. *And this is the writing . . . MENE, MENE, TEKEL, UPHARSIN.*

Daniel 5:26. *This is the interpretation . . . MENE; God hath numbered thy kingdom, and finished it.*

Daniel 5:27. *TEKEL; Thou art weighed in the balances, and found wanting.*

Daniel 5:28. *PERES; Thy kingdom is divided, and given to the Medes and the Persians.*

The actual meaning of Mene, Mene, Tekel, Upharsin is uncertain. The words are apparently Aramaean and may represent the names of weights. Mene is the "mina," which is roughly equivalent to the modern pound, and Tekel is the "shekel," which is one fiftieth of a mina, or a third of an ounce. Upharsin is more puzzling. The Revised Standard Version changes it to "parsin" and it may be a pun on "Parsa," the native word for what we call Persia. Some think that Upharsin is a form of a word that originally meant a half shekel.

In any case, an inscription made up of the names of weights might give the impression of God weighing the worth of Chaldea in comparison with Persia and finding Chaldea "wanting"—that is, the lighter of the two. This is reminiscent of the scenes in the Greek epic, the *Iliad*, in which Zeus consults the Fates by placing the lots of two fighters in separate balances of the scale to see which one outweighs the other. This may be the source of the vision of God weighing Belshazzar in the balance.

It is this dramatic incident that has given rise to the common phrase "the handwriting on the wall" to signify a certain indication of imminent disaster even amid apparent success.

Darius the Median

Certainly, what followed the episode was dramatic enough, according to the Book of Daniel:

Daniel 5:30. *In that night was Belshazzar . . . slain.*
Daniel 5:31. *And Darius the Median took the kingdom, being about threescore and two years old.*

It was in 538 B.C. that Gobryas, a general of Cyrus the Persian, led an army into the city of Babylon and Cyrus was indeed about sixty-two years old at the time. Babylon itself offered no resistance. Belshazzar, maintaining a last-ditch struggle at some point outside Babylon, was slain.

But what is this about Darius the Median? Who was he? No one, apparently. He arises, apparently, out of the conviction that the four great empires appeared consecutively: Chaldean, Median, Persian, Greek (see page 602); whereas actually Chaldean and Median existed together and both fell to the Persian. The writer's conviction of consecutive empires leads him to suppose that Babylon had to fall to a Mede and that it was only afterward that Cyrus supplanted the Mede.

As for the name Darius, given to the mythical Median conqueror of Babylon, this must be drawn from the Darius who came to the Persian throne in 521 B.C., seventeen years after the fall of Babylon, and the most capable and renowned of all the Persian monarchs.

The rest of the Book of Daniel dates itself sometimes in the reign of Cyrus, sometimes in the reign of Darius the Mede, and no useful purpose can be gained from trying to place actual dates to the chapters. The writer was not describing actual incidents and had no specific dates in mind.

At one point, he gives the name of the father of Darius the Mede:

Daniel 9:1. *In the first year of Darius the son of Ahasuerus, of the seed of the Medes* . . .

The father of the real Darius the Persian was Hystaspes. If Ahasuerus is Xerxes I of Persia (see page 463), then he was the son of Darius, not the father.

The famous story is then told of Daniel being thrown into a den of lions because he violated an edict (which Darius was tricked into signing) forbidding anyone to address any petition to anyone but himself. Daniel's open prayers to God were construed as a violation of this edict. Nevertheless, an angel was sent to protect him from the lions and he remained unharmed. Again, it is the Seleucid monarchs that are really meant and the reader is assured of God's care at all times.

Daniel 6:28. *So . . . Daniel prospered in the reign of Darius, and in the reign of Cyrus the Persian.*

Thus, Darius the Median is described as being followed by Cyrus the Persian in line with the writer's mistaken view of history.

The Little Horn

The remainder of the Book of Daniel is a series of apocalyptic visions, with the facts of human history (as the writer saw them) disguised in the form of mystic symbolism, presumably to avoid trouble with the authorities. The first vision described is that of four beasts, representing the four kingdoms, arising, in succession, out of the sea:

Daniel 7:4. *The first was like a lion, and had eagle's wings* . . .
Daniel 7:5. *. . . a second, like to a bear* . . .
Daniel 7:6. *. . . another, like a leopard . . . the beast had four heads* . . .
Daniel 7:7. *After this . . . behold a fourth beast, dreadful and terrible, and strong exceedingly; and it had great iron teeth . . . and it had ten horns.*
Daniel 7:8. *I considered the horns, and behold, there came up among them another little horn, before whom there were three of the first horns plucked up by the roots* . . .

The first beast is clearly the winged lion that gave rise to the notion that Nebuchadnezzar ate grass (see page 605) and represents the Chal-

dean Empire. The bear is the Median Empire, and the leopard the
Persian Empire. The leopard's four heads are the four monarchs of the
Persians whom the writer will mention again later in the book. The
fourth beast is the Macedonian Empire set up by Alexander the
Great, whose enormous feats of conquest astonished all beholders and
have steadily remained a wonder of history through succeeding ages.

To the writer, that portion of Alexander's empire which came under
the rule of his general Seleucus and his descendants is the important
part, for it is under these Seleucids that the Jews were suffering persecution. The prime persecutor, in particular, was Antiochus IV, the
eighth reigning monarch of the line, who came to the throne in 175 B.C.

The symbolism of the ten horns and the additional "little horn"
seems clear. Each horn is a king of the Seleucid line and Antiochus
himself is the little horn. He apparently became king only after a short
civil war between rival factions. Antiochus was victorious, uprooting
three horns, leaving seven, and making himself the eighth king.

The Ancient of Days

Daniel then saw the beasts slain before the judgment seat of God:

Daniel 7:9. . . . *the thrones were cast down, and the Ancient of
days did sit, whose garment was white as snow, and the hair of his
head like the pure wool* . . .

The "Ancient of days" is, of course, God, visualized as an old man
since he existed from the beginning of time and even before. The Revised Standard Version removes the effect of "Ancient" as a capitalized noun and has the phrase read: "one that was ancient of days
took his seat."

In place of the destroyed beasts, a new kingdom was set up:

Daniel 7:13. . . . *behold, one like the Son of man . . . came to
the Ancient of days* . . .
Daniel 7:14. *And there was given him dominion, and glory, and a
kingdom . . . which shall not pass away* . . .

It is sometimes suggested that this is a Messianic utterance; that the
fourth kingdom is the Roman Empire and that the Son of man represents Jesus. (That is why the King James Version capitalizes "Son"; the

Revised Standard Version does not.) It seems much more likely, though, that what is meant here is that a new and eternal kingdom is given to the ideal Jewish state, represented here in the likeness of a man rather than in the likeness of the beasts that represented the various heathen and idolatrous kingdoms.

Gabriel

The last five chapters of Daniel are in Hebrew. This may mean that they were written by a different hand than those that wrote the six preceding chapters. Or, perhaps, the shift to Hebrew is to further disguise the treasonable meaning of the visions described in those chapters.

Another vision is described. A ram with two horns (Media and Persia) is destroyed by a goat with one large horn (Macedon under Alexander the Great). The goat then develops several horns from among which a little horn appears—again a reference to the Seleucid kings and to Antiochus IV. The meaning of the vision was explained to Daniel through supernatural means:

Daniel 8:16. *And I heard a man's voice . . . which called, and said, Gabriel, make this man to understand the vision.*

Gabriel ("hero of God") is a product of the development of the Jewish view of angels under Persian influence. Gabriel is one of the four archangels (chief angels)—or of the seven, or twelve, or seventy, depending on the writer who is working out the mystical interrelationships.

Perhaps because of his role in the Book of Daniel, Gabriel is usually thought of as God's messenger, explaining divine meanings to selected human beings. In the New Testament it is Gabriel who explains to Mary that she is to bear Jesus, and in Mohammedan legends, it is Gabriel who takes Mohammed to Heaven and dictates the Koran to him.

In later Jewish legends, intended to fill out the details omitted in the earlier Biblical books, it was the angel Gabriel who supposedly took on the guise of a man and directed the young Joseph to the place where his brethren were pasturing their sheep. Gabriel was also, according to legend, one of those who buried Moses, and one of those who destroyed the army of Sennacherib.

Daniel is the only book in the Jewish canon in which angels are given names. Elsewhere the names of the angels appear only in the Apocrypha and in the New Testament. This is another sign of the late composition of Daniel.

Seventy Weeks

The writer then represents Daniel as considering Jeremiah's prediction that the kingdom of Judah would be restored, presumably in ideal form, after seventy years from the time of the destruction of the Temple. In the time of Zerubbabel and Nehemiah, it must have seemed to Jews, generally, that the prophecy was coming true. After all, Jews again controlled Jerusalem and the second Temple was opened to worship just seventy years after the destruction of the first Temple (see page 449).

To later Jews, though, particularly to those living under the Seleucids, there must have seemed a bitter irony in the prediction. The restored state of Jerusalem had remained under the firm control of first the Persians, then the Ptolemies, then the Seleucids. Not only did it never become the ideal Israel dominating the world, but it was actually being threatened under the Seleucids with utter extinction. How could all this be squared with Jeremiah's prediction?

A modification of that prediction had to be made and the writer of Daniel turned to the mystic lore of numbers. The Jews, like many of the ancient peoples (even certain of the Greek philosophers), felt there were all sorts of hidden meaning in numbers and that special numbers had special characters.

Seven, for instance, was a number of peculiar significance. This might be traced back to the seventh day being the Sabbath, but this in turn seems to be of Babylonian origin, where the seven-day week rose from the fact that there were seven "planets" in the heavens. Each of the planets was in charge of a particular day of the week. We still have a remnant of this in Sunday (the sun), Monday (the moon), and Saturday (Saturn). In the Romance languages the other days are similarly identified. In French, for instance, Tuesday, Wednesday, Thursday, and Friday are *mardi* (Mars), *mercredi* (Mercury), *jeudi* (Jupiter), and *vendredi* (Venus).

But whatever the origin of the special characteristics of seven, to

Daniel seven was a sacred number. The seventy years of Jeremiah were really seven decades, and might not the sacred significance of that be increased further by an additional multiplication by seven? Instead of seventy years, there would be seventy weeks (seventy times seven) of years. Gabriel explains this to Daniel:

Daniel 9:24. *Seventy weeks are determined upon thy people and upon thy holy city, to finish the transgression and to make an end of sins.*

The phrase "seventy weeks" is expanded to "seventy weeks of years" in the Revised Standard Version.

Seventy weeks of years, or 490 years, counting from the destruction of the first Temple in 586 B.C., would carry matters to 96 B.C., a date safely in the writer's future. (As it turns out, of course, the ideal Jewish state was not established in 96 B.C., either, and that date has no particular significance in Jewish history.)

Messiah the Prince

Daniel's vision goes into greater detail:

Daniel 9:25. . . . *from the going forth of the commandment to restore and to build Jerusalem unto the Messiah the Prince shall be seven weeks, and threescore and two weeks: the street shall be built again . . .*

Daniel 9:26. *And after threescore and two weeks shall Messiah be cut off . . .*

One might see in this a reference to Jesus, particularly since the King James Version capitalizes "Messiah" and "Prince." The Revised Standard Version does not, however. The phrase in 9:25 is rendered "an anointed one, a prince," and in 9:26, "an anointed one." And we must remember that the writer of Daniel is speaking obscurely, at least to us. His original readers would have had no trouble.

What the twenty-fifth verse seems to say is that seven weeks of years (forty-nine years) will pass from Jeremiah's prediction, or from the fall of the first Temple in 586 B.C. to the coming of an anointed king who will make it possible to rebuild. A passage of forty-nine years (seven times seven, a sacred number indeed) brings us to 537 B.C., which is indeed within a year of the time (538 B.C.) when Cyrus granted Jews permission to rebuild; and remember that Cyrus is specifically spoken of by the Second Isaiah as one whose hand God holds and therefore as an anointed king (see page 549).

It is completely reasonable, then, to understand "Messiah the Prince" to signify Cyrus of Persia. Following Cyrus are sixty-two weeks of years (434 years) during which Jerusalem exists as a city. At the end of that time, 104 B.C., "shall Messiah be cut off."

This can't be the same Messiah spoken of in the verse before. In the first place, four and a third centuries have passed, and in the second, the first is a prince, a secular leader, and the second is not. The second is merely "an anointed one"; that is, a High Priest.

As a matter of fact, there was a High Priest in the time that Daniel was probably written who was a champion of Judaism against the Seleucids and against those Jews who advocated a compromise with Seleucid views. He was Onias III, the son of that Simon II who was praised so highly by Jesus, son of Sirach (see page 516). Onias III became High Priest in 198 B.C. When Antiochus IV became king, Onias III was first deposed, then imprisoned, and finally, in 171 B.C., executed. This quickly led to the final crisis that brought on a Jewish revolt against the Seleucids. The killing of Onias III can therefore be looked upon as a turning point.

It may, therefore, be Onias III who is the Messiah that is cut off, although the date given in Daniel misses the actual date by sixty-six years. (However, no one has been able to make the dates given in Daniel's vision come out both significantly and accurately.)

The peak of persecution that follows on the death of Onias III is also described:

> Daniel 9:26. . . . *the prince that shall come shall destroy the city and the sanctuary . . .*
> Daniel 9:27. . . . *for one week: and in the midst of the week he shall cause the sacrifice and the oblation to cease, and for the overspreading of abominations he shall make it desolate . . .*

The language as the writer approaches his own time becomes more carefully obscure. Apparently, he speaks now of the final week—the seven-year period after the death of Onias III in which Seleucid persecution is at its height—from 171 to 165 B.C.

In the "midst of the week," or in 168 B.C., Antiochus IV took Jerusalem and pillaged it. He outlawed Judaism and ordered the Temple to be profaned and dedicated to Zeus. Swine were deliberately sacrificed on the altar in order to subject it to the most vile desecration possible in the eyes of pious Jews. Such sacrifices were "abominations" and the Temple was rendered so unclean that it had to be abandoned, or made "desolate" till it could be cleansed again by painstaking ritual. These idolatrous sacrifices are sometimes spoken of as "the abomination of desolation."

The final cleansing and rededication of the Temple did take place in 165 B.C. at the end of the week of years and Antiochus IV died in 163 B.C.

Michael

In Daniel's next vision, he is helped by a heavenly messenger who reaches him only after resistance from one angel and help from another:

> Daniel 10:13. . . . *the prince of the kingdom of Persia withstood me one and twenty days: but, lo, Michael, one of the chief princes, came to help me . . .*

Here we have the late Jewish view that each nation had a guardian angel of its own (a kind of henotheism reduced to a subsidiary level). Michael ("who is like God?") is the guardian angel of Judah. The angel tells Daniel:

> Daniel 10:20. . . . *now will I return to fight with the prince of Persia: and . . . lo, the prince of Grecia shall come.*
> Daniel 10:21. . . . *there is none that holdeth with me in these things, but Michael your prince.*

Naturally, in his capacity as the guardian angel of Judah, Michael is considered by the Jews to be the greatest of the angels. In the legends concerning the fall of Satan from Heaven (see page 540), Michael is viewed as the leader of the loyal angels, fighting for God against the devil. This is mentioned in Revelation:

> Revelation 12:7. *And there was war in heaven: Michael and his angels fought against the dragon: and the dragon . . .*
> Revelation 12:8. . . . *prevailed not . . .*
> Revelation 12:9. *And the great dragon was cast out . . . into the earth, and his angels were cast out with him.*

Another mention of Michael and the devil, contending on earth, is to be found in the New Testament Book of Jude:

> Jude 1:9. . . . *Michael the archangel* . . . *contending with the devil* . . . *about the body of Moses* . . .

Grecia

Daniel is told:

> Daniel 11:2. . . . *Behold there shall stand up* . . . *three kings in Persia; and the fourth shall be far richer than they all: and* . . . *shall stir up all against the realm of Grecia.*

The four kings of Persia are foreshadowed earlier by the leopard with four heads that represented that empire (see page 609). Presumably, the four kings of Persia are Cyrus, Cambyses, Darius, and Xerxes. That the fourth is Xerxes is indicated by the fact that his famous expedition against Greece is mentioned.

The King of the South

In guarded language, Daniel is told of the coming of Alexander the Great and of the breakup of Alexander's empire; then, of the history of the fragments of importance to Jewish history:

> Daniel 11:5. *And the king of the south shall be strong* . . .
> Daniel 11:6. . . . *the king's daughter of the south shall come to the king of the north to make an agreement* . . .

The two fragments of importance are Ptolemaic Egypt and the Seleucid Empire. Egypt lies to the south and west of Judah, and the Seleucid Empire to the north and east. The "king of the south" refers to the Ptolemies, and the "king of the north" to the Seleucids.

These verses and those that follow refer to the continuing wars between the Ptolemies and the Seleucids for the control of what had once been the land of Canaan. The early Ptolemies were victorious:

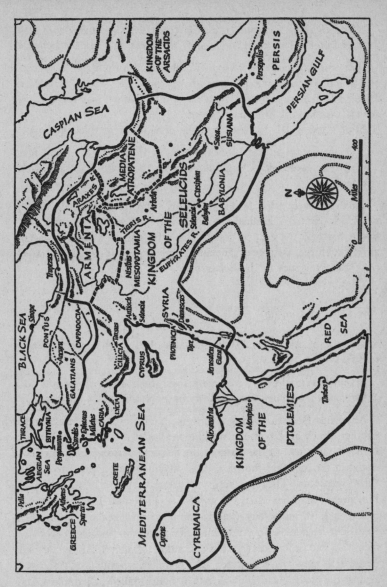

Kingdoms of the Ptolemies and the Seleucids

Daniel 11:7. . . . *one . . . shall come with an army, and shall*
enter into the fortress of the king of the north . . . and shall prevail:

This probably refers to Ptolemy III, who reigned from 246 to 221 B.C.
and who defeated the Seleucids in what is called the Third Syrian War,
taking all of Syria and even sections of Asia Minor. His reign represented the peak of Ptolemaic power.

After Ptolemy III, however, a series of weak kings ruled in Egypt:

Daniel 11:15. *So the king of the north shall come . . . and take*
the most fenced cities: and the arms of the south shall not with-
stand . . .

This very likely refers to Antiochus III, who ruled from 223 to 187
B.C. Under him the Seleucid Empire was at the peak of its power. Between 201 and 195 B.C., he fought the Fifth Syrian War with Egypt
and took all the Asian coast, including Judah. With that, Judah passed
from the Ptolemies to the Seleucids.

The Ships of Chittim

The rise of Antiochus IV is then described in the most insulting
terms:

Daniel 11:21. *And in his estate shall stand up a vile person . . .*
he shall . . . obtain the kingdom by flatteries.

Antiochus IV became king in 175 B.C. and in 171 B.C. he launched
another attack on Egypt, against the weak and cowardly Ptolemy VI.
It may be that part of the cause of the Seleucid persecution of the Jews
rested in the fact that the Jews, in all likelihood, were pro-Egyptian in
their sympathies. They had been well treated, by and large, under the
Ptolemies, and Alexandria, the capital of Ptolemaic Egypt, may well
have contained more Jews (and certainly more prosperous Jews) than
Jerusalem itself did. To Antiochus, the attack on Judaism may have
seemed a political necessity. His execution of Onias III in 171 B.C.
(page 614) may have been intended to remove a possible rallying point
against the pro-Seleucid High Priests he had installed in Jerusalem, and
to prevent a rising in his rear while he was busy in Egypt.

Antiochus won his war—but times had changed. There was a new

power in the world now; that of Rome. The Roman Republic had no
desire to see any eastern kingdom grow strong enough to dispute overlordship of the Mediterranean world. They ordered the victorious
Antiochus out of Egypt, and Antiochus, very much against his will,
had to leave. He could beat the Egyptians but he knew he could not
beat the Romans.

> Daniel 11:30. *For the ships of Chittim shall come against him:
> therefore he shall be grieved, and return, and have indignation
> against the holy covenant . . .*

Chittim is Cyprus (page 201). The writer of Daniel is rather vague
on the geography of the mysterious regions out past the Mediterranean
shores and this would be his way of saying "the ships from the western
islands." Of course, it is the Roman power that he means and this is
the only reference to Rome in the Old Testament.

Antiochus IV, unbearably humiliated by this treatment from Rome,
must have felt the need for some victory, however small, with which to
save his face before his people and himself. No doubt, the Jews were
openly jubilant at the way in which Antiochus had been made to crawl
before the Romans, and this caused him to "have indignation against
the holy covenant" and helped drive him on to occupy Jerusalem and
profane the Temple.

> Daniel 12:2. . . . *there shall be a time of trouble, such as never
> was . . .*
> . . . .
> Daniel 12:7. . . . *it shall be for a time, times, and an half . . .*
> . . . .
> Daniel 12:11. . . . *from the time that . . . the abomination that
> maketh desolate* [was] *set up, there shall be a thousand two hun-
> dred and ninety days.*

The reference to "time, times, and an half" is taken to mean one
year plus two years plus half a year, or three and a half years. And, of
course, 1290 days is also equal to about three and a half years, and it
did take about that long after the profanation of the Temple before
the Jewish rebels could retake and repurify it.

Susanna

The canonical Book of Daniel ends with the twelfth chapter, but there are, in addition, several short legends told of Daniel, stressing his wisdom and cleverness. Three of them are included in the Apocrypha and these are considered canonical by the Catholic Church.

The first is "The History of Susanna," which appears as the thirteenth chapter of Daniel in the Catholic versions of the Bible.

The book is titled after its heroine, whose name means "lily." It is what we would today call a detective story and, considering the time of its composition, it is an excellent one and has been sufficiently popular, as a result, to make the name Susanna and Susan common among young ladies even today.

The setting is in Babylon during the Exile:

> Susanna 1:1. *There dwelt a man in Babylon, called Joacim:*
> Susanna 1:2. *And he took a wife, whose name was Susanna . . .*

Quickly, the two villains are introduced:

> Susanna 1:5. *The same year were appointed two of the ancients of the people to be judges . . .*

The "ancients," or elders, proved to be wicked, and Jewish tradition identified them, therefore, with two prophets denounced as false by Jeremiah:

> Jeremiah 29:21. *Thus saith the Lord . . . of Ahab . . . and . . . Zedekiah . . . which prophesy a lie unto you in my name; Behold, I will deliver them into the hand of Nebuchadrezzar . . .*

But since Susanna is generally considered a work of fiction, such an identification need not be taken seriously.

The two elders lusted after Susanna and tried to seduce her. Her virtue was proof against their elderly charms and they conspired to accuse her of adultery, in order to punish her for her refusal. They stated they had seen her intimate with a young man whom they had not been strong enough to arrest. The assembly, impressed by the word of the elders, condemned Susanna to death.

At this point Daniel enters:

Susanna 1:45. . . . *when she was led to be put to death, the Lord raised up the holy spirit of a young youth, whose name was Daniel:*

Daniel's youth, at the time of this event, has led some old editions of the Bible to place this story at the beginning of the Book of Daniel rather than at the end. Certainly there is some sense to this.

Daniel demanded the right to cross-examine the elders separately before the council. He asked each the name of the tree under which he had seen the criminal intimacy take place. Each named a different tree and it was plain that they were lying. Susanna was freed and, presumably, lived happily ever after, while the elders were put to death for bearing false witness.

Bel and the Dragon

The two remaining legends of Daniel are combined under the title of "Bel and the Dragon." These are included as the fourteenth chapter of Daniel in the Catholic versions of the Bible. Both tales are designed to show the folly of idolatry.

The tales are laid in the time of Cyrus:

Bel and the Dragon 1:1. *And king Astyages was gathered to his fathers, and Cyrus of Persia received his kingdom.*

This apocryphal tale is more accurate, at this point, than the canonical Book of Daniel. Here there is no mention of "Darius the Median." Astyages was, indeed, the last king of the Medes. He was defeated by Cyrus, who ruled in his place and who then went on to conquer Lydia and Babylonia.

In the first short tale, Daniel got into trouble with Cyrus because he would not worship the idol Bel (or Marduk), to which every day the Babylonians devoted twelve bushels of flour, forty sheep, and fifty gallons of wine.

Daniel maintained that Bel was a false god, and Cyrus pointed out how much he ate and drank. Daniel therefore secretly arranged to have the floor of the room in which the idol stood covered with fine ashes and the doors sealed after the offerings had been made. The next morning, footsteps were found in the ashes and it turned out there was a secret room to which the priests of Bel, with their families, took the food and ate it. The priests were therefore killed and the temple destroyed.

As a matter of fact, the great Babylonian temple of Marduk was indeed destroyed by a Persian king, but for strictly secular reasons. It was Xerxes who razed it in punishment for a Babylonian rebellion against his rule, and as part of a general sack of the city.

In the second tale Cyrus orders Daniel to worship a dragon (probably a large snake). Daniel refuses, pointing out that the dragon can easily be killed, so that it is no god. He then proceeds to feed it a concoction that kills it.

The king was forced to hand over Daniel to the indignant Babylonians and they threw him into a lion's den. Here, as in the canonical book, Daniel is saved by divine intervention, but with an added feature, for another prophet is introduced.

> Bel and the Dragon 1:33. *Now there was in Jewry a prophet, called Habbacuc . . .*

or, as the Revised Standard Version has it: "Now the prophet Habakkuk was in Judea."

There was indeed a prophet by that name in Judah, and he was the author of one of the canonical prophetic books. Undoubtedly, the writer of Bel and the Dragon meant this Habakkuk, but if so, he missed out a bit chronologically. Habakkuk was active in the reign of Josiah and shortly afterward, or over half a century before the time of Cyrus. He was not likely to be alive at the time of this tale.

But putting this small matter to one side, the prophet Habakkuk fed Daniel after he was miraculously transported from Judea to Babylon. Daniel was then freed unharmed and once again was triumphant over all his enemies.

28. HOSEA

HOSEA • JEZREEL • JAREB • SHALMAN • DAVID

Hosea

The final twelve canonical books of the Old Testament are twelve relatively short prophetic works, which, for convenience' sake, were combined into a single scroll in ancient times. One might therefore speak of a "book of the twelve."

Indeed, Jesus, son of Sirach, implies just that. In his memorial to the famous men of Biblical history (see page 516) he goes through the books of the Bible in order (and thus shows which were accepted as canonical in the Judea of his day). Having spoken of Isaiah, Jeremiah, and Ezekiel, the major prophets, he does not list the remaining prophets separately, but merely says:

Ecclesiasticus 49:10. *And of the twelve prophets let the memorial be blessed . . .*

(Be it noted that there is no mention of Daniel, a book very likely composed after his time.)

The twelve prophets are sometimes called the "minor prophets," not because their teachings are necessarily unimportant from a religious standpoint, but simply because their messages are much shorter than those included under the names of Isaiah, Jeremiah, and Ezekiel.

The twelve minor prophets do not occur in chronological order, though this may have been the original intention. Unfortunately, the traditional period of activity of the individual prophets does not always agree with the one determined by modern scholarship.

Hosea, who heads the list, is indeed one of the earlier ones of the twelve, but he is not the earliest. He is the only one of the twelve

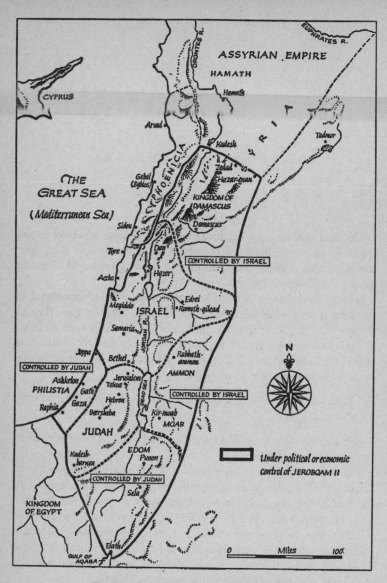

Israel and Judah at the Time of Hosea

to be a man of Israel, a northerner, rather than a man of Judah. Indeed, although there were northern prophets who, in later times, were greatly honored by the Jews (Elijah, for instance), Hosea is the only northerner whose utterances are collected into a formal and separate book.

That Hosea is a northerner is not specifically stated, but it is deduced from the fact that virtually all his speeches are addressed to Israel rather than Judah. In addition, he refers to the Israelite monarch in a possessive that includes himself:

Hosea 7:5. *In the day of our king . . .*

The book begins by dating itself:

Hosea 1:1. *The word of the Lord that came unto Hosea . . . in the days of Uzziah, Jotham, Ahaz, and Hezekiah, kings of Judah, and in the days of Jeroboam, . . . king of Israel.*

This introductory verse is probably by the later hand of a Judean editor anxious to date the book in Judean terms.

Uzziah became king in 780 B.C. and Hezekiah died in 692 B.C. As for Jeroboam II, he ruled from 785 to 745 B.C. The book gives clear evidence of knowledge of the near anarchy that pervaded Israel in the quarter century between Jeroboam's death and the destruction of Israel by Assyria. If, then, we were to guess that various parts of the book represent utterances made between 750 and 720 B.C., Hosea would have preached from the last years of Jeroboam II to the destruction of Israel. In Judean terms, that would date him from the final years of Uzziah through the reigns of Jotham and Ahaz and into the beginning of the reign of Hezekiah. This would account for the dating of the first verse and would make Hosea an older contemporary of Isaiah.

The name Hosea, by the way, is a version of the more correct Hoshea, the name borne by the last king of Israel.

Jezreel

The first three chapters of Hosea are taken by most commentators to be autobiographical and to relate the story of Hosea's marriage. Hosea's wife proved unfaithful but the prophet found he loved her

anyway and took her back. In this, he discovered a symbolic reference
to God's love for Israel and God's willingness to forgive Israel her
transgressions.

As was true of Isaiah at roughly the same point in history, Hosea
gave his children symbolic names:

> Hosea 1:3. . . . he went and took Gomer . . . which conceived,
> and bare him a son.
>
> Hosea 1:4. And the Lord said unto him, Call his name Jezreel;
> for yet a little while, and I will avenge the blood of Jezreel upon
> the house of Jehu . . .

A century earlier, Jehu had overthrown the reigning house of Omri
and had established himself on the throne (see page 364). The prophetic party had justified this result, since it overthrew an idolatrous
line of kings who were attempting to introduce Tyrian worship, and
who were energetically persecuting the Yahvists. Nevertheless, even the
Yahvist editors of the material in the Second Book of Kings could not
hide the fact that the revolution had been carried through very bloodily
and that Jehu had remorselessly killed a large number of helpless
people.

The murder of an anointed king, regardless of the personal characteristics of that king, is bound to be looked upon with horror by
people taught to believe that the anointment represented the adoption
of the monarch by a deity. This quasi-holy character of the kingship
served to protect kings from assassination down to modern times, and
explains some of the horror produced in conservative minds by the
British execution of Charles I in 1649 and the French execution of
Louis XVI in 1793.

There is bound to be a feeling, therefore, that an act of regicide
will have its consequences, even though these may be delayed. Thus,
Shakespeare, in his historical plays, sees some of the disasters befalling
England in the fifteenth century as being the consequence of the forced
deposition and later murder of Richard II (even though Shakespeare
recognizes him as an unworthy king).

Similarly, there could well have been a feeling in Israel that the
horrors that Jehu carried through in Jezreel (where Jezebel was among
those killed) would come back to haunt his descendants. So far, Jehu,
his son, his grandson, and Jeroboam II, his great-grandson, had reigned

for a century of reasonable peace. Indeed, under Jeroboam II, Israel reached a peak of power. Nevertheless, Hosea foresees the coming disaster and with the king's death in 740 B.C., that disaster begins. Jeroboam's son Zachariah succeeds to the throne as the fifth member of the dynasty of Jehu, but he is assassinated almost at once and then comes the downward spiral.

The accession of Tiglath-Pileser III to the Assyrian throne in 745 B.C. and the quick evidences that here was a strong, warlike monarch who was sure to engage in westward aggressions must have made it clear to Hosea, as to Isaiah, that the time was running out for the little kingdoms.

Jareb

It seemed to Hosea that even submission to Assyria would not cure the general decay sweeping over Israel and Judah:

Hosea 5:13. *When Ephraim saw his sickness and Judah saw his wound, then went Ephraim to the Assyrian, and sent to king Jareb: yet could he not heal you, nor cure you of your wound.*

There is no Assyrian king named Jareb, so it must be a nickname. It is associated with a Hebrew word meaning "to strive" or "to fight." Perhaps it might be translated as "the fighting king" or "the warlike king" and in either case it is obviously Tiglath-Pileser III of Assyria. The Revised Standard Version translates "king Jareb" as "the great king," a common title for the king of the Middle Eastern empires of ancient times.

In the event, Hosea's judgment proved correct. Submission to Assyria did not save the kingdoms for each rebelled, until the former was finally crushed by Assyria and the latter by the successor kingdom of Chaldea.

Shalman

The disaster Hosea predicts is expressed in a number of ways, including the very familiar:

Hosea 8:7. *For they have sown the wind, and they shall reap the whirlwind . . .*

and the less poetic, but more specific:

Hosea 10:14. *. . . all thy fortresses shall be spoiled, as Shalman spoiled Beth-arbel . . .*

Hosea 10:15. *. . . in a morning shall the king of Israel utterly be cut off.*

Neither Shalman nor Beth-arbel can be certainly identified, nor can the incident be pin-pointed. Some suggest that Shalman is a king of Moab, contemporary to Hosea (one such is referred to as Salamanu in Assyrian inscription) and to some local victory in the Trans-Jordan which he won just before the time of the prophet's utterance.

Another possibility is that the verse refers to Shalmaneser V, who succeeded Tiglath-Pileser III in 727 B.C. In this case, Hosea may be speaking as Shalmaneser is marching to the siege of Samaria and be referring to a victory won by him en route. It is this siege which led to the fall of Samaria and the destruction of Israel even though Shalmaneser V did not live to see its conclusion.

David

As is usually true of the prophets, however, Hosea sees beyond the immediate destruction to an ideal future:

Hosea 3:5. *Afterward shall the children of Israel return, and see the Lord their God, and David their king . . . in the latter days.*

This sounds as though it was uttered after Sargon's carrying off of the Israelites into captivity, but of course those exiles never returned. The mention of David himself rather than a descendant of his may be simply symbolic, but it may also reflect an early notion among the Jews, predating the development of the Messianic notion.

It is an attractive idea, for a nation which has experienced greater times in its past (or imagines it has) sometimes dreams that some powerful king, whom it magnifies in tradition, is not really dead. Thus, king Arthur sleeps in Avalon, waiting to return on some day when his country really needs him. Similarly, the twelfth-century German emperor, Frederick Barbarossa, sleeps under the Kyffhäuser mountain, likewise awaiting his country's call.

Perhaps, then, this verse is a reflection of a time when Jews expected the return of David himself.

Of course, it is odd to have a northerner say this. The northern kingdom had been only uneasily subject to David and Solomon at the best of times and had revolted from the Judean dynasty immediately after Solomon's death, showing no signs, thereafter, of any longing to return to its original allegiance. Would Hosea dream of the return of David, or could the verse be the addition of a later Judean hand?

29. JOEL

Joel

Joel ("Yahveh is God") is the first of the eleven minor prophets of Judah. The collection of his utterances bears no dates but begins merely:

Joel 1:1. *The word of the Lord that came to Joel . . .*

Since the book makes no mention of the Assyrian or Babylonian menace, it would seem that Joel either spoke before those menaces had made themselves plain or after they had passed. In other words, the book must be dated either before 750 B.C. or after 500 B.C.

At the time the Jewish canon was being established, it was the first alternative that seemed to attract the scribes, and for that reason Joel was placed early in the group of minor prophets.

This, however, is extremely unlikely and modern commentators seem certain that the book was written after the return from exile. There are, after all, no references to kings, or to the idolatries that were so prevalent during the kingdom. There is, on the other hand, mention of the deportation of the Jews and the scattering that followed the destruction of Jerusalem:

Joel 3:2. *. . . my people . . . whom they have scattered among the nations.*

There is even a reference to the Greeks, who did not come into the Jewish ken until well along in the Persian period:

Joel 3:6. *. . . the children of Jerusalem have ye* [Tyre and Sidon] *sold unto the Grecians . . .*

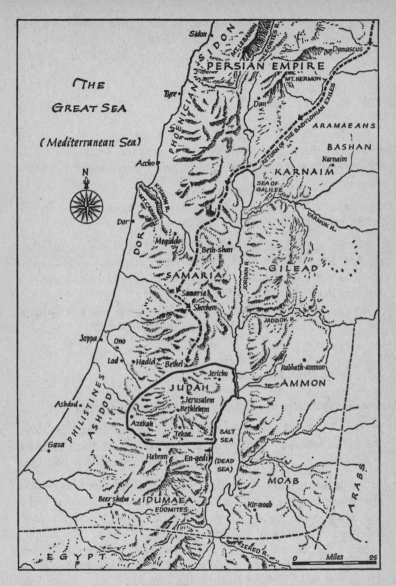

Judah at the Time of Joel

The reference here is undoubtedly to the lucrative slave trade carried on by the Phoenicians in ancient times.

Consequently, the Book of Joel is usually dated about 400 B.C.

The Day of the Lord

Joel begins by describing a plague of locusts and then moves on to consider this a disaster symbolizing a much more awful event that will strike the world as the equivalent many times over of the locust plague:

> Joel 1:15. . . . *for the day of the Lord is at hand, and as a destruction from the Almighty shall it come.*

The day of the Lord, to which Joel refers, is, of course, the apocalyptic final accounting (see page 543) at which the tyrants who oppress the Jews will be punished, while the Jews themselves will be compensated with an ideal state and eternal security.

Because the day of the Lord is viewed as a day on which the nations are judged, it has come to be called "Judgment Day."

The Valley of Jehoshaphat

God is quoted as describing the events of Judgment Day:

> Joel 3:2. *I will also gather all nations, and will bring them down into the valley of Jehoshaphat, and will plead with them there for my people . . . whom they have scattered among the nations . . .*

God is not pictured as pleading like a suppliant but rather like a prosecuting attorney and judge. The Revised Standard Version makes this clearer by translating this portion of the verse "I will enter into judgement with them there, on account of my people."

No one has succeeded in definitely identifying the valley of Jehoshaphat and it is probably not a real place. The word Jehoshaphat means "Yahveh has judged" and perhaps the verse does not refer to king Jehoshaphat of Judah but should be translated "and will bring them down into the valley of the judgment of the Lord."

Joel pictures the judgment as involving nations as a whole and the punishment as being made to fit the crime:

Joel 3:4. . . . *what have ye to do with me, O Tyre and Zidon . . .*
. . . .

Joel 3:6. *The children . . . of Jerusalem have ye sold unto the Grecians . . .*

Joel 3:7. *Behold, I will raise them out of the place whither ye have sold them, and will return your recompence upon your own head:*

Joel 3:8. *And I will sell your sons and your daughters into the hand of the children of Judah, and they shall sell them . . . to a people far off.*

Gradually, this notion of judgment by nations was still further etherealized to the point where judgment became individual and personal. This is expressed, for instance, in the final verse of Ecclesiastes, a late addition to a book that is itself post-Exilic:

Ecclesiastes 12:14. *For God shall bring every work into judgment, with every secret thing, whether it be good, or whether it be evil.*

The notion of individual judgment is also implied in the late-written Book of Daniel:

Daniel 12:2. *And many of them that sleep in the dust of the earth shall awake, some to everlasting life, and some to shame and everlasting contempt.*

AMOS • CHIUN • AMAZIAH

Amos

The third of the twelve minor prophets is Amos and he seems to be, in actual fact, the oldest (chronologically) of the group. Indeed, he was the first example of a new phenomenon in the history of Judaism: the inspired visionary whose words were preserved in writing.

Amos and those who followed are generally called prophets, but there are many differences between the new breed and the old bands of prophets led by men such as Samuel and Elisha. The latter were ecstatics who in their fits were thought to be mystically close to God. Amos, on the other hand, was a lone wolf, who needed no fits or seizures but spoke in plain language on what he considered the important problems of the day. Indeed, on being questioned, he denies that he is a prophet (in the old sense):

Amos 7:14. *Then answered Amos and said . . . I was no prophet, neither was I a prophet's son; but I was an herdman . . .*

The Book of Amos is dated in the first verse:

Amos 1:1. *The words of Amos, who was among the herdmen of Tekoa . . . in the days of Uzziah king of Judah, and in the days of Jeroboam . . . king of Israel, two years before the earthquake.*

When the earthquake referred to might be is unknown. There is no mention of an earthquake in the reign of Uzziah or of Jeroboam in the Books of Kings or Chronicles. Rabbinic tradition states that it took place when Uzziah was stricken with leprosy for attempting to officiate

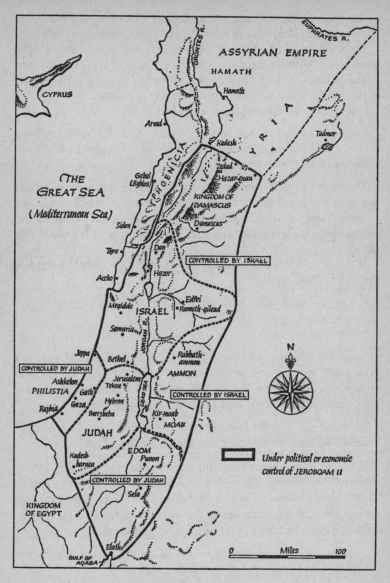

Israel and Judah

at the Temple rites. This is merely legend, of course, but even if it were true, the exact year in which Uzziah was stricken is unknown.

Some scholars find reason to believe that the leprosy struck eight years before Uzziah's death; that is, in 748 B.C. If that was the year of the earthquake, then Amos prophesied in 750 B.C. and, actually, that is the usual estimate of the date of Amos's discourses.

One of Amos's apocalyptic visions states:

> Amos 8:9. And it shall come to pass in that day, saith the Lord God, that I will cause the sun to go down at noon, and I will darken the earth in the clear day.

This seems to be a reference to a solar eclipse and such an eclipse was visible in Israel and Judah in 763 B.C. If Amos indeed prophesied in 750 B.C. then it is quite reasonable to expect he had witnessed the eclipse thirteen years earlier and that his impression of it colored this verse.

If this is so, Amos is a contemporary of Hosea and Isaiah, perhaps a little older than either.

Chiun

Amos was a Judean, a native of Tekoa, which was a village some ten miles south of Jerusalem. Nevertheless, although the book records brief warnings of destruction against the nations surrounding Judah, and even against Judah itself, Amos's chief target was Israel:

> Amos 7:15. . . . the Lord took me as I followed the flock, and the Lord said unto me, Go, prophesy unto my people Israel.

It was to Bethel he traveled: the southern outpost of Israel, twenty miles north of Tekoa. There he preached against the Israelite custom of worshiping at the shrines of Bethel and Dan (see page 339) and against the idolatrous manner of the worship there. For instance, he refers (rather obscurely) to some form of star-worship:

> Amos 5:26. . . . ye have borne the tabernacle of your Moloch and Chiun your images, the star of your god.

The Revised Standard Version clarifies this somewhat by leaving "tabernacle" untranslated and translating Moloch instead. The verse becomes: "You shall take up Sakkuth your king, and Kaiwan your star-god, your images." Apparently, then, Amos is referring to two idols, Sakkuth and Kaiwan (Chiun); or perhaps they are alternate names of the same deity, expressed in poetic parallelism. Neither is mentioned anywhere else in the Bible but Kaiwan may be a form of the Babylonian Kaiman, a deity representing the planet Saturn. If so, this is one of the only two references to the planets in the Bible; the other involves Lucifer, that is, Venus, in the Book of Isaiah (see page 538).

Amaziah

Amos also inveighed against the injustices in Israel, against the luxury of the few and the poverty of the many, against the harshness of the rich toward the poor. Like the later prophets Isaiah and Jeremiah he denounced mere ritual and demanded ethical behavior. He quotes God:

Amos 5:21. *I hate, I despise your feast days . . .*
Amos 5:22. *Though ye offer me burnt offerings . . . I will not accept them . . .*
Amos 5:23. *Take thou away from me the noise of thy songs . . .*
Amos 5:24. *But let judgment run down as waters, and righteousness as a mighty stream.*

With this view it is reasonable to suppose that Amos did not believe that the day of the Lord ("Judgment Day") could possibly be a day of great joy for all Jews alike; since he could not believe that all Jews alike would be saved by the mere existence of the Temple ritual. Righteousness was required and for those in whom it was absent all the ritual in the world would not help. Therefore he warned:

Amos 5:18. *Woe unto you that desire the day of the Lord! to what end is it for you? the day of the Lord is darkness and not light.*

This seems to foreshadow the notion of individual judgment and salvation, rather than national judgment.

For the nation's failure to bring about a thoroughgoing moral reform, Amos quotes God as predicting certain disaster:

Amos 7:9. . . . *I will rise against the house of Jeroboam with the sword.*

Here, apparently, Amos went too far. He might denounce idolatry and demand justice all he wished and he could be dismissed as a mere dreamer and ranter. When he spoke of rising against the king, however, he was announcing rebellion and was speaking treason. Amaziah, the Israelite priest officiating at Bethel, had no choice but to consider it that:

Amos 7:10. *Then Amaziah the priest of Bethel sent to Jeroboam king of Israel, saying, Amos hath conspired against thee . . .*

. . . .

Amos 7:12. *Also Amaziah said unto Amos, O thou seer, go, flee thee away into the land of Judah, and there eat bread, and prophesy there:*

Amos 7:13. *But prophesy not again any more at Bethel . . .*

Amos returned a spirited answer and predicted an evil end for Amaziah (whether such an end came to pass the Bible does not say). However, Amos presumably returned to Judah, for had he stayed in Israel he would very likely have been convicted of treason and executed and there is no tradition concerning his martyrdom.

31. OBADIAH

OBADIAH * SEPHARAD

Obadiah

The Book of Obadiah is the shortest book in the Old Testament, consisting as it does of a single chapter made up of twenty-one verses. Nothing about its author is known for the book starts off with nothing more than the author's name:

Obadiah 1:1. *The vision of Obadiah* . . .

There are a dozen Obadiahs mentioned in the Bible outside this book, the most notable of whom appears in the First Book of Kings. This Obadiah was an important official in the palace of Ahab of Israel:

1 Kings 18:3. *And Ahab called Obadiah which was the governor of his house. (Now Obadiah feared the Lord greatly:*
1 Kings 18:4. *For . . . when Jezebel cut off the prophets . . . Obadiah took an hundred prophets, and hid them by fifty in a cave and fed them . . .*

Obadiah, for performing such a dangerous feat, in the very midst of a notoriously idolatrous court, was looked up to by later Jews, and the first-century Jewish historian Josephus maintained it was this Obadiah who was the prophet and who wrote the short book that goes by that name.

This, however, would date the book about 860 B.C., which seems to be impossible. In this book, Edom is anthematized for its crime in joining the invaders who destroyed Jerusalem:

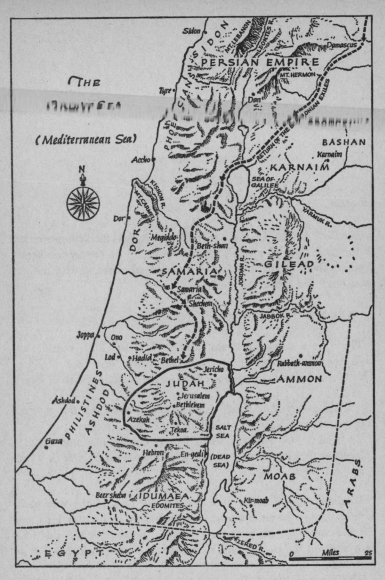

Judah

Obadiah 1:11. . . . *thou stoodest on the other side, in the day that the strangers carried away captive his [Judah's] forces, and foreigners entered into his gates, and cast lots upon Jerusalem, even thou wast as one of them.*

This, it is generally agreed, is a reference to the destruction of Jerusalem by Nebuchadnezzar in 586 B.C., so that it would seem that the book cannot be earlier than that.

It cannot be too late, either. In the final verses, Obadiah seems to expect a restoration of Israel as well as Judah:

Obadiah 1:20. . . . *the captivity . . . of the children of Israel shall possess . . . [the land] of the Canaanites . . . and the captivity of Jerusalem . . . shall possess the cities of the south.*

Since the Israelites never returned and did not participate in the reoccupation of the land, it may well be that the Book of Obadiah was written before the Return, or at least so early after the Return that the non-return of Israel had not yet been accepted. At a guess, the book may be dated 500 B.C.

Sepharad

The final verses also place the exiled Jews in a spot otherwise unmentioned in the Bible:

Obadiah 1:20. . . . *and the captivity of Jerusalem, which is in Sepharad . . .*

No one knows the locality which is here identified as Sepharad. It does not seem to fit the name of any place in Babylonia, where the Jews were in exile, and the word may be a corruption of an original which is now impossible to recover.

One speculation has been that the word refers to Sardis, the capital of Lydia, in western Asia Minor. There is, however, no reason to think that there was any notable Jewish colony in that city in Exilic times.

During the Middle Ages, Jews flourished in Moslem Spain and the rabbis of the day decided, quite without justification, that Sepharad was a reference to Spain. As a result the Jews of Spain and Portugal, together with their descendants down to the present day, are referred to as Sephardim, as opposed to the Ashkenazim (see page 47), which include the Jews from northern and eastern Europe.

These two groups remained distinct in certain aspects of ritual as well as in ancestry. The Sephardim inherited details of their ritual from the Babylonian school since Moslem rule extended over both Spain and Babylonia (or Iraq, as we now call it) and communications across the width of their elliptic remained possible and easy for many centuries. The Ashkenazim, however, were descendants of those Jews who, both before and after the Roman destruction of Jerusalem, had maintained themselves in Europe and, eventually, came under Christian rule. They had no contact with Babylonia and inherited the ritual of Judea.

The Sephardic Jews were evicted from Spain in 1492 and were scattered over North Africa and the Middle East. An important community of Sephardim remained in Salonika, Greece, and was not finally destroyed until 1941, when the Nazis occupied the land.

Some of the Sephardim found their way to Holland, England, and, eventually, the United States. The early Jewish migrants to the United States were Sephardim. Benjamin Disraeli, a Prime Minister of England in the 1870's, and Benjamin Cardozo, an American Supreme Court Justice of the 1930's, were of Sephardic origin.

The common language of the Sephardim is Ladino, a mixture of Hebrew and Spanish, whereas that of the Ashkenazim is Yiddish, closely related to medieval German. Each has its own rules for pronouncing Hebrew and the modern nation of Israel has adopted the Sephardic pronunciation, although the Sephardim make up only a small percentage (perhaps one sixth) of the total Jewish population of the world.

32. JONAH

Jonah

The Book of Jonah is unlike any of the other prophetic books in that it is not primarily a record of the utterances of the prophet. Rather it is a short story, clearly fictional. The hallmarks of fiction rest in its anachronisms and its elements of fantasy.

It is included in the books of the prophets because its protagonist, Jonah, would seem to be a man who lived in the time of the kingdoms and who is mentioned in the reliable historical section of the Bible:

> 2 Kings 14:25. He [Jeroboam II] *restored the coast of Israel . . . according to the word of the Lord . . . which he spake by the hand of his servant Jonah, the son of Amittai . . . of Gath-hepher.*

Gath-hepher is a town in Israel, in the section which, by Roman times, had come to be called Galilee. Indeed, it is only about three miles northeast of Nazareth, and the traditional tomb of Jonah is still to be found there. The real Jonah might, therefore, like Hosea, be viewed as an Israelite rather than a man of Judah.

Jonah (the real man) flourished in the early part of the reign of Jeroboam II, for the verse records that he predicted the successful outcome of the king's plans for territorial expansion. That would make the prophet active about 780 B.C. Scholars agree that the book cannot be that early, so that it was not written by Jonah himself or even by one of his immediate disciples. The book makes use of the phraseology of some of the later psalms; its language shows similarities to that used in the time of Ezra and Nehemiah; and its teachings have particular meaning for the time of the return from exile.

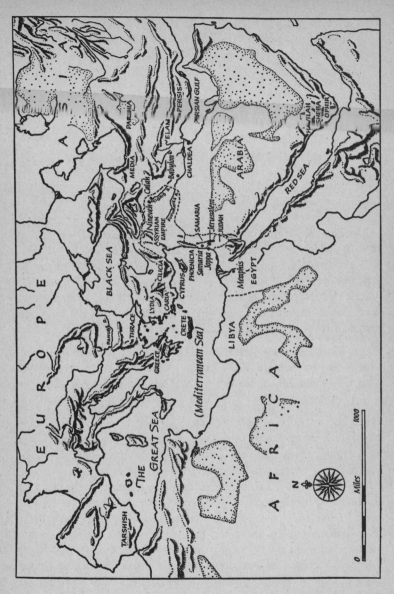

The Mediterranean World in the time of Jonah

A reasonable guess is that the book was written about 300 B.C. by some anonymous Judean. The book, although dealing with an Israelite prophet, is not an Israelite production in the sense that the Book of Hosea is.

Nineveh

The Book of Jonah begins with God's instructions to Jonah:

Jonah 1:1. *Now the word of the Lord came unto Jonah, the son of Amittai, saying,*

Jonah 1:2. *Arise, go to Nineveh, that great city, and cry against it; for their wickedness is come up before me.*

Here is an anachronism. Nineveh is treated as "that great city," the capital of the Assyrian Empire; and, of course, so it was during the time when Judah, under Manasseh, was an Assyrian tributary. Then it was indeed "that great city," the most powerful and dreaded military center in the world.

However, the real Jonah was active about 780 B.C. and at that time Assyria was in a period of decay and was no threat to anyone. (How else could Jeroboam II have created his short-lived empire?) Moreover, Nineveh was then only a small provincial town. The capital of Assyria in Jonah's day was Calah, as it had been for five centuries, from the reign of Shalmaneser I in 1270 B.C.

It was Sennacherib who established the royal residence at Nineveh nearly a century after the time of the real Jonah, and Nineveh remained a world-conquering city for only about three quarters of a century. Its fame far outshadows that of Calah, partly because it was when Nineveh was capital that the Assyrian Empire reached its maximum extent; and partly because it was when Nineveh was capital that the Assyrian Empire was mistress over Judea, so that the city was rewarded by ample mention in the Bible.

Later in the book, the writer refers to Nineveh in the past tense:

Jonah 3:3. . . . *Now Nineveh was an exceeding great city . . .*

The use of the past tense is an indication that the book had been written (or at least reached its final form) not only after 612 B.C., when Nineveh was destroyed, but long after, so that even its memory had grown faint and could stand refreshing.

The Great Fish

Jonah was not willing to preach in Nineveh and perhaps we can sympathize with him in this. A Jew asked to preach repentance to the city of Berlin in the time of Hitler's ascendancy might have suffered similar pangs of reluctance.

Jonah therefore took passage in a ship to Tarshish at the western edge of the Mediterranean (see page 332). There is here a bit of henotheism on the part of Jonah, for his action can only be understood if he felt that God was not powerful outside Israel and that the greater the distance from Israel, the weaker the hand of God.

The writer himself is not, however, a henotheist, and he makes it plain that God cannot be escaped by mere physical distance. The ship is struck by a storm and the mariners attempt to save themselves by lightening the ship and throwing unnecessary cargo overboard. They also cast lots to find out who among them had angered the gods, and the lot fell upon Jonah, who was promptly thrown overboard. (Ever since, a person or object that is believed to cause bad luck to those about him has been called a "jonah." The slang equivalent, "jinx," is not derived from Jonah despite the common possession of "j" and "n.")

Once in the water, Jonah underwent a most unusual experience:

> Jonah 1:17. Now the Lord had prepared a great fish to swallow up Jonah. And Jonah was in the belly of the fish three days and three nights.

Since the book is fiction, it would be best to consider the "great fish" an element of fantasy, a mythological monster, and let it go at that. Nevertheless, the popularity of the tale and the long centuries during which it was considered to describe actual history have led to endless discussions of the creature.

Popularly, Jonah's fish is considered to have been a whale. Nor can one counter this by saying that the whale is not a fish, for this is the case only according to the classification schemes of modern biologists, who recognize the whale to be a mammal with warm blood and lungs, rather than a true fish with cold blood and gills. Before the rise of modern biology, however, fish (or the equivalent word in other languages) would be applied to any sea creature. We recognize this in such common words as "shellfish," "jellyfish," and "starfish," none of which represent what the modern biologist would consider a fish. In Biblical times, therefore, a great fish could very easily signify a whale.

The suggestion that the fish is a whale is strengthened in the minds of Christians by the fact that Jesus is quoted as referring to it as such:

> Matthew 12:40. . . . *Jonas* [Jonah] *was three days and three nights in the whale's belly* . . .

If it was a whale that swallowed Jonah, then we are left with the fact that the only type of whale with a throat large enough to swallow a man intact is the sperm whale—the largest of the toothed whales. (There are larger whales which have whalebone strands or "baleen" in their mouths. These strands serve to strain out the tiny creatures on which the huge whales feed. Such baleen whales have throats suited to the size of the creatures they eat and could not swallow a man's hand, let alone a man.)

Sperm whales are not found in the Mediterranean and, in the course of nature, it is completely unlikely that a man should be swallowed by one there, or, still further, survive three days and nights of such incarceration. All difficulties disappear, however, if it is remembered that the Book of Jonah is a fantasy.

The Gourd

Jonah repented and was cast out upon dry land by the fish. The order to go to Nineveh was now repeated and this time Jonah obeyed. Through the city he went, proclaiming that Nineveh would be destroyed in forty days.

Whereupon, to Jonah's surprise, apparently, all of Nineveh repented, from the king on downward. All sat in sackcloth and fasted. This, in itself, is as great a miracle as the three-day stay in the fish and, of course, there is no record of such a remarkable occurrence anywhere in secular history. Indeed, what is even more significant, there is no mention of such an unusual Yahvistic victory in the historical books of the Bible itself. Clearly this is another element of fantasy.

But to continue. As a result of Nineveh's mass repentance, God decided not to destroy Nineveh after all. The city was spared.

At this unexpected turn, Jonah was furious. He had not wanted to undertake the perilous mission but had tried to escape and been swallowed by a fish for his pains. Now, after all he had gone through, all had come to nothing. (One must assume he did not consider repentance an achievement, but only the city's destruction.) Presumably, Jonah, he harbored hopes that God might destroy the city after all:

> Jonah 4:5. So Jonah went out of the city, and sat on the east side . . . till he might see what would become of the city.
> Jonah 4:6. And the Lord God prepared a gourd, and made it to come up over Jonah, that it might be a shadow over his head . . .

"Gourd" is the translation of the Hebrew word *kikayon* and is, it would seem, a poor translation. The Revised Standard Version satisfies itself with the more general "And the Lord God appointed a plant." The best guess is that by the *kikayon* is meant the castor-oil plant which is common in tropical countries and which can grow to tree size.

God, however, causes the gourd to die the next day, and Jonah, finding a sudden absence of shade, is furious once more. Then comes the climax and the moral of the tale:

> Jonah 4:10. Then said the Lord, Thou hast had pity on the gourd, for the which thou hast not laboured, neither madest it grow . . .
> Jonah 4:11. And should not I spare Nineveh, that great city, wherein are more than sixscore thousand persons that cannot discern between their right hand and their left hand; and also much cattle.

Jonah is thus taught a lesson in mercy and pity and the writer emphasizes the care of God for all His creatures and rebukes the narrow views of the nationalists. Even if the men of Nineveh are sinners, they have repented; and aside from that, there are children in Nineveh who are too young yet even to have learned to tell their right hand from their left and surely they cannot be considered sinners worthy of death. And in a final phrase Jonah is reminded of the innocent animals in the city—virtually the only place in the Bible where a love of animals is clearly displayed.

(This is the very reverse of the primitive conception of God as evidenced by Samuel's insistence on the complete extermination of the Amalekites down to their cattle and his denunciation of Saul for attempting to set limits to the destruction—see page 283.)

Clearly, the Book of Jonah, like that of Ruth, is the product of that school of Jewish thought which was universalist and which opposed the nationalist views of Ezra and his followers (see page 451). It is the universality of God and the attribute of divine mercy that are the lessons of Jonah. Those who think of the book as nothing more than the story of a man and a whale miss the whole point.

Micah

The name Micah is a shortened form of Micaiah ("who is like Yahveh?"). The most important Micaiah in the Bible is a prophet of Ahab's time. Before the battle of Ramoth-gilead (see page 351) Ahab arranged to have his court prophets predict victory. His ally, Jehoshaphat of Judah, requested that a prophet of Yahveh also be consulted:

> 1 Kings 22:8. *And the king of Israel said unto Jehoshaphat, There is yet one man, Micaiah the son of Imlah, by whom we may inquire of the Lord: but I hate him; for he doth not prophesy good concerning me, but evil . . .*

Micaiah is called but he prophesies defeat and disaster. He is mocked by the other prophets and is ordered off into imprisonment.

There is no chance at all, of course, that this Micaiah is the author of the Book of Micah. Micaiah is an Israelite and the time of the battle of Ramoth-gilead is 854 B.C. As the first verse of the Book of Micah proclaims, the author is a Judean who preached over a century after the time of Ahab's death:

> Micah 1:1. *The word of the Lord that came to Micah the Morasthite in the days of Jotham, Ahaz and Hezekiah . . .*

Micah was thus the fourth of the great prophets of the eighth century B.C., a contemporary of Isaiah, Hosea, and Amos. Whereas Hosea was a northerner, and Isaiah an aristocrat of Jerusalem, Micah, like Amos, was a Judean provincial. His description as a Morasthite in-

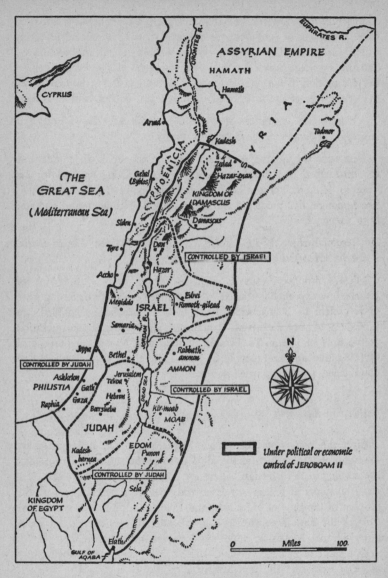

Israel and Judah

dicates him to be a native of Moresheth-gath, a town about twenty-five miles southwest of Jerusalem, near the borders of Philistine territory.

The fact that Micah begins with a warning of the destruction of Samaria would indicate that the early passages of the book antedate the destruction of that city by Sargon in 722 B.C. Later, he denounces the corruption of the priesthood of Judah and quotes God as saying:

Micah 3:12. *Therefore shall Zion for your sake be plowed as a field, and Jerusalem shall become heaps . . .*

This verse was quoted, a century later, in the Book of Jeremiah, at the time when that prophet was in danger of being lynched for his Temple Sermon. Those who defended him pointed out that Micah, like Jeremiah, had predicted the destruction of Jerusalem and had not been executed.

Jeremiah 26:19. *Did Hezekiah . . . put him* [Micah] *. . . to death? did he* [Hezekiah] *not fear the Lord . . .*

Micah's prophecy, thus specified as having been in the time of Hezekiah, was probably uttered with reference to the forthcoming siege of Jerusalem by Sennacherib. If so, it was not entirely fulfilled, for Jerusalem was not destroyed. It may be that the use of the quotation at the time of Jeremiah's Temple Sermon also served the purpose of soothing the indignant people by reminding them that prophecies of doom need not be regarded too seriously.

Bethlehem Ephratah

After the visions of destruction, Micah passes on, as is customary for the prophets, to picture the ideal state of the future and to predict the coming of the Messiah. There are some suggestions that the Messianic chapters of Micah are later additions to the utterances of the prophet of the time of Hezekiah; and that the additions date from the time of the Exile a century and a half later. It was during the Exile, after all, that Messianic hope and longings grew intense.

One piece of evidence in favor of this is a mention of Babylon as a place of exile for "the daughter of Zion":

Micah 4:10. *. . . thou shalt go even to Babylon . . . there the Lord shall redeem thee . . .*

In Micah's time, it was Nineveh, not Babylon, that was the enemy. If this reference is not accepted as a divinely inspired prophetic vision of the future, then it must be taken to indicate, for that verse at least, a later origin than the time of Micah.

Micah refers to the Messiah in a verse that became famous in later centuries:

> Micah 5:2. *But thou, Beth-lehem Ephratah, though thou be little among the thousands of Judah, yet out of thee shall he come forth unto me that is to be ruler in Israel; whose goings forth have been from of old, from everlasting.*

If this verse is of Exilic origin then it may well be that Bethlehem Ephratah is deliberately used as a symbolic way of referring to the house of David by way of its ancestral town of origin. Any direct mention of the coming of a new king of the Davidic line might have brought down Babylonian suspicion of attempted treason. If so, this prediction would be one of an ideal king arising from the Davidic line, which had now, through dethronement and imprisonment, become "little among the thousands of Judah." (The Revised Standard Version has it read "little . . . among the clans of Judah.")

The "goings forth" which "have been from of old, from everlasting" would refer to the fact that the line was an ancient one, stretching back to the beginnings of the monarchy centuries earlier. The term "everlasting" gives one the impression of eternal existence, and, therefore, of a Messiah who existed coevally with God. However, "everlasting" seems to be a poor translation, and the Revised Standard Version has the passage read "whose origin is from of old, from ancient days" with no implication of a more-than-historic origin.

Despite the interpretation I suggest here, the fact is that Micah 5:2 came to be interpreted literally as describing the place where the Messiah was to be born. It came to be expected that the Messiah, like his ancestor David, was to be born in Bethlehem.

Isaiah

Micah, in his vision of the Messianic future, is quoted as predicting a time when swords would be beaten into plowshares and war would cease in almost the precise words Isaiah used (see page 535).

Since the two prophets are contemporaries, it is difficult to argue that Isaiah was quoting Micah or that Micah was quoting Isaiah. Perhaps the passage is the Exilic utterance of some anonymous person which later editors placed in the Bible in different manners; one attributing it to Isaiah and one to Micah, with the resulting discrepancy never having been smoothed out.

The Book of Micah, like that of Isaiah, denounced the injustices practiced by the rich upon the poor and upheld the view that religion is not essentially ritual. In a very famous passage, the Book of Micah defines what it considers to be the essence of true religion:

> Micah 6:7. *Will the Lord be pleased with thousands of rams, or with ten thousands of rivers of oil? . . .*
> Micah 6:8. *He hath shewed thee, O man, what is good; and what doth the Lord require of thee, but to do justly, and to love mercy, and to walk humbly with thy God?*

34. NAHUM

Nahum

This book of three chapters is devoted to a paean of joy over the forthcoming destruction of Nineveh:

Nahum 1:1. *The burden of Nineveh. The book of the vision of Nahum the Elkoshite.*

(or, as the Revised Standard Version has it: "An oracle concerning Nineveh. The book of the vision of Nahum of Elkosh.")

The location of the town of Elkosh is unknown, though some have suggested it to be southwest of Jerusalem in the neighborhood of Moresheth-gath, the home town of Micah (see page 652).

The book, which treats Nineveh's fall as a matter of inevitability, was probably written not long before 612 B.C., when the city was taken by the allied forces of Chaldea and Media.

Nahum 2:4. *The chariots shall rage in the streets* [of Nineveh] . . .
. . . .
Nahum 2:6. *The gates of the rivers shall be opened, and the palace shall be dissolved.*
Nahum 2:7. *And Huzzab shall be led away captive* . . .

The meaning of Huzzab is uncertain. If it is not some sort of copyist's error, then it may be a symbolic name for Nineveh; or it may refer to some Assyrian goddess and idol; or even to the Ninevite queen. The Revised Standard Version has the passage read, ". . . the palace is in dismay; its mistress is stripped . . ."

The Assyrian Empire

35. HABAKKUK

Habakkuk

Nothing is known of the prophet, for the first verse of this book simply says:

Habakkuk 1:1. *The burden which Habakkuk the prophet did see.*

The reference to Habakkuk in Bel and the Dragon (see page 622) can be completely discounted, of course.

This brief book must, apparently, be dated shortly after that of Nahum, perhaps about 605 B.C. Nineveh has fallen for now it is the Chaldeans who represent the great danger and against whom the wrath of God is promised. This view rests, actually, upon a single verse. When Habakkuk complains to God about the evils being practiced in Judah, he is assured that there will be a punishment:

Habakkuk 1:6. *For lo, I raise up the Chaldeans* . . .

Zephaniah

Zephaniah is given the longest genealogy of any of the prophets:

> Zephaniah 1:1. *The word of the Lord which came unto Zephaniah, the son of Cushi, the son of Gedaliah, the son of Amariah, the son of Hizkiah* . . .

Hizkiah is a form of Hezekiah, and the name is given as Hezekiah in the Revised Standard Version. It is very tempting to suppose that the genealogy is stretched through four generations in order that it be made to reach a particularly important person. If so, it could be that by Hezekiah is meant the king of Judah, and that Zephaniah is therefore the great-grandson of that king.

This would fit, without distortion, the dating of the book, which is given as:

> Zephaniah 1:1. . . . *in the days of Josiah . . . king of Judah.*

Josiah is also the great-grandson of Hezekiah and it might be, then, that Zephaniah (like Isaiah; see page 527) is a member of the royal family and is, indeed, second cousin of the reigning king.

Zephaniah denounces idolatry and quotes God as saying:

> Zephaniah 1:4. . . . *I will cut off the remnant of Baal from this place* . . .

This passage, at least, would seem to be dated earlier than Josiah's reformation of 621 B.C. The utterances of Zephaniah must be viewed against the background of the beginning of Assyria's rapid fall and the quickly gathering anarchy that sweeps over western Asia, compounded, perhaps, by the final raids of the nomadic Cimmerians (see page 558).

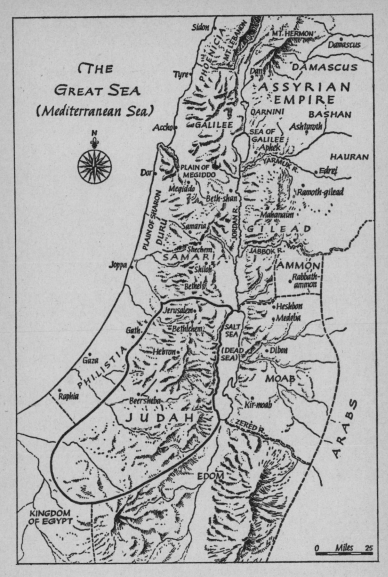

Judah

The prophet sees in all this a foretaste of the coming day of the Lord and a sample of its nature:

> Zephaniah 1:14. *The great day of the Lord is near* . . .
> Zephaniah 1:15. *That day is a day of wrath, a day of trouble and distress, a day of wasteness and desolation, a day of darkness and gloominess, a day of clouds and thick darkness.*

37. HAGGAI

Haggai

The Book of Haggai is dated quite specifically:

> Haggai 1:1. *In the second year of Darius . . . came the word of the Lord by Haggai the prophet unto Zerubbabel . . . governor of Judah, and to Joshua . . . the high priest . . .*

Darius ascended the throne of Persia in 521 B.C. and Haggai's message was therefore advanced in 520 B.C.

The Jewish exiles had returned to Jerusalem seventeen years earlier and yet the Temple had not been rebuilt (owing largely to the hostility of the people of the land; see page 441). It was Haggai's task, therefore, to spur on Zerubbabel and Joshua, the political and religious leaders of the returnees, to complete the task. With renewed vigor (and with the patronage of Darius; see page 448), the Jews bent to the task and the Temple was rebuilt.

Zerubbabel

The final short speech attributed to Haggai is Messianic in character. What's more, the Messiah is named, for Haggai quotes God as saying:

> Haggai 2:22. *. . . I will overthrow the throne of kingdoms . . .*
> Haggai 2:23. *In that day . . . will I take thee, O Zerubbabel, my servant . . . and will make thee as a signet: for I have chosen thee . . .*

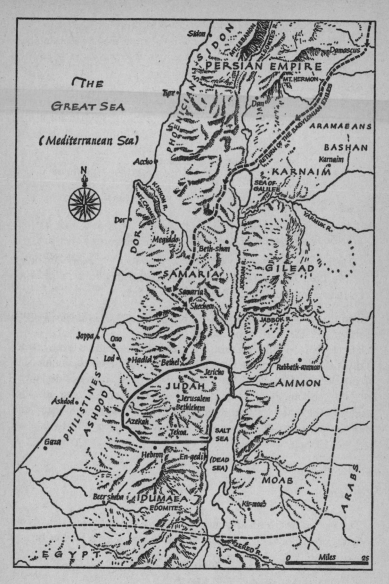

THE
GREAT SEA
(Mediterranean Sea)

Sidon

PERSIAN EMPIRE

MT. HERMON

Tyre

Dan

ARAMAEANS

BASHAN

Karnaim

KARNAIM

Accho

SEA OF
GALILEE

YARMUK R.

Dor

Megiddo

Beth-shan

GILEAD

SAMARIA

Samaria
Shechem

JABBOK

Joppa

Ono

Lod

Hadid

Bethel

Jericho

Rabbath-ammon

JUDAH

Jerusalem
Bethlehem

AMMON

Ashdod

Azekah

Tekoa

SALT
SEA

Gaza

Hebron

En-gedi

(DEAD
SEA)

MOAB

Beersheba

IDUMAEA
EDOMITES

Kir-moab

ARABS

EGYPT

ZERED R.

0   Miles   25

Judah

Since Zerubbabel was of Davidic descent (see page 405) and since he was in charge of the Jewish community at the time of the restoration of the Temple, it would seem natural to consider him as a possible Messiah, but the hope came to nothing.

Haggai is not heard of after 520 B.C. and may well have died a natural death shortly after his emergence on the stage of Jewish history. There is, after all, some reason to consider him an old man for at one point he asks, with reference to the second Temple as it is under construction:

> Haggai 2:3. *Who is left among you that saw this house in her first glory: and how do ye see it now? is it not in your eyes in comparison of it as nothing?*

If one accepts the implication that Haggai did see the first Temple and could make the comparison (and was challenging other ancients to do the same), then he was of advanced age. Even if he were only fourteen at the time of the destruction of the Temple in 586 B.C., he would be eighty in 520 B.C. A natural death at that age would not be surprising.

Zerubbabel also disappears from history. It is reasonable to suppose that being made the object of Messianic prophecies was fatal to his usefulness as a Judean governor, at least as far as the Persians were concerned. After this time, in fact, the leader of the Jewish community was the High Priest alone. It was as though the Persians had decided it would be too dangerous to allow the Jews a secular ruler as well.

The Jews were to continue to remain without a secular ruler for four centuries thereafter, until the time of the Maccabees.

30. ZECHARIAH

Zechariah

Zechariah is a contemporary of Haggai and the prophetic activity of the two began in the same year, 520 B.C.

> Zechariah 1:1. *In the . . . second year of Darius, came the word of the Lord unto Zechariah . . .*

The two prophets are even mentioned together in the Book of Ezra:

> Ezra 5:2. *Then the prophets, Haggai . . . and Zechariah . . . prophesied unto the Jews that were in Judah . . .*

However, whereas Haggai's work ended the year it began, Zechariah continued to prophesy at least as late as 518 B.C.:

> Zechariah 7:1. *And it came to pass in the fourth year of king Darius, that the word of the Lord came unto Zechariah . . .*

It was Zechariah, therefore, who (as possibly much the younger man of the two) continued the task of encouraging the rebuilding of the Temple after Haggai's voice had fallen mute.

Satan

Zechariah speaks of the sufferings and defeats of Judah and of the coming restoration of the kingdom in a series of visions granted him by an angel (rather like those in the later Book of Daniel). At one point, the change in Judah's fortunes is described as follows:

Zechariah 3:1. *And he shewed me Joshua the high priest standing before the angel of the Lord, and Satan standing at his right hand to resist him.*

Zechariah 3:2. *And the Lord said unto Satan, the Lord rebuke thee, O Satan* . . .

Zechariah 3:3. *Now Joshua was clothed with filthy garments* . . .

Zechariah 3:4. *And he [the Lord]* . . . *spake* . . . *saying, Take away the filthy garments.* . . . *I will clothe thee with change of raiment.*

Joshua here represents, apparently, the Jewish nation, clothed in the sins of its fathers, but now rescued and promoted into grace and virtue (as symbolized by the new clothing).

The Jews of Babylonia had come under Persian influence only in 538 B.C. when Cyrus conquered Babylon, but already, less than twenty years later, Persian dualism had affected Judaism to the point where Satan began to play a part. Here Satan fulfills his early role (also shown in the Book of Job (see page 478), which was written perhaps a century after Zechariah's time) as a kind of prosecuting attorney against mankind and, particularly, against the Jewish people.

The Branch

To Zechariah, as to Haggai, the prospect of the completion of the second Temple was a clear indication of the coming of the Messiah, the predicted scion of the Davidic line, who would rule over an ideal Jerusalem. Thus, after Joshua is attired in clean garments, he is told, in Zechariah's vision:

Zechariah 3:8. *Hear now, O Joshua* . . . *behold, I will bring forth my servant the Branch.*

Here, Isaiah's metaphor of the Messiah, as the fresh branch arising out of the withered stock of the Davidic line, is used.

Nor does the Branch, in this case at least, refer merely to some indefinite ideal king of the future. He is named:

Zechariah 6:9. *And the word of the Lord came unto me saying,* . . . .

Zechariah 6:11. . . . *take silver and gold, and make crowns, and set them upon the head of Joshua . . . the high priest;*

Zechariah 6:12. *And speak unto him, saying . . . Behold the man whose name is The Branch; and he shall . . . build the temple of the Lord.*

Originally, this passage seems to have referred to two men, for Zechariah describes himself as being instructed to make "crowns" (in the plural), which would mean two of them at least. Rather than suppose that both were placed on Joshua's head, it would be more reasonable to suppose that one was set on Joshua and the other on a second person, and that this second person is introduced to Joshua as "The Branch." The Branch is described as someone who will "build the temple of the Lord" and this can only be Zerubbabel. Zechariah is thus, like Haggai, naming Zerubbabel as the Messiah.

He goes on:

Zechariah 6:13. *Even he* [The Branch, or Zerubbabel] *shall build the temple of the Lord and he shall bear the glory, and shall sit and rule upon the throne; and he* [Joshua] *shall be a priest upon his throne; and the council of peace shall be between them both.*

A later editor seems to have tampered with this passage by removing actual reference to Zerubbabel, since this portion of the prophecy was quickly shown to be untrue, and the secular rule vanished. On the other hand, the High Priesthood continued unbroken throughout the succeeding centuries, so that Joshua's name might be allowed to stay.

Hadrach

The last six chapters of this book do not appear to be from the hand of the Zechariah who is the author of the first eight. The style of the language alters; the background against which the language is spoken seems to have changed radically; and there are references to events that don't fit in with the time of the immediate return from exile.

This later section of the book begins:

Zechariah 9:1. *The burden of the word of the Lord in the land of Hadrach, and Damascus . . .*

This section of the book is not carefully dated, as is the earlier section (in two different places); nor is the prophet's name mentioned.

Hadrach, unmentioned elsewhere in the Bible, is apparently a town in northern Syria and the first verses of the ninth chapter describe the passage of a conquering army down the length of Syria and Philistia:

Zechariah 9:3. . . . *Tyrus did build herself a strong hold* . . .
Zechariah 9:4. *Behold, the Lord will cast her out* . . . *and she shall be devoured with fire.*
Zechariah 9:5. . . . *and the king shall perish from Gaza* . . .

It is tempting to see in this passage a reference to the career of Alexander the Great as he impinged upon that area of the world inhabited by the Jews. In 333 B.C., Alexander defeated Darius III of Persia at the battle of Issus at the northeastern corner of the Mediterranean Sea, some four hundred miles north of Jerusalem. He then proceeded to march southward, taking all of Syria (Hadrach and Damascus) without a fight. Phoenicia, all but Tyre, capitulated. Tyre, undoubtedly remembering its heroic defense against Nebuchadnezzar (see page 588) fortified itself and held out.

Alexander the Great, however, was a far more deadly opponent than Nebuchadnezzar. The siege lasted seven months of desperate attack and defense and in the end Alexander won and Tyre was destroyed, in 332 B.C. Alexander also reduced Gaza after a stubborn siege, executing its Persian governor.

Those astonishing victories over a Persian Empire which, for two centuries, the Jews must have considered invincible could not help but seem supernatural in character. Alexander must be a tool in the hand of God, overturning the great kingdoms of the earth in order to prepare the way for the coming of the Messianic kingdom. Certainly, the Jews did not attempt to join in any resistance against Alexander and the armies of that mighty conqueror moved harmlessly past them.

If it is indeed the career of Alexander the Great that inspires this passage, the writer might have taken the view that the great military power attributed to the Messiah by earlier prophets was fulfilled in the form of a heathen king. The true Messiah might now appear in quite other guise to bring about the state of ideal peace associated with him. With military affairs taken care of, the non-military aspect, the humility, the peaceful nature of the Messiah could be emphasized:

Zechariah 9:9. *Rejoice greatly, O daughter of Zion; shout, O daughter of Jerusalem: behold, thy King cometh unto thee: he is just, and having salvation; lowly, and riding upon an ass, and upon a colt the foal of an ass.*

Zechariah 9:10. *. . . and he shall speak peace unto the heathen: and his dominion shall be from sea even to sea, and from the river even to the ends of the earth.*

The Shepherds

If this peaceful picture arises in the immediate aftermath of Alexander's victory, it is followed at once by a series of strenuous and obscure passages that seem to date later still, from the period of Seleucid persecution, when the Jews rose in revolt against their Greek-speaking masters. Thus, immediately after the picture of the humble Messiah riding upon an ass, there is a picture of war:

Zechariah 9:13. *. . . I have . . . raised up thy sons, O Zion, against thy sons, O Greece . . .*

Again, there is hostility toward other nations, rather than the notion of a Messiah who "shall speak peace unto the heathen." Thus:

Zechariah 10:11. *. . . the pride of Assyria shall be brought down, and the sceptre of Egypt shall depart away.*

The reference here seems to be to the two portions of Alexander's broken empire which were of particular interest to the Jews: Ptolemaic Egypt and the Seleucid kingdom. The latter was commonly known as Syria because its Syrian centers of power were nearest the Jews, and this Syria is here converted, presumably by a copyist's error, to Assyria.

There follow passages concerning shepherds which defy intrepreta-tion. The shepherds can well refer to the various High Priests of the Temple during the period of the Seleucid persecution, and to the struggle for power among them as some supported compromise with Greek culture while others held out for firm adherence to the principles of Judaism. The events of the time, known in full detail to the original readers of the passage, are known only sketchily to us and this leaves us confused. Thus:

Zechariah 11:8. *Three shepherds also I cut off in one month . . .*

This may be a reference to three High Priests deposed in a short space of time owing to the strife of contending factions, but the details are unknown.

The writer seems to be speaking of himself as one of the shepherds:

Zechariah 11:4. *Thus saith the Lord my God; Feed the flock . . .*
. . . .
Zechariah 11:7. *. . . and I fed the flock.*

For some reason not made plain to us, but probably clear to the original readers, the shepherd resigned from his position and asked for his wages:

Zechariah 11:12. *. . . So they weighed for my price thirty pieces of silver.*
Zechariah 11:13. *. . . And I took the thirty pieces of silver, and cast them to the potter in the house of the Lord.*

The shepherd considers this payment to be insultingly small and it may even have been meant as a deliberate insult, since thirty pieces of silver is set in the Mosaic law as the compensation for an injury to a slave:

Exodus 22:32. *If the ox shall push a manservant or a maidservant; he* [the owner of the ox] *shall give unto their master thirty shekels of silver . . .*

The word "potter" seems to be a mistranslation of the Hebrew word, which really means "treasury." The Revised Standard Version has Zechariah 11:13 read "I took the thirty shekels of silver and cast them into the treasury in the house of the Lord." It is as though, disdaining to bother with so small a sum, the shepherd donated it to the Temple.

The book ends with an apocalyptic picture of the final battle of the heathen against Jerusalem, their defeat, and the establishment of the ideal Messianic kingdom.

Malachi

The author's name is given in the first verse of the book:

Malachi 1:1. *The burden of the word of the Lord to Israel by Malachi.*

The name Malachi means "my messenger" and it is possible that it does not represent the actual name of the author but arises out of a misunderstanding on the part of a later editor.

Later in the book there occurs the verse:

Malachi 3:1. *Behold I* [God] *will send my messenger, and he shall prepare the way before me . . .*

the messenger being one who prepares the world for the day of the Lord.

If the editor assumed that the messenger had come and was the author of the book, he would naturally place "my messenger" or, in Hebrew, Malachi, in the superscription.

But if this is indeed the origin of the reputed name of the author of the book, it would seem to be a mistake. Later in the book, there is mention again of someone to be sent to prepare the way, and this time the messenger is named:

Malachi 4:5. *Behold I will send you Elijah the prophet before the coming of the great and dreadful day of the Lord:*

It is difficult to tell when the book was written but the best estimate seems to be about 460 B.C. At that time, the second Temple had already been built but Jerusalem was still without walls and helpless, and the people were despondent and apathetic.

It could already be seen that the prophecies of Haggi and Zechariah, two generations earlier, had not come to pass, for Zerubbabel had faded out in most un-Messiahlike fashion. What's more, the inspiring presence of Nehemiah (see page 456) had not yet made itself felt. It was Malachi's task, therefore, to assure the despondent Jews (and threaten them, too) that the day of the Lord would nevertheless come and that they had better be ready for that coming.

DATES OF INTEREST
IN BIBLICAL HISTORY

NOTE: Many of the dates given in this table are approximate, or controversial.

B.C.

8500	First cities established in Middle East.
5000	Jericho already existing.
4004	Archbishop Ussher's date of creation.
3761	Traditional Jewish date of creation.
3600	Sumerian city-states in existence.
3100	Egypt united under single rule, 1st dynasty founded.
3000	Canaanites enter Canaan.
2700	Assyrian cities come into existence.
2570	Great Pyramid built in Egypt.
2500	Bronze Age reaches Canaan.
2264	Sargon of Agade founds Akkadian Empire.
2050	11th dynasty rules Egypt; 3rd dynasty rules Ur.
2000	Beginning of patriarchal age in Canaan (Abraham).
1971	Sesostris I rules Egypt.
1900	Babylon begins to dominate Tigris-Euphrates valley; Sumerian city-states decline.
1730	Hyksos enter Egypt.
1700	Hammurabi rules Babylon.
1650	Israelites in Egypt (Jacob, Joseph).
1570	Hyksos expelled from Egypt.
1500	Assyria becomes independent kingdom.
1490	Thutmose III rules Egypt.
1479	Thutmose III defeats Canaanites at Megiddo.
1475	Mitanni kingdom flourishing.
1450	Tyre founded by colonists from Sidon.
1400	Mycenaean Greeks at height of power.

1397 Amenhotep III rules Egypt, which is at height of its prosperity.
1390 Hittites at height of their power.
1370 Ikhnaton rules Egypt; attempts monotheistic reform; Egyptian power begins to decline; kingdoms of Moab, Ammon, and Edom established.
1290 Rameses II rules Egypt; oppression of the Israelites.
1275 Assyria conquers the Mitanni kingdom, as Assyria enters its first period of strength.
1250 Shalmaneser I rules Assyria.
1235 Tukulti-Ninurta I [Nimrod] rules Assyria.
1223 Merneptah rules Egypt; ancient world convulsed by migrations of peoples.
1211 Death of Merneptah; possibly time of Exodus (Moses).
1200 Hittite kingdom destroyed. Tarshish founded by colonists from Tyre.
1190 Rameses III rules Egypt and defeats Philistines.
1184 Trojan War.
1170 Israelites enter Canaan; Philistines settle coast (Joshua).
1150 Barak and Deborah defeat Sisera; period of judges.
1116 Tiglath-Pileser I rules Assyria.
1100 Gideon defeats Midianites; Greeks begin to settle Asia Minor coast.
1093 Death of Tiglath-Pileser I; Assyria in decline.
1080 Philistines defeat Israelites at Aphek; Shiloh destroyed.
1040 Samuel judges the tribes.
1028 Saul rules Israel.
1013 Philistines defeat Israelites at Mount Gilboa; Saul and Jonathan killed; David rules Judah.
1006 David rules united Israel-Judah.
1000 David establishes capital at Jerusalem; Aramaeans begin infiltration of Syria.
980 David's empire at peak.
973 Death of David; Solomon rules united Israel-Judah.
969 Hiram rules Tyre.
962 Completion of Temple by Solomon.
950 Rezin founds kingdom of Damascus (Syria).
933 Death of Solomon; breakup of Israel-Judah; Jeroboam I rules Israel; Rehoboam rules Judah.

928   Shishak of Egypt loots Jerusalem.

917   Abijam rules Judah.

915   Asa rules Judah.

912   Nadab rules Israel.

911   Baasha overthrows Nadab, seizes rule of Israel.

889   Elah rules Israel; overthrown by Zimri.

887   Omri rules Israel, founds Samaria.

883   Asshurnasirpal rules Assyria, which experiences revival.

880   Omri conquers Moab.

875   Ahab rules Israel; Jehoshaphat rules Judah; career of Elijah.

859   Shalmaneser III rules Assyria.

858   Ahab wars with Syrians.

854   Syrian-Israelite coalition holds off Assyria at Karkar.

853   Battle of Ramoth-gilead; death of Ahab; Ahaziah rules Israel.

852   Jehoram rules Israel; career of Elisha.

851   Jehoram (of Judah) rules Judah; J document in written form.

850   Mesha of Moab gains independence.

844   Ahaziah rules Judah.

843   Jehu rebels successfully and rules Israel; Athaliah usurps power in Judah; Hazael rules Syria and brings it to height of its power.

842   Jehu pays tribute to Assyria.

837   Jehoash rules Judah.

824   Death of Shalmaneser III of Assyria, which enters another period of decline.

816   Jehoahaz rules Israel.

814   Carthage founded by colonists from Tyre.

800   Jehoash (of Israel) rules Israel; death of Elisha.

797   Amaziah rules Judah.

785   Jeroboam II rules Israel; Israel at height of its power.

780   Azariah (Uzziah) rules Judah; Judah at height of its power.

760   Amos prophesies.

753   Rome founded.

750   Hosea prophesies; E document in written form.

745   Tiglath-Pileser III (Pul) rules Assyria; its power revives.

744   Death of Jeroboam II; gathering anarchy in Israel.

743   Tiglath-Pileser III conquers Urartu (Ararat).

740   Jotham rules Judah; Isaiah begins prophesying.

738 Pekahiah rules Israel, which is now tributary to Assyria.

737 Pekah rules Israel.

736 Ahaz rules Judah.

734 Pekah attempts to form coalition against Assyria; attacks Judah.

732 Hoshea rules Israel; Tiglath-Pileser III takes Damascus and brings Syrian kingdom to an end.

730 Micah prophesies.

726 Shalmaneser V rules Assyria.

725 Shalmaneser V lays siege to Samaria.

722 Sargon II usurps throne of Assyria and takes Samaria; Israelites carried off into exile; northern kingdom comes to an end.

720 Hezekiah rules Judah.

705 Sennacherib rules Assyria, makes Nineveh his capital.

703 Babylon under Merodach-baladan rebels against Assyria.

701 Sennacherib lays siege to Jerusalem.

700 Deioces founds Median kingdom.

693 Manasseh rules Judah, which is now tributary to Assyria.

681 Sennacherib assassinated; Esarhaddon rules Assyria and brings it to the peak of its power.

671 Esarhaddon invades and controls Egypt.

668 Asshurbanipal rules Assyria; establishes library at Nineveh.

663 Asshurbanipal sacks Thebes, ancient Egyptian capital.

652 Psamtik I rules Egypt, which is now free of Assyria.

640 Asshurbanipal defeats and destroys Elam.

638 Josiah rules Judah.

631 Cyrene founded by colonists from Greece.

630 Zephaniah prophesies.

626 Jeremiah begins to prophesy.

625 Asshurbanipal dies; gathering anarchy in Assyria and Nabopolassar seizes control of Babylonia.

620 Discovery of Book of Deuteronomy in the Temple followed by Yahvist reform in Judah; beginnings of Greek philosophy in Miletus.

615 Nahum prophesies.

612 Nabopolassar takes Nineveh; last Assyrian holdouts at Haran.

610 Necho (Pharaoh-nechoh) rules Egypt.

608 Necho defeats Judah at Megiddo; Josiah killed and Jehoiakim rules Judah; Jeremiah delivers Temple Sermon.

605 Babylonians defeat Necho at Carchemish; Nabopolassar dies; Nebuchadnezzar rules Babylonia and crushes last Assyrian stronghold; Habakkuk prophesies.

597 Judean rebellion crushed by Nebuchadnezzar; first Babylonian exile; Zedekiah rules Judah.

593 Ezekiel begins to prophesy in captivity; Psamtik II rules Egypt and places Jewish garrison at Elephantine; Astyages rules Media.

588 Apries (Pharaoh-hophra) rules Egypt.

587 Zedekiah rebels against Nebuchadnezzar.

586 Nebuchadnezzar takes Jerusalem and destroys the Temple; second Babylonian exile; Davidic dynasty comes to an end; Gedaliah assassinated; Book of Lamentations written.

585 Nebuchadnezzar lays siege to Tyre.

573 Nebuchadnezzar raises siege of Tyre.

569 Aahmes rules Egypt.

568 Nebuchadnezzar invades Egypt unsuccessfully.

562 Death of Nebuchadnezzar; Evil-merodach rules Babylonia; various documents being combined by Jewish scribes in Babylon to form the historical books of the Old Testament.

560 Amel-Marduk assassinated; Nergal-ashur-usur rules Babylonia; Croesus rules Lydia, which is at its peak of power.

556 Nabonidus rules Babylonia; his son, Belshazzar, is co-ruler.

550 Cyrus overthrows Astyages of Media; founds Persian Empire.

546 Cyrus conquers Lydia; brings Lydian kingdom to an end.

540 Second Isaiah prophesies.

538 Cyrus takes Babylon and ends Babylonian kingdom; Jews allowed to return to Judea and first group under Sheshbazzar does so.

530 Death of Cyrus; Cambyses rules Persia.

525 Cambyses invades and conquers Egypt.

521 Darius I rules Persia.

520 Haggai and Zechariah prophesy; Zerubbabel takes over leadership of Jewish returnees.

516 Second Temple dedicated.

509 Rome evicts last king; Republic founded.

500 Obadiah prophesies; Greek cities of Asia Minor revolt against Persia.

490   Persian expedition defeated at Marathon by Athens.
486   Death of Darius I; Xerxes I (Ahasuerus) rules Persia.
480   Persian expedition defeated at Salamis by united Greece; Tarshish destroyed by Carthage.
465   Xerxes I assassinated; Artaxerxes I rules Persia.
460   Malachi prophesies.
459   Ezra in Jerusalem; historical books in final form.
450   Book of Ruth written; Third Isaiah prophesies.
440   Nehemiah in Jerusalem.
437   Walls of Jerusalem completed.
407   Jewish Temple at Elephantine destroyed by Egypt.
400   Books of Chronicles, Ezra, and Nehemiah written; Joel prophesies.
300   Book of Song of Solomon and Book of Jonah written.
275   Apocalyptic portion of Book of Zechariah written.
250   Book of Ecclesiastes written; Book of Proverbs reaches final form; Septuagint in preparation in Alexandria.
180   Book of Ecclesiasticus written.
165   Book of Daniel written.
150   Book of Esther written; Book of Psalms reaches present form.

INDEX OF BIBLICAL VERSES

* Main treatment in Volume 2.

INDEX OF SUBJECTS

sale of, 106
triumph of, 113–14
Joseph tribes, 206
bull worship and, 152
Josephus, 109, 127, 129, 379, 456, 461, 639
Joshua (general), 146–47, 168
commander in chief, 208
death of, 224
sun and, 216
Joshua (High Priest), 661, 665–66
Joshua ben Sira, 516
Joshua, Book of, 208–25
Josiah, 388–90, 427–28, 534, 658
death of, 392, 559, 568, 581
Deuteronomy and, 195
sons of, 402–4
Jotham (son of Gideon), 197
Jotham (king), 374, 423, 530, 625
Jozadak, 440
Jubile, 163–64
Jubiles, Book of, 164
Jubyl, 589
Judah (eponym), 95
Benjamin and, 113
children of, 106–7
Joseph and, 106
Judah (kingdom), 338
Chaldeans and, 576
Egypt and, 392–93, 568–69
guardian angel of, 615
Jeroboam II and, 371
kings of, 402
Nebuchadnezzar and, 394–96
Seleucids and, 618
tribal makeup of, 340
Judah (tribe), 166, 284–85
Canaan conquest by, 226–28
Deborah's song and, 240
Edomite components in, 169
Jacob's blessing and, 116–17
Moses' blessing and, 206
Philistines and, 255
territorial allotment of, 222
Judaism, 195, 390, 460
Ezekiel and, 595

Jude, 184
Judges, 230
Judges, Book of, 226–60
chronology of, 230–31
Judgment Day, 632–33

Kadesh, 170–71
battle of, 123
Kadmonites, 75–77
Kagera River, 111
Kaiwan, 637
Karkar, battle of, 349, 372
Karkor, 243
Kassites, 30, 51–52
Kedar, 505
Kedesh-naphtali, 238
Kenaz, 169
Kenezite, 168–69
Kenites, 75–77
Kenezzites, 75–77
Khabur River, 379
Khartoum, 112
Khufu, 63
Kidron valley, 315
Kings, First Book of, 320–52
Kings, Second Book of, 353–96
Kirisha, 471
Kirjath-arba, 68, 89
Kirjath-jearim, 273, 305–6
Kishon River, 238
Kition, 47, 201
Kitron, 229
Kittim, 47, 201
Klein, F. A., 358
Kohath, 136
Kohathites, 270
Korah, 136, 171–72
Korahites, 136, 498
Koran, 331, 611
Krakatoa, 82

Laban, 91, 96, 179
Labashi-Marduk, 606
Ladino, 642
Lahmi, 288
Laish, 254
Lamentations, Book of, 581–82

Language families, 44
Larsa, 68
Last Supper, 156
Law, The, 17
League of Nations, 196
Leah, 94–95
  burial of, 117
Leaven, 154–56
Lebanon, 196–97
Lemuel, 511
Levi (eponym), 95
  death of, 120
  descendants of, 136
  Shechem and, 100–1
Levi (tribe), 167
  Jacob's blessing and, 116
  Moses' blessing and, 206
  territorial allotments of, 224
Leviathan, 485–87, 501
Levites, 135, 154, 417
Leviticus, Book of, 154–64
Libanus, 196
Libyans, 48, 335
Lightning, 530
Lilith, 545–46
Lion of Judah, 332
Little Ararat, 42
London, 595
Lord God, 19–20
Lot, 65–67
  capture of, 73
  daughters of, 83–84
Lots, casting of, 150
Louis XIV, 326, 539
Louis XVI, 626
Lower Egypt, 62
Lubim, 418
Lucifer, 538–40
Lud, 54
Lugal-Zaggisi, 50
Lydia, 46, 54, 594, 607, 641
Lysimachus, 472

Maachah, 419
Macedon, 285
Macedonian Empire, 602–3, 610
Macedonians, 473

Machir, 239–40
Machpelah, cave of, 89–90
Madai, 46
Magadalous, 592
Magog, 46, 594–95
Mahanaim, 298–99
Maher-shalal-hash-baz, 533
Mahlon, 263
Malachi, 357
Malachi, Book of, 670–71
Mamre, 67–68
Man, creation of, 21
Manasseh (eponym), 113–16
Manasseh (king), 388, 424–27, 557, 645
  captivity and reform of, 425–26
  Isaiah and, 546–47
Manasseh (tribe), 166
  Deborah's song and, 239–40
  Midianite raids against, 241
  Moses' blessing and, 206
  tribal territory of, 190–91, 224
Manasses, 427
Manetho, 109
Manna, 143
Manoah, 249
Marathon, battle of, 444
Marduk, 467, 486, 552–53, 621–22
Marduk-apal-iddin, 387
Mari, 368
Maronites, 196
Martyrdom of Isaiah, Book of the, 547
Mary, Virgin, 611
Maschil, 496
Mass, Catholic, 156
Massa, 92, 510
Mattaniah, 404
Mazzaroth, 484
Medes, 391, 434
Media, 46
Median Empire, 434, 549, 602, 610
  capital of, 448
  fall of, 435
Megiddo, battle of (Josiah), 392, 568